D1118570

ONE AND INSEPARABLE

Daniel Webster, by Francis Alexander, 1835

ONE AND INSEPARABLE
DANIEL WEBSTER
AND THE UNION

MAURICE G. BAXTER

THE BELKNAP PRESS OF
HARVARD UNIVERSITY PRESS
Cambridge, Massachusetts, and London, England
1984

This book is printed on acid-free paper, and its binding materials
have been chosen for strength and durability.

Library of Congress Cataloging in Publication Data

Baxter, Maurice G. (Maurice Glen), 1920–
  One and inseparable.

  Includes bibliographical references and index.
  1. Webster, Daniel, 1782–1852.   2. United States—
Politics and government—1815–1861.   3. Legislators—
United States—Biography.   4. United States. Congress.
Senate—Biography.   I. Title.
E340.W4B297   1984   973.5′092′4   [B]   83-26597
ISBN 0-674-63821-2

PREFACE

Many Americans are likely to call up a certain image upon mention of the name of Daniel Webster. They will remember him as the supreme nationalist at a time of growing sectional strife, as a defender of the Union against nullifiers and secessionists in magnificent Senate speeches; Healy's panoramic painting in Faneuil Hall in Boston shows just such an occasion, Webster's reply to Robert Hayne in 1830. They will probably remember a few other things about the famous New Englander: his tireless opposition to Andrew Jackson, his perennial quest for the presidency, and his unforgettable speech on March 7, 1850, for compromise on the issue of slavery. As for his personal character, they will visualize an imposing physical appearance, an unusual eloquence, an overpowering demeanor. No doubt, too, there will be a negative dimension: human frailties concerning money and drinking, lack of interest in social problems, and great caution about slavery.

Yet many significant features of a long, eventful life remain. Innumerable authors have written about both his public and private characters, providing many details and useful insights; but as in almost all topics of history, new evidence has become available. A project at Dartmouth College, directed by Charles Wiltse, has gathered copies of all surviving manuscripts by and to Webster, wherever located. This collection is an invaluable resource for a fresh biography. Other relevant materials are available: newspapers, government documents (both archival and published), and an enormous amount of recent historical writings.

Through the years there have been two comprehensive lives of Webster: the first by George Ticknor Curtis (1870) and the most recent by

Claude Fuess (1930). Both two-volume sets are unvaryingly sympathetic to Webster's national conservatism. As an intimate friend and literary executor, Curtis drew upon personal knowledge and a wealth of sources untapped until then. Fuess produced an elegantly written portrait based upon printed sources and interesting for its New England context. Between 1870 and 1930 there were many popular publications, mostly laudatory, although a few, such as one by Henry Cabot Lodge, emphasized defects. In the last fifty years still more books and articles have appeared, with liberal orientation and more critical evaluations. Lately several important studies of special features or periods of Webster's life have come out. Added to these is a large body of writings on his times, which decidedly enlarges the base for a new full-scale biography. I have profited from this literature, though not accepting some interpretations found there.

My principal strategy has been to bring together all parts of Webster's life—personal, legal, diplomatic, oratorical, and political—and by relating each to the others to throw light on all. This approach ought to be productive because one is dealing with the whole person of Webster, whose actions in one of these areas did in fact affect all the rest. The reader will notice that Webster's role as a lawyer is given greater attention here than elsewhere, and its interaction with his other concerns yields an improved view of Webster as a public figure.

Beyond merely reporting new and old facts, I have addressed a number of broad issues raised by Webster's behavior. Most of the questions are not so much novel as they are resistant to conclusive answers. Though not deluding myself that this book provides final solutions, I trust the discussion will move toward them.

One such question is whether Webster was an effective politician. In the struggles between Federalists and Republicans, then between National Republican–Whigs and Democrats, with an anomalous one-party situation intervening in the 1820s, politicians aimed at winning elections with techniques of organization and communication that assumed a popularized cast. Did Webster, often depicted as aloof from or hostile toward such a trend, weaken himself and his collaborators by maintaining such an attitude? There are other large questions too. What was the impact of his personal traits and professional activity upon his public career? Why did his effort toward adoption of a program of economic nationalism fail? Finally, were concessions to the slavery interest in 1850 consistent with the principles of Union and liberty for which he had stood? The answers depend upon further consideration of his many years on the American scene.

PREFACE

I must express my indebtedness to several persons: to Aida Donald and her associates at Harvard University Press for their efficient editorial assistance; to Harold Moser, Mary Virginia Anstruther, and others of the Webster Papers project at Dartmouth College for guiding me to needed materials; to Howard Jones and Kenneth Stevens, former students whose own work has improved my understanding of diplomatic aspects; to officers at depositories for permission to use illustrations, as listed on p. xi; and especially to Cynthia Lewis Baxter, who was actively involved in every phase of producing this book.

CONTENTS

CONTENTS

ILLUSTRATIONS

ONE AND INSEPARABLE

Chapter 1

PREPARATION

In his mature years, after he had reached great prominence in national affairs, Daniel Webster's thoughts often ran to the earliest part of life he could remember. The time was the late 1780s, when the Constitution was adopted; and the scene centered on a country tavern in New Hampshire. A sizable structure of two and a half stories with more than a dozen rooms, the tavern sat close to the highway, its wide front porch nearly touching the road's edge. Here at Ebenezer Webster's place in tiny Salisbury Lower Village, travelers frequently stopped on their way up the Merrimack Valley from Concord, some fifteen miles south, or down from the Connecticut River towns in the northwest. Around the fireplace in the evening when conversation and storytelling reached a peak, Daniel could learn a good deal of the outer world. Whether the topic was the latest news from some far-off city, a political controversy at the state capital, the prospects of farmers and merchants, or a recollection of times past, none quite so fascinated the lad as tales of the French and Indian War and of the Revolution, which his father could tell better than anyone else. After all, he spoke from firsthand experience.

Around the tavern were fertile fields, which Ebenezer farmed with the help of his older sons. The land was more favorable for agriculture than most in this granite-based state because it was located on a small alluvial plain extending from the west bank of the nearby Merrimack River. Just three miles north of the tavern, the river began at the junction of two streams, the Pemigewasset hurrying in a course from the mountains and the winding Winnipesaukee from the lake of that name. To the west, at the Salisbury town line, Mount Kearsarge was visible; and when the sky

1

was clear, one could see Ascutney in Vermont and towering Washington in the White Mountains on the northeastern horizon.[1]

The Websters had first settled along Punch Brook, starting less than three miles west and emptying into the Merrimack at the Lower Village. There by the head of the brook, Ebenezer had built a log house in 1762 at the close of the French and Indian War; and there most of his children had been born, except Daniel and his youngest sister, Sarah. By the time of Daniel's birth, on January 18, 1782, his father had constructed a modest frame house nearby; but the next year he had abandoned this isolated, rugged area for a more promising farm along the river. So the environs of his birthplace made no impression on Daniel, though long afterward it would be a spot of historical interest because of his fame.[2]

Memories of his father ran back to the days when he was about fifty. Six feet tall, powerfully built though tending to take on too much weight, markedly erect, perhaps owing to his military service, Ebenezer was a commanding figure. His thick hair was jet black, his forehead broad, his complexion decidedly swarthy (inherited from his mother, Susan Bachelder, it was said), his eyes and heavy brows also very dark. Young Daniel strongly resembled his father, although it appeared he would be slender, indeed frail. Ebenezer's natural disposition and the innumerable obstacles he had faced caused him to be stern when he had to be. Yet ordinarily everyone found him congenial, fair-minded, with an engaging sense of humor. Entirely self-educated and a man of the soil, he displayed a dignity and a self-assurance attributable to long experience of leadership. And a basic resource was his deep religious convictions, orthodox Congregationalist.

Ebenezer's great-grandfather, Thomas, had come from England to Dedham, Massachusetts, as a young child around 1636. The father of Thomas, with the same name, had died previously, and his mother, Margery Godfrey, had remarried. Twelve years later the Godfreys took Thomas Webster, then in his teens, with them into New Hampshire, where they settled in the coastal town of Hampton, a bit south of Portsmouth. The son of Thomas, first in a line of Ebenezers, was one of the grantees opening up the new town of Kingston, a short distance inland; and it was here that Daniel's father, the third Ebenezer, was born and grew to manhood.[3] Having had no formal schooling and having left home as an adolescent for a period of apprenticeship, he volunteered at the age of twenty for service with Rogers' Rangers in the French and Indian War. This was 1759. These troops, noted for their ingenuity and aggressiveness, took part in the invasion of Canada under General Jeffrey Amherst. Ebenezer had been equal to the challenge of warfare; and when the fighting ended, he was a captain. Now he felt ready to put his energy and self-reliance to use in private affairs.

Upon his return to Kingston in 1762 Ebenezer married Mehitable Smith and with some neighbors decided to move to a new town on the New Hampshire frontier at the head of the Merrimack. The land granted to him lay along Punch Brook, where he set up first a gristmill and then a sawmill to supplement what he could earn from farming his marginal tract. From the beginning, he was active in town government and held various offices, selectman, moderator, justice of the peace. When the Revolution broke out, he raised a company and fought at Bennington, White Plains, and elsewhere. After the war he went to the legislature, was a delegate to the state convention called to ratify the Constitution, and from 1791 onward served as a lay justice of the county court of common pleas. His character and ability kept him in a position of local prominence the rest of his life.[4]

Daniel's mother, Nabby, was Ebenezer's second wife, whom he married in 1774, a few months after the death of Mehitable. Both parents were then thirty-five. Previously unmarried, Nabby took charge of three young children and in the next ten years gave birth to five more. Plain-featured, dark-complexioned, and stout, she was a conscientious mother, though less of an influence upon Daniel than the father. His mother's parents, Gerusha and Roger Eastman, lived with the family through his boyhood. During the French and Indian War Major Eastman had lost a leg but remained hearty to an old age. Grandmother Gerusha lived past ninety, until nearly the time Daniel went off to college. Like her husband, she was of Welsh stock and, as her grandson later remembered her, an unusually attractive person.[5]

In a day when families were large, the Webster household was no exception. Ebenezer and his first wife had five children; two died young, one moved to Canada as an adult, and two, Susannah and Joseph, lived in the vicinity all their lives. From the second marriage with Nabby there were also five—three girls and two boys. Daniel was the second youngest, Ezekiel two years older.[6] His closest relationship by far was with Ezekiel, not only in his youth but in adulthood. Both resembled their father physically, though Ezekiel was more robust and therefore busier with farm work than his somewhat frail brother.[7]

There were many interesting things for a boy to see and do. Along the road near the tavern his schoolmaster, William Hoyt, had a shop, and Daniel would long remember buying a cotton handerkerchief there with the text of the Constitution printed on it, the first time he ever read the great document.[8] Another neighbor was the young lawyer Thomas

Thompson, who had set up his office in the Lower Village and from the first took an interest in the development of this bright lad. Across the road Daniel's sister Abigail and her husband, William Haddock, lived in a house called the Elms until they exchanged places with Ebenezer in 1799.[9] Ezekiel and Daniel would keep this house after their parents' death. Near the Elms farmhouse were the remnants of a cabin once occupied by Philip Call's family. Daniel was fascinated by stories about an Indian raid there in the fifties when Mrs. Call had been slain. As a reminder of these perilous days, a log fort still stood on the property.[10] But best of all, he could go down to the riverside cottage of a friendly old soldier, Robert Wise. The youth and the veteran got along famously: both enjoyed fishing, boating, walking through the hills and woods, and just sitting on the doorstep talking. Wise had served with the British army in European campaigns but had deserted to the American side during the Revolution. So he had an endless supply of adventures to recount to his eager listener. In turn, Daniel obliged the old man by reading newspapers and books to him by the hour.[11]

Ebenezer accepted with equanimity Daniel's lack of interest in farming. Indeed, he hoped his son would get the kind of education he had missed. In the beginning it was a matter of sending the boy to a town school, which for a brief time each winter haphazardly exposed pupils to rudiments of learning. Better progress came independently. His mother taught him to read when he was quite young, with the Bible usually serving as text. And Ebenezer and others started a circulating library offering a few staples which the youngster reread until he could repeat long passages from memory. Daniel's favorites were Addison's *Spectator*, Pope's *Essay on Man*, Cervantes' *Don Quixote*, and especially Watt's psalms and hymns. A standby was the latest almanac giving all sorts of information.[12]

When he was fourteen, in the spring of 1796, his father decided he must move on to a school of higher quality, to Phillips Academy. So they mounted horses and rode east to Exeter, located between Kingston and Portsmouth. Already the academy had gained a good reputation, mainly because of the expert leadership of Benjamin Abbott, then in the early phase of a fifty-year tenure as principal. Abbott and a tutor handled the instruction of some ninety boys, over half from New Hampshire and many headed for college. Daniel's primitive manners, homespun clothing, and self-doubts did not prevent his performing well in his studies from May to December, which was the extent of his stay at Exeter. His work was mainly in English grammar, writing, and arithmetic, with a bare beginning in Latin and a frightening introduction to declamation. Strange to say, he showed little promise of becoming an orator. But he was deeply thankful for encouragement from the twelve-year-old-tutor, Joseph Stevens Buckminster, who, though two years younger than his pupil, handled the situation deftly. Other students at the academy were Lewis Cass and two boys who would be college classmates, Joseph Brackett and James Hervey Bingham.[13]

Daniel had to return home in December 1796 to earn some money by teaching in the district school for a couple of months. Then his father arranged for Samuel Wood, the minister in Boscawen, a few miles south on the Concord Road, to prepare Daniel further for college. Under Wood's supervision, he concentrated upon Vergil and Cicero to improve his Latin and scouted Greek hesitantly. After six months the kindly Wood felt sufficiently satisfied to write a strong recommendation for his admission to college, stronger, no doubt, than his fifteen-year-old charge had earned.[14]

Naturally, the college was Dartmouth. In August 1797 he rode over to Hanover to begin four years of study that would profoundly affect his future. The little village was situated on a plain elevated from the banks of the Connecticut River to the west and surrounded by hills and pine forests in other directions. Reflecting the original reason for its settlement in the 1760s, all aspects of life in the town continued to focus upon the presence of the college. At the center was the green, a large quadrangle with college buildings, some houses, a tavern, and a few stores on the perimeter. On the eastern edge was Dartmouth Hall, a white, three-story structure with a Georgian flavor and a bright dome. Here many students had dormitory rooms and attended recitations in classrooms crudely equipped with stoves and wooden benches. Alongside this hall was an unimposing chapel, and next in line to the south was the president's house. This was the extent of the campus.[15]

When Daniel arrived, commencement week activities were in progress. His first step was to appear before faculty members in a cursory examination for admission. One examiner was Bezaleel Woodward, son-in-law of the founding president, Eleazar Wheelock, and professor of mathematics and natural philosophy, though his more important responsibility, it seemed, was to carry out the duties of treasurer. Another examiner was John Smith, a shy scholar burdened with an unbelievable range of assignments: professor of Greek, Latin, and Hebrew; librarian; acting professor of theology; and minister of the church.[16]

At the head of this modest faculty was John Wheelock. At forty-three, he was in his eighteenth year as president. His father had established a wilderness college in 1769, with help from English donors, from the province of New Hampshire, and occasionally thereafter from local and state sources. In the beginning, the purpose had been to conduct a school for instructing Indian youth, but soon that mission had virtually disappeared. As his father had done before him, but with a heavier hand, John Wheelock ran the college like a petty monarchy. The faculty, students, and even the board of trustees knew him to be a strict disciplinarian, deciding all questions large and small according to his own lights. A tall, stately figure, he dressed in smallclothes and three-cornered hat; and the most striking feature of his somber face was an extraordinarily long nose—a perfect quadrant, it was remarked. From daybreak, when he read prayers in the bleak, unheated chapel, until evening, when he appeared in a student's room to enforce one of the myriad rules of behavior, he was, if nothing else, very industrious. The principal difficulty was that he lacked the desired intellect; yet he handled all instruction of the senior class, whether in moral philosophy, natural law, or history. Behind his back the young men of Dartmouth ridiculed his meaningless prayers and speeches, malapropisms, and strange falsetto voice.[17]

There were less than a hundred and fifty students altogether, mostly New Englanders, and more from New Hampshire than from any other state. Webster's class of 1801 graduated thirty, a little below the average at the time.[18] Despite a self-consciousness due to his rustic background, he was more typical of the student body than he first realized. Almost everyone entered with minimal academic preparation and had trouble paying bills, including a little over a dollar a week to a boardinghouse for food and twenty-five or thirty a year for tuition and room. Much as others did, Webster ran up a sizable debt by his senior year. Socially, he gained confidence and polish along with the rest. He cultivated friendships easily and valued them greatly.[19] Among his special friends were Samuel Bradley, George Herbert, and Weld Fuller, all with similar interests and all later to become successful lawyers. Then there was Thomas Merrill, the highest-ranking student in the college, who would have a long career as a clergyman in Middlebury, Vermont. When Webster arrived he found two whom he already knew: Joseph Brackett and Hervey Bingham, both from Phillips Exeter. Bingham became his closest friend and would maintain lifelong contact with him.

Webster's course of study was narrow, rigid, and rather superficial. It consisted preponderantly of Latin and Greek, with less attention to mathematics, English, and science. In his senior year, under Wheelock's tutelage, he would deal with a variety of philosophical and political topics as treated by a few respected authors. Though generally conscientious in his courses, he progressed much further in Latin, English literature, and politics than in Greek and mathematics. His entire class attended the same recitations from early morning to late afternoon, found it necessary to memorize and accept what authorities laid down, seldom dared to venture independent judgments. To some extent, he compensated for defects in the system by his individual reading, which was substantial; but his choices were quite limited because of the inferior quality of the college library. Indeed, like some of his classmates, he depended chiefly on the better library of the literary society to which he belonged, the United Fraternity; others drew from the rival society, the Social Friends.[20] These organizations were also a valuable feature of academic life because of their emphasis upon declamation. Speeches and debates provided the main activities of the societies; and so-called oratorical exhibitions were highlights of college courses and exercises. He soon developed his extraordinary talent for oratory and was acknowledged by everyone to be the best speaker in the college. If the intellectual results of four years at Dartmouth were unspectacular, he and his fellow students were still intensely interested in recognition, particularly in their class standing. He graduated near the top of his class and was elected to Phi Beta Kappa.[21]

In his junior year he began contributing many poems and essays to the *Dartmouth Gazette,* a Hanover newspaper founded by young Moses Davis. "Should you think the productions of my puerile pen worthy a place in your new 'vehicle of Knowledge,' you may depend on a number weekly," Webster assured the editor.[22] Fulfilling his pledge to "range the whole field of nature," he published essays on hope, fear, charity, deception, the horrors of war, Napoleon, and so forth, all signed with the pen name Icarus. He interspersed his prose with poems and such themes as winter and spring, none of which showed unusual aptitude in that branch of literature. In any case, he continued writing for the *Gazette* for several years, even after graduation. And at one period he took charge of the paper during Davis' extended absence. At least there was a financial reward, enough to pay one year's expenses.[23]

Weaknesses are apparent also in the surviving texts of his orations, drafted before delivery but put aside when he spoke. They, too, tended to be extravagant and florid. Yet when one allows for his age (eighteen or nineteen), and for contemporary rhetorical patterns, these efforts reveal the qualities of conceptualization and expression that would one day make him the greatest orator of his era. He had opportunities to strengthen his skills by giving numerous speeches to the United Fraternity and by judging those presented by other members. An example is his short oration on ambition delivered in October 1800. It is the "grand nerve of human exertion," he said, producing both good and evil. The achievements of Cromwell, Chatham, and Caesar sprang from ambition; but in contrast to the pure-hearted Washington, they did not al-

7

ways keep their ambitions subservient to integrity. An interesting theme, if pretentiously constructed.[24] As he gained experience, he would learn the value of directness and simplicity.

Each year, student oratory reached its zenith during commencement week in late August. Among his class of 1801, it was natural for Webster to expect a major assignment, probably the valedictory, since the leading scholar, Merrill, would have the salutatory. It had been the custom for the students to select the person to give the valedictory; but a controversy had arisen between the societies on this matter, and the faculty had taken over the power to decide. Discontented with the rule, the United Fraternity decided not to participate in the main commencement exercise. And Webster, failing to get the role he wished, followed his friends and declined a minor part. As usual, the two societies held their own ceremonies earlier in the week, so that Webster at least had a chance to speak before the Fraternity.[25]

The manuscript of his oration is extant and provides the best specimen of his rhetoric thus far in his life. He discussed the importance of opinion in human affairs, in philosophy, education, politics, religion. Though still unsophisticated and overdrawn, the address must have strongly moved his auditors as they were about to leave their alma mater. He charged the seniors to emulate those outstanding alumni then serving God and country to their capacity. They must beware of fashions in opinion with deplorable tendencies, he warned. Critical of modern philosophers such as Hume, he recommended Plato instead. Innovators in various fields, captivated by passing fads, were dangerous because of the impracticality of their ideas. In this category he included Mary Wollstonecraft because of her unworkable notions on women's rights. It was better to energize opinion in the proper direction. As for religion, Webster espoused the old doctrines, not novelties that might win popularity. "The existence of God," he asserted, "and some other propositions are as clearly demonstrable as any theorem in Euclid."[26] On this subject he had more to say the next day, when he delivered a highly sentimental eulogy on his classmate Ephraim Simonds, who had died that spring. The comfort of all men as they contemplated tragedy and death must be their religious faith, tried and true, he concluded.[27] Basically, the mind of the young graduate from Salisbury was sober and conservative.

Some months before Daniel departed from Hanover in August 1801 with diploma in hand, his brother Ezekiel had matriculated there. Though he was two years older, Ezekiel had not at first expected to go to college, for their father needed help on the farm. Being the only son at home and better suited physically for this labor than Daniel, he had had little education. But during a visit to the Elms in the spring of 1799, Daniel had convinced Ezekiel that he, too, ought to go to Dartmouth and had then persuaded his parents to that view. So Ezekiel had attended the local academy and, like his brother, had been prepared for college by Samuel Wood.[28]

Though Daniel began studying law in Salisbury after graduation, within a few months he had to teach school for a time to raise money for Ezekiel's expenses. During his time as a college student Ezekiel was hard pressed, spending half of each year as schoolmaster, first near home and then in Boston. Since even this did not bring in enough, Daniel, too, scratched for whatever he could. Once he wrote that the family had had a conference, found they could not raise any cash, but perhaps could send Ezekiel two cents next week to buy a pipe and become philosophical about his straits.[29] "Money, Daniel, money," exclaimed the worried student. "As I was walking down to the office after a letter, I happened to find one cent, which is the only money I have had since the second day after I came on. It is a fact, Dan, that I was called on for a dollar, where I owed it, and borrowed it, and have borrowed it four times since, to pay those I borrowed of."[30] The Websters would be in a dense financial thicket until Ezekiel completed his three-year legal apprenticeship in 1807.

To assist Ezekiel, from January to September 1802 Daniel taught at the academy in Fryeburg, Maine, a village just across the New Hampshire line in the White Mountain region. The eight months he spent there were pleasant and moderately rewarding financially.[31] Added to the compensation for teaching were a few dollars he earned each month by copying deeds for his landlord, James Osgood, the county register. It was tedious work over many long evenings—he later remarked that "the ache is not yet out of my fingers."[32] But there were enjoyable moments because of a circle of good friends, particularly his fellow boarder, Jacob McGaw, also a Dartmouth graduate and a former law student with Thomas Thompson at Salisbury. This relationship with McGaw was close. They would ride their spirited horses the dozen miles to Conway or play cribbage for hours after dinner and exchange humorous stories as well as serious-minded speculations about the future.[33] Though he made a desultory effort to continue reading law, more often he picked up a book at the circulating library for amusement or general instruction. In September he felt he must refuse an offer from the trustees of the academy for reappointment at a higher salary and return home to prepare full-time for a career as a lawyer.

For the next two years, until mid-1804, he lived with his parents at the Elms and walked down the road each day to Thompson's law office for seemingly endless encounters with legal treatises and the dull routine of a country lawyer. His father, now in failing health, was thankful to have him there. Ebenezer continued to farm and to serve as a lay judge in the county court; and though constantly troubled with debts, he insisted that Daniel persist in his training.[34] There were four sisters and a brother at home or in the neighborhood. Among them, Sally best understood his moods and aspirations because, as the two youngest children, they had been together so much while growing up. Another sister of whom he was fond was Nabby, living with her family in the nearby tavern house.[35]

To relieve the tedium he depended not only upon relatives but also upon former classmates now scattered throughout New England. In fact he felt a compulsion to maintain intimate connections with them. His letters to Bingham, Fuller, Merrill, and several others relayed the latest gossip and unhurriedly rambled through a maze of trivia that amounted to little more than filling the pages. Through the lighthearted banter and self-deprecation, however, his friends could see his impatience, anxieties, ambitions.[36] An indicator of this comradeship was his habit of returning to Hanover whenever possible. Once or more each year, nearly always at August commencement, he rode over to visit with those graduates whom he could persuade to join him. For a while, Ezekiel was a student and provided a special reason for a homecoming; and a further attraction was the presence of his classmate Tommy Merrill, who had stayed on as a tutor. Besides these periodic reunions, he enjoyed getting acquainted with the younger men currently in residence; it was on such occasions that he improved his friendship with the precocious George Ticknor.[37] The best visit was the one in the summer of 1806, when he delivered an enthusiastically received address before the Phi Beta Kappa Society.[38]

If he could not look to his family and friends to make life interesting, he drew upon his own resources by turning to literary pursuits. Since his student days he had had a powerful motive to read, chiefly English authors, some Latin classics, very few American writings except those of a political character. But regularly he tried his own hand, amateurish though it was, at poetry and prose. He wrote poetry, he said, "not from any wish to show my productions to the world, but for amusement, and to keep alive some taste for the *Belles lettres*. The Law is certainly, as it seems to me, rather hard study, & to mollify it with some literary amusements I should think profitable."[39] Often his object was to compose a piece as a communication to a friend, sometimes to help himself develop an idea or express his feelings. Like many young men of the day, he might select a romantic theme, with allusions to women. Yet the topics were various: Jeffersonian politics, the Napoleonic wars, philosophy, nature, and human behavior in general. During his time in Fryeburg he composed a number of essays and verses, entitled "Sports of Pequawket." Although they remained justifiably unpublished, they reveal something about their fearless author. A short poem about a lady who made a purse for him in return for some rhymes ended: "Pope wrote for bags of glittering gold, I, for an *empty* purse." A long essay entitled "Women," laden with quotations, metaphors, and satirical comment, closed with the comment, "The common adage is 'fruit that falls without shaking is too ripe.' "[40] Yet some items did appear in print, such as "The News Boy's Message to the Patrons of the *Dartmouth Gazette,* January 1, 1803," written for his editorial friend, Moses Davis. Here he emphasized the alarmingly radical tendencies of President Jefferson and his colleagues. [41] Several pieces went to Peter Thacher's *Monthly Anthology* in Boston, mostly review essays showing a respectable acquaintance with things cultural and pleading for American literary progress.[42]

When he could not follow his sociable inclinations or amuse himself with literature, he enjoyed a foray outdoors to fish, shoot, or ride, often alone. Beyond the recreation of these solitary expeditions, he liked "to contemplate nature, & to hold communion, unbroken by the presence of human beings, with 'this universal frame, thus wondrous fair.' " Then one could think, truly know oneself, decide what to do about some specific task, or chart a course for the years ahead.[43] This early habit, though not dominating his behavior, proved to be a permanent characteristic.

Though acknowledging the pleasure of solitude, he could not accept a bachelor's life as ideal. He had a keen interest in marriage, and the sooner the better. In his chatty letters to former classmates, he dwelt upon the subject, albeit in a humorous vein, to an extent that made it appear a primary concern. While a student at Hanover, he found competition for the scarce females of that village to be formidable; but during the months of schoolteaching in Fryeburg, the ratio was more favorable. He broke the monotony of an instructor's duties by rides into the countryside and by evenings of dancing and backgammon with various young women, some of them his students at the academy.[44] Afterward, when he returned to the law, his search for female companionship and a marriage partner did not flag, though he remained single. Fortunately he did not usually take the whole matter too seriously and could always resort to the self-therapy of poetry. Thus after a woman he knew cut her foot and could not attend a dancing party, he wrote:

> But Clara, Clara! were thy heart
> As tender as thy *pedal* part;
> From thy sweet lips did love but flow,
> Swift as blood gushes from *thy toe*,
> So many Beaus would not complain
> That all their bows & vows were vain![45]

Nor did he have any principles against stooping for a pun. As for a certain Miss Paine, "She might perhaps write her name upon my heart as fairly as I can write it upon paper. Yet that would not be a singular case, for there has been many a lover before me, who has had Pain in his heart."[46]

His surviving correspondence is uninformative about the identity of women to whom he was attracted. Friends who received his letters referring to them by one or more initials of course knew whom he had in mind, but curious historians remain frustrated. About the only exception is Mary, daughter of Professor Bezaleel Woodward of Dartmouth. Long after his student days Webster remained interested in her but knew that a number of others were too.[47] To Merrill, still a college tutor and possibly a rival, he once remarked upon the desirability of visiting the "Queen of Hearts"; but eventually he realized that someone else would win Mary's hand, and that is what happened.[48]

Within a year after graduation, in the Fryeburg period, he confided to Hervey Bingham that he contemplated setting his "bachelor friends a laudable example," which was shorthand for an intention to marry. Who the prospective bride was is unknown, but in any case he did not take her to the altar.[49] And it was

> For those blest fields, where Love's gay Graces reign
> I once have tried, and tried, Alas! in vain![50]

As the months and years passed, a single existence seemed to be his destiny. So he thought when he was twenty-two.[51] And at twenty-four he complained to Bingham, "The example of my friends sometimes excites me, and certain narratives I hear of you, induce me to inquire why the deuce female flesh and blood was not made for me as well as others; but reasons, good or bad, suppress hope and stifle incipient resolution."[52]

His thoughts about marriage were merely part of his general state of mind concerning the future. Impatient with the delay in entering his chosen profession, indeed not altogether sure he should have chosen it, undecided where he should locate permanently, filled with a mixture of doubts and ardent ambition, he was given to somewhat discomforting

12

introspective moods. Outwardly he professed only modest hopes of what his fate would be, but in the very statement of them he implied they were a great deal higher. It would be his aim, he said, to attain a local respectability, to earn enough to be reasonably secure, and to find happiness among his friends. Perhaps settling in Cheshire County over on the Connecticut in company with Bingham would be just right—still, it might be better to move on to Portsmouth or even Boston, where one could get ahead more rapidly.[53] "Depend on it, however, James, that I shall sometime avail myself of more advantages than this smoky village affords," he promised.[54]

The apprenticeship with Thompson, from August 1801 to July 1804 except for his eight months of schoolteaching in Fryeburg, introduced him to the law but hardly promised to make him a great lawyer. Thompson was a fairly well-equipped practitioner; yet like others who had apprentices, he paid little attention to their instruction. Mainly, Webster was left alone to confront an array of books on the office shelves when he was not performing some clerical task. It was easy enough, and more interesting too, to pick up a volume of history or literature instead and on a pleasant day to persuade fellow students Daniel Abbott and Parker Noyes to join him for a few hours of fishing or hunting. Nevertheless, he moved resolutely through such staples as Vattel's *Law of Nations*, Bacon's *Pleas and Pleadings*, and especially Blackstone's *Commentaries*. When he first encountered Coke's intricacies on the common law, he despaired. Legal study ought to be more practical, he concluded, and so Espinasse's *Nisi Prius* seemed a more profitable guide to handling daily problems of the profession.[55]

The fact was he had continuing reservations about the law. As for the materials with which he struggled, he found not a "single author who pretends to elegance of style or sweetness of observation. The language of the law is dry, hard, stubborn as an old maid. Murdered Latin bleeds through every page." Not only this, there was also a question of moral standards, for too often lawyers seemed to sacrifice all other considerations in order to make money. And pressed as he and his family were, he felt he himself was pursuing his present goal chiefly for financial reasons. To do so could compromise one's integrity, for temptations abounded. After all, "the business of an office is conducted with the very refuse and remnant of mankind."[56] Fortunately, when he became depressed he found relief in his sense of humor. "Heigho!" he wrote Bingham. "A man wants a remedy against his neighbor, whose lips were found damage feasant on his, the plaintiff's wife's cheek! What is to be done? But you have not read the law about kissing."[57]

As he neared the end of his required three-year period of study, he saw

13

the desirability of leaving Salisbury for a place better suited to completing his preparation. In early 1804 that place seemed to be Boston. One powerful attraction was Ezekiel's presence there as teacher in a small private school, a position Webster had obtained for him by arrangement with their college friend Cyrus Perkins.[58] Letters from Ezekiel poured forth praise of the city, "a world in miniature and a world alive, resounding with the 'busy hum of men.' " It was truly the "focus of information," said Ezekiel, the perfect spot for Daniel to learn what he needed to know; furthermore, he could help with the schoolteaching and earn a little cash.[59] Consult father and your friends, Zeke advised, and then "decamp immediately with all your baggage, from Salisbury, and march directly to this place."[60]

In mid-July Webster did decamp and went to Boston in search of an accomplished lawyer who might take him on as a clerk. The outcome was even better than he had dared to hope. Christopher Gore, a distinguished attorney and diplomat, had recently returned from an extended mission to England concerning the Jay Treaty, and perhaps for this reason found room for the brash young man from the New Hampshire hills who entered his office on Tremont Street on a summer's day. His friend Samuel Bradley, who accompanied him but also did not know Gore, boldly introduced himself and then Webster to the Federalist aristocrat. Without delay he began work and felt entirely pleased with a situation providing valuable training by a man of such eminence.[61] Whether this opportunity resulted from sheer luck or from help by Thompson is uncertain, but his Salisbury sponsor had recommended him through an intermediary. Gore probably had known more about him than he realized.[62]

During the fall and winter of 1804 he concentrated upon his professional development as he never had before. With some regularity he kept a journal of what he read, observed, and thought. He continued to study the common law—Coke, Viner, and other commentators, as well as such reports of cases as were available, for example those of Saunders—but now, no doubt because of Gore's expertise, he spent many hours with volumes on international law and maritime law. As he progressed he made notes, set forth propositions, raised queries, all reflecting a highly serious purpose. Often he went into the state and federal courts sitting in Boston, where he briefed the cases he heard and was fascinated by arguments of counsel. Theophilus Parsons and Samuel Dexter, the most prominent members of the bar, impressed him so much that he returned to his journal in the evening to sketch their special qualities.[63] An enlarged view of the legal profession moderated his severe opinions about it. Of course, his admiration of Gore, "a deep and various scholar," had a good deal to do with this shift in his thinking. "He has great amenity of manners," Webster remarked, "is easy, accessible, and communicative, and take him all in all, I could not wish a better preceptor."[64] Still, the overriding consideration was material rather than intellectual. In this respect, too, he now felt he was going in the right direction, for though lawyers hardly ever acquired as much wealth as merchants, their income was steadier, less subject to the oscillations characteristic of the business world. And outstanding attorneys such as Gore and Parsons (whose reputed earnings he recorded in his journal) fared well indeed.[65]

Though absorbed in his labors at the office, he was not oblivious of the city about him. He found time to develop a number of friendships within a few months. With the help of Gore, he became acquainted with some established families in Boston and tended to prefer their company to that of recent arrivals, whose every move seemed calculated for self-advancement.[66] As it turned out, the two persons with whom he would have closest connections in later life were then mere boys. One, ten-year-old Edward Everett, was a pupil in Ezekiel's school on Short Street; and for a week, while his brother was out of town, Webster took over instruction of this prodigy. The other youth was George Ticknor, whom Ezekiel was tutoring in Greek as preparation for Dartmouth.[67] A friend at Webster's boardinghouse, wealthy and eccentric Taylor Baldwin, provided him with the most exciting experience, a trip through the Berkshires to Albany and Saratoga in November. What he saw in these parts interested him very much: the stately homes of aristocrats, the crowded sections of the New York capital, occupied by people of various ethnic backgrounds, the fashionable visitors at the springs, taking the medicinal waters and displaying their affluence as they relaxed. All quite different from rural New Hampshire.[68]

In anticipation of finishing his study, he continued to think about the nagging question of where to settle. Though several possibilities were attractive—Portsmouth, the Connecticut Valley, Concord, even Boston—there were strong reasons to return to Salisbury, the strongest being the responsibility he felt to be near his parents. But could an enterprising young man make enough money there? Perhaps so, if he could get an appointment as clerk of the Hillsborough County Court of Common Pleas, for this would pay fifteen hundred dollars a year. The previous summer, just before he came to Boston, his father, a lay judge of the court, had begun trying to obtain the post for him; and Webster himself had let the chief judge, Timothy Farrar, know that he was interested.[69]

15

Finally, in January 1805 his mail brought an offer of the appointment. When he proudly told Gore of his good fortune, he was surprised by an unenthusiastic reaction. Gore declared that of course he must decline. He must aim for a higher station, the older man insisted, something better than recording the words and actions of others. He must practice law himself, exploit the unusual ability and training he had. Persuaded, but embarrassed by the circumstances, Webster hurried to the Elms to tell his father he had changed his mind. Ebenezer accepted the decision more calmly than his son had expected, despite tempting visions of a clerk's salary.[70]

Meanwhile Webster impatiently awaited the end of his apprenticeship. As early as November he had asked Thompson to certify that he had spent the necessary three-year time of preparation.[71] And to Judah Dana in Fryeburg he had written an apologetic request for a letter saying he had read law in Dana's office while he taught at the academy.[72] From both he promptly received what he wished.[73] Then Gore, with these papers on hand, petitioned the court in Boston to waive the extra year required in Massachusetts of all those who were not Harvard graduates. In March 1805 it was done. Webster gained admission to the bar, then immediately left the city for home.[74]

He still felt he must live near his family and, for the time being, resisted an inclination to go to Portsmouth. Six miles south of the Elms on the Concord Road was the village of Boscawen, claiming a population of fourteen hundred but aspiring to greater importance; and here he decided to open his first law office. Timothy Dix, a merchant there, agreed to add a room to his house for the purpose, so that Webster soon had "a shop," he remarked, "for the manufacture of justice writs."[75] Sometimes he also slept there on a cot behind his desk. At first the new attorney's place must not have impressed his clients much, for the walls were bare where ordinarily they might have expected shelves of books to assure them that legal lore would be handy to help their cases. As a matter of fact, Webster had sent eighty-five dollars to Boston by way of a friend to buy books, only to learn that his messenger had lost the money. A flurry of correspondence with Ezekiel, still in the city, at last brought the arrival of a few volumes, most of them on credit.[76]

Much of his business was petty, uninspiring, and not very profitable. Typical of that time and place, it consisted largely of debt-collection cases in the court of common pleas. Having arrangements with some mercantile and banking firms in Boston and Portsmouth, he acted as local agent to keep pressure on defaulters, one of whom regrettably was his landlord, Dix, and to sue when necessary. Yet he also represented debtors, as when Dix sought to extricate himself from financial difficulty by suing his own debtors. Dependent upon a fairly loose credit system, this preindustrial society used legal proceedings to make the system work; but they were often an informal variation on the strict law. Though this kind of practice could pose ethical questions and might also create hostility toward the young attorney, he managed very well. People expected the law to operate the way it did. Overall, his success rate in court was high, even for clients who were debtors, for he was enterprising and well grounded in the common-law principles underlying the more than 260 cases he had over a two-year period in his Boscawen office. He felt much of his activity was mere money catching, however, a routine he could not tolerate indefinitely.[77]

Traveling the circuit in several counties, he followed a pattern characterizing the profession in early America: uncomfortable travel over poor roads in bad weather as well as good, many nights in crowded and filthy inns, inadequate time and resources to prepare for whatever cases came up on the docket. To be sure, there were interesting highlights when on court day a town would fill with people from the countryside to hear an oratorical display by these legal gladiators. Such was true in one of Webster's cases on a murder charge. Defending the accused, Josiah Burnham, he made an unusual if unsuccessful effort, even arguing against the inherent justice of the death penalty.[78] He was gaining a reputation as the most promising lawyer in the area; yet his annual income amounted to only a few hundred dollars. Whether he could continue in those circumstances seemed doubtful. At least a consolation was that if he had to move, "the disagreeable incumbrances of houses, lands, and property need not delay me for a moment. Nor shall I be hindered by love, nor fastened to Boscawen by the power of beauty."[79]

Still, he did not confine his thoughts only to moving ahead in his legal practice, for he had a growing interest in politics. Indeed this had been true ever since his student days at Dartmouth. As a sophomore, he had taken the lead in organizing the Federal Club to gather published materials on political questions and to discuss them, naturally from the perspective the club's name announced.[80] And there were opportunities to express his views to a wider audience when he was called upon to give orations. An early instance was his address on the Fourth of July of 1800 in Hanover; and nearly every year, it seems he spoke someplace on Independence Day—at Fryeburg in 1802, at Salisbury in 1803 and 1805, at Concord in 1806. Though florid and ultrapatriotic, these speeches revealed a good deal about his opinions. Equally revealing were the numerous pieces he published in newspapers, periodicals, and pamphlets.

Davis, editor of the *Dartmouth Gazette,* often included Webster's comments and poetry of a political complexion in his paper, among which the "News Boy's Message" of January 1, 1803, was as bold and ambitious as any. While studying law with Gore in Boston, he contributed political items to the newspapers there.[81] Later he began writing review essays for the *Monthly Anthology,* one of which, in October 1806, focused upon and wholly approved the controversial Sedition Act of 1798.[82] A Fourth of July address and a lively campaign tract of 1805 were also published as pamphlets. By this time he had become fairly active in state and local politics.

He was a wholehearted Federalist. He belonged, he said, to the Washington school of politics, which meant approval of the Hamiltonian system and unqualified support of President Adams in the late nineties. If he had to choose between Hamilton and Adams, as many did when the two disagreed on foreign policy or quarreled personally, he would go for Adams as the upholder of Washington's principles.[83] An outright partisan, he saw nothing in Jeffersonianism that was safe and satisfactory. He deplored the Virginian's election as a triumph of unstable democracy, atheism, and Jacobinism, all to be countered with utmost vigor.[84] Though a committed Federalist enlisting for war against Republicans, he looked upon parties in a general sense much as others of the time did, as dangerous factions to be eliminated for the survival of the republic. If not, the day would come "when the banner of civil war shall be unfurled; when Discord's hydra form shall set up her hideous yell, and from her hundred mouths shall howl destruction through our empire; and when American blood shall be made to flow in rivers, by American swords!"[85]

Central to his political faith was an intense patriotism. In his Fourth of July speeches he gave it full play, expounding a nationalism that must be the foundation of American growth and prosperity. His expository vehicle was historical: contributions of sturdy settlers in the colonies, glorious achievements of Revolutionary heroes, wisdom and foresight of framers of the Constitution, constructive policies of Federalist administrations, each a part of the present generation's precious heritage. And for each he employed ideological symbols already familiar to his fellow countrymen. Thus the Declaration of Independence and the Constitution were not only great documents of government but also sacred testaments of the nation. They united the people and charted their future progress; they inspired as well as instructed. No personality better symbolized American values and expectations than Washington, the father of his country, intrepid and skillful general of the Revolutionary War, indispensable leader during the formative years under the Constitution. Neither a monarch nor a god, the first president filled their places to some extent in a republican society.[86] Finally, this brand of patriotism rested upon the belief that the United States and Europe stood in contrast to one another. In his first Independence Day oration, at Dartmouth in 1800, he developed this theme, which he and his contemporaries would often reiterate. Behold ancient Europe, he said, burdened by oppressive institutions and now mortally imperiled by French aggression sweeping across the continent. In contrast, young America lived in peace, enjoyed a free system of government, steadily became more prosperous, flourished as science and education advanced. Such a nationalistic credo had its uses for a young man like Webster.[87]

Despite his youth, he never once inclined toward ideas of abrupt change from established political truths as he understood them. He was an unwavering conservative, opposed to extremes whether of left or right. If he classified his position, he called it republican, with a small *r* and not to be confused with the title claimed by these Jeffersonian radical democrats. When Jefferson came to power in 1801, Webster was only nineteen but had the same kind of worries about trends that an older, disillusioned person might have had. In the next few years he found no cause to be more sanguine. The ascendant party was pushing the nation toward despotism and ruin through a deceitful, false appeal to popular rule, "through the mire and dirt of uncontrolled democracy."[88] As he wrote in the "News Boy's Message,"

> Democracy is a true Fury,
> Whose snaky hair and savage yell,
> Bespeak *Alecto* fresh from Hell.[89]

Tyranny, he felt, could come from that quarter quite as easily as from an arbitrary monarchy such as threatened America on the eve of the Revolution.

Republicanism, correctly practiced, therefore demanded preservation of much of the existing order. Thus the Constitution, which he deemed threatened by this Virginia Jacobin, must not be destroyed by piecemeal alteration, for it was the palladium of American liberty. To protect it, America must hold to a virtuous course, to a strict morality that would ensure civic responsibility.[90] And he did not doubt for a moment that virtue, in turn, depended absolutely upon religion. "The altar of our freedom," he declared, "should be placed near the altar of our religion. Thus shall the same Almighty Power who protects his own worship, protect also our liberties."[91] An atheistic president could not subscribe to this maxim. It was a matter, as Hamilton had said, of entrusting power to the wise and the good, which to Webster meant following Federalist leadership. That party, he thought, "unites in its support more than two thirds of the talent, the character, and the property of the nation."[92]

He was eager to help the Federalist cause. Beginning in his student days at Dartmouth, through the period of studying law, and during the first phase of his career as lawyer, he moved into party politics with enthusiasm. In New Hampshire there were frequent elections for governor and legislature, congressmen, and the presidency, not to mention town contests, so that the politically minded had plenty to do and to talk about. His correspondence was full of plans and comment about unceasing party rivalry. An important spur to this activity was the improving fortunes of the Republicans in a state that had long been Federalist territory. In 1804 the Jeffersonians won the presidential contest and elected a majority in the legislature—in fact they nearly captured the governorship.[93] Thomas Thompson did gain a seat in Congress, however, and later from Washington exchanged information and views with his former student about political conditions at the national capital and back home.[94]

The impending annual election of a governor in March 1805 stimulated both parties to even greater exertions. In January while Webster was home from Boston on a brief visit, he complied with his friends' request to write a pamphlet in behalf of the Federalist candidate John Gilman, challenged, as usual, by the Republican John Langdon. Entitled "Appeal to the Old Whigs," it was an outright diatribe against Langdon, depicted as driven by ambition and base factionalism. To prove his argument, Webster connected the gubernatorial aspirant with Republicanism in general, with Jefferson's administration of the past four years. Langdon, he asserted, resembled his party associates not only in opposing the adoption of the Constitution but in undermining it afterward. The specific charges against Republicans included obstructionist opposition to Washington's sound policies, later unwarranted attacks upon the federal judiciary (including the current impeachment trial of Justice Samuel Chase), and such ill-advised measures as repeal of internal taxes, reduction of the nation's naval forces, and ratification of the Twelfth Amendment to the Constitution to perpetuate a Virginia dynasty in the executive office. In New Hampshire, he concluded, good citizens could help avert catastrophe by casting Federalist ballots. If they did not, the pamphleteer hoped that the republic would not collapse, at least not until the Revolutionary fathers had gone to their graves and "could no longer reproach the apostasy of their sons."[95] In

March not enough voters sensed the danger, and Langdon won the governor's chair. Disappointed though he was, Webster felt proud of his role in that election and believed New Hampshire to be a suitable base for a young lawyer-politician. He would remain in the Merrimack Valley for the time being.

Chapter 2
PORTSMOUTH

The rustic village of Boscawen offered the restless young lawyer neither social nor professional advantages. Less than two years after setting up practice, he was thinking of moving. "A little money might be made there," he later recalled, "but no pleasure, of a social sort enjoyed." Presently Ezekiel gained admission to the bar and could assume responsibility to assist the family. So in 1807 Webster turned over his law office and interest in the farm to his brother, who would be much more content in handling both than he had ever been. In September the arrangement was complete, though they continued to collaborate in legal business and had a close, flexible financial relationship, usually, it appears, to the advantage of the always out-of-pocket Daniel.[1]

A logical place in which to relocate was Portsmouth, the focal point of business activity in the state. It was here that the sign of a new attorney appeared one day at the window of a modest office over Wilkins' dry-goods store. Webster's friend Nathaniel Adams, the clerk of the New Hampshire supreme court had found the space for him and had even reserved a room in a near y boardinghouse to encourage him to come. As further help, Adams identified some clients with cases in his court.[2]

Portsmouth was one of New England's most active seaports. In the 1620s settlers had sailed up the estuary of the Piscataqua River and landed at a point where wild strawberries spread along the south bank. At first appropriately named Strawbery Banke and then Portsmouth because of the breadth of its harbor, the town flourished in the next two centuries as its commerce rivaled that of Salem and Newburyport, if not of Boston itself. When Webster moved there, wharves and warehouses lined the waterfront, and everywhere there was evidence of mercantile energy. Daily, two or three ships arrived with cargoes of tea, rum, broadcloth, calico, silk, and a variety of other goods for auction sales and distribution into the agricultural interior.

Despite removal of the capital to Concord, Portsmouth remained pre-eminent in New Hampshire politics and society. Like other towns in early America, it suffered from a perennial urban lag—muddy and filthy streets, rowdyism, burglaries, assaults, inadequate or nonexistent fire and police protection. Nonetheless, there were many pleasing features. Around Market Square among the shops were churches, an athenaeum, and the Assembly House. Facing the tree-lined streets were handsome mansions of Georgian architecture with gambrel roofs. Inside these homes of retired sea captains, wealthy merchants, and the current generation of prominent families, one could admire luxurious furnishings, expensive art objects, ornate wood carving, and a general flavor of elegance and social grace.[3]

A widening circle of friends enriched Webster's life in Portsmouth. The closest of these was Jeremiah Mason, whom he had known for some time on the circuit. A huge, stoop-shouldered figure, Mason was fourteen years older than Webster and already ranked at the head of the New Hampshire bar. His homespun appearance, simplicity of habits and speech, and unaffected manners at first impression concealed his well-cultivated mind and aristocratic tendencies. After graduation from Yale and a short period of country practice, this Connecticut Yankee had come to Portsmouth. He now lived in an imposing house with an attractive garden, had a substantial income in a commercial town that generated an endless amount of litigation, and commanded respect for his ability and integrity. Webster often said that all things considered, Mason was the best lawyer he ever knew. Politically, the two men thought alike: both were committed Federalists, vocal critics of Jeffersonian trends, reliable friends of the business interests for which they spoke and acted.[4]

Another close friend was Joseph Buckminster, pastor of the Old North Church and father of his onetime tutor in the academy at Exeter, Joseph Stevens Buckminster. From the time that the elder Buckminster introduced him to the congregation on a September morning, Webster enjoyed very amicable relations with the minister and his family. To strengthen his somewhat frail constitution, he could be found sawing wood with Buckminster in the morning before breakfast; and in the evenings he often visited his friend's home for conversation and relaxation. The member of the family who most admired him was undoubtedly Buckminster's daughter, Eliza, who would be an unfailing friend in the years ahead.[5]

Old associations continued as new ones developed. He maintained contacts with several Dartmouth classmates through frequent letters and occasional visits. Some, like Webster, were rising lawyers—Weld Fuller, Samuel Bradley, Jacob McGaw—scattered throughout the state. In Boston there was Peter Oxenbridge Thacher, a lawyer, editor of the *Monthly Anthology*, and a connection with affairs in that city. And the amazing young graduate of Dartmouth, George Ticknor, who would become the arbiter of brahmin society, was beginning a lifelong friendship with him which both valued highly. Though Webster may have seemed aloof, perhaps arrogant, to many people, these characteristics were absent from his private relationships.

Nor did he forget his family back in Salisbury. His aging, widowed mother at Elms farm survived for some time, but soon his sister Sally and brother Joseph would die.[6] As always, the main link was Ezekiel, rapidly becoming the squire of Boscawen and a leading figure of the Merrimack Valley. Letters about law cases, financial arrangements, and personal matters moved constantly between them. Ezekiel was always the steady, sensible person in whom he could confide his troubles and his expansive expectations.

Still, a bachelor's existence seemed incomplete. "If the fates are propitious," Webster observed to a friend a few months after coming to Portsmouth, "I hope I shall be able to afford you a shelter, in a year or two. I have been a young dog long enough, and now think of joining myself, as soon as convenient, to that happy and honorable society of which you are one; the society of married men." He had long shown a keen interest in marriage generally, and over the past couple of years had narrowed his attention to one woman particularly.[7]

She was Grace Fletcher, schoolmistress in Salisbury and sister-in-law of the county sheriff, Israel Webster Kelly, in whose home she then lived. Daughter of a Hopkinton minister and graduate of an academy, she had had more than the usual cultural and intellectual opportunities open to women. Now, at twenty-seven, she was poised and attractive, if not beautiful. Since both her father and stepfather were churchmen, it was not surprising that she was deeply religious. Her perspective was Calvinistic, with all the fatalism and solemnity one might find in a devout Congregationalist. But she kept her gloomy, pessimistic moods in tight check and was complimented for her kindness and pleasant manner.[8]

Webster had known Grace for quite some time; and before he left Boscawen in September 1807, the two probably had an understanding that they would be married.[9] The slow-moving courtship met further delay until the following spring, when one day he rode off without saying anything to his Portsmouth friends about his intentions. On May 29, 1808,

Grace Fletcher Webster, by Chester Harding, 1827

they were married in Kelly's house in Salisbury Center. Like a number of husbands, he later had a little difficulty in remembering the anniversary—he would record an incorrect date in his autobiography.[10]

The Websters settled into a rented house on Vaughan Street, once occupied by Mason. Across the street from the Assembly House, it was a respectable two-story structure, with an interior ornamented by handsome woodwork, a gambrel roof then so popular, and a well-planted garden that extended back to the next street. Shortly, they decided to buy a house, similar but smaller, on the corner of Court and Pleasant. From the front, one could see the carved posts of the fence along the sidewalk and a heavily paneled door bordered by decorative windows on either side. Unfortunately, a fire destroyed their home, along with many others, in a town disaster in December 1813. They then moved to a modest house on High Street behind Buckminster's church.[11]

Each home in turn became a center of social activity. Guests—the Masons, Buckminsters, Havens, young Ticknor, and others—enjoyed the genial hospitality, flowing conversation, and generous spread of food and expensive wines whenever they visited. Their host was relaxed and good-humored, attentive, often fascinating with his stories and observations. The Webster household grew with the birth of a daughter in 1810. Named after her mother, she was a beautiful, appealing child. Three years later there was a boy, Daniel Fletcher. Whether entertaining visitors or playing with the children, Webster could push away his daily concerns for a satisfying evening's interlude. But he had a limit. Typically an early riser, he was also ready for sleep earlier than many of those around him; then he would lapse into quiet and detachment.[12]

His physical appearance made a strong impression. Early portraits confirm Eliza Buckminster's recollection of him as "slender, and apparently of delicate organization." She recalled that "his large eyes and massive brow seemed very predominant above the other features, which were sharply cut, refined, and delicate. The paleness of his complexion was heightened by hair as black as a raven's wing." As time passed, he assumed the stouter proportions which seemed to accompany maturity and success. His bearing became more imposing and his style more self-assured, perhaps to the critical eye a bit pompous. In any event, he was a person neither to be overlooked nor forgotten.[13]

His intellectual qualities were more noteworthy than his appearance. Equipped with an uncommon mental capacity, he could absorb a wide array of information, recruit it when needed, and express his thinking with remarkable effectiveness. His range of reading reached well beyond legal subjects to literature and history, reflected in an expanding library of books along the walls of home and office.[14] Indeed he felt comfortable enough in the field of literature to deliver the Phi Beta Kappa lecture at the Dartmouth commencement of 1809. Deploring the paltry contributions of America thus far, he urged a literary nationalism such as his friend Noah Webster envisioned.[15] Perhaps he felt he could help redress the shortage with his essays and reviews in the *Monthly Anthology*.[16] But the foundation of a respectable literature, he realized, depended upon educational progress; and this would be a recurrent theme in his writings and speeches. One sign of this commitment was elected service on the town school committee.[17]

As for religion, Webster felt this was more a matter of faith than of reason. Rationalistic trends such as Unitarianism, Universalism, and deism were unattractive; he subscribed to the old doctrines. He preferred the theological position of the orthodox elder Buckminster to the disturbing departures from it by the minister's son, now called to the pulpit of the Brattle Square Church in Boston. At about the time he came to Portsmouth, Webster wrote out a statement of his religious tenets, all of them axiomatic among New England Congregationalists. In this confession of beliefs he affirmed his adherence to trinitarianism, the complete authority of the Bible, and predestination. "I do not believe in those doctrines," he declared, "as imposing any fatality or necesssity on men's actions, or any way infringing free agency." Yet he saw "the utter inability of any human being to work out his own salvation without the constant aids of the Spirit of grace." A divine providence governed the world, but one did not prove its existence by intellectual inquiry and logic. He knew this great truth because the Bible revealed it.[18]

His thoughts ran more often, of course, to his legal practice. Steadily he acquired treatises and reports and gained expertise in various branches of the law. As his reputation rose, there was no shortage of clients in local and state courts, especially the New Hampshire supreme court, which moved on circuit from county to county. Some business consisted of criminal cases, in which Webster's role as defense counsel was so skillful that observers recollected them long afterward; but mainly he handled commercial cases for merchants and traders as plaintiffs. The trend was now gradually away from old common-law actions on debt and toward modified procedures under the developing law of contracts suitable to a market economy. During the decade of his Portsmouth practice, he had more than seventeen hundred cases, with a success rate well over 50 percent.[19] His connection with his brother continued to be very close, so that Ezekiel looked after some of the business in the interior. His pattern of work changed somewhat when he went off to Congress in 1813 and attended the United States Supreme Court's term for a few weeks each year.

Income from fees, about two thousand dollars annually, never seemed enough.[20] Having a boundless need for more funds and accelerating his rate of spending, Webster sent constant appeals to Ezekiel. "Money I have none—I shall certainly be hanged before three weeks, if I cannot get some," he wrote. "What can be done?"[21] One solution, enticing to many people, might be a windfall in land speculation. He was increasingly interested in a large tract in Coos County, granted by the state at a bargain price to his onetime landlord, Timothy Dix of Boscawen. As surety for Dix's note, together with others, he paid installments on the principal for some time; but it is doubtful he profited much from such projects.[22] This seems to have been true also of land he held in Grafton County, some of it acquired in payment of legal services and the rest by the kind of mysterious manipulations of credit so characteristic of the day.[23] Besides land, he dabbled in stock of corporations, notably the Lower Concord Bank. His friends Peter Thacher and Cyrus Perkins in Boston thought his influence with the bank's officers was considerable for a while; but after leaving the area, he lost interest in the institution.[24] Generally, he seldom owed less than he owned; and often he was hard pressed. Late in 1810, for example, he found it necessary to mortgage the Salisbury property and had to ask Ezekiel and his sisters to consent to this unpalatable step.[25]

Public affairs frequently overshadowed such private concerns. Like many other lawyers, he moved quite naturally into politics, and did so with zest. His unusual talents joined with his keen interest in things political to draw him into the world of speeches, pamphlets, mass meetings, and elections. Although he never gave up his law practice, he would be better known as an unceasingly active politician. The excitement of the contest, the warmth of popular admiration, and the fascinating possibilities of achievement were powerfully magnetic forces. Undeniably, besides these self-serving elements, he felt a civic responsibility to influence the future character of the young republic.

As a matter of fact, the direction of the country seemed very uncertain and perilous. Nearly as long as Webster could remember, Europe, and to some extent the United States, had been suffering the anxieties and damages arising from the French Revolution and the Napoleonic wars. And in 1807 the outcome was never more doubtful for the belligerents, Britain and France, or for America, clinging to a precarious neutrality. The network of British orders in council and French decrees, both intended to deliver a mortal blow in this war of attrition, had developed fully. Complaining of violation of neutral rights according to its reading of international law—paper blockades, arbitrary seizures of ships, impressment of American sailors—the nation seemed unsure how to maintain its honor without resort to outright warfare.

New England Federalists such as Webster believed the Republican administrations of Jefferson and Madison incapable of providing a practical and just solution. A fatal defect, they thought, in Jeffersonian policies was the demonstration of stubborn favoritism to France, or, expressed the other way, of doctrinaire hostility toward Britain. But what else could be expected of visionaries and demagogues? Since Jefferson's "Revolution of 1800," a series of measures had not only discriminated against New England but had also been highly injurious to the nation's general welfare and security. One of these had been the Louisiana Purchase of 1803, tending toward a South-West coalition to the disadvan-

28

tage of the northeastern states. A Union of this sort might not survive. Another Federalist indictment of the "Demos" charged that they had corrupted the national character by base appeals to popular prejudice. The republic, dependent upon virtue and respectability, was in serious danger.[26] And presently the danger became more ominous when Jefferson and his successor Madison experimented with the entirely misguided policy of economic coercion, of cutting off American trade with Europe, to win recognition of neutral rights. This move merely helped Napoleonic France, the greatest menace to civilization in modern history, while ruining New England's more valuable economic interest, foreign commerce.

These were the feelings and assumptions of New Hampshire Federalists during the decade in which Webster was closely involved in party politics there. All too often they more than met their match in a continuing duel with the Jeffersonian Republicans. Despite an early ascendancy, Federalists faced ever stronger opposition in the annual spring elections for governor and legislature and in fall elections for congressmen and president. For years, each party ran the old reliables for governor: the Federalist John Gilman and the Republican John Langdon. The longtime Federalist dominance had cracked in 1805, when Langdon won; and except in 1809, when the former chief justice Jeremiah Smith was elected, Republicans prevailed in New Hampshire through 1812. In the subsequent war years Gilman returned for three terms, but these would mark the end of the Federalists as a majority party in the state. Thereafter Republicans under the leadership of Governor William Plumer, editor Isaac Hill, and the precocious Levi Woodbury prevailed.[27]

The Federalist problem was even greater in Portsmouth, for strange to say, this commercial town was a Republican stronghold. Repeatedly, when inland districts of the Merrimack and Connecticut valleys stayed loyal to Federalism, the Jeffersonians carried Portsmouth. Here prospects both for Webster's party and for his own advancement were dim. Nevertheless, after he arrived in the fall of 1807, he entered local politics without delay. In an extensive correspondence with friends in other towns, such as Bradley and Thompson, he pleaded for maximum effort.[28] Shaken by the reelection of the irrepressible Governor Langdon in March 1808, by the alarming Republican strength in and around Portsmouth, as well as by news from the national capital, he saw the coming presidential contest as crucial. He concluded, if reluctantly, that his party must use the same tactics as the opposition: thorough organization, a coordinated newspaper campaign, wide distribution of circulars

and pamphlets, mass meetings, even the somewhat disreputable caucuses, all to improve Federalist communications with voters at large.[29]

Webster's own appeal to the people, a pamphlet attacking the embargo, went out just before they voted. In effect for nearly a year, the law
prohibiting all American exports had encountered discontent and eva-
sion, nowhere more serious than in New England. This was the most
vulnerable point in the Republican position, now personified by James
Madison, secretary of state and presidential candidate. Hurried off the
press and into as many hands as possible, the pamphlet advanced constitutional, economic, and altogether partisan arguments. Whatever effect it may have had on the outcome of voting in the state, the "little
book," as he called it, was at least an interesting reflection of Webster's
political thinking.[30]

Beginning with constitutional theory, he wrote: "The Government of
the United States is a delegated, *limited* Government. Congress does not
possess *all* the powers of Legislation. The individual States were originally complete sovereignties. They were so many distinct nations, rightfully possessing and exercising, each within its own jurisdiction, all the
attributes of supreme power." The Constitution rested on mutual agreement of these states, but they surrendered only "a part of their powers,
not the whole," to the general government. One of these delegated
powers was the regulation of commerce, claimed now as justification for
an embargo. Webster objected to this interpretation, on the ground that
regulation of commerce did not encompass its destruction. "When we
send our watches to be regulated, our intention is, not that their motion
be altogether stopped, but that it be corrected," he contended. Thus, as
other Federalists were saying, the principal fault of the existing statute
was its silence on a terminal date, in contrast to the sixty-day embargo of
1794 (a Federalist measure), which specifically aimed at protecting
American shipping from capture and confiscation. Now the policy was
not protective. The unexplained but actual purpose was to force Britain
and France to recognize maritime rights. In constitutional terms, Congress had wrongly expanded a fairly limited power conferred upon it by
the states.

Not only was the purpose of the embargo insupportable, he continued, but its effect was highly injurious to merchants, sailors, and farmers
of this country, and it offered no hope of achieving the diplomatic objective. To demonstrate the large amount of trade sacrificed, he included
a statistical table on exports. Of this figure, a major share consisted of
re-exports carried by American ships. This meant that the embargo
choked commerce, not merely with the belligerents but with many other

30

areas as well—with Latin America, Africa, the Far East, and particularly with Canada, affected by a recent amendment to the law. Such folly reminded him of the story of a dentist who, after pulling a tooth on one side, pulled a second one on the other side so that the suffering would be equal. Besides, there were no benefits to offset these self-inflicted difficulties. The French could get along quite well without this denial of commerce and were, in fact, helped by the Americans' doing what they could not: weakening the British. It really seemed to Webster that the administration was dragging the nation into an alliance with France. Such a move could be expected from Jeffersonian Francophiles.

New Hampshire was receptive to arguments of this sort, no doubt because of spreading economic troubles. When votes were totaled, Federalists found the results gratifying. They elected their slate of congressmen and delivered the state's presidential electoral votes to Charles Cotesworth Pinckney. Even though Madison would become president, the people had shown their dissatisfaction with conditions as they were; and the party seemed to be recovering.

As usual, Portsmouth was obstinate. Through the next several local and state elections, Republicans prevailed here. Webster felt all the more uncomfortable because of setbacks in his first efforts to gain elective office. In four consecutive years, beginning March 1809, he was a candidate for the state legislature from Portsmouth. Each time Webster and the other Federalists lost, though a consolation perhaps was the thin margin by which he did so in 1812—532 to 512.[31] Outwardly, he did not make much of these early attempts—there is no mention of them in surviving letters, and none of his biographers has referred to them. But he did worry as the town repeatedly voted for a Republican governor and other officers.[32]

Despite disappointments, the persisting trend of foreign affairs and of Madisonian stategy pushed him to greater exertion. Successive commercial policies in various forms after repeal of the embargo had undesirable effects. While Napoleon maneuvered the administration into opening trade with France and closing it with Britain, in Webster's opinion, the United States suffered ever more acutely and drifted toward war. Only "a respectable federal minority" could check this reckless course of the "imperial Democrats," he wrote.[33] But a lively correspondence with connections in other towns, numerous meetings, and a stream of Federalist print seemed insufficient to turn the Republicans out of power.

To stimulate party enthusiasm in 1811, Portsmouth Federalists combined patriotism with politics in a celebration of the Fourth of July. In the morning a procession formed at the Washington Reading Room

31

and, preceded by a band and escorted by a company of "Gilman's Blues," moved to North Meetinghouse. Here they sang odes—one an original composition for the occasion—and heard a prayer by the Reverend Dr. Buckminster, followed by an "elegant," patriotic oration by John Lord. Then everyone returned to the Reading Room for what a friendly reporter described as a "handsome collation." All this was just prelude to a sumptuous dinner in the afternoon at the Assembly Room for a hundred "disciples of Washington," who enjoyed the "feast of reason and the flow of soul." Webster was a vice-president of the proceedings and offered one of the seventeen toasts, each laced with partisanship.[34]

As late as the spring elections of 1812, the Republicans held on, however precariously. In March at a heavily attended town meeting, Webster narrowly won election as moderator, the first Federalist to do so in thirteen years. But such satisfaction as this may have given him dwindled when the meeting cast a few more votes for the Republican William Plumer than for the Federalist John Gilman for governor.[35] The statewide popular vote was very close: Gilman, 15,612; Plumer, 15,492. Because there were enough votes scattered among other candidates to deny Gilman the required popular majority, the decision went to the Republican-controlled legislature, which predictably elected Plumer. Webster experienced another frustration by again losing the contest for a legislative seat, this time by only a handful of votes.[36]

By the end of June, news arrived from Washington that Congress had at last declared war against Britain. After years of complaint about violations of neutral maritime rights and after a long sequence of commercial restrictions to stop the violations, many Americans now felt that war was the only available means to vindicate national honor. It was true that those favoring war did so for different reasons—some saw tempting possibilities for annexing Canada and Florida, and others worried about the economic hardships of farmer, planter, or merchant. On the other hand, a large number of people, many of them New England Federalists, opposed war in any event. Typical of these dissenters was Webster.[37]

An opportunity to express his opposition soon came. On the Fourth of July the Washington Benevolent Society of Portsmouth conducted an elaborate celebration. Established after Washington's death as a patriotic and charitable organization, the society had chapters in dozens of communities across the land. Actually it became a favorite Federalist vehicle, whose motive power was limitless adulation of the Father of the Country.[38] On this day, members and recruits of the society gathered at the Washington Reading Room, moved in procession to Hosea Ballou's meetinghouse, were inspired by song, prayer, and customary reading of the Farewell Address, and listened approvingly to the principal oration. The speaker was Webster.

His theme was the contrast between Washington's achievements and recent Republican mistakes. The first president had handled the commercial and diplomatic problems of his time effectively and justly, Webster observed, because as a framer of the Constitution he realized that this more perfect Union was formed to eliminate the commercial distress of an earlier period. He resorted to a short-term embargo only to preserve and protect commerce, an entirely proper regulation. His path was "illuminated with all the light of heaven." Yet the current administration was destroying commerce; and instead of showing impartiality to all nations, as Washington had, it made war against one and aided another.

What should Federalists do? "With respect to the war, in which we are now involved, the course which our principles require us to pursue cannot be doubtful. It is now the law of the land, and as such we are bound to regard it. Resistance and insurrection form no parts of our creed." As citizens opposing the war, they would fulfill their obligations by paying taxes and rendering personal services, though there were constitutional limits to the latter, he hinted. But they would freely express their opinions, exercise their right of suffrage, and seek to restore correct policies. Never would they approve alignment with the tyrannical, infidel French regime. In his soaring peroration, he predicted the sons of New England would embrace martyrdom before they would consent to that.

The crowd responded enthusiastically. It was the most eloquent oration the town had ever heard, the *Oracle* reported. Undeterred by a rival Republican meeting at Frost's Hotel, the society rounded out a festive day by adjourning to Underwood's ropewalk for food and drink, with the customary toasts declaring their determined sentiments. For Webster, it was a glorious moment, promising much for both his party and himself.[39]

Hoping to maintain momentum, the Federalists decided to hold a county convention the next month to protest the war. The place they selected was Brentwood, a few miles west of Exeter, and a call went out to all "Friends of Peace" in Rockingham County to send delegates. They hoped to attract antiwar Republicans as well, a promising strategy in view of the rising dissatisfaction with the war. On August 5 about two thousand people arrived in the village, too many for the meetinghouse. They gathered at an open-air site where speeches and resolutions, interspersed with refreshments, were the bill of fare. Congressman George Sullivan, the leading speaker, criticized the administration for poor judgment in diplomacy and for pro-French tendencies. Then the convention authorized a committee of fifteen to prepare a memorial to the president on grievances requiring redress.[40]

While the convention enjoyed an intermission of lunch and relaxation, the committee met to endorse what had already been decided: it would report a memorial drafted by Webster some weeks earlier.[41] Though others on the committee, such as Sullivan, Thompson, and Nathaniel Gilman, may have made some last-minute changes, the document seems to have been chiefly Webster's own production. Known as the "Rockingham Memorial" and circulated widely, it assembled the standard arguments of the time in persuasive form.[42]

An introductory part of the memorial deplored the commercial distress caused by the embargo and later legislation. The right to engage in commerce, secured by the Constitution, must not be infringed. Pulling out of context a statement by Jefferson that Americans must provide for themselves and not "recur to distant countries," Webster called it shockingly arrogant. Clearly, the economic basis of the young Federalist's politics was the commercial interest of the voters in his section.

The main body of the appeal to Madison refuted each of the asserted reasons for declaring war. The charge that the British navy had impressed thousands of American sailors was a gross exaggeration. Actually the mercantile states, such as New Hampshire, knew that very few citizens of the United States had been impressed, notwithstanding complaints from states not involved in shipping. The real problem was, in Webster's judgment, that many British subjects, including deserters from the British navy, had been signed on American ships; and Britain had a perfect right to the services of its own citizens. Certainly war was not the remedy, for Britain had always been willing to negotiate a settlement on impressment (to what extent he did not specify).

Nor was the complaint against British orders blockading trade with Europe justified. They had remained in effect, he contended, in retaliation against French decrees, which were rigorously enforced despite Napoleon's pretenses of revocation. He argued that as a result of a congressional law of 1810, the United States had been deceived by these pretenses, then had carried on commerce with France while stopping it with Britain. But the British government had not been deceived and continued its orders through 1811 and early 1812. In any case, the memorialist declared, Britain had now repealed its orders, and there was consequently no valid American grievance.

A further defect in current policy was the lack of preparation for war. The sea frontier was very extensive, many coastal towns were utterly

unprotected, essential navigation was endangered. Under the Constitution, the government must protect the members of the Union, as the
president himself had said years ago in the *Federalist* essays. But the navy
had been neglected and was obviously incapable of providing that protection. Federalists had been firm advocates of a strong navy and were
now saying, "I told you so."

Despite all these mistakes, the northeastern states were strongly attached to the Union, the paper concluded. Though giving such assurances, it implied a reduced patience. "We shrink from a separation of
the States," it warned, but the recent measures of the administration
had a "very dangerous and alarming bearing on such an event." If a separation ever occurred, it would come when one part of the Union sacrificed the interests of another. "It shall be our most fervent supplication
to Heaven to avert both the event and the occasion; and the Government may be assured, that the tie that binds us to the Union, will never
be broken, by us." This veiled threat seemed to derive nearly as much
from a revulsion against a French connection as from commercial
wrongs, however iniquitous they may have been. "No pressure, domestic
or foreign, shall ever compel us to connect our interests with those of the
house of Corsica"; this position, said the memorial, was "deep, fixed, and
unchangeable."

The impact of the protest was perhaps to exhort Webster's own ranks
more than to convert his adversaries. Both his Federalist friends and the
author himself seemed highly pleased with it—indeed, twenty years
later, in different circumstances altogether, he reread it with approval.[43]
As a partisan document, however, it had the opposite effect upon Republicans. Governor Plumer saw Federalist opposition to war as obstructionist, perhaps even seditious and treasonable. Party motives, he
thought, shaped their behavior entirely. Their sole purpose, therefore,
was to turn out the president and regain power by demagoguery and
manipulation.[44] Even harsher were the reactions of editor Isaac Hill of
the *Patriot*, who gave over column after column to counterattacking each
point of the memorial. It was a flagrant untruth, he declared, for Webster to say that reports of British impressments could not be verified—
the names of forty victims, including seventeen from Portsmouth, had
been published. Hill believed Britain had committed a long series of injustices against American shipping and seamen, injustices stubbornly
ignored by Federalists. Typically, the fiery journalist directly attacked
the good faith of his opponents by doubting the memorialist's sincerity
on the matter of state secession.[45]

Whether he was right or wrong, Webster's standing had decidedly risen as a result of the summer's activity. So he was a prominent figure in the Federalist state convention, meeting in Gilmanton on October 7. Over two thousand Friends of Peace gathered again to hammer Madison and the war, to hear speeches, to draft more resolutions and memorials, and to nominate candidates for Congress. This year there would be six representatives from New Hampshire, all to be elected on a general ticket. One of the nominees, recommended by committee and heartily ratified by the convention, was Webster. Within a month, he would learn if this was another unimportant gesture by the party or if this time he would win an election.[46]

Through October 1812 the campaign was intense. Both parties descended to a low level of argument, impugning personal motives and character as well as discussing the issue of war and peace. The Portsmouth *Gazette* even revived old charges against the Federalist elder Timothy Pickering of Massachusetts for being traitorous in the 1790s. Webster offered to represent Pickering in a libel suit. His party had poor prospects as far as the presidential contest was concerned, and so it turned to an independent Republican, De Witt Clinton, to oppose Madison. Though futile, the strategy did deliver a good many electoral votes to Clinton throughout the Northeast. As for the state's congressional seats, all the Federalist candidates, including Webster, won election. His margin of victory was more than 15 percent. In general, the outcome revealed a Federalist trend in New Hampshire which would soon put them in control of the governorship and the legislature.[47]

All this did not help much, however, when he looked at the state of the nation. Continuously, the trend of affairs drove him to the conclusion that this could be a long, very costly war. The year 1812 had been a sobering one for those believing that military victory along the Canadian frontier would be easy. Defeats and stalemate were the highlights of the early fighting, and nothing indicated that next year would be different. Trade languished and avoided a worse condition only because of illegal commerce with the enemy; merchants were in an angry mood; and ordinary people felt keenly the heavy costs of war.[48] Was there any possibility that the special session of Congress, called for May 1813, might provide some relief?

Chapter 3
ANTIWAR CONGRESSMAN

When Webster arrived for the opening of Congress on May 24, 1813, he saw Washington for the first time. Though over the preceding twenty years planners and promoters had envisioned a beautiful metropolis, the young city of a few thousand inhabitants had not yet attained that status. The center of interest was the Capitol, actually two separate buildings to accommodate House and Senate, connected only by a rough boarded passageway instead of the contemplated gallery and dome. Looking to the northwest down broad but muddy Pennsylvania Avenue, lined by Jefferson's Lombardy poplars, one could see aspiring shops, some houses, even three hotels, notably the Indian Queen. More than a mile away stood the president's house, only recently completed and still more severe than elegant. To the south across the Potomac was Alexandria; westward, up the river, Georgetown. Along the grids of streets and diagonal avenues there was still only a scattering of buildings. In the southeastern section of the capital, the Navy Yard bordered the Anacostia, with the quarters of laborers, white and black, nearby. Altogether, living conditions were primitive, rather disagreeable. Waste was dumped into the streets to be scavenged by hogs, and water came chiefly from public pumps. To guarantee the unhealthfulness of the place, the terrain was low and swampy; and the humidity of the summer months was notorious.[1]

No wonder, then, that Webster decided against taking a room in one of the numerous boardinghouses near the Capitol and moved into Crawford's Hotel in Georgetown. Here he found the congenial company of Rufus King, Christopher Gore, and their wives. King, perhaps the foremost Federalist in the nation, had just won election to the Senate after his party had made a strong recovery in New York. And Gore, veteran lawyer, diplomat, and Webster's mentor in Boston, brought ability to the antiwar cause, despite his aristocratic proclivities. In their parlor, the Kings and Gores gathered friends and followers for diverting social hours; and congressional events and strategy were analyzed daily at this headquarters of the opposition. Within a few weeks a delightful addition was Jeremiah Mason, sent to the Senate by a new Federalist legislature of New Hampshire.[2] All this typified Washington's political society, fragmented as it was into many boardinghouse messes, but each internally homogenous as to opinion and interest. In the currently fluid situation of parties, such groups not only demonstrated a deep aversion to centralized power and direction but also performed political functions of no little importance.[3]

The Thirteenth Congress, now assembling for the first time, had a decidedly Republican profile. In the House, the administration's party outnumbered Federalists 114 to 68; in the Senate, 26 to 10. But Republican prospects were not as bright as these bare figures suggested. Their dominance, sustained through the Jeffersonian years, seemed to be slipping, for there were now twice as many Federalists in this Congress as in the preceding one, including three more in the Senate. In the Northeast, as far down as New York and even in Maryland, Federalists had either gained control or were very close to it. In nearly half of the states of the Union, in some of which they drew support from dissatisfied Republicans, they were a major force, growing rather than declining. If the administration was to get Congress to do the numerous things it must to carry the war forward, Republicans would have to stand fast against both their opponents and an exasperating band of dissidents and independents within the party. The first test of strength in the House was the election of a Speaker. Comfortably enough, 89 to 54, Henry Clay defeated the Federalist Timothy Pitkin of Connecticut, and the Kentucky War Hawk reoccupied the chair he had filled with so much effect in his first term.[4]

The magnetic young Speaker could rely upon several members to lead the majority. Preeminent was another War Hawk, John C. Calhoun, also beginning a long career on the national scene. As chairman of the Committee on Foreign Relations, Calhoun brought power, logic, and boundless zeal to the task. The South Carolinian, probably the foremost spokesman of nationalism, could be independent on some topics (such as banking), but he was often the central personality in a wartime Congress which gave as much attention to international relations as to military operations. Another member of that committee, with a sure politician's touch, was Felix Grundy of Tennessee, who spoke for the new West as

38

convincingly as Clay himself. To guide essential financial measures through the House, there was John W. Eppes, the son-in-law of Jefferson and chairman of the Committee on Ways and Means, who, among other contributions to the administration, had dispatched the troublesome John Randolph in the last Virginia election.

On the other side were Webster and his determined friends. They looked upon the stalwart conservative from Salem, Timothy Pickering, as the exemplar of the "Washington school of politics." Given to extremism, Pickering worried his opponents with the possibility of New England secession if sectional tension continued. In day-to-day proceedings, however, more practical heads prevailed. Assignment to the Committee on Foreign Relations enabled Webster to launch an embarrassing offensive against the president's diplomacy. One after another, Federalists delivered heavy blows: Thomas J. Oakley of New York, Daniel Sheffey of Virginia, William Gaston of North Carolina, Richard Stockton of New Jersey. But the most passionate was Alexander Hanson from Maryland. This Baltimore editor of the *Federal Republican* had vehemently criticized the decision for war a year earlier; and the horrifying result had been a brutal mob attack upon him and his sympathizers. Then, as martyred defender of freedom of the press, he had won his seat in Congress, the better to carry on his campaign. Over in the Senate the opposition was even stronger, for it could depend not only upon King, Gore, Mason, and others of the party but also upon some influential anti-Madison Republicans, such as the Virginian William Branch Giles and Samuel Smith, former editor of the *National Intelligencer* and a resourceful manipulator.[5]

As soon as Congress had organized, the president sent up his message. It was a rosier report of the nation's condition than a detached examination might have provided. Dwelling upon achievements of the navy, he predicted equal success for the army. His purpose was to exhort a strenuous, patriotic prosecution of the war. Such menaces as the presence of British ships in the Chesapeake, just below Washington, which he did not emphasize, certainly called for greater effort. But peace might come without much more fighting; and in fact that possibility was Madison's principal reason for convoking the legislators. On the basis of an offer by the czar to mediate a British-American settlement, he was nominating a three-man peace commission, for which he sought approval. He insisted that the outcome must be recognition of this country's rights under international law. The most serious violation of these rights, after the repeal of the orders in council, remained impressment; and the president left no doubt that a treaty would have to deal with this issue. Apart from such long-range hopes, the message addressed the immediate problem of

39

how to finance the war. He recommended an internal-tax program already developed by Secretary of the Treasury Albert Gallatin, who had escaped the discomfort of its adoption by leaving on the peace mission to Russia.[6]

While committees began considering various segments of the message and Clay stirred his colleagues with what Webster called a "furious speech," the New Hampshire congressman nourished complete contempt toward the chief executive, personally as well as politically.[7] The same day the message was read, he called at the White House, and his first impression was quite unfavorable. "I did not like his looks," Webster observed, "any better than I like his Administration." He could see "clearly eno in his features, Embargo, Non-Intercourse & War."[8] Through the summer he seldom returned, certainly not for the Madisons' "drawing rooms," which he found very uncomfortable. Indeed he soon became dissatisfied with Washington, with its oppressive heat, its scarcity of shade trees and feminine society, and its unpleasant quarrels (to which he contributed considerably).[9] An escape to Mount Vernon, along with his friend Pickering, to visit Justice Bushrod Washington allowed a day's respite.[10] But generally his mood was sour. He seemed to translate some of these feelings into personal hostility toward the president, who lay in bed seriously ill with influenza during much of June. Willing to believe the worst, he doubted that Madison would recover and showed no regret that he might not.

Regarding matters of policy Webster's opinion of the administration was no higher. He thought it weak, divided, and always wrong on both foreign and domestic questions. Though predicting that some taxes would be laid, he believed Republican factionalism would prevent full acceptance of the president's proposals. Westerners would probably support a comprehensive program, except for an unpopular whiskey tax, but other Demos, as he continued to call them, were not enthusiastic about either excise or direct taxes. Since many of them felt that peace was imminent, why bother, they asked, with such disagreeable steps? For his part, Webster had no intention of voting for new taxes but seemed to wish they would be levied, a move that would add to the administration's unpopularity.[11] Yet as weeks passed, nothing was done. The majority party, he remarked disdainfully, "cannot raise a Caucus, as yet, even, to agree what they will do. They are in a sad pickle. Who cares?"[12]

To report events and to circulate his opinions, he carried on an active correspondence—with Ezekiel, now in the legislature at Concord, with friends in Portsmouth and throughout New England. The most frequent exchange of letters involved Charles March, a New York City merchant formerly of New Hampshire. Here was an instance of his tendency to mix politics and personal affairs without restraint. Hard pressed for cash, as usual, he repeatedly drew upon March to supply it until something turned up. And he looked to March not only in an emergency but in the long run as well. "You must contrive some way for me to get rich," he wrote, "as soon as there is peace."[13] March had no complaint about the relationship, for he felt equally obliged to Webster. Especially interesting to the merchant and his Wall Street circle were Webster's assessments of the possibility that Congress would reopen foreign commerce, repealing nonintercourse. After all, it was vital that Britain and the United States resume their mutually advantageous commerce. Best of all would be an end to the war. What were the prospects of that, March asked? Meanwhile, he was pleased with the several ways in which Webster and other Federalists compounded Madison's misery.[14]

The strategy to do just this surfaced at the end of May, within a week after Congress gathered. The emphasis would be upon the timing of French revocation of decrees and British repeal of orders in council. In response to the American law of 1810 (Macon's Bill No. 2), Napoleon, through his foreign minister, the Duke of Cadore, announced that he would revoke his decrees if Britain repealed her orders. Madison seized upon this chance to close trade with Britain, under terms of the law, until she respected American maritime rights. But Britain would not accept such an informal, conditional revocation by France as proof that it was genuine. Thus things stood until May 1812, when the French foreign minister Bassano showed the American representative in Paris, Joel Barlow, a decree dated April 1811 formally revoking the decrees of Berlin and Milan. The astounded Barlow was told that his predecessor, Jonathan Russell, had been informed of it a year earlier. Neither Russell, now in Britain as chargé, nor Secretary of State Monroe had any prior knowledge of the document of 1811, they said. The consensus was that Bassano was producing a predated decree. At any rate, Britain used this latest French move as excuse to repeal its orders in council in June, a few weeks too late to be communicated to the United States before the declaration of war. The question Federalists raised was: if Britain had learned of the French revocation in 1811, would she not have acted at that time and thus forestalled war? Furthermore, had Russell or the Madison administration concealed this information from Britain? Most Federalists understood that the newly discovered decree was spurious and really wished to put blame on the president, the secretary of state, and the chargé for allowing the French maneuvers. All of which, the opposition declared, proved they were too sympathetic toward that nation.

The issue had partially developed in the preceding session, closing in March, when Madison answered a congressional inquiry about the decrees as briefly and noncommitally as he could. Now the Federalists followed up with more exacting questions. They began in the Senate, which could properly probe Russell's conduct because the president had just nominated him as minister to Sweden. King and Robert Goldsborough introduced a resolution requesting the president to inform the Senate if Russell had ever affirmed or denied Bassano's contention that he had been informed of the revocation in 1811. In a few days the answer came that Russell had indeed denied prior knowledge of the decree in a private letter to Monroe.[15] Still, King and a good many other senators thought the response evasive; and they later showed their dissatisfaction by rejecting Russell's nomination. In the same uncooperative spirit, they also refused to confirm appointment of Secretary of the Treasury Gallatin to the peace mission, as long as he kept his cabinet post. Both decisions were perhaps less disapproval of the nominees' qualifications than partisan harassment of the chief executive.[16]

As Madison's response to the Senate query arrived, Webster was poised to raise even more searching resolutions in the House. Waiting a few days until Alexander Hanson, the fiery congressman-editor, took his seat, he moved five resolutions: (1) when and how did the administration learn of the revoking decree of April 1811? (2) had Russell ever admitted or denied the truth of Bassano's assertion of informing him of it? (3) had the French minister to the United States notified the administration? (4) what other information did the president have? and (5) had the administration asked the French government for an explanation or complained of any delay in communicating the decree?[17] For the moment, Webster spoke only briefly. After reviewing the salient facts, he contended that if Britain had learned of the French revocation earlier, she would also have repealed the orders in council earlier. Then the United States would not have declared war. The honor of this country and the character of her officers, he said, demanded that the whole truth be known.[18]

Beginning June 16, a five-day debate on the background of the war erupted. Though Webster was silent, the Federalist position did not lack advocates. Alexander Hanson, Thomas Oakley, Daniel Sheffey, Zebulon Shipherd, and others assailed Madisonian diplomacy mercilessly. Their point of departure was the perfect right of the House to have, at last, all the information withheld so long. Once the full story was told, they believed, the president would be proved guilty either of having concealed knowledge of French revocation in order to start a war with Britain or of having been repeatedly exploited by Napoleon, with the same result. Most speeches at least implied that the second case was more probable.[19] Oakley, with a lawyer's powerful logic, forced this unpleasant dilemma upon the administration more insistently than anyone else. Surely Madison would wish to absolve himself, both before the public generally and before his party in Congress, of suspicion of suppressing information. But a complete disclosure, Oakley thought, would convict the administration by its own acts. Had it not been duped by the slippery Cadore letter, and must it not now, to be consistent, admit the validity of the revocation of 1811? The New Yorker, of course, was not as interested in establishing that validity as he was in demonstrating that the president's pro-French feelings had made him continuously vulnerable to the emperor's duplicity. The tragic consequences were delay of British repeal and American declaration of war.[20] All the Federalist speakers agreed that if the orders blockading Europe had been abandoned in time, the United States would not have gone to war on the sole remaining grievance, impressment of sailors. More painful to Republicans than this line of reasoning were the bare-knuckled blows of Hanson, who charged that the president had been compelled by his own party leaders to recommend a declaration of war as the price of his reelection; and that he had done so on the basis of an "undeniable, authenticated falsehood" of the French government.[21]

Members of the majority returned fire on every issue. As chairman of the Committee on Foreign Relations, Calhoun began by challenging the form more than the substance of Webster's resolutions. He had no objections to an inquiry, he said, if the request for information was proper, if it did not address the president disrespectfully and imply wrongdoing. During the debates, he waited for an opportunity to propose amendments.[22] But the most adept Republican speaker was Felix Grundy, also of the committee. The Tennessean, too, wanted amendments, but he would vote for the resolutions in any event to dispel misunderstanding. His principal argument, repeated by others, was that British repeal had not hinged upon French revocation, as announced. Referring to the prince regent's declaration of April 1812, Grundy said that Britain had demanded total revocation of the decrees affecting all neutral, not merely American, commerce (France did not do so). The result would have been to open commerce with the Continent to Britain as well as to the United States. When repeal had come in June, he continued, it had derived from internal pressures of British industrial interests, then in acute economic distress, and not from any action by Napoleon. The reason given by the ministry in Parliament was therefore not the real motive for the repeal.

Together with his associates, Grundy believed that Federalists such as Webster were dangerously disloyal. "To my mind," he declared, "it is impossible to draw a line of distinction between adding to the strength of the enemy and taking from the strength of his own country." The Friends of Peace were quite inconsistent: they would not repel the British invasion, and they would not support the peace mission to Russia. What would they gain from the current inquiry? Even if they proved that France had acted despicably, would they declare war against her too? Their previous voting showed they would not, he concluded.[23]

Finally, on June 21, the talking stopped. The tax bills were ready, and the administration wished to move them forward. So Calhoun suddenly dropped his amendments and agreed to vote for the resolutions. Most Republicans agreed that this was the only way to quiet the opposition and to get on with essential business. Primed with a set speech, Webster found no need for it now and gleefully watched as each resolution passed by a large majority.[24] The other side had acted very strangely, he observed. "A dozen Motions, made & withdrawn, some pulling one way, some another. They do not manage like so many Solomons."[25]

The next day, Webster and John Rhea, selected by the House to present the resolutions, called at the White House. "The Presdt was in his bed," Webster wrote, "sick of a fever—his night cap on his head—his wife attending to him &c &c. I think he will find *no relief* from my prescription." There was no discussion. Madison tersely promised that the resolutions would be attended to, whereupon Webster and Rhea left.[26]

Attending to them required three weeks. In early July, Webster tired of congressional proceedings and stayed in Washington just to hear the president's reply. Even this incentive ultimately failed to keep him from heading homeward before it came to the Capitol on July 12. This time Madison gave a much fuller report. Put together chiefly by Secretary of State Monroe, it was an extended statement attempting to refute charges and insinuations of improper conduct. The central position on decrees and orders in council was identical to the Republican version during the House debates. But Monroe's paper plainly reflected the administration's worries about being indicted by Federalists for partiality to, if not alliance with, France. No such thing was intended or had occurred, the secretary insisted. Copies of various documents and correspondence (involving the French government, Barlow, Russell, and Monroe) accompanied the report. Together, these items conveyed the impression that Bassano had fabricated and antedated the revoking decree, that Barlow and Russell had been surprised by its belated appearance, and that they had received no satisfactory explanation of the affair.[27]

Within twenty-four hours Calhoun brought in a committee report expressing entire satisfaction with the response and commending the administration's policy and conduct. French behavior had had no effect upon the arrogant British, the report declared; and the United States had had no alternative to declaring war to maintain its honor. The South Carolinian met with disappointment, however, when on the twentieth the House voted down his motion to consider the committee report, seventy-four to sixty-two.[28]

Like the controversy itself, final reactions were partisan. Pickering felt that "the most influential members of the ruling power" were "insensible to shame" and would therefore be unaffected by the probe; yet he thought the broad impact would be beneficial. Another archconservative, Jedidiah Morse, complimented Webster profusely for such telling opposition to the war. It was the highlight of the congressional session, he believed. Typical of Federalists in Congress, Richard Stockton discounted Monroe's statement as unconvincing, particularly as to the relation between French revocation and British repeal. In New Hampshire as well, appraisal depended upon party: the *Oracle* described the administration's answer as tortuous and evasive, while the *Patriot* derided "the great Mr. Webster" for cutting such "a sorry figure" in the capital.[29]

Webster's resolutions had been a piece of the general antiwar strategy. To be sure, they were also an obstructive device, employed for petty, vindictive purposes. From that viewpoint, the considerable diversion and lingering doubts which they created indicated their effectiveness. This is not to say that many people fully accepted the allegation that the administration had sought to conceal early knowledge of the French decree to justify going to war. Obviously, the revoking decree was fictitious. Americans knew it; so did the British; and the French realized that they knew it. Everyone also knew that notwithstanding his decrees in 1810 or 1811, Napoleon had continued to seize ships and to interfere with maritime commerce. Undoubtedly Webster was aware of all this. But his larger aim was to discredit past diplomatic policies, to prove bias for France and against Britain. If Madison had accepted the Cadore letter at face value, or, as was more likely, if he had used it as leverage against Britain and failed, then he had been nearly helpless when the French government resorted to the sham of the revoking decree. He had been pushed along by events, and by his missteps, into war. So Webster reasoned. The great advantage of unmasking Madisonian ineptitude would be to stop a ruinous war. Although the opposition did not accomplish this objective for the time being, they would keep trying.[30]

While the House debated the resolutions on the French decree, the Committee on Ways and Means was preparing a tax bill. Debate ended when the committee, through Chairman Eppes, reported the bill to be ready. Much like Gallatin's plan of a year earlier, the measure proposed internal taxes on numerous items as well as a direct tax on land. The treasury badly needed revenue and had to resort to loans for most of the expenses of prosecuting the war, but found borrowing, especially in the uncooperative Northeast, very difficult. So the president had called upon Congress in his message of May to vote taxes for the duration of the conflict. As presented to the House, the bill would levy taxes upon carriages, sugar, salt, distilled liquor, and bank notes and would apportion the direct tax on land among the states according to population, as required by the Constitution.[31] Through late June and early July, the House in committee of the whole waded through provision after provision. The discussion was not as animated as expected, less so than on Webster's resolutions.[32]

At first Webster predicted that the revenue program might not pass, though somewhat perversely he said he hoped it would because of the political liabilities it would impose on the administration. Daily he was on hand as the House voted on each section, and on every one he cast his nay. The only tax which he might have supported was one on distilled liquor, probably because this would affect the West. But the bill was changed to tax the capacity, not the output, of large stills only. And this modification he also opposed, because it could be evaded.[33]

When the two houses were in the last stage of reconciling differences, he had already left Washington. On July 9 he received a leave of absence and thus missed the last three weeks of the session. The hot, humid climate of the capital oppressed him, he remarked, and he was "out of sorts."[34] Even his selection as a member of a Federalist steering committee for party strategy did not deter him from fleeing the dispiriting scene.[35] His first experience in Congress had thrown him briefly into the center of a stormy discussion of national policy, he had immediately become prominent on his side of the House, but he had made few speeches and had accomplished nothing constructive so far.

No doubt the main reason for hurrying home was Grace's pregnancy. He barely arrived in Portsmouth before their second child, Daniel Fletcher, was born on July 23. Through the summer and fall he gave his attention to his growing family and to his law office, which his young partner, Timothy Farrar, Jr., had capably overseen during his absence. Too soon, in early December, he had to return to Washington. His reluctance was so great that he did not set out until after the session had begun and arrived at Crawford's in Georgetown on December 28. He was three weeks late.[36]

Letters with shocking news from his wife and Farrar awaited him. There had been a devastating fire in Portsmouth on the twenty-second. A large part of the town was burned to the ground, his house was destroyed, but fortunately Grace and the children, as well as the other people in the area, had escaped. From the letters and later reports he could reconstruct a frightening scene. Early on a cold evening, flames burst forth from Woodward's barn, just to the rear of Webster's home on Pleasant and Court streets. Relentlessly the fire swept across many blocks of houses and shops as far as the waterfront. The wooden construction of many buildings, a long drought, strong winds, confusion, and the primitive equipment of valiant fire fighters allowed the disaster to spread all night. Miles away, as far as Boston, it was said, the sky was lighted by the fire. Now hundreds were homeless, and the town faced an enormous, expensive task of reconstruction.[37]

His impulse was to leave for home immediately. But a combination of his wife's assurances and his own feeling that the times required his attendance at this session prevailed.[38] A comforting thought was that his family could stay with Mrs. Mason—Mason himself was at the capital with Webster—for this house on the edge of town was untouched. Within a few weeks Grace decided to go to Boscawen to spend the rest of the winter with Ezekiel's family.[39] Still, his dismay at his overwhelming financial loss persisted. The house, valued at six thousand dollars, and all its contents were lost; and improvidently he had bought no insurance.[40]

Many people in the stricken seaport hoped for relief from the national government. A town meeting of January 15, 1814, petitioned Congress to apply revenue from Portsmouth's federal taxes to help the more than one thousand homeless persons. Webster presented the request to the House, and it was referred to committee. Later he brought in another petition, asking for an exception to the current embargo on coastal traffic so that lime for bricklaying could be shipped from Maine. Both appeals failed: the House tabled a committee report on allocating tax revenues; and when the question on transportation of lime came up, it was moot because the embargo had been abandoned.[41]

Disappointments on other, general issues seemed, in Webster's judgment, characteristic of this session. An instance was the adoption of an

47

embargo and its repeal four months afterward—a turnaround, however welcome it was, that illustrated unsettling, fluctuating policies. Other measures to raise money and recruit men would pass, but only after heated oratory from both sides. And prospects of peace were still slight, Webster feared. Britain had vetoed Russian mediation, and a new mission departed for the Continent.[42] One of the American negotiators would be the hawkish Clay, who resigned as speaker in mid-January. Federalists found some consolation, but not much, in the choice of Langdon Cheves rather than Felix Grundy, Madison's preference, for the House leadership.[43]

When Webster had returned in late December, he learned that the embargo had already passed. The president had recommended the law, which forbade all exports, in order to stop trade that was reaching Britain. There had been brief but lively debate, in which opponents demanded proof of such commerce. Though they failed to require Madison to supply information, the fact was that the traffic did exist; and for that matter, it would continue after adoption of the bill.[44] Presently Webster had a chance to express his entire dissatisfaction with the embargo. In January and February 1814 he criticized it as both unjust and unconstitutional. He compared it to the hated British acts on colonial trade before the Revolution. Under color of regulating commerce (the only possible constitutional authority), the statute was annihilating commerce. This perversion of power, he said, hurt maritime New England more than any other section.[45] His disapproval was so categorical that he was one of only seven representatives voting nay when an exception for the stranded island of Nantucket carried. He thought this provision countenanced the embargo itself by implication.[46]

In this session Webster sought to revive his charges in the resolutions on the French decree. Absent when Madison's reply had arrived in August and upset because the House had taken no further action, he moved on January 3 for discussion of the message and of Calhoun's committee report on it. If the president's "elaborate argument" went unchallenged, he asserted, the assumption would prevail that it was correct. Yet the gloomy news from the field of battle reflected popular belief that this was a useless war, "ill-judged and ill-timed in the beginning, as well as ill-conducted since." After Republican complaints, such as Robert Wright's call for an end to this *"petit guerre"* against the administration and for support of the main war, Calhoun reluctantly agreed to a consideration of message and report. The House never got around to it, however, and Webster's last-minute effort in April to bring up the issue collapsed under a two-to-one vote.[47]

There were other opportunities to attack war policies. In January

1814 Congress considered bills to fill the sparse ranks of the army, but most speakers gave far more attention to the causes and progress of the war than to the specific proposals before them. Though earlier legislation had authorized nearly sixty thousand troops, less than half that number were actually in service at the moment. Secretary of War John Armstrong, already criticized by both Madison and Monroe for feeble performance, was lobbying for conscription on his own initiative—he was less alive to the political explosiveness of the idea than were the president and secretary of state.[48] Webster assailed this proposition and published an alarm in the New England press when he heard of it.[49] But the principal question before the House was how to make voluntary enlistment more attractive. On the fourteenth, debate began on a bill to increase bounties for recruits, to give the same benefits to soldiers who reenlisted, and to reward persons who persuaded men to sign up. Hardly anything relating to the war escaped notice.[50]

Federalist criticism emerged when Daniel Sheffey moved a rider that these recruits could be used only for defense. The motion failed, largely on a party vote.[51] Then Webster gained the floor to unburden his antiwar feelings.[52] More troops were unnecessary, he contended, unless the coming campaign followed the same foolish pattern of the previous two years. The vote just taken proved to him that the dream of taking Canada still influenced American strategy. Instead of protecting its own seacoast and truly maintaining maritime rights, for which the existing size of the army was ample, the government would resort to desperate means to build an invasion force. He predicted another failure, for the people could see neither the justice nor the object of this conflict. Once convinced of a broad moral purpose in the war, the nation would readily unite to prosecute it, he reasoned. He could not accept the widespread notion that military operations went badly because of negativism by the minority. This was an old refrain that had been sung throughout history when those in responsible positions were ineffective (an example was Lord North during the Revolution). He, for one, would never give up his constitutional right to expose anything destructive of popular interests. Nevertheless, those in opposition, he promised, were "not of a school, in which insurrection is taught as a virtue. They will not seek promotion through the paths of sedition, nor qualify themselves to serve their country in any of the high departments of its Government, by making rebellion the first element in their political science."[53] In rounding out his argument, Webster offered his prescription for the future: repeal the embargo, protect the coast with a stronger navy, seek peace at the earliest possible date.

Whatever persuasive effect the speech may have had was probably more apparent outside than within the walls of the Capitol. He sent copies to New Hampshire and elsewhere to aid the antiwar cause; and at least Federalist readers admired the eloquence and vigor of this new voice in Washington.[54] William Plumer, ever aware of Webster's ability if not agreeing with his judgment, sourly remarked that he saw "too much of egotism & rant of conscience in it."[55] In the House of Representatives the vote to pass the enlistment bill was a decisive ninety-seven to fifty-eight.[56] After more disputation about the war in the next few days, another bill to extend the term of enlistments also passed.[57] Republicans such as Calhoun thought Webster and his friends were not only wrong about policy but were very close to treason as well. It was "factious opposition," said the Carolinian. It was "moral treason," cried Grundy.[58]

While Congress quarreled over issues of money and troops and the very nature of the war, important events were occurring in Europe. Early in January news of Napoleon's defeat at Leipzig arrived in Washington. After the battle in October 1813, the emperor retreated to France, and in the next few months an allied invasion forced his abdication. At last Britain and her allies were victorious, the Continent was liberated from French domination, and its ports were open to world commerce. Implications for the war in America were large. With an end to hostilities in Europe, British resources could now be funneled into the campaign against this country, with ominous possibilities for the republic's fate. Furthermore, Britain would be less troubled by the embargo than would the United States; trade with Europe was much more accessible to the former, whereas the latter would deny itself valuable commerce if the embargo continued. As long as American commerce was slight, whether because of embargo or British blockade, desperately needed revenue from duties would be correspondingly small. In addition to relieving these difficulties, repeal of the embargo might somewhat placate Britain and encourage her to agree to a favorable treaty at the forthcoming peace conference in the Low Countries.[59]

Such thoughts were in Madison's mind by March 1814, though he hesitated to abandon a measure so recently adopted. His followers in Congress had not yet received any signal of a reversal as late as the middle of the month and therefore beat off an attempt to repeal.[60] Two weeks later, the president decided to change course and sent a brief message recommending an end to the embargo and partial repeal of nonimportation of British goods (if carried by neutral vessels).[61] Swiftly the Committee on Foreign Relations endorsed these recommendations and reported a bill. Speaking for the committee on April 6, Calhoun summarized the new situation in Europe, which made embargo undesirable now that trade was open there. He found it easy to push repeal, for he had only reluctantly acquiesced in the restrictions in December.[62]

Webster followed with an abrasive speech, which of course approved repeal but capitalized on the administration's embarrassing twists and turns. He was happy, he said, to be present at these funeral ceremonies. Sarcastically, he extended his condolences to the mourners at the final rites of a system they had embraced as an article of faith. To explain this sudden switch, he recurred to a favorite theme, the Republican habit of connecting American policy to the French cause. While Napoleon closed the continent to imports, the United States assisted him with embargoes and nonintercourse acts; and when French control ceased, these laws must go.[63]

Calhoun could not endure this silently. Interjecting with some spirit, he repelled a charge of Franco-American collaboration. This country had been protecting her own interests. What had previously been advantageous, he countered, was no longer so because of completely different circumstances. It would be foolish to ignore this fact. Readjustment was, in short, wise statesmanship. Well, Webster replied, he did not intend to impugn anyone's motives, did not charge that the purpose was necessarily to aid France, but did believe that the effects had been just that. Calhoun could understandably doubt the sincerity of this explanation.[64]

After a number of speeches, nearly all favoring either full or partial repeal of the restrictive laws, the main substance of the original bill passed both houses by a sizable margin.[65] Federalists were in good humor, while Republicans were not. They felt "a little sore under Webster's rubs," thought Nathaniel Macon.[66] Apart from this bright spot late in the session, Webster found little else to cheer him. He could foresee neither peace nor improvement in public affairs as a result of anything this discredited executive would do.

Chapter 4

PEACE

Soon after repeal of the embargo, in mid-April 1814, Congress adjourned; and Webster returned to Portsmouth. One of his main concerns for the next few months was the congressional election, to be held in New Hampshire in late August. The outcome would not only indicate how people there were reacting to news from the capital, but along with voting throughout the country, it would also determine whether Federalist opposition would continue to be chiefly a nuisance or would become decisive in national politics. An encouraging sign was the party unity demonstrated early in the contest. At Concord on June 22, 1814, a mixed caucus of members of the legislature and of leaders across the state renominated Webster and all but one of the other incumbent representatives.[1]

Republican spokesmen such as Isaac Hill and William Plumer had a large target as they took aim at the candidates. During the summer, Hill's *Patriot* fired rounds in quick succession. And Plumer, narrowly defeated for the governorship in the spring, turned his ever-ready pen to work in a series of aggressive essays by "A Farmer."[2] As expected, their principal charge was Webster's obstruction of essential steps to win the war: votes against military and financial bills, near-treasonous harangues in the House, and the shameful resolutions on French decrees. If he and the other congressmen would give the support they owed their government, the United States would be victorious. As it was, weak popular commitment to that goal was attributable to petty politicking or worse. Hill also found much in Webster's personal character to attack. This puffed-up graduate of the "Hanover Indian school," the editor declared, did not pay his debts, was often absent in the House, and, when present, talked too often. In short, he was a "cold blooded wretch."[3]

Probably the most effective Federalist paper was the Portsmouth *Oracle,* to which Webster contributed freewheeling pieces.[4] In syrupy phrases this party organ voiced its thankfulness that the state so fortunately had illustrious statesmen like Webster and Mason. Hill's ridicule, it observed, was typical Jeffersonian leveling, an unwillingness to recognize unusual talent. But voters would not allow passions to prevail over understanding. Their cool judgment would approve an informed resistance to "Madison's war." Releasing a passion which it had deplored, the *Oracle* proclaimed that "the members of the FEDERAL REPUBLICAN TICKET, wish for peace, and to close this scene of blood. They will use their *united exertions* to shut the TEMPLE OF JANUS and to bind in chains the dogs of war."[5]

On election day, August 29, Federalist candidates held on to the slight edge their party had had in preceding campaigns: Webster and the other five, all on a general ticket, received a little over 18,000 votes to about 16,500 for Republicans. Throughout New England nine new Federalist congressmen won election, and six in other states. Still, in the nation as a whole, Republicans offset these losses and looked forward to a somewhat larger majority in the House of Representatives than before.[6]

Not much time—less than three weeks—passed before Congress began its new session, called by the president to handle acute war problems. But Webster, recently criticized for absenteeism, would be absent again, for in Portsmouth an alarm had swept across the town. The British, now on the offensive, had raided a number of places along the coast, including a destructive though brief occupation of Washington. British ships were dangerously close to the Portsmouth Navy Yard, where several vessels were berthed. People worried even more about loss of their own property, perhaps lives. At a meeting on September 3 called to organize local defense, residents exchanged ideas on what to do and selected a committee to coordinate action.[7] As chairman of this committee, Webster sent Governor Gilman an appeal for troops, who soon arrived and may have been a deterrent. A printed handbill, signed by Webster, summoned men from the town itself to muster on the parade ground; and circular letters alerted nearby places.[8] No doubt, as he stopped on the street to talk about the crisis, he freely blamed the administration for not listening to Federalist advice that the coast ought to be better protected. Not until early October did he feel easy enough to leave for Washington.

On the evening of the fourteenth, as the coach carrying Webster and other passengers moved along the streets of the capital, he was dismayed at what he saw. The destruction by the British raid of August 24 was a depressing sight: the interior of the Capitol gutted by fire, the outside still standing but flame-blackened, other public buildings—the Treasury and the War Department—badly damaged, the White House uninhabitable, the president now occupying a private house up the avenue. On the other side of the city, the Navy Yard had been burned at the order of the secretary of the navy to deny it to the British. A consolation was that the enemy commander, General Robert Ross, had spared most private dwellings and even one government building, the Office of Patents, on Eighth and E. It was into this crowded structure, the temporary meetingplace of Congress, that Webster went the next morning. He could not fail to notice as he read the *National Intelligencer* that the typeface was different and rather primitive, the result of Admiral Cockburn's order to break up the press of Joe Gales, English-born but an irritating exponent of American nationalism.[9]

As Congress sat through the late months of 1814, many representatives besides those on the minority side worried about the course of events. Free of demands upon its military resources in Europe, Britain could give more attention to the American theater. In addition to raiding the coast, it tightened the blockade, now extended to New England. Thousands of troops, some of them veterans of the Napoleonic campaigns, were sent over to mount offensive operations—from Kingston on Lake Ontario, from northern New York and Vermont along Lake Champlain, and from the sea toward New Orleans. Notwithstanding the continuation of peace talks at Ghent, it seemed quite possible that British terms would be severe, perhaps requiring a territorial cession in the North and West, terminating fishing rights dating back to the Revolution, and rejecting every argument about maritime law. Yet news was not entirely bad. Just as Congress assembled on September 19, reports of a brilliant American victory at Plattsburgh came. A large British invasion force turned around after the costly loss of its gunboat fleet on Lake Champlain. It was on such aspects of the war that Madison dwelt in his message of the twentieth, reiterating that the just cause of the United States must prevail. But a close reading of that message left no doubt that even the cheerful president thought that Congress must provide more men and money for that to happen.[10]

Instead of specifying how much and in what manner, Madison left the details to his cabinet officers. Having assumed the duties of secretary of war, Monroe presented several options for strengthening the army on October 14, the day of Webster's arrival. The first of these, and the most distasteful, was conscription. To bring regular forces at least up to the authorized sixty-two thousand, he proposed dividing the adult male population into groups of one hundred and requiring them to furnish four recruits; if they did not, four would be drafted. A second plan would conscript portions of the state militia. A third would exempt persons from militia service if they supplied men for the national service. And the fourth, an extension of existing policy, would accelerate volunteering by doubling the land bounty to 320 acres and by lowering the enlistment age from twenty-one to eighteen.[11]

Into December, these options were framed into bills by committees, repeatedly amended, tediously parsed by some, and excitedly attacked by others. The outcome was failure of everything except stimulation of voluntary enlistment. Federalists Timothy Pitkin and Cyrus King deplored enlistment of minors without parental consent as immoral and oppressive. Webster sought to delete an increase in the land bounty. Nevertheless the bill passed, and the president signed it into law on December 10. Connecticut and Massachusetts were so inflamed that they empowered their state judges to issue writs of habeas corpus releasing enlisted minors.[12]

Monroe's first conscription proposal had no chance of adoption whatever. Though he personally approved it, George Troup, chairman of the Military Affairs Committee, decided it was useless to report a bill. As for the idea of drafting the state militia, Troup and others in the House disliked it so much that they refused to initiate the measure. The Senate, however, did pass such a bill, and the result was an extended debate in the House through mid-December.[13]

At this point many representatives realized that a militia draft was the only system that might be accepted, however undesirable it was in comparison to conscripting men directly into the army. Their contention was that the need for more troops in the next campaign would be desperate, that volunteering was insufficient, particularly because of competition by states in organizing their own forces.[14] They saw no difficulty in justifying the constitutionality of a draft. Resorting to Hamiltonian theory, as Secretary Monroe had in his recommendations, they connected a draft with raising an army, an enumerated power in the Constitution.[15]

Joining a progression of congressmen speaking against the militia draft, Webster's turn came on December 9.[16] Like them, he emphasized its unconstitutionality. Reflecting the political circumstances of the Jeffersonian era more than the ideological heritage of his party from the previous Federalist decade, he reasoned like a strict-constructionist states' righter, as he often had on the embargo and other subjects. This bill, he contended, would employ national powers unwarranted by the militia clauses of the Constitution: the authority to call forth the militia to execute the laws, suppress insurrections, and repel invasions (Article I, section 8). The present intention was to do something different from any of these; it was to draft a federal army for general purposes, including invasion of foreign soil, for a period longer than the traditional six to nine months. Emotion rivaled philosophy as he warmed to the theme. "Anticipate the scene, sir, when the class shall assemble to stand its draft, and to throw the dice for blood." He could see the families of draftees tearfully watching husbands and fathers compelled to march off to a distant battlefield, many of them never to return. "May God, in his compassion, shield me from any participation in the enormity of this guilt."[17]

Much of what Webster said was familiar to his listeners, who by now were accustomed to the usual review of diplomatic, financial, and military mistakes of the administration. What must have drawn their particular attention was his warning that New England did not lack remedies for its afflictions. They were quite aware that in a few days an ominous meeting would occur in Hartford to make decisions that could threaten the Union itself. Although he did not specifically refer to this regional convention, he obviously was thinking about it and, by implication, approved it. A state must resist conscription, he declared, by every constitutional and legal means available. "It will be the solemn duty of the State Governments to protect their own authority over their own Militia, & to interpose between their citizens & arbitrary power... Their highest obligations bind them to the preservation of their own rights & the liberties of their people."[18] Then, alluding to the "state of things in New England," he denied the charge that these states intended to secede. Attachment to the nation was too strong for that. The real danger, in his opinion, lay in the probability that if measures such as this one were adopted, the national government would collapse.[19]

After more oratory and repeated attempts at amendment (Webster's proposal to reduce service from a year to six months failed by one vote), the House passed the bill on the fourteenth.[20] But it was the end of the month before the question was finally resolved. Since House and Senate disagreed on the length of service—one year as against two—a conference committee met and compromised, but the House refused to concur.[21] Undoubtedly the general nervousness about conscription, rather than a fixation on this specific point, prevented enactment of a law.

The reliably proadministration *National Intelligencer* vehemently disapproved the position of the bill's opponents. Their motive, thought the editor, was not to criticize honestly a legislative proposal but to stimulate the lagging courage of delegates then assembling in Hartford. "A member from New-Hampshire [Webster] has said, he will advise the resistance of the execution of the Militia Draft," the newspaper observed, but such threats would be futile; and in the future, historians would surely condemn those who tried to provoke a civil war while their country was imperiled by a brutal foreign power.[22] Whether Webster was worrying about some future historian or about the immediate impact, he decided not to give the reporter the manuscript of his speech, and it does not appear in the *Annals of Congress*. This omission would spare him some embarrassment in later years when southern nullifiers ransacked the records for his early advocacy of interposition.

Throughout the session, the House was as much involved in raising money as in recruiting men. Estimates by the new secretary of the treasury, Alexander Dallas, were that current taxes would be entirely inadequate for the coming year. And loans, the main device to pay for the war, were sadly undersubscribed; or, when subscribed, heavily discounted. So beginning in October, the representatives spent long hours discussing proposals by Dallas and Eppes to increase revenue. They would double various excises and the direct levy upon land, as well as add new taxes. Remaining deficiencies would be met by large issues of treasury notes.[23]

Early Federalist reception of these recommendations was surprisingly mild. A group from that party, including King, Gore, Pickering, and Oakley, circulated a paper saying the enemy threat was so serious that the minority had an obligation to support essential steps to repel it. Some Federalists did so.[24] Webster, however, stood firm.[25] On October 24, 1814, during debate on the direct tax, he countered with a strange speech. If provisions for revenue depended upon his vote, he said, he would not withhold necessary military supplies; but inasmuch as the bill would pass anyway, he would cast a nay. His conscience would not allow him to approve, even implicitly, this unjust, poorly managed war. Supporting this charge with details led him through familiar territory: disordered public finance, ruined commerce, military disaster. Besides, he could not understand the stall of peace negotiations. It must be caused by a lack of realism and clarity in the American position, he felt, and by a lingering lust for Canada.[26]

Again Republicans could see nothing less than obstructionism and faltering patriotism in this kind of reasoning. Calhoun replied the next day by staunch advocacy of intensified effort in the next campaign, since dependence upon British generosity would be very risky.[27] The *Intelligencer* also reacted by condemning Webster's speech as wholly insincere, as demonstrating his party's disappointment in not getting "a share in the *offices* of the government."[28] At least Webster was correct in believing the tax bill would easily pass without his support, for late in December the House approved it by a large majority.

Everyone knew that whatever Congress decided about taxation, the desperate condition of the treasury dictated that much more be done. Quite aware of this, Secretary Dallas began pressing for a national bank in October as the central part of his fiscal strategy. After the expiration of the first national bank's charter in 1811, currency and credit had deteriorated badly; and the demands of war had enormously magnified problems in public and private sectors. In his recommendations, however, Dallas offered primarily a formula for a bank to help the government obtain funds instead of a blueprint of an ideal institution to operate with maximum efficiency and dependability. Elements of his plan were a large capitalization of fifty millions, all but six millions in United States stock, the presence of governmental appointees on the board of directors, an obligation of the bank to loan the treasury up to thirty millions, and presidential authority to approve suspension of specie payment of bank notes.

Party ranks fragmented on the bank question. Some Republicans, such as Eppes, had pristine Jeffersonian objections to almost any kind of a national bank on constitutional grounds. Calhoun, normally a mainstay in forwarding administration programs, disagreed with Dallas on certain fundamentals—he preferred smaller capitalization, subscription in treasury notes instead of bonds or stock, less obligation by the bank to lend to the government, and requirement of specie payment. Federalists tended to collaborate with Calhoun; but they were unsteady, and more than once they deserted him just as it seemed he would prevail. After clearing early hurdles, Calhoun's version stumbled in late November. Then a bill incorporating Dallas' recommendations passed the Senate and came before the House during Christmas week.[29]

After so many encounters with Calhoun, Webster found himself on common ground with the South Carolinian. He made this plain in his speech of January 2.[30] His preference, he said, was for capitalization of twenty-five or at most thirty millions, deletion of the provision obligating the bank to lend to the government, and strict provision for specie payment. If a system like the one proposed by the administration were adopted, he warned, a government debt of seventy-five millions (in stock and loans) would attach to the bank. The immediate consequence would be a gigantic overissue of worthless, irredeemable bank notes. To him, a corporation in this situation looked "less like a bank than a department of government. It will be properly the paper-money department."[31] Even if one agreed that this was desirable, the policy would inevitably disappoint its friends by worsening rather than removing existing difficulties. Further depreciation of currency and decline of confidence in all financial arrangements would hardly help the country. Better to charter a sound, conservative bank free of political manipulation.

Whether owing to such arguments or to the intangibles of politics, the bill did not attract quite enough support. The division was eighty-one to eighty for it, whereupon Speaker Cheves voted no, making a tie and defeating it. Within a few days Calhoun revived his plan after consulting Webster; and both houses finally approved it in a form agreeable to the two men. The only remaining worry was how Madison would react. Webster predicted that the president would sign the bill because of the desperate fiscal situation.[32]

His forecast was wrong. On January 30 Madison returned the bill with an unswerving veto message. The chief executive objected to nearly every feature inserted by Calhoun; it would not meet the needs of the government, he concluded.[33] Interestingly, the Father of the Constitution and custodian of Jeffersonian Republicanism had no constitutional objections to a national bank; neither did Calhoun nor Webster. Opinions were not altogether stable on this subject. Following the veto, another try for an administration model began, got through the Senate, but fizzled in the House when news of peace arrived.[34] The question carried over to the next session.

While Congress struggled with issues of military recruitment, taxation, and banking, events even more interesting to the opposition were occurring in New England. From December 15 to January 5, a convention of discontented Federalists met in Hartford to discuss grievances and means of redress. This gathering turned out to be a highlight not only of the last winter of the war but also of American political history. Over the previous decade the trend of affairs had seemed to Federalists of this section very unsatisfactory—Jeffersonian ascendancy, annexation of Louisiana, embargo, war—all making them victims of exploitation and discrimination. There had been several proposals for a convention of these states, but not until late 1814 was the idea translated into action. Various long-standing complaints such as those expressed by Webster were common among the advocates of a convention, though some, such as Pickering, would take bolder steps than others.[35]

When the convention met, the dominant mood was gloomy. Coastal raids, predictions of an attack upon New Orleans, slow peace negotiations, and discouraging news from Congress could have brought extreme decisions. But moderates, principally Harrison Gray Otis and George Cabot, were in control. Consequently, the resolutions set forth well-known Federalist views: requests for regional autonomy in military defense and for use of federal tax revenue by the states for that purpose. As for the long-range remedy, constitutional amendments were proposed to end the Virginia dynasty in the White House and to require two-thirds approval, instead of a majority vote, for admitting new states, imposing embargoes, and declaring war.[36] The convention also approved a committee report that implied the states' right to nullify a federal law and even to secede from the Union, but nothing so bold was to be done for the time being. "A severance of the Union by one or more States against the will of the rest, and especially in time of war, can be justified only by absolute necessity," the report said, but a state must "interpose its authority" to protect its citizens against unconstitutional measures, such as conscription, of the general government.[37]

It was the fate of the Hartford Convention to announce its protests just as the war closed and to appear the more disloyal, perhaps disunionist, to an America moving toward nationalism. The secrecy of its proceedings cast further suspicion on its deliberations. Those who had had any connection with the convention, not merely delegates, later suffered scarred reputations.

Was Webster culpable of some close relationship to the convention? This question pursued him for years; and notwithstanding his frequent denials, he could never put it to rest. In the 1830s, when he was the supreme nationalist combating advocates of nullification and defenders of slavery, his adversaries probed past inconsistencies and forced him to put out unqualified disclaimers of involvement. "I was not a member of the Hartford Convention, and had no agency in it, nor any correspondence with any of its members," he would declare. Emphasizing that he attended Congress from October until well after adjournment of the convention, he detached himself from it completely.[38]

These statements were literally correct but misleading. An important fact was that New Hampshire did not send delegates, because the council, unlike the governor and the assembly, was Republican. So no delegates were officially appointed, although two counties sent unofficial representatives. Indeed Webster seems to have advised Governor Gilman not to ask approval to send a delegation, for this practical reason.[39] It was probably the only reason and did not derive from disapproval of the convention itself. His correspondence before and after the meeting reveals keen interest and satisfaction in what was happening. On October 17 he wrote from the capital that he was "disappointed" to hear that the convention had been postponed, and on the same day sent a second letter saying he was glad to learn it was not. "That the States must defend themselves, or be undefended is clear with me—and the sooner they prepare themselves the better."[40] After he had reports of what the meeting decided in January 1815, he praised the resolutions as "moderate, temperate, & judicious."[41] Well he might, for they laid down precisely the sentiments he and fellow congressmen had been elaborating ever since the war began. The truth is that though he was not a radical disunionist, he did concur, however circumspectly, with this regional protest both in form and in substance.

His belief that New England must resort to a convention was rooted in an intensifying pessimism about public affairs. As he had from his first day in Congress, he saw nothing but ruin coming out of the war and no promise whatever that the Madison administration could do anything about it. Through the months of this session, while Congress fumbled with taxes, enlistment, and other issues, he concluded that the day of doom for the republic could be near at hand. In January Dallas found he could not meet drafts on the treasury to cover military operations. Much of the forty millions needed for next year's expenses would have to be raised by loans; and if they were subscribed, that would be a miracle. Monroe visited the banks in Washington and Georgetown and gave his personal surety (none too sound) for advances to the government.[42] Webster believed that the nation would soon be bankrupt and the offices of the departments would close.[43] Madison, whom Webster characterized as a "faint hearted, lily livered runaway" for having fled the capital before British occupation, seemed helpless in the crisis.[44] Military prospects, in his judgment, were discouraging because of the probable loss of New Orleans, and diplomatic prospects were no better because of the ineptitude of American negotiators.[45]

In an age of slow communications, Webster and his fellow citizens endured a bleak January worrying about obsolete problems. Unknown to them, the Treaty of Ghent had been concluded in Europe on Christmas Eve, and Andrew Jackson's defenders at New Orleans had slaughtered a British assault force on January 8. It was February 4 when news of the battle arrived in Washington, and the thirteenth when a messenger from New York brought a copy of the treaty.[46] Then feelings throughout the land approached ecstasy. The *Intelligencer* swelled with pride as it described an honorable peace achieved by this determined nation in conflict with a powerful foe. Even in the hour of celebration, the editor could not withhold a jab at domestic malcontents: "Federalists, rejoice! For that your opposition has been unavailing in checking the measures

61

of your government; and that your Hartford Conventions, your plots and counter plots, have not arrested the march of the Republic to the heights of Fame and Glory."[47] There was indeed much rejoicing. When people at Portsmouth learned of the treaty from a British vessel arriving there, they raised flags over all public buildings, and the *Oracle* spread the "joyful news of PEACE" to the interior by handbills.[48] On the sixteenth, the day before the Senate overwhelmingly agreed to the treaty, Webster headed homeward.[49]

The close of the war caused many politically minded persons to look back over this time of trial and to assess the record of the Federalist party. Blamed for sheer obstructionism, disloyalty, and possible disunionism, Federalists assumed an ugly image. Mere mention of the Hartford Convention brought to mind the whole range of events and behavior deserving condemnation. It looked very much as if the party would never be resuscitated.[50] Yet Federalists themselves, and some historians afterward, found a basis for approving the positions they had taken.[51] The question whether war had been necessary to defend national interest and honor remained fairly open, with a credible answer being that the United States had been quite close to maintaining, without resort to arms, most of the neutral rights for which it went to war in June 1812. Besides, it was hard to praise an outcome that was status quo ante bellum. As for Federalist wartime negativism, the administration itself had been far from free of mistakes in its confused handling of major problems; and generally it had got the congressional legislation it thought essential because it had always had a sizable majority despite Federalists and maverick Republicans. One would have to look at the nation at large, at the lack of commitment everywhere to provide soldiers and money, to explain chronic difficulties in prosecuting an effective war. South as well as North, Republicans as well as Federalists, had to bear responsibility for the country's embarrassment and peril. But conceding such an argument would help Webster's party very little, at least outside New England, where it had had a heartening if brief renaissance.

After returning home in late February 1815, Webster spent the rest of the year practicing law, with occasional interludes of local political activity. He was happy to do so, for he had had his fill of a congressman's life. "I do not intend spending another winter in this Great Dismal," he wrote shortly before he left Washington. As a change of pace, he was interested, perhaps just mildly, in appointment as state attorney general; and it was later thought that Governor Gilman did nominate him for that office in December but was rebuffed by the Republican council.[52]

There was also a faint possibility of his becoming governor in the follow-ing year, though that never amounted to much.[53]

As usual, Congress would meet in early December; but Webster, al-ready known for late arrivals and early departures, delayed even longer this time in going to the capital. The reason was a critical campaign for the New Hampshire election in March 1816, to which he was giving close attention. Beyond established party differences, the leading issue involved his alma mater, Dartmouth College, which was entering the greatest ordeal of its history. The despotic president, John Wheelock, had at last met his match in his board of trustees during the summer of 1815, and the entire state was treated to a thorough ventilation of their disputes about the college government, Congregationalism versus Pres-byterianism in the Hanover church, and ultimately the political impli-cations of those questions. Pamphlets by the Wheelock side were countered by the trustees. What had first been a simple rebellion of an ordinarily obedient board against the president spread to broader issues. Nearly all members of the board were firm Congregationalists and Fed-eralists. After a quarrel with them over the appointment of a theological professor and minister of the church, Wheelock, a stern Calvinistic Pres-byterian, allied himself with those in the neighborhood and throughout the state who attacked Congregational sectarianism as having been in-tolerant, as well as unpatriotic in the late war. Ike Hill of the *Patriot* op-portunely portrayed the college controversy this way. And Wheelock, until then a dedicated Federalist, found his main support in Republican ranks, including the current candidate for governor, William Plumer. So it happened that this election would focus on the future of the college, which might become a more liberal, state institution if Plumer's Jeffer-sonian ideas prevailed, and on the future of the Federalist establishment, whether in Concord or in the Connecticut Valley.[54]

Some of the trustees were Webster's intimate friends, and he was therefore carefully following these developments and calculating their effects. It was imperative but difficult to choose the strongest possible candidate to oppose Plumer. Gilman, a fixture for years, had been abandoned in the summer for Timothy Farrar, Sr., a college trustee vul-nerable to attacks such as Hill had mounted. Webster and other leaders decided that a less controversial person was preferable. At a party con-vention in December, they substituted John Goddard. The question re-mained whether Goddard, who had declined various nominations in the past, would accept; and after long hesitation, he did refuse. Reportedly, several other men did too before James Sheafe, a prominent Portsmouth merchant, agreed to run. It was now February, and Webster finally felt

63

he could leave for Washington. The next month, after a scurrilous contest, Plumer and other Republicans won impressively and threw the future of New Hampshire Federalism into serious doubt.[55]

When Webster took his seat in the House on February 7, 1816, he noticed a decided change in the prevalent spirit there. Postwar viewpoints expressed a buoyant nationalism which the war had never allowed. The president had struck the keynote in his annual message, calling for a series of policies to bring the country together and to stimulate its growth: a national bank, a protective tariff, an adequate military force, and perhaps a transportation system sponsored by the government. Clay was back in the Speaker's chair. Calhoun was constantly visible as the spokesman of a loose-constructionist, optimistic outlook and as the strategist to translate it into legislation. Some Federalists, such as Thomas Grosvener of New York, seemed receptive, while Old Republican John Randolph, returning to Congress, was as excitable as ever and smelled trouble.

Webster learned at once that the most important bill awaiting House debate was one to charter a national bank, a proposal inherited from the two previous sessions. This time Calhoun not only had the initiative at an early stage but kept it throughout, for Secretary Dallas no longer had a different plan. The two agreed on a measure providing for capitalization of thirty-five millions, of which the government would subscribe seven, and for twenty-five directors, of whom five would be governmental appointees, as well as for familiar functions of central banking. Because the wartime urgency of lending to the treasury had subsided, Calhoun emphasized another goal: the necessity of improving the currency system, now tangled by a vast overissue of state bank notes. He argued that resort to national bank notes would solve the problem.[56] Almost all those supporting the bill discussed the problem of the currency but had little to say about the question of constitutionality—they believed time had settled it.[57] Clay, for example, descending from the rostrum to speak with characteristic eloquence, conceded he had changed his mind since 1811, when he had voted against rechartering the first bank, because of the "force of circumstances" and "the lights of experience."[58]

Webster disliked a Republican bank even more than he had a year ago. Too large a capitalization, he contended; ten millions, enough for Hamilton's institution, was enough for this one. And he was absolutely rigid on the relation between bank and government. Any governmental subscription of stock or representation on the board of directors whatever would preclude the corporation's being a true bank. It was not that he doubted the constitutional power to act on this subject, he insisted, but unless a bill met his specifications, he preferred no bank at all. Furthermore, it was far more necessary to reform the currency by stopping wild issues of irredeemable state bank notes, which Congress could do without setting up a bank. So he concurred with Calhoun and the majority that unsound money was the disease, while distrusting their prescription for it.[59] By early April, however, he could see that his objections were futile; and on the fifth, a conference bill carried and went to the president.[60]

Calhoun was very interested in restraining non-specie-paying banks and later came in with a bill for the purpose. After failing by one vote to get it through, he had a conversation with Webster; and the next day, the twenty-sixth, the New Englander offered a resolution, rather than a bill, to require the treasury to give fuller effect to existing laws. After February 20, 1817, according to his resolution, payments to the government, such as duties and taxes, must be in legal currency (gold or silver) or in notes redeemable in legal currency. The House decisively approved, by a two-thirds vote.[61] Quite pleased with this success, Webster would recall it in the years ahead as the foundation of an efficient system of money and banking. Actually, though it did eventually help the new Bank of the United States, its impact upon state bank notes was modest.[62]

The other nationalistic policy which was affirmed in this session involved the tariff. An early decision was to discontinue the wartime double duties by mid-1816. Since they had operated not only to supply revenue but to protect young manufacturing enterprises from foreign competition, Congress had to decide how much of each of these purposes it wished to incorporate in postwar policy. After exhaustive debate through March and April, it adopted a moderate tariff, one that had protective features but would bring in much of the revenue needed by the government.[63]

Again Calhoun led the nationalists. His enthusiasm for a protective system was large, indeed larger than he would one day like to remember. Economic interests in all sections of the country were interdependent, he argued; and of these, manufacturing was so undeveloped that it required encouragement through the tariff. Remembering the unpleasant experience of the late war, Calhoun also believed a balanced economy was essential for real independence from Britain, still regarded more as a threat than as a friend. Above all, a self-sufficient economy would strengthen the political Union, upon which the liberty of every American depended. Liberty and Union—a sentiment he would later hear Webster express under different circumstances.[64]

At the moment, Webster was ambivalent about the tariff. Receptive

65

to the aggressive lobbying of the textile pioneer Francis Cabot Lowell, who spent a good deal of time with him in the capital that winter, he proposed a protective rate of 25 percent on cottons for a time, to be reduced to 20 percent. "Something should be done" for this industry, he said. With slight modification this provision carried.[65] His mercantile attachments were strained by a section for minimum valuation at twenty-five cents a square yard, very damaging to importers of cheap cloth. But he did not resist it except to vote for a delay in putting it into effect.[66] On other items, such as iron, raw wool, and brown sugar, he voted with the majority to reduce rates.[67] Thus he remained more favorable to fairly low duties as a means of helping shipping than to a protective system. Where he assented to a degree of protection, he insisted on a steady schedule that would avoid business uncertainty arising from frequent and precipitate fluctuations. In the last stage of the discussion, he took no clear overall position: he made no speeches, did not vote on complete parts of the bill, and in fact did not vote on it as a whole when it passed on April 8.[68]

Instead of sober economic arguments, the aspect of the tariff debate he would remember most vividly was personal friction with the volatile Randolph. The Virginian's quick temper exploded during a clash with Webster over the sugar duty, and Randolph characteristically interpreted it as a personal affront. Flinging a challenge, he demanded satisfaction on the field of honor. Webster demurred. He refused to duel because Randolph had no right, he wrote, "to call me to the field to answer what you may please to consider an insult to your feelings." He did not feel bound to accept such an invitation "from any man, who shall choose to risk his own life," but he was prepared to "repel in a suitable manner the aggression of any man who may presume upon such a refusal." Then mediators smoothed out the affair. On the last day of the session, April 30, Randolph felt remarkably satisfied with a "polite and friendly note" from Webster and told him so in a cordial reply.[69]

The trends so evident in this Congress caused Webster as a prominent young Federalist to reflect deeply upon the future of politics in America. His party was in a discouraging, precarious position, fast losing ground in many states and ineffectual on the national scene. And it was less and less homogeneous and unified, in spite of what one might expect of a defensive minority. Divisions on bank and tariff diverged from party lines, with many Federalists voting for and many Republicans voting against those measures.[70] "Whether all our party distinctions are not breaking up, I cannot say," he observed. "Appearances are very much in favor of such a supposition ... I believe we are all to be thrown into new forms, &

new associations."[71] If he foresaw the imminent collapse of his party, as he seemed to, he inclined toward rejection of a two-party system altogether. Like many contemporaries, particularly fellow Federalists, he had often related party loyalty and behavior to undesirable factionalism, which he hoped could be eliminated for the general good. In an essay written in this period, he warned against the "fury of party" and selfish office seekers. "In times of high party feeling," he reasoned, "there is no such thing as free and conscientious choice of rulers."[72] Such thinking was understandable in the context of widespread doubts about the usefulness of a party system, but it suggested trouble for Federalist candidates in coming elections.

Webster himself would not be a candidate this fall. Having decided to move from Portsmouth, he left the battle in New Hampshire to others, though he followed events closely. It turned out that the Republicans swept the state. For the short congressional session from December to March 1817 he was at the capital, giving only slight attention to business there. The only noteworthy question involved presidential veto of a federal internal-improvement bill, for which he voted without comment. No doubt he was true to his prediction that he would "see the sun go down on the third of March with unusual cheerfulness" as he set out for home.[73]

Chapter 5

BOSTON

After the War of 1812, Webster began to think of moving from Portsmouth to a place offering better opportunities. "Our New England prosperity and importance are passing away," he said. "This is fact. The events of the times, the policy of England, the consequences of our war, and the Ghent Treaty, have bereft us of our commerce, the great source of our wealth." He was tempted to go to Albany or New York City, in a state where, he predicted, the "great scenes are to be acted in this country within the next twenty years."[1] But the attraction of Boston proved stronger. Influenced and helped by friends to come there, he decided upon it by mid-1816; in June, he and Grace were in the city to find a house. During the visit he also completed arrangements with young Alexander Bliss to set up a law office in Court Street. An unostentatious graduate of Yale, Bliss would manage day-to-day business reliably, one of his first tasks being to receive and shelve books shipped from Portsmouth a few weeks later. On August 16 the Websters arrived and took rooms at a boardinghouse for the time being.[2]

Boston had some interesting features, not least of which were topographical. Nearly two hundred years old, it sat on a small peninsula bounded by the Charles River to the north, bays to the west and south, and the harbor to the east. Crossing the Charles by way of the bridge with which Webster would be much involved legally and politically, one came to Charlestown. Here at Bunker Hill, scene of an early battle of the Revolution, he would deliver a well-known oration. Up the river was Cambridge, whose main importance derived from the presence of Harvard College. The only access to Boston by land was from the west, across a narrow neck from Roxbury and Brookline, though a bridge did connect the city with Dorchester to the south. Limited to a small, irregular area as it was, the early town had a maze of short, narrow streets haphazardly laid out and quite bewildering to the stranger. Another physical characteristic had been the three hills that rose from an otherwise low terrain (one of the principal streets was named Tremont); a few years after the Websters' arrival, a slow process of leveling these heights ended. Even in 1816, Beacon Hill had long ago lost its light to aid navigators and had shrunk to an ugly core as excavators cut into its slopes and hauled away the soil to fill the now useless Mill Pond.

Boston's general appearance reflected the fact that a primary interest was still commerce. Along the waterfront there was constant activity at the docks and warehouses, where goods from all over the world were landed and sold. On the important wharves—India, Central, and Long—wholesale merchants dealt in sugar, rice, china, flour, coffee, whale oil, fish, hardware. The shipbuilding and ropemaking industries employed many workingmen, and masters of the vessels that filled the harbor signed others to go to sea. Nearby, Faneuil Hall, the pre-Revolutionary structure of widespread fame, was a market whose ground-floor shops and stalls distributed goods to townspeople; the second floor continued to be the meeting place for public occasions, often of a political cast. Up State Street were banks, mercantile firms, and insurance companies, with which Webster would be associated as a lawyer. His office was close at hand, in Court Street curling beyond the Old State House, a landmark topped with handsome figures of lion and unicorn but no longer serving as the capitol.

A short distance westward lay the Common, set aside for civic use, its rail fence a necessary restraint on the cattle grazing there. Not until 1829 did the city discontinue the privilege of citizens to use it for their livestock. At one corner the new State House, designed in 1798 by the busy architect Charles Bulfinch, rose impressively above the neighborhood. Along Beacon Street, on the northern edge of the Common, lived some of the most prominent families, such as those of Harrison Gray Otis, David Sears, and John Phillips.[3]

Above Beacon, another fashionable street was Mt. Vernon, where the Websters soon set up housekeeping in an elegant house rented from Jonathan Mason. This four-story, brick and stone building, at number 57 in the shadow of the State House, had majestic lines enhanced by balcony and grillwork. A short walk took the lawyer to his office and the commercial section. After three years he bought a house at 37 Somerset, still closer to the center of the city. Then from 1822 to late 1824 the family lived most of each year in rustic Dorchester, with Webster and, at times, his wife and children going to Washington during the winters.[4]

At last, in November 1824, he found a more permanent home a few blocks south of State Street on Summer, where Federal, High, and South came together in a delightful open square. Israel Thorndike, the wealthy merchant-manufacturer, had owned this house and lived in the one adjacent; in fact the two buildings were connected by a door which could be opened when either occupant needed more room for a social affair. Like others in the neighborhood built by Thorndike, Webster's house was a three-story structure set close to the street, with space for a stable and an extensive garden in the rear; soon he enlarged his property by buying additional small lots. The architectural style was late Georgian, with modest columns at the doorway, the familiar balcony and metalwork, paned windows flanked with shutters, and a general impression of dignity. The attractiveness of the place derived more from the setting, however, for in these days Summer was a beautiful street, lined by tall horse-chestnut trees providing deep shade and suggesting a lingering rural atmosphere. Here affluent, proper people enjoyed a haven from some of the disturbing and unpleasant aspects of an emerging urban environment.[5]

In fact, the city as a whole seemed to want to hold to its established ways. Still fairly homogeneous ethnically and culturally, predominantly Anglo-Saxon and Protestant, it adhered to many deep-rooted values. A stout conservatism emphasized order in the community and respectability of the individual, with the two characteristics dependent upon one another. Caution and moderation were desirable traits of the good citizen. These demanded conformity to accepted standards of behavior, set at the upper level of society. Virtue and intelligence counted heavily but appeared to be identifiable with material success. Thus the great merchants and the new textile entrepreneurs (often the same people) were at the center of power, shared though it might be by lawyers, clergymen, college professors, newspaper editors, and politicians. The result was a remarkable stability, achieved by a continuity of leadership and by a surprisingly low degree of economic mobility.[6]

Nevertheless, the current of change was irresistible. With a population of about forty thousand in 1816, Boston was growing at the rate of 50 percent each decade. In addition to the swelling numbers coming to the city from surrounding towns, the influx of foreign immigrants, especially the Irish, accelerated. So at least in a demographic sense, a great deal of mobility did exist and increased in subsequent years. The consequences of urbanization for Boston resembled those in other places and at other times: inescapable problems of housing, labor conditions, municipal government, and more than a little social tension. Reformers would respond to the situation, sometimes in a manner that further alarmed upholders of the old order.[7]

However much he may have thought about these trends, Webster was of course more directly concerned with his own household, with a growing, satisfying family that brought moments of hope, joy, and sorrow. When the Websters arrived in Boston in 1816, they had two children: Grace, then six, and Daniel Fletcher, three. Julia was born in 1818, Edward in 1820, and the youngest, Charles, in 1821.[8] It was a contented family, its members closely linked by affection. Mrs. Webster strongly inclined to concentrate her attention upon their home and children instead of the outside world of social relations and public affairs. And this inclination became firmer because of Webster's frequent absences on legal business and later in congressional service. Though helped by Hannah, a maid who remained with the family for years, she had the main responsibility for guidance of the children. Like other youngsters, they learned the kind of conduct expected of them, including deference and respect toward their parents.

There were times of sorrow too. One of these occurred the first winter after the family moved to Boston, during one of the few occasions when Mrs. Webster accompanied her husband to Washington for a session of Congress. Leaving Grace and Fletcher with a friend in Cambridge when they set out in November 1816, they had no sooner arrived at the capital than they heard that their little daughter was seriously ill. What had earlier seemed a minor ailment turned out to be an advanced case of tuberculosis. In the second week of January the worried Websters traveled homeward as rapidly as they could, only to find Grace's condition hopeless. She died on the twenty-third.[9] As Eliza Buckminster recalled, Webster "turned away from the bed, and great tears coursed down his cheeks." His wife was so shaken that she would not leave the house for weeks.[10]

Later, the impact of Charles's death was also painful. In Washington in December 1824 Webster received letters telling of a persistently high fever afflicting the three-year-old boy.[11] Their friend, the highly reputable Dr. John Warren, attended the child tirelessly but was pessimistic. A flurry of similar cases about town amounted to an epidemic, he thought; but he could not deal with it effectively.[12] For a while Webster heard little more, because he left on a trip into Virginia. Then on Christmas Eve, a few days after his return, the mail brought news that Charles had died on December 19.[13] Finding it impractical to go to Boston, he felt frustrated. As an outlet for his distress, and in an effort to console Grace, he wrote a poem to Charles's memory. Interesting for their religious sentiment more than for literary qualities, his hymnlike lines closed:

> My Father, I beheld thee born,
> And led thy tottering steps with care;
> Before me risen to Heaven's bright morn,
> My Son! My Father! Guide me there—[14]

He could find solace in submission to the will of providence, mysterious as it might be; but Grace, though subscribing to the same article of faith, was less resilient. The effects of Charles's death upon her were severe and enduring. She mourned deeply through that winter, seemed somewhat withdrawn, and fell into moods of gloomy introspection, toward which she had tended anyway. A long-range result was reinforcement of her habit of worrying about sickness or death. The experience also seemed to undermine her confidence in overseeing the children's behavior and development.[15]

Such periods of trouble probably brought Daniel and Grace closer together in a marriage that was always stable. Their relationship rested not only on love but on mutual respect—in many ways, he benefited from her good sense and moral character. According to social norms, as his wife she dutifully subordinated herself to him, to his aspirations and advancement on the public scene. She often alluded to the dullness and triviality of her letters, which reflected, she confessed, her own narrow interests. Describing herself as "the daughter of a poor Country clergyman," she felt it "mortifying to reflect how much I am behind you in every thing. I know no one respects, but rather despises, those, they consider very much their inferiors." This she regretted "more on your account than any other."[16] But her self-image was incorrect, for she was an intelligent, cultivated woman with more knowledge of human affairs, including political events, than she might display. Occasionally she dropped her reserve and commented quite perceptively about current topics, only to apologize for intruding her opinions. On the whole, Webster had no reason to regret he had married the daughter of a poor country clergyman.

Of Grace's relatives, the one with whom Webster had the closest relationship was William Paige, her half brother. Much younger than Grace, Paige was a bachelor until nearly forty and was therefore drawn into the circle of the family as soon as they came to Boston. He was in the early phase of a long career as a merchant and textile manufacturer in the town, a partner of Nathan Appleton. Living in a house on Summer Street close to the Websters, he shared their happy moments and became a mainstay whenever needed. Webster called upon Paige frequently to handle his recurrent financial problems, to assist Grace in his absence, and often to take charge of the children, who were quite attached to Uncle William.

As for his own relatives, most of whom were back in New Hampshire in and around Salisbury, Webster visited them from time to time but was not especially close to any except Ezekiel. The thinking and values of the brothers were very similar, despite the fact that Daniel had left tiny Boscawen for a more complicated life in the city while Ezekiel was comfortably established in the village. In 1825, after an interval as a widower, Ezekiel married Achsah Pollard, a young woman of Concord, New Hampshire, who became a capable stepmother to his two little daughters and a sister-in-law warmly welcomed by the Websters of Boston.[17]

Besides his family, an increasing number of friends enriched his life. He was a sociable person who thoroughly enjoyed companionship during hours of leisure, in conversation or recreation; and in business and politics, he relied upon others regularly. Seldom did he depend upon his own resources alone, however much his ability and reputation suggested he might. Two of his most valued friends were George Ticknor and Edward Everett, both exemplars of New England conservatism and culture. Endowed with brilliant talents, the two young scholars had left for several years of study in Europe just before the Websters moved to Boston; and after returning in 1819, both were professors at Harvard. Soon Everett gravitated toward politics, while Ticknor became the arbiter of the city's intellectual community, at least its genteel branch. Webster's attachment to Everett and Ticknor grew even stronger as the years passed. They responded with a loyalty approaching adulation and helped him with advice and with the cheerful performance of innumerable chores. Elsewhere, other steady friends, less deferential because of their age and experience, were Joseph Story, Jeremiah Mason, and Joseph Hopkinson. To all three, entirely congenial as they were, Webster could confide his thoughts and feelings freely.

Although his association with the state's most prominent men in business and government was very amicable, he did not develop the kind of comradeship with any of them that one might predict. He stood on excellent terms with his neighbors Thomas Handasyd Perkins and Israel Thorndike, with Everett's wealthy father-in-law, Peter Brooks, with the Appletons, the Lowells, Josiah Quincy, and Levi Lincoln. But as a companion for hunting and fishing, for an interlude of recreation, he turned to George Blake, also a resident of Summer Street. United States attorney for Massachusetts in the twenties, Blake appeared in court there with Webster and accompanied him to Washington for some cases.

When their wives came to the capital, the Blakes and the Websters spent many pleasant hours together. Though an able lawyer, the easygoing Blake did not let his work interfere with the lighter side of life; and nothing interested him more than a holiday on the Cape with rod and gun. That exactly suited his crony Webster too.[18]

In August the Blakes and Websters would head for Sandwich, where they stayed at a boardinghouse and enjoyed the beach and excursions into an area that was still mainly in its natural state. The two men spent long days tramping through the marshes to hunt birds and working slowly down the brooks to cast for trout. Proud of his skills as a sportsman, Webster felt exhilarated by a successful expedition. No doubt he found as much satisfaction as if he had achieved some political triumph or won an important legal case.[19] He never tired of telling the story that he composed a much-quoted part of his Bunker Hill oration while fishing in Mashpee Brook. One can picture him standing hip deep in a tree-shaded pool with rod in hand and addressing the elusive trout as if they were ancient survivors of the Revolutionary War: "Venerable Men! you have come down to us from a former generation."[20]

His affairs at home were improving but required all the attention he could give them, more than he usually managed. Since coming to Boston in 1816, his income had dramatically increased and promised to continue doing so. In his first month there, he received legal fees totaling more than two thousand dollars; in the next few years his clients on State Street, the merchant capitalists, insurance companies, and banks, paid him very well for his valuable services. His account book, whose accuracy was less than perfect, showed annual incomes averaging from ten to fifteen thousand, several times that of the Portsmouth period. Important cases could bring in a thousand dollars—one, *McCulloch* v. *Maryland* (1819), twice that amount. And the greatest single source of earnings was the batch of Spanish claims before the commission established under the Florida treaty in 1822 and 1823. For his extensive work on them, commissions exceeded seventy thousand.[21]

However handsome a lawyer's fees might be, they were never enough for Webster. As he had from the start of his career, he searched for money elsewhere. An attractive possibility was to reap spectacular profits from buying and selling land, for he saw many men rising rapidly by shrewd or fortunate investments of that sort. In the dynamic economy of this young country, fortune seemed to await those who were enterprising. Whether that would be true in his case remained undetermined, but he believed it would. His landholdings in New Hampshire, particularly in the northern, sparsely populated part of the state, were substantial if unprofitable, while he frequently obtained and disposed of other parcels of real estate in both the Connecticut and Merrimack valleys. Some property came as fees from clients; a good deal of it was encumbered by mortgages to such generous creditors as Nathaniel Haven, the Portsmouth merchant; and nearly all the transactions depended upn Ezekiel's collaboration.[22] Off and on, the brothers shared ownership of the family farm in Salisbury, to which Webster added several neighboring pieces. In the 1820s he also acquired town lots in Boston, chiefly near his house on Summer Street, and in Cambridge.[23]

In addition to land, he owned a modest amount of corporate stock. For a long while he held shares in the Concord Bank, and briefly in a Portsmouth institution. In 1822, when the Boston Associates incorporated the Merrimack Manufacturing Company for cotton-textile production, his friend Nathan Appleton arranged for him to buy a little stock in it, a valuable privilege in light of the sizable dividends regularly paid.[24] The next year he subscribed sixty thousand dollars for the newly organized mill in Nashua, New Hampshire, but apparently failed to raise the necessary money.[25] The corporation which interested him most, however, was the Bank of the United States. Never a large stockholder, he did have a few shares as early as 1819.[26] More lucrative were his retainers, on a steady basis, as the national bank's eminent attorney from his arguments of the *McCulloch* case that year onward. Beginning in 1825 he was elected for several terms as a director on the main board in Philadelphia, having previously been on the board of the Boston branch.[27] His special relationship to the corporation's president, Nicholas Biddle, enabled him to install his brother-in-law Paige as a director in Boston and to place Mason in office as president of the Portsmouth branch.[28] How much all this helped him financially is unclear, yet he did find the bank receptive and very patient with respect to his numerous notes and drafts.[29]

In truth, the story of his personal finances concerns credit more than anything else. Life seemed to be an unending sequence of due dates on his notes to banks and friends, whose sympathy must often have changed to irritation. His correspondence, particularly with his partners, Alexander Bliss and later Henry Kinsman, is full of instructions about payments and renewals, usually the latter. Paige, Blake, and Nathan Hale were faithful agents and endorsers to pacify creditors, just as others had been earlier and more would be in the future.[30] He wrote and talked as if he was systematic about these matters—he did keep intricate records—but his visions, lack of discipline in spending, and general impracticality kept him in hot water. What saved him from disaster was the unfailing presence of some "angel," ever prepared to extend further aid. Already there was a widely accepted idea that this great man deserved compensation for making heavy financial sacrifices by serving in public office instead of devoting his unique talents to material goals.[31]

Though Webster's primary concerns were politics, law, and, to a lesser degree, money, he did not lack intellectual interests. Justifiably, he thought of himself as an educated man. As a youth, he had acquired a good foundation in Latin language and literature, a familiarity with modern English authors, and a modest acquaintance with works in philosophy and science. Now, in his mature years, he occasionally turned to these for leisure or instruction, a tendency reflected in his private conversations, writings, and public speeches. Yet he had little taste for contemporary American fiction and poetry in a period when they were gaining popularity and distinction for the first time. He did read books and essays from both sides of the Atlantic in history, biography, political economy. Thus his orientation was pragmatic rather than speculative or artistic.[32]

In the late 1820s a good many other people had similar preferences, a fact illustrated by the remarkable popularity of the lyceum. This movement, begun in Millbury, Massachusetts, in 1826, soon spread through the land with the aim of educating the common man. Lecturers, including such eminent figures as Edward Everett and Ralph Waldo Emerson, were active in their own communities or on the circuit. In November 1828 Webster helped organize the Boston Society for the Diffusion of Useful Knowledge and served as its president the following year.[33] His introductory lecture emphasized the applications of science throughout history. Taking as an example the principles of motion, he traced efforts to discover easier and more efficient means of producing it for industrial progress and therefore the well-being of mankind. Though not profound, his discussion seemed to hit the right note: it was solidly informed and not so theoretical as to lose the interest of workingmen in his audience.[34]

Like most other Americans, Webster joined a number of associations for social improvement. Often the mail brought him an invitation to become a member of some society, to pay his dues, and perhaps to address a future meeting. In Boston, the American Academy of Arts and Sciences elected him a fellow, a distinction which obligated him to purchase the academy's publications as they appeared.[35] Along with friends in the city's intellectual and business circles, he supported the development of the Athenaeum. To the American Antiquarian Society in Worcester he sent off his annual dues as a new member in 1820.[36] Indeed, it was frequently a historical society which attracted his interest, with the organization capitalizing upon his reputation, sometimes benefiting from a speech before one of its meetings.[37] A connection of this kind pleased him too, more than endorsing a movement whose purpose might be dangerously radical. There was an oversupply of these groups, he believed.

Basic to his structure of values, then, was a view that human advancement depended upon the slow, sober process of education, not upon a dramatic breakthrough by agitation or a magical formula of the dreamer. Typical of his generation, he thought that effective education would enable the next generation to preserve the best of the old institutions while promoting the progress of the republic. Although he never contributed much concretely to the establishment of a modern public school system, then in an early stage, he wholly approved what was occurring.[38]

His direct involvement was with higher education, especially with Dartmouth. Handling the famous case against state control brought him into intimate contact with the college's affairs, and afterward he was idolized as a veritable savior. Then he sought to help the institution recover from its ordeal: financially, by publishing a report of the case to improve public relations and by encouraging alumni contributions (he himself contributed very little); internally, by urging the distinguished chancellor James Kent to take over the presidency (Kent declined).[39] His brother Ezekiel was a trustee through these years, and two of his nephews would later become professors there. During visits to New Hampshire he could keep in touch with the situation in Hanover. So his relationship with the onetime Indian school remained close.

Not long after moving to Boston, Webster became increasingly interested in Harvard. In the state constitutional convention he wrote a succinct but informative report on the history and current status of the university, together with mild recommendations for change which that body approved but the voters subsequently rejected. A year later, in 1822, he accepted appointment as an overseer, one among a large board of state officers, Congregational ministers, and laymen.[40] And in August 1824, when Lafayette was the guest of honor at commencement, Webster received an honorary LL.D., a token of the university's friendliness toward him as well as an acknowledgment of his achievements in public life.[41] In general, he wished to see Harvard become a true university instead of a struggling college such as it had been. His friends Ticknor and Everett initiated a plan for academic reform toward that goal in 1825, proposals supported by Webster and Story but abandoned by Everett after second thought. Ticknor, as professor of French and Spanish literature, was really slapping the wrists of fellow faculty members by insist-

77

ing upon specialization by departments and upon higher intellectual standards. The faculty, now backed by Everett, complained that such decisions were theirs to make, not to be assumed by the governing bodies of corporation and overseers. But Ticknor, with legal and other advice from Story and Webster, gained acceptance of his plan by those governors—a rather superficial victory, it appeared, if the faculty continued its opposition.[42] Perhaps a more vigorous president could counter that obstacle, the reformers concluded; and when the harried John T. Kirkland resigned in 1828, Webster led a move to put Ticknor into that office. By this time there was too much opposition to the learned professor, and so the always popular Josiah Quincy was chosen.[43] Disappointed but not upset, Webster soon found great satisfaction in the appointment of Story as the first Dane Professor of Law, an event quite as important to the university's progress as the selection of a president.[44]

Though somewhat involved with problems of education, he would not overlook society's dependence also upon religion. Nowhere was there wider agreement upon that point than in Boston, as its two-century history showed. Even the capital of American Puritanism, however, had recently witnessed changes in long-established patterns. One by one, beginning with King's Chapel, the city's churches abandoned many Calvinistic doctrines to adopt Unitarianism.[45] The shift was neither sudden nor complete, the Congregational form of government usually remained, and the theological positions of its minister influenced the current status of a church. But the general effect was to replace the severe implications of predestination and regeneration with a more buoyant, optimistic outlook.

Webster must have found this trend somewhat disturbing. Although he was friendly with William Ellery Channing, foremost Unitarian clergyman of this generation and occupant of the pulpit in the Federal Street Church near his house, Webster had not changed his beliefs since his close association with the orthodox Joseph Buckminster in Portsmouth.[46] When he came to Boston, he regularly attended the Brattle Square Church (a few steps away from his law office), where young Joseph Stevens Buckminster had been pastor until an early death, to be succeeded briefly by nineteen-year-old Edward Everett and later by John Gorham Palfrey. All were Unitarians. The Websters' relations with Palfrey during the 1820s while he was their minister were outwardly smooth, sometimes warm. But Grace, who worried about theological matters more than her husband did, preferred old-style trinitarianism regardless of what Channing and Palfrey expounded. "I cannot but fear we are wrong to appear to be of that [Unitarian] sect," she scolded Daniel. "I am anxious that our children should be taught the right way if it be possible to ascertain what that is. I fear my dear Husband that you have not sufficiently considered the subject and I have been myself too easy."[47]

The difficulty of the subject may have accounted for the fact that the family owned pews not only in Brattle Square but also in St. Paul's Episcopal.[48] When the latter church, a striking Grecian temple on Tremont, was under construction in 1820, Webster served on the building committee.[49] Though their connection with St. Paul's was not as strong as it was with Palfrey's congregation, they did attend services sometimes; and there they interred the two children who died during this period. To what extent they accepted Episcopalian dogma is uncertain, but no doubt they did so with reservations.

Webster's approval of much of the old Puritan faith is attested in one of his best known orations, "The First Settlement of New England," delivered on the bicentennial of Plymouth, December 22, 1820. In this occasional speech, he explored the foundations of Puritanism in the New World, the history of its expansion, and its effects upon American society and government. The opportunity to articulate these ideas came from an invitation by the newly organized Pilgrim Society to deliver an address that would be the most famous of a series reaching back to the 1770s and extending annually into the twentieth century.[50] With grandiloquent phrases, he expressed a reverence of the past and an inspirational forecast of the future altogether agreeable to his eager audience.

Taking brief leave from his work in the Massachusetts constitutional convention, he set out on December 21 for the day-long journey of forty miles to the Old Colony. His traveling companions, including his wife, Ticknor, and several other friends, joined an almost continuous column of people on their way to a keenly anticipated celebration. Upon arrival he found the town full of animated visitors, some anxiously searching for lodging in private homes because the inns were overflowing, others listening to music of a military band tirelessly marching to and fro, many being drawn, as if by a magnet, down to the renowned rock first touched by the Pilgrim fathers two hundred years before.[51]

The next afternoon a procession led by the selectmen, members of the clergy, and the orator passed through snowy streets to the meetinghouse, packed to capacity well ahead of time. Inside, the ceremony opened with a hymn, prayers, and a specially composed ode, after which President Kirkland of Harvard introduced him. Webster stood at the deacon's station beside a table covered with green cloth and for a minute ran his eyes over his receptive audience. Dressed in smallclothes, black silk stockings, buckled shoes, and silk gown, his figure matched a commanding countenance to set the desired mood.[52] "Let us rejoice that we behold this day," he began. "Let us be thankful that we have lived to see the bright and happy breaking of the auspicious morn, which commences the third century of the history of New England."[53]

In a well-prepared historical review, he characterized the founding of Plymouth as a turning point in human affairs. This colony was distinctive, he believed, for it had developed its own ideals and free institutions, not mere extensions of those in the mother country, from which the Pilgrims had fled to escape suppression of their religious freedom. Here in the American wilderness they had broken away from old restraints, in contrast to the closely controlled colonies of ancient Greece and Rome or even of Britain in the West Indies. Courageously, these hardy settlers prevailed over the enormous obstacles they faced; and this experience in a common cause nourished sturdy self-reliance and pride, resisting any threat to their liberties.[54] Thus in the next century and a half New England (he now broadened the discussion beyond Plymouth) was alive to such moves to oppress it as installation of the hated Andros as governor, unfair navigation acts, and pre-Revolutionary tax measures. New England's religious principles, moral habits, public school system, thriving commerce, and contributions to western migration not only reflected its remarkable progress but also enabled it to strike the first blow for independence in 1775.

Developing his theme, the orator then explained those features of New England society and government deserving praise. One was the freehold system of land tenure, embodying a rejection of old feudal rules, such as primogeniture and entail, and assuring the right of alienation. As a result, property was widely distributed. The extent to which a government rests upon just conditions of property holding always determines the extent to which it is free, he contended. Very similar to the position he was taking in the constitutional convention, the argument derived from a central premise in his political thought. Another strong support to this well-ordered society, he continued, was the public school system, which virtually eliminated illiteracy while fostering sound morality, an achievement equaled nowhere in Europe. But this would not have occurred, he reasoned, had not all institutions rested upon true Christian principles, upon the church, vital to every stage of improvement from the days of William Bradford to the present moment. Near the end, Webster made a foray against the illegal, evil slave trade to arouse the nobler sentiments of his audience, perhaps to capitalize on feelings precipitated by the recent Missouri debates. Whatever the problems encountered in the years ahead, the correct course must be to carry forward those precepts inherited from the founders. "Advance, then, ye future generations!" he exclaimed. "We welcome you to the immeasurable blessings of rational existence, the immortal hope of Christianity, and the light of everlasting truth!"

Following the oration came a public dinner, attended by more than four hundred and highlighted by interminable toasts. The language was occasionally unwieldy, if elevating. The last one, for example, declared, "The mineralogy of *Forefathers' Rock* of the *primitive* formation—*in place*—the *base* of all formations—like the forefathers—not easily broken—let it be crowned by the *transition* MARBLE."[55] In the evening, an even larger number gathered for more entertainment at a ball until long after midnight. Webster participated in these festivities lightheartedly, glowing with satisfaction derived from compliments on his oratory.

His speech at Bunker Hill in June 1825 also illustrated his rhetorical talent. Fifty years had passed since the famous battle on the Charlestown peninsula. On the seventeenth, the people of Boston and vicinity witnessed the laying of the cornerstone for a monument at the site and celebrated the day by marching, singing, eating, and listening. As principal speaker, Webster faced an enormous audience and expressed in moving words the memories and ideals of these many thousands. His use of history and his view of the present very much resembled what he had said at Plymouth, though not equaling the intellectual quality of the previous effort. But this occasion aroused more popular interest and was therefore more significant.

The idea of a monument dated back to the immediate aftermath of the battle as a way to honor the fallen defenders, notably General Joseph Warren, who had been buried on the hill. Finally, in 1823, leading men of the city—William Tudor, Thomas Perkins, John Warren, George Ticknor, Edward Everett, Webster, and others—organized the Bunker Hill Monument Association to bring the idea to reality, at least to begin construction two years hence. Then the association launched a subscription campaign to raise money. One could become a member by paying five dollars and, it was hoped, a good deal more.[56] The visit of Lafayette to Boston in August 1824 during his tour of the country gave a strong stimulus to achieving the goal, for the profuse admiration shown him naturally recalled the sacrifices of his fellow soldiers during the Revolutionary War. Furthermore, the old general promised to return the following June when the cornerstone would be laid.[57] So there would be an elaborate ceremony, requiring an appropriate oration.

It was spring before Webster accepted an invitation to speak. Through early March he was in Washington, so much involved with congressional business that he gave little thought to the matter; indeed he was still unsure whether an address was necessary. Besides, he had become president of the monument association, which perhaps made it improper for him to be the principal orator as well. He did not overcome these doubts and begin preparation until June, completing the speech just before the appointed day.[58] Writing to Ticknor, who had pressed him to go ahead with the speech, he revealed more than ordinary modesty about what he had composed. "I am pretty well persuaded," he complained, "it is a speech that will *finish* me—as far as reputation is concerned."[59] The only part pleasing him related to the surviving Revolutionary veterans, a passage he conceived while trout fishing at Sandwich.[60] Yet it would be a mistake to say that all was last-minute effort, for he had long had an interest in the history of the battle of Bunker Hill, in fact had published an article on it in the *North American Review;* and his thinking on American society and government, which infused the oration, had also been well settled.[61]

By midmorning of the seventeenth, the procession was forming on the Common across from the State House and moving through the streets of Boston to Charles River Bridge and over to Bunker Hill. Never had inhabitants of the city, many of them massed on the sidewalks and some watching from windows of shops and houses, seen anything like it. At the head of a seemingly endless line were the old men who had fought in the battle, as well as other veterans of the war; then there were military escorts, several thousand members of the monument association, almost as many Masons, and, toward the end, public officers and other prominent figures, including Webster and Lafayette. Arriving at the top of the hill, this last group performed the ceremony of laying the cornerstone. Afterward they moved from the northern slope to a stage, flanked and fronted with seats for spectators. It was a natural amphitheater, with about twenty thousand people on the hillside looking upon the speaker and various notables, the latter sheltered from a relentless sun by awnings. Despite detailed arrangements, the vastness of the affair brought on confusion—such as the collapse of a section of seats for which competition may have been too zealous. But nothing seriously interfered with the business at hand, as a veteran chaplain gave the invocation in trembling words and the throng joined in a hymn, "O, is not this a holy spot?" Now attention centered upon the robed orator, whose customary self-confidence seemed sufficient to a test that would shake most mortals. Any initial uneasiness he may have felt as he gazed at this awesome field of faces did not show; and for a little more than a hour, the magnificent voice, keyed high for the purpose, carried across the vast audience.[62]

First he called attention to the occasion, the work begun upon a monument to perpetuate the memory of bravery and patriotism displayed here fifty years ago, the inspiration which recollection of the nation's early history provided. Turning to the little band of survivors, he cried, "Venerable Men! You have come down to us from a former generation." They had undergone the ordeal of a war precipitated by the bloody battle on this spot, he said. In contrast to the anxiety and suffering they had once felt, today they could view a scene of peace and plenty and enjoy their reward.[63] Further connecting the past and present and recognizing those being honored, he also addressed Lafayette in highly complimentary fashion. As a young man, the general had an "interesting relation to this country," for heaven had ordained that "the electric spark of liberty should be conducted through you, from the New World to the Old."[64]

The keynote of the speech was human progress. And his point of departure was the Revolution, building upon an earlier American experience in self-government and providing the basis for growth and improvement. How satisfying it was, he observed, to contemplate the increase of population, the geographic expansion of this republic, its achievements in economic enterprise, its cultural advances. And in broader perspective, the United States had influenced other people, both in Europe and South America, in a corresponding transformation. "We live in a most extraordinary age," he declared. Public opinion everywhere dictated regard for civil liberty and peace among nations. To assure continuance of this happy trend, he called upon America to maintain its example to the world: "The last hopes of mankind, therefore, rest with us." Superpatriotic and ultraromantic emotion peaked with this charge, "Let our object be, our country, our whole country, and nothing but our country."[65]

The next year, in August 1826, Webster delivered another speech, which in substance and theme surpassed both the Plymouth and Bunker Hill orations. It was his eulogy of Adams and Jefferson, whose deaths on the Fourth of July were a remarkable coincidence, not only because their lives ended within a few hours of each other but also because this occurred precisely fifty years after the adoption of the Declaration of Independence. Not long after the news of these deaths arrived in Boston, Webster began work on the eulogy, to be given at Faneuil Hall in accordance with resolutions adopted by the city council. His materials were historical, drawn from public documents, correspondence, histories such as David Ramsay's on the Revolution and John Marshall's life of Washington, as well as his own rather full knowledge gathered through the years.[66] His approach was necessarily biographical and for that reason had the advantage of broad human interest. Though he prepared what he would say with uncommon care and skill, he did not finish his final draft until the day before the occasion.

At midday on August 2 he accompanied a procession through town to Faneuil Hall, where four thousand fortunate people had squeezed into the meeting room while many others stood disappointed in the market-place or reached only the stairway. With Webster on the stage were President Adams, Governor Lincoln, Mayor Quincy, and other leading men. The hall was darkened, draped in black, and quiet, at least after those on the outside pressing to enter were satisfied that there was abso-lutely no more space available. Dressed again in smallclothes and gown, the orator placed his manuscript on a small table beside him but hardly looked at it while he spoke deliberately yet smoothly for about two hours. Because of the solemnity of the ceremony, his listeners kept their reactions to a subdued level.[67]

After allusion to the striking circumstance of the deaths of Adams and Jefferson and to generalities about their long, fruitful lives, he traced the careers of each in some detail up to 1776. But he focused upon the Dec-laration of Independence, with which both men were very much con-cerned. His description and analysis of the Declaration were thorough, as sound as one would find in later scholarly treatments. Jefferson, he said, did not attempt any novelty, for he was restating well-known American positions to justify the crucial step to be taken. The Virginian directed his list of grievances against the king, the only connection be-tween Britain and the colonies, and not against Parliament, whose legis-lative power did not extend to these provinces. So Jefferson rested his case, Webster observed, on a foundation of established American self-government.

Deferring to his southern colleague in the drafting of this document, Adams took the lead in debating the issue on the floor of the Continental Congress. Here Webster admitted that texts of speeches had not been reported, but the Massachusetts delegate and other prominent figures had so often and so openly expressed their thinking that there could be no doubt about the main outlines of this discussion. The orator therefore felt justified in re-creating the scene and the arguments for and against a declaration—a technique to attain dramatic effect. An opponent, ac-cording to this narrative, urged, "Let us pause! This step, once taken, cannot be retraced." America did not yet have the strength, military or diplomatic, to risk revolution. The public mind was not ready for it. If the powerful mother country overwhelmed resistance, all would be lost, no just reconciliation of existing differences would then be possible, and the worst kind of despotism would inevitably follow.

Adams rejected this cautious counsel, Webster continued. "Sink or swim, live or die, survive or perish, I give my hand and my heart to this vote." Reconciliation was impossible, and submission unthinkable. "The war, then, must go on. We must fight it through." As for himself, Adams declared that his judgment drove him to this measure, and he was willing to stake his life and fortune upon it. "I am for the Declaration. It is my living sentiment, and by the blessing of God it shall be my dying sentiment. Independence *now,* and Independence forever."[68] Such a powerful statement, direct and courageous as it was, carried the day, Webster concluded; and joined with Jefferson's authorship of the famous document, Adams' vigorous role formed a collaboration that ought never to be forgotten.

He then lightly outlined a few facts about later phases of the two men's lives. Their services were quite comparable, in terms of the high offices they held; their long years of retirement were unusually happy and filled with constructive pursuits, especially of an intellectual character. Conceding their disagreements on many political topics, he chose not to elaborate on them. Nor did he notice, perhaps did not know about, the reestablishment of friendly relations in a correspondence between the two old men. Instead, he moved to his peroration, emphasizing the duties devolving on the living to acknowledge their debt to those departed patriots, to uphold the virtue and liberty they had transmitted. "America, America," he exclaimed, "our country, fellow-citizens, our own dear and native land, is inseparably connected, fast bound up, in fortune and by fate, with these great interests."[69]

In his occasional speeches of the twenties, Webster showed an extraordinary ability to express the ideals of his contemporaries. Such discourses took the shape that they did from what his audiences wished to hear; in this sense, they were a dialogue between him and his listeners. It was a time when a certain pattern of oratory had become popular. Elevated patriotism, moral inspiration, and an expansive optimism were essential elements, regardless of topic or setting. The ornate, urbane style of Everett, the popular though scholarly lyceum lectures of Emerson, all reflected the mind and feelings of their America. And so Webster, too, whether talking of Puritanism or the American Revolution, was sensitive to the public pulse. He was superbly equipped for the task. His "God-like" presence, his command of the classics and history, his habit of careful preparation, his clear and direct diction—varied by long periods—his magnificent elocution that could reach out to the thousands were constant assets. By today's standards, he might appear too grandiloquent and too prone to cater to the sophisticated; but by the standards of the early nineteenth century, he personified much of what his fellow citizens admired.[70]

Participation in such public affairs had given his individual characteristics more definite shape. Entering his middle years, he was not moving in new directions but was becoming the kind of person one would have predicted he would be, given his natural talents and the social setting in which he lived. Intelligent, educated, ambitious, he found outlets for his energy in a society whose values were both conservative and dynamic—conservative in holding to old articles of faith and norms of behavior, dynamic in aspiring to new levels of human progress. Of course he and his associates within Boston's most influential circle encountered uncomfortable contradictions in this system of values. Still, in his first decade of residence there, he found ways of reconciling them so that they had very broad appeal.

Chapter 6

MASSACHUSETTS POLITICIAN

After his term as congressman ended in early 1817, Webster was less involved in national politics for several years. Having moved to Boston the preceding summer, he gave more attention to his law practice and personal concerns, both of which decidedly benefited from the change of scene. It was a relative matter, for his interest in issues and events remained very much alive, though often centering on state and local politics. Regarded as a party leader in Massachusetts, he was fairly active in Federalist councils and by the early twenties would again return to an important role at the national level.

He found Boston's political environment quite hospitable. Though his party was ailing, maybe moribund, in the country as a whole, it continued for some time to be dominant here. In the years following the Treaty of Ghent, Federalists regularly elected the governor and a majority in the legislature against a mounting Republican challenge. Perhaps the events and behavior which had damaged the party nationally had temporarily strengthened it locally. To advocate its cause and to defend its interests, it had adapted its techniques and organization to the demands of popular politics. In the city, its leadership could depend upon well-disciplined workers in the several wards and upon committees and caucuses to determine and execute Federalist strategy. Very helpful too were loyal newspapers, such as the *Columbian Centinel* and the *Advertiser*. And frequently, always on the eve of elections but whenever an exciting issue arose as well, there were mass meetings at Faneuil Hall or the Exchange Coffee House to hear partisan speeches. Beyond Boston, conceded to be the center of power, the party was also vigorous in towns and counties throughout the state. Though Federalism may have held true to its original principles and may have had the same social and economic orientation it had in Hamilton's day, it adjusted its tactics for practical purposes.[1]

Unlike Federalists elsewhere, until the mid-1820s Massachusetts men did not feel compelled to ally with Republican factions to win elections or to share patronage within the state. They were seldom reluctant to use the names "Federalist" and "Federal." Yet they faced a more difficult problem having national implications. Rigid distinctions between parties would of course be disadvantageous while Republican supremacy in Washington was so complete. On that level, they hoped that old labels would be discarded and that the Monroe administration would be nonpartisan and magnanimous, particularly in appointments to office. Would not an exclusionary policy be unfair, indeed vindictive?

Bay State Federalists had reason to believe the answer would be favorable. At the outset of his presidency Monroe talked of harmony now that the nation had emerged from a divisive war, and he pledged that he would do all he could to promote it. Such was the spirit that pervaded his goodwill tour of the northern states in the summer of 1817. A later story was that Webster had urged the president to visit New England, where he was promised a cordial reception.[2] Whether true or not, the report did reflect a Federalist eagerness for smooth relations, an eagerness that seemed quite unrestrained during Monroe's triumphal visit to Boston in early July. For six days the chief executive was honored by processions, speeches, admiring crowds, elaborate entertainment by such Federalist aristocrats as Thomas Perkins and Harrison Otis, and glowing predictions of a new "era of good feelings."[3] That their hospitality was not entirely selfless is suggested by a plea from George Sullivan to Monroe to confirm his harmonious intentions by bringing Webster into his cabinet as attorney general. But the president was not that generous and did not seriously contemplate anything of the kind—he gave the post to William Wirt. Party considerations could not be ignored.[4]

Webster was neither disappointed nor angry. The next year, when he was in Washington, he accepted a dinner invitation at the executive mansion and found the occasion interesting and pleasant.[5] More than this, he joined the Massachusetts leadership in endorsing Monroe's reelection in 1820. When electors were chosen, he was one of eight Federalists, with seven Republicans, who pledged themselves to cast a unanimous vote for the president's continuance in office. Though they cheerfully did this, the Federalist electors, including Webster, could not approve the return of Vice-President Daniel D. Tompkins for another four years and therefore threw away their votes on Richard Stockton, a stalwart of their own party.[6]

Despite this gesture of independence, Webster was moving remarkably far toward reconciliation with former Republican adversaries. In September, shortly before the presidential election, he was the genial host for none other than Calhoun, his old congressional antagonist, now making a tour of military sites as secretary of war. All day, people across the town could see the two men riding about in a light carriage and carrying on an animated conversation. And in the evening many guests attended a dinner party at which the cordial New Englander seemed delighted to introduce his southern friend to the young men present. The inescapable inference was that Webster would be glad to see Calhoun succeed to the presidency four years hence.[7]

Webster's newfound cooperativeness did not extend to the subject of slavery. This was a period of protracted debate over the admission of Missouri to the Union, with or without slavery as Congress might decide. Northeastern Federalists like Webster could not repress a decided sectional answer to the question; and indeed the suspicion was that their antislavery position revealed a reviving party spirit as well. In addition to sectional and partisan elements, there was also a moral dimension, to a degree somewhat difficult to assess.

About the time the crucial congressional session to resolve the issue began in December 1819, Bostonians held a large meeting at the State House to ventilate their opinions. After speechmaking, in which Webster joined, the assemblage selected a five-man committee to prepare a memorial against any concession to the slavery interest. As chairman of the committee, Webster drafted a document, later circulated as a pamphlet. It was a forcible argument, closely resembling those being heard in Washington and emphasizing a constitutional power to prevent the spread of slavery into the West.[8]

The central point was that Congress could set conditions on Missouri's admission as a state, including a prohibition of slavery there. This was so, the memorial said, because the constitutional grant of congressional authority to make rules and regulations for the territories was a plenary, unqualified authority. Missouri, then a territory, was covered by this clause at the moment the national legislature passed an act enabling it to draw up a state constitution. Webster's committee said nothing about one feature of the coming compromise, a provision against slavery in the rest of the Louisiana territory (north of 36°30′ latitude), which would become very controversial in the future.[9] Further to justify national power to attach conditions to statehood, Webster advanced the reasoning already developed by his fellow Federalist Rufus King in the Senate: the Constitution prescribes that Congress can admit new states; and this comprehends the collateral power to say on what terms admission will occur.[10] There were several historical precedents, such as legislation on the new states of Ohio, Kentucky, Tennessee, Alabama, and Louisiana, all cited as proof. To round out the constitutional argument, Webster hurriedly suggested that the commerce power was also available as a means of forbidding the entry of slaves into Missouri. His view of that power had expanded since embargo days and would be reiterated in some of his commerce cases in the Supreme Court.[11]

Sectional interest was another consideration. For years the three-fifths ratio, which the Constitution allowed in counting slaves into population totals for apportionment of representation, had bothered New Englanders. They had repeatedly complained—for example, in resolutions of the Hartford Convention—about an unjust southern advantage. The Boston memorial contended that to admit another slave state would magnify this injustice.[12] Fundamental here was a sectional rivalry for the balance of power, which seemed more serious to the nonslaveholding area than it really was. Even now, compromisers at the capital were reducing the threat perceived in the North by admitting Maine and thus maintaining numerical equality between free and slave states. Afterward, Webster said that *"equal weight in the political power of the Government,"* not northern political dominance, was one of his principal objectives; and he hoped to see a diminution of long-standing southern ascendancy in the national government.[13]

Apart from constitutional and political viewpoints, the protest lightly touched the moral issue. Largely, the sentiment that slavery was an evil to be strenuously opposed and somehow abolished appeared by implication only. Neither then nor later was Webster known for bold action or statement on this problem. His position in 1819 was as far as he would ever go, and that was basically nonextensionist, with some tentative gradualist thoughts about long-range solutions.[14]

One feature of the Missouri Compromise, the separation of Maine from Massachusetts and its admission as a state, helped bring on another event that soon occupied Webster's attention. This was a Massachusetts constitutional convention, meeting from mid-November 1820 to early the following January, called ostensibly for legislative reapportionment because of the detachment of the district to the north. The necessity of amending the constitution seems unclear in light of the constitutional provision empowering the General Court to reapportion from time to time. As a matter of fact, the move for a convention arose chiefly for other reasons, to liberalize and modernize various parts of the constitution. Despite the reformist, perhaps radical motives of the pro-convention forces, it would soon become apparent that Webster and his conservative friends did not have to worry about any drastic remodeling.

In June 1820 the legislature adopted an act to refer to the voters the question of convoking a convention. The referendum passed by a two-to-one margin; and on October 16 the towns throughout the state selected delegates, 490 altogether, who would assemble at the State House on November 15. Notwithstanding an effort to stimulate popular interest, voting was light, indicating either lukewarm consensus or widespread apathy. The subsequent election of delegates seemed also to be a drowsy affair.[15] A meeting in Boston, with conservative William Sullivan presiding, chose a slate of 46 delegates (by far the largest contingent sent by any town), nearly all of whom were elected a few days later. Webster was one of that number, together with such well-known persons as Isaac Parker, Lemuel Shaw, Josiah Quincy, George Blake, James T. Austin, and two newspaper editors, Benjamin Russell of the *Centinel* and Nathan Hale of the *Advertiser*.[16]

When the convention was called to order the first day, organizational work proceeded rapidly, thanks to preliminary decisions made by those in control. Almost unanimously the delegates chose ancient John Adams as presiding officer as a mark of respect for his eminent services, which had included drafting the existing state constitution during the Revolution. After Adams declined because of his age, they selected Chief Justice Parker of the state supreme court, whose prestige and stability would inspire the desired caution. Soon William Prescott moved that the existing constitution be divided into ten parts, each to be examined for possible revision by committees, with general discussion of their reports to follow. The motion readily passed.[17] All this exactly suited Webster's thinking; and he said so in an early speech. He had already reflected upon a proper course for the convention and had exchanged ideas on it with Jeremiah Mason and with leading delegates, among them Justice Joseph Story of Salem. In the weeks ahead, he was ever alert to parliamentary twists and turns and seemed to be at the center of decision making.[18]

In an era of democratizing government, the question of broadening the voting franchise arose early in the proceedings. Like other older states, Massachusetts then had a property qualification, an estate valued at sixty pounds or an annual income of three pounds from a freehold. Though first inclining toward universal manhood suffrage, the convention instead adopted a nominal taxpaying requirement. Some members, including Blake, the mover of the final resolution, had had second thoughts and retreated from complete abandonment of economic restrictions. Webster did not have to think twice, for he opposed universal manhood suffrage from the start. But he spoke very little on the point and was satisfied with this revision of the old qualification. In fact the whole subject did not ignite much debate, probably because the state had laxly enforced property requirements. In short, law adjusted to practice.[19]

A fuller discussion of republican theory focused on legislative apportionment, especially of the senate. Henry A. S. Dearborn, son of the Jeffersonian secretary of war and successor to his father as collector of the port of Boston, led a liberal effort to abolish the existing method of apportionment on the basis of tax assessments in districts. With unexpected ease, his resolution to apportion according to population carried. Aided by another second-generation Jeffersonian, Levi Lincoln, and by Henry Childs, the most articulate reformer in the convention, the younger Dearborn attacked the property-weighted sytem as aristocratic—a system found in no other state in the Union.[20]

Then the tide began running the other way. A motion to reconsider Dearborn's resolution passed, and a sequence of powerful speeches defended the status quo. Blake, Prescott, William Sullivan, Leverett Saltonstall, even old Adams emphasized the desirability of maintaining a check by a senate reflecting property interests against the more popularly oriented house. Keep a time-proven institution, they contended. There was no danger of favoritism toward the wealthy in a society where property was so broadly distributed and where there was so much mobility. Such was also the theme of Story, who wrote out his speech with his customary thoroughness and delivered it with conviction, if not eloquence. A number of those wishing to leave the prevailing formula alone were delegates from Boston (Suffolk County), whose representation by six senators was further out of proportion to population than that of any other district, because of the larger amount of taxes it paid.[21]

A highlight of the debate was Webster's argument against revision.[22] It was a penetrating inquiry into the relationship of property and government, which he found both intimate and beneficial. As for the pending issue, he saw a property-based senate as an essential check against the other chamber, not against the people but against their agent, the house of representatives. In his judgment, satisfactory long experience under the existing provision was proof enough of the inadvisability of implementing something different. Still, he thought it helpful to explore the philosophers and commentators of the past to reinforce his opinion. Spicing his exposition with references to Aristotle, Montesquieu, Grotius, Hamilton, and Madison, he did not forget Adams himself, the author of this section of the Massachusetts constitution. The principle he saw in all these authorities was that political influence must be proportionate to the holding of property. Many delegates must have nodded in agreement when he referred to James Harrington's *Oceana* as showing that "power *naturally* and *necessarily* follows property."[23] Interest in property did not undermine republicanism, he continued, for in a commonwealth it would have an extensive popular basis. "In my judgment, therefore, a republican form of government rests, not more on political constitutions, than on those laws which regulate the descent and transmission of property."[24] If protected by law, property would, in turn, be the means of protecting life and liberty. Referring to the English revolution of 1688 and to the American Revolution, he observed that men of property had undertaken them to secure liberty.

The debate on apportionment resulted in only minor modifications. Most counties, including Suffolk, kept the same number of senators they had had.[25] For the house, the decision was to reduce sharply the total number of representatives but to continue to apportion them among the towns, with additional legislators assigned to more populous places.[26] Webster and other opponents of change felt relieved. Yet how long would the older order survive? In this matter, twenty years. In 1840 a constitutional amendment abolished the property basis of the senate; thereafter both chambers were apportioned solely by population and were supposed to be reapportioned regularly after each census.[27]

Those wishing reform by this convention also hoped to separate church and state completely. As the "Bible Commonwealth" in the seventeenth century and as a Puritan bastion into the nineteenth, Massachusetts had held out against the trend toward disestablishment of the church. Now it appeared to be making its last stand in behalf of Congregationalism, whether of trinitarian or unitarian persuasion. Not that the constitution of 1780 had completely overlooked religious liberty, for its bill of rights had provided that "no subject shall be hurt, molested, or restrained, in his person, liberty, or estate, for worshipping God in the manner and season most agreeable to the dictates of his own conscience; or for his religious profession or sentiments." Nevertheless, it had further provided that towns and parishes levy taxes for the support of public worship, though a statute of 1811 allowed individuals to request that their tax money be allotted to churches of their own choice. There was another vestige of establishment in the constitutional requirement that elective officeholders affirm by oath their belief in the Christian religion, an oath that more and more liberals found offensive.

Webster was involved directly in handling this last issue. As chairman of a committee, he reported an amendment which would eliminate this test oath and require officials merely to swear their allegiance to the state and their support of the constitution. In a curious speech he explained in some detail why the state could require the kind of oath currently prescribed, following which he also explained why it was no longer expedient to do so. Public office, he believed, was "in the free gift of the people," and no citizen had a right to hold it. This being true, government could set any qualification deemed necesary: age, wealth, residence, even religious belief. A religious oath therefore had "nothing to do with any man's conscience. If he dislike the condition, he may decline the office." If Webster had had his way in the committee, he would have stopped here; but being outnumbered by those opposing the old oath, he was prepared to abandon it on the ground of expediency. After all, he said, ninety-nine out of every hundred inhabitants were Christians, and it was superfluous to insist on their swearing they were. Nor would he press the point in the case of those few persons who might have some finespun reason to refuse taking the oath. There were enough delegates who concurred with this pragmatic viewpoint, joined with others who had definite conscientious objections to a religious test oath, to adopt his amendment easily.[28]

Of greater interest to Webster was the role of the judiciary in government. And it was on this subject that he delivered his best-remembered speech of the convention. Story had reported committee recommendations concerning the courts: to create new tribunals of equity and appeal, to abolish the practice of advisory opinions rendered by the supreme court on request, and to make it more difficult for the legislature to remove judges merely by address. As a firm believer in a strong judiciary, Webster welcomed all these revisions. His remarks centered on the proposal to require a two-thirds instead of a majority vote for removal. This was a separate procedure from impeachment (spelled out in another part of the constitution) and had not obligated the legislature to state the cause of removal or to grant a hearing. Typically, he drew upon history for authority. He recalled the problem of weak judges subservient to the crown before the English revolution of 1688. And he found similar instances in Scottish and American colonial history. To function effectively, to maintain basic rights always vulnerable to legislative abuse, courts must be independent. Then they could fearlessly and impartially interpret the constitution and, when necessary, invalidate unconstitutional laws. Judicial review was indispensable to good government. It protected liberty and property, which otherwise might be undermined by oppressive or confiscatory acts, frequently private laws. On this head, he foreshadowed a doctrine which would later be known as substantive due process of law. Despite defeat of the two-thirds proposition, Webster managed to get through a substitute provision that the legislature must make known to an accused judge the specific causes of removal and allow him a hearing.[29]

In addition to these large questions of the relationship of one branch of government to another and of government to individuals, there were several lesser issues with which he was concerned in the convention. From committees to which he had been assigned came reports the convention approved: slight alteration in the administration of Harvard, change of Boston's form of government from town to city, and provision for future constitutional amendments.[30]

On a January evening in 1821, the State House filled with delegates and townspeople to close the convention. One by one, the fourteen amendments to be submitted to the people for ratification were read and voted. After the appropriate prayer by one of the delegates, the Reverend Edmund Foster, giving thanks to God and congratulating his colleagues, Chief Justice Parker declared the assemblage adjourned.[31] Except for a small minority of disappointed reformers, the departing members felt quite satisfied with what they had done, or perhaps to a greater extent with what they had prevented from being done. As Webster said, notwithstanding "a good deal of inflammable matter" in the proceedings, "we were extremely fortunate, in finding a considerable number of Gentlemen well disposed."[32] He was doubtless conscious of his own heightened reputation as a result of helping to hold the line through his parliamentary skill and oratory. In the words of his warm friend Story, he had " now secured the title of an eminent and enlightened statesman."[33]

Voting on ratification came on April 9. Newspapers had carried the convention's "Address to the People" and editorials explaining each proposition. Nathan Hale, editor of the *Advertiser* as well as a delegate, had told his readers they should exercise their own judgment but, if in doubt, should remember that well-informed and highly respectable men had framed the propositions before them.[34] In fact, voters exercised their judgment more than they deferred to the convention's wisdom. They approved the measures for broader suffrage, city government, deletion of a religious test in oaths of office, and procedures for amendments. But they rejected five of the fourteen proposals, some of which had been exhaustively debated: slight changes in religious support of churches, comparably small alterations in legislative apportionment, the modest requirement of tighter procedure for removing judges, and even the light

95

repair of the structure of Harvard's board of overseers.[35] No one knew, nor can any one now safely say, why so many very restrained modifications were repudiated. One possible reason is that the changes were too mild. If this was the case, then many people were thinking that it would be better to wait for meaningful reform rather than take the crust of the loaf.[36] That might have been some voters' reasoning, but it is more likely that, at the moment, public opinion and politics generally in Massachusetts remained conservative and that most voters wanted few alterations in the constitution.

Within a year, Federalist power in the state seemed to be splintering. When Boston held its first mayoral election under the new city form of government in April 1822, two prominent Federalists confronted each other. Resigning his seat in the United States Senate, Harrison Gray Otis would have easily become the first mayor if he had not been challenged by another aristocrat, Josiah Quincy. After party leaders nominated Otis, Quincy stubbornly stayed in the race and recruited support from many in the ranks as well as from Republicans. A coalition formed around a momentary issue, which would not ordinarily have been important enough to affect party alignments. This was a question on materials for constructing buildings, limited by statute mainly to brick in order to prevent or control the fires that were so destructive in early American cities. In behalf of freer enterprise and smaller capitalists, the "Middling Interest," as it was called, advocated revision of the statute to permit construction of less expensive wooden buildings. And opportunistic Quincy allowed his candidacy to be linked with it. The result was that neither Otis nor Quincy received a majority, and both withdrew in favor of Federalist John Phillips, who became mayor.[37]

The following month there were elections for representatives from Boston to the state legislature, with opposing slates of twenty-five men each, one Federalist and the other Middling Interest. At the head of the former list was Webster. The *Advertiser*, speaking for the loyalist Federalist organization, deplored such factionalism, given that there was no substantial difference between the slates. The trouble, too, was that the "Democrats" were exploiting the situation. All but eight of the twenty-five Federalists won—Webster was near the top in the totals; but a run-off for the eight seats went to the Middling Interest.[38]

Attendance at the legislative session in early June was Webster's only service in state office and hardly notable. Many years later, he recalled that his only achievement was sponsorship of a statute prohibiting the taking of fish from Massachusetts streams with anything but hook and line—something to be expected of the ardent fisherman he was, but not of the distinguished statesman he was becoming. It was necessary, however, to take a stand on the matter of wooden buildings; and without much of a stir, he followed Federalists in soothing feelings by voting for a measure that allowed some wooden structures.[39]

A decision that affected him more directly was the selection of a successor to Otis in the Senate. He was tempted when his fellow legislators began suggesting his name; but either because he was not yet ready to commit himself again to the demands of congressional politics or, more probably, because James Lloyd had prior claim to the post, he declined to be a candidate.[40] Nevertheless, it seemed to be only a question of how soon he would return to Washington.

It would be very soon, in fact. Congressman Benjamin Gorham of the Boston district had tired of his duties and refused to run again. Now the Federalist establishment, acting through Thomas Perkins and others, earnestly pressed Webster to sacrifice his personal interests and to go to the House. He agreed with outward reluctance but also with real pleasure.[41] Through the latter half of October 1822, a brisk contest between Webster and the nominee of the Middling Interest, the merchant Jesse Putnam, ensued. With no genuine points of disagreement between the two, the campaign seemed to pivot on whether Webster was too ambitious and on whether a lawyer rather than a merchant could best represent the commercial community of Suffolk County. Friends of Webster explained away these issues by saying that the opposition was criticizing him chiefly because he was too qualified.[42] Yet Putnam never had much of a chance; he lost by 2,633 to 1,557.[43] Modestly, Webster remarked, "I intend to discharge my two-year duty, if I live & enjoy health, punctually & assiduously, & then consider that I have discharged my debt."[44]

Chapter 7

SECTIONALISM

In those days a congressman-elect had to wait more than a year after election to take his seat, with incumbents holding on through a lame-duck session. It was December 1, 1823, when Webster arrived for the opening of the Eighteenth Congress in the recently renovated House chamber. From his mahogany desk he looked upon the Speaker's imposing station, soon to be occupied again by the seasoned Henry Clay, who had had an interval away from Washington after the Missouri Compromise. On the periphery of the domed, semicircular room there were beautiful marble pillars providing recesses where representatives and visitors could gather for conversation or could lounge during a somnolent speech. Webster's unusual promptitude was probably the result of Grace's having come to Washington with him for the long session of six months. Leaving two children behind and bringing the two others, the Websters passed an interesting winter, surrounded as they were by friends such as George Blake and his wife and by such legislators as John W. Taylor, James Buchanan, Louis McLane, John Forsyth, Joel Poinsett, and the unstable John Randolph—all colleagues in the House.[1]

Historians would remember this session for President Monroe's exposition of a Latin American policy that endured over the next century. In his annual message, the chief executive discussed the newly independent condition of the former Spanish colonies in South and Central America. These nations of the Western Hemisphere, the president declared, must be free of intervention by European powers—he had in mind France especially, which seemed poised to help restore Spain's empire. And as quid pro quo, Monroe laid down another principle: the United States would continue to avoid involvement in the internal affairs of Europe.

This part of the Monroe Doctrine would not be as well known as the other, though it touched upon a matter with which Webster was just now very much concerned.

This was the situation in Greece, where fierce revolution against the ruling Turks kept that area in upheaval for most of the 1820s. Already the Greeks seemed likely to achieve independence, though rebels and faltering Turkey alike had suffered heavy casualties in a war brutally prosecuted by both sides. In the United States a so-called Greek fever spread through the land. Mass meetings, sermons, publications, fund raisings brought widespread sympathy for a people depicted as heirs of a rich civilization and as valiant defenders of Christianity against the oppressive, barbaric infidel. In a draft of his message Monroe had planned to come out vigorously for the Greek cause and even to recommend sending a minister there; but Secretary of State Adams convinced him this would be inconsistent with the two-spheres position on Latin America. So the president limited his comment on Greece to a restrained note of encouragement. "A strong hope has been entertained," he wrote, "founded on the heroic struggle of the Greeks, that they would succeed in their contest, and resume their equal station among the nations of the earth." It was an "object of our most ardent wishes."[2]

To Webster this lofty statement seemed insufficient. Before he left Boston he had been thinking of a major move, possibly a set speech, to commit Congress in behalf of the Greeks. No doubt he was inclined to do so because of the prevalent enthusiasm for this cause, not to mention possible political and personal motives. But another reason was persuasion by Edward Everett, professor of Greek literature at Harvard, who as a brilliant young scholar had traveled to Greece during the years of his study in Europe. Since his return, despite spectacular social and academic advancement, Everett had wearied of the routine and sought something more exciting. The restless professor now had an overpowering desire to gain appointment as American minister, or at least commissioner, to Greece.[3] With characteristic energy and intellectual capacity, he had investigated the background and current progress of the Greek revolution, had taken this as his topic in some of his public lectures in Boston, and in the issue of the *North American Review* for October 1823 had published a long article on the subject.[4] Webster was quite impressed by this piece, which reinforced what his friend had been telling him. If the United States recognized and supported the Latin American revolutions (a rather "miserable" cause, he thought), did not the fate of the Greeks also compel attention?

On his way to the capital in November and after his arrival, Webster wrote a series of letters to Everett repeating his intention to "say some-thing of the Greeks" in the House.[5] Typically, he looked to his friend for help. In addition to the essay of October, he received one in manuscript intended for the next number in January and another, a narrative of the war, that would later appear in the press. Reading these carefully and checking details against maps, he enthusiastically reported to Everett that he had "mastered the campaigns of 1821–1822, historically & topo-graphically."[6] Though he knew the administration had backed away from sending an agent to Greece, he felt optimistic about congressional approval and confident that Everett would be the person chosen. To fa-cilitate this and to maintain his supply of information, Webster urged him to come to Washington as soon as possible.[7]

The first thing to do was to introduce a resolution in the House: "That provision ought to be made, by law, for defraying the expense incident to the appointment of an agent, or commissioner, to Greece, whenever the President shall deem it expedient to make such an appointment." After presenting the resolution on December 8, Webster spoke only briefly. He merely wished, he remarked, to be responsive to the presi-dent's message expressing the hopes of the civilized world that the Greeks would succeed in throwing off Turkish dominion. The House, too, should record its sympathy for that "heroic people" who had suf-fered under a "system of foulest atrocity." Webster intended to call up the resolution for debate within two weeks and predicted that it would pass nearly unanimously.[8]

There was more difficulty than he had anticipated. Whether to delay consideration of the question to a calmer moment or to mobilize opposi-tion to Webster's motion, other resolutions appeared. One of them asked the president for copies of relevant diplomatic correspondence; and it was the end of the month before this arrived. Included was correspon-dence involving Minister Richard Rush in England, John Forsyth of the House, Secretary Adams, and Andreas Luriottis, the Greek agent in London. It was the exchange between the last two that was most inter-esting. In February 1823 Luriottis had written Adams about the jus-tice of the Greek cause and called upon the United States to remember its own revolutionary past and to support the new nation by recognition and otherwise. Adams' reply, in August, must have seemed coldhearted to Luriottis; the secretary promised no official assistance, because of America's long-standing attitude of nonintervention in Europe. So op-ponents of Webster's measure had the negative administration policy out in the open.[9]

Another resolution, adopted on January 2, 1824, requested the secre-tary of the treasury to provide information on the volume of trade with the eastern Mediterranean area. Those who spoke for this inquiry reasoned that Congress should be aware of how much commerce might be lost if Webster's resolution were passed and antagonized Turkey.[10] Unquestionably, an economic dimension did exist. For example, one of Webster's most ardent admirers was merchant Thomas Perkins, whose fortune had been built upon a very profitable trade with China, including shipping opium there from Turkey. In Perkins' opinion, American partiality for Greece would precipitate Turkish retaliation. Understandably, Perkins disapproved pro-Greek meetings in Boston.[11] And Adams himself, though evoking nonentanglement in diplomatic terms, was thinking of commercial implications. In a private conversation, he pointed out that there was then an American negotiator at Constantinople whose errand to obtain a trade agreement might suffer if Webster's resolution passed.[12]

At last, on January 19, Webster began debate on his resolution. He had carefully prepared for this effort, as his detailed notes of over forty pages of historical allusions, statistics, and ideas show.[13] Despite the opportunity to make the speech a grandiloquent foray into the rich past of Greece as well as into the current crisis there, he resisted extravagances while dealing with those themes. Characteristically, he opened in a low key, with only brief references to the contributions of classical Greece and with a plea to the House to support the president's position favorable to the heroic Greeks striving for independence. Disclaiming either radical or quixotic motives, he called upon the United States as a uniquely free country to voice the "prevailing spirit of the age" against oppression and bloody war. All he asked, he insisted, was a modest step of congressional declaration of sentiment, to be followed by an agency, not a ministerial mission, to the Mediterranean country.

The core of the speech closely resembled the thinking of Adams and Monroe in its criticism of the Holy Alliance (Russia, Prussia, and Austria), which, he charged, had inverted the true principles of government when it had recently asserted that rights and justice were concessions by sovereign monarchs. This declaration was plainly contrary to the Anglo-American principle of popular rights, he observed, so correctly laid down in the documents of the English revolution of 1688 and embedded in the American experience. Equally dangerous, he contended, were the alliance's pronouncements that it had the responsibility to interfere in the affairs of other states to maintain order, when in fact its purpose was to maintain the status of its own rulers. This nation must oppose that pernicious policy both in Latin America and Europe. But this did not mean that the United States should proceed by intervening in Latin America itself; nor did it mean that it should leave

Europe open to the alliance's intervention without strong protest or other peaceful action. His application of the Monroe-Adams doctrine might differ somewhat from that of others, even though he shared its antipathy toward the Holy Alliance. In both spheres, Europe and Latin America, he favored active diplomacy while opposing military intervention.[14]

There were no other speeches until the next day, the twentieth, when Joel Poinsett, a member of the Committee on Foreign Relations, led off with counterargument and a substitute resolution. Although Poinsett agreed with most of Webster's views and was friendly with him personally, the South Carolinian opposed sending an agent. It was well known that he was speaking for the administration, for in the preceding weeks he had been conferring with the president, the secretary of state, and others. On January 4 Adams had told Poinsett that an agency to Greece would ruin the possibility of negotiating a commercial agreement with Turkey; besides, he had said, Everett, the prospective agent, was too much "a partisan." Both Monroe and Adams believed that Webster's legislative resolution encroached upon executive discretion. At a cabinet meeting on January 10, the president posed the question whether Poinsett could say on the House floor that he was expressing the position of the administration. The cabinet did not approve, chiefly because Calhoun and Samuel Southard objected—well they might, inasmuch as they had been encouraging Webster—yet it did not disapprove.[15] It was generally understood at the Capitol, if not specifically said, that the executive disliked Webster's proposition.

The ground Poinsett assumed in his speech did not reveal all that had been discussed at the executive mansion but consisted mainly of a warning that the presence of an American agent could incite Turkey or a European power to war against this country. Or what if the agent were captured and cruelly handled? Would this not drive the nation into war? Poinsett's substitute would thus simply support Monroe in extending sympathy and would avoid such risks.[16]

In the week-long debate several options were thoroughly explored. Some representatives followed Poinsett in preferring a mere declaration of legislative sentiment, while a number would do nothing at all because even a declaration would be dangerous involvement, contrary to the tested rule of neutrality toward European conflicts as set forth by the great Washington and his successors.[17] John Randolph launched his oratorical rockets to attack the foolish notion of foreign involvement. He called for preservation of America's resources and character. Impugning Webster's motives (as Adams had in private conversation), he speculated that they were only to attract attention by making speeches.[18] Still, there were some substantial arguments supporting Webster, the most notable being those of Speaker Clay, who endorsed a bold pro-Greek policy to match his "American System" of relations with the former Spanish colonies. He had a resolution on that subject, which he hoped to get through too.[19]

Quite possibly, Clay was politically courting Webster in light of the coming election. He suspected, he said, that some congressmen opposed the proposal on Greece solely because it came from a Federalist. If his own party took such a narrow position, Clay vowed, "I for one, should cease to be a Republican, and would become a Federalist."[20] And he joined a secondary skirmish between Webster and Ichabod Bartlett of New Hampshire, who obliquely compared his longtime antagonist to Don Quixote ostentatiously tilting against a windmill. Indeed Clay and Bartlett arrived at a point where it was feared there would be trouble between them outside the House.[21] Webster himself had a chance to reply to Bartlett toward the end of the debates by injecting some sarcasm: "If I should happen in my course to meet with a *wind—mill,* why, sir, I must take a tilt with it, whether it be large or small, unless, indeed, I should conclude to have a little patience, and to wait a while, till the motion and the noise shall die of themselves, for a slight puff is generally soon over."[22]

On January 26, the final word had been said; the House, sitting as committee of the whole, rose without action; and it was clear that Webster would not carry his resolution.[23] As he looked back on the issue, he concluded that Adams' opposition had been the "most formidable obstacle."[24] Enough votes were diverted because of the desire to be consistent and safe on the policy of nonintervention, by Europe in America and by America in Europe. In any event, Bartlett, despite his obnoxious slurs, made a solid point when he observed that sending an agent to Greece was useless anyhow, for the United States could find out about conditions there well enough without one. The only loss was that felt by Everett, yearning for travel to a favorite land. As for announcing American sympathy, that had already been accomplished—by Monroe's message, by the congressional debate, including Webster's stirring prose, and by the numerous public movements in behalf of Greece.[25]

One can interpret Webster's strategy in several ways. An explanation accepted by some contemporaries is that he hoped to rejuvenate the Federalist party. Surviving evidence does not support this view. Webster knew that the party was no longer capable of reviving. Another explanation would attribute to him a desire to allay party and factional strife.[26] Again there is little to document that idea, except his tendency now toward romantic nationalism, toward a pride in country and its institutions, in contrast with those of decrepit Europe. If he connected a reduction in party strife with his thoughts on the Greek issue, it was only in this general sense of American nationality.[27] A more convincing explanation would be that Webster was searching for a personal platform, a prominent place in the congressional politics to which he was then returning. And the current Greek fever across the country provided the occasion.

Soon after the Greek debate closed, attention shifted to the tariff issue. In early February the House, in committee of the whole, was debating a bill to raise rates imposed in 1816 but now unsatisfactory to the numerous advocates of a protective system. In the lead was Clay, inspirational spokesman for such a system and, more than incidentally, prominent presidential candidate. The irrepressible Kentuckian spoke not only for western agricultural interests but also for manufacturers of both East and West. In fact Clay announced that he spoke for the whole country and all interests, for the adoption of an American System of interdependent and concurrently developing parts. As Speaker, he naturally had seen to it that committee appointments conformed with his plans; and out of the Committee on Manufactures had come the present bill, with much higher duties on hemp, iron, wheat, raw wool, woolen textiles, and other items. In the House until the measure's passage in mid-April, and in the Senate for another month, there was little evidence of the attitude of mutual concession so fervently invoked by Clay. On each provision, immediate advantage prevailed over economic theory in determining voting patterns. Despite these variations, the alignments for and against more protection were remarkably sectional: the middle states and the Northwest in support, the south opposed, and New England divided but with a majority opposed. It was basically a coalition of northern manufacturers and western farmers confronting another of northern merchants and southern planters.[28]

When the bill came out of committee in January, Webster sensed at once the threat to his constituents' interests. Sending copies to influential men back home, he solicited their opinions, in detail, on the probable effects of the proposed upward revision.[29] His friend Nathan Hale, editor of the *Advertiser*, shared his alarm and published many columns explaining the injurious impact such alterations would have on specific industries and on the entire economy.[30] From Portsmouth, Mason wrote that woolen manufacturers would lose more than they would gain because of the projected increase in duties on raw wool.[31] Nathan Appleton, whose wealth had been built upon commerce and was now being invested in cotton-textile manufacturing, saw no need for added protection of that industry, for the law of 1816 had provided substantial help and New England factories had reached a high level of efficiency.[32] And of course the preeminent maritime shipper, Thomas Perkins, opposed more barriers to foreign commerce.[33]

In Boston on January 26 an antitariff meeting convened at the Exchange Coffee House, with Israel Thorndike, Amos Lawrence, Appleton, and Perkins among those guiding the proceedings. From this group a committee was appointed to prepare a memorial of protest to Congress.[34] The committee rushed its report, with a thousand signatures, to Webster, who presented it to the House on February 9.

The protest began with a brief statement of objections to the bill and then referred to an attached document, an earlier memorial, for a fuller explanation. Webster had probably been the principal author of this document, drafted in 1820 at a meeting of antiprotectionists from all parts of the state to oppose a congressional bill.[35] Although that measure had been defeated by a single vote in the Senate, the same arguments applied to the current proposal.[36]

The memorial reveals the antiprotective feelings of the period, especially when one considers the document in relation to Webster's speech in the meeting adopting it on October 2, 1820.[37] Both memorial and speech had criticized the protective principle on nearly every possible ground. A fiscal objection emphasized the loss of revenue if rates were higher, owing to a predicted decline in imports, and warned of onerous internal taxes to make up the deficit. In the economy as a whole, Webster, Perkins, and the others perceived nothing but damage resulting from the projected schedule. Consumers would have to pay more for the goods they bought—here there was a little demagoguery in a charge that the rich would become richer, and the poor poorer. Manufacturers and artisans would be hurt by an increase in rates on the raw materials they used because of higher duties on iron, hemp, molasses, hardwood, and wool. Even textile companies, both cotton and woolen, would lose more than they would gain. And labor in all industries would therefore suffer too, contrary to claims that wages would increase. Equally deplorable would be the impact upon agriculture, for farmers would encounter higher costs while their market contracted. Would not many be driven to some occupation in the cities and, as in England, sink into a condition of exploitation, vice, and crime? An interesting Jeffersonian argument by Federalists!

In thinking of unfortunate consequences, the petitioners were naturally most worried about commerce, still dominant in their financial and political world, notwithstanding the industrialization now in progress. A protective policy would wrongly force men and capital into new pursuits. There was, Webster had declared in his speech, a natural order of society, best left alone by legislation. "Excess corrects itself. If there be too much commerce, it will be diminished. If there be too few manufactures, they will be increased with but ordinary care and protection." Thus "we could no more improve the order and habit and composition of society by an artificial balancing of trades and occupations, than we could improve the natural atmosphere by means of the condensers and rarefiers of the chemists."[38] Attempting to do so, he suggested, violated not only sound rules of political economy (essentially the theory of laissez faire) but perhaps also the Constitution. Inconsistent with "the spirit and intention" of that document, a protective system forcing "great and sudden changes, both of occupation and property," could not be justified "as incidental to the exercise of any other power."[39] How much might Webster later wish to obliterate any memory of such arguments.

But now, in 1824 during the tariff debate, he had not yet changed his economic thinking even though he was silent about the constitutional issue. Through February and March the House proceeded unhurriedly from item to item in the bill, with protectionists prevailing in each instance. Repeatedly Webster spoke and voted against higher duties on iron, hemp, wheat, tallow. The first two materials were necessary to shipping, particularly hemp for ropemaking. Though larger imposts on tallow were supposed to help Massachusetts whalers, who produced oil for illumination in competition with chandlers making candles out of imported tallow, he opposed revision because he was unconvinced it would have that effect. In general, he was dissatisfied with what he saw and heard, found it tedious, and hoped that somehow the whole measure would die.[40]

Clay would not let that happen. At the end of March, the nationalistic Speaker expounded his American System in an impressive two-day oration. His themes were national growth and unity. At present, he said, the United States suffered from a depression in every phase of business and agriculture. Debts, bankruptcies, stunted trade, agricultural distress, unemployment of labor, all required a more vigorous national policy, one calculated to develop a balanced, self-sufficient economy no longer dependent upon Europe. As he had often argued before, a high tariff, stimulating American manufacturing, would provide a home market for American farmers and planters, who would also constitute a market for the increasing volume of industrial goods. All sections and industries would benefit by recognizing their mutual interest.[41]

As Webster would remember it, Clay's speech goaded him out of his heretofore inconspicuous role in the discussion. Quickly he scratched out some notes in the evening, and on April 1 and 2 he had the floor for a long rebuttal to the Kentuckian.[42] It was an exposition of free-trade ideas in opposition to a system of industrial development and national self-sufficiency. The economic situation was not nearly as bleak as Clay portrayed it, he thought, and anyway could be remedied by depending upon freedom of enterprise, not by more generosity toward manufacturing. Above all, he counseled, do not cripple commerce—the new rates on hemp and iron, he estimated, would add one-third to the costs of American shipping. He had much to say about comparative features of American and English policies. Denying the truth of Clay's argument that this country would merely be retaliating against similar English restrictions, Webster saw England as presently moving toward free trade under the leadership of Lord Liverpool and William Huskisson. Besides, how could one call any system American which imitated that of a foreign nation? Discounting old mercantilistic notions of balance of trade, flow of specie, and ultranationalist economics, he declared that the "general sense of this age sets, with strong current, in favor of freedom of commercial intercourse, and unrestrained individual action."

However interesting his audience in Congress or readers of published reports may have found his speech to be, the defender of New England commerce discovered that the current in Washington was not now setting in his direction. With Webster voting nay, the tariff bill passed the House in mid-April. Despite some moderating amendments in the Senate, he was still dissatisfied with the law as enacted.[43] In trying to explain the setback, he thought he saw a reason: "There are members who are influenced by their instructions, or afraid of their constituents." Politicians lacked the backbone to adhere to their own convictions. What could be expected after the coming election? Very little. Clay had sponsored the tariff law, Senator Andrew Jackson had voted for it, and "J. Q. [Adams] is as bad upon it as any of the rest."[44] Still, in the aftermath he paid little attention to the tariff, would in the not distant future be reconciled to it, and would ultimately go for even higher walls of protection.

During the last months of the session, the House faced a controversy more politically inflamed than the intricate question of a tariff. It involved a charge by Ninian Edwards of Illinois that Secretary of the Treasury Crawford had wrongfully handled governmental funds deposited in western banks. Early in 1823 Edwards had published a series of anonymous letters, signed "A. B.," to this effect; and Crawford had had to defend his conduct in responses to House inquiries. The matter now revived in April 1824 when Edwards revealed his authorship of the letters. So the House appointed a committee of investigation, to which a reluctant Webster was appointed. He and his colleagues were aware how explosive the dispute was and therefore dealt with Crawford with maximum generosity in their report, believing Edwards' conduct to have been improper. Though hurt a little by the episode, Crawford emerged in better shape than Edwards, who was forced out of his new post as minister to Mexico. For Webster, in addition to some discomfort about the political implications, the A. B. controversy precipitated another quarrel with fellow committee member John Randolph, who took offense at some remarks he made on the floor and resorted to his favorite remedy of issuing a challenge to a duel. No more willing to fight the Virginian now than he had been in 1816, Webster managed to extricate himself by a vague but conciliatory explanation.[45]

Though few persons dwelt upon the point, everyone knew that the Edwards-Crawford controversy had assumed the importance it had because of its bearing upon the current presidential contest. As one of several variables, it could affect the decision in the fall election, which would probably be the most complicated and the most criticized of any in all American history: complicated, because the breakdown of the two-party system opened a ruthless competition for the succession among a number of Republican aspirants, each with his separate sectional and personal following; criticized, because victory went to a candidate who received a minority of both popular and electoral college votes, yet who won after some suspicious maneuvers.

Despite signs ominous to his cause, Crawford seemed to be leading until early 1824. A handsome person and a veteran in the public service as senator, minister to France, and secretary of the treasury, the Georgian was a wily politician, armed with an extensive patronage and a claim to custody of the Jeffersonian tradition. His support was strongest in the South, but it extended to Isaac Hill's camp in New Hampshire, to a band of high-toned Federalists in Massachusetts, and to the potent Albany Regency in New York. In Washington, the *National Intelligencer* consistently portrayed him as the official candidate. Still, his prospects shrank when in September 1823 he suffered a stroke and was left nearly incapacitated through the crucial months ahead.[46]

Even if Crawford had maintained his former excellent health and had escaped all the bad luck which dogged him, he would have had reason to worry about a field of formidable opponents. An early rival was his colleague, Secretary of War Calhoun, well known as a nationalist since his wartime service in Congress with Webster but silently reorienting his thinking toward states' rights. Intense, efficient, and very ambitious, he seemed determined to thwart Crawford's progress toward the executive mansion. Another challenger, somewhat difficult to assess, was General Andrew Jackson, hero of the battle of New Orleans, chastiser of Indians and Spaniards in Florida, and currently the new senator from Tennessee. Deprecated as a mere military chieftain and portrayed as something of a wild man, Jackson was surprising the establishment in Washington with his charm and self-control. Would he be the man of the people? Easier to classify was Clay, experienced congressional leader and unreserved spokesman of economic nationalism. His supreme confidence and limitless capacity made him look and feel like presidential timber. Then there was the secretary of state, the incomparable diplomat Adams. Son of a president, hungry for that office himself though lecturing himself in his massive diary for such frailty, he had the intellectual and technical qualities of brilliant statesmanship. The question was whether he also had practical skills to survive in the jungle of politics.

One might have expected Webster to glide easily into the Adams fold, but that was not the case. Unable to forget Adams' apostasy from the Federalist party in embargo days and alienated by the cold, disagreeable manner of this New England Puritan, he could not accept Adams as first choice, notwithstanding the likelihood that he would eventually have to go along with his section in voting for one of its own. He tended to concur with his brother Ezekiel, who, two years before, had declared, "I never did like John Q. Adams. He must have a very objectionable rival whose election I should not prefer . . . yet it seems to be in some degree a matter of necessity to support him, if any man is to be taken from the land of the *Pilgrims.*"[47] Overtly Webster and Adams maintained correct, respectful relations, even socially, but each habitually gave the other little benefit of the doubt in his private judgments. "My impression of that Gentleman's character," said Webster, "though high and favorable, in some respects, is, in others so little satisfactory, that I hardly know what to *wish,* in regard to the future."[48]

In the first stage of the contest, he seemed to wish that Calhoun would prevail. It appeared then that the South Carolinian would be the principal contender against the Crawford movement; and Webster's attitude toward Calhoun had grown friendlier with the passing years, an attitude well illustrated by the hearty reception of the secretary of war during his visit to Boston in 1820. He was a southerner, it was true, but a man without a trace of sectional bias, a genuinely national statesman. Translated, this meant that the Northeast would be safe under his care.

Through 1823 Calhoun believed he could count on Webster's support and that this could be decisive in Massachusetts and adjacent states. But both men were cautious, for they knew that Adams had a natural advantage there and that they must patiently await the collapse of the secretary of state's candidacy. "D Webster is still with me; and is quite certain," wrote Calhoun in March, "that if Mr. Adams does not take New York, that New England will not rally on him but myself."[49] Webster's determination to remain publicly uncommitted, regardless of his inner sympathies, was firm when Calhoun tried to persuade him to write a pamphlet for his candidacy in September. He could not do this, Webster explained, for Adams was still New England's favorite, despite Calhoun's rapidly rising popularity.[50] Six months later, on March 4, 1824, a Pennsylvania convention smashed these prospects by declaring its preference for Jackson instead of Calhoun. Thereafter, the latter would have to be consoled with the vice-presidency, a position for which Webster thought him well fitted. "He is a true man, and will do good to the country in that situation," he concluded. [51]

Never showing much interest in Crawford's candidacy, Webster believed it was declining late in 1823 when rumors of the Georgian's illness began circulating.[52] But neither doubts about Crawford's physical condition nor dissatisfaction with his political opinions appeared decisive to Webster. The point he emphasized was the use of a congressional nominating caucus in behalf of the secretary. For practical reasons, he was among the increasing numbers opposing a caucus as outmoded and undemocratic. He recognized the disadvantage to a party and to a nominee relying upon it. "It is time to put an end to caucuses," he declared. "They make great men little, & little men great. The true source of power is the *People*. The Democrats are not Democratic enough. They are real aristocrats. Their leaders wish to govern by a combination among themselves, & they think they have a fee simple in the people's suffrage."[53] Regardless of the unpopularity of this device, the Crawfordites in Congress pressed ahead and held a caucus on February 14, 1824, but were badly shaken when only a rump attended and endorsed the debilitated cabinet member. Afterward, Crawford's cause shriveled. It was becoming clear that no one would obtain a majority of the electoral votes, that the decision would have to go to the House, and that the House was hardly pro-Crawford.[54]

The person gaining ground was Andrew Jackson. His enormous popularity was telling, and his efficient organization had established valuable connections across the land. Of course, the general was not the kind of man Webster preferred as president of the United States, but he now took the candidacy seriously and estimated that Old Hickory had moved up to first or second place. In the Senate, as well as in Washington society, Jackson revealed a dignity and self-command of which few had thought him capable. "General Jackson's *manners* are more Presidential than those of any of the Candidates," Webster conceded. "He is grave, mild, & reserved. My wife is for him decidedly."[55]

In his correspondence Webster exchanged views on the status of the candidates in various parts of the Union and tried to assess the fluid situation. He was friendly toward Clay, perhaps more so after their collaboration during the Greek debate and after other marks of the Speaker's kindness, such as appointment to the chairmanship of the House Judiciary Committee. Yet the Kentuckian did not seem to be generating more than secondary strength, derived from a few states. He could be third highest in the electoral vote, entitling him to later consideration by the House; but Webster thought of him only in terms of the effect on the other candidates.[56] Largely this was true of De Witt Clinton, currently reviving after a conflict in New York with Van Buren on the Erie Canal issue. A movement for Clinton could hurt others but could not affect him.[57] Similarly, Calhoun and the declining Crawford were important factors in the equation only insofar as their constituencies could influence a developing duel between Jackson and Adams.

The direction Massachusetts would take was highly important, for there would not be much of a duel if Adams could not carry his own state. Many people there disliked Adams even more than Webster did. For example, the arch-Federalist Timothy Pickering would have none of Adams because John Quincy was too much like his father, who had broken with Pickering's idol, Alexander Hamilton. And Theodore Lyman, Jr., the son of another Hartford Conventioner, would never forgive Adams for having deserted his party and then impugned its loyalty during the late war. Both Lyman and Pickering entered a strange collaboration with the Democrats David Henshaw and Marcus Morton to support Crawford.[58] Then too, some Federalists moved toward Jackson. That movement picked up when, in May 1824, the press published a correspondence between Jackson and Monroe, written in 1816, about the patronage. The general had urged Monroe to appoint some Federalists, even to his cabinet, to heal old wounds. Now in 1824, the Federalists, interested in getting a share of offices in the next administration, envisioned Jackson's accession to the presidency as a good opportunity. Indeed the Federalist traffic toward the Jacksonian banner was fairly heavy throughout the country.[59]

To numerous Massachusetts Federalists the question came down to what Adams would do about the patronage, specifically whether he would proscribe them because of past party loyalty. Certainly this worried Webster a good deal more than what the view of Adams or other candidates might be on the issues of the day. In May two congressmen, after talking with Webster, conversed with Adams on this very matter. John Reed of Massachusetts extracted a reassurance from the secretary of state that he would not systematically exclude Federalists from office. And William Plumer, Jr., of New Hampshire got much the same answer. These discussions became specific to the level of Adams' visitors mentioning names, such as Jeremiah Mason and Joseph Hopkinson. Though not promising to bring them into his administration, Adams let it be known that he would not arbitrarily exclude persons of this type.[60]

Whether or not such conversation had an effect, it seemed quite probable that Massachusetts would go for Adams. However grudging and detached many political leaders may have been, a decided majority, in the end, would accept him in preference to any other. Observing this, Webster would do likewise—he would ultimately conform and feel comfortable about it. He thought he saw Adams' stock rising strongly, while Jackson's had peaked and was falling.[61] All New England and at least two or three other states would vote for Adams, he estimated, and the choice would be made in the House of Representatives from among the top three men. None of them, he complained, had the distinction and character for which one would hope; "local considerations, personal considerations & a hundred other *small* considerations will have their influence."[62] So it was still undesirable to announce his intentions until they did. After all, he would be in the House when the day of decision arrived.

Up to election day a sizable bloc of Massachusetts Federalists remained cautious or neutral. The *Advertiser,* which usually spoke the same language as Webster, and often spoke for him, approved a strategy of choosing uncommitted presidential electors, who might then either vote for Adams or not vote at all as the situation might invite. Hale, the editor, insisted that this noncommital course was the one Webster had pursued since he had been elected to Congress, and argued against any other move now. Nevertheless there were two electoral tickets, one pledged to Adams and the other unpledged. On the former were Republicans and some old Federalists; on the latter, mostly Federalists.[63] This division of opinion did not operate against Webster himself, for he could expect overwhelming support from both groups for his own reelection to the House.[64] But he made no speeches and wrote no letters for publication on the presidential question. This was a moment for quiet.

In November the results of popular voting in the country showed Jackson getting about 153,000 votes, Adams 114,000, Crawford 47,000, and Clay approximately the same. As for electoral votes (counting splits in individual states and selection of electors by several legislatures rather than by the people), Jackson received ninety-nine, Adams eighty-four, Crawford forty-one, and Clay thirty-seven.[65] Jackson, though definitely the leader, did not have a majority of either popular or electoral votes; and in accordance with the Twelfth Amendment, the House would select a president, with Clay excluded from the list.

Despite the advice of the *Advertiser* and the silence of Webster, Massachusetts went to Adams: 30,637 for pledged electors and only 6,616 for unpledged ones. In Boston, pledged electors defeated the unpledged slate two to one.[66] All five other New England states joined Massachusetts in the Adams column, and New York, Delaware, Maryland, and Louisiana also contributed some electoral votes. In New York, the foxy Van Buren had been outfoxed. His failure to manipulate proceedings in the legislature the way he had planned hurt Van Buren's favorite, Crawford, badly and in an unplanned aftermath hurt Clay still more, so that the Kentuckian dropped to fourth in the national totals.[67]

When Congress reassembled in December 1824, the precise count of electoral votes was still uncertain; but it was obvious that the main business of the House would be to choose the next chief executive. In the intervening months it handled some other matters. The first of these was to give an enthusiastic reception to Lafayette, currently on a triumphal tour of the United States and now invited to address the legislators. Webster was absent, visiting Jefferson at Monticello. Following this pleasurable interlude he passed through a period of grief over the death of his son Charles. It was January before he began serious work.[68]

Regardless of how the people had voted or how the electoral college had divided on the presidency, the decision rested with the House, each of the twenty-four states' delegations having one vote to give to Jackson, Adams, or Crawford. Of the three, Crawford's prospects were minimal, dependent upon repeated balloting and upon some piece of good fortune, or more probably upon some arrangement by the politicians. Though Jackson had received more popular and electoral votes than either of the other two, he seemed to have no better chance of success, perhaps less, than Adams, particularly if Clay, now out of consideration, threw his support to the New Englander. Would not this legislative veteran, the Speaker of the House, play the part of president maker with customary skill?

That Webster's course might be just as influential he only vaguely

113

realized when he arrived in Washington in December 1824, but began to understand as he surveyed the terrain on which a complicated game was being played. At first cautious and publicly noncommittal, as he had been from the start, he did intend to vote for Adams while avoiding anything offensive to Jackson. His friend Plumer paraphrased his remark: "If Adams succeeded all was well; if Jackson, the North by not quarrelling with him would come in for her share in the Administration." The New Hampshire congressman believed Webster was thinking not only of Federalists generally but of his own future, which might involve an appointment as minister to England. Not until the new year did he become more active in Adams' cause, and even then carefully.[69] Counting the probable total of state votes Adams could expect, he optimistically predicted it could be the required thirteen, or more. Meanwhile he detected a rising "reaction agt. Genl. Jackson—a feeling, somewhat adverse to giving the Presidency to *mere* military character."[70] As a matter of fact, at the moment Adams could not quite depend upon getting thirteen states' votes on the first ballot; and in a more sober mood Webster knew this. Even if Clay could deliver Kentucky, Ohio, and Missouri to Adams, the necessary two additional states, New York and Maryland, were still doubtful. Here was an opportunity for Webster to contribute something and, in the process, obtain assurances.

He decided to discuss the subject with Adams. On January 19 he and Congressman John Reed of Massachusetts called upon the secretary of state and, in Adams' words, "conversed upon the topic which absorbs all others."[71] It would be informative to know what was said; but concerning the discussion there is one of those intriguing gaps, intentional or not, in the famous diary. Probably its tenor resembled that of the talk two days later between Adams and Reed, who returned by himself. Adams assured Reed, as he had the previous May, that in his appointments as president he would "exclude no person for political opinions, or for personal opposition to me."[72] The two men clearly understood that this statement referred to Webster's fear that Federalists would be proscribed. These soundings of intentions must have been satisfactory to Webster, who remarked that "our Eastern candidate grows a little stronger."[73] Day by day, the outlook was improving.[74] At the end of the month, Clay finally announced what had long been his purpose: he was supporting Adams. On the twenty-ninth the Speaker had a frank conversation with Adams, one topic being the desirability of conciliating Webster.[75] The secretary felt he had taken care of that.

He was correct, for Webster was already moving to align the votes of Maryland and New York. Probably by previous agreement, he exchanged letters with Henry Warfield, the Federalist congressman from Maryland and one of a delegation of nine then divided between Adams and Jackson. Warfield may have been uncertain how to vote, though this is questionable; but more important, there were others from the state, John Lee and George Mitchell, who were doubtful and might be persuaded to come over to Adams. At any rate, on February 3 Warfield wrote Webster that he was undecided, wondered how Adams would treat Federalists in his administration, and sought advice. Webster skillfully phrased his reply. Disclaiming any intimate relationship with the candidate or authority to speak in Adams' behalf, he said he had worried about this very question and had concluded that Adams would be liberal-minded in regard to old party distinctions. All men would stand "according to their individual merits." While he did not wish or expect to see any apportionment of offices according to party affiliation, he did think "that by some one clear & distinct case, it may be shown, that the distinction alluded to does not operate as a cause of exclusion."[76]

Before sending the letter to Warfield, Webster went to Adams' house on the evening of the fourth and showed him the draft. After giving it a very close reading, Adams had one reservation. It must not be inferred, he warned, that he promised to appoint a Federalist to his cabinet; whereupon Webster assured him he did not have that in mind at all. Some high office, say a judgeship, would do. Then Adams said he "approved altogether of the general spirit of his answer, and should consider it as one of the objects nearest to my heart to bring the whole people of the Union to harmonize together."[77] The next day, Webster added a note to his letter outlining this discussion and sent it to Warfield.

To reinforce the understanding, Webster arranged for Warfield to call upon Adams on the seventh; and the latter told the Maryland congressman face to face the same thing he had told Webster. Warfield, the secretary thought, was "perfectly satisfied."[78] Meanwhile Warfield was using Webster's letter to advantage among his colleagues, both from his state and elsewhere, as February 9, the day of balloting in the House, approached. Webster also was active.

At this point the main concern was New York, whose large delegation was almost evenly divided between those committed to Adams and those going for Jackson or Crawford. If Adams did not get at least one more than half the votes of New York congressmen, the state's ballot could not be cast. Van Buren, a confirmed Crawfordite, was desperately trying to prevent an early selection of Adams in the hope that something would turn up. On the edge was the Federalist patron Stephen Van Rensselaer, who was receiving a great deal of attention from his messmate Van Buren and also from other quarters. Well aware of this, Webster had referred to Van Rensselaer's crucial position when he spoke with Adams on the fourth and had arranged for the New Yorker to talk with the secretary of state the following morning. The meeting occurred, and Adams attempted to allay Van Rensselaer's uneasiness in the same way he had with Webster, he hoped with equal success.[79] Chiefly to stiffen the malleable Van Rensselaer's own resolution, Webster enlisted his aid in recruiting the vote of Marylander John Lee.[80]

Concurrently another problem emerged. George Kremer, a Pennsylvania congressman, charged that Clay had bargained with Adams to support him for president in return for the promise of appointment as secretary of state. Angrily Clay branded this a lie, flung a challenge to duel, and then had to be satisfied with a committee inquiry when it seemed ridiculous to call the eccentric Kremer to the field of honor. On February 3 the committee, including Webster, began an investigation but soon found that Kremer would neither testify nor apologize to Clay.[81] A credible story later circulated that Webster went to Kremer's room, strenuously urged him to smooth over relations with Clay, but failed.[82] It was not until the very morning of balloting in the House that the committee reported its inability to question Kremer. Though there was no finding adverse to Clay, the allegations themselves were damaging enough. More would follow.

At noon on February 9, the senators and representatives solemnly filed into the House chamber for a joint session to receive returns from the electoral college. Ordinarily such proceedings would have gone unnoticed; but their unusual character on this day had excited intense interest and had drawn a large crowd to the Capitol to observe a suspenseful scene. There was no surprise at first; none of the candidates for president had received a majority of electoral votes, but Calhoun was overwhelmingly elected vice-president. Then the senators retired so that the representatives could select one of the leading three men as chief executive. Speaker Clay ordered a roll call; and one by one, each state announced to the tellers the tally of its delegation's votes. Maryland went to Adams on the basis of a five-to-four division. Warfield and George Mitchell, but not Lee, were among the five. The highlight was New York's decision for Adams, also by the narrowest margin—Van Rensselaer had cast his ballot for the New Englander. At the close, Adams had the necessary thirteen states, Jackson seven, and Crawford four. Applause and confusion erupted in the galleries, which Clay ordered cleared; but no one cared about that now.[83]

Van Rensselaer's ballot, tipping New York's vote and providing the thirteenth state for Adams, was therefore decisive, but no surprise to Webster. For days the patroon had been the object of pressure from all sides, by Webster for the Adams candidacy, by Van Buren for Crawford, by Clinton for Jackson; and finally Webster's pressure was the most effective. Bringing him in to confer with Adams to quiet his Federalist nervousness, recruiting him to talk with others, such as Lee, and emphasizing the importance of political and economic stability as promised by an Adams administration, all brought the desired result. Then on the morning of the House election, when he arrived at the Capitol, he encountered Webster and Clay, who escorted him into the Speaker's room for an earnest conversation. Here again he heard warnings of dire consequences if this election were deadlocked or if it went for the unpredictable Jackson, warnings that apparently stirred him deeply.[84] Earlier he had given Van Buren the impression that he would not vote for Adams, at least on the first ballot, in order to accommodate the New York leader's strategy of prolonging the voting. And he may have believed that his vote for Adams would not decide the contest, since he was not aware of how Maryland would go. In any case, Van Buren was furious with the old man. To justify his conduct, Van Rensselaer later told the story that just before casting his ballot he prayed for divine guidance and, glancing at the floor, saw an Adams ticket lying there. He picked it up, he recalled, and cast it as his vote as if this were the will of providence. Van Buren, who surely believed that political behavior is usually shaped more by human management than by divine direction, repeated this story in his autobiography; and historians have fastened on it as an interesting, perhaps true, explanation. In light of what had preceded Van Rensselaer's prayer, this interpretation is dubious.[85]

In the immediate aftermath of these extraordinary events, Webster was understandably happy about the victory. On the evening of the ninth he joined many guests at a reception at the White House, where he saw both Adams and Jackson, correct and courteous toward each other, and could hope that the loser would gracefully acquiesce in the recent decision. The next day, with others of a committee, he called upon Adams to notify him officially of his selection and received a written reply to the House.[86] He read reassuring items in the press: the *National Intelligencer*, for example, though a Crawford paper, doubted there had been any improper combinations before the voting.[87] And as mail arrived from home, papers and friends there reported an expansive pride that one of New England's sons would succeed to the highest office of the country.[88]

In the days before Adams' inauguration in March, Webster was also sanguine about the probable direction of the new administration. He felt confident that the new president would do what he had promised with respect to appointments and policies. Writing Jeremiah Mason in Portsmouth, he recalled the Warfield letter: "I was very distinct, & distinctly answered; & have the means of showing, *precisely*, what was said. My own hopes, at present, are strong that Mr. Adams will pursue an honorable, liberal, magnanimous policy. If he does not, I shall be disappointed, as well as others;—& *he will be ruined.*"[89] Quite so, replied Mason; Adams must not exclude Federalists from office, including a cabinet post. Federalists "ought not, & I trust will not be satisfied with mere empty declarations of liberality in his inaugural speech."[90] To keep Adams alert to his obligations, Webster sent him Mason's letter; and there was no demurrer. But, as Mason said, the measure of the new president's liberality would be action, not words—action dependent upon both political circumstances and his principles.[91]

Chapter 8

FRIEND OF THE ADMINISTRATION

Even before Adams' election, Webster knew it was unlikely that the incoming chief executive's liberality would extend to him personally. He had had notions, as early as the preceding summer, of appointment as minister to England, whose society, law, and politics interested him.[1] But he revealed these thoughts to only a few friends. One of them was his fellow congressman William Plumer, Jr., with whom he had a free conversation in December 1824. Perhaps by arrangement, Plumer relayed what he had learned to Adams a few days later. Straightaway, the suspicious secretary was on guard and disparagingly referred in his diary to Webster's "panting for the mission to London." In another discussion with Plumer on January 17, 1825, Adams made it quite clear that this ambition to go to England "might be gratified hereafter, but not immediately."[2] So before the Warfield correspondence and the House balloting in early February, Webster knew he would have to be patient if he were to share the rewards of this election. To avoid misunderstanding, before his inauguration Adams got Webster's assurance he would return to Congress and, as Adams put it, wait until "a proper time, to go abroad."[3] Nevertheless, the taste lingered. Through the spring the congressman gave more than passing notice to the selection of Rufus King for the post—Adams was fulfilling his promise to show by a distinct case that he would do justice to Federalists. To Webster, the attractiveness of King's appointment was that the old man's health would probably not allow an extended stay in England. But when King resigned a year later, his replacement was Albert Gallatin, not Webster.[4]

If he stayed in the House, there was the possibility of becoming

Speaker now that Clay was secretary of state; but Adams closed that off too. At the same time that he promised to postpone the ministry to England, he also agreed to defer to Adams' preference for Speaker, John W. Taylor.[5] At the opening of the congressional session in December 1825, he squirmed a bit in the bonds of that pledge when opposition to Taylor developed and his friends mentioned him as a candidate. Promptly the president reminded him of the arrangement, to which Webster had no outward complaint.[6] After all, leadership in the House could come from the floor, and that is what happened. He was soon recognized as the administration's spokesman and tactician, bringing to the role impressive oratorical and parliamentary talents. Now his relationship with the president was much friendlier than it had been or would later be. There were frequent visits to the White House; and very cordially, Adams invited him "to come and spend the evening . . . whenever it might suit his leisure and convenience."[7] His standing in Congress was so prominent his friend Chief Justice Isaac Parker characterized him as the "Premier of the House of Commons."[8] And Clay, despite firmly opposing a diplomatic assignment for him, valued his legislative leadership highly.

His capacity as a leader would be severely tested. The issue around which a protracted controversy swirled was whether to send delegates to a pan-American congress, the first such meeting in history. Conceived by the hero of the South American revolution, Simón Bolívar, the congress was to meet in Panama to discuss common problems of nations in the hemisphere. Secretary of State Clay, ever enthusiastic about closer relations with Latin America, persuaded Adams to accept an invitation to the United States to participate; and the president sent nominations of two ministers to the Senate on December 26. Both here and in the House there were months of speech making on resolutions and amendments before belated approval in May 1826. What would ordinarily have been a fairly noncontroversial proposal became the target of a coalescing opposition to the administration, handicapped as it was by the unusual circumstances of the past election.

This opposition was nothing less than a combination of all those who had supported other presidential candidates. Already the movement was under way to vindicate in 1828 the people's choice of Jackson and to expose thoroughly the "corrupt bargain" by which it had lately been thwarted. In Congress the direction of that movement fell into the hands, strangely enough, of the senator from New York, Martin Van Buren, now realizing the political potency of Old Hickory after a vain effort to win with Crawford. Though he was not prepared to come out openly for Jackson until he felt reassured about the principles and strategy of the movement, Van Buren began by talking with Vice-President Calhoun. Leaving other subjects for future discussion, the two readily agreed that opposition to the project of the Panama Congress ought to be the first step.[9] Thus in the subsequent debates most of the Jacksonians, Crawfordites, and Calhounites united in an attempt to defeat, or at least delay, the mission. In their oratory they ranged across the whole field of politics.

Through January, senators spoke on and on about the desirability or, more often, the undesirability of representation at the Panama Congress; and Adams, Clay, Webster, and others on the side of the administration soon understood that a decision would be tardy and possibly negative. In the House, it was believed, the prospect was better. Why not put through a resolution there to approve the policy of participation and of appropriating funds for it? This might give "the spur," as Clay said, to the procrastinating upper chamber.[10] Overcoming an initial nervousness about offending the Senate, Adams consented; and at the end of the month Webster received a plea to act.[11]

The first move was a resolution requesting information from the president about the objects of the mission, thus getting the question of appropriations before the House. For several days, until approval on February 3, Webster, with the assistance of Everett (the new congressman from Cambridge), Edward Livingston, and Rollin Mallary, fought off repeated amendments to extend the call for information to instructions to be given to American delegates. This demand, they contended, would be an improper legislative infringement of executive powers; and though they did not say so, it would also provide a better handle for the opposition to attack every particular of the convocation. Webster's version, which left to the president's judgment what information could be transmitted, prevailed.[12]

The Senate was not easily shaken, and debate there on confirming the nominations dragged into mid-March. The turning point was rejection of Van Buren's resolution that accepting the invitation to Panama was inexpedient, twenty-four to nineteen. Among the innumerable words uttered by the opposition were many playing upon the theme of the corrupt bargain, more important to them than the pending question. The most strident complaint came from Randolph, now a senator, who compared Adams and Clay to the hypocritical Puritan and the swindler in *Tom Jones*. In response to this offensive language, the secretary of state brought Randolph to the dueling field, fortunately unstained with blood.[13]

On April 4 attention shifted back to the House, which for the next three weeks discussed the expediency of appropriating funds. Amendments to the resolution came from Louis McLane, James Buchanan, and John Forsyth to guard against entangling alliances, against entering into any agreements, even against talking about agreements. Loquacious advocates of these amendments professed, unconvincingly, to have no partisan motives; and many of them, more convincingly, also professed approval of attendance at the Panama Congress within proper limits. Constitutionally, they argued, the House could appropriate money with conditions attached. The power to grant therefore implied the power to lay down the terms of use. Fundamentally, of course, the opposition distrusted both Adams and Clay. Their reasoning was that the president had already exceeded his authority by accepting the invitation to send ministers before communicating with Congress; besides, they well recalled Clay's long-standing interest in close commercial and political relations with Latin America. Diplomatically, their position was that the established American policy of neutrality forbade anything with the color of an entangling alliance. The repeated appeal was to Washington's proclamation of neutrality in 1793 and his Farewell Address. Monroe's doctrine could not change that policy: there must be no commitment to collective enforcement of its principle of nonintervention. Hovering over the whole debate was the subject of slavery and especially its fate in Cuba. Spanish control of the island was currently wavering, France had a fleet in the area that might intervene, and Mexico and Colombia showed signs of intervening too. The result might be emancipation of slaves and, even worse, repetition of the rebellion occurring in Haiti. With some reason, critics warned that the nations to the south meant to use the congress to meddle in Cuba.[14]

Midway in the debate, on April 14, Webster spoke in favor of approving the mission without congressional provisos. Have confidence in the president, he urged. In charge of conducting foreign relations, the chief executive must not be restricted by McLane's amendment, which really undertook to instruct him on how to do so. Thus the House could not intrude in the diplomatic field under cover of its financial powers. Fully endorsing the principle of no entangling alliances, he foresaw no commitment in Panama that could depart from it. Perhaps his strongest point was to demonstrate the value of discussing various problems—of neutral maritime rights, of commerce, of possible intervention in Cuba, or of any other threat to Latin American stability. Discussion did not require entering an alliance, he continued; in fact it would be desirable to explain to other nations the traditional policy of the United States. As for the Monroe Doctrine, he would adhere to it completely as a counterweight against European adventures in this hemisphere, but by this country's own decision and not in alliance with others. Topping off his speech with some inspirational sentiments, Webster voiced hope that the rise of republican government in South and Central America would promote civil liberty in place of religious intolerance and political oppression. What better way to nourish this tendency than to participate in the conference? The United States, "the great Northern light," would be encouraging its neighbors' progress toward freedom and justice.[15]

Though supported throughout the debate by a proadministration contingent saying much the same things he had, Webster had to sit through interminable argument and assault by the new Jacksonian combination. Some remarks became very personal. His opponents recalled his own obstructionism during the late war: he had been the "Magnus Apollo" among the "domestic enemies of his country," one of them exclaimed. His magnificent oratory at Bunker Hill last year, it was observed, had strangely passed over the military heroism of that war (best illustrated by Jackson at New Orleans, of course). And now his exposition of an expanded Latin American policy too much resembled his forensic display in behalf of the Greeks not long ago.[16]

In committee of the whole, the House rejected amendments to the administration's resolution, but the leading one failed by only one vote.[17] In formal session, however, the representatives approved McLane's amendment for nonentanglement, 99 to 95. It is impossible to account for the switch; but whatever the reason, Webster and other administration men would not accept the resolution in its revised form. So it was defeated.[18] They now decided to endorse the expediency of participation in the conference by passing a straight appropriations bill (out of a different committee) which said nothing about policy explicitly. In this way, both revisionists and unreserved advocates could join in approving the measure. And in fact the list of the yea votes shows such amenders as Buchanan and McLane in the majority of 134. Among the minority of 60 were other, perhaps more determined Jacksonians such as Forsyth, Samuel Ingham, George McDuffie, and James K. Polk. A strange and delayed victory it was when the bill was sent to the Senate on April 23.[19]

It was the third of May before the Senate passed this appropriations bill and at last the two American delegates could head for Panama. One of them, Richard Anderson, then the minister to Colombia, died en route; and the other, John Sergeant, who would not risk his health to go there during the summer months, missed the meeting. The United States was therefore not represented, but contemporaries and later scholars believed that not much was lost anyhow, owing not only to the unproductive work of the Panama Congress but also to the energetic activity of a British agent, who would have thwarted the Americans if they

had been there. The importance of the whole affair was not so much diplomatic as it was political, with more effect upon partisan controversy in
this country than upon foreign relations.[20]

Intensifying party feeling spread to nearly every question, including a
bill to reorganize the federal judicial system, with which Webster, as
chairman of the Judiciary Committee, was involved. The problem addressed by this bill was the inadequacy of the system in the growing
West, where there were too few circuit courts. These tribunals, presided
over by a traveling Supreme Court justice and the federal district judge
of the place, remained much the same despite the movement of the
frontier and the admission of new states to the Union. Webster got a bill
through the House, adding three western circuits and thereby increasing
the number of Supreme Court justices from seven to ten, while in the
Senate Van Buren reported a similar bill but with different circuit
boundaries. On this minor point the legislation stalled, indeed did not
go to conference, owing to Van Buren's inflexibility. Obviously the
Jacksonian opposition adopted this tactic to block any reform and
thereby to deprive the administration of an opportunity of making some
choice appointments.[21]

The second session of the Nineteenth Congress, December 1826 to
March 1827, was more of the same. A principal topic of controversy was
the tariff, with much rhetoric, maneuvering, voting, but no change. Despite the protectionism of the law of 1824, there were some unsatisfied
interests, notably wool growers and woolen manufacturers. From his
committee, Rollin Mallary introduced a bill to raise rates on raw wool
and woolen textiles and to make certain they were higher by requiring
minimum valuations instead of the existing *ad valorem* system. After three
weeks of intermittent discussion, the bill passed on February 10.[22] Webster said not a word. Never known for his silence, he had good reason to
stay clear. From his first years in politics, and as recently as the tariff debate of 1824, he had opposed a protective policy; yet he was now convinced that the economic trend was irrevocably toward manufacturing.
Capital flowing into the mills of New England required protection from
foreign competitors.[23] Still, he was probably not quite ready to ruffle his
many mercantile friends unnecessarily. So he made no speeches, but he
did vote more than once to move Mallary's bill through the House.

In the Senate there were others in an equally delicate situation. Van
Buren, caught in the vise of high-tariff opinion in New York and low-
tariff opinion among his allies in the South, could not afford just now to
antagonize either. As the clerk called the roll for yeas and nays, the Magician was not in his seat.[24] Because of his conspicuous position in the

vice-president's chair, Calhoun on the other hand had no place to hide when the voting ended with a tie, perhaps not by mere chance. He broke the tie by casting a nay, and that stopped the Mallary bill.[25]

To keep the tariff movement alive, a convention met at Harrisburg that summer. Called by the Pennsylvania Society for the Promotion of Manufacturers, strongly encouraged by Clay, and guided by publicists Hezekiah Niles and Mathew Carey, the convention brought together delegates from thirteen states and formulated a stiff high-tariff plan designed especially to help wool farmers and the woolen industry. Clay and Webster had recognized the political implications: this move could promote an administration party to reelect Adams. Jacksonians declared that was exactly what it was trying to do, but there was no overt commitment to such a purpose by the convention's leadership.[26] Webster approved the proceedings; and though he did not attend, his brother Ezekiel did.[27] It seemed clear that the next Congress would have to deal with this tariff issue, however uncomfortable the task might be.

In the coming session, the new alignments in American politics would be even more visible. As a result of the recent congressional elections, the Jacksonians would have a majority, could replace Taylor as Speaker and therefore frame the kind of committee report on the tariff they wished, and could exploit the subject to their advantage. Yet they were aware of the perils of handling the topic, for it could seriously damage the combination of sectional and ideological elements they were forming. The object must be to achieve unity while discrediting the administration.

Over the preceding two years, they had achieved considerable progress toward that goal. At the capital they had begun with an energetic resistance to the Panama mission that stalled the entire first congressional session of Adams' term. Then they had successfully opposed nearly every other administration measure so that what emerged was not much significant legislation but an absorbing discussion of the president's political morality. Meanwhile the personality around whom they rallied was Andrew Jackson, the wronged hero who must finally prevail.

Jackson himself was determined that would happen. Soon after inauguration of his New England opponent in March 1825, Old Hickory had returned to his plantation in Tennessee, with numerous conversations and public receptions en route. He left no doubt in anyone's mind that the late transactions in Washington had thwarted the popular will—the new secretary of state, he said, was the Judas of the West, gaining office by a corrupt bargain with a hungry presidential candidate. Unhesitatingly, he welcomed a movement to put things right in 1828. In October 1825 he appeared before the state legislature to resign as senator, to urge constitutional amendments to prevent recurrence of electoral abuses, and to witness his nomination for the presidency.[28] A dedicated, efficient circle of his friends and advisers was working for the cause. Known as the "Nashville Junto" and including Senator John Eaton, Judge John Overton, former congressman Felix Grundy, crony William B. Lewis, and protégé Sam Houston, it was the center of information and strategy for a campaign that covered the country and operated up to the election.

The theme continued to be the corrupt bargain. By the summer of 1827, Jackson was publicly charging that just before the House elected Adams, Buchanan (then a Clay man, though currently a Jacksonian) had approached him with an oblique offer to throw Clay's support to him in return for appointing Clay to the State Department. This proposal he had instantly rejected, said Jackson. Presumably, Clay then made a deal with Adams. Jackson's charges, brought forward in a letter to Carter Beverley of Virginia, were now unequivocal and completely in the open. It was no help to the administration, it seemed, for the embarrassed Buchanan and the furious Clay to deny these allegations. Had not Adams awarded the office to Clay?[29]

Webster gave not the slightest credence to any story of a corrupt bargain. As member of the House committee investigating the Kremer charges in February 1825, he and his associates had rejected the first version to appear. And in April he praised Clay's address to his constituents for its convincing explanation of the Kentuckian's reasons for preferring Adams to Jackson.[30] As months passed, Webster thought he saw throughout the Northeast a general approval of "the events of last winter" and of Clay's "agency" in producing them.[31] Hardly an impartial judge in view of his current close political collaboration with the secretary of state, Webster wrote Clay letters saturated with cordiality and praise whenever, as frequently happened, the latter issued still more denials.[32] In July 1827 he thought Clay's refutation of Jackson's Beverley letter was "admirable" and had put the general in an uncomfortable position whichever way he turned. Indeed, he later remarked, Jackson would never "recover from the blow which he has received."[33] His advice to Clay was to consider the matter settled and to waste no more attention on it.

By 1827, the opposition had other resources besides indignation about corruption. The mobilizer was Van Buren, New York senator and politician extraordinary, who made a series of brilliant moves that year to lay a foundation for the rising Jacksonian party. Actually, the preliminary had been the helpful, if open-ended, arrangement with the vice-president early the preceding year—the decision to oppose the Panama mission. Then at the beginning of the short session in December 1826, he had further conversations with Calhoun, in which the two set forth their ideas in greater detail. Like Thomas Jefferson and Aaron Burr, the Magician believed the keystone in party structure was a North-South alliance, and plans to assure it had high priority. As for principles, they must also be Jeffersonian, with due attention to states' rights and to the doctrines of '98 (the Virginia and Kentucky resolutions of 1798), as Van Buren would so often reiterate. No room here for a resurgent Hamiltonian Federalism with consolidating tendencies to the detriment of state interests. Though an avid nationalist in the past, Calhoun now fully concurred. The issue on which the two men did not think identically was the long-range indispensability of parties in government, for the New Yorker attached great value to parties in democratic politics, while the South Carolinian never abandoned his view that parties per se were corrupting, factional forces. There was no use in debating that point, however, for the two talked of immediate strategy, of the need to combine all pro-Jackson elements, of assuring a friendly newspaper press, of a variety of practical things to be done to elect the Old Hero.[34]

One of these chores Van Buren attended to right away. In January 1827 he was cementing a relationship with Thomas Ritchie, editor of the Richmond *Enquirer* and leader of the so-called Junto there. In language that would become a veritable Van Burenite slogan, the senator called for an alliance of the planters of the South and the plain Republicans of the North.[35] His belief in the editor's ability to bring this about was so firm that he had attempted to bring Ritchie to Washington to edit the main opposition newspaper. But Calhoun had vetoed that idea on the ground that there was already such a paper, the new *United States Telegraph,* run by Calhoun's admirer, Duff Green.[36]

As soon as Congress adjourned in March, Van Buren left on a political tour of the South, through Virginia, into the Carolinas, and as far as Savannah. With characteristic urbanity, he charmed his hosts and received enthusiastic greetings everywhere. There were many private talks with leaders in these states about ways of putting Jackson in the White House. No doubt the most important conference occurred in Georgia with William H. Crawford, Van Buren's candidate in the election of 1824. Though no longer having any hope for the presidency himself, Crawford still had excellent currency among those known as Radicals, chiefly southern states' righters. He assured Van Buren of his decided preference of Jackson to Adams, despite his irreconcilable opposition to Calhoun's continuing as vice-president.[37] With such highly desired connections as those with Ritchie, Calhoun, and Crawford, the wily senator could believe that he would have the planters of the South with him but must see what further needed to be done about the plain Republicans of the North.

A fundamental in Van Buren's thinking was the absolute necessity of sound organization in one's own state. For years he had practiced that principle, and his Albany Regency was the ideal type of state machine. His cohorts, among them Silas Wright, Benjamin Butler, and Azariah Flagg, dependably superintended a pyramidal edifice based upon workers and followers in all counties and districts, held together with rigorous discipline and discriminating patronage, and supported by loyal newspapers such as the Albany *Argus* and New York *Courier and Enquirer*. Until the election in late 1828, Van Buren worked unceasingly to maintain the Regency's efficiency. One problem was the alarming Antimasonic movement, which had sprung up in 1826 and threatened havoc to old patterns of political behavior. If the movement helped either presidential candidate, it would be Adams, who disliked Masonry, and not Jackson, who was a Mason. On this and other matters Van Buren acted skillfully; but to ensure that New York would deliver its vote to Jackson, the Fox of Kinderhook decided that he himself must run for governor. Even so, the administration party had reasonably good prospects in the state.[38]

To this many-sided challenge of the Jacksonian opposition across the nation, the Adams-Clay "coalition," as its foes had labeled it, had to respond. The president, to tell the truth, was not much help. Steadfastly refusing the electioneer, a term then connoting an entirely unworthy pursuit of the chief executive's office, Adams took no part in directing his party's operations, would not hear of using the patronage for his own advantage, and refused to be involved in any fund raising or to contribute anything himself. Like most of his generation, he felt that parties were intrinsically undesirable, were factions divisive to the Union and subversive of the public good. Regardless of this general question, his conception of the presidency dictated self-restraint. Thus his proper role was to behave as a latter-day Washington might, remaining above parties and petty disputes. Clay, on the other hand, was a born party politician. Early in life a Jeffersonian Republican, he had moved toward a neo-Federalist position in advocating national economic policies and was ready to employ partisan techniques to advance them. By this time, he welcomed all available aid from old Federalists as well as from fellow Republicans; but he saw the opposition as a menacing states' rights combination trying to lift a military hero to the presidency. In behalf of the American System and of his own future, he would use patronage, the press, money, and organization to defeat that combination.[39]

Ever since the Treaty of Ghent, there had been a strain of ambivalence in Webster's relationship to parties. As a zealous Federalist of the Washington school, as he expressed it, he had fought the Jeffersonian Republicans strenuously before and during the War of 1812. And as a recent writer has pointed out, he had had the reputation of a young Federalist, holding to that party's credo but adjusting to the realities of an increasingly popular political environment, specifically by resorting to much the same tactics as the Republicans in reaching the voting public.[40] But at the war's end, he could see clearly enough that old party distinctions were fading: Federalism was decrepit, probably moribund, and Republicanism, though triumphant, was heading toward a nationalist consensus. He had had high hopes that Monroe's administration would truly be an Era of Good Feelings. The fact was that Monroe was still very conscious of party distinctions, particularly in his appointments to office. Webster himself had been slow to shed his Federalist coat, for the state and local context in which he moved forbade it. In 1823 he had said, "We must divide, into Republicans, & Radicals; comprising, in the last class, not merely the reformers, in Congress, but the *intriguers*—the caucus men—the hot & Exclusive party men."[41] But a bit later, during the Greek debate in Congress, a friendly Clay had classified him as a Federalist.[42] And throughout the process of electing Adams, his overriding aim had been to protect the interests of Federalists, to guarantee they would not be proscribed in the dispensation of patronage. Perhaps one can encapsulate his attitude toward parties by saying that like so many others of the time, he often deplored their dangerous features in a good and just society but more often acted otherwise.

Now, halfway through Adams' term, it was obvious there were two parties well on the way toward solidification, but how they should be described and how long they would last were open questions. "We are foolish enough, some of us, to talk still about Federalists & Democrats," Webster observed, "but the general sentiment is favorable to the Administration, & opposition can make no progress."[43] Whether that prediction would be vindicated or not, he had to recognize the fact of a new division of political opinion: the "Friends of the Administration" (whatever their previous party affiliations) and the opposition (Jacksonians, Radicals, Calhounites, Richmond Junto, Albany Regency, and so forth). Though hoping that this division was a passing phenomenon, he knew better than to ignore it.

The administration party needed as much Federalist support as it could get. Gaining it would be difficult, for large numbers had been joining the Jacksonians. Webster felt a special responsibility to minimize this defection as far as possible. In the first months of Adams' presidency, the Massachusetts congressman joined an effort, known as amalgamation, to recruit Federalists as a block in the new coalition.[44] Much depended, he believed, upon a favorable perception of the Federalists' record so that they would no longer suffer unfair condemnation and consequent proscription from their deserved role in public affairs. The basis of their union with Adams-Clay Republicans must therefore be mutual respect. To promote that kind of relationship, Webster helped plan the publication of a history of the years 1797 to 1817 to put Federalist behavior in a true light. After a promise of money from a group in New York and on advice from Joseph Hopkinson, he arranged for Robert Walsh, editor of the Philadelphia *Gazette,* to write this apologia. In mid-1825 Walsh reported his determination to complete the project, despite criticism that he would malign the old Hamiltonian Federalists while praising the Adams wing. Actually the history never appeared, but the effort for amalgamation would continue.[45]

After Adams took office, two years passed before Webster fully understood the character of the opposition. In the first session of Congress, while speakers on the Panama mission droned on endlessly, he knew, of course, that they had subtler motives than merely to discuss the merits of this question. Perhaps they wished to vent dissatisfaction with the election, still fresh in their memory; yet "a good degree of civility & kind feeling prevails," he thought. He hoped that "time and events may abate the malignity that still rages in some quarters."[46] In a few weeks, by March 1826, he detected an opportunistic opposition to the administration forming under Calhoun's leadership. The vice-president had simply capitalized upon long-standing sectional prejudices, upon the South's unwillingness to "acquiesce in the administration of any President on our side [of] the Potomac." His object in obstructing the mission, Webster suspected, was to put Adams in his power. "Mr. Adams, then, would have been obliged to make terms, or he could not get on with the Government & those terms would have been *the dismissal of Mr. Clay.*" Beyond that, he saw little evidence that the disparate elements of the opposition could hold together.[47] At the close of the next congressional session of early 1827, however, the Jackson movement had crystalized, Van Buren was off on his southern tour, and the president's adversaries were gaining unity and confidence. Neither privately nor publicly would he admit that this challenge to Adams' reelection could succeed. Counting states that would remain loyal, he listed all in New England, some in the Ohio Valley, and Louisiana. The South and parts of the Southwest could blindly follow Jackson, but their loyalty would be fruitless.[48]

Webster was cooperating closely with Clay in leading the Friends of the Administration throughout the country. In Washington, they frequently talked about legislative strategy and party affairs; and when he returned home, Webster exchanged many letters with the secretary on the political situation in states of every section. Clay felt optimistic, too, about the next election and entirely agreed that the West and the Northeast would be safe, with excellent prospects in Pennsylvania, if it pursued its true interest on the tariff as it seemed to be doing, and in New York, if the substantial pro-Adams forces there thwarted Van Buren and Clinton, which seemed to be happening. Clay's connections with the South were good, so that he could report promising developments in Virginia and Louisiana. The two also agreed on indispensable measures: improved party organization in each state, plenty of campaign funds, an active partisan press, and realistic handling of patronage. They thought alike, furthermore, on the condition of party alignments. Old distinctions between Federalists and Republicans were meaningless, but a new one, for or against the administration, had unfortunately emerged.[49]

Political developments in Webster's Massachusetts illustrate what had happened. After collapsing in other parts of the country, the Federalist party remained paramount there for a time and annually elected its candidates for governor and the state legislature. In 1822, however, the challenge by the Middling Interest, though largely unsuccessful, frightened party leaders by revealing factionalism and weakness. The Republicans gained strength, electing their candidate for governor in 1823 and 1824. The state's vote for the Republican Adams for president in 1824 contributed to this trend. Support for Crawford by a number of Federalists, such as Theodore Lyman and Timothy Pickering, alongside democratically minded David Henshaw and Marcus Morton, compounded the confusion. At the outset of this disruptive process, Webster worried about the "miserable, dirty squabble of local politics," involving several narrow interests but "no national interest, nor any national feeling."[50] His role in the effort toward amalgamation represented an attempt to unify these narrow interests.

On April 4, 1825, just a month after Adams' inauguration, Massachusetts held its election for governor and state senators, the first test of amalgamation here. A coalition of the two old parties presented a common slate of candidates. For governor, it nominated moderate Republican Levi Lincoln; and for lieutenant governor, the incumbent Marcus Morton, a strongly partisan Republican. Three of the six persons on the list for senators from Suffolk County were Federalists, the other three Republicans.[51]

Recently arrived from Washington, Webster attended a huge, enthusiastic meeting in Faneuil Hall on the day before the election and set forth the amalgamationist rationale. Endorsing the Union ticket ratified by the meeting, he called for abandonment of previous party distinctions, now that the old issues causing them had disappeared. It was time for reconciliation, for national development, he announced. His theme resembled Clay's American System: internal improvements for the West, encouragement of eastern commerce and manufacturing, greater prosperity for southern planters. All sections would benefit from unity; all would share in exploiting the promise of America, a land of enterprise and liberty. In the course of his argument, he depicted political parties as always undesirable, often factional, and now wholly unnecessary. His plea was to continue the nonpartisan mood of Monroe's administration. Inescapably, he had to mention the suspected Clay-Adams bargain. There had been no bargain, he insisted; Clay's conduct had been pure and straightforward, and the president had naturally turned to him as highly qualified for his post. In any case, that matter was no reason to revive party warfare.[52]

The election did not go uncontested. Another slate with a Federalist label entered the campaign, demonstrating that reconciliation was not yet at hand. True enough, Lincoln and the rest of the Union ticket prevailed. But a soft spot in amalgamation, in addition to some Federalist recalcitrance, was exposed when Morton had second thoughts about collaboration and resigned as lieutenant governor to take Lincoln's former place on the supreme court.[53]

Two years later, the outcome was similar. In Boston, Lincoln and most of a Union slate of state senators led in the voting but separate Republican and Federalist slates appeared. These also supported both national and state administrations and included a majority of the same names found on the amalgamationist list, with some differences. On the Federalist list only, for example, were Theodore Lyman and Benjamin Gorham. This circumstance apparently left many people uncertain as to who preferred to be on which list, a technicality in one sense but also an indication of fluidity in party identification.

In this contest of 1827 a more formidable problem involved the Charles River Bridge. Complaints had mounted against this toll bridge, connecting Charlestown and Boston since the 1780s, because of the company's enormous profits and exploitation of an important line of traffic. At least that is what an active group in Charlestown contended; and it found supporters in Boston itself, notably opportunistic David Henshaw, wholesale druggist and would-be party boss. Only weeks before the election, those who had criticized the bridge as a privileged monopoly unacceptable to a democratic society finally got a bill through the legislature to build another bridge, this one to be toll free. On that issue, Webster and his friends took a firm position in behalf of property rights. Though they would compromise to the extent of giving up the old bridge if the state compensated the stockholders, they believed the current bill was confiscatory, and thus contrary to federal and state constitutions. So Governor Lincoln refused to sign the bill. The aroused free-bridge advocates thereupon held a meeting to nominate their own slate of senatorial candidates and William C. Jarvis of Charlestown, then the house speaker, as governor. Jarvis formally declined the nomination but received a substantial vote anyway. Generally, the bridge controversy strengthened antiamalgamationist opinion and helped form a Jacksonian party.[54]

Despite hortatory editorials in the *Advertiser* and valiant efforts by unionists, fragmentation pervaded the May election of state representatives too. Five slates of thirty candidates each, again with much overlapping, competed for the bewildered voter's ballot. Amalgamationist, Federalist, Republican, free-bridge, and pro-lottery nominees were available if one could sort them out. A Union meeting called by Hale and Perkins assembled in Faneuil Hall on April 20, heard resolutions proposed by David Child (editor of a new Webster-sponsored newspaper) and authorized a committee to choose candidates for the Massachusetts house. On May 8 another meeting approved the committee's list of thirty, the president's son George, Nathan Appleton, and Israel Thorndike among them.[55]

At the first of these gatherings (April 20), Webster spoke as a staunch friend of the administration, his first opportunity in the city since the close of the congressional session. In a historical review he found that parties had arisen in the era of European war from the 1790s to 1815, when Americans disagreed about foreign policy and United States involvement in the conflict. Afterward, he said, old questions had disappeared, and so had any justification for parties. Accordingly, during Monroe's administration New England Federalists had joined men of other sections and backgrounds in affirming national unity. Recently, the unusual circumstances of Adams' election angered the opposition; but, he contended, this situation was no excuse for adhering to anachronistic parties or for creating new ones. When he finished, he had doubtless invigorated the spirit of his audience. Yet his history was faulty; his hopes for a no-party republic were visionary; and his own actions, partisan as they had been, proved it.[56]

The results of the election were curious. Only eight candidates, all amalgamationists, were elected by the required majority vote; however, the entire Union ticket got twice as many votes as any of the other four. In a second election a week later (May 17) to fill the remaining twenty-two places, the nonamalgamating groups stood their ground so that the offices remained vacant; and Suffolk County sent eight instead of thirty representatives to the legislature.[57] Heartened by a good showing, Webster nevertheless had to face the fact that a menacing opposition continued.

Meanwhile he followed events in New Hampshire with deep interest. There were two elements of the Republican party: one, led by Levi Woodbury and Ike Hill, comprised Jacksonians; the other, led by Senator Samuel Bell, supported Adams' reelection. Also favoring Adams, the dwindling number of Federalists, including Ezekiel Webster and Jeremiah Mason, hoped for an amalgamationist position of Adams men, Republican and Federalist. For a time, the Bell forces felt they could not risk such an association, much to the disgust of people like Ezekiel. In Washington, Webster kept in touch with what was occurring and urged Ezekiel to swallow his pride and join in a declaration under the Republican name if necessary. At last Bell soothed Federalist feelings and agreed to a unionist strategy, with mixed meetings, a combined convention, and promised patronage.[58]

Just as Webster and his friends hoped to surpass the Jacksonian effort of Van Buren and others in efficient organization at the state level, so they entered the savage war of the newspaper press for the same purpose. Even in a day of highly politicized, unrestrained journalism, the administration found such papers as the Regency's Albany *Argus,* the New York *Post* (now under the practical management of William Cullen Byrant), Ritchie's Richmond *Enquirer,* Henshaw's *Statesman* in Boston, and dozens of others to be irritating and alarming. As the election campaign progressed, they, too, concluded that success absolutely depended upon reaching the people by way of a friendly press.

If there was one paper which invariably mirrored Webster's opinions through his forty years in national politics, it was the Boston *Advertiser,* edited by his faithful friend Nathan Hale. Everyone knew that Hale's editorial columns, especially in reference to the congressman, could just as well have been written by Webster himself; in fact some of them were. The two belonged to the same social circle, had a personal relationship involving both their families and their money, and thought as one about politics. When Webster took new positions, the *Advertiser* would explain and commend them. Hale played an active role in Federalist and then in proadministration politics of the city, in supervising work in the wards, calling meetings, writing and publishing public addresses. Like Webster, he now felt very uneasy about the opposition's appeal to emotion, prejudice, and hero worship. But the respectable editor printed his share of inflammatory comment, only in retaliation of course.

To aid the Friends of the Administration, as early as the summer of 1825 Webster was trying to establish another paper in Boston, the *Massachusetts Journal*. Together with Edward and Alexander Everett, he sought capital and a dependable editor, both somewhat scarce it seemed, until the paper began publication a year later. How much of his own money he gave to the project is unclear. He did assist it, but noiselessly, by promoting subscriptions, raising funds, obtaining public documents, and providing valuable political information.[59] David Child, the editor, announced that the *Journal* would be independent of party and would strive for literary quality and good taste.[60] What he produced was another partisan paper, for the administration and for Webster in season and out, with a veneer of elevation and detachment that must not have deceived many readers. Webster was satisfied. "It is . . . well disposed, occasionally able . . . and for the Administration, & all its great measures," he observed.[61] He backed it through the election of 1828; but when Child asked if he was willing to continue his "distinguished favor," he answered no.[62]

In cooperation with Clay, who agreed that it was imperative to counter every journalistic blow by the opposition, Webster collected a sizable sum from well-to-do friends in Boston, New York, and elsewhere to subsidize a friendly press. A beneficiary was Charles Hammond of the Cincinnati *Gazette,* who later published merciless allegations about irregularities in Jackson's marriage. At Clay's suggestion, Webster promised to draw upon his fund to buy a new set of type for Hammond.[63] To John Pleasants of the Richmond *Whig* he pledged as much as one thousand dollars.[64] For these and other papers substantial sums came, at Webster's solicitation, from wealthy men at home, Perkins, Amos and Abbott Lawrence, Israel Thorndike, David Sears.[65]

A different strategy to stimulate editorial activity seemed necessary in Philadelphia. In passing through that city in late March 1827, Webster found the press too quiescent, hardly stirring for the administration's cause. Robert Walsh, editor of the *National Gazette* and an old-line Federalist, was inclined toward Adams but showed minimal enthusiasm. After a conversation with Walsh, he believed the main problem lay with the president's passivity on the patronage. The remedy was to appoint some Federalists to important offices, a step which would mollify the editor and, through him, enliven numerous other Federalists in the state. The office Walsh and Webster had in mind especially was the federal district judgeship in Pennsylvania, likely to be vacant soon; and the appointee, they thought, ought to be Joseph Hopkinson. In letters to Clay and Adams, Webster urged that this be done and said that Walsh would visit Washington to talk about it.[66] The Philadelphia journalist found Adams noncommittal and Clay much less receptive.[67] In any event, the matter would have to rest until there was a vacancy.

The center of any network of party newspapers had to be in Washington, of course, and both sides knew it. By 1826 the Jacksonians had the new, aggressive *United States Telegraph,* Duff Green, proprietor. A model for all-out partisan editors, Green would be primarily loyal to Calhoun, with whom he was connected not only by political cords but also by the marriage of his daughter to the South Carolinian's son. As long as the Calhoun-Jackson alliance lasted, he would provide a sturdy voice for the entire Jacksonian party.[68] In his ferocious way, Green gave Webster extraordinary attention, perhaps owing to the influence of his rash young coeditor, Russell Jarvis of Massachusetts, and to his increasingly friendly relations with David Henshaw there.[69]

The Friends of the Administration had greater firepower in the Washington press but tended to muzzle it in the name of propriety. One organ was the *National Journal,* helped with printing jobs for Clay's State Department and edited by the capable Peter Force. His tone of respectability and profession of impartiality gave way, at times, to the exigencies of superheated politics; and he dependably expressed pro-Adams viewpoints, still in a literate, rational style. Webster's relationship to the paper was close because of his friendliness with Force's associate, the English-born John Agg. A popular figure in the capital's social life, having unusual talent for writing and for dissecting a political problem, Agg often passed the hours with Webster, discussing literature, a recent Washington party, or campaign tactics.[70] A more durable paper was the *National Intelligencer,* published from 1800 until after the Civil War. Its perennial editors, Joseph Gales and William Seaton, also were intelligent men striving for good taste in journalism; but they, too, frequently became entangled in controversy. The *Intelligencer* had been the official newspaper, more or less, during the Virginia dynasty of Jefferson, Madison, and Monroe—in those days Webster received rough treatment in its pages. After a futile effort for Crawford in 1824, Gales and Seaton came over to Adams, no doubt with an eye toward their printing contracts. From the mid-1820s onward, with few exceptions, Webster enjoyed the *Intelligencer*'s aid and approval. How many pieces he himself drafted for publication in the paper will never be exactly known; sufficient to say, a good many.[71]

Besides the press, a useful instrument available to the administration was patronage. Long recognized as a powerful cohesive agent, it was not yet generally accepted as a positive good instead of an evil to be avoided, concealed, or explained away. Van Buren and a number of Jacksonians did recognize its value, indeed indispensability, to the party system they were developing. Adams, on the other hand, did not. Qualification must be the sole standard for appointments, he believed; and if this policy hampered the growth of parties, so much the better. Thus Postmaster General John McLean, who said he opposed a spoils system but inclined toward Jackson, remained in office, untouched by the president because he had a reputation for efficiency. Clay concluded that Adams' position was suicidal and ought to be reversed without delay. Victimized himself by the corrupt-bargain charge, he could see that the president had satisfied no one—to his enemies he projected the image of spoilsman and to his friends, a timid, aloof leader.[72]

Webster perfectly agreed with the secretary of state. To turn back the Jacksonian attack, it was imperative, he thought, to reward supporters of the administration, perhaps also those who were potential supporters, and to weed out the rabid Jackson men from federal office. As he surveyed the current appointive policy, he felt dismay about the lethargy and the fumbling which debilitated it as a positive factor in the next election. Still, he expressed this opinion only in private conversations and letters, not for public circulation. Partisan appointments were sometimes necessary, though in principle difficult to defend.[73]

During Adams' years in the White House, Webster had only a limited influence upon appointments.[74] The selection of King as minister to Britain was, in a sense, fulfillment of the Warfield pledge—the so-called distinct case. His pressure to place Hopkinson in the district judgeship gave the impression of collecting another election debt in behalf of old Federalists. He finally succeeded, in the twilight of the presidential term. Adams was wary, however, of rewarding Federalist friends; like Monroe, he did not wish to incur probable Republican criticism and defection.[75] And eventually it did not matter what he preferred, because the opposition dominated the Senate and could reject his nominees.[76]

But now, in the spring of 1827, when the forces of the administration and of its opponents were yet forming for the battle of the next quadrennial election, Webster had to decide about his own political future. His alternatives, at the moment, were to stay in the House, leading his incipient party there, or to shift to the Senate, where his influence at first

might be less substantial. The previous year, he had taken the first option. After James Lloyd had resigned from the Senate, Webster had
thought about the change, had heard hints of support, and had received
one-third of the votes of the state house of representatives when merchant Nathaniel Silsbee of Salem won the post. His interest had been
tentative, however, and the outcome had caused him no ostensible disappointment.[77] In the fall of 1826, his reelection to Congress had been
overwhelming: 1,545 votes to 98 for his Jacksonian opponent. An important feature of that one-sided contest had been his nomination as the
Republican candidate (with Federalist cooperation, of course). This
abandonment of an old party name had pleased the amalgamationist-
minded congressman.[78]

The term of the other Massachusetts senator, Elijah H. Mills, a reliable but colorless upholder of the administration, would soon expire;
therefore, the legislature through January and February 1827 began a
long series of ballots. Repeatedly, the house favored Elijah Mills, the
senate John Mills of Springfield, who was more satisfactory to Jacksonians. To avoid an impasse, the senate tried Governor Levi Lincoln; but
before the house could act, Lincoln declined. So the business was carried
over to the May session.[79]

After returning to Boston at the close of Congress in March, Webster
talked and wrote to a number of people about the senatorship. Having
cheerfully approved the effort to reelect Elijah Mills, he discovered that
the senator's ill health forbade his serving again. Mills let it be known
that he thought so too.[80] What of Lincoln? Would he change his mind?
If not, should he himself go after the position? In a letter of early May,
he reviewed the situation and posed the last question to Clay, and
through the secretary to the president as well. Saying Lincoln would be
an excellent choice but would probably not consent, Webster insisted he
preferred to stay in the House. It was nevertheless essential, he declared,
that the next senator add strength to the administration's ranks.[81] Clay
answered promptly. The Kentuckian obviously hoped that Webster
would remain in the lower house, as he had said a year ago concerning
the other Senate seat, when he had emphasized the "strong and commanding ground" Webster had assumed in the House as the administration's spokesman. It might be safe now for Webster to change if other
persons, such as John Sergeant and Thomas Oakley, would come in to
assume the leadership, though he feared they would not. Adams also
would be happier if Webster stayed where he was and if Lincoln, in
whom he had the greatest confidence, would reconsider. Nonetheless,
Clay, with the president concurring, obligingly concluded that Webster
should go to the Senate if, as seemed likely, Lincoln stood fast.[82]

Encouraged by this and other advice, he was abandoning his stance of reluctance as the legislative session approached.[83] On May 22 he confronted the problem of Lincoln directly by a final appeal to the governor. Again Webster explained that his own contributions would probably be greater in the House but asked for a reply by way of Nathan Appleton, who, they both knew, could use it in the legislature to remove any uncertainty. Conveniently, Webster would be out of town and would leave the affair to others.[84] Lincoln's answer came two days later. He could not give up his current responsibilities, he said; furthermore, it would be better for someone (such as Webster) with more experience in Washington to take the office.[85] Additional considerations, unmentioned by the governor, must have influenced him. The fragile Federalist-Republican coalition which had elected him a few weeks earlier would crumble if he left now. Specifically, the wrench to that relationship might be even more damaging if the next governor should be William C. Jarvis, a leader of the free-bridge party. It would be interesting to know who had talked to Lincoln and what they had said about the sensitive issue of the Charles River bridges.[86]

The stage was ready for Webster's election. On May 30 he wrote to Lincoln, Appleton, and Joseph Sprague, a political organizer and the key figure in the proceedings, and announced to each his availability. Assuring them he could be spared in the House, he was "content the Legislature shall act as its own sense of public interest may dictate."[87] In the balloting of June 7 he got two-thirds of the votes of both houses, with most of the remainder going to the two Millses.[88] As he received the predictable but welcome letters of congratulations, he displayed no great elation but was determined to use his new position as effectively as he could in the decisive phase of national politics that was imminent. He could not know how intimately his reputation in history would be connected with events in the Senate.[89]

Chapter 9

SENATOR

When the Senate convened in early December 1827, Webster had not yet arrived at the capital. His reason for being late was better than usual, for he and Grace were in New York, where they had had to stop because both were ill. Webster's illness, a cold and an attack of rheumatism, was not serious; but his wife's malady alarmed him. It was the middle of the month before he dared leave her at the home of Cyrus Perkins and travel to Washington alone. In the next two weeks news about Grace was still discouraging; so after New Year's he hurried northward, not to return to the legislative scene until February 18. This period of worry and, finally, anguish about Grace's death consumed nearly half the session.[1] The other half was a time of continuing gloom and uncertainty.

In the Senate, he had to adjust to new circumstances. Its forty-eight members constituted a much smaller body than the House. Each senator had an assigned place among the three rows of desks compactly arranged in a chamber of modest size—Webster's was a few feet away from the vice-president's chair in front of the windows. It was "Hobson's choice," he said, "left by 47 wiser heads than mine." The galleries around the semicircular room could accommodate a few hundred spectators when they crowded in to hear the solons debate an interesting question. There was larger scope for individuality than in the other house, more opportunity for the oratory in which Webster excelled. But the Senate seemed "new & strange," he said, and he needed time "to feel at home" here. Besides, the opposition had command. "I think the true course is to let them exercise it, as seems to them good. Why should *we* be responsible for what we cannot control?"[2]

The Jacksonians did have the upper hand. They could now, it seemed, deal with the tariff question as they saw fit. In the House they installed a friendly Speaker, made committee assignments suited to their strategy, and moved ahead with determination. On the Committee on Manufactures, they allowed proadministration Rollin Mallary to remain as chairman but otherwise loaded it with their own men, chief of whom was Van Buren's agent, Silas Wright. So Mallary had the embarrassing responsibility of reporting a bill largely drafted by Wright and entirely contrary to his own ideas. Intended to appeal to middle and western states at the expense of New England manufacturers, the measure would raise duties on hemp, iron, molasses, and raw wool but very little on woolen textiles. The bill passed without significant change and came before the Senate in late April and early May.

Here Van Buren could manage the business directly. If the Friends of the Administration felt uncomfortable, the Magician had worries too. Genuinely favoring some higher rates, such as those on raw materials covered by the bill, he recognized that his opponents could defeat it unless he made concessions. Thus he decided to prevent all amendments lowering the proposed schedule on these items, particularly on raw wool, but to allow somewhat larger increases on woolens. It might be a bitter pill for the senators from the Northeast to take; yet take it they would in order to get the increases. An added advantage would be to pacify protectionist sentiment in his own state. The South would be disgruntled with a higher tariff, but Van Buren knew it was safely in the Jackson fold in any event. And he weighed everything in terms of victory in the coming election.[3]

Webster's mail from home amply revealed opinion on the subject. Many constituents expressed dissatisfaction with high duties on hemp, iron, and molasses, which would hamper shipping and other commercial enterprise. Incoming correspondence generally did urge more protection for raw wool, despite additional costs to woolen-mill owners. Wool growers and woolen manufacturers in Massachusetts, as in the Harrisburg convention, accommodated their inherently conflicting interests. But the House bill's low rates on woolen textiles drew the heaviest criticism.[4] It was this opposition which Van Buren softened by concessions in the Senate amendments. By the first week in May, Webster's correspondents were saying that all things considered, the amended version ought to pass. "New England would reap a great harvest by having the bill adopted as it now is," Abbott Lawrence wrote.[5] Editor Joseph Buckingham of the Boston *Courier* reported that manufacturers found the revised schedule "satisfactory and advantageous." In light of later political events, Buckingham gave an interesting piece of advice: "It is, perhaps,

141

better that the Jacksonians of the south and middle States should not know that the bill has been made acceptable to the people of New-England."[6] Even merchants such as Perkins and Thorndike who staunchly opposed higher levies on raw materials did not complain about provisions on wool and woolens.[7]

Webster's speech of May 9 registered the varied sentiments of his constituents.[8] Though later believed to have been his first important statement as a converted protectionist, it actually mixed old and new views. He still argued for justice to maritime industries. A number of the proposed duties were truly abominable, he contended, as others had already characterized them. Ropemakers (and, in turn, shipowners) would needlessly suffer from inflated prices of imported hemp, because the domestic dew-rotted product was unsatisfactory for their purpose. They had to buy foreign, water-rotted hemp, now unavailable from American growers in the quality and quantity required. An indirect subsidy to encourage these growers through preferential purchasing by the navy would be more desirable than imposing such a ruinous rate as was prescribed in the bill. Another abomination, in his judgment, was the unreasonable duty on molasses. Although friends of grain distillers depicted it as a necessary offset to rum distilled from West Indies molasses, Webster cited figures to show that less than 25 percent of that commodity went into rum, while the rest was consumed as food. Objectionable sections had been included in the bill, he suspected, "for the very purpose of destroying the bill altogether" or of hurting those interests which might reluctantly accept them because of other, more favorable provisions. He accused southerners, especially, of keeping all the abominations in the bill so that New England would defeat it. If that did not happen, the master strategist Van Buren would push through an unfair bill.

While denouncing higher duties on hemp and molasses, he saw a legitimate demand for them on woolens. In this respect, he spoke as a protectionist recruit. Freely admitting his region's long-standing dislike of high tariffs, committed as it had been to freedom of foreign commerce, Webster explained why it was changing its mind, and implicitly why he also was reconsidering. When New England resisted the rise of rates in 1816 and 1824, it wished to go slowly and self-reliantly toward manufacturing without depending upon a tariff which could be terminated at any time.[9] After 1824, the policy of protection appeared permanent; and having the requisite capital, labor, and general capacity, it naturally committed them to the new industry. Different economic circumstances therefore dictated a different political opinion. The leading problem had become inadequate protection for woolen textiles, a problem publicized by the recent Harrisburg convention and only partially addressed by the pending bill. The senator preferred still higher rates on woolens, with several categories of minimum valuations and with specific instead of *ad valorem* duties, but no increase in rates on other goods.[10] The outlook for this kind of law, at the moment, was poor.

A week after Webster's speech, the bill passed.[11] His amendments on hemp, molasses, flax, and sail duck failed; and Van Buren's abominable combination, slightly sweetened with revised woolen rates, attracted votes of the Northeast and the Ohio Valley. Southerners unwittingly helped by defeating Webster's amendments, following which they were shocked to learn that he and enough others would swallow the abominations. They were understandably surprised, for up to the last minute senators such as Webster were indeed undecided.[12] Their greatest miscalculation probably concerned Van Buren, who, they supposed, intended that the bill be defeated—thus to array disappointed westerners against the Adams following of the North. Though this strange measure was enacted and he had voted for it, Van Buren and other Jacksonians came out of the affair in a strengthened position for the approaching election. A cost they incurred, postponed though it might be, was a discontented southern branch of their party. Soon afterward, a disturbing sign of trouble was the appearance of Calhoun's "Exposition and Protest," the cornerstone of southern sectionalism and nullification.

Apart from the tariff, which was undoubtedly the principal enactment of the session, little else worth remembering came out of this stymied Congress. Wrangles broke out over Thomas Hart Benton's advocacy of reduced prices on unsold millions of acres of public land. In an effort to conciliate the West and in line with his own growing interest in that section, Webster spoke for governmental generosity, but not as much as Benton wished.[13] Familiar questions on internal improvements also arose; and again Webster took a nationalistic position.[14] But, on the whole, there was more talk than action.

After adjournment, Webster accepted an invitation to a public dinner in his honor at Boston on June 5. Organized to approve his services, the meeting provided him an opportunity to pacify those merchants dissatisfied with the new tariff. Managing this rather well, he proceeded to expound the benefits of a nationalistic economic program of protection and internal improvements. Naturally, when Clay heard about the occasion he was pleased.[15]

A reason for the public dinner was to encourage Webster to remain in the Senate. It was well known that the impact of his wife's death and concern about the children and personal affairs caused him to be uncertain about the future.[16] Reflecting this state of indecision, thoughts of an appointment as minister to Britain had again been much on his mind. Letters from friends referred to the possibility of appointment and were giving him advice one way or the other.[17]

At the capital, many people understood that he was one of two or three men whom the president was considering for the post. So Adams, who was taking his time to act, also received advice, some of it unsolicited. In addition to Webster, other possible appointees were Secretary of the Treasury Richard Rush and Secretary of War James Barbour. Rush was eliminated first, for he was slated to be the vice-presidential candidate in the fall. But the choice between Webster and Barbour was difficult. In several conversations with the president, Clay expressed a preference for Barbour; and to settle it, the secretary had discussed the matter with Webster. The New Englander wanted the appointment, Clay said, but was willing to defer to Barbour, who could probably stay in England only a year or two, after which the administration could accommodate Webster's wishes. Of course, Clay was assuming that Adams would still be president in 1829 or 1830, a dubious assumption. The chief executive agreed that Webster earnestly desired the assignment, probably, he uncharitably suspected, to escape the storm raging around the administration. "In fitness for the office Mr. Webster stands pre-eminent," Adams concluded. Yet "political considerations at the present moment are unfavorable to his appointment."[18]

Politics did forbid it. Currently, the opposition was busy exposing what it called the Adams pledge, the understanding of February 1825 between Webster and Adams that Federalists would not be proscribed from office. Laid down in Webster's letter to Henry Warfield, the promise sealed another corrupt bargain, the Jacksonians declared. Though confused about the precise form and circumstances in which the pledge was given, they knew some basic facts and now demanded publication of the letter. Their demands were ignored; but if Webster got this appointment, they would have proof enough to demolish Adams' chance of reelection. This is what the president heard from several visitors, among them Samuel Bell of New Hampshire, who pleaded with him to bypass Webster. At the end of the congressional session, in late May, Adams named Barbour to the office.[19]

Whatever disappointment Webster may have felt was muted by strong practical arguments against the change. Not only would an appointment have made Adams more vulnerable to the charge of corrupt bargain, but it would also have deprived the administration of an able leader in the current campaign for reelection. And his contributions to national development would doubtless be larger as a senator than as a minister abroad. As a result, his own reputation and influence would advance farther and faster in Washington. This was what Story and Mason counseled when he asked their opinions.[20] Besides, the confusion of his personal affairs would have worsened rather than disappeared if he went to England. When he compared an American minister's income with the enormous expenses at the English capital, for example, the prospect of going there seemed less desirable.[21]

Discussion about this ministerial appointment neither began nor ended the running controversy about the Warfield pledge, but was merely one incident in it. Ever since early 1827, Green's *Telegraph* had been contending that Webster had extracted a pledge from Adams in February 1825 that if elected president, he would appoint Federalists to office. The pledge appeared in a letter with interlineations by Adams himself, it charged. This "attorney of the Hartford Convention" thus held "Mr. Adams' bond, his *corrected* letter in behalf of Northern traitors."[22] Then in October 1827, the Philadelphia *National Palladium* published a more specific story: John Bailey, the president's intimate friend, had written the letter to Webster, with Adams' own revisions, and Webster had then shown it to pivotal congressmen from Maryland and New York to influence the pending House election. Other papers reprinted the item from the *Palladium;* however, the administration may have felt some relief when a convincing denial by Bailey of his involvement quickly came out. Nonetheless, said the New York *Post,* the essential fact of a Webster-Adams understanding remained. The Boston *Advertiser,* probably speaking for Webster, observed that it was unnecessary for him to respond to such careless allegations, for the burden of proof was upon the accusers.[23] Clay also preferred silence and told Warfield he should not publish his correspondence.[24]

In the spring of 1828, while the president pondered whom to appoint as minister to England, Jacksonian editors added fuel to the fire. Now it was Richard Stockton of New Jersey, who, they said, had confirmed their suspicions. According to this version, Stockton had been in a group, including Hopkinson and Walsh, to whom Webster had shown the pledge. An ardent supporter of the president, Stockton had later become disillusioned because he had not received a desired appointment as a district judge. Apparently he had not kept his displeasure to himself. He died in March 1828; and within the month, opposition newspapers carried accounts of his firsthand knowledge of an Adams-Webster agreement.[25]

Despite denials of the truth of certain details, Webster and his friends

145

never quashed the main indictment. With Webster's advice, Hopkinson published an effective piece to show that the critics were wrong about who had met with Webster and where, what had been written, and to whom it had been shown. Privately, Hopkinson remarked that he did remember Webster's having spoken about the Warfield correspondence to him alone, though he had never seen it.[26] Walsh in his *Gazette* rejected many features of the Jacksonian accounts; but he did say that the president had assured someone, possibly Webster, that there would be no proscription of Federalists in his administration. His explanation really admitted the central point of the charges while putting it in the best possible light, and it may have come indirectly from Adams.[27] Stockton's son, Robert, also challenged the accuracy of parts of the story, yet urged that the Warfield correspondence itself be brought forward.[28] But Webster, Clay, and Adams published nothing and said little. The *Telegraph* was pleased as it could be. A very corrupt transaction, Green concluded, and Webster's silence admitted that it had occurred. Produce the letter, he demanded.[29] Finally, in September, Webster decided it would be wise to do so, recommended that course to the president but did not get his consent, and thereby allowed the opposition to exploit the issue in the November election.[30]

Success in this election would depend heavily upon strong organization by Friends of the Administration in each state; and for Webster, that had to start with Massachusetts. Here early in the year, prospects were very good. The amalgamation of Federalists and Republicans held up well, with Lincoln again elected governor and the legislature favorably disposed. In June a state convention met, selected a central committee (led by Joseph Sprague), and also chose Adams electors.[31] As he watched events with approval but seldom participated in them directly, Webster's chief contribution was to draft "An Address to the Citizens of the Commonwealth of Massachusetts," which the state committee revised and broadcast in October.[32] The Jacksonian party, led by Henshaw and Morton, was an active but minority movement. It did have help from a band of Federalists, including patrician Theodore Lyman, who began publishing a newspaper, the *Jackson Republican,* much to the discomfort of many old friends.[33] As election day approached, however, the administration counted Massachusetts as safe.

In fact it counted all of New England. And to Webster, the other state having special significance in that region was New Hampshire. So he closely followed developments there, mainly by way of Ezekiel and Mason. In March 1828, excellent news arrived. Friends of the Administration, old Federalists and Senator Samuel Bell's wing of the Republicans now collaborating smoothly, elected the governor (John Bell, the senator's brother) and majority of the legislature.[34] Quite elated, Webster predicted this splendid victory would influence the fall elections both in New Hampshire and in other parts of the nation. "Depend upon it," he vowed, "with proper exertions, we may yet save the Country."[35] Indispensable to that end, he believed, was an early announcement by Ezekiel that he would run for Congress, even though that election was a year off and thus after the presidential contest. Actually, the personal satisfaction Ezekiel's presence at the capital would bring must have been a stronger motive to press him to do so.[36] To assess the situation in his native state, Webster traveled with his brother through most of the districts in July. Greater effort to communicate with the outlying towns was necessary, he reported to Samuel Bell. Hill's *Patriot* and the powerful organization of that editor and Levi Woodbury ought to be countered promptly.[37] The next month, possibly with an eye to political implications, he helped put Mason into the presidency of the national bank's branch at Portsmouth.[38]

In his estimates of the outcome nationally, he remained optimistic until the fall elections. Realistic enough to see Jackson's enormous popularity and the skillful techniques of the general's party, Webster still thought Adams would win, if by a scanty margin.[39] From March to November 1828 he maintained contacts with friends in many states, raised money, advised strategy, always exhorted maximum commitment to the effort.

As in 1824, he felt New York would be a decisive state. Here the Antimasonic agitation should help immensely, for Jackson was a known Mason, and the energy of leaders such as Thurlow Weed promised a number of electoral votes for the president.[40] What effect the recent death of De Witt Clinton, who had inclined toward Jackson, would have was unclear; but it might encourage his followers, who tended to be for Adams, to come out more boldly.[41] Webster himself could assist through his close relations with affluent businessmen in New York City. Though conscious of Van Buren's zealous work, he did not despair. In a somewhat facetious rejoinder to the Magician's teasing, he remarked that the political health of administration forces there did not need either "prescription or nursing."[42]

Through the spring and summer, Webster worried about Kentucky as much as about any other state. Obviously, the connection with Clay, the alleged corrupt bargain, and associated complaints against the administration brought it to the foreground. As a westerner, Jackson could attract its vote (its legislature vainly instructed Clay to vote for him in the

House election of 1825); and a victory here might influence the entire Ohio Valley. An indicator of what Kentucky would do in the fall was the election of governor and legislature in August. Clay's man, Thomas Metcalfe, opposed William T. Barry, the former chief justice of the now defunct New Court for debtor relief. If Barry won, Webster feared, Adams could hardly hope for reelection.[43] In March he conveyed this disagreeable thought to the president by way of John Bailey, with the bald request that Adams help his own cause by contributing five to ten thousand dollars in behalf of Metcalfe. The chief executive did not have to meditate about that—he briskly retorted he did not believe in paying money for an office. Anyway, he could not afford it.[44] Metcalfe did win, without a presidential subsidy; still, Kentucky was not safe.

To respond to alarming challenges in New York, Kentucky, and elsewhere, Webster continued to act as a de facto party treasurer by raising funds to be rushed to a troubled state organization or an embattled newspaper. In September he obtained pledges amounting to four thousand dollars from merchants and manufacturers in Boston, from Everett's father-in-law, Peter Brooks, from the Appletons and the Lawrences; and he hoped for more from Thorndike, Sears, and Perkins.[45] A letter from Clay suggests that some of this money did go westward: "What you sent was safely received in Kentucky," wrote the secretary.[46]

Toward the end of the preelection period, Webster remained confident. As information from states came in, he calculated and recalculated probable electoral votes, each time arriving at an encouraging result. His forecast included a sweep of New England; the votes of Kentucky, Ohio, and Indiana in the West; none in the South except Louisiana; and, in the Middle Atlantic region, New Jersey and Delaware. This estimate brought him to a situation very much like that in the House election of Adams in 1825. New York and Maryland must deliver the necessary remainder, and he bravely concluded they would.[47] But there was no room for a misstep. His deepest concern in the last days was Kentucky, where Clay must see that the administration's case was as strong as possible. The secretary of state should send out a final round of letters presenting the facts to the public, he said.[48] Clay replied that all looked promising in Kentucky, Ohio, and other places, but it was "mortifying" that the election would be so close.[49]

Like so many others in the nation's history but to a greater extent than most, this campaign focused less on great issues than on personalities. And the emphasis by each side was quite as much upon the grave defects of the opposing candidate as upon the merits of its own nominee.

Indeed the level of discussion degenerated to slurs of the most vicious sort upon the moral character of both.

Not content with classifying Jackson as a mere military chieftain unequipped for the presidency, administration men revived the most damaging chapters of his past. He had lived as an adulterer with Mrs. Jackson for some time before they were legally married, it was asserted, and had admitted his sinful behavior by a later wedding. He was not only unprincipled but also cruel, as illustrated by his heartless, unjustified order for the execution of six militiamen during the late war. Newspapers and broadsides developed this charge down to the smallest detail, even picturing the victims' coffins.[50]

Nor did Jacksonians scruple to assail Adams' honor and integrity. Beginning with the corrupt-bargain charge in 1825, they never tired of it in the next four years. Meanwhile, to sharpen the administration's image of corruptness, they picked up the story of the Adams pledge in the Warfield correspondence. Outdoing this extravagant portrayal of the president as a spoilsman was the incredible tale of his procuring a young American girl for the czar's pleasure when he was minister to Russia. And if that did not totally disqualify him for another term, then there was the strange allegation that this Puritan in the White House was also a gambler, buying billiard tables and other gaming devices with public money.[51]

Webster did not personally resort to these tactics either for attack or defense, so far as his speeches and correspondence show; still, he did not condemn them. Furthermore, he willingly raised money for some of the most aggressive journalists (including Charles Hammond of the Cincinnati *Gazette*).

Webster and other old Federalist allies of the president did not escape low blows. Within a month of election day, an ugly quarrel broke out about the New England record before and during the War of 1812. A letter by Jefferson, written in 1825, now appeared in the press, saying that in a conversation with him while the embargo was in effect, Adams had reported possible secessionism in that region. Though correcting some points in Jefferson's letter, Adams let it be known through the *Intelligencer* that there had been sufficient grounds in 1808 to worry about New England's separatism, perhaps with British help.[52] Jacksonians asked how the chief executive could now embrace as political friends the same men whose loyalty he had once indicted.[53] This was the very question that Theodore Lyman asked about Webster in his paper, the *Jackson Republican*. So on the eve of the election, hard feeling abounded in Boston. The complaint was that Adams' comments were ill timed and absolutely untrue. The *Advertiser* and the *Massachusetts Journal*, both all-out Webster papers, reprimanded the president, said they would still support him, but added that if he should be defeated, their regret would not be as great as it might otherwise have been.[54]

Adams was defeated, and more decisively than Webster had thought possible. Jackson received 178 electoral votes, Adams 83. The president did carry all New England (with the exception of one electoral district in Maine), New Jersey and Delaware, and about half the districts in New York and Maryland. Despite a good showing in the Ohio Valley, he lost every state in the West; and he failed completely in the South too, even in Louisiana, where he had had strong hopes. Jackson took 56 percent of the popular vote, more than any other presidential candidate in the remainder of the nineteenth century.[55]

"We are beaten," Clay wrote Webster. He thought it useless to inquire into the causes of defeat and inexpedient to say much of anything. Wait quietly for Jacksonian measures to appear, he advised, and for an inevitable disintegration of the political conglomeration which had put Old Hickory into power. After six years of agitation, the country required a respite, concluded the Kentuckian. As for himself, he intended to return to Lexington and to take his time about deciding his future course.[56]

Surviving evidence does not indicate precisely what Webster's reactions were, but a fair guess is that they were not much different from Clay's. Never an admirer of Adams, he must have had some uncomplimentary thoughts about the president's qualities as a politician. In the years ahead, he would maintain polite relations with Adams, often collaborate with him in congressional affairs, but look upon him as a maverick deserving whatever might happen to him as a result. If he did not concur entirely, his feelings may have been similar to those of Ezekiel, who lamented, "If there had been at the head of affairs a man of popular character like Mr. Clay, or any man whom we were not compelled by our natures—instincts & fixed fate to hate, the result would have been different."[57]

During the interregnum, while Jackson prepared for his triumphal march to the capital to take power, Webster had little to do in the Senate, even when he did appear. His only satisfaction was to see Hopkinson's nomination as district judge confirmed, a delayed installment of the Adams pledge. Otherwise it was a time of reviewing the past and speculating about the future. Neither gave him any great pleasure. He could recall his valiant but largely unsuccessful advocacy of the administration's policies in Congress. Still, his own standing as a political leader had risen, in a general sense, for along with Clay he had helped build a new party in competition with Jacksonian Democrats, despite his own intellectual disapproval of political parties in the United States. While doing so he had moved, along with his section, toward nationalistic positions on important subjects, particularly on the tariff; and this shift coincided with the prevailing ideology of the party with which he was connected. He had no notion, at the moment, of gaining the presidency with the aid of the party—Clay, he felt, had prior claim to that.[58] But four or eight years hence, no office would be out of reach. One thing was quite clear: Adams could be counted out.

If 1828 was a year of disappointment in politics, it had been even worse in his private life. Just as he had begun his first term in the Senate and entered the crucial period of the presidential contest in December 1827, the fatal illness of his wife tested his courage as nothing else had before.

Grace had decided to go to Washington with him this session; but with their children Julia and Edward, they had to stop in New York on the first of December because Webster was debilitated with a cold and rheumatism and Grace suffered from a painful tumor on her leg. Staying at the home of Dr. Cyrus Perkins, he soon felt well enough to continue the journey, but Grace's trouble was far more serious.[59] What it was exactly experts in medical science could not determine. Perkins consulted other doctors in the city and even the noted Dr. Philip Physick of Philadelphia. Webster asked his friend Dr. John Warren to come from Boston. There was no confident diagnosis by any of these physicians and no surgical procedure possible in the case. The disease may have been cancer, for in a month it had spread to vital organs, a condition which revealed its deadly progress. From mid-December to early January Webster was in Washington, very despondent and aware of what the outcome would be.[60] His brother-in-law, William Paige, had fortunately come down to be with Grace; but on January third he was back in New York himself. Unselfish and devout to the last, Grace faced death as the will of providence; Webster, too, found consolation in his religious faith. Finally, on January 21, she died.[61]

He and his children accompanied the body on a sorrowful trip to Boston for the funeral on the twenty-sixth.[62] Before the ceremony Ticknor found him quite fatigued and brokenhearted, almost disengaged from the scene about him. But he insisted upon walking behind the coffin in the procession from Summer Street to St. Paul's instead of riding in a carriage. Hand in hand with Fletcher and Julia, he moved slowly through the cold dampness of a winter's day to the church where his wife was to be interred in a crypt alongside the two children he had also lost. "It was a touching and solemn sight," said Ticknor.[63]

Ten days later he departed for Washington. He had found it difficult to do anything, to rouse himself from a lethargy induced by grief, to attend to personal affairs, to feel any enthusiasm about political and professional business. Yet relatives and numerous friends had been ready to help with necessary arrangements at home. Paige would keep young Edward, Julia would stay with Eliza Buckminster Lee, and Fletcher would remain with his schoolmaster in Boston. The Ticknors and Hales would also assist—in the spring Julia lived for a while with the editor's family.[64] After Webster arrived at the capital, his mood persisted. "I feel very little zeal or spirit in regard to the passing affairs," he wrote. "My most strong propensity is to sit down, and sit still."[65] Here also his friends lent aid. From Story he received not only sympathy but advice to plunge into his work as a way of conquering gloom. Still, Story observed, when he did this, he soon succumbed "to exhaustion and despondency; and his mental distress, and his struggles, sometimes to disguise and sometimes to overcome it, are not a little embarrassing."[66]

The passage of time helped, of course, and no doubt problems and details of the presidential contest diverted his mind from such depressing thoughts. Then too, his interest in the children was an important healer, as frequent letters back and forth indicated.[67] After returning home in June, he and Paige and the two boys were together in his reopened house; and during the summer, the family traveled to New Hampshire for a vacation. Ezekiel and his wife kept Julia and Edward in Boscawen afterward until December, when Achsah, with her stepdaughters, came to Boston and cared for them over the winter while he was attending Congress.[68]

No sooner had he returned home in April 1829 than shocking news arrived. At three o'clock in the morning of the eleventh, a messenger woke the household to report that on the previous afternoon Ezekiel had died of a heart attack. He had been addressing a jury at the courthouse in Concord and without warning fell to the floor dead. Webster and Achsah, who was still with him, could hardly believe what they heard. Then forty-nine and very active, Ezekiel had been unexpectedly stricken at a time when his family and his brother depended upon him in many ways. The impact upon Webster was nearly as great as that of losing Grace.[69] "He has been my reliance, through life," he lamented, "and I have derived much of its happiness from his fraternal affection. I am left the sole survivor of my family."[70] Here he referred to the deaths of all his brothers and sisters, as well as his parents. The passing of Ezekiel and Grace not only left him dispirited but, by removing two steady influences on him, had important long-standing effects on his life, not all of them for the better.

Through the summer and fall, he was even more unsettled than he had been. He had a nagging problem of arrangements for the children. Eliza Lee cheerfully assumed the main responsibility of Julia; he and Paige tried as best they could to take care of Edward; and Fletcher stayed with his schoolmaster, who was preparing him to enter college soon. Yet these were temporary solutions. Because of his absences from home for several months each year to attend Congress, and at other times to try legal cases, not to mention his habit of taking trips to New Hampshire and to the Cape for a respite, he knew that his family required a situation more permanent and practical than they now had. Furthermore, the fact was that he was lonely, altogether dissatisfied.[71]

These circumstances led him to think of finding a wife. In May, a month after Ezekiel's death, he made a specific move in that direction. His political friend, the New York patroon Stephen Van Rensselaer, had a daughter, Catherine, who struck his fancy. In a carefully phrased letter to the old aristocrat, he expressed his interest in the young woman and asked permission to visit Albany to improve his acquaintance with her. "I think it right to say, frankly," he wrote, "that from the time I first saw her, I have admired her character & manner; and can add, with entire truth, that since I have brought myself to think on the subject of a change in my own condition, she has been the leading object of my reflections." Admitting that Catherine knew little about him, he hoped she was "not unwilling to know more."[72] What Van Rensselaer answered and precisely what happened are unknown, except that Webster did spend a day in Albany that summer; possibly it did improve his acquaintance.[73] Meanwhile, there was a hint now and then that he might marry someone else.[74]

The someone turned out to be Caroline Le Roy, daughter of a prominent New York City merchant. He had known her for some time, but how well is unclear; in surviving correspondence, the first reference to her appears in a letter of November 18, 1829. "The affair is not of long standing," he confessed, "but it looks so much like terminating in a marriage, that I may venture to mention it to you."[75] At thirty-two, Caroline was neither very young nor very beautiful. He found her "amiable, discreet, prudent, with enough of personal comeliness to satisfy me, & of the most excellent character & principles." Her father was reputable and, though Webster did not say it, wealthy. On December 12 they were married in the parlor of the Eastern Hotel near the Battery in New York.[76]

Though he could confidently expect this marriage to be a good one, it would differ decidedly from his first. Fifteen years younger than her husband, accustomed to an elegant style of living and the highest social circles, Caroline had neither Grace's depth of character nor her caliber of mind. She would be less interested than Grace in the daily concerns of her husband, however much loyalty and affection she felt toward him. But she did become a conscientious stepmother for the children. Instead of leaving Julia back in Boston, Caroline insisted on taking her to Washington with them for the winter. And Fletcher, at his father's prompting, wrote her a warm letter, which began a close relationship with him too.[77]

With his family in a happier state, Webster could begin the first congressional session of the Jackson administration in an improved mood. Political combat, however, would soon put his resiliency and renewed energy to the test.

Chapter 10

LAWYER

Although Webster gave over a great deal of his time to politics and public affairs, he was a lawyer by occupation, a fact that significantly affected his life. It was because of better professional opportunities in a flourishing commercial center that he moved to Boston, where he prospered and attained a stature exceeding even his own hopes. Business flowed into his office in Court Street from merchants, shipowners, insurance brokers, and bankers, all able to pay liberally for expert assistance. Then every winter he attended the Supreme Court, where he argued many cases, including leading constitutional controversies, in larger numbers and over a longer period than almost any contemporary. Thus for much of each year he was practicing law in state and federal courts, trial and appellate.

Like others who were officeholders and had additional interests as well, he required an associate, someone to handle practical matters and to carry on the work in his absence. These persons were younger, satisfied to stay at home rather than going off to Washington. During his first eleven years in the city, it was Alexander Bliss, a congenial, efficient collaborator upon whom Webster depended heavily. After the untimely death of Bliss in 1827, Henry Kinsman, a former student, joined him in the practice and remained for fourteen years. Both Bliss and Kinsman were no mere clerks but took charge of as many cases as their senior colleague, though naturally leaving to him those that were most intricate or remunerative.[1]

In a day when most young men learned the law as apprentices to a practitioner rather than attending a university law school, Webster

155

usually had two or three students under his wing and gave them nominal instruction. A few of them became notable in later life, including Charles Francis Adams and Robert Winthrop, although they are better known for illustrious public careers than for legal attainments. Another clerk, in the 1830s, was John Healy, Dartmouth graduate and son of one of Webster's New Hampshire friends. He would be Kinsman's successor in 1841.[2]

Whoever tended the office—Bliss, Kinsman, or Healy—found that a major duty was to struggle with Webster's unceasing financial problems, to look after his notes and drafts, often to arrange something with the banks and his friends for more cash or credit. Receipts, seemingly never enough, were nonetheless substantial. Webster's personal accounting showed that his annual income from legal work ordinarily amounted to between ten and fifteen thousand, with lows of around five and highs of over twenty. Important constitutional cases before the Supreme Court sometimes brought in as much as two thousand; but land-title and claims cases turned out to be the most lucrative. A typical client might pay around a hundred dollars, though many only ten, twenty-five, or fifty.[3] In addition to fees for taking suits to court, he received permanent retainers to ensure his availability to give opinions and to represent an individual or a company in litigation. A number of Boston capitalists, such as Thomas H. Perkins, and various institutions (the national bank, the English House of Baring, and others) sent him retainers regularly.[4]

In Boston Webster's practice continued to center on commercial law. There were still many cases of debt involving mercantile relations, such as problems of insolvent retailers unable to meet obligations to large-scale merchants of the city. Increasingly, he went into court to handle these matters rather than relying upon informal settlement by parties, upon agreement to voluntary arbitration by referee, for example. Usually representing large firms or prominent individuals, he preferred more dependable judicial rulings when it was a question of interpreting the terms of a contract. In one interesting instance he was retained by his friend, the wealthy Israel Thorndike, in a dispute over construction of houses in Summer Street. Though Thorndike ultimately had to pay more than he thought fair to a mason, Webster and his client resorted to litigation as the best way to resolve the disagreement.[5] That strategy was now typical among lawyers and their businessmen clients.

Much work concerned the rapidly developing banking system. To supply capital necessary for economic growth, an ever-larger number of banks supplied credit and issued notes in large quantity. Their complex operations posed novel questions. Webster appeared in a number of

cases which arose, some against these corporations but more in their behalf. For the Dedham Bank, he successfully defended circulation of bills
of exchange which looked like notes but were more difficult for holders
to redeem. But he failed to win a suit by another institution against the
Gloucester Bank, whose notes carried the forged signature of its dead
president. A transformation of the financial world led to new economic
crimes eluding punishment. Embezzlement, for example, was not specifically a crime in Massachusetts until 1824 and was often immune from
effective prosecution afterward. Generally, the courts permitted freewheeling, dubious behavior in the area of private enterprise.[6]

Commercial expansion, industrialization, and financial change generated new legal issues with which lawyers of Webster's ability dealt. Indeed these economic conditions were moving American law from
ethically grounded and relatively stable principles to an instrumental-
ism favoring initiative, growth, and an extended market. Both bench
and bar had to innovate, to adapt established doctrines and procedures
of the common law to fit different circumstances.[7]

Whether Webster entirely understood and accepted what was occurring is doubtful. Not that he was uninformed about legal and economic
trends, for he was well schooled in the leading branches of jurisprudence
and was intimately connected with men of business. Furthermore, on
the political scene he eloquently advocated dynamic public policies. But
he never abandoned the view that the law was primarily a science, a
body of wisdom inherited from respected authorities rather than in-
vented for present convenience. Great truths, derived by learned men
from natural law, had penetrated this science and assured its applicability to problems of later generations.[8] A large gap existed between that
theory and what he was actually doing. Still, the analyst can identify a
common denominator of philosophy and behavior: it was a firm belief in
the timeless sanctity of property rights as the basis of growth and
progress, as the source of confidence in an age of burgeoning enterprise.
Of course the question remains: whose property rights deserved the
greater protection, those well settled by contract or grant or those
claimed in the name of a free economy, those of the old order or the
new? The location of power and influence could determine the answer.[9]

Not a specialist in criminal practice, Webster did occasionally take a
case in that branch of law with no less effectiveness than in others. Alive
to the dramatic aspects of a crime exciting public attention and skillful
in moving summation to a jury, he showed that he could have been a
prominent criminal lawyer, had his interests run in that direction. For
example, in the spring of 1817 he defended two young men, Levi and
Laban Kenniston, against charges of assault and robbery. Their alleged

victim was Elijah P. Goodridge, a person of reputable standing, at least
till then. On a wintry evening while traveling near the toll bridge at
Newburyport, according to Goodridge, he encountered his assailants
who beat, shot, and robbed him. Afterward, he conducted a personal
search for the villains and the seventeen hundred dollars in gold he said
they had taken from him. One after another, he identified several sus-
pects on whose premises he uncovered incriminating evidence, wrappers
for his money and a few coins. The chief perpetrators, he charged, were
the Kenniston brothers. As defense counsel at the trial of the Kennistons,
Webster shifted attention from the accused to the accuser by rigorous
cross-examination. Systematically he exposed Goodridge's story as a
wild fabrication. His address to the jury, one of the few such items now
extant, was a model of logic and clear statement. He offered the jurors
another theory of the case: embarrassed by large debts, Goodridge had
falsified a robbery to evade his creditors; along the lonely road the traveler had scattered papers and personal possessions to simulate evidence
of an attack; to make his tale more credible, he had sought to shoot a
hole in his own coat sleeve but had the bad luck of wounding his hand;
and finally he had planted the wrappers and coins at the houses of the
accused. The jury preferred Webster's theory to the testimony for the
prosecution and found the Kennistons not guilty. After further setbacks,
the discredited Goodridge departed for points west.[10]

A criminal case arousing even greater popular excitement concerned
the brutal murder of Joseph White, a retired and wealthy merchant of
Salem. At night, on April 6, 1830, while the old man slept, the murderer
entered White's house through an unlocked window, crept silently upstairs to the bedside, and dispatched his victim with club and dirk.[11]
Shocked and bewildered, people in Salem and the surrounding area
nervously speculated who could have committed such a cold-blooded
crime, as weeks passed without solution of the mystery. Organized to
apprehend the assassin and to protect the town against his striking
again, a committee of vigilance began an aggressive search which at last
brought results. A prime suspect was Dick Crowninshield, who, it appeared, had been hired to kill White. But who were the others impli-
cated in the foul plot? One seemed to be Crowninshield's brother,
George; and so both young men, black sheep of a prominent family,
waited in jail while the hunt continued. By way of information supplied
by another shady character, the committee identified Joe and Frank
Knapp as the persons who had planned the deed and procured Crowninshield to do it. The Knapps were also errant offspring of a reputable
family of the community. Joe, in fact, had married the grandniece of
White in the face of the latter's strong disapproval. Now the following

hypothesis developed. Dissatisfied with White's will leaving a large estate mainly to nephew Stephen White, Joe had destroyed the document to augment his inheritance through his mother-in-law. Then he felt he had to dispose of White so that the money would come his way. In execution of Joe's plan, Frank Knapp paid Dick Crowninshield to commit the murder—indeed Frank stood on a nearby street to make sure he did.[12]

What might have been a simple matter of convicting the culprits became difficult when Dick hanged himself in the cell. Under the law of Massachusetts a court had first to establish the guilt of a principal to a crime (the late Dick) before doing so for accessories (Joe Knapp and possibly the others), and one could not try a dead man. Still, if he had been in the vicinity of the crime ready to assist Dick, Frank Knapp might also be considered a principal. Or Joe and Frank, or one of them, might confess. In either event, prosecutions would succeed. With this in mind, the committee of vigilance and the state attorney general sent a local minister, Henry Colman, to talk with the Knapps. Carrying a promise of immunity in exchange for a confession and representing himself as a friend of the Knapp family, Colman induced Joe to sign a statement describing the conspiracy and admitting his role in the murder. Conversations with Frank reinforced the minister's belief in the Knapps' guilt. To expedite proceedings, the legislature enacted a statute providing for a special term of the supreme court. But before the court sat, Joe had retracted his confession and upset hopes for a swift disposition of the case.[13]

These strange events captured public attention, and the entrance of a special prosecutor added an unusual feature. By request of the attorney general and fresh from his oratorical duel with Hayne in the Senate, Webster joined the prosecution when the trial of Frank Knapp began on August 3. Of the three attorneys on that side, the senator assumed chief responsibility for proving that Frank was a principal in the crime. In taking testimony, conducting cross-examination, and presenting argument, he expertly displayed a lawyer's skills. Whether he pressed the law and influenced the jury beyond fair limits was a question that lingered long afterward.

It took more than two weeks to obtain a verdict in Frank's case. The large number of witnesses, intricate points of law, and verbosity of counsel accounted for slow progress. More important than these reasons was the necessity of conducting a second trial after the jury could not agree at the end of the first week. Generally the testimony, arguments, and rulings were the same in both hearings; and variations are obscure in the histories describing them. Contemporary pamphlets mingled the records of each, while the best-known parts, Webster's two summations, have been combined into one speech in his published works, with additional and substantial changes by the lawyer himself in preparing them for print.[14]

At any rate, it is clear that the special prosecutor focused upon two main points: (1) Frank was a principal to the crime because he stood on a nearby street ready to aid Dick Crowninshield at the moment of the murder; and (2) Frank had confessed in conversations with the Reverend Henry Colman. To establish his first point, Webster had to build his case on somewhat shaky, conflicting testimony, but the court helped a great deal by its loose construction of common-law and statutory rules. As for the confession, he encountered more difficulty, for twice the judges (two to one) excluded it on the ground that the defendant did not give it freely but hoped for a pardon. The persistent attorney finally prevailed upon the court to allow the minister's testimony about the jailhouse interviews and to leave the question of its weight to the jury.[15]

Besides these legal arguments, his oratory contributed heavily to Frank's conviction. Perhaps the most telling passage of his summation graphically reconstructed the scene of the bloody deed. The jury must have been horrified as Webster described the murderer's stealthy progress through White's house to the bedchamber, the cool and heartless efficiency with which Dick bludgeoned and stabbed his victim, the silent departure without detection. Yet the culprit made a "dreadful mistake," he reminded his audience. "Though he take the wings of the morning and fly to the uttermost part of the seas, human murder to human vision will be known. A thousand eyes, a thousand ears are marking and listening, and thousands of excited beings are watching his bloodstained step." In the end, his conscience would no longer permit him to keep the secret. "His guilty soul is relieved by suicide or confession, and suicide is confession." Altogether he spoke for eight hours, alternating between emotion-laden rhetoric and painstaking commentary on the admittedly circumstantial evidence of Frank's complicity. The effect upon his listeners was powerful.[16]

Not long after convicting and executing Frank Knapp, the state proceeded with the trial of Joe, the mastermind and would-be beneficiary of White's murder. The chief question at the hearing of his case in November was the admissibility of Joe's retracted confession. In it, he had revealed his motive of ultimately enlarging his inheritance by destroying the will kept in the old man's trunk, his arrangement (by way of Frank) with Dick Crowninshield to kill the victim, and his unlocking a first-floor window beforehand to help Dick enter the house. Adopting Webster's position, the judges admitted the confession; and this, as well as the fact of Frank's guilt, doomed Joe's case. By the end of the year, Joe too was hanged.[17]

It was the consensus then and later that despite some possible irregularities in the Knapp cases, moral justice was done. And that interpretation may well be correct. Nevertheless, at least according to modern standards of criminal law, irregularities appear substantial. One was the influence of highly excited public opinion upon the proceedings—the sensational aspects of the crime and the vigilante atmosphere prevailing after its commission, all affecting the trials at the time and place in which they occurred. Webster's participation doubtless further unbalanced the scales of justice, for his vast prestige and golden oratory made the task of defense counsel the more difficult, as they repeatedly contended. In fact, they objected to his role also because of a statutory prohibition against public prosecutors enlisting aid of private individuals. To this, during Joe's trial Webster answered that he appeared without fee "in this case." Though literally true, his earnest assertion bypassed the pertinent fact that he had received a handsome fee from his friend Stephen White, nephew and principal heir of the slain shipmaster, to prosecute Frank in the preceding and closely related case.[18] Finally, the ruling to allow the confessions as evidence, both of them induced by hopes of immunity or pardon, seems defective even by the standards of that day. If Joe and Frank retracted, of course, they had no claim to immunity conditionally offered; yet the state hardly had a right to use the confessions to convict them. Defense arguments on that issue seem more convincing than Webster's.[19]

Rather than such exceptional instances, Webster's practice in Boston and its vicinity normally involved civil cases, among which quite a number related to admiralty law. Constitutionally, these questions fell under the jurisdiction of the lower federal courts, district and circuit; and here, as in the Supreme Court, the attorney found himself in an important legal area during the decade after the War of 1812. International law and English precedents applicable to a maritime age supplied the context of this business and therefore were a subject to be mastered.

An example is marine insurance. In circuit court, Justice Story was eager to expand federal admiralty jurisdiction over that kind of litigation, and Webster preferred this forum over state tribunals resisting a trend toward rules generous to insured claimants. His clients, at first, tended to be shipowners seeking compensation from insurers, who were either merchant groups pooling capital to cover a given voyage or new companies entering the field; later, he preferred to represent the insuring corporations because of more attractive fees. For the owners of a ship deviating from a route specified to insurers and then taken prize by the British, he persuaded Story to hand down a permissive ruling in his favor. And in another claim he got a broad decision upholding federal admiralty jurisdiction over marine insurance. The justice readily departed from the old doctrine that only contracts made on the sea came within the cognizance of admiralty. That principle, if followed, would have excluded insurance written on land. It was not the place where the contract was made but the subject matter that gave access to an admiralty court, Story held. Thus insurance of shipping was a maritime question.[20]

In Story's court, *La Jeune Eugénie* (1822) also tested Webster's expertise in the law of the sea. The principal actor in events leading to the case was Lieutenant Robert Stockton, a son of Webster's political friend and captain of the naval vessel *Alligator*. While cruising off the African coast the young officer encountered a ship equipped for slave trading and brought it into the port of Boston to be condemned for violating national and international rules against that traffic. The aggressive, anti-slavery-minded Stockton drew praise from all those who looked upon the slave trade as highly deplorable morally, while more cautious people, including President Monroe, wished the case handled delicately. As a further complication, the nationality of the actual owners of *La Jeune Eugénie* was unclear: built in the United States, the ship carried papers declaring it belonged to two French citizens, but that could well have been a subterfuge.

So Webster thought when he argued the case. If the documents were false, American laws treated slave trading by American citizens as a serious crime. Still, assuming French ownership, the lawyer urged the court to condemn the vessel because French law also prohibited that traffic; and thus the seizure merely enforced the policy of that country. And an even stronger justification lay in the law of nations, whose natural-law principles classified the trade as an atrocious, barbarous crime, "an insurmountable barrier to the advancement of civilization and virtue."[21] Story's opinion incorporated each of these points, even the moral disquisition; but once announcing his holding, the judge backed away and approved a request by the United States district attorney (instructed by the president) to turn the ship over to the French consul for proceedings.[22] Whether in the future an American court could enforce another nation's laws and whether the slave trade indeed violated international law were continuing issues, not to be resolved until the Supreme Court later answered no to both questions.[23]

Of his extensive business involving maritime law, the most profitable turned out to be his agency for claimants under the Florida Treaty in the early twenties. Soon after ratification of that treaty with Spain in 1821, he began preparing and then presenting memorials before a commission in Washington, established to make awards totaling five million dollars to those whose ships and cargoes had been confiscated in Spain during the Napoleonic wars. His diligence and skill immensely benefited both his clients and himself.

From the moment that Secretary Adams and Minister de Onís put their pens to the document of 1819 ceding Florida and providing for assumption by the United States of its citizens' claims against Spain, Webster had the idea of exploiting this opportunity. Sounding out prospective claimants, he conceded he was a bit embarrassed; "I do not remember that I ever before sought any employment with a view to pecuniary profit."[24] Though faintly tempted to accept an appointment as a member of the commission, he quickly concluded that he could do "infinitely better with the agency for the claimants."[25] By mid-1821, when the newly appointed commissioners assembled, he was arranging to represent insurance companies, merchants, and executors of estates not only of Boston but also of Salem, Portsmouth, and other New England towns.[26] Shortly he entered agreements with nearly all those Bostonians wishing to forward their cases that he would represent them for a fee of 5 percent of such awards as they might win. Foremost among those signing the papers was Peter Brooks, who hoped to get around two hundred thousand in compensation and helped recruit dozens of other clients too. The list included Thomas H. Perkins, Thomas Wren Ward, and numerous notables of the financial community.[27] By way of Joseph Hopkinson, Webster also acquired a good many cases from Philadelphia, especially those of the Insurance Company of North America, for very large amounts. From whatever awards he gained for these claimants he would get 1 percent.[28]

For three years, until the commission's final report of June 1824, he gave the major share of his professional attention to the Spanish claims. Each January he came to Washington to file and argue cases on through the winter; and at other times he had to return for the same purpose. When he could not do so himself, he sent his partner, Alexander Bliss, but was often busy at home assembling documents of proof or drafting memorials. On the whole, his efforts brought favorable results, owing to his careful preparation and to fairly lenient adjustment of rules by the commission. On the points on which he failed, the main obstacle arose from the fact that during their long occupation of Spain, the French had seized American property. Here he had the difficult task of showing that the Spaniards had knowingly approved condemnations.[29]

The last phase began in May 1824. To carry out the treaty, Congress had to enact a law appropriating five millions, a measure which Webster, at that time a representative, actively promoted. Though taking the floor only once during debate, either for reasons of delicacy or strategy, he supplied information to others, such as James Buchanan, for speeches. Against worrisome opposition, even by Speaker Clay, a bill passed at the end of the month.[30] Then he hurried to Philadelphia to draw upon the fund set up at the office of the national bank. His own account book listed payments in the period from June 9 to July 7, with his fees totaling $62,000. Other payments raised the amount to over $70,000. The largest award went to the Insurance Company of North America for $332,993 (giving him 1 percent, $3,329); his largest fee came from Peter Brooks, $8,640 on a 5 percent basis. These sums provided a marked contrast to his income from well-known but less remunerative cases in the Supreme Court.[31]

It was before that tribunal, of course, that he attained the reputation which has placed him in the highest rank of the American bar throughout the nation's history. During the two decades from his first appearance in the Court in 1814 as a young congressman until 1835, he helped formulate a system of constitutional law. With other lawyers, such as William Pinkney and William Wirt, he argued path-marking cases delineating the powers of national and state governments and the relationship of individual rights to both. There were very few important decisions in these areas to which he did not contribute by his briefs and oral presentations.

That he could do so is understandable when one looks at the justices sitting on this bench. Chief Justice John Marshall was the dominant figure, a confirmed nationalist unfriendly to claims of states' rights and a tireless protector of property rights, amazingly effective in holding his associates together as a unit and in developing the Court's responsibility to interpret the Constitution. True Federalist that he was, he unfailingly admired Webster both as politician and as legal counselor. Beside Marshall sat the attorney's intimate friend Joseph Story. Sharing the chief justice's constitutional and economic views, he brought to the task a brilliant mind, profound learning, and unreserved attachment to principles of the common law. Webster returned Story's esteem in full measure and repeatedly showed it by calling upon him for advice on a variety of subjects, some of them political. As for the other five justices, Webster's relations with them were not as close, but he found them receptive to his reasoning and eloquence.[32]

In the early phase of his practice at the capital, Webster handled many admiralty cases, just as he did in lower federal courts. In addition to litigation, generated by the country's active maritime commerce, there was more caused by special circumstances of the time: questions of trading with the enemy and of widespread restrictive systems during the War of 1812; problems of neutrality toward Spain and her Latin American colonies while their revolutions were in progress; and cases of prize and piracy arising from that upheaval. Much of it required tedious work, but a constructive outcome was adaptation of old rules of jurisprudence to fit new conditions and to conform to statutory and constitutional provision in the United States.

A typical case was the *Divina Pastora* (1819). A Spanish consul sought to recover property seized by a privateer commissioned by the United Provinces of Rio de la Plata. The legality of the seizure depended upon whether the United States neutrality law of 1817 and subsequent presidential proclamations applied to this former Spanish colony now asserting its independence. Was it really a nation, having the right under international law to commission privateers; and had the American government so regarded it? Had U.S. citizens had some connection with the privateer and therefore compromised American neutrality? Representing the Spanish consul, Webster did not get the decree he wished but did have the case remanded to the lower court for further proceedings to determine additional facts.[33] In a similar case later, the *Santissima Trinidad* (1822), again appearing for a Spanish consul, he prevailed, for this time there was proof that a vessel of the United Provinces had been manned and supplied at Baltimore, much as many others had been, in violation of the neutrality law.[34]

Often ships that roamed the seas had only fictitious commissions identifying them as privateers, or they had none at all. International law and American statutes classified these marauders as piratical, punishable by death. By 1820 a batch of cases on this crime had come to the Supreme Court from federal districts and circuits; and in that term the justices attempted to dispose of the legal questions once and for all, to put an end to the frightful problem itself. When the chief justice ordered a hearing on various points raised in the conviction of about fifty pirates, he found they had no counsel and therefore appointed Webster to represent them. How much he extended himself in this unpalatable assignment is unclear, but he did attack the vagueness of the Piracy Act of 1819, broadly defining the crime in terms of the law of nations. Unconvinced by that argument, the Court upheld the convictions, and soon many of Webster's clients went to the gallows.[35]

Beginning in the term of 1819, the Court handed down the first of a series of constitutional decisions that became fundamental precedents in American law and government. The case was *Dartmouth College* v. *Woodward*. As a loyal Dartmouth alumnus, he helped save his alma mater from state intervention in its affairs, gained a victory for conservative political forces in New Hampshire after protracted controversy, and by a renowned argument contributed to a judicial doctrine protecting corporations from unlimited state regulation.

At issue were statutes passed by the state legislature in 1816 reorganizing the college board of trustees by adding enough gubernatorial appointees to dominate the previously private, self-perpetuating body. The effect would be to transform the institution into a state university, which indeed it was now called. Chartered in 1769, Dartmouth had operated for many years under the autocratic leadership of its first president Eleazar Wheelock and his son, John, both of whom had little trouble with acquiescent trustees. Then, beginning in the 1790s, new members of the board challenged the strong-willed John Wheelock on a variety of questions, some large and others petty. A late episode in this running dispute concerned the call of the theological professor to the pulpit of the Hanover church, with the president being defeated in an argument with the board. To vent his frustration and counteract his adversaries, Wheelock precipitated a pamphlet war in which he, his friends, and the trustees carried their viewpoints to the public. And in the summer of 1815 he appealed to the legislature to investigate the inflamed situation at the college. Though rebuffed by a committee report on the subject, he did attract support, chiefly from Republican ranks in New Hampshire—most of the trustees were Federalist stalwarts, such as Timothy Farrar and Thomas Thompson.[36] That the battle had assumed a political complexion became very clear when Ike Hill's *Patriot* savagely attacked the trustees with charges of partisan conspiracy and religious intolerance.[37] In the spring 1816 election the Wheelock forces connected themselves with William Plumer, Republican candidate for governor, a propitious move because of the sweeping victory of that party. So the new governor, erstwhile Federalist turned Republican and advocate of Jeffersonian principles of religious toleration and expanded public education, put bills through the legislature changing the status of Dartmouth College. True enough, Plumer's liberal objectives of social policy differed from those of Wheelock, until now a liberal neither in politics nor in religion; yet Wheelock, having been evicted as president by the trustees, calculated that in the new order he could recapture his authority.[38]

Not if they could prevent it, vowed the trustees. They refused to meet with the new members packing their board, and they maintained the separate existence of Dartmouth College alongside the state's university by holding student loyalty though losing the institution's buildings. They were determined to test the validity of the distasteful statutes in the courts.[39] Initially their counsel were Jeremiah Mason and Jeremiah Smith, two Federalists at the head of the New Hampshire bar. They initiated a suit in the county court to recover college records in the possession of William H. Woodward, former secretary-treasurer, who had taken them with him when he assumed that office in the university. Without delay the case went up to the superior court on a special verdict with a bare-bones statement of facts. Here Mason and Smith made long and able arguments at the terms of May and September 1817.[40]

Webster had followed all these events closely because of his attachment to Dartmouth, his intimate friendship with the college party, and of course the important political facets of the controversy. In the early phase of the case, however, he had not participated as an attorney. Only at the second hearing in September did he appear for a relatively brief, one-hour argument to supplement those of Mason and Smith.[41] He had hardly any hope of success in the superior court, for the three judges, each of them a Republican, had only recently taken their seats on the bench as a result of one of the periodic, politically inspired reorganizations of the judiciary. Through Chief Justice William Richardson, in November the court upheld the validity of the state legislation.[42]

From the start, Webster and his associates knew they would have to appeal their cause to the Supreme Court if they were to prevail; and this they now set about doing. Having moved his residence to Boston and given up his congressional seat, Webster still went to the capital early each year to attend to legal business there. So he agreed to take the main responsibility for the appeal, after being assured of a thousand-dollar fee.[43] Mason and Smith would not go; but their thorough briefs were available to him, and he used them very extensively, in fact added little, beyond his incomparable oratory.[44] As colleague, Joseph Hopkinson would also be helpful. His opponents, Attorney General William Wirt and Congressman John Holmes of Maine, found themselves at a disadvantage due to late arrival of materials from the New Hampshire counsel, not to mention their cursory preparation.[45]

Argument of the case before the Supreme Court began on March 10, 1818, and ran for three days. In a four-hour presentation which would become a classic in legal history, Webster opened for the college trustees.[46] Characteristically, he first reviewed the facts and stated the issues in systematic, low-keyed fashion. In 1769, Eleazar Wheelock had re-

167

ceived a royal charter as founder of Dartmouth College for instructing Indian and white youths. Upon his death a decade later, his supervisory rights (that is, his rights as visitor) devolved upon the board of trustees, though the office of president went to his son. For thirty-five years the trustees governed the institution as a private, charitable (eleemosynary) corporation until the legislature enacted the laws of 1816 changing it to a state university. Did New Hampshire have the constitutional power to do this?

No, he answered. The main grounds for his position were: (1) the nature of such private corporations at common law; (2) the bill of rights in the New Hampshire constitution; and (3) the contract clause of the national Constitution. Probably because he followed Mason's brief so closely, he emphasized these points in descending order of importance, despite the fact that in cases coming from a high state tribunal the Supreme Court had jurisdiction only over those involving federal questions—in this instance, the interpretation of the contract clause.

There was no room for doubt, he contended, that the common law classified chartered franchises of those who founded colleges as private property. Thus the state court had erred in approving the laws, because they looked to the school's public uses rather than the trustees' visitorial rights gained from the founder. No matter that the public benefited from the operation of the college; to encourage creation of eleemosynary enterprises, rights once vested must be inviolate. All such corporations, he insisted, were private, not public, and therefore free from public regulation.[47]

Turning to the state constitution, he contended that the statutes conflicted with the article prohibiting deprivation of property except by the law of the land. Derived from an ancient constitutional concept as far back as Magna Charta, the law-of-the-land clause, he continued, required judicial proceedings to revoke vested rights unless the holder consented. Legislative enactments were too arbitrary. In this branch of his argument, Webster's reasoning meshed with the principle of separation of powers in American government and presaged what would one day become the far-reaching doctrine of substantive due process of law.[48]

Finally, he came to the contract clause of the federal Constitution, technically the only basis on which this Court could invalidate the statutes. He cited the two relevant previous decisions, one holding state grants to be contracts, and another upholding vested rights on general principles of common and natural law.[49] Logically he could urge the Court to build on these and to declare a corporate charter a contract free from state impairment. Actually, the New Hampshire court had not denied that corporations were covered, only that this one, being public rather than private, was not.

In closing, the attorney coated his legal discussion with a moving peroration. The exact text has eluded historians, but a dependable version of its general character exists.[50] With unconcealed feeling, he appealed to the justices' sympathies for this small New England college, whose very survival hinged upon their decision. Indeed the whole cause of higher education was at stake. As so many orators of the early nineteenth century habitually did, he finished with an allusion to classical history. "Sir, I know not how others may feel, but, for myself, when I see my Alma Mater surrounded like Caesar in the senate-house, by those who are reiterating stab upon stab, I would not, for this right hand, have her turn to me, and say, . . . And thou too, my son!"[51] Justice Story later recalled: "The whole audience had been wrought up to the highest excitement; many were dissolved in tears; many betrayed the most agitating mental struggles; many were sinking under exhausting efforts to conceal their own emotions."[52]

When both parties had finished argument, the Court's term was closing; and since some justices were still pondering the issues, the chief justice announced a delay of the decision until the next term. Neither side felt altogether disappointed by the postponement, for each had hoped to present its case more effectively than it had. Webster and his friends wished to broaden the questions beyond the contract clause, to general principles of law—something they could better do if they carried a case to the Supreme Court from a federal circuit, where, unlike the circumstances in *Woodward,* jurisdiction lay in suits involving citizens of different states. Accordingly they had such litigation in process and could push it if needed.[53] For their part, supporters of the university (that is, of the New Hampshire policy) felt entirely dissatisfied with the performance of Wirt and Holmes as counsel. Would it not be possible to reargue their cause next time with greater vigor if they brought in the brilliant William Pinkney to represent them?[54] Through the ensuing months, both college and university people were busy with these plans. Furthermore, both hoped to influence the undecided judges somehow, perhaps by propagandizing their points of view before the public, perhaps by swaying the judges privately through an intermediary such as Chancellor James Kent. They used these tactics too.[55]

All the maneuvers had little effect upon the outcome. Supplied with an array of new facts about the early history of Dartmouth to prove that it was a public institution supported by the state through the years and now rightfully regulated by the state, Pinkney did not even have a chance to make a second argument at the term of February 1819. The chief justice abruptly began delivering his opinion without recognizing the lawyer as he stood before the bench.[56] And the college move to bring up other cases allowing a broader approach proved to be unnecessary, for these suits were left pending until disposition of *Woodward*, which would then determine what would be done with them.[57] Furthermore, it is doubtful that attempts by Webster's friends to influence the justices caused a reversal of their thinking. Two among the five in the majority holding for the trustees' appeal may have been initially unsure about some specifics of the case, but one and probably both would have concurred with Marshall's ruling in any event.[58]

The chief justice accepted Webster's argument. He dwelt upon the nature of corporations at the common law, particularly charitable trusts for educational purposes. According to well-established rules, these eleemosynary corporations created by private donors, he held, were private. To encourage founders of colleges, the law must protect their right of visitation. Such was true of Dartmouth College, he concluded, after reviewing the text of its charter. Conceding that the public benefited from the operation of the college, he could not agree that this factor justified public regulation, such as the New Hampshire statutes. The trustees' chartered rights, which derived from donors and founder, were therefore valuable property which the state must respect. In the United States even more than in England, there were limits upon governmental power, for here the contract clause of the Constitution prohibited state impairment of contractual obligations. And though he did not make any great effort to support his reasoning, he did not hesitate to classify the college's corporate charter as a contract, constitutionally speaking.[59]

The *Dartmouth College* case had far-reaching effects. To be sure, it immediately advanced Webster's reputation as a constitutional lawyer of the first rank during this formative period of American law. And it created in the minds of generations of Dartmouth men a heroic image of the silver-tongued attorney as their valiant advocate.[60] In the broader sense, however, its importance lies in the enduring principle it helped to establish: the Constitution protects fundamental rights from arbitrary legislative infringement.[61] That principle, of course, has had a varied history in the century and a half since John Marshall's decision. For years, such rights attached to corporations as well as to individuals, on the business scene more often than in the field of higher education. The rights therefore related to the use of property in the economy, sometimes at the expense of the public interest.[62] The time would come when these vested rights would lose a good deal of their immunity; yet essentially the same principle, strengthened by the Fourteenth Amendment, would serve the cause of civil liberty, of personal freedom instead of corporate privilege.

As favorable to property rights as this ruling was, even more judicial protection was possible. In numerous cases, Webster sought it with some success. The doctrine of *Dartmouth College* invoked the contract clause as a shield for corporations chartered prior to state legislation, logically following previous decisions that other types of grants were safe from retrospective statutes. What of laws operating prospectively, affecting *future* public or private contracts? Were they, too, invalid if they impaired an obligation? Such was the question in an interesting case involving state systems of bankruptcy. *Ogden* v. *Saunders* (1827) determined whether the Court would extend its oversight of that specific subject and of economic policies generally.[63] Though historians have not emphasized *Ogden* as much as a number of better-known cases of Marshall's time, it was in fact pivotal. The chief justice himself thought so—during his thirty-four years on the bench it was the only constitutional case in which he dissented.

Marshall would have liked to have incorporated Webster's argument into a majority opinion, for he found the lawyer's reasoning quite sound. As counsel for the creditor, Webster attacked a New York insolvency act upon which the debtor relied for release from a contract dated after passage of the statute. Now for the first time the Court squarely faced the issue of constitutionality of the prospective reach of a state measure (it had earlier invalidated another law applied retrospectively).[64] The contract clause, he contended, forbade all such state bankruptcy laws, retrospective or prospective; however, he looked upon all of them as necessarily retrospective in their impact. Underlying his argument was a conception of natural law which, Webster explained, created the obligation of every contract even in the absence of positive law. So statutes and Constitution merely affirmed this universal truth and could in no circumstances allow impairment of an obligation.[65]

Four of the seven justices would not go as far as Webster wished, upheld the New York statute, and ruled that a bankruptcy law was a condition always implicit in contracts subsequently made. Parties accepted this condition when they made an agreement.[66] Practical considerations probably led the majority to that conclusion, inasmuch as there had long been a mass of colonial and state statutes for debtor relief and creditor rights. Since there was then no national legislation on the subject, a rapidly developing economy required a policy somewhere. Naturally those judges with states' rights preferences felt content that the states continue to lay down that policy. Webster believed otherwise. Congress should enter the field; indeed he was currently trying to get a bankruptcy bill through that body. But except for brief periods, efforts of this kind failed throughout the nineteenth century; and a maze of state systems, handicapped by limited jurisdictions, had to serve the purpose.[67]

The setback in *Ogden* v. *Saunders* extended beyond the matter of bankruptcy to the fundamental question of the Court's power to protect property rights in the fullest sense, perhaps on extraconstitutional grounds of natural justice or the common law. Yet the question persisted despite the decision, with Webster repeatedly striving to expand judicial power to that end in other cases. For example, in the same term of 1827 when *Ogden* was decided, he expressed the position plainly in *Mason* v. *Haile,* testing a Rhode Island statute which had released a debtor from imprisonment. In addition to the contract clause of the Constitution, he looked to natural law: acts of this description, he insisted, "might even be considered void on general principles, independent of the positive prohibition in the Constitution, as being retrospective laws interfering with vested rights."[68] Still more forcefully, in *Wilkinson* v. *Leland* (1829), he called for the Court to strike down a state statute authorizing the sale of a deceased person's property to satisfy creditors' claims. Such authorization was not within the scope of legislative power, he urged, for it bypassed indispensable judicial procedures and amounted to confiscation of property claimed by the heirs. He did not contend that the law violated the contract clause. "Though there may be no prohibition in the Constitution," he said, "the legislature is restrained from committing flagrant acts, from acts subverting the great principles of republican liberty, and of the social compact; such as giving the property of A to B."[69] Neither in *Mason* nor in *Wilkinson* did the Court base its decision on such argument. But some justices—Story and Marshall and William Johnson—thought much as Webster did. Sometimes they incorporated that kind of thinking in opinions, though they usually found a constitutional clause with which to connect it.

The common law also provided fertile soil in which vested rights could thrive. Despite opposition in early America to adoption of the common law because of its alleged anachronistic and unrepublican character, bench and bar drew upon it freely. In this country a legal system developed from its rules dating back through the centuries, albeit selectively in order to adapt past wisdom to changing conditions. That process therefore allowed judges, aided by the lawyers, to build a defense around property more dependable than might have been possible on strict statutory or constitutional grounds. The extent to which they could do so varied from subject to subject and case to case; and well into the nineteenth century the boundaries were unstable. In the 1830s, however, the Court confronted the question head-on.

An instance was *Wheaton* v. *Peters* (1834).[70] Here the specific issue was whether the common law, instead of an existing federal statute, protected literary property. If it did, the rights of authors and publishers could be more secure under the wing of judgemade law. Henry Wheaton, prominent legal commentator and able reporter of Supreme Court cases, had sought an injunction against Richard Peters, his successor as reporter, to prevent republication of materials (mainly judicial opinions) from his annual volumes.[71] There was a federal copyright law to which authors could resort, but Wheaton had not complied with all the procedural requirements to be assured of its protection, and he therefore turned to more flexible common-law rules to assert his rights. An additional attraction was a perpetual copyright at common law, in contrast to a limited period of exclusive use under the statute.[72] Webster was Wheaton's counsel in arguing the case on appeal to the Supreme Court.

His brief reviewed the English background from early monopolies conferred upon publishers, supported at times by censorship, to cases there in the late eighteenth century—one upholding a common-law copyright despite a parliamentary statute and another deciding the opposite. He could also cite a few American decisions and laws, as well as the constitutional clause conferring power upon Congress to legislate in the field. But basically, *Wheaton* presented a new question, certainly before the Supreme Court, with the answer likely to have broad implications.[73]

They turned out to be negative, much to the disappointment of the attorney and his client. In an opinion for the majority, John McLean flatly rejected the existence of a federal common law concerning such private rights and insisted that Wheaton had to rely only upon the congressional statute.[74] Although Webster had not gone so far as to contend there was a federal common law, separate from and superior to state systems, he certainly hoped a body of rules of that kind would evolve. So did Justice Story, who would soon seize an opportunity to expound the principle with great effect.[75]

While most of Webster's cases, *Ogden, Wheaton,* and others, may have contributed in some fashion to the development of American law, the reader of general history seldom encounters them. But one always found in the basic literature is the well-known national bank case, *McCulloch* v. *Maryland* (1819). Not only did the Court decide that the congressional charter of the Bank of the United States was constitutional, but it laid down in classic form a nationalistic theory of the Union. As an attorney still in the first phase of a long career at the Washington bar, Webster represented the bank in this case.

Ever since Secretary of the Treasury Alexander Hamilton had succeeded in establishing a national bank in 1791, the power to create such an institution had been a controversial subject. Soon after the second Bank of the United States began operations in 1817, several states hostile to it laid heavy taxes on its branches to drive them out of their jurisdictions. One of these states was Maryland. James McCulloch, cashier of the Baltimore branch, refused to pay a tax, and as a result a case testing the bank's congressional charter came to the Supreme Court in February 1819.[76] Extended, brilliant arguments highlighted the hearing, the most memorable being that of William Pinkney, and to a lesser degree one by Webster, for the BUS.

Opening for his side, Webster dealt with two questions: (1) could Congress incorporate a bank; and (2) could a state levy a tax upon it? In addressing the first, he traveled a familiar route—loose construction of the Constitution, implied powers of Congress justified by the ends-and-means rationale. Hamilton had stated the position long ago; as Webster's associate Pinkney remarked, it was a threadbare topic. Webster's discussion of the second point (state taxing power) entered less explored territory. Here he relied upon Article VI of the Constitution, providing that national statutes were the supreme law of the land, state laws to the contrary notwithstanding. Though both nation and states could lay taxes, he conceded, a state tax could not impede functions of the national bank set up by the federal act of 1816.[77] In phrases often quoted afterward, he said: "If the State may tax the bank, to what extent shall they tax it, and where shall they stop? An unlimited power to tax involves, necessarily, a power to destroy; because there is a limit beyond which no institution and no property can bear taxation. A question of constitutional power can hardly be made to depend on a question of more or less."[78]

For a unanimous Court, Marshall delivered an opinion corresponding closely to arguments by BUS counsel. In concept and expression it resembled Pinkney's definition of the Union, formed, he said, by the sovereign people and not by sovereign states.[79] Thus the government of this Union was one of the people. "In form and substance it emanates from them. Its powers are granted by them, and are to be exercised directly on them, and for their benefit." Such a government must therefore have adequate power to accomplish its great objectives—in this instance to charter a banking corporation for fiscal and commercial purposes. Good Hamiltonian theory.[80] Then the chief justice turned to the question of

174

state taxing power and liberally borrowed from Webster: "The power to tax involves the power to destroy . . . [and] the power to destroy may defeat and render useless the power to create."[81] The scope of the principle could be large, seemingly even to the point of establishing a rule of intergovernmental tax immunity for states and nation.[82]

That Marshall meant what he had said soon became clear. Facing a defiance of the *McCulloch* decision in an appeal coming up from the federal circuit court of Ohio, he reaffirmed it in unqualified terms. In that state, the auditor Osborn had forcibly collected a tax on the BUS branches and resisted a judicial order to return the funds.[83] Neither Webster as one of the bank's attorneys nor the chief justice in his opinion wasted much time in reiterating the doctrine of tax immunity. But an important new aspect now appeared. Could the bank go into the federal courts in the first instance for a remedy against such state action? Yes, Marshall held. Congress had constitutionally conferred jurisdiction upon tribunals of the United States in cases in which the BUS was a party, because the questions were federal. The law of 1816 chartering the institution made them so.[84] Though one might think this point to be merely a technical sidelight, the bank actually won a valuable concession. Instead of having to maintain its rights originally in state courts, frequently unfriendly as they were, the corporation could turn to more impartial, if not sympathetic, federal courts. *Osborn* v. *BUS* could be a judicial subsidy of major proportions.

Through the twenties and thirties, as a standing counsel of the bank, Webster found the Supreme Court to be a congenial forum in a variety of controversies involving his powerful client. None was as crucial as *McCulloch,* but taken together they represented a trend toward a new body of law helpful to the corporate form of business as well as to the BUS itself.[85]

Even more than the cases involving the national bank or Dartmouth College, *Gibbons* v. *Ogden* was the one Webster argued in the Marshall era with the broadest effects. It was the first and best-known of all Supreme Court decisions on the commerce clause of the Constitution. And that clause would become the center of never-failing debate about the nature of American federalism, the distribution of powers between states and nation. With sweeping strokes, the chief justice's opinion, much like Webster's brief, depicted federal authority as comprehensive and sufficient to the changing needs and circumstances of a growing republic, despite a reservoir of state powers applicable to the same circumstances. Admittedly, he left the dividing line between the two spheres of government vague, to be more precisely defined in later years; but Marshall's exposition of the commerce clause created possibilities for Congress to legislate in many fields—transportation, communications, industry, labor, agriculture, even civil liberties.

The origins of *Gibbons* v. *Ogden* involve the development of the steamboat in America. By the late eighteenth century the idea of using steam engines to propel vessels appeared practical to a number of entrepreneurs, inventors, and dabblers. One such person was the eminent chancellor of New York, Robert Livingston, who capitalized on his political standing to get measures through the legislature granting him exclusive rights to operate steamboats in the state if he could run a craft at a certain speed a certain distance within a certain number of years. Subsidizing policies of this kind were already familiar throughout the country, based on the notion that social benefits were likely to follow encouragement of enterprise.

Livingston soon entered partnership with Robert Fulton, much to the advantage of both; and after the famed trial run of their boat up the Hudson in 1807, they established a monopoly of the increasingly popular steamboat traffic in New York. For a time they also dominated the business in a number of other states. Repeatedly there were challenges to the monopoly, particularly in the neighboring states of New Jersey and Connecticut, resulting in a great deal of litigation to protect the monopolists' rights.[86] From 1812 onward in case after case, the New York courts upheld their claim to exclusive control of this form of transportation. Judges such as James Kent found nothing in the Constitution or in congressional statutes forbidding the state's commercial policy.[87] Undeterred, one of the challengers, Thomas Gibbons of New Jersey, defied these decisions and persisted in running his boat from Elizabethtown to New York City, which was of course an interstate route. Aaron Ogden, who had reluctantly paid for a license from the Livingston-Fulton company, felt sorely injured by Gibbons' competition and therefore got Kent to issue injunctions to put a stop to it. For his part, Gibbons refused to give up, even in face of a ruling by the court of errors in 1820.[88] So his appeal, *Gibbons* v. *Ogden*, went to the Supreme Court.

Gibbons vowed he would kill the monopoly and was prepared to spend whatever necessary to present his cause most effectively. What better counsel could he employ than Attorney General William Wirt and Webster, by this time a highly reputable constitutional lawyer? This he promptly did. But there was a delay in the hearing, far too much for the impatient client, until argument came on in the term of 1824.[89] These were the circumstances surrounding the Court's consideration of the first commerce case in constitutional history and, in many ways, the most noteworthy to the present day.

Opening for the appellant Gibbons and in opposition to the steam-

boat monopoly, Webster spoke for two and a half hours, defining terms
and expounding a nationalistic interpretation of the commerce clause
that would recur often in the years ahead.[90] "I shall contend," he began,
"that the power of Congress to regulate commerce is complete and entire, and to a certain extent, necessarily exclusive; that the acts in question are regulations of commerce, in a most important particular,
affecting it in those respects in which it is under the exclusive authority
of Congress."[91] Conceding that commerce included many subjects,
whose character changed as the nation grew and whose importance differed, he argued that there were "higher branches" of commercial regulation open only to congressional action. Surely, he reasoned, steamboat
transportation had become a higher branch, significantly affecting business and the daily concerns of people across the land.[92] To allow state
regulation would be to revert to the confusion of the Confederation era
and to suffer "perpetual jarring" of conflicting policies. Indeed such a
condition now prevailed, with New York, New Jersey, Connecticut, and
other states arrayed against each other.[93] One can visualize the chief
justice, remembering as he did the post-Revolutionary tangle of commerce, listening with unconcealed approval. Pushing his argument further, Webster would deny state power over the higher branches even if
Congress had not regulated them. "All useful regulation does not consist
in restraint; and that which Congress sees fit to leave free is a part of its
regulation, as much as the rest." Such an idea, known as the silence of
Congress, would become an accepted doctrine of constitutional law.[94]

With respect to the issue before the Court, he saw no need to apply the
doctrine, for Congress had legislated. The federal coasting act of 1793
had established a licensing system for shipping, his client Gibbons held a
license, and the New York statutes interfered with the licensee's rights
and privileges. Here was a direct conflict of state and national laws, re-
solvable by Article VI of the Constitution, which affirmed the supremacy of federal over conflicting state laws.[95] Webster's reading of the
coasting act seems weak in light of its background, since its obvious purpose was merely to confer advantages upon American-owned vessels over
foreign shipping within the revenue system, not to prohibit any state action whatsoever. Such was the construction Chancellor Kent had given
the act in his earlier decisions; still, the option Webster offered the
Court, secondary though it was, could help his cause.[96]

It did. In his opinion Marshall invalidated the New York legislation
on the ground that it conflicted with the federal coasting act and therefore was in violation of the supremacy clause.[97] Because he did not emphasize this decisive point much more than Webster had nor support it
with more thorough reasoning, contemporaries and later commentators

were either mistaken or puzzled about the character of *Gibbons* v. *Ogden* as precedent. The tendency was to think that the chief justice held that congressional power over interstate commerce was exclusive, with nothing left to the states in a concurrent sense.[98]

This misconception is understandable, for the more prominent part of the judicial opinion laid down broad definitions of words in the commerce clause. Comprehensive and flexible, the language of the provision must not be narrowly interpreted. Beyond the sale and exchange of goods, navigation and passenger traffic in both old and new forms were aspects of "commercial intercourse" covered by the clause, Marshall said. And the constitutional phrase "among the states" authorized Congress to regulate commerce "intermingled" with them, affecting more states than one, not stopping at the state's external boundaries. Despite the innumerable possibilities for national action which this exegesis suggested, nowhere did the opinion rule specifically that national power was exclusive. The implications were strong that Marshall believed it was, especially since he adopted Webster's classification of many instances in which states had regulated interstate commerce as exercise of a different power altogether, the police power over health and safety. Besides, in approving state power over what became known as intrastate commerce, while denying it to Congress, he seemed to be constructing mutually exclusive compartments in the federal system of government. Nevertheless, he did not carry these implications to the logical conclusion by resting his holding on them and so left the matter open to be determined at a later day.[99] Along with other lawyers, Webster would be involved in several cases in the next quarter-century finally leading to a formula for the divisibility of state and national powers.

In the two decades after 1815 Webster had attained a high professional standing and gained an ample income from his legal practice. Over a large part of every year he brought cases into courts of varied jurisdictions—local, state, and federal, criminal and civil, law and equity, admiralty and constitutional. Most of the business, however, had a commercial cast, for the American bar, in which he had become so prominent, was reshaping the law to promote the economic growth of the United States. Particularly in the great constitutional controversies decided by the high court in Washington, he expounded a system of law favoring enterprise: encouragement of the corporate form of business; firm protection of property rights from governmental restrictions; and assertion of national power, not so much to regulate as to stimulate a developing economy.

Chapter 11

LIBERTY AND UNION

In a sense, the year 1829 was a watershed in Webster's life. At forty-seven, he could see his progress from modest beginnings in rural New Hampshire to a standing in Boston's society equal to any and superior to most. With a sizable income and an established reputation, he could count numerous friends among the city's elite. For twenty years, his marriage to Grace had been uncommonly satisfying as they shared the good fortune which had come their way and as they found so much happiness in their household. In his legal career and in public affairs, the theme was unqualified success. As for politics, he had become an influential figure of his region and party, at last reaching the Senate where he became a very visible spokesman of national conservatism.

Then the shape of things changed. Grace had died the previous year; and soon afterward he keenly felt the loss of Ezekiel, ever his strong support. In December 1829 his personal life took another turn when he married Caroline Le Roy, a younger woman whose background and character differed from Grace's. Her aristocratic connections and her detachment from many of Webster's everyday concerns provided a new domestic relationship. The political scene, always an absorbing interest, assumed a different aspect as well. Webster's hopes of promoting a system of economic nationalism dimmed when Andrew Jackson came to power. He would again, as he had throughout much of his time in Washington, find himself on the minority side and could only trust that all would turn out better in a future election. Yet events in the Jacksonian period revised the old issues and brought on others which proved unusually controversial.

At the outset of this administration, Webster could hardly contain his

Webster Replying to Hayne in 1830, by George P. A. Healy, 1851

dissatisfaction. On March 4 he watched the disorderly inaugural proceedings with a critical eye. "I never saw anything like it before," he lamented. This "monstrous crowd" had collected to see the new president
and appeared to believe that the country had been "rescued from some
dreadful danger."[1] Perhaps he ought to resign from the Senate and have
nothing further to do with the deplorable state of affairs in Washington.[2]
But second thought and probably his improved personal circumstances
dissuaded him from such withdrawal.

So after his wedding in December 1829 he and Caroline slowly prepared to leave New York. At the end of the month they shipped boxes of
her clothes and headed south so that Webster could return to the Senate
on New Year's Day, more than three weeks late. His wife felt greater excitement about what she saw and heard than he, especially at the president's dinner party, where Jackson, escorting her to the table, seemed
amiable and attentive.[3]

Neither Webster nor Jackson could have predicted the interesting direction the first congressional session would take. In the following weeks
a great debate on constitutional theory and public policy unfolded. The
Senate provided a forum for display of various sectional viewpoints, but
the common denominator became the definition of the Union's true
character.

Just before Webster arrived at the capital, on December 29, an unspectacular prologue to the forensic drama took the form of an obscure
senator's offering a resolution for a committee inquiry which could have
led to nothing worth remembering. Samuel Foot of Connecticut moved
that the Committee on Public Lands inquire into the expediency of limiting land sales to those areas previously surveyed but unsold. Millions of
acres of land were now on the market, Foot remarked, enough to meet
the demand for years to come. The next day, Thomas Hart Benton vehemently attacked the resolution as a further instance of eastern prejudice against the West.[4] On this sectional note, a protracted debate began
not only about land policy but also about the tariff, internal improvements, slavery, and the very nature of the federal republic. Despite in-
tervals of varying length in between, flurries of speech making
dominated the entire session. From a parliamentary viewpoint, all the
talk concerned whether to refer the resolution to a committee, with no
inquiry or bill ever resulting. On May 21 the debate ended without a
vote, even to table the motion.

The best-known part of the debate came in late January. On one side
were Benton and Robert Hayne of South Carolina; on the other, Webster. From the eighteenth to the twenty-seventh, the three spoke repeat-

181

edly: first Benton, followed by Hayne, Webster's first reply, Benton and Hayne in rebuttal, then Webster's second reply, and concluding efforts by each.

Benton seized the lead in opposing Foot's resolution. The mere proposal to consider restricting land survey and sale inflamed the Missourian. "It is never right to inquire into the expediency of doing wrong," he exclaimed. Such a measure would check western settlement, for public lands now on the market were scraps and leavings, many of them valued at less than the minimum auction price. And that was what the East wished, he charged, in order to keep low-paid laborers in its factories. Benton cited many instances of eastern unfriendliness toward the West from the 1780s onward: Jay's antiwestern diplomacy during the Confederation period; New England's disloyal opposition during the War of 1812, culminating in the notorious Hartford Convention; false sympathy for blacks at the time of Missouri's admission as a state; inequitable distribution of federal money for internal improvements; and an exploitative protective tariff in behalf of eastern capital. In his later speeches Benton increasingly focused on Webster's record to illustrate sectional injustice. As remedy, he called for an alliance of South and West; and to encourage that alignment he said a few things sympathetic to states' rights and slavery. Still, he avoided any mention of interposition, nullification, and secession.[5]

Endorsing Benton's complaints against the East, the urbane, eloquent Hayne at first confined his attention mainly to the subject of land policy and thus extended a southern hand to his friend from the West. He, too, spoke of eastern determination to keep the "paupers" of factory towns from migrating to the agricultural frontier. For the moment he alluded only to dangers to state sovereignty posed by high land prices and a bloated national treasury.[6]

After Webster's first reply, the South Carolinian carried his argument across the entire political landscape. The protective tariff and federal internal improvements had been unjust to the southern states and violated their constitutional rights. Now menaces against slavery intensified, illustrated by Webster's laudatory references to the antislavery sections of the Northwest Ordinance. Indeed Hayne revealed more sensitivity on this point than on any other. On every issue, the discussion descended to personal confrontation, with a review of Webster's career to demonstrate inconsistencies, such as his switch on the tariff and particularly his reprehensible opposition to the War of 1812.[7] Hayne's indictments were specific, for he drew upon a mass of material supplied straight from New England.[8] Highlights were the Hartford Convention and an antitariff meeting of 1820 in Faneuil Hall, to both of which he connected his adversary. Ironically, he reproached Webster for attacking him and for not forthrightly responding to Benton. Toward the end, Hayne laid down his own constitutional ideas (that is, those widely associated with the presiding Vice-President Calhoun, who seemed to nod approvingly if cautiously). Fully sovereign states had acceded to a compact, which was the basis of the Union and the prime feature of the Constitution. Remaining sovereign, they could prevent unjustified expansion of strictly limited federal powers. One state could interpose against the operation of an unconstitutional measure. This would be a peaceful, regular procedure, not a resort to revolution. And the federal government must respect interposition unless and until three-fourths of the other states ratified a clarifying amendment to the Constitution. The South Carolinian stayed clear of secession as an extreme remedy, instead portraying interposition as the best means of preserving the Union. To counter an allegation of radicalism, to place his doctrine in the political mainstream, he dwelt upon its Jeffersonian heritage. Like many other states' righters of the day, Hayne adhered admiringly to the Virginia and Kentucky resolutions of 1798 as authority for state sovereignty, compact, and interposition.[9]

Perhaps to a greater degree than some other participants in the debate, Webster became involved unintentionally. On January 19, as Hayne rose to speak for the first time, the New Englander happened to come into the Senate from business in the Supreme Court, where he had been spending much of his time. When Hayne finished, Webster, by his own later account, decided to answer him after some urging by friends.[10] His reply the next day and his second on the twenty-sixth rested mainly on notes he managed to take while listening, supplemented by last-minute thoughts and topical headings.

Word of the oratorical combat soon spread. The Senate chamber filled with spectators, no doubt more interested in the clash of personalities than in profound constitutional principles. In the area of the senators' desks, according to one report, there were three hundred women—six times the number of senators, if the count was accurate. Just where the lawmakers were is unclear; but a journalist remarked that they were driven from their "cerulean chairs."[11] Another observer described the contest as a "moral gladiatorship, in which characters are torn to pieces, and arrows, yes, poisoned arrows, which tho' not seen, are deeply felt, are hurled by the combatants against each other."[12]

Webster's first reply stayed within fairly limited bounds. He gave a good deal of attention to the subject of Foot's resolution, land policy.

Though indicating some approval of Foot's objective to assure an orderly sale of land at a reasonable price, he doubted it was necessary to direct a committee inquiry. Later he moved to table the resolution. Generally, he was satisfied with the existing system, wishing neither to impose new restrictions which might make land prices rise nor to resort to give-away prices. Benton's notion of graduating prices of unsold tracts downward from the minimum of $1.25 an acre to nearly nothing seemed to Webster to be a waste of a national resource belonging to all the people. Besides, Benton's proposal would play into the hands of speculators to the detriment of actual settlers. Not much time would pass before Webster would see the merits of a homestead, free-land policy. And before long, he himself would be an active speculator.

The senator now turned to his main task: exonerating the East from charges of discouraging western settlement. From the Confederation period onward, he said, the East had aided western development. The ordinance of 1785 drew from eastern experience and received eastern support—the township system, prior survey, generous terms of sale, all resembled earlier New England practice. And the Northwest Ordinance of 1787, with its liberal plan of government and its antislavery provision, came chiefly from the pen of Nathan Dane of Massachusetts. As for the tariff, not until 1828, when a protective policy had become fixed, did Webster and others from his state concur in it. If the South had not voted for the rising tariffs of 1816 and 1824, they would not have passed. Furthermore, eastern votes had made possible national aid for roads and canals in the West. No better example of this positive attitude could be found, the senator felt, than his own exchange with George McDuffie of South Carolina in House debates of 1825. While the southerner had deplored low land prices which drained population to the West, Webster had argued that the nation as a whole benefited from settlements there.[13]

Just as Hayne had dealt with a number of issues besides land policy in his second speech, so did Webster in his elaborate reply of the twenty-sixth and twenty-seventh.[14] Nonetheless, he began by chastising his opponent for wandering from the main question: "When the mariner has been tossed for many days in thick weather, and on an unknown sea, he naturally avails himself of the first pause in the storm, the earliest glance of the sun, to take his latitude, and ascertain how far the elements have driven him from his true course." Calling upon the secretary to read aloud Foot's resolution, he appeared to be insisting that the discussion remain on track. Nevertheless, he covered the same broad ground as Hayne had. A comparison of Webster's notes and the text of his speech shows that he took up each item in turn to refute what his opponent had said. Notwithstanding the resulting haphazard character of the speech, two broad categories emerge: (1) a further defense of New England and of himself concerning past positions on economic and political questions; and (2) a notable exposition of the nature of the Union to combat the doctrine of interposition.

First, Webster extended his argument to counter Hayne's blows. Recurring to land policy, he again explained his cautious view favoring prices neither so high as to discourage western migration nor so low as to squander a national treasure. Specifically, he praised the record of New England congressmen in voting more decidedly than southerners had for the liberalizing land acts of 1820 and 1821. Here was his answer to Hayne's questions about when, how, and why his region had shown its friendliness to the West. He also amplified his discussion of internal improvements and the tariff in self-justifying terms. While referring to these points, he rapped South Carolinians (obviously including Calhoun) for abandoning earlier nationalistic goals. Why, then, should he be criticized for being inconsistent, Webster wondered, when he had always favored internal improvements and had voted for a protective tariff only after it had become a permanent policy? Among other things, he talked about slavery. He still credited Nathan Dane for adoption of an antislavery clause in the Northwest Ordinance, despite a different explanation by Benton and Hayne.[15] They should not worry about slavery in the states, however, for that institution was constitutionally immune from congressional action, he assured them.

Second, and more important in the long run, came his discourse on the nature of the Union. Recapitulating the South Carolina doctrine, which defined the Union as a compact of sovereign states creating a general government as their agent, he underscored the claim of a state's constitutional right to nullify a national measure thought to be unwarranted by the Constitution. After interjections by Hayne, the New Englander distinguished the theory of interposition or nullification from the conceded right of revolution in all instances of tyranny. He then attempted to discredit the notion that the former was a peaceful, lawful process. Nullification was a wholly impractical, absurd theory, he declared. South Carolina would nullify the tariff, as it had threatened to do in the Exposition of 1828; but this action would violate the rights of other states taking a different view. What would happen then? The nullifying state would prohibit collection of customs and call out the militia to execute its decision. In command would be the honorable member himself (who was currently a high-ranking officer). When Hayne's followers asked about the consequences if the tariff act turned out to be constitutional, he would have to answer that those resisting the law were guilty of treason, the penalty for which was hanging. Such must be the case, Webster contended, "or else we have no constitution of general government, and are thrust back again to the days of the Confederation."

He found Hayne's reliance upon the Virginia and Kentucky resolutions of Madison and Jefferson in 1798 no more convincing than the rest of his argument. Rather than asserting a state's right of nullification, these resolutions were probably only a remonstrance, looking toward repeal of legislation or amendment to the Constitution. If Madison were now cited as authority on the tariff question, it was essential to remember that the retired president had conclusively argued in a recent statement that the protective system was constitutional.

In contrast to a loose compact of fully sovereign states, Webster's Union derived from popular consent. Instead of being an agent of the states, the general government of the Union exercised its own powers just as the states exercised others. By distributing these powers, the Constitution provided the nation with a federal system. Restating the Supreme Court's opinion in *McCulloch* v. *Maryland* a decade earlier, he expressed the idea concisely: "It is, sir, the people's Constitution, the people's government, made for the people, made by the people, and answerable to the people." Quite apart from that sphere in which the states acted, the national government related directly to all citizens in areas of their common interest. "In war and peace we are one; in commerce we are one," he said.[16]

Who should determine the dividing line between state and national powers? Certainly not the states. The Constitution itself unequivocally answered that question, he believed. Article VI provides that the Constitution, laws and treaties of the United States are the supreme law of the land, state laws to the contrary notwithstanding. And to give effect to that clause, Article III extends the federal judicial power to all cases arising under the Constitution and laws of the United States. So the Supreme Court must be the arbiter of constitutional questions concerning conflicts of state and national powers. "These two provisions cover the whole ground. They are, in truth, the keystone of the arch! With these it is a government; without them it is a confederation."[17]

At the close, he expressed complete satisfaction with this Union, with its utility to the country's commerce, financial system, and general development. He would not look beyond the Union, he declared, or inquire how it could be broken. The emotion-laden words of his peroration would be a legacy to generations after him: "When my eyes shall be turned to behold for the last time the sun in heaven, may I not see him shining on the broken and dishonored fragments of a once glorious Union; on States dissevered, discordant, belligerent; on a land rent with civil feuds, or drenched, it may be, in fraternal blood! Let their last feeble and lingering glance rather behold the gorgeous ensign of the republic, now known and honored throughout the earth, still full high advanced, its arms and trophies streaming in their original lustre, not a stripe erased or polluted, not a single star obscured, bearing for its motto, no such miserable interrogatory as 'What is all this worth?' nor those other words of delusion and folly, 'Liberty first and Union afterwards'; but everywhere, spread all over in characters of living light, blazing on all its ample folds, as they float over the sea and over the land, and in every wind under the whole heavens, that other sentiment, dear to every true American heart,—Liberty *and* Union, now and forever, one and inseparable!"

The usual historical account of the so-called Webster-Hayne debate centers on these two figures, often with Hayne portrayed as a foil for the Massachusetts senator, now known as the Defender of the Constitution. One reason this has been so is that the development of American institutions seemed eventually to vindicate Webster's nationalist exposition. Yet some time passed before that became clear. At the moment and for the next thirty years, the cluster of states' rights beliefs evoked by Hayne occupied an important place in political thought and behavior.

The speeches of the numerous senators participating in these debates reveal the wide spectrum of contemporary constitutional ideas. Though differing with his colleague on the land question, William Smith of South Carolina subscribed fully to the concept of state sovereignty, indeed advanced the right of secession, which Hayne did not.[18] John Rowan of Kentucky, a tireless critic of the Supreme Court, aligned himself with Hayne and freely attacked Webster on every issue.[19] No doubt Hayne felt the greatest satisfaction with the remarks of Felix Grundy, Jackson's loyal friend from Tennessee, who agreed with him on the formation of the Union by sovereign states and on their right to interpose against unconstitutional federal laws. As a refinement of the doctrine, Grundy would look to a state convention, not its legislature, to interpose.[20] Could he be expressing the president's own sentiments?

A larger number of senators did not endorse the Carolina argument for interposition. Peleg Sprague and John Holmes, both of New England, concurred with Webster, though they were more interested in defending their section against criticism than in expounding constitutional law.[21] John Clayton upheld the Supreme Court's role as constitutional interpreter quite emphatically while tilting in partisan fashion with Benton and other Jacksonians.[22] Many of Webster's allies preferred to direct their fire chiefly at the Missourian.[23]

In the context of later events, the middle position of Edward Livingston of Louisiana merits notice. He disagreed with Webster on the formation of the Union—it was a compact by the people of the states, not by the people of the nation as a whole, he said. Such phrasing could reconcile the view that the people were the source of power with the view that the states had entered a compact. Livingston felt he was accurately restating Madison's resolutions of '98, and his reason for this belief rested on his private correspondence with the former president. But he saw nothing in the resolutions to justify the novelty of nullification, for they had called upon states to remonstrate against an unconstitutional act, never to resist it forcibly. The president must enforce the laws, insisted this influential Jacksonian, until they were repealed.[24] Livingston's mix of Unionism and states' rights resembled the opinions of a number of administration men, including Benton and Levi Woodbury.[25]

Meanwhile copies of Webster's speeches of January were coming off the press and going out to the country. A month afterward, the texts were first reported in the Washington *Intelligencer.* Editor Joseph Gales had taken shorthand notes in the Senate, his wife had transcribed them, and the senator had revised before printing.[26] By late February 1830, newspapers across the land were reprinting his speeches and those of other participants in the debate.[27] The next step, according to practice, was to publish pamphlet editions. In this instance, publication occurred on large scale. "We are just completing an edition of twenty thousand copies, which, added to former editions, will make an aggregate of very nearly forty thousand copies that will have been printed in this Office alone," Gales remarked in the *Intelligencer* on May 21, the day the Senate debate stopped. "There have been printed also, at other different places throughout the United States, perhaps twenty different editions of these speeches. It is hardly too much to say, that no speech in the English language has ever been so universally diffused, or so generally read."

Some readers found little to approve. One was Duff Green of the *Telegraph,* the recognized editorial spokesman for Calhoun. Subscribing to the doctrine of nullification while hoping it would never bring on secession, Green concentrated upon the political implications of the debate, which, he charged, reflected a dangerous attempt by the old Federalists to upset the administration. Careful to avoid any mention of possible disagreement among Democrats themselves, which would be likely to alienate Calhounites from Jackson, he preferred not to explore constitutional theory in much detail.[28]   An exception was his assertion that Webster advocated "unlimited" national powers over the states; and for that he suffered some scratches when Webster moved, though unsuccessfully, to replace him as printer to the Senate.[29] On the whole, the *Telegraph* confined its comment to derogatory items about Webster's connections with the Hartford Convention and with the late Adams-Clay "coalition."

Newspapers friendly to the senator were just as partisan. Despite its normally bland character, the *Intelligencer* cheered him on. A little later, the heading of its news column regularly carried Webster's call for "Liberty and Union."[30] In Boston, the *Advertiser* unreservedly applauded his noble defense of New England, his authoritative command of constitutional principles, his "sublime" peroration.[31] Elsewhere, papers such as the New York *Journal of Commerce* and the Richmond *Whig* concurred.[32]

The historian must naturally be careful in inferring from a person's incoming correspondence anything about the degrees of approval and disapproval of that person's conduct. Nevertheless, given that a politician's correspondents tend to agree rather than disagree and that disapproving letters may disappear over the years, surviving manuscripts at least show the enthusiasm of Webster's admirers after reading his reply to Hayne. Henry A. S. Dearborn of Boston, editor of the Philadelphia *Gazette* Robert Walsh, Henry Warfield of Maryland, William Plumer, Levi Lincoln, Warren Dutton, John Davis—all long-standing friends— were profuse in their superlatives.[33] "Your speeches, on this occasion," wrote fellow Bostonian William Sullivan, "not only excel all former ones, made by you, but by Every other man, in our country; . . . we must go to the days of Burke, Chatham, &c. to find objects of comparison."[34] A letter from Jeremiah Mason, whose judgment he always respected, must have been satisfying, for it remarked on his correct interpretation of the Virginia and Kentucky Resolutions, a pivotal issue.[35] A review of all his correspondence uncovers only one substantial dissent, from George Hay, Monroe's son-in-law. Notwithstanding his general praise of the speeches, Hay thought states could secede from the Union, even if they could not nullify laws. Should they dare to nullify, he continued, at least their citizens could not be punished for treason. Of course, Webster did not assent to either of these propositions.[36]

Often in his lifetime he returned home after a noteworthy congressional session and received plaudits from the city. The current situation seemed to call for something of that kind. During the period between his reply to Hayne and his arrival in Boston, the preliminaries took shape: in February, members of the Massachusetts legislature adopted resolutions of thanks for "vindicating the State from undeserved and unfounded charges"; a meeting in Faneuil Hall in April commended his position on the Union; and Amos Lawrence, representing numerous friends, had the idea of honoring him with a ball or a dinner. Already a veteran of such occasions, Webster declined with more modesty than usual. Yet he did accept the gift of a small service of silver plate, to be appropriately inscribed with words of gratitude.[37]

Approval by those knowledgeable about constitutional law especially pleased him. Nathan Dane, whom he credited with launching a liberal western policy in the Northwest Ordinance, expressed objections to nullification similar to those of Webster when he brought out an appendix to his *Abridgement of American Law* that year.[38] Francis Lieber, the South Carolina scholar with nationalist convictions, invited Webster to contribute an article on nullification to his encyclopedia.[39] Story, learned commentator on the Constitution as well as Supreme Court justice, thought the effects of the senator's speeches were gratifying: "There never was a triumph more complete & to all appearance more undisputed."[40] Ex-president John Quincy Adams, never generous with praise, privately approved the counterblows against Hayne and publicly affirmed national sovereign powers in an address on the Fourth of July, 1831.[41] James Kent, eminent jurist, applauded Webster's refutations of the doctrine of nullification; and to show appreciation, he organized a public dinner in New York City in March 1831. As honored guest, Webster spoke at length about states' rights errors in constitutional construction. The federal judicial power, he contended, was coextensive with national laws and with the Constitution, which it must authoritatively interpret and safeguard.[42]

Of all constitutional authorities whose opinions on nullification were most eagerly sought, Madison was the most prominent. Both nullifiers and nationalists felt certain that the Father of the Constitution could vindicate their positions and were beseeching him to do so. For a while the ex-president restricted his answers to private correspondence with Hayne, Livingston, Everett, Webster, and others. He rejected the doctrine of nullification and approved the main outline of Webster's argument, though with some reservations.[43] Then, a few months after the congressional session, in October, he allowed his views to appear in print, as part of an article by Everett in the *North American Review*. The Union, he wrote, was not a compact of sovereign state governments. Though he would not altogether endorse Webster's assertion that the people of the whole nation established it, he thought the people of the states did. At any rate, under the Constitution the people of the nation were one people for certain purposes and had entrusted the national government with important national powers. Holding other powers themselves, the states could not decide upon the dividing line nor nullify a national law. At most, they could remonstrate against a questionable measure. And he believed that was all that the Virginia and Kentucky resolutions had claimed.[44]

Though a good many contemporaries and some later commentators did not react so favorably to Webster's exposition, he had made a solid case for constitutional nationalism.[45] The history upon which he relied was fundamentally sound: a long-standing common interest of Americans both before and after the constitutional convention; a substantial sense of nationality; the firm belief that all governments rest on the consent of the people, not on that of other governments; the forty years of development of political institutions in the United States; the repeated rejection of claims of state interposition in that period. He could bring to his argument not only extensive knowledge of the nation's history but also much experience as a constitutional lawyer. To these he added clear, powerful rhetoric, infused with deep feeling and understandable by the public.

The fact remains that the debate with Hayne, indeed the rhetoric of the entire session, became just one episode, however dramatic, in a continuing story of conflict. Party warfare and rising sectional tensions would not permit the Websterian exegesis to attain a definitive status, at least for some time to come. In ascendancy at Washington were Andrew Jackson and his Democratic coalition rather than Webster's National Republican friends. No one could be certain how the president would react to nullification should it be tested, nor predict how long his Democratic following would hold together. As the most formidable exponent of nullification, Vice-President Calhoun had been silent during the Senate debate; but soon his connection with the Old Hero would be strained. Soon also he would issue a vigorous address to the people from his Carolina plantation restating the doctrine of interposition, a prelude to still bolder challenges to Webster's concept of nationalism.[46]

From the start, the administration had depended upon a fragile combination of rival elements. In forming his cabinet, Jackson had naturally recognized Van Buren's contributions by appointing him to State, had brought in his fellow Tennessean John Eaton to War, and had selected two others friendly to Eaton and Van Buren. But two of the initial group were closer to Calhoun. When the secretary of state and the vice-president escalated their competition for the succession, Jackson's inner council showed the strain. That situation worsened when a seemingly petty matter promoted discord. Eaton's wife, daughter of a Washington tavern keeper with a dubious reputation, suffered a snub by the other cabinet wives and Mrs. Calhoun, while Van Buren, a widower and consummate politician too, stayed clear of the bickering. That diffidence recommended him all the more to Jackson, who fumed at the treatment of Peggy Eaton. Then the president and the South Carolinian had further differences after the Webster-Hayne debate, highlighted by Jackson's nationalistic toast at a banquet. And to complete the rupture, the two men flung themselves into a quarrel, made public in the press, about Calhoun's criticism of Jackson's conduct in the Florida invasion of 1818. The result was that in the spring of 1831, after the astute Van Buren resigned, the entire cabinet did so, necessitating a complete overhaul of the administration.[47]

All this seemed to verify Webster's idea of desirable strategy. Let the Democrats destroy themselves, he reasoned. National Republicans should be quiet, permit the administration to play its hand, speak out only when a vital interest such as the protective tariff was endangered, and stay clear of the factionalism within Jacksonian ranks. As for a presidential nomination, though he would support Clay, he counseled delay through 1831, for he feared that the chief executive was still prohibitively popular and would probably be reelected unless conditions changed still more. This attitude caused many of his associates to suspect his loyalty to Clay, indeed to guess he might make an attempt himself.[48]

Besides Jackson's strength, a surge of Antimasonry dampened Clay's prospects. Originating a few years earlier, this peculiar movement gained substantial support in the Northeast, now especially in New York and Pennsylvania. Capitalizing on what first appeared to be a passing craze, professionals such as Thurlow Weed, William Seward, and Thad Stevens transformed it into a political party with which both Democrats and National Republicans had to reckon. The Antimasons broke ground in developing the national convention as a party device when their delegates gathered in September 1830. After discussing ways of improving their organization, they postponed a presidential nomination. When another convention met a year later, Justice John McLean led the list of candidates; Webster got two votes and had received tentative support from others. But McLean decided to withdraw because he could not expect the National Republican nomination as well. Then the convention named William Wirt, who reluctantly accepted, despite his own preference for Clay as the best challenger to Jackson.[49] Webster thought so too and criticized the Antimasons for putting forward a separate nominee who would simply split the antiadministration vote and probably ensure the president's reelection. Nor would he approve dropping Clay in deference to the choice of this new party which was unlikely ever to become the voice of a national majority.[50]

Though holding fast in public to Clay's candidacy, Webster had private doubts. Could the Kentuckian carry his own section, even his own state? There had been delay and uncertainty before the legislature selected Clay to return to Washington as senator. Webster detected "something hollow, in Mr. Clay's western support."[51] All the while, he could not suppress thoughts that he himself might be the logical man behind whom the opposition could unite. At the height of favorable comment on his reply to Hayne, a selection of his public speeches and legal arguments was being prepared for publication— one means of bringing him before the public.[52] In early 1831 he considered taking a trip to the West, a tactic which could also increase his visibility. Yet he decided not to go, he explained, for fear it would be misconstrued as an unfriendly move against Clay.[53] In October he put aside whatever temptations he may have felt and urged Clay to assume party leadership in the next session of Congress.[54] That leadership would undoubtedly be reaffirmed in the forthcoming National Republican convention.

This is what happened. In Baltimore, delegates from most of the states met for five days in mid-December 1831 to select presidential and vice-presidential candidates, to send out an address criticizing the administration, and to stimulate enthusiasm for their cause. It was the first major-party, national convention in American hsitory but drew from local and state development and from the precedent of the two earlier Antimason gatherings. Webster's friend John Agg, editor of the *National Journal,* had promoted the idea of a convention; and he himself had concluded it was the best strategy. Webster did not take an active part in the proceedings, though he probably did visit the convention hall for a few hours toward the end. As expected, Clay became the nearly unanimous choice for president in balloting which amounted to formal ratification rather than the result of deliberation by delegates.[55]

Whether Clay had much of a chance to displace Jackson depended a good deal upon the course of politics in the next few months, in part upon the resolution of issues confronted by Congress, just now beginning an important session. For the Kentucky senator to succeed, the position of his party in relation to that of its Democratic opponents would have to improve materially. Above all, the image of the Old Hero would somehow have to be reduced to mere human dimensions.

Chapter 12

KILLING
THE MONSTER

The halls of Congress now provided an arena for the forces competing to control the presidency. In the long session from December 1831 to July 1832, Democrats and National Republicans divided on several issues. One inflammatory question was the confirmation or rejection of Van Buren's nomination as minister to England; another, on which party alignments seemed somewhat less distinct, was revision of the protective tariff; a third, the most controversial, was whether to renew the charter of the Bank of the United States. The last of these helped define conflicting viewpoints on economic policy, governmental powers, and individual rights. In fact it became the dominant, most persistent subject of dispute, to the extent that a politician's opinions on a national bank usually affirmed his party allegiance and influenced his ideas about many topics of public interest.

Established by congressional legislation in 1816, the Bank of the United States had a charter extending to 1836 and authorizing important operations. It was mainly a privately owned and directed corporation, since most of its capital stock was subscribed by investors and most of its board of directors were elected by those stockholders. As minority partner, the federal government owned only one-fifth of the stock and appointed only one-fifth of the directors. In one sense it was just another commercial bank, though the largest in the country, with active involvement in every part of the economy. More significantly, it did some things associated with central banking. It monitored state-chartered banks by its leverage upon their loans and note issues, for it could set the discount on paper it acquired and could present these notes for redemption in specie. Furthermore, it substantially affected the flow and rate of domestic and foreign exchange, the principal means of transferring funds from place to place. As fiscal agent of the Treasury, the BUS also held and moved governmental deposits, a service which increased its working capital. But the most critical function proved to be its creation of currency, either at the home office in Philadelphia or at branches throughout the Union, by circulating its notes.[1]

From his desk in the Greek temple on Chestnut Street in Philadelphia, Nicholas Biddle wielded immense power as the bank's president. This handsome intellectual had held the post for nine years, ever since appointment by his friend President Monroe. He managed the institution's business as expertly as he read the classical authors, wrote essays or poetry, and managed his estate on the edge of the city. His greatest defect lay not in capacity to make decisions about loans and exchange but in his supreme self-assurance, one may say arrogance. If true, such an assessment would not rest solely on his personality but also on the characteristics of his position. The board of directors paid only casual attention to workings of the bank, left most decisions on credit policy and note issue to the president, and merely assented to his actions as a matter of form. Neither by terms of the charter nor by way of its few representatives on the board did the government have much to say. And Biddle oversaw the operations of the branch offices without contradiction because, in effect, he selected the inactive branch presidents and directors, as well as the cashiers, who carried out his will.[2]

During the first three years of his administration Jackson had made it quite plain that he disliked many features of Biddle's bank. In each annual message to Congress he referred to the institution in negative terms. "Both the constitutionality and the expediency of the law creating the bank," he said in December 1829, "are well questioned by a large portion of our fellow-citizens; and it must be admitted by all, that it has failed in the great end of establishing a uniform and sound currency." His later messages showed no change of mind. The bank, as "at present organized," had defects demanding congressional study, he reiterated. Those who had known the president before he took office could have predicted such statements, consistent as they were with his opposition to the BUS as early as 1817. In Tennessee he had then objected to the proposal to establish a branch office in Nashville and continued to do so through 1827, when it occurred. In part, his reason seems to have been rooted in suspicion of all banks because of their tendency to take unfair advantage of their debtors while favoring certain clients. He himself had had some troublesome experience feeding that belief. As for this particular bank, his view was the more inimical because of its vast power over the nation's credit and currency, its unjustified immunity from state regulation, its connection with a moneyed elite. Most of all, evidence that the bank meddled in politics, too often on the side of his adversaries, disturbed him profoundly. Reports that branches in Kentucky, New Hampshire, and elsewhere had been National Republican allies filled a receptive ear.[3]

Friends of the BUS had attempted to counter Jackson's predisposition as best they could. Congressional committees, such as McDuffie's Ways and Means in the House, responded to the president's messages with endorsements of the bank's constitutionality, usefulness, and probity, largely with information supplied by Biddle.[4] In the cabinet, most members were supportive of the corporation or at least rather passive (Van Buren played a typically noncommital role). After the shake-up in the spring of 1831, new cabinet officers were also pro-BUS: Edward Livingston in the State Department, Lewis Cass in War, and especially Louis McLane in the Treasury. A former Federalist of a nationalist persuasion but now Van Buren's protégé, McLane might reconcile differences between the administration and the bank. If so, he would have to prevail over the new attorney general, Roger Taney, who disapproved everything he saw in Biddle's corporation. McLane and Taney, flatly disagreeing about policy as well as suspecting each other's ambitions, argued their respective cases before Jackson while he prepared his message to Congress in late 1831; both gained a little, for the time being.[5]

Party politics brought the festering problem to a head. At their convention in December, the National Republicans approved an address critical of the president's hostility toward the BUS, a misguided and ominous attitude, they asserted.[6] That the question would be a highlight of the campaign became probable after the nomination of Clay, who began urging early recharter, despite his opposite opinion previously. Would not pressure of the election force Old Hickory to sign such a measure; or if he vetoed it, would such a move not contribute mightily to a National Republican victory?[7] Biddle had always said he did not wish the bank to be politicized, for that could interfere with its operations touching every interest in the country and could damage its relationship to the government. But if political involvement had to come, he would look to National Republican leaders for help, a preference understandable in light of his past association with conservatives. He not only admired Clay as a public man but had employed him as an attorney. With Webster, his relations had been closer: the Massachusetts senator had been a special friend, a regularly retained BUS counsel, and a member of the board of directors. At the outset of the congressional session, Webster joined Clay in favoring immediate petition for recharter. Do not wait until the charter expires, even until after the coming election, Webster advised, because if Jackson remained in office, the national bank would have a "poor chance" of surviving. Instead of vainly hoping to bring the president around, confront and defeat him.[8]

After surveying congressional opinion, Biddle concluded that a recharter bill would pass comfortably, though it would almost certainly encounter a presidential veto. Perhaps McLane could help find a compromise. If Jackson remained adamant, the only hope lay in gathering enough votes to override a veto, either by converting reluctant incumbents or by turning them out at the next election. On January 9, 1832, McDuffie in the House and George Dallas in the Senate introduced the bank's petition for renewal of its charter. In the following months, Biddle employed a diversified strategy to promote the corporation's cause. By way of the branches he generated a stream of petitions from state banks, legislatures, and groups for passage of the bill; published supportive arguments in newspapers and pamphlets; and allegedly extended generous loans to influential politicians and journalists. Despite earlier disclaimers of political entanglement, that was the course Biddle pursued.[9]

Resisting each move, the antibank men looked to Benton for leadership. The fiery senator inexorably opposed the "Eastern Monster" as a monopoly wielding uncontrolled power over the economic life of the nation (particularly honest farmers of the West), corrupting institutions of government, and establishing a privileged class. In the preceding session, the Missourian had begun his own offensive with a long speech asking the Senate to declare that the charter ought not to be renewed. Webster and other supporters of the bank were not then ready to open the question and killed Benton's motion without debate.[10] Now that the recharter bill had been introduced, Benton could speak often and exhaustively upon his favorite theme, the abuses of circulating paper money. Gaining the sobriquet "Old Bullion," he described the dangers of paper bank notes, displacing the true "constitutional" currency of the republic, gold and silver. On January 20 he held the floor for several hours to attack the circulation of branch drafts by BUS offices, plainly illegal under the charter, he charged, but a way of expanding a paper medium of exchange. A vote refusing leave to introduce a resolution against branch drafts, twenty-five to sixteen, pleased Webster and indicated the relative strength of the two sides on the bank question.[11]

Undeterred, Benton tried a more promising approach: a request for committee inquiry into the bank's affairs before acting on the recharter bill. Such an investigation could both reveal some irregularities and perhaps delay consideration of the measure until the next Congress. Knowing that refusal to investigate would be impolitic, pro-BUS Senators agreed to the inquiry. A select committee of five, chaired by Dallas and including Webster, carried out its task perfunctorily. Knowing that a committee could not have been friendlier, Biddle cooperated fully; his letter promising to do so was an exact copy of Webster's draft.[12] The committee report incorporated the bank president's own suggestions, which Webster had solicited.[13] But in the House another committee, with an antibank majority, was less sympathetic. Going to Philadelphia and scrutinizing what records it could wrest from Biddle, it perceived numerous wrongdoings. The majority of four in the seven-man panel emphasized unjustifiable loans to newspaper editors, including Watson Webb and Mordecai Noah of the New York *Courier and Enquirer,* to reward them for supporting the BUS. Although the majority report did not probe deeply into generous loans to congressmen, it said enough in general terms to cause nervousness in Washington. John Quincy Adams' brisk dissent criticized his colleagues for improperly discussing private affairs of individuals and for imperiling the freedom of the press, but he could not wholly repair the damage to the bank's reputation.[14] The appearance of these reports put an end to any inclination Jackson might have had to compromise with Biddle.

The Senate took the initiative in debating and revising the recharter bill, with the House acting on it afterward. Webster guided it through the upper body not only by speech making but also by managing the give-and-take of amendment.[15] Benton fought at each stage and prolonged the discussion, hoping for postponement. Even if the bill passed, it was essential to keep the margin as small as possible, for a presidential veto was probable, and he wished to prevent an override.

On May 25 Webster opened debate with a reasoned, conciliatory argument. His principal theme was the utility of the national bank in providing a safe, adequate medium of exchange. A disordered currency consisting of unrestrained issue of state bank notes, he said, inflicted a great evil upon the country. "It was against industry, frugality, and economy." His preference would have been to abolish all such local paper; but in any event, Congress must fulfill its constitutional responsibility by authorizing a national bank to circulate a convertible paper currency. Understanding the strength of sentiment for a specie basis, he suggested prohibiting notes of small denomination, say under twenty dollars. Turning to other functions of a bank, he praised its exchange operations, which facilitated foreign and domestic commerce by assuring low, uniform rates. The cost of domestic exchange was now less than one percent instead of former levels as high as six. As for foreign bills, the existing favorable rates, he said, helped the plantation South, since it was an exporting section depending upon brokers who dealt in exchange. Here he sought to placate those who might most strongly oppose a bank. Similarly, he contended that the West, as well as the South, derived advantages from a bank which could provide a large amount of capital, through loans and discounts, for a rapidly growing economy. All interests, agricultural, commercial, industrial, in all regions benefited from the financial services provided by the corporation. In fact, he concluded, the East did not need them as much as other sections, because it had a more satisfactory state banking system.[16]

The Senate debated the recharter bill for more than two weeks. Much of the discussion related to amendments to reduce the institution's powers and privileges; and Webster continued to be conciliatory, willing to accept a number of changes. Among them, he voted for raising the amount of the bonus paid to the government, for prohibiting note issues under twenty dollars, and for restricting the bank's right to hold real estate. He proposed some amendments himself to meet past criticism of the corporation's conduct.[17] Yet his flexibility did not extend to points he considered vital, such as deleting the provision that Congress could set up no other national bank during the period of the charter. The failure of this amendment and the rejection of a proposal to allow states to exclude branches must have filled him with relief.[18]

No motion aroused him more than the one to permit state taxation of the branches according to the amount of their loans and notes. This levy would be patently unconstitutional, he declared, because the states would be taxing the currency of the country (bank notes) and therefore interfering with congressional power over that subject. In words reminiscent of his arguments in *McCulloch* v. *Maryland,* he asserted that taxation involves "a power to embarrass, a power to oppress, a power to expel, a power to destroy." The Supreme Court had so decided, he continued, in two cases in which states had attempted to tax. From the rule of state noninterference with national action on the currency he deduced a corollary that Congress could not surrender its power to the states. A statute consenting to state taxation would violate the Constitution, as judicially interpreted.[19] Whether in response to the constitutional problem or not, the Senate rejected the amendment by about the same margin as on the other questions.[20]

After all amendments had been approved or defeated, opponents of recharter delivered long speeches to make the best of the situation. Benton, Ike Hill, and Hugh White were trying either to get postponement until the next session or to persuade as many to their view as possible so that they could later uphold a presidential veto.[21] On June 11 the Senate passed the bill 28 to 20, 4 votes short of a two-thirds majority. On July 3 the House approved the measure without amendment, 107 to 85, 20 votes under a two-thirds majority.[22]

Meanwhile Jackson was not spending his time deciding whether he would sign the bill but was thinking of what he would say in his veto. In late June he received a detailed opinion from Attorney General Taney, advancing legal and political reasons for refusing renewal. The principal draftsman of the veto message, however, was Amos Kendall, a dedicated foe of the national bank since his editorial warfare against it in Kentucky. An influential counselor to the president, Kendall blended his own settled thoughts about the corporation with Taney's views but always subject to Jackson's careful oversight. Refinements of the draft came from other White House advisers, including Taney. Out of this collaboration emerged a definitive statement of the Jacksonian faith.[23]

The message contained two classes of presidential objections to the bill: it conferred unjust privileges upon a select group, and it violated the Constitution. To support the first claim Jackson set forth several specific objections relating to the general category of "gratuity." Recharter would immediately cause the value of BUS stock to rise by as much as 50 percent, thus unfairly rewarding current stockholders, most of them in the East and in foreign countries, to the detriment of the South, the West, and the government. He considered modifications in the existing charter to be inadequate safeguards against favoritism to the few who controlled a powerful, profitable corporation. Most of the alleged constitutional flaws, previously outlined in Taney's opinion, related to the clause authorizing Congress to pass "necessary and proper" laws to carry out enumerated powers. Incorporating such a bank as this was not necessary or proper. It was unnecessary to prohibit future congressional action by granting a "monopoly," to abdicate governmental power over the currency to a private institution, to give it discretion in setting up branches wherever it pleased, to shield it from the vital state taxing power. Who should determine whether a law was constitutionally necessary? At this juncture the courts could not, despite their earlier decisions approving a bank, because at this point the problem was legislative, demanding congressional and executive judgment. When a president decides whether to sign or veto a bill, he is acting in a "legislative capacity" and must therefore pass upon "the degree of necessity."

No other part of the message would later provoke more criticism and misunderstanding than this one.

Jackson concluded in a populistic key. When government makes the "rich richer, and the potent more powerful—the humbler members of society . . . have a right to complain of the injustice." Every citizen of the United States deserves equal protection of the law; in this instance such protection consisted in a fundamental guarantee against monopolistic privilege. Webster must have felt the irony of the Old Hero's appeal to providence to aid the nation in preserving "liberty and Union." But he certainly concurred in the call for the people themselves to resolve the dispute when they elected representatives to the next Congress.[24]

The day after announcement of the veto, July 11, Webster led off debate on the question of sustaining or overriding it. His speech was a point-by-point refutation of the president's message. To the argument that extending the life of the bank would suddenly enrich the stockholders, he responded that Jackson had furnished no proof whatever that the value of stock would rise. And to the assertion that foreign stockholders could exercise dangerous control, he replied that the charter forbade them to serve as directors or even to participate in electing directors. Foreign capital was an asset to the economy, a fact already demonstrated by its flow to America in other ways, such as extensive loans to states for internal development. Furthermore, the chief executive ought not to have portrayed the South and West as potential victims of exploitation, for they tended to be debtor sections. The large volume of loans and exchange there, about thirty millions, did reflect heavy borrowing, but it was beneficial because it opened up the land and promoted enterprise. If the national bank closed down, he predicted, farmers and planters would suffer disaster.

Not only had the president erred on the matter of expediency, Webster continued, he had also put forward constitutional opinions without any plausible foundation. In the senator's opinion, congressional and judicial action had absolutely settled the question of constitutionality. Reviewing the legislative history of the two national banks, he discovered no evidence that Congress had ever decided that incorporating a bank was unconstitutional; and the current bill was almost entirely a reenactment. As the body principally responsible for interpreting the Constitution, the Supreme Court had unreservedly affirmed the power to create a bank. Contemptuous of all these precedents, the president claimed authority belonging to a despot, to a James II or a Louis XIV. "If that which Congress has enacted, and the Supreme Court has sanctioned, be not the law of the land, then the reign of individual opinion

201

has already begun." As for Jackson's particular constitutional reasons, Webster brushed them aside as having no merit. Granting an exclusive right to a national bank did not wrongly divest future legislative authority, for it was an essential contract to protect investors taking a risk. Nor did the bank's immunity from taxation by states invade their sphere of reserved powers, for, as an instrument of the national government, the corporation must be free of that kind of obstruction.

On one point Webster and Jackson could agree: the bank controversy involved first principles of American politics, the relationship of branches of government to each other and the relationship of government to the people. Jackson would augment presidential power, his opponents would support congressional and judicial powers against it, and both sides would appeal to the people at the next election for a mandate. Naturally, each side felt that it alone had stated its own case fairly. Webster, for example, complained that the president had appealed to popular prejudices by inciting the poor against the rich.[25]

Long-winded debate ensued, seemingly so that the record might be laid before the electorate, since friends of the BUS could not now recruit a two-thirds vote.[26] Oratory reached a climax with an excited exchange between Clay and Benton. As the Kentuckian's vehemence mounted, he dwelt upon Jackson's eagerness for power. Benton deplored such disrespect for the president; Clay retorted that he would not look to the Missouri senator for instruction in courtesy, especially from a person who had brawled with Jackson years ago and had himself predicted during the presidential election of 1824 that if Old Hickory were elected, congressmen would be compelled to conduct business with dirks and pistols at their sides. "False, false," Benton shouted. To quiet the turmoil, the presiding officer called Clay to order; and after he and Benton apologized to the Senate (but not to each other), a vote on overriding the veto came. It failed, twenty-two to nineteen.[27]

Jackson had won the first battle of the Bank War. Although Biddle headed a powerful corporation, indeed exerted total control over it, he should have understood long beforehand that he confronted an immovable, very popular opponent. Hoping to conciliate the president with some concessions or with the help of McLane, Livingston, Lewis, and others, he badly miscalculated the odds for victory. Certainly he had reason to believe that the proven usefulness of his institution to the economy would build support during the recharter controversy; but as the issue assumed a political cast, his difficulties deepened. While a good many congressional Democrats at first approved retention of the bank, they soon felt the force of Benton's scolding: "They might continue to be for a bank and for Jackson; but they could not be for *this* bank, and for Jackson."[28] The bank's future hinged upon a National Republican ascendancy after the next election. And Biddle would have to depend upon political tactics, arm in arm with leaders of that party.

Collaboration between Biddle and Webster involved more than their common goal of recharter. Over a long period, they had developed a solid friendship. The banker and the senator had much in common: their cultivated tastes and breadth of information, their images as both country squires and men of affairs. There were frequent visits and conversations, often when Webster stopped at Philadelphia on his way to or from Washington. Surviving manuscript collections include a huge number of letters between the two on a range of topics, though politics and banking predominate. Despite his reluctance to admit it, Biddle was a thoroughgoing National Republican–Whig with regard to all political matters. He believed his New England friend was a great statesman whose correct views and enormous ability ought to find a just reward in the White House. For his part, Webster admired the banker's eminence in the financial world.

Webster would doubtless have advocated the bank's cause as a straight political matter if he had had no personal connections with it. But that was not the case, as his critics since then have emphasized. For years he was the corporation's most reliable counsel before the Supreme Court. At the very time the Senate began debate on recharter, he sent Biddle a bill for legal services.[29] Later, during the Bank War, he wrote, "Since I arrived here, I have had an application to be concerned, professionally, against the Bank, which I have declined, of course, although I believe my retainer has not been renewed, or *refreshed,* as usual. If it be wished that my relation to the Bank be continued, it may be well to send me the usual retainer." Sensitive to the charge that the institution bought more than his legal services, he suggested that his request not go before the board of directors, for he knew that government members would promptly report whatever they learned to the administration for publication in Blair's *Globe.*[30]

He was even more sensitive about his situation as perennial debtor to the bank. Was it not imprudent or worse for him to seek credit at the main and Boston offices while he spoke at the Capitol to save the corporation's life? True enough, prominent men of both parties borrowed too; yet some of his arrangements seemed especially lenient. Just as Jackson was sending up his veto message, Webster requested a BUS loan of ten thousand on a shaky security of notes by merchant John Connell in anticipation of awards for pending French claims. Worried about criticism, he asked the cashier to set up the transaction indirectly through other Philadelphia sources so that his name would not appear on the books where unfriendly directors or congressional investigators could discover it.[31] His uneasiness in the matter led him to seek repeatedly to clear all his debts to the bank.[32] But the best he could do was to deny any irregularity. In April 1834 he gave Everett a statement for public use: "If in the course of yr investigation, the [House] Commee, should incline to notice my name, I wish you to state, as on my authority;— That I never had any particular or unusual accommodations from the Bank, to the amt. of a single dollar;—that since I went to Boston, in 1817, I have kept my account, & done my necessary banking business at the Boston office; & notes, bills of exchange &c, &c have been with my name on them collected, & discounted, &c as often as occasion required, precisely as would have been done in the case of any other person, & not otherwise. I have reports of mortgages, standing loans, &c &c between the Bank & myself, in all which there is not a single word of truth. I never gave the Bank any mortgage, & never had any standing loan, or any other accommodation, except in the way of discount of bills & notes, as at other Banks."[33] Even allowing for the well-known flexibility of public ethics of that day, it is difficult to reconcile Webster's intimate relationship to the BUS with his conduct in Congress.

After returning to Boston at the end of the session, he began preparing for publication his speech against the veto. Typical of general practice, what he had said in the Senate and what appeared in print were not the same, and in fact several versions appeared in various pamphlet editions. He used his own notes, those of a reporter, and probably some suggestions of friends.[34] He invited Story to look over the constitutional "trash" in Jackson's message and to give him "in a letter of three pages, a close & conclusive confutation, in your way, of all its nonsense, in this particular. It will take you less than half an hour."[35] To improve other parts, he urged Biddle to revise further before sending it to the printer. In September Biddle was circulating the speech in quantity as a campaign document at the bank's expense. A political abuse, exclaimed the Jacksonians.[36]

During this session, Congress struggled not only with the bank question but also with the tariff, an issue soon to precipitate a national crisis. The existing schedule of import rates, adopted four years earlier in that strange enactment known as the Tariff of Abominations, had satisfied no one. New England felt it got too little protection for some manufactures and had to pay too much for some raw materials. Other sections, particularly the offended South, felt they paid too much for imported goods, as Calhoun and Hayne had strenuously argued. After saying or doing little on the subject through much of his term, the president indicated in his message of December 1831 (doubtless with the coming election in mind) that there ought to be relief from high rates and that the government would need less revenue because retirement of the public debt was imminent. Congressional committees and the secretary of the treasury devoted a great deal of time to the subject through winter and spring; debate on bills took place in May and June, interspersed with discussion on the BUS; and the law, viewed hopefully as a permanent compromise, passed in early June at the close of the session.

At the center of these events was ex-president John Quincy Adams, beginning a long, unprecedented period as a representative in the House. His background and convictions would have led him to oppose any tampering with the protective system, except to make it more protective. But he found himself, as chairman of the Committee on Manufactures, having to subordinate his own ideas to those of colleagues, the administration, and opposing sections of the country, playing the role of disinterested elder statesman in an evenhanded placation of North and South, high- and low-tariff exponents. Ordinarily, a tariff bill would come out of the Committee on Ways and Means, whose chairman, George McDuffie, shared Calhoun's intense dislike of protectionism; and so, for the sake of moderation, the assignment went to Adams' committee, reluctant though he was. His task was to steer a dangerous course between the McDuffies and the Clays, to reduce the tariff but not too much.[37]

If he were to succeed, Adams quickly recognized, he had to have the administration's cooperation. He therefore worked closely with Secretary of the Treasury Louis McLane, who gathered a mass of economic information and drafted proposals for a bill which Adams largely accepted as his own. McLane, like Adams, believed it indispensable to accommodate his protective orientation to the Jacksonian thrust for reduction—but not so far as to surrender to South Carolina.[38] Adams himself considered the measure he reported to be an administration bill. Average rates would go down from 45 to 27 percent and would be strictly *ad valorem*, with no classification of minimum valuation, which presently increased actual levies. Was this not such a generous concession that all talk of nullification would cease?[39]

By late June, with adjournment not far off, the Adams bill had won House approval and moved to the Senate. Here the guardian of the American System, Henry Clay, vowed he would not yield to the nullifiers, abandon a policy of fostering industrial enterprise, or abjectly follow

205

the Democratic lead. On foreign goods not competitive with American products he would consent to reductions, which would cut the revenue enough to satisfy economizers, though he saw no merit in their plea. This concession would, however, improve his chances of keeping land prices high as a counterweight, with proceeds being spent for internal improvements. This sort of packaging suited Clay's nationalistic aims, but the reduction of duties must be selective and nowise endanger those manufacturing interests needing federal encouragement.[40]

Webster agreed. There could be no retreat, he thought, from the general lines of present policy, for otherwise vital interests would be ruined. Of this he was the more certain as he read his mail from home. Harrison Gray Otis, Jeremiah Mason, and others in Boston wrote him about objectionable features of the Adams bill, chiefly the continued neglect of woolen manufacturers and the abandonment of minimum duties for a pure *ad valorem* schedule. Above all, they cautioned against radical fluctuations in the tariff, for businessmen with large commitments of capital required a stable policy. To advance their argument, they sent Abbott Lawrence to lobby in Congress (and to supply Webster with facts) during debate.[41]

Webster joined Clay in demanding a number of amendments to the bill in the Senate and generally succeeded in getting them by a two-to-one margin. Increases in woolen rates and restoration of minimum duties stood out as the most important changes, to which they hoped the House would agree. In conference committee, however, senators yielded everything to congressmen. Then, despite a tongue-lashing by Clay and Webster of William Wilkins, who headed the Senate conferees, the upper chamber agreed to recede from every one of its amendments. Nevertheless, the two National Republican leaders allowed the final bill to pass, and on July 14 Jackson signed it.[42]

Throughout 1832, politicians assessed each issue in terms of the coming election. Relatively unimportant questions became partisanly charged, and one such topic was Van Buren's appointment as minister to England. The Senate did not get around to acting on the nomination until January 1832, well after he had gone to his post. But then the National Republicans went after their target with zeal. Van Buren, they contended, was unfit for the office because he had mixed politics with diplomacy while he had been secretary of state. He had written instructions to the American representative in London to take a new approach to the long-standing problem of trade with the British West Indies; and in doing so, he had implicitly criticized previous policies of Adams and Clay. The objection here really lay in Van Buren's strengthened position in the administration and in his excellent prospects for the succession. At any rate, with Vice-President Calhoun breaking the tie, the Senate rejected the nomination; whereupon the furious president was all the more determined that his injured friend would be just the person to take over after the second term. Meanwhile, with Jackson's decisive endorsement, Van Buren was nominated for the vice-presidency.[43]

As the election approached, Clay, of course, projected confidence, a good deal more than circumstances justified. Again he could not be sure of his own state, where the governorship went to his opponents in August.[44] In the Northeast, there was the continuing problem of the Antimasons. Would not Wirt divert votes which would otherwise be National Republican? Here and there, anti-Jacksonian leaders talked of combining forces, of getting Wirt's withdrawal from the campaign, of uniting behind a fusion candidate instead of Clay or Wirt, perhaps the ever available John McLean. Yet that strategy never matured.[45]

The only thing to do was to attack the president on the main issues. Since Clay, like other candidates for the presidency, could not properly make electioneering speeches, the logical National Republican spokesman was Webster. Yet he remained inactive, except for an appearance at a state convention in Worcester on October 12. In a long, carefully prepared address he scored the administration for its missteps and for the dangers they posed to the Constitution. It was a comprehensive bill of indictments, omitting nothing of importance on the political scene. Probably organized according to his own sense of priorities, his list of complaints began with the tariff. Events during the past congressional session, he said, showed that the protective system could soon collapse, for the president had shifted to a negative outlook as was evident in an allusion to his bank veto. Opposition to exclusive privileges, as Jackson defined them, might lead to further and drastic reduction of rates beyond the new statute. Or if he faced state nullification of the tariff, would he enforce the law? His refusal to do so in the Georgia-Cherokee controversy suggested that he would not. Then, on the issue of the BUS, Webster summarized his criticism of the recharter veto in the Senate. His listeners already knew his views on that topic because copies of his speeches had circulated widely. He also laid down party positions on public lands (maintenance of existing prices, with distribution of proceeds to the states), on federal internal improvements, and on excessive executive power. With respect to the last of these, he portrayed Jackson as trampling on the Constitution in many ways, such as rewarding party hacks by appointment to office, subsidizing editors, and resorting to the veto on an unprecedented scale. The speech was precisely what the convention wished to hear and shortly reached a much larger audience through the press.[46]

Far from a majority of the voters in November shared Webster's dissatisfaction with the Democratic record. Jackson won reelection decisively—Clay carried only six states, and Wirt only one. Obviously the main element in Old Hickory's victory was his enormous personal popularity. Whether those who voted for him endorsed his judgment on specific issues seemed secondary to his overall reputation as a fearless representative of the common man.[47] The president's own reaction was to consider the result a mandate to continue his firm resistance to all the elements of evil surrounding him, to BUS minions, to nullifiers, to subverters of equal rights. Soon he would have more encounters with each of them.

Chapter 13

NULLIFICATION

Immediately after Jackson's reelection, events in South Carolina precipitated a crisis that not only troubled the administration but alarmed the entire nation. Though the lowered tariff rates of the recently enacted law may have seemed a sensible, durable settlement of a vexatious question, the Palmetto State did not consider it so. A nullification party had prevailed over Unionists to control the legislature, which then called a convention to decide upon a strategy of resisting national tariff policy. At the convention in late November 1832, the nullifiers had little difficulty in adopting an ordinance declaring the tariff unconstitutional and therefore unenforceable in South Carolina. To make certain it was not, the ordinance prescribed a test oath for state officials, even juries, not to allow collection of duties; and other provisions set up legal barriers against action by federal customs officers and judges, including the Supreme Court. Any congressional effort to apply force would be "inconsistent with the longer continuance of South Carolina in the Union."[1]

In his annual message of December 4, Jackson appeared unworried about this unprecedented challenge, for, he said, he had sufficient authority to handle the situation. Still, he recommended further downward revision of the tariff because the Treasury now needed less revenue. His calm exterior concealed boiling anger at the threat against both the Union and his position as president. Hoping to undermine the "Nullies" by an appeal to the patriotic sentiment of fellow citizens in his native state, he ordered Secretary of State Edward Livingston to draft a proclamation.[2] Veteran constitutional lawyer that he was, Livingston lacked nothing for the task. The secretary, who had fully expressed his opinions

209

in the Webster-Hayne debates, opposed the state-sovereignty idea, occupied moderate ground in the dispute about who formed the Union, but repudiated the novelty of interposition.

The proclamation to the people of South Carolina, on December 10, was a mixture of constitutional discourse and firm resolve to enforce the law. After summarizing the ordinance of nullification, Jackson rejected the state's right to judge the constitutionality of federal laws as impractical and absurd. The Union, he continued, could never have survived if discontented states had attempted to nullify national measures deemed ruinous and invalid. In no previous instance, even when New England opposed the embargo, had any state gone as far as South Carolina. History would not justify an invention of this kind, for the Constitution, from the time of its adoption, had secured a "more perfect Union" above local interest or party strife. As for particular objections to the tariff, such as those protesting its protective purpose and uneven impact, the president viewed each of them as very weak. At any rate, these were questions not to be left to every state's judgment. Undoubtedly, Congress had power to lay duties and could pass laws necessary and proper to carry that power into execution. Whether a revenue act was enforceable must be ultimately decided by courts of the United States, despite the current obstruction of appeals to the federal judiciary. Nor could a state resort to secession as the ultimate remedy. Accepting Livingston's draft, Jackson argued, much as Webster had, that the Constitution formed a government relating directly to the people rather than to the states. This was truly the government of a single nation indissoluble by any pretended right to secede. Their leaders had misled them if South Carolinians thought they could constitutionally and peacefully break up what was purported to be a weak league of sovereign states. They ought to reconsider the idea of separation, because that would be revolution. "Disunion by armed force is *treason*," the president declared, and he would deal with it accordingly.[3]

News of the developing confrontation did not surprise Webster. He had believed for some time that the nullification movement was reaching a dangerous stage requiring vigorous response. In October he decided to publish a reply to Calhoun's most recent exposition of states' rights theory, but he had not managed to do so before South Carolina translated theory into practice.[4] After adoption of the ordinance, he felt that armed conflict was bound to follow. "I have not the slightest doubt," he said, "that both Genl. Jackson & Govr. Hamilton [of South Carolina] fully expect a decision by the sword."[5] Still at home through early December after the beginning of the congressional session, he read

Jackson's proclamation approvingly. Friends of the Union must stand together, he thought, regardless of party differences. Across the country, many others agreed and demonstrated their patriotism at this critical hour by mass meetings. In Faneuil Hall on the seventeenth, notables of the city addressed a large assembly for that purpose. T. H. Perkins presented resolutions sustaining Jackson's position, affirming national sovereignty, condemning interposition and secession. The old Hartford Conventioner, Harrison Gray Otis, shared the platform to explain the difference between New England's earlier complaints and the unprecedented boldness of present-day nullifiers. Highlighting proceedings, Webster's speech endorsed the resolutions and called upon everyone to rally around the president, for if South Carolina should prevail, the Union would collapse. With his best flourish, the senator vowed that "when the standard of the Union is raised and waves over my head—the standard which Washington planted on the ramparts of the Constitution—God forbid that I should inquire whom the people have commissioned to unfurl it and bear it up; I only ask in what manner, as a humble individual, I can best discharge my duty in defending it."[6]

On his way to the capital Webster stopped briefly in Philadelphia, where he encountered Clay. They talked about the explosive condition of political affairs and how Congress could defuse it. Webster discovered, to his dismay, that their ideas differed. While the Kentuckian disapproved the doctrine of interposition, he had already concluded that Congress would have to make some concessions to South Carolina. His diagnosis led him to favor a compromise on the tariff as the only means of preventing civil war, and a number of National Republican businessmen with whom he conferred said the same thing. A preliminary plan, now taking shape, would cut rates to 20 percent but delay reduction until 1840, when the protective policy would give way to one of revenue primarily. This apparent surrender to nullifiers worried Webster.[7]

Arriving in Washington, he found the mood of Congress to be tense indeed. Attention centered upon Calhoun, now a senator after resigning as vice-president and replacing Hayne, who had taken over as governor in the excited southern state. The Carolinian's colleagues could plainly see by the set of his jaw that he intended to test the case for nullification; and everything he said in conversations along the corridors confirmed that impression. The outcome seemed dependent upon which of two irresistible forces would be stronger, the aroused general in the White House or the stern logician in the Senate. Could the politicians save the Union by some formula combining principle and accommodation?

Without delay, there emerged a formula to lower the tariff more drastically than Clay's preliminary plan. At the end of December the chairman of the House Ways and Means Committee, Gulian Verplanck, proposed to cut rates within three years to an average well below 20 percent. Devised by Secretary of the Treasury Louis McLane and promoted by Secretary of War Lewis Cass, the bill reflected a prescription favored by Verplanck's fellow New Yorker, Martin Van Buren, and a powerful wing of the Democratic party following the vice-president-elect. The measure would probably pass in the lower house, especially if the president himself got behind it, but what the Senate would do was uncertain. So it seemed to Webster. Through the first two weeks of January, therefore, he was doing what he could to quash the Verplanck bill by private talk, correspondence, and meetings with groups of congressmen. He felt encouraged when the Massachusetts delegation agreed that such an abandonment of the protective system would be ruinous.[8]

Congress considered both tariff revision and enforcement. Debate in both houses mingled the two issues and various proposals to resolve them; but all the speeches, spun out to the end of February, sought to identify the boundary of national power, which of course involved the extent of state power too. On January 16 the president sent up a message asking for legislation to assist him in executing laws of the United States: use of forts and naval vessels to collect customs duties; removal of cases on the subject from state to federal courts; and deployment of troops, if necessary, to maintain order.[9] Quickly the Senate Judiciary Committee, of which Webster was a member, reported what was called the force bill to give Jackson the authority he wanted. Just as quickly, Calhoun presented resolutions laying down his doctrine of state sovereignty in the vain hope that discussion would shift from the force bill to them. Amid this oratory, Clay introduced a new compromise on the tariff to replace Verplanck's plan. House and Senate acted on each at different times, with passage of a combination of statutes on March 1, near the end of the session.

Supporters of the force bill in the Senate stood together on the necessity of meeting South Carolina's defiance directly, for they saw it as a wholly revolutionary threat to the Union. William Wilkins, chairman of the Judiciary Committee, recommended it on that ground; and others, including George Dallas and John Clayton, insisted that the emergency demanded firmness.[10] John Forsyth, the Jacksonian Democrat from Georgia, concurred, though trying to obtain moderating amendments on judicial appeals.[11] Most senators speaking for the bill contended that the sovereign people, not the state governments, created the Union, that

federal power reached the people without going through states as intermediaries, and that the right to judge the constitutionality of congressional statutes belonged to the Supreme Court, not to states.[12]

Opposition to the force bill came from a southern minority who disagreed among themselves about constitutional principles. Very few endorsed the South Carolina ordinance. There were those who, though
unwilling to embrace nullification as a logical weapon of sovereign
states, thought the pending measure too drastic; they would reduce the
tariff and, if imperative, resort only to action that was already available
to put down any disorder. They worried about giving still more power to
Jackson, dangerously inclined as he was to expand presidential authority.[13] Future president John Tyler, somewhat cautious about the
exact scope of nullification, unhesitatingly condemned the use of force
now proposed.[14] His colleague from Virginia, William C. Rives, while
believing military provisions of the force bill to be unnecessary, preferred to expose the errors of present-day nullifiers. Rives's position
bothered Calhoun much more than that of outright advocates of national coercion. Characterizing current exponents of interposition as a
"new" school of constitutional law, Rives distinguished their ideas from
Jeffersonian tenets in the Virginia and Kentucky resolutions of 1798. A
state, possessing substantial rights though not complete sovereignty,
could follow the precedent of '98 by "moral" interposition, he said.[15] In
Calhoun's judgment, this was an unpromising prescription, certainly
nothing approximating the help offered by George Poindexter. In a
long-winded speech, the volatile Mississippian slashed at both Jackson
and Webster, the former for seeking dictatorial power and the latter for
luring the president into the consolidationist camp. Yet what a contrast
there had been, he declared, between Calhoun's patriotism and Webster's localism during the late war.[16] But as the Senate listened to every
reason presented for rejecting the force bill, the prospect of passage appeared strong.

To prevent it, Calhoun would have to be extraordinarily persuasive.
He sat impatiently while argumentation continued, often interjecting
comment or contradiction, waiting for the best time for a set speech,
preferably after Webster had showed his hand. But, except to speak
briefly for the force bill when it was reported out of committee, Webster,
too, was waiting for the most advantageous moment. Deciding not to
delay any longer, Calhoun took the floor on February 15 and again the
next day. At the beginning, he sought to correct "misrepresentations"
against South Carolina and himself. In a painstaking historical review of
tariff policy, he depicted his state as a long-suffering victim of unconsti-

213

tutional exploitation. Though he conceded that he had voted for the law of 1816, he described it as an essential postwar revenue act; then in the twenties he had sensed the threat of protectionism and had voted against the bill of 1827 while vice-president. Soon the Tariff of Abominations passed; and more recently, the so-called adjustment of 1832 promised to make its inequity permanent. Insisting that he had always opposed such a system, he concluded the time had come for the state to exercise its right to judge whether its reserved powers were infringed. If Congress should adopt this oppressive, unconstitutional force bill, he warned, thousands of the state's brave sons were prepared to lay down their lives to preserve its rights. But he did not mention secession anywhere in his speech.

From this background, he moved to political theory. As he had often contended, he repeated his view that the Union was a compact of sovereign states, responsible for defending the liberty of their citizens against consolidation of national power. In defining true federalism, he drew little from American history but much from that of other people, such as the Hebrew and Germanic tribes. For the existing problem in the United States, he proposed as a solution the doctrine of concurrent majority. He attributed many evils to dominance by an absolute majority. Minorities suffered from protective tariffs benefiting industrialists, even encouraging monopoly; too much revenue in the Treasury fostered abuses; excessive presidential authority (to be expanded by the bill under consideration) corrupted government, particularly through a vast patronage dispensed by the chief executive. No provision of the Constitution could check these consequences of rule by an absolute majority. All interests, some inevitably in a minority, must be secure; and at last, he alluded to the South as a distinct interest of that kind. Constitutionally, the doctrine would operate by way of the sovereign states. When a state found a minority interest endangered, it must interpose, a peaceful, legitimate process. If other states disagreed, they could adopt a constitutional amendment, to which Calhoun expected the nullifying state would defer. Still, he left practical aspects of the concurrent-majority idea undeveloped, for he did not reconcile the right of a fully sovereign state to interpose and the right of three-fourths of the states to overrule. Thus the concepts of nullification and concurrent majority could be incompatible, short of state submission or secession. Furthermore, he did not address possible defects of absolute-majority government within a state, nor explain how to determine fairly either type of majority in one like South Carolina with malapportioned legislative districts and numerous filters between popular will and decision making.[17]

When Calhoun finished, Webster took the floor. For several hours in the afternoon and during an evening session, he made a full-scale speech that he had been preparing for some time. He had looked over his reply to Hayne of 1830, then had searched for relevant items on the constitutional convention, state ratification, and the first Congress of 1789. These, together with last-minute notes on Calhoun's remarks, provided the materials with which he organized his argument. But he had waited to make it until his opponent made the first move. Other than saying a few words on the force bill, which he described as an administration measure, he had remained silent.[18] The effect was to heighten the expectations of his listeners, who filled every corner of the Senate chamber.

Webster first concentrated on Calhoun's resolutions, introduced coincidentally with the force bill and intended to defeat it. They had defined the Union as a constitutional compact of people of sovereign states and had asserted a state's right to judge instances of national invasion of reserved powers.[19] Altogether untenable opinions, Webster declared. Feigning regret that the South Carolinian had placed himself in such a treacherous, hopeless position, he remarked, "He is like a strong man struggling in a morass; every effort to extract himself only sinks him deeper and deeper." Calhoun had based his theories on the false premise that sovereign states had *acceded* to a compact, or league, Webster contended, whereas the people had actually *ratified* a constitution and thereby created a government. Indeed well before 1787, as early as 1774, they had formed a union to oppose British measures, had strengthened it by the Articles of Confederation in 1781, and had perfected it with the Constitution. If one were to accept the term *accede*, then logically a state could secede as well. And the notion that nullification was a cushion against secession amounted to the "wildest illusion, and the most extravagant folly." Nullification with the avowed purpose of not proceeding to secession resembled taking the plunge over Niagara and trying to stop halfway down.[20]

Then Webster laid down his own propositions: (1) the Constitution is not a compact of states but an instrument of government created by the people; (2) a state cannot secede without precipitating a revolution; (3) the Constitution is the supreme law of the land, to be interpreted by Congress or the Supreme Court; and (4) nullification is therefore a revolutionary usurpation of power.[21] In that order, he expanded upon each proposition.

Instead of a compact, the framers had established a national government, having a relationship to individuals on such subjects as taxes, military service, and criminal justice. Here he restated what he had often

215

said and what the Supreme Court had held: "As to certain purposes, the people of the United States are one people. They are one in making war, and one in making peace; they are one in regulating commerce, and one in laying duties of imposts."[22] In contrast to the Articles of Confederation, the Constitution and statutes pursuant to it affected the citizens of the country directly and did not depend entirely upon state enforcement. All the materials of constitutional history, some of which he cited and quoted, showed the creation of a new federal system of this sort, he thought. If the system arose from a compact of states, why does the preamble of the Constitution say, "We the people of the United States do ordain and establish this Constitution"? His answer was that the sovereign people lived under two governments, state and national, both responsible to them. One was the government of a perpetual Union; the other of states, which had not entered into a temporary partnership, terminable by unilateral decision to secede. This, his second proposition, was a corollary to the first.[23]

In the event of conflict between governments of the two spheres, a state could not be the arbiter. To a large degree, Congress must determine the extent of its own powers, for its statutes were the supreme law of the land (Constitution, Article VI), and it must interpret the "necessary and proper" clause (Article I, section 8) in carrying out enumerated powers. But when a question could assume the shape of a lawsuit, then the Supreme Court had jurisdiction (Article III) and must define the law of the land. If state nullification could override congressional and judicial interpretation, then there might be twenty-four different versions of the Constitution, destructive of essential uniformity.

While explaining his last two propositions, Webster took notice of the concurrent-majority doctrine. It violated the great principle of majority rule, he believed. It would in fact countenance minority rule. Conceding the importance of protecting minority rights, the senator saw abundant checks and balances in the Constitution for that purpose. And how incongruous it was for South Carolina to advance the doctrine while it acted harshly against rights of a respectable minority, the Unionists, at home.[24]

Nullification, an extraconstitutional, impractical absurdity, would depend upon forcible state resistance to legitimate authority, inevitably fragmenting the Union. It would lead to secession, and secession would be outright revolution. Though the right of revolution always existed, there must be proof of unbearable injustice for which the Constitution could not afford remedy.[25]

In the present situation, however, the South Carolina ordinance posed force against a perfectly valid law. The words of the Constitution and more than forty years of history after the document's adoption convinced Webster that Congress had authority to pass a protective tariff. The power to lay duties was explicitly granted without qualification, and by implication these duties could be discriminatory in order to encourage manufacturing. All tariffs, ever since the first statute of 1789, reflected mixed purposes, partly to raise revenue, partly to protect American industry. Quoting the preamble of the act approved in the first congressional session and Madison's speech on its desirability, the senator seemed to score an important point. More telling, perhaps, was his reference to the law of 1816, endorsed by Representative Calhoun and others from South Carolina. He could not resist the temptation, any more than his adversaries, to probe for personal inconsistencies.[26]

Now, Webster concluded, the government must put down the current challenge by nullifiers, must prevent commotion and maintain peace. For his part, he pledged his help wherever needed. Even if the Constitution fell before its assailants, he fervently declared, "I will still, with a voice feeble, perhaps, but earnest as ever issued from human lips, and with fidelity and zeal which nothing shall extinguish, call on the PEOPLE to come to its rescue."[27] When he finished, the chamber resounded with predictable applause from the crowded galleries.

Calhoun and Webster, in turn, had ably set forth states' rights and nationalist definitions of the Union. Both positions attracted a following among contemporaries, and both remained valid to some Americans for years to come. Although no state would again attempt nullification in such an advanced form as South Carolina did in 1833, the doctrine of state sovereignty proved to be a formidable political idea for the next thirty years. And many historians continue to find features of Calhoun's argument superior to that of Webster.[28] Viewed on pragmatic grounds, however, in the context of national experience, the formula of state sovereignty has been associated with lost causes, while Webster's constitutional nationalism has been more durable.

Calhoun's view of the formation of a union in 1787 was plausible, for the Articles of Confederation declared the states to be sovereign, the new Constitution rested on acceptance in those states, and afterward a states' rights persuasion flourished. A relatively inactive central government left much for the states to do, and a fear of consolidated power persisted. Even the firmest advocates of a strong Union referred to the republic as an uncertain experiment instead of as a perpetual entity. Then too, a fundamental attachment to the idea of limited government, connected as it was by the South Carolinian to minority rights, cast the states in the role of trustworthy guardians of liberty.

Perceiving the compact theory to be unsupported by the history of the

217

United States over the preceding half-century and more, Webster contended that the people, not the states, formed the Union and adopted the Constitution. Thus the source of power was not state governments but the people, who had created them as well as the national government. Undeniably, the concept of popular sovereignty had deep roots— the Declaration of Independence affirmed it. Besides, the troubles of the Confederation era led the American people to reject a system of dominant state legislatures and to distribute authority between two levels, national and state. This was a sovereign decision, implemented by the people's delegates at the federal convention and by the people's conventions in the states. Use of the device of a convention was a function of popular sovereignty.[29]

More important than the question of how the Union was formed, in Webster's opinion, was that of how the government under the Constitution had later operated. From its first session to this one, Congress had passed statutes supreme over those of the states and affecting the people directly. Though some laws had provoked complaints and threats, prevailing sentiment had always rejected a state's right to judge whether those measures were constitutional. Long ago the Supreme Court had assumed a major responsibility of doing so, and it was too late now to abolish judicial review. Nullification amounted to usurpation, with no foundation in practice; secession was worse, wholly revolutionary.

So Madison thought as he read reports of the debates in the Senate. Almost immediately after receiving a copy of Webster's speech, on March 15, the former president wrote the senator a long letter, fully agreeing that the history of the country since 1787 vindicated his argument, leaving little or nothing for Calhoun's side. Madison's only concession to the compact interpretation was to say that people of the states had ratified the Constitution. Regardless of this point, he believed the relationship of all the people to their national government, as it developed subsequently, was the more significant fact.[30]

In the next few days after Webster spoke, discussion of the force bill was winding down. Whether for or against it, those having the floor retraced well-marked paths already taken, with only the question of parliamentary strategy in doubt. Administration men and National Republicans favoring the bill had a majority of at least two to one, and all that Calhoun and his friends could reasonably expect was to obtain amendments or delay. But motions to amend, to postpone, and to adjourn failed. At last, on February 20, the exasperated Calhoun and a little band of allies, as well as Clay, Benton, and others evading the embarrassment of voting, left the room. The bill passed, thirty-two to one. The minority of one consisted of John Tyler, very anxious to record this protest against an odious policy of presidential coercion. On second thought, upon returning to their desks the following day, some absentees sought to register their disapproval too. Yet they had to have unanimous consent, according to a rule of the house, and several of the majority were unwilling. None was less generous than the stouthearted Virginian, who declared that "he felt a little pride in this matter. He stood single in his negative to the bill; and he was not desirous to lose this proud position, and to share the honor he now enjoyed alone with any others."[31]

In a trailer to proceedings on the force bill, Calhoun revived his resolutions. Again he explained his constitutional principles emphatically and exhaustively; and again Webster returned fire by repeating essentials of his earlier speech. Seeing that a vote would certainly go against him, Calhoun allowed his resolutions to be tabled and looked for consolation elsewhere.[32]

He had, indeed, reason to feel he had not lost everything in this legislative conflict. Though he had not recruited sufficient support to defeat the force bill or to endorse nullification, he gained concrete concessions on the tariff. On February 26, the very day he gave up on his resolutions, news came over from the House that a bill lowering rates had passed there. It was in fact Clay's compromise, which had supplanted the Verplanck bill and which the Senate had been discussing for two weeks. In a ten-year period, duties would gradually decrease to a maximum of 20 percent with an understanding that they would probably not exceed that level afterward. When he introduced his measure in the Senate on the twelfth, Clay assured his colleagues that his object was not a long-range abandonment of a protective policy. Mainly, he said, he wished to calm the country and save the Union. Though disapproving nullification in a few gentle words, he recognized that South Carolina had legitimate grievances; and he proposed to redress them by moderate, gradual adjustments while preserving necessary protection for manufacturers.[33] Before offering his prescription for peace, he had cleared it with Calhoun and with certain businessmen as well. He then persuaded the Senate to establish a select committee (including himself as chairman and Calhoun as member) to bring in the proposal. But in addition to opposition by staunch protectionists, he encountered complaints by others that the Senate could not constitutionally initiate money bills. To solve that problem he handed a copy to his friend Robert Letcher, who managed to get it through the House in one day, without any amendment.[34]

Webster resisted the progress of Clay's bill from beginning to end. When the Kentuckian introduced it, he countered with resolutions laying down his own views on the tariff;[35] and as discussion continued, the highlight became an unreserved exchange of arguments between the two. He did not object to cutting rates where necessary, he said, but he did oppose flat reductions by an equal percentage on all articles. That would amount to surrender of the protective principle, to giving up the existing policy of discriminating against foreign goods in favor of those manufactured at home. Not only would American industrial interests suffer, but the laboring man would lose a fair wage. Worst of all, as a result of the 20 percent ceiling on duties after 1842 Congress would abdicate much of its indispensable power to regulate commerce and thereby to foster national economic development. Passage would also signal a surrender to demands by nullifiers.[36]

To Clay, this last point appeared to be the heart of the matter. He insisted that the compromise was wholly a political reconciliation of divergent sectional interests, not an abandonment of protection. Only an inflexible man could dissent from it. How deplorable, he lamented, that Webster "opposed this proposition of peace and harmony, and wished to send forth the measure of force alone." "The gentleman has no authority for making that assertion," Webster muttered, whereupon Clay exclaimed he "would not submit to interruption." Later, during a long rejoinder, Webster disclaimed an unreasonable posture. Had he not also introduced resolutions accepting the idea of adjustments? And as for criticism of his pushing through the force bill, he had simply helped the administration pass it. Both senators did not hide their personal feelings any more than their disagreement about the tariff issue.[37]

Clay prevailed. Some protectionists concluded that the dangerous situation demanded accommodation and therefore voted for his plan. If the Senate had not already passed the force bill, these protectionists would probably not have agreed to a reduced tariff, for the two measures were packaged as a way out of the difficulty. Low-tariff men saw this solution as the best they could get; and, of course, the administration's approval made it possible.[38] On March 1 the bill passed, twenty-nine to sixteen, with Webster voting nay. Then force and tariff bills went to the executive mansion together, to be signed promptly by the president.[39] South Carolina receded from nullification of the tariff but registered lingering discontent by nullifying the force act.

In weathering the storm of constitutional dispute, the administration had to look for help beyond the ranks of its own party, to Webster to check an extravagant states' rights movement and to Clay to find an acceptable revision of the tariff. As a result, speculation about political realignments mounted. One possibility, unlikely as it might once have seemed, would be a unionist party led by Jackson and Webster, arrayed against an anti-Jackson coalition of Clay and Calhoun. Undoubtedly the rupture between president and chief nullifier was permanent; and it was unthinkable that Jackson and Clay, adversaries in the recent election, could find much common ground. Perhaps Old Hickory might find collaboration with Webster useful again if the challenge of nullification recurred. He was well aware of Webster's undeniable ambition for higher honors and of his disagreement with Clay.

During the session there had been hints of such a shift. Secretary of State Livingston repeatedly conferred with Webster about speeches on the force bill, relayed Jackson's gratitude for the role he had assumed, and perhaps explored others as well.[40] John Tyler suspected that something odd was happening. After visiting the White House, he concluded that Jackson and Webster "must come into the closest and more fraternal embrace. I dined at the Palace, yes, palace, a few days since, and found Mr. W. there in all his glory."[41] When Webster replied to Calhoun on February 16, Jackson did not conceal his satisfaction—indeed, according to one recollection, sent his carriage over to Webster's quarters to take him to the Senate.[42] Afterward, the president remarked: "Mr. Webster replied to Mr. Calhoun yesterday, and, it is said, demolished him. It is believed by more than one that Mr. Calhoun is in a state of dementation,—his speech was a perfect failure; and Mr. Webster handled him as a child."[43] Was there not some truth in an item by the fictional Major Jack Downing, having Jackson declare that if, after he left office, the nullifiers made another try, Webster should talk and Downing should fight to save the Constitution?[44] Calhoun's advocate, Duff Green, also detected a Jackson-Webster alliance, but in a different light. Instead of Webster going over to the Jacksonian camp, he contended, it was just the reverse. The chief executive had subscribed to the old Federalist tenets of Webster and his Hartford Convention friends.[45]

Even Benton, a Jacksonian stalwart, noted a warmer Jackson-Webster relationship. The Missourian, silent during the nullification debate, did not vote on the force bill, apparently because he did not wish to antagonize southerners who might help revise the tariff lower than Clay's proposals. Nevertheless, he did welcome the president's stern response to Calhoun's doctrines, praised the proclamation to the people of South Carolina, and felt that Webster substantially contributed to the administration's success. "Released from the bonds of party, and from the narrow confines of class and corporation advocacy," Benton observed, Webster's "colossal intellect expanded to its full proportions in the field of patriotism, luminous with the fires of genius; and commanding the

221

homage, not of party, but of country." Jackson "threw out the right hand of fellowship" to Webster, to the extent that the public thought the New Englander might be appointed to the cabinet or some other high office. Alas, Benton concluded, Webster lacked the strength of character, the will, to take a new direction, so that the opportunity disappeared.[46]

Van Buren, too, believed the nullification controversy brought Jackson and Webster closer, much to his discomfort. Unhappy with the expansive nationalism of the presidential proclamation, he correctly assigned its theory to Livingston and other executive advisers, who unfortunately entertained old Federalist ideas. In other words, it sounded too much like Webster. To soften the damage to the party throughout the South, Van Buren wrote and put through the New York legislature a long statement warning against consolidationist implications of the proclamation. And he set about rebuffing moves to associate Webster with the Old Hero. On the other hand, finding that the Verplanck bill could not pass, he was happy that Clay's compromise did. What a shame that Webster had been so stubborn about these necessary concessions to the South.[47]

In fact Van Buren represented the power center of the Democratic party more accurately than Benton did. The Washington *Globe,* identified with Van Buren's interest, reported congressional proceedings exhaustively but rarely mentioned Webster, except to criticize him for being unyielding on the tariff.[48] And Ike Hill, an influential voice in party affairs, was equally negative about any understanding with the Massachusetts senator: "Nothing lacks now to complete the love-feast, but for Jackson and Webster to solemnize the coalition with a few mint-juleps . . . But never fear, my friend. This mixing of oil and water is only the temporary shake-up of Nullification. Wait till Jackson gets at the Bank again, and then the scalping knives will glisten once more."[49]

What the effects of the Clay-Webster disagreement might be upon the two men themselves remained unclear after the close of the session. The Kentuckian discounted the probability of permanent hostility, saying "there is no breach between Webster and me. We had some friendly passes, and there the matter ended. Since, we have occasionally met on friendly terms. I think (of course I do not know) that if he had to go over again the work of the last few weeks, he would have been for the compromise."[50] Still, he appreciated an effort by Biddle to mute any hard feelings on Webster's part, quite desirable, of course, when the bank issue should return to the foreground. It would then be essential, Biddle knew, for all three anti-Jackson leaders, Clay, Calhoun, and Webster, to unite in the common cause.[51]

Just as Clay and Webster diverged on the tariff, so did other National Republicans. Webster's incoming mail included complaints about the compromise, the strongest being against maximum rates of 20 percent after 1842. In the judgment of some of his friends, Congress had repudiated the protective principle, its power to encourage domestic industry.[52] But others reported that the sentiment of businessmen tended to be favorable. After all, they could depend upon a known system for the next decade; and for most of that time, rates would decline only moderately. Undoubtedly, a feeling of relief that the national crisis had subsided induced their satisfaction with the compromise.[53] Webster must have wondered why even Mathew Carey, the most active protectionist propagandist in the nation, seemed untroubled by the new policy.[54]

After enactment of the tariff compromise, however, no one could be certain that nullification would not revive. Webster could see several possibilities that it would. In Georgia the long-standing problem of state defiance of national authority on the Indian question might precipitate another crisis, which South Carolina extremists could exploit.[55] Or instead of the tariff, slavery might become the paramount issue emphasized by nullifiers. The South Carolina unionists Benjamin Perry and Joel Poinsett expressed deep concern about this eventuality, telling him that Calhounites still meant to disrupt the Union and form a southern confederacy. Believing the danger to be real, Webster assured the South that slavery was secure from federal intervention. In a letter published in newspapers during May 1833, he said that though slavery was a great moral and political evil, Congress lacked power to touch it within the states. Already such a statement was a staple antidote to calm the slaveholding interest.[56] Yet he would not count entirely upon soothing words and good will. If nullifiers pressed the issue by attempting to repeal the force act, he would resist it to thwart those contemplating treasonous projects.

Chapter 14

BANK WAR

Through the remaining months of 1833, Webster's behavior seemed tentative and exploratory, understandably so, in an unstable political situation full of uncertainties. Calhoun and a small southern contingent had broken with the Democratic party, at least while Jackson presided over it. There could be further erosion when the bank question recurred, as it surely would. And the tariff controversy had, to an extent, blurred party lines; during the nullification crisis a good many National Republican protectionists had supported reductions. Having opposed Clay on that issue and supported Jackson on the force act, Webster was tempted to use whatever leverage he had with the administration to save the BUS. Moreover, it was not too soon to be thinking about the next presidential election, when voters might prefer him to Clay or Van Buren.

Perhaps he could have clarified matters a bit in June, when the president came to Boston on a northern tour; but he was absent, despite a declared intention to be on hand to welcome Jackson. His friends Stephen White, Edward Everett, Josiah Quincy, and others joined people of every class and persuasion in entertaining their honored visitor. After arrival on June 21 Jackson had a grueling schedule of parades, receptions, speeches, tours, and assorted ceremonies, which proved too much for his precarious health. For three days he was shut up in his rooms at the Tremont House, an interval between preceding events at the Common, Faneuil Hall, and the State House and others at Harvard, Bunker Hill, and the Navy Yard.[1] The future would disclose whether all this had any political significance.

Webster found it impossible (some said inconvenient) to be present for a personal estimate of the implications. In late May he set out on a trip to the West, through upper New York and as far as Ohio, not to return home until July 20. He probably had several purposes, not all of them easy to document. One, no doubt, was to take his wife as far as the Genesee country to visit her brothers who owned extensive farms there. Another was to fulfill a long-felt desire to see the rapidly growing area of the Ohio Valley, whose development he had often extolled. And another may have been to test the mood of the West, possibly with thoughts about the next presidential election.[2]

Travel was fatiguing and slow, owing to the poor condition of the roads and torrential rains along the way; nevertheless, an enthusiastic reception at place after place warmed his heart. Invitations came for him to visit this town and that, to receive approval of his contributions as expounder of the Constitution and defender of the Union, usually to address the citizenry at dinner meetings. Though not objecting to such adulation, he did try to avoid as many formal affairs as possible in favor of discussions with small groups or an open-air speech to the public. The principal points where he broke his journey were Buffalo, Columbus, Cincinnati, and Pittsburgh.[3] Wishing to go farther south or west, he decided against it, he said, for fear of "giving offence." Exactly what he meant is obscure, but he may have worried about creating the impression that his tour amounted to electioneering in his own behalf. This was the part of the country where National Republicans had often expressed their allegiance to Clay, and a suspicion that he was searching for votes in the Kentuckian's territory could cause embarrassment. At any rate, an outbreak of cholera in Lexington provided a handy excuse for not going down to visit Clay. It is impossible to say whether the hazard of the disease or his still ruffled feelings accounted for his decision.[4]

In Pittsburgh on a hot July afternoon he spoke to a large crowd gathered in a spacious grove. Touching upon a number of current topics, he soon got to the tariff question. Protection of American industry was imperative, he reasoned, chiefly to benefit the laborer, who must have good wages and the opportunity to acquire property, to share in the nation's prosperity, and, above all, to gain an education. Regardless of its validity, this was a protectionist argument with more popular appeal than one looking merely to the advantage of business. In any event, he was surely telling his audience that he did not support reductions like those voted at the last congressional session. But the most noteworthy feature of his speech was his high praise of Jackson's response to the nullifiers. Characterizing the proclamation to the people of South Carolina as able and patriotic, full of constitutional truth, he declared, "Gentlemen, the

President of the United States was, as it seemed to me, at this eventful crisis, true to his duty. He comprehended and understood the case, and met it as it was proper to meet it." Webster conceded that he differed with the chief executive on many issues, but on nullification he had given his "vigorous and cordial support" and obviously meant to continue giving it.[5] No wonder that this passage captured the attention of the press and the politicians.

Proof that Webster was moving toward a complete rapprochement with the administration would depend upon scattered beliefs, suppositions, and inferences. They suggest, but do not establish, that he was invited to advise on the patronage, that he might have joined the cabinet, and that maybe he hoped to become president with Jackson's blessing.[6] The most credible piece of evidence has been Webster's own account of a meeting with Edward Livingston in New York on July 18, upon his return from the western trip.[7] Leaving the State Department to become minister to France, Livingston was about to depart for his new post. As early as March, Webster had had the idea of a "confidential interchange of opinions upon topics which must arise, in the course of a short time, & on which public men will be obliged to act."[8] Failing then to arrange a conference, he had postponed it until summer. The two men had known and respected each other for a long while, though their party associations had been different. Now they occupied common ground in opposition to nullification; and Webster had complimented Livingston for his ability and patriotism in the recent crisis, chiefly for drafting the proclamation to South Carolina. Unfortunately the specifics of their conversation in July are unknown, allowing speculation that Webster sought to cement a Jacksonian alliance. Yet the outgoing secretary of state would not have been helpful on everyday politics, appointments, and elections, for he had never had that kind of influence even when he belonged to the cabinet. Given the context of general circumstances, it seems likely that the meeting focused on the bank question. It was no secret that Jackson was seriously considering removal of the government's deposits from the BUS, if he had not already decided upon it. Biddle continually pressed Webster to prevent this from happening at all costs. The senator's recollection of his discussion with Livingston indicates he tried to capitalize upon his collaboration with the president in upholding the Union by reaching an understanding about the bank, a more limited objective than joining the administration in some important role. As Webster recalled, Livingston told him Jackson would appreciate his continuing support; but, in Webster's words, "there was an irreconcilable difference on the great question of the currency."[9] If so, he negotiated with the wrong person on that subject.

The most influential presidential advisers on the bank question were Attorney General Taney and Amos Kendall. The latter, though only a minor official in the Treasury Department, was a leading member of the so-called Kitchen Cabinet. By the time Webster talked with Livingston, they had already convinced Jackson he must remove government deposits from the BUS. For a long while, since almost immediately after the veto of recharter a year earlier, there had been frequent discussions at the White House about taking this serious step. Despite a contrary opinion among all members of the cabinet except Taney and despite Van Buren's caution and reservations, the president strongly leaned toward it and revealed as much in messages to Congress and in public statements. The Kendall-Taney argument that the deposits were unsafe in custody of this "moneyed monopoly" triumphed. But throughout the summer of 1833 Jackson had immense trouble with his new secretary of the treasury, William J. Duane, who absolutely opposed removal of the public funds.

Jackson's uncharacteristic patience with the adamant Duane ended in late September when the secretary refused to carry out a direct order to relocate the deposits in state banks, now arranged by Kendall's tour of eastern cities. So the president dismissed Duane, appointed Taney, who was poised to execute the plan, and prepared to wage war with the opposition in the coming congressional session. When the legislators assembled in December, the new system was in place. Jackson and Taney informed Congress what they had done and why, thereby setting the stage for an acrimonious, protracted discussion of the country's financial policy.[10]

In the Senate the result of that discussion would partly depend upon the composition of committees now to be organized; and Clay, wielding substantial control over these decisions, gave them a great deal of attention. The sooner these arrangements were made the better, the Kentuckian thought, certainly before the vice-president arrived at the Capitol, for Van Buren could influence the Senate's election of committee members. Felix Grundy, an administration leader, wished just the opposite and moved to delay selection. To Clay's displeasure, Webster supported the motion. Was this an olive branch the New Englander extended to the Democrats? Van Buren believed Webster was courting a coalition with the Jacksonians to gain a cabinet post and then to become president in 1836. Upon returning to Washington, the vice-president anxiously conferred with Jackson and Grundy about the situation, for he had his own hopes of the presidential succession. Whether Webster or Jackson ever envisioned a coalition is doubtful, but after this meeting Van Buren felt he had quashed any such notions. As for the committees,

' Clay succeeded in getting his slate elected, one of whom was Webster as chairman of the Finance Committee, obviously an important assignment during a session in which the deposit issue would be dominant. Both Van Buren and Clay concluded that placing Webster at the head of this committee would soon underline his fundamental differences with the administration.[11] They apparently did not understand that he was not at all reluctant, indeed was eager, to become committee chairman.[12]

For some weeks Webster's intended political course continued to provide a favorite topic of conversation. The idea that he sought a basis of collaboration with Jackson persisted because of his strained relations with Clay and because of his growing interest in the presidency. Some Democrats would settle for his benevolent neutrality—Webster himself expressed such an inclination. He would support the president "on proper measures," he had written, as long as they did not conflict with the essentials of tariff protection and a safe currency. "I came here, as you know, with a strong desire to avoid taking any course, particularly one hostile to the Administration."[13] After he found conflict inescapable, he clung to the possibility of eventual compromise on the bank question. Or a middle position could lead to establishing an independent party to uphold the Constitution and the Union, with himself at its head.[14] In fact the National Republicans were in disarray, there had been some splintering of Democratic ranks, and in a few months the new Whig party would emerge. If Webster was rethinking his relationship to parties, so was Calhoun, now an aroused foe of the Old Hero. Could Webster and Calhoun join hands? Biddle hoped so, for the sake of the BUS. An anti-Jacksonian alliance between an ultra nationalist and an ultra states' righter, however, would be difficult to hold together.[15]

Clay insisted upon counterattacking against removal of the deposits at every point, whereas Webster preferred a more cautious response as the best means of saving the bank. For example, they reacted differently to presidential nominations of four government directors. Mobilizing a majority of the Senate to reject their reappointment, Clay shared Biddle's view that they had obstructed the work of the BUS board for partisan reasons. Webster believed it better to concentrate on the fundamental problem before Congress rather than on one that the public might interpret as a petty quarrel. But he had to acquiesce in this confrontation with the determined chief executive. Twice the Senate rejected Jackson's appointments, and the prospects of an accommodation dwindled.[16] Similarly, Clay launched a resolution requesting Jackson to send up the text of the paper on removal that he had read to the cabinet in September; an unnecessary irritant and premature as well, thought Webster. Again he had to fall in line by voting for Clay's resolution, which produced nothing except an answer from the president that what he said to his executive advisers was privileged, none of the Senate's business.[17]

Finally Webster found the occasion for which he had been waiting to strike directly at the removal policy, "the experiment" of deposit in "pet" state banks, in the phraseology of the day. Silas Wright, Van Buren's lieutenant, brought into the Senate from the New York legislature resolutions approving removal, opposing any type of national bank, and favoring state banks as fiscal agents of the government. In speeches on January 30 and 31, 1834, Webster deplored and condemned these resolutions, presented as they were by Wright, a well-known spokesman of the administration. He was discouraged, he said, by this authoritative pronouncement of an uncompromising position on the financial system.

How unfortunate, he declared, that the government seemed unmindful of the distress throughout the land. The recent attack upon the Bank of the United States had forced it to curtail its loans, had weakened confidence in it at home and abroad, and had disarranged economic life generally. When state banks became depositories for the Treasury, they overissued notes and failed to provide a safe, uniform medium of exchange. And credit, increasingly left to these institutions, was either inadequate or unreliable. So Webster urged restoring the bank as fiscal agent, an entirely constitutional and quite desirable remedy for the afflictions of the economy.

To achieve this goal, the senator would depend upon public opinion. Already he detected numerous signs of dissatisfaction with existing measures. The whole South, he unconvincingly asserted, disapproved removal of the deposits. Everywhere persons who opposed rechartering the national bank also opposed withdrawing government funds from it— even some of the president's closest associates; excessive executive power over the purse alarmed those who, like himself, sensed a usurpation of congressional power.

An appeal to the public was possible on either side of the issue. In Webster's judgment, antibank forces put their case before the people unfairly by stirring up class prejudice, by inciting hatred of the poor against the rich. But Americans would not be driven around in herds. They would not accept such a dishonorable blot on the right of self-government. Those with the greatest need for a sound currency, such as that supplied by the BUS, were laboring men, for they realized that depreciated money helped only greedy speculators, cheated common folk of their daily bread.[18] "Sir, the great interest of this great country, the producing cause of all the prosperity, is labor! labor! labor! We are a laboring community. A vast majority of us all live by industry and actual employment in some of their forms. The Constitution was made to protect this industry, to give it both encouragement and security; but, above all, security."[19]

In early February, as the Senate focused on the main issue of removing deposits, Webster cooperated with Clay in an offensive against Jacksonian policy. One tactic was to report out of the Finance Committee an endorsement of the Kentuckian's resolution disapproving Taney's reasons for removal. For weeks the legislators had been discussing the secretary's report to Congress and the condemnatory resolution on that subject. Though Biddle and Clay believed a vote on the floor of the Senate could now dispose of the question, Webster felt his committee should first lay down a specific statement upon which the opposition could unify, and he had long since drafted such a paper.[20] He had looked into the legal background and the history of government deposits in the BUS and had asked his friends for their advice. Both Joseph Story and Joseph Hopkinson offered disappointing opinions that the secretary of the treasury had very broad authority to order removal, though such action was, of course, subject to review by Congress. A conversation with Adams, however, reassured him that Taney's action had violated the law.[21] When the Senate ultimately agreed to refer the question to his committee on February 4, Webster said he would report the next day, thereby in effect admitting that the document was already written.[22]

On the fifth he did present it. Spectators crowded into the chamber to see and listen as he read his detailed reprimand, running on for an hour and a half. At the beginning, he quoted the statute chartering the bank which provided that public funds be deposited there "unless the Secretary of the Treasury shall at any time otherwise order and direct" and that he lay before Congress "the reasons for such order." In Webster's judgment, the clause requiring the secretary to give reasons confined his discretion to a sudden, unforeseen situation in which the very safety of the funds was endangered. Here the senator had to base his argument on inference instead of on explicit language in the statute. If one accepted this approach, his subsequent points seemed fairly credible.

In turn, he summarized and rejected each of Taney's reasons for removal. First, the fact that the current bank charter would expire in two years was in itself no justification for an executive decision, because Congress, the appropriate body, had plenty of time to decide what to do about deposits. The government had left deposits in the old national bank until its charter ran out in 1811. Second, he saw no merit in

Taney's criticism of a small exchange committee making day-to-day decisions rather than the full board of twenty-five directors, thus shutting out the five government appointees from participation. This was a general practice of all banks, Webster remarked. In any case, he added weakly, government directors were no different from the others except for the manner in which they were chosen, an assertion not borne out by the past relationship of the two types of directors. Third, he defended the bank against Taney's complaint about its handling of a bill of exchange for the receipt of claims from France. Though the bank had charged substantial damages against the United States government because France had dishonored the bill, he said, that procedure was normal for commercial transactions. Fourth, the bank was not culpable of meddling in politics or manipulating its credit for partisan purposes. Who could say that the secretary himself was not partisan in making such allegations? All these particulars, as well as Taney's underlying beliefs that the BUS had been unconstitutionally chartered and had become a moneyed monopoly, were perversions of the statutory requirement for an order to withdraw deposits. To correct these errors, the Senate ought to vote for Clay's resolution saying as much. It did.[23]

Throughout the congressional session, probank forces also sought to reverse the administration's policy by flooding the two houses with memorials from cities and villages across the country. Their aim was to demonstrate public dissatisfaction with the presidential veto of recharter, removal of deposits, and consequent economic distress. The movement assumed such a pattern as to indicate organization by political leadership or perhaps by the bank itself. A local meeting attended by large numbers of people (always described as respectable voters) provided a platform for speeches and adoption of a memorial urging abandonment of the "experiment" in order to alleviate depressing conditions. Then the memorial went to Washington, often carried by a citizens' committee, to be presented to House or Senate, sometimes to the president. Invariably the complaints cited derangement of currency, exchange, and credit, pointed to stagnation of enterprise in business and agriculture, reported steep declines in prices and employment. If the warfare against the BUS would cease, the nation could surely recover the prosperity it had enjoyed before this crisis.

In the Senate Webster presented memorials from Boston, New York City, Albany, and elsewhere. Others from Pennsylvania came to him rather than to its senators, because they opposed the bank. Often he said something complimentary about the industry and patriotism of those living where the petition had originated, and he usually elaborated upon the theme of distress, which demanded relief from the party in power. As time passed, he feared that the House and the president were determined not to give in, so that the only realistic goal would be an appeal for the voters to speak at the next election. Other senators added their views, either in support or rebuttal. Then the memorials were routinely referred to committee for burial.[24]

Argument about a memorial could strain senatorial courtesy. Because signatures totaled in the hundreds, even thousands, suspicion about their authenticity abounded. When Webster announced that twenty-eight hundred people had signed the Albany petition, the *Globe*, prompted by Silas Wright, counted the names at thirteen hundred, fewer than those on Wright's probank memorial from the same place. Rarely would a Jacksonian concede that these protests truly represented public opinion, generated as they were for political effect.[25]

Defenders of the administration's actions thought that complaints of distress were misdirected, that they ought to have been brought against the bank itself for needlessly and harshly curtailing credit, for inducing a recession, and for attempting to coerce the president into reversing his position. This was the usual response to memorials in Congress and at the White House too. When delegations called upon Jackson to present their case, he crisply told them to go to Nicholas Biddle. The expression "Biddle's panic," circulated widely. It is true that the BUS did drastically reduce its loans and exchange operations from the summer of 1833 through the first half of 1834: and it called upon state banks for all balances due. These were essential steps, Biddle said, because the bank had to prepare for the time when the charter would expire. In the Senate Webster answered the bank's critics in the same fashion. Tighter credit and higher rates of exchange, he explained, necessarily followed massive removal of government deposits, together with resulting withdrawal of individual deposits.[26] But privately he feared that Biddle had gone too far, may have been so vindictive as to alienate the business community. His incoming correspondence and visits of protesting committees from Boston and New York made him uneasy, and he let the bank president know he was worried.[27] At first, Biddle seemed relentless—"your Boston friends are a little impatient," he wrote to the senator.[28] After a while, he realized that severe curtailment was counterproductive, since it undermined his own base of support; and he therefore relaxed pressure. In July he had abandoned a strategy which had certainly exceeded what circumstances required.[29]

Although Webster had now joined the Clay-Biddle offensive against Jackson's financial policy, through March he still hoped for constructive compromise. His aim was to assure a commitment to some kind of national bank, whether it was the existing corporation or another which would quiet the constitutional, economic, and political objections so rampant at the moment. Only such an institution, he firmly believed, could relieve the nation from its economic malady by restoring a dependable system of currency and credit. To accomplish his purpose, he had to take into account the fact that opponents of the BUS controlled the House and the probability that he would need a two-thirds vote in Congress to override a presidential veto. As early as January 20, he spoke favorably of a proposal by his friend Stephen White, a member of the Massachusetts legislature, to establish a new bank, taking over the stock of the Bank of the United States with additional subscriptions by the states for fifteen millions. White would make further concessions to the states to allow them to regulate branches within their jurisdiction.[30] Eleven days later Webster announced his intention of introducing a bank bill in the Senate.[31] He delayed doing so, however, for several weeks because of continued debate on removal and because he wanted to see what direction the House would take. As he reflected on a permanent solution to the banking problem, he realized that the only step possible during this session was to extend the bank's charter for a few years. He might get the deposits returned, though that was questionable, and at least buy some time until the next presidential election brought a better opportunity.[32]

At last, on March 18, he had the floor to describe his proposal.[33] He began with a familiar recitation of all the troubles besetting the country—the poor condition of currency and credit, high interest rates, rising unemployment, a predicted loss of public revenue. Congress must do something this session; it must not delay when so many people were suffering. Fundamental to any remedy must be a more intelligent outlook on the subject of banking, on its usefulness to the population as a whole. Too often, politicians whipped up fear and prejudice, an entirely wrong notion of the practices of banks. History showed, he said, that a well-established system of credit developed after the breakdown of feudalism, the coming of capitalism, and the rise of a middle class. In the United States this had occurred during the nation's recent remarkable economic growth. "The history of banks," he observed, "belongs to the history of commerce and the general history of liberty." Both rich and poor benefited from the operation of a bank such as the one now chartered; indeed persons of modest means held substantial amounts of its stock. Parenthetically, he jabbed at the state banks, supposedly more trustworthy; in particular, he cited the New York system. Was it not also powerful and

233

open to the same criticism that its Jacksonian friends were directing against a national bank? Having attempted to counter a general suspicion of banking, he briefly touched upon the constitutional question by reiterating the usual justifications of a bank.[34] Anyway, he urged those who had constitutional reservations to put them aside in existing circumstances out of respect for the judgment of lawmakers and courts over the past forty years.

If opponents would moderate their thinking, he would as well. The bill he wished to present was just an interim measure. Continue the Bank of the United States for six years (to 1842) or less; prohibit note issue in denominations less than twenty dollars; perhaps add more provisos. But he would require the return of government deposits unless Congress itself decided to the contrary. Candor and common sense dictated some relief in this emergency.

Rather than grant Webster leave to report his bill, senators preferred to discuss it immediately. Over the following week many spoke, some at length and nearly all with disapproval. He could expect stalwarts like Wright and Benton to reject his proposal, and so they did with much rhetoric.[35] But a critical question was what the reaction of Clay and other probank men would be—and critical too, the reaction of Calhoun.[36] The South Carolinian veered off on his own course, independent of everyone. Though he had attacked Jackson for executive high-handedness in removing the deposits and had been counted by Biddle as a converted friend of the corporation, he prescribed a remedy intended eventually to kill the patient.[37] He would "unbank the banks," he declared. All these institutions, state and national, had the common fault of pouring out paper notes, whereas gold was the only sound medium of exchange. On this issue he sounded like Benton. To reform the currency, he would extend the BUS charter for twelve, not six, years and require its aid in shifting wholly to gold. Afterward, he hoped to eliminate all banks. Naturally Benton and Wright would not give the bank one extra day beyond its present charter. And Calhoun's antibank argument detached him from Webster and Clay and so neutralized whatever influence he may have had either for or against the bank.[38]

Webster should not have been surprised in failing to get help from his perennial adversary, but he found Clay, who commanded the majority, also aloof. The Kentuckian really did not want any recharter bill passed—the House and the president stood in the way—and he was absorbed with his effort to chastise Jackson for his reprehensible conduct.[39] Undoubtedly another element affecting his attitude was the absence of any pressure from Biddle to support Webster. Though the bank president had commented politely on Webster's plan, he did not lift a finger to push it in Congress.[40]

On March 25 Webster decided to shelve his idea. He explained he did not wish to consume too much time while debate on Clay's resolution on removal pended. That may have been true, but he also saw that Clay had no interest in his compromise.[41]

Three days later, on the twenty-eighth, the speeches on Clay's resolution censuring Jackson reached a climax. Introduced in late December, it had provided the point of departure for venting every thought and feeling about the president's controversial order to remove the deposits. Placing the greatest importance upon its passage, Clay lectured his colleagues on the dangers of excessive executive power at the expense of Congress, on the union of the purse and the sword. Jackson was comparable to Caesar when he demanded that a tribune hand over the key to the treasury, Clay exclaimed. Calhoun freely lent his support to the resolution, for he felt that removal had been another proof of the president's abuse of power, similar to his behavior during the tariff crisis. Webster seemed detached and said nothing as the time for voting approached. Now the question was put: "Resolved, That the President, in the late executive proceedings in relation to the public revenue, has assumed upon himself authority and power not conferred by the Constitution and the laws, but in derogation of both." Approved, twenty-six to twenty, with Webster voting yea.[42]

At this point Webster felt discouraged. Economic conditions were bad and becoming worse. Jackson was winning the Bank War, and nothing the opposition attempted seemed effective. Scold and censure though it did, the majority in the Senate encountered a proadministration House and a determined president. Webster's hope for a compromise collapsed without support from even his own party. And his pessimism about public affairs intensified a restlessness he often experienced after a period of congressional and legal work.

Flight from this dispiriting scene for a visit home ought to lift his mood, permit him to transact some personal business, give him an opportunity to speak to the public, who, in the long run, must return government to its true course. Soon after the vote to censure, he took leave from the Senate for the greater part of April. He spent time trying to rehabilitate his sagging financial condition and overseeing extensive improvements at his farm.[43] On the way back to the capital, he stopped at New York, Philadelphia, and Baltimore, where he addressed large gatherings, numbering in the thousands according to friendly reports, with an emphasis upon the economic distress caused by Jacksonian missteps.

His listeners in these cities appeared to respond more positively than his colleagues in Washington as he outlined what must be done to restore prosperity. At any rate, he returned to his seat with a fresh outlook.[44]

On his first day back in the Senate, April 21, he found that discussion centered on a counteroffensive unleashed by the president. Irritated by the censure resolution, Jackson had just sent up a protest defending his policy and denying the right of this body to invade the executive domain. In requiring the secretary of the treasury to remove deposits, he said, he had correctly exercised his control of a cabinet officer (Duane), whom he could always remove in case of nonconformity. Besides, he continued, the Senate was a constitutional court of impeachment and therefore could not prejudge a presidential act as illegal prior to a regular trial. Benton and others had been saying exactly the same thing, but now the question was whether the Senate would pass a motion not to receive the protest on grounds of impropriety.[45]

During this sustained debate, Webster spoke twice: once on the day he returned and two weeks later, on May 7. His theme was that Jackson had assumed an erroneous, dangerous position concerning the dividing line between executive and legislative powers. Conceding that the president could dismiss the secretary of the treasury, he argued that this fact did not empower him to order removal of deposits, as he had in a paper read to the cabinet in September 1833. It was a tenuous distinction the senator was making: you can dismiss the secretary, but you cannot control his functions. Nevertheless, he believed that the new secretary (Taney), carrying out Jackson's will, had violated the bank charter, a statute of Congress, by removal for unauthorized reasons. As for the right to censure, Webster based it on the Senate's representative character. Being a legislative body, it must protect popular liberty against arbitrary executive acts. In so fulfilling its duty, the Senate had not subverted the impeachment process but only expressed its opinion on an important constitutional matter. History demonstrated, in his view, that the great danger in all governments had been the tendency of executive power toward despotism. In this instance, Jackson had advanced the faulty rationalization that he was the direct representative of all the people. Not true. This chief executive reminded Webster much more of the Stuart kings or, in America, an aspiring elective monarch.[46]

The opposition maintained the same margin of votes it had throughout the session, so that the motion not to receive the protest carried. Benton declared he would continue his effort to repudiate the censure and vowed he would have this blot on the Senate journal expunged, however distant that day of vindication might be.[47]

236

Whereas the protest justified previous antibank measures, the Jacksonians did respond, to some extent, to the cry for a constructive approach to financial problems. What emerged as a main feature of their program was a hard-money policy. Many of them disagreed with supporters of the bank that to be adequate, the currency of this growing nation must consist chiefly of redeemable bank notes. Excessive issues, too frequently manipulated at the expense of the common man, increasingly came under their attack. Why not eventually ban all paper money, starting with small denominations, and move to specie only? This was Benton's thesis. The people, he contended, believed that "money which would jingle in the pocket was the right money for them"—it was the only currency authorized by the Constitution, he reasoned.[48]

Though Webster thought Benton deserved his sobriquet of "gold humbug," he would compromise on the question by eliminating small notes while retaining essential larger ones. He had recorded his ideas on this subject ever since the recharter debate two years earlier. Yet he would not go as far as Benton or indeed Calhoun, who called for elimination of all paper and all banks within an appointed time.[49] So when Democrats in both Houses proposed an act to increase specie by bringing more gold into circulation, Webster cooperated. The outcome was a law to raise the value of gold at the mint, achieved through a change of its ratio to silver from one to fifteen to one to sixteen. Needless to say, he did not share Jacksonian expectations that this was the first step toward a currency consisting entirely of hard money.[50]

Another administration response to the clamor for relief was a plan to supervise the network of state banks holding government deposits. A House bill, incorporating Taney's recommendations, would have empowered the secretary of the treasury to select depository banks according to their financial condition as determined by governmental inspection and to report to Congress on the status of the operation. Despite congressional failure to pass this bill, the Treasury substantially followed these procedures anyhow. An aspect which bothered Webster, apart from the general idea of using state banks, involved the arrangement for inspecting banks. Compensation of the inspector currently came from the banks themselves, he said. But Taney denied that charge. Regardless of these details, the principal fact was that Jackson meant to continue his deposit system.[51]

By late June, near the close of the session, relations between the two sides in the Bank War had become quite inflamed. Seven months of contention had not only sharpened political differences but had also heightened personal hostility. Such was the situation when Jackson finally submitted his long delayed nomination of Taney as secretary of the treasury a few days before adjournment. Knowing the Senate might well vote against that appointment, the president had allowed Taney to continue on an interim basis for nine months. The opinions of the senators were so fixed that they did not even debate the nomination, rejecting it twenty-eight to eighteen and giving no reason for their decision. Afterward Webster revealed his own feelings when he referred to Taney as Jackson's "pliant instrument," a remark inciting the ex-secretary's rejoinder that the senator was the bank's pliant instrument.[52]

If the bank's supporters in the Senate took satisfaction in denying Taney his post, as they had in sniping at the administration throughout the removal controversy, they had little reason to suppose that the corporation would ever regain its previous status. Old Hickory would fulfill his intention to kill the Monster of Chestnut Street and to entrust deposits to the "pets." About the only thing Webster and the others could do, beyond waiting until Jackson left the White House, was to carry their case to the public. Someday, a new approach might succeed.

They felt a need to set the record right, to exculpate the BUS, to verify their own arguments. On the last day of the session, June 30, 1834, they authorized Webster's committee during the summer and fall to investigate bank operations and to report when they reassembled in December. A motion instructed the committee to inquire whether the bank had violated its charter, whether public funds deposited there had been safe, and how the institution had managed its credit and exchange functions. Such thorny items as unnecessary curtailment of loans, the corporation's service to the Treasury on debts and claims, and allegations of its involvement in politics would have to be explored. The members of the committee, with Webster as chairman and including Willie Mangum, Thomas Ewing, and John Tyler, were thoroughgoing opponents of the administration; the body became still more homogeneous when a fifth member and the lone Jacksonian, William Wilkins, refused to serve.[53]

Webster's role was slight. Early on, he wrote out the heads of committee inquiry, then a letter to Biddle requesting cooperation, and, in fact, Biddle's response promising to do so.[54] Except for occasional consultation with a committee member and brief talks with the cashier of the Boston branch, he left the work to the others, chiefly Tyler, who wrote the report and read it to the Senate on December 18. Just before the document was presented, Webster assured Biddle that everything was going to turn out all right. The bank president already felt easy, knowing that the committee had accepted the information and advice he had provided.[55]

The report presented the BUS almost without blemish. Each criticism of its operations was unfounded, Tyler concluded: financial management had been sound; loans had been curtailed only as removal of deposits required; relations with editors and congressmen were proper. Only one hint of disapproval was discernible. The bank ought not have spent funds to circulate materials for political purposes.[56] In general, the report may have been a comforting exercise in justification, may have indeed had a good bit of truth in it, but it was largely an epilogue in the story of the Bank War. Other issues would assume importance in the year ahead.

Chapter 15

JACKSON'S VINDICATION

From the climax of the Bank War in 1834 until the election of 1840, the Democrats remained ascendant. Holding on to the presidency and generally controlling Congress, they could search for a fiscal system free from a monopolistic central bank and compatible with Jacksonian ideals of equal rights and limited involvement of the national government in the economy. But they found this to be no easy task. Reliance upon state-chartered banks created endless problems; and disengagement from all banks, though increasingly appealing, was both questionable and difficult. Meanwhile they encountered one political hazard after another. A rising antislavery movement threatened Democratic unity. And the opposition, now building a formidable Whig party, could win any election if conditions worsened. By the late 1830s, as the nation slid into a depression, that prospect seemed likely.

Added to these concerns was one relating to foreign affairs. Indeed, during the congressional session beginning in December 1834, a diplomatic crisis worried Jackson more than anything else. In his annual message the president reported a breakdown in lengthy negotiations with France for payment of American claims against that country's spoliations to commerce in the Napoleonic period. Three years had passed since France had agreed to a settlement, but the Chamber of Deputies had refused to appropriate the money. After patiently waiting for it to act and receiving ineffectual assurances by King Louis Philippe that it would, Jackson felt that the time for firmness had come. He requested congressional authorization to seize French property to the amount of the claims, if required to uphold American honor; and that, of course, could lead to a serious situation.[1]

240

Webster and most other Whigs opposed such an extreme measure. Concurring with recommendations from Clay's Foreign Affairs Committee against reprisals, yet recognizing that United States grievances were substantial, the Massachusetts senator preferred to avoid precipitate action. Both chambers passed his resolution that it was "inexpedient at present to adopt any legislative measure" concerning the negotiations.[2] Nevertheless, would it not be prudent to strengthen defenses in case the dispute led to war? A majority of the House thought so. That body voted to amend the annual fortifications bill by providing three millions, to be spent at the president's discretion, for military readiness. Quite unnecessary, in fact dangerous, said Webster, for Jackson had not asked for anything of the kind; and if he had, giving him such broad discretionary power would violate the constitutional requirement that appropriations be specific. In this view he reflected the dominant sentiment of the Senate. Then on the eve of adjournment, March 3, 1835, a conference committee came up with a compromise, which Webster as a member had proposed. The amount for defense would be reduced to eight hundred thousand, and there would be much less executive latitude. This version died when the House learned that the president would not sign any more last-minute bills.[3]

By early 1836 the danger of armed conflict had disappeared, following renewed diplomacy and the long-anticipated French appropriation.[4] Whatever bellicose spirit remained took the form of political recriminations inside Congress. To justify his position on the fortifications bill in answer to a number of critical speeches, Webster reviewed the whole story on January 14. Contrary to what administration men were saying, he declared, the blame for failure to pass a defense bill lay with the House not the Senate, with Democrats not Whigs, with others not himself, and mainly with the president, who had never sent Congress a specific request and had angrily closed off the midnight effort to do something. He reiterated his opposition to delegating undefined powers to the executive, for this amounted to "fantastical man worship." The Constitution must be preserved: "If the proposition were now before us, and the guns of the enemy were battering against the walls of the Capitol, I would not agree to it."[5] Over in the House, Adams, an advocate of legislative collaboration with Jackson during the crisis, was shocked by that statement. In a three-hour rejoinder he also reviewed events of the preceding session and concluded that the conduct of senators such as Webster had been deplorable. The next step after allowing the enemy to move guns against the Capitol, Adams sarcastically remarked, would be helping to do it. Hard feeling between Adams and Webster would not subside for a long while, and meantime there was a sizable effect upon Massachusetts politics.[6]

Except for the Franco-American controversy, the principal topics of congressional business were domestic; and of these, several were financial. Democrats and even most Whigs felt that rechartering the Bank of the United States was highly improbable in the foreseeable future, but there were loose ends left by the recent struggle. Benton believed that one of them was the resolution of March 1834 censuring Jackson for removing the government's deposits, a slur upon the Old Hero's reputation and a misuse of senatorial power. He tirelessly sought to remove every trace of the resolution by pressing the Senate to expunge it from the journal. In the sessions of 1835 and 1836 he failed by decisive margins.[7] The standard argument against expunging, strained though it was, emphasized the Senate's obligation to keep a record of its proceedings. After beating down an attempt by the Missourian, Webster said, "The record remains, neither blurred, blotted, nor disgraced."[8]

Though Webster saw no way, at the moment, to recharter the national bank, he missed no opportunity to attack the depository banks. The truth would eventually prevail, he hoped, if the public understood the unsound practices and corrupt tendencies of the "pets." As chairman of the Finance Committee, he carefully read reports by the Treasury Department on the deposits, frequently requested more information, and introduced bills to regulate the system. The banks were pouring forth their notes and otherwise expanding their obligations at an alarming rate, he complained. Now that the treasury's surplus was mounting, the impetus to a flood of paper had become stronger. It was imperative, he concluded (and Secretary Levi Woodbury did too), that notes of depository banks, at least those handled by the government, be redeemable in gold or silver. He wished to guard the deposits against those unsound banking operations, but he thought that difficulties would inevitably persist as long as the "experiment" continued.[9]

Inherent in the system, too, he reasoned, was its connection with the fortunes of the administration party. Selection of the banks that would receive deposits seemed to be more a political than a fiscal decision. Still worse, he found regulation of these institutions lax and partisan. An example he liked to give involved Reuben Whitney, an acknowledged agent of the banks, paid by them but used by the Treasury Department in overseeing his clients. Though Taney and Woodbury vehemently denied that Whitney had any supervisory role, they did not convince Webster. He could see an insidious growth of a Democratic network.[10]

A variety of proposals addressed the condition of public finance in the mid-thirties—to dispose of a growing treasury surplus, to monitor the banks, to regulate the currency. Ideas differed as much as the constitutional and economic persuasions of leading figures at the capital. As for the surplus, Benton wished to eliminate it, while stimulating western settlement, by reducing, or "graduating" downward, prices of government land. Clay and Webster preferred to maintain prices but to "distribute" the proceeds to the states, which could use them for internal improvements. Van Buren and Jackson disliked Clay's purposes, first because they were nationalizing and second because they involved high tariff rates to raise revenue lost by distribution. If they had to go along with distribution, they would give states the surplus coming from all sources, such as the tariff, not merely that from land sales. Calhoun typically stood apart from the others. Abandoning opposition to distribution, he would now accept it but called for a constitutional amendment.[11] As for depository banks, everyone recognized the desirability of changing their relationship to the government but had disparate views on how to assure the safety and proper status of the deposits. Concerning currency, opinion ranged from a hard-money group to those favoring wholly redeemable bank notes and to many others with a permissive attitude toward paper money.

Webster introduced a bill on May 31, 1836, dealing with two of these issues: regulation of depository banks and distribution of the surplus. To reform the deposit system, he proposed minimal reserve requirements, payment of interest on treasury funds, and detailed reporting of operations. Turning to the problem of surplus, he explained the causes—mistakes in setting tariff rates, dramatic expansion of cotton production, a boom in western land sales, a flurry of state internal-improvement projects, an immense influx of foreign capital. To make available the money needed by business but locked up in the form of mushrooming federal deposits and to deprive the administration of vast funds for patronage and other political ends (though he did not now elaborate that point), he proposed four installments of "deposits" with the states during 1837.[12] The Senate then referred the bill with numerous amendments to a select committee, chaired by Silas Wright and including Webster.[13]

Out of this committee came a measure enacted with Jackson's reluctant approval on June 23, 1836, and resembling what Webster had put forward. It required depository banks to make systematic reports, redeem treasury drafts in specie upon demand, pay interest on government funds, and comply with new rules on note issue. Better known were the sections of the statute distributing the surplus above five millions to the states in quarterly installments the following year. Characterized as deposits, they were really permanent loans which nobody expected to be repaid; although the secretary of the treasury could demand repayment, this never happened.[14]

Meanwhile Benton maintained his hard-money campaign. In his judgment, overissued bank notes and overextended credit posed great danger; and the current land boom, accelerated by a multitude of unsound practices and arrangements, exacerbated the problem. He therefore offered a resolution limiting payment for public lands to specie. This move could open the way to a policy of total reliance on gold and silver, he believed. What a "visionary" idea, charged Webster. He predicted that specie would be transported at high cost back and forth between western land offices and eastern banks with more negative than positive results. Thwarted in the Senate, Old Bullion found another way. After adjournment, he convinced Jackson that the proposal could be implemented by executive order; as a matter of fact, he would be happy to draft one. In July the president, liking this advice, issued his "Specie Circular" with much the same contents as Benton's defeated resolution. The impact would be significant.[15]

Although the Senate spent more time on financial questions than on any other, slavery was becoming a more important subject in each session. An abolitionist movement, rooted deeply in the moral convictions of reformers, forced the issue before the public. It grew by way of local, regional, and national societies, editors and pamphleteers, and some clergymen, but very few politicians. In Congress, southerners uniformly found abolitionist agitation a radical peril to their section, and northerners found it an embarrassing fact which they had to recognize.

One antislavery tactic was to force congressional attention through petitions. From 1832 onward, Webster's mail brought increasing numbers of memorials and requests that he present them to the Senate. Many consisted of printed forms (supplied by antislavery societies), with names of places and petitioners written in. They urged prohibition of slavery and the slave trade in the District of Columbia and of traffic in slaves across state lines, though acknowledging that Congress could not constitutionally act against this great evil in the states in which it already existed. A steady stream came from Massachusetts, one of the earliest from William Lloyd Garrison's New England Antislavery Society; yet some came from as far west as Michigan. Conscientiously he did present them, insisted upon the right of petition, and said that Congress had power to legislate on slavery in the District and on the interstate trade, notwithstanding the dubious expediency of doing so.[16] In March 1836 and again in February 1837, the Senate excitedly debated the whole matter of abolitionist petitions, to which southerners objected because they could incite a slave rebellion. Alfred Cuthbert of Georgia vigorously reproved Webster for bringing in these materials, then said he was not surprised in light of the New Englander's well-known memorial on Missouri in 1819, taking the same ground as the present agitators. Cuthbert was substantially correct, but Webster retorted that he could not remember what he had written so long ago and that, in any event, he now defended the right of petition. The outcome was that the Senate established a precedent for future procedure by voting to table the question of receiving such petitions.[17] It was a sophistic, ultracautious solution, effectively stopping both reception of petitions and their reference to committee. Webster's minority position was similar to that assumed by Adams in a celebrated eight-year crusade against the House gag rule.

Meanwhile a revived opposition was gaining confidence that it could defeat the Democratic nominee, Van Buren, in the next election. After losing twice in contests against Jackson in 1828 and 1832, the party of Adams, Clay, and Webster meant to capitalize upon what it believed to be serious Democratic abuses. Its theme became limitation of executive power. Presidential authority, it charged, had grown at the expense of liberty and representative government by improper veto of legislation, dictatorial control of the financial system, and introduction of the spoils principle. Lately, the most notorious examples of this trend were the disastrous removal of deposits from the national bank and a bellicose approach to the French crisis. To popularize their message, opponents of the administration called themselves Whigs. Just when the new name first appeared is uncertain, but in several places politicians and editors were using it in the early thirties; and in spring 1834 Clay and Webster adopted it in Senate speeches. The parallel, they thought, between King Andrew and earlier British monarchs, both claiming absolute power, was obvious. If those resisting that claim were Whigs, then Jacksonians were Tories. Whigs were largely National Republicans renamed. Yet they also recruited those disaffected for one reason or another—some disappointed office seekers, some BUS Democrats, some states' righters during nullification days, such as John Tyler.[18] Whether Calhoun himself would enlist remained unclear; still, he inclined to collaborate with the Whigs against a common enemy.[19] This negative dimension of the party, its cohesiveness dependent upon a personal target or upon mere electoral success, diluted its ideological purity.

The Antimasons could become a significant element in the Whig coalition. Since the late twenties they had waged a zealous campaign to destroy the institution of Freemasonry because of its secrecy ensured by oaths, its alleged unrepublican, repressive character. In the election of 1832 they had tried for the presidency by nominating William Wirt and still had substantial strength in the Northeast and the Ohio Valley. In Vermont they were dominant. In western New York they continued to thrive, with leadership by the able political practitioners Thurlow Weed, William Seward, and Francis Granger. In Pennsylvania also they were active, holding the balance of power between Whigs and Democrats and including influential figures such as Thad Stevens and Joseph Ritner, the governor for a time. From the beginning, however, many Antimasons leaned toward an alliance, if not a merger, with the National Republicans and Whigs.[20] As the election of 1836 approached, Webster hoped they would abandon their status as an independent party, support Whig candidates, and definitely stay away from the Democrats. To fulfill that hope, it would be necessary to treat them generously.

Understandably, Webster was more interested in the political scene in Massachusetts than in any other state. Here the Whigs inherited the controlling position which Federalists and National Republicans had long occupied. They had to reckon, however, with a competitive Democratic party, marshaled by the enterprising boss David Henshaw. In the mid-1830s young George Bancroft, pushing Henshaw aside as the premier Jacksonian, became a formidable adversary.

At the moment, Antimasons aspired to be the pivotal factor in the state's elections. And it looked very much as if they would when they turned to Adams as their candidate for governor in 1833. Ever an independent spirit, Adams combined a newfound commitment to Antimasonry with his basic National Republican–Whig viewpoint. Though failing to get the National Republican nomination too—he believed Webster had promised it—he showed his popularity by gaining the second highest vote, eighteen thousand, compared with twenty-five thousand for National Republican John Davis and fifteen thousand for Democrat Marcus Morton. Because no one had a majority, the election had to be decided by the legislature, whereupon Adams, offended by the conduct of the Webster group, withdrew from the contest to allow Davis to take the office.[21] Two years later, in 1835, there was a similar scenario concerning a seat in the Senate. The ex-president came very close to winning it, but Davis, with Webster's backing, again prevailed.[22] Given these circumstances, it is little wonder that Adams and Webster magnified their dispute over the French crisis into a personal matter.

Pragmatically, Webster was willing to make concessions to the Antimasons. He concurred with fellow Whigs in Massachusetts on the policy forbidding extrajudicial oaths (that is, Masonic oaths) and urging lodges to surrender their charters voluntarily. What he would not approve was a statutory prohibition of the organization altogether. Nor would he bar Masons from public office. Believing a separate Antimasonic party to be entirely unjustified, he depended upon conciliatory general statements and moderate specific commitments, perhaps some appointments of Antimasons, to persuade them to endorse Whig candidates. At first the strategy seemed to succeed—they solidly supported his reelection to the Senate in 1833. But a number of his friends, including Levi Lincoln and John Davis, were less friendly to the movement; in fact a good many Whigs were Masons. So by 1835 Antimasons in this state were listening to the advice of Benjamin Hallett, editor of the *Advocate,* to join the Democrats.[23] If they did, the Whigs could probably still carry Massachusetts; yet the effects elsewhere might be harmful.

Throughout the country, anti-Jacksonian interest in finding the best route to victory in 1836 developed without delay. As soon as Clay lost his presidential bid in 1832, his admirers could not help but speculate about his chances next time. His defeat had been so decisive, however, and his liabilities derived from past conflicts so numerous that he had no taste for an active effort. If the party should agree that his candidacy was essential, he would answer its call; but Whig leaders, Webster included, thought it was not essential.[24] An early bird was Justice John McLean of the Supreme Court, who would spend the better part of his life dreaming of the presidency. An Ohioan with political convictions very difficult to classify, McLean would eventually be known as an antislavery, conservative nationalist, though his flirtations had extended to Calhoun, Jackson, and Antimasons. Now Webster protested that McLean would be the poorest choice imaginable, and he expressed that opinion through 1833 and 1834, when the judge's name circulated widely. He would rather have Van Buren, he declared.[25] Then a more attractive option appeared: put forward Hugh White, Tennessee senator and disenchanted Jacksonian Democrat. White appealed to southerners, for a while to Calhounite Duff Green of the *Telegraph,* and to opportunists wishing to split the Democratic vote. That he was the same kind of Whig as Clay and Webster was doubtful, but he could be more than a thorn in Van Buren's side. He could detach enough electoral votes to throw the election into the House.[26]

Webster needed no reminder that, everything considered, he might be the best Whig candidate. Did he not have a superior claim because of public service as well as personal attainments? Had he not been in the forefront in defending the Union and expounding the Constitution against nullifiers and bank radicals alike? One of the first indications of a Webster movement was the establishment of a newspaper, the Washington *Examiner,* on the Fourth of July, 1833. The editor, largely acting on his own initiative, at once extolled Webster's qualifications.[27] In conversations and correspondence the senator nourished the idea, but guardedly, as if to test the water.[28] His trip to the West that summer also provided a reading of sentiment, mainly encouraging, on his standing as a national statesman. In April 1834, in a respite from the deposit-removal debates, he spoke in eastern cities with an eye to public opinion. He gave special attention to New York City, where local elections were under way and where merchants and bankers could provide the backing he would need.[29] In October he went to Concord, New Hampshire, to help honor Senator Samuel Bell and incidentally to help his own plans. Here he gave a major speech, dealing with all the topics of the day, banking, public lands, tariff, and the patronage.[30] If his audience had read their current number of the *New England Magazine,* they would have been informed about his character and career in an article by Justice Story, "Statemen—Their Rareness and Importance."[31]

When 1835 arrived, Webster in Washington and his advisers in Boston felt the time had come for formal action. The legislature was in session, so that Whig members could nominate him, the procedure then generally used. His letters to people back home revealed with increasing clarity his wish that this be done. On New Year's Day he wrote to Mason, saying that the legislature should move ahead speedily, but that he would be passive and "satisfied with any result."[32] Within a week he was thinking of the best language for the nominating resolutions. His impatience mounted as the business proceeded slowly, for Massachusetts ought to influence other states. In Ohio especially, a critical stage had come because there were signs that William Henry Harrison might replace the faltering McLean as nominee. In frequent reports from Boston, Webster learned that a cautious segment of the party worried that he might be less popular than Clay, who had not explicitly withdrawn, or than other possible candidates.[33] Finally, on January 21, the caucus did nominate him. Pleased with the outcome, he felt optimistic that a ripple effect would occur in several states, though he understood the difficulty of predicting the course of events in a long preelection period.[34]

The men seeking to expand the Webster movement were in Massachusetts, where it originated. Of these, Edward Everett stood out as most important. A lifelong, intimate friend, cultivated and tactful, always willing to take on a task, whether drafting a paper or corresponding with politicians across the land, Everett also played a leading role on his own. Having tired of a decade's service in Congress, he searched for something different to do. An opportunity appeared at the very time of Webster's nomination. It involved a reshuffle of officeholders: Governor

Davis would move into a vacant Senate seat, despite Adams' competition for it; and Everett would replace Davis in the fall election. This arrangement suited Webster very well—indeed his agreement made it possible—for Everett had a following among Antimasons, who might also vote Whig in the presidential election.[35] Another mainstay was Caleb Cushing, currently beginning a congressional career and loyally advancing Webster's interests, public and private. He cheerfully took care of details and saw that pro-Webster information got into print.[36] Rufus Choate and Robert Winthrop, also young lawyer-politicians, attached themselves to Webster's cause and would be valued associates for years to come.[37] Friends Mason and Story, businessmen Abbott Lawrence and Nathan Appleton, politicians Lincoln and Davis, all viewed the senator's success as vital.

Essential to attaining the goal was a favorable press. In Boston, the *Advertiser* supplied that need to an extent. Always portraying Webster as a faultless statesman, editor Nathan Hale predictably supported his nomination. Months beforehand, Hale laid the foundation with numerous items in his columns, then worked with Whig legislators in January to obtain the appropriate resolutions.[38] Yet the newspaper's bland, stuffy character and its skimpy coverage of politics did not deliver the desired impact.[39] So with the help of Everett, Choate, and Cushing, Webster turned to another organ, the Boston *Atlas*. First they had to bring in a new editor, young John Sargent, to replace Richard Hildreth, who had been a bit too independent, particularly on the matter of uniting with Antimasons. Next they had to raise money needed for the transformation, and they regularly had to provide the new management with materials and ideas for effective political coverage.[40] As he did for other papers, Webster himself wrote some editorials, as clear and lively as one would find in the press of that day. Readers knew that on all questions relating to the senator, the *Atlas* spoke with authority.[41]

Among New York papers, James Watson Webb's *Courier and Enquirer* became Webster's most enthusiastic advocate. Previously a Jacksonian Democrat, the proud, strong-willed editor became an arch-Whig—his paper was one of the first to use the name. Typically, Webb's politics became entangled with his personal finances, as when he asked Webster's assistance in floating a loan of fifty thousand at Boston. Mingled in this correspondence were the editor's assurances on the presidential contest—he had resisted earlier approaches by McLean men, he added. Somehow, though probably with less help from Webster than he hoped, Webb kept his press running and called upon the Northeast to vote for the New Englander.[42]

Other important papers adopted the same position: Whigs should support different candidates in each section of the country, Webster in the Northeast, White in the South, someone else in the West. However well-disposed the Washington *National Intelligencer* was toward Webster, it concurred in advising such strategy, and so did the Philadelphia *National Gazette.* This approach did not exactly confirm Webster's claim that he was a man for the whole nation. Rather, it rested on the assumption the only way to defeat Van Buren was to make different appeals to different sections, get enough scattered votes to throw the election into the House, and then hope for the best.[43]

In any event Webster knew that 1835 would be the critical year. Since a national Whig convention seemed unlikely, he must have nominations from individual states, at least in his section but preferably in others as well. Custom and circumstances would not permit extensive canvassing by a candidate himself; in such a decentralized setting, he could at best make only a few appearances and must be mindful of proprieties. Beyond that, he had to depend upon a network of friends, encouraged and guided by the written or printed word. Altogether, it was largely a matter of passive waiting, not of active campaigning.

An opportunity for action arose in Pennsylvania. When Congress adjourned in March, he stopped there for several days on his way home. Concerned about both the three-party situation, arising from Antimason strength, and the uncertain shape of opinion in that state, he sought to solidify support by dinner speeches in York, Lancaster, and Philadelphia.[44] The best opening proved to be a chance to address the legislators at Harrisburg. Afterward he felt dissatisfied with the indecision prevailing in Pennsylvania. It must speak out, he told Biddle, because its example could have national significance. Furthermore, if Whigs did not resist the lure of men such as White, who was really not one of them, they would surely lose to Van Buren, now rapidly moving ahead. Why did not Pennsylvania second the known sentiment of Massachusetts? Such a move would be bound to influence other states.[45]

Though he made few speeches, there were other vehicles for electioneering. Off the press came a second volume and a new edition of the first of his speeches and forensic arguments. Everett kept busy sending letters to supporters and prospective supporters. And Cushing brought out a well-written sketch of Webster's career in the *National Intelligencer.* This piece described his humble origins in New Hampshire, his rise to fame in law and politics, his eminent fitness for the presidency. It also emphasized the falsity of recurrent assertions about Webster's obstructionism during the War of 1812 and his involvement in the Hartford Convention.[46]

This biographical article might promote Webster's nomination in

Pennsylvania, where Antimasons and Whigs would soon hold conventions. Scheduled for mid-December 1835, they could materially advance or demolish his prospects generally, for a number of still-undeclared states were watching closely. The convention of Antimasons was more important because they were stronger than the Whigs, who inclined to fall in step with them. But Webster's main competitor there, William Henry Harrison, now threatened to win a joint Antimason-Whig endorsement. In Ohio and elsewhere, McLean had collapsed; Clay no longer seemed a possibility; and as a favorite of the West, Harrison looked like a new model of the military hero in politics. Perhaps the general's modest victories in the War of 1812 and his public service, ranging from governorship of the Indiana Territory, periods in Congress, and the American ministry to Colombia, to his current clerkship in a county court at Cincinnati, did not match Jackson's exciting record. Nevertheless, the new governor, Joseph Ritner, and many other Pennsylvania Antimasons were definitely interested in him as a probable vote getter in the presidential election, much as Thurlow Weed and William Seward were in New York.[47]

For a while it appeared that Webster could turn back the accelerating Harrison movement. Antimasons in Pittsburgh announced a county nomination of Webster. In the East, Thad Stevens, a powerful party figure, preferred him to Harrison. And the rival Ritner group received strenuous pleas in letters from Everett.[48] Finally, Webster sensed the degree of danger posed by Harrison. Though he had earlier visualized Old Tippecanoe as merely an ornamental vice-presidential choice, by November he understood the challenge to be serious.[49] First, he had to dispel the ideas that he himself lacked popular appeal and that despite his brilliance in law and government he remained an aristocratic Federalist. Second, he had to convince Antimasons that his views on questions vital to them were sound.

The second task proved easier than the first. He corresponded with Harmar Denny of Pittsburgh and other Antimasons to establish his acceptibility at the forthcoming state convention. With the help of a draft by Everett, on November 20 he sent off carefully phrased statements disapproving secret societies and oaths as incompatible with popular institutions. When requested to revise his letters for a clearer, more comprehensive answer to questions put to him, he did so within a few days. He deleted the words "as I understand them" after referring to Antimasonic principles, said he thought it a constitutional right of voters to use the ballot to combat Masonry, but balked at an outright pledge as president to appoint only Antimasons to office. He would naturally keep in mind

251

the principles of those who had supported him, he said vaguely.[50] Harrison also had to try twice to answer the same questions satisfactorily and said about the same things Webster did.[51] With two candidates having reached a standoff on the Masonic issue, it would have very little bearing on what the state convention would do.

The chief issue therefore was whether Webster or Harrison would attract more voters. Americans had developed a political culture in which the test of availability often decided whom they would select as their leaders. Popularity and freedom from liabilities could count more heavily than experience or intelligence. At the Antimason convention in Harrisburg, beginning December 14, 1835, that axiom seemed operative. Throughout the sessions, the Ritner groups, feeling that Webster's image forbade his election, defeated Denny, Stevens, and a small faction supporting the Massachusetts senator. Old charges about his war record twenty years previously and a perception of his outlook as elitist, whether true or not, were simply too burdensome, at least compared to the attributes of this popular, relatively uncommitted western soldier. Denny and Stevens desperately attempted to postpone a decision by urging delegates not to nominate anyone but to call for a later national convention. They failed by ninety-eight to thirty-six votes. On the question of a nominee, the division favored Harrison ninety-eight to twenty-nine. Enraged, as he could easily be, Stevens walked out in protest; and a few on his side followed.[52]

Deeply disappointed, hardly able to believe that opponents of Jackson would imitate Democrats by choosing another military chieftain, Webster realized that the odds against success were now high. Still, his wounded pride and obligations to his constituency did not allow him to withdraw. What of the other state nominations due soon? If some went to him, just possibly he might finally draw enough Whig and Antimasonic votes from the Northeast to send the election into the House.[53]

During the winter that hope faded. A nomination in New York could have more than offset his failure in Pennsylvania, and there had been reasons to expect it. He had devoted friends in the City, especially on Wall Street; he had spoken there frequently; and he was very familiar with the state's political scene. Early in December, before the Pennsylvania convention, a large meeting in Manhattan enthusiastically resolved that Webster had every qualification for the presidency. With the rise of Harrison, however, New York moved toward the Ohioan, in large part because Seward and Weed quickly recognized his potential for victory in the coming election. This gain was all Harrison needed to get the state's nomination.[54] Another setback to Webster occurred in Maryland, where he had anticipated help. Though his connections with prominent Whigs were very good and though people across the state admired his talents and achievements, a Maryland convention declared for Harrison on December 23, only a week after the Pennsylvania decision.[55] Here, as in a number of other places, the ripples from Harrisburg had an effect. In western states, such as Indiana and of course Ohio, in New Jersey, even in Vermont and Maine, supposedly Webster territory, the trend continued. Everywhere there was praise of Webster's contributions but preference for Harrison as candidate.[56] The only state safe for Webster was Massachusetts, and this despite an Antimason shift to Van Buren.

Early in 1836 he knew his effort had failed. He not only recognized the hopelessness of the cause but translated that fact into gloomy predictions of a "complete dismemberment of the Whig party." He told Everett that "there seems little now left for us, but to hold on upon Massachusetts. We must retreat into that Citadel and defend it." Both the Senate and the Supreme Court were also succumbing to Democratic control, he added.[57] As for himself, he was ready to withdraw his candidacy. On February 27 he wrote Henry Kinsman, his law partner and member of the legislature, that his "personal wishes" were to withdraw but that he would comply with whatever the party in Massachusetts decided to do. Nothing ought to be done harmful to the Whig interest in the state. This letter or its substance could be made public, he directed.[58] But Kinsman did not make it public for some time, and a Whig caucus of March 10 reaffirmed his nomination.[59] When Kinsman did give the letter to another meeting of legislators and town delegates on the twenty-fourth, they also adhered to the original declaration of the preceding year.[60] The state stood behind the senator, with support by the congressional delegation (except Adams) and by a later convention in September.[61]

Victory in the fall went to Van Buren, who won with 170 electoral votes over opponents with 124; the margin of popular votes, however, was less than a percentage point. Webster won only Massachusetts, 42,247 to Van Buren's 35,474.[62] Though he did not persuade the state's electors, he told them they were free to cast their votes for another candidate, meaning Harrison. This number would not have been enough to elect the general, who nevertheless had made an excellent showing and had emerged as a likely candidate next time.[63]

Right then, that possibility seemed somewhat distant, for the Democrats were still in power; indeed the last congressional session of Jackson's presidency was just beginning. It dealt primarily with continuing questions of public finance. Now that the administration controlled the

Senate, Benton could take the lead on this subject; and he knew which aspect was the most urgent. The censure of the president for removing the deposits must be not only repudiated, but also expunged from the record. At the start of this session in December 1836, Benton announced his intention to introduce his familiar resolution to achieve that end. Impatiently he watched the days pass before he could get the item up for debate and vote, not until the middle of January. The speeches began on the thirteenth and fourteenth; and on Saturday evening, the fourteenth, he brought his Democratic colleagues together for a caucus to agree upon strategy. Next Monday they would press the resolution through without further delay and then order the secretary of the Senate to expunge the words of censure from the journal that very day.[64]

Everything went according to plan. Speeches by the majority demanded vindication of the Old Hero, whose wisdom and courage had upheld the rights of his fellow citizens by defeating the bank. In his final months of office he deserved this elementary act of justice. On the other side the argument centered on the constitutional requirement that the Senate keep a journal, which expunging would violate. For that reason, at least one member who had voted against censure three years earlier opposed expunging. But Benton's forces blocked any effort to adjourn and postpone, insisting upon staying in session through the evening. Contemporary witnesses draw a dramatic picture of the solons exchanging verbal volleys under the great chandelier before a crowded gallery. At last, seeing that the deed would be done, Calhoun and Clay spoke in bitter mood.[65] And then Webster closed. "We collect ourselves to look on, in silence," he solemnly observed, "while a scene is exhibited which, if we did not regard it as a ruthless violation of a sacred instrument, would appear to us to be little elevated above the character of a contemptible farce."[66] The resolution passed, twenty-four to nineteen.

The secretary bent over the manuscript journal, open to the page for March 28, 1834, drew black lines around the words of censure, and wrote across them, "Expunged by order of the Senate, this 16th day of January, 1837." Commotion broke out among the spectators. Benton, feeling menaced by an especially noisy group, demanded that the sergeant at arms seize them and bring them to the bar. "Here is one just above me, that may easily be identified—the bank ruffians!" The person he pointed out was brought forward but released after a parliamentary mix-up, neither quizzed nor disciplined.

During these final weeks of Jackson's term Webster considered resignation. From time to time he had felt that it was a sacrifice for him to serve as senator at the expense of his legal practice and private affairs; in fact many of his friends agreed; and this view had induced some of them to make various financial arrangements, mostly easy credit, to persuade him to advance a cause in which they believed. Undoubtedly, disappointment with the outcome of the recent election gave him another strong reason to be casting about for alternatives. But as he turned the question over in his mind, he had to confess that he liked a life in politics more than in law, often a rather dull occupation. Despite the present setback, he still had a taste for the presidency, and it would not go away easily. He must think of those who had supported him and who would do so again. He should not alienate them by an impulsive act, for he was under an obligation to them, which he translated into an obligation to the people of his state, that is, the general interest. Perhaps there was a middle way. His term would expire in 1839, two years hence, so that he might be able to resign with a commitment to return to his seat then. Meanwhile he could carry out his plan to travel to the West again, probably also to Europe (now an attractive thought), and could rehabilitate his personal finances.[67]

Through January and February 1837 he had a lively correspondence about what he should do. To Mason, Winthrop, Kinsman, and Paige at home and to Hiram Ketchum in New York he wrote about the options and gradually settled upon a course. All of them pleaded with him not to resign, not to ignore his large public responsibilities. Whig legislators in Boston concurred with this argument in resolutions, which Winthrop sent on to him. So he agreed to postpone a decision at least until fall, when voters of the state would elect a new legislature. By inaugural day, March 4, the word went out that he would not resign, at least for the time being.[68]

During this period of indecision he maintained his pursuit of the presidency. At his request, his friends in New York arranged for him to give a major speech in the City after adjournment. One of the persons he had been consulting about his future was Hiram Ketchum, a Wall Street lawyer who had become a dedicated promoter of his candidacy. To Ketchum's original suggestion that he deliver a kind of farewell address in the Senate, he replied that, considering the immense importance of New York in national politics, he preferred to speak there.[69] So Ketchum, Chancellor Kent, David Ogden, merchant Philip Hone, and other Whigs invited him to appear before a gathering on March 15. Meanwhile Webster had decided not to resign, so that the meeting became an occasion to honor him for his services and to assist him to assume a larger role.[70]

New Yorkers gave him an enthusiastic reception. On the afternoon of

March fifteenth a committee escorted him across the bay from Perth Amboy on a steamboat with flying streamers to a pier where a procession had formed to move up Broadway to his hotel. Along the way as he stood in his barouche, he waved to people lining the street and watching from windows. All in all, it seemed like a hero's triumph rather than the visit of a recently defeated candidate of the minority party. In the evening he went to Niblo's Saloon on Prince Street to speak to several thousands who had squeezed into that popular theater to hear the famous senator.[71]

If one were to select a single speech as his most effective statement criticizing Jackson's record and laying down Whig principles, it would be this one. For more than two hours he reviewed the political battles of the preceding eight years. His audience, living in a busy port city linked to the West by internal waterways, cheered as he took issue with Democrats on the need for national development of transportation, particularly on rivers and in harbors. Commercial prosperity and the unity of the country depended upon it, he insisted. Then he connected land policy to these internal improvements. Ceding the public domain to certain states, as the Jacksonians recommended, would be unfair to other states (such as New York), for lands sold at reasonable prices to western settlers could yield funds for internal improvements that would benefit everyone. This revenue should be equitably distributed among all states. Similarly, on the tariff he set forth the rationale of protectionism in broad terms, vital to the interests of all sections and classes, including mechanics and unskilled workers. A tariff must protect America against the pauper labor of Europe. Shifting to the slavery question, he spiritedly attacked expansionists now crying for the annexation of Texas. He objected on both moral and constitutional grounds to taking more slave states into the Union. As usual, he conceded that Congress could not abolish slavery in the states in which it already existed.[72]

Of all topics, he had the most to say about public finance. His detailed argument amounted to a recent financial history of the United States according to Daniel Webster. Upon assuming office in March 1829, Jackson revealed no hostility toward the national bank. But within a few months he had dragged the institution into politics, because he was annoyed with the selection of branch officials, such as Mason at Portsmouth, who were not good Democrats. Antipathy led to the veto of recharter in 1832, denying the proof of experience and defying congressional will. From that point, Jackson stretched executive power dangerously, notably by removing deposits the following year and in mid-1836 by issuing the notorious Specie Circular. What Benton had failed to achieve in a legislative bill, the president had done by mere decree. The country was now suffering from the consequences: specie was scarce where it was needed, it moved westward to the land offices, currency and credit were alarmingly disarranged. High interest rates, inflated prices, expensive exchange portended trouble. Webster implied that the country would soon pay for Jackson's mistakes by facing a much deeper financial crisis. The first remedy must be repeal of the Specie Circular, which an arbitrary pocket veto had just prevented.[73]

Bankers in New York City agreed with Webster's prescription to abandon the specie policy. They had come to that conclusion before his speech at Niblo's Saloon, but perhaps it stimulated them to action. In any event, soon afterward bankers and merchants convoked a large meeting to explore measures of relief, including revocation of the Specie Circular. A delegation of fifty took the meeting's resolutions to Washington as a petition to President Van Buren, who, needless to say, felt little pleasure when they called at the White House. Indeed, he told them they must put their plea in writing so that he could answer it on paper too. When they did, Van Buren's response rejected their estimate of the situation and refused to reverse what had become a symbolic political as well as economic commitment. In early May banks in the city felt so hard pressed that they contemplated suspension of specie payment for notes presented to them; and on the tenth, by agreement, they did so.[74] In a sense, the country had arrived at a turning point in its economic history, for a panic occurred. It was the end of Jackson's struggle with the national bank and the beginning of trouble that would last several years.

Chapter 16
DEPRESSION

The financial panic in the spring of 1837 signaled a long period of difficulty in the American economy. At first it seemed possible that only bankers, merchants, and speculators would feel the impact of suspension of specie payment and contraction of credit at the banks across the land; and when these institutions resumed redemption of notes the next year, that theory appeared valid. But general conditions, which had been deteriorating anyway, grew worse in 1839 and stayed poor into the early forties. Businessmen, planters, farmers, and laborers became victims of this depression. Factories slowed production or shut down, corporations and individuals faced bankruptcy, mortgages were foreclosed, workers lost their jobs, even state governments became insolvent. Meanwhile politicians wrangled about the causes and cure of the malady, with inconclusive results.

Regardless of their party allegiance, people agreed that a significant source of the problem had been overexpansion of industry in the East, of cotton plantations in the South, and of land buying there and in the West, all encouraged by bloated credit. State governments went heavily into debt while launching a welter of internal-improvements projects. Construction of canals and railroads was carelessly financed, often by each state's favorite bank especially chartered for the purpose. For more credit, these governments marketed huge quantities of their bonds in England.[1]

Had Jacksonian policy precipitated the distress? On this point, disagreement abounded. Democrats, replying no, emphasized their party's battle against paper money and easy credit. The Bank of the United States, they asserted, had been a principal villain; and though it was now only a frantic Pennsylvania state bank, it continued its devious manipulations. Old Hickory had pointed the way toward a sound monetary system with his Specie Circular; and now a good many hard-money Democrats talked of a day when the nation could get along better without banks. Whigs saw the matter quite differently. They believed that the crisis sprang primarily from ruinous missteps by Jackson. Without a central bank as a stabilizing force, currency, credit, and exchange were deranged. By failing to assume its constitutional responsibility in these areas, government had allowed excesses of economic behavior to push the republic over the precipice.[2]

When he arrived in Wheeling, Virginia, on the first leg of a long trip through the West, Webster learned that New York had suspended specie payments. Just what he had predicted, the senator remarked. In a speech there on May 17, 1837, he laid responsibility for the panic upon the Jackson administration, which by its financial policy since 1832 had "brought us where we are." The unsound practices of depository state banks, which had unfortunately been substituted for the BUS, had disastrous consequences, intensified by the Specie Circular. "I would not say," he continued, "that other causes, at home and abroad, had not had an agency in bringing about the derangement." Yet when government withdrew from its rightful role of providing a uniform currency, it had encouraged overexpansion in business and agriculture.[3]

Over the next two months he had many opportunities to elaborate upon his diagnosis, for in his circuit through the Mississippi Valley he was often the honored guest at public dinners, open-air meetings, and barbecues. Moving down the Ohio from Wheeling, he disembarked at Maysville, Kentucky, rode to Lexington to meet his host Clay, returned to the river at Louisville at the end of May. Again by boat, he proceeded to Madison, Indiana, was welcomed by Senator William Hendricks, a resident, and gave an address in the square. He continued up the river to North Bend and Cincinnati for a friendly visit with Harrison and a round of entertainment. Traveling by carriage across Indiana and Illinois, he reached St. Louis on June 9 for a stop of several days. Clay, now visiting his son there, participated in another reception for his fellow Whig and heard him speak. Through June he proceeded northeastward to the new Illinois capital of Springfield—local politician Abraham Lincoln had some time with him—and to his farm at Peru. Ten miles from his next destination, the small city of Chicago, a mounted troop met him; and he entered town in a barouche drawn by four handsome, cream-colored horses. Heading back in July, he stopped at Toledo, Detroit, Buffalo, and Rochester.[4]

Webster's party included his wife Caroline, daughter Julia, and a

young friend, William Fessenden of Portland. Along the way others fell
in with him, among them his son Fletcher, who joined the group at St.
Louis.[5] Everywhere people, hearing of his progress, invited him to visit
their communities and to speak on some public occasion. His fame excited adulation in many who knew of his accomplishments; those who
did not were curious to see and to hear him.[6] His admirers in Ohio gave
him an inscribed buckeye cane; citizens in Buffalo organized a steamboat regatta in his honor; in Louisville there was a barbecue of oxen
with a good supply of bourbon to wash it down.[7]

He thoroughly enjoyed this tour. Social approval filled him with deep
pleasure. Aside from that and from political considerations, there was
the chance to see the West. His limited sweep as far as Ohio four years
earlier had only encouraged him to travel further. Besides, he was currently acquiring vast land holdings in the area, in fact was one of the
speculators to whom he often alluded. He saw some of his property, in
Peru, Detroit, Michigan City, and Toledo, though he had to give up a
plan to go to Rock Island and Galena, in northwestern Illinois.[8] So he
spoke from his pocketbook as well as from general convictions when he
opened each speech along the route with complimentary words about
the promise and growth of the place, whether Chicago or Buffalo or
Madison, Indiana. He reached his audience not only because he was an
effective orator but also because he shared their aspirations concretely.

Every address emphasized the financial crisis, why it had come and
who was to blame. Disclaiming any intention to be partisan, he nonetheless made a true Whig speech. The pattern was fixed: a review of the
Bank War, the damage inflicted by an arbitrary executive, the need to
restore a national bank. He characterized currency as a vital instrument
of commerce, which Congress could and must regulate on the basis of
the constitutional commerce clause. Neither exclusive metallic currency
nor irredeemable paper money would do.[9] "I hardly know which *is* the
worst—the humbug of the one, or the fraud of the other."[10] And a sound
credit system must also be a great national concern. At Rochester he declared, "Credit, reasonable and just credit, has cleared these forests,
opened these roads, constructed this canal, built these mills, erected
these palaces, and given being to this important city, hardly reduced
from the wilderness thirty years ago."[11]

Soon he would see what the Van Buren administration meant to do to
ease the nation's problems. While he was in Illinois, news arrived that
the president had called a special session of Congress to meet in September. He had to abbreviate his stay in the West and by late July was in
New York City briefly, then in Marshfield in August before returning to
Washington.

Van Buren had summoned the special session, beginning on September 4, 1837, to deal with a serious situation faced by the Treasury after the onset of the panic in May. The law of 1836 required the government to stop using the depository banks to handle public funds when they suspended specie payment. Since then, federal officers had themselves been responsible for the safekeeping of money they collected, an ad hoc arrangement. Furthermore, over the summer, revenue had drastically declined because of sluggish business at land offices and customhouses. Instead of worrying about a surplus, the government now needed a substantial amount to carry it through the year; and ironically it was obligated to pay another installment of a nonexistent surplus to the states.

In his message to Congress the president reviewed these difficulties and recommended measures to counteract them. His remedy was what would soon be called an independent treasury, a separation of the government's fiscal operations from all banks. History showed, Van Buren said, that mingling them always brought abuses. Whenever banks held public deposits, they overissued notes and extended too much credit. Such had recently happened, with the results being reckless speculation and unsound commercial practices. His indictment covered all banks, state and national—he repeated the settled Jacksonian objection to a national bank. In his opinion, the obvious option was to continue the existing system of entrusting public officers with responsibility for handling the funds they collected. Presented in this light, the idea of an independent treasury grew out of past practice. But in fact Van Buren had been aware of scattered proposals in the preceding two or three years to adopt that kind of permanent policy. Experience had convinced him of its utility.[12]

If an independent treasury would be safer for fiscal operations of the Treasury, what should be done to help the economy generally? Very little, the president answered. Jeffersonian strict constructionist that he was, he lectured Congress on the limited powers of the national government to meddle in the concerns of business and agriculture. Here he disagreed with Whigs such as Webster, for he held that intervention was neither constitutional nor desirable. Let those guilty of overtrading learn their lesson and help themselves. Thus beyond an independent treasury, the agenda for Congress must be short: amend the deposit act to stop the last installment to the states; authorize issuance of treasury notes to provide governmental funds; assist hard-pressed merchants by modest concessions on customs bonds, perhaps by a narrowly restricted bankruptcy law; then adjourn.[13]

Master politician Van Buren was losing his touch. Fellow Democrats criticized the plan for an independent treasury because it threatened the interests of state banks, a matter of considerable concern to states' righters. As long as the party had fought a national bank, there was a good chance of maintaining unity, but now solidarity eroded. And the national party, fashioned by Van Buren himself more than anyone, had depended heavily upon a coalition of separate party organizations in each state, such as the powerful machines in New York and Virginia. Not surprisingly, in New York the editor of the Albany *Argus* and Governor William Marcy did not welcome the assault on state banks depriving them of federal deposits. Even Van Buren's closest political friend, Senator Silas Wright, hesitated before agreeing to promote the new plan. Senator Nathaniel Tallmadge did not concur and would vote with Whigs in opposition. In Virginia, too, the Democratic leadership balked. Thomas Ritchie and William Rives, both stalwarts in the national party, opposed this thrust at the state's financial system. In Washington, Frank Blair, editor of the *Globe* and a Jacksonian high priest, initially questioned the proposal but later expounded it with customary partisanship.[14]

While committee work and debate on the independent treasury continued during the month-long session, the Senate also took up and passed most of the less controversial parts of the president's program. Amendments to the deposit law postponing the last installment to the states, due October 1, passed comfortably, though Webster and a Whig group opposed it. The states had already calculated their budgets on the basis of receiving the funds, they said. Wright convincingly replied that it did not make sense for the government to borrow several million dollars, as it would have to do, to distribute a so-called surplus.[15] Moving next to the request for issuance of ten millions in treasury notes, the legislators approved it after some disagreement on details. Webster did not like the first version of the bill at all; it would authorize non-interest-bearing notes with no maturity date in denominations as low as twenty dollars. Just the same as worthless continentals of the Confederation, the New Englander complained. How inconsistent for professed hard-money men to resort to that extreme. The law in amended form did provide for interest and raised the minimum denomination to fifty dollars so that the notes would probably not circulate as fiat money.[16] Another enactment provided a little relief to merchants on customs bonds; but a bankruptcy bill, mainly for banks, failed.[17]

Attention centered, however, on the proposed independent treasury, discussed simultaneously with the rest of these measures. Against it, Webster spoke long and often.[18] He gave his standard résumé of recent financial history, the foolish Jacksonian experiment of depository state banks, and the dead end finally reached by the administration. Through the years, he contended, there had been a continuing consensus of the obligation to provide reliable circulating media, regardless of differences of opinion on the means of doing so. The framers of the Constitution, Hamilton in the 1790s, President Madison in 1815, even Jackson himself in the 1830s, all had agreed on that. Webster recalled that Calhoun had spoken warmly for a national bank in 1816. Here Calhoun interjected he had really had doubts about that earlier measure and now believed Congress lacked the power to create one. At any rate, Webster retorted, the South Carolinian had maintained the necessity of a uniform system of money; and that was exactly what he himself was seeking, one way or another, because he recognized that establishment of a bank was unlikely in existing circumstances.[19]

From Webster's perspective, the president, by proposing detachment from all banks, was recommending an unprecedented retreat from the accepted responsibility for a sound currency. Van Buren would look after the safety of public funds and leave the people to take care of themselves. "Divorce" was the appropriate term for such a policy. At a time of commercial distress, the people's own government would coldheartedly claim that it had no constitutional or moral duty to do anything to help them. Calhoun, he noted, supported this idea, indeed went further by urging an amendment to the pending bill to require that by 1841 payments be made to the government in specie only. Private transactions could be conducted in any medium, safe or unsafe, while collection of public dues would be strictly regulated. To this charge, Webster added his well-known argument that constructive action on currency was vital to every phase of economic life and would be a valid exercise of the commerce power.

Countering objections of the opposition and recruiting most Democrats to support the proposal, Wright skillfully pushed the bill through the Senate by early October. Calhoun decided to back the administration, a move which, in contrast to his previous collaboration with Whigs, had an even broader significance. Yet his independence was apparent when he insisted upon his amendment requiring specie payment to the Treasury. Webster, Clay, and the Whig minority stoutly resisted. They received help from Democrats Rives and Tallmadge; and that link would remain firm in the future. On October 4, however, the bill, with Calhoun's amendment, passed twenty-six to twenty. Webster could take consolation in the vote of the House to postpone the bill, but Van Buren would determinedly try again.[20]

When the administration continued its effort to pass an independent-treasury bill during the session opening in December 1837, it had trouble keeping the issue in the foreground. Its new ally, Calhoun, diverted the Senate's attention from financial questions to slavery. Introducing a series of resolutions on the subject, he asked for a national commitment to protect slavery where it existed and to encourage its expansion into western territories. In the ensuing angry debate Clay and Calhoun exchanged recriminations, now that the latter had deserted to the Democrats. Webster said little, though voting against the resolutions, certainly the one declaring the Union to be a compact of sovereign states. When he did speak, it was to reassure the South that its peculiar institution was safe in the older states and that even if Congress had power over some other aspects of slavery, it should be very cautious about using it.[21]

Because of the long discussion of slavery, it was late in the session of 1838 before the Senate seriously considered the acute financial problems of the country. Among them the question of rescinding the Specie Circular required prompt action, Webster felt. That order by the Treasury, according to bankers whose assertions he believed, had caused a currency crisis, forced them to suspend specie payment on their notes, and paralyzed land transactions. Earlier attempts to repeal the order had failed—first in March 1837 when Jackson had pocket vetoed a bill and then in the special session of September as a result of entanglement with the independent-treasury proposal. On April 30, 1838, Clay introduced a resolution in effect forcing the administration to withdraw the Specie Circular by prohibiting discrimination in the modes of all payments to the government. If specie were demanded for land sales, it must be required also for taxes and customs, an utterly impractical course, so that insistence upon gold and silver for land purchases would have to be abandoned. Clay's resolution, amended but supported by Webster, passed both houses the end of May; and on June 1 a new Treasury order went out allowing receipt of redeemable bank notes. Thus ended, the *Intelligencer* observed, experiment number two.[22]

Through the remainder of Van Buren's term, to March 1841, more economic trouble brought more argument about how to alleviate it. After a brief recovery, banks again suspended in late 1839, industry and labor experienced a decline, at least a deflation, and the government sought first aid for its fiscal condition. Webster continued to blame all these developments on Democratic mistakes and to call for a national bank as a long-range solution. The status of the currency remained his central concern. If redeemable in specie, bank notes must be a major medium, he contended, for the idea of exclusive use of hard money, expounded by many of his opponents, was nothing less than visionary. He

264

roundly attacked the latter for their inconsistency in requesting issuance of ever-larger amounts of treasury notes. Furthermore, these notes represented a rising national debt. Better to revise the tariff upward, particularly on luxury items such as silk and wine, and thereby raise more revenue. In short, the country's descent into a depression demanded a general overhaul of financial policy.[23]

The administration insisted that the principal reform must be adoption of its proposal of an independent treasury. Put forward by the president in September 1837 as his formula for guaranteeing the fiscal security of the government, the idea of separating Treasury Department functions from all banks did not die with defeat of a bill in that special session. Wright revived it in January 1838, and Congress deliberated upon it through June. Calhoun backed the measure in his own fashion, to the extent that it was compatible with his objectives of protecting southern rights and of shifting to an exclusive specie medium. Conservative Democrats such as Rives and Tallmadge still disliked it, despite Van Buren's offer to compromise by allowing some deposits to remain in state banks. A solid Whig aggregation maintained a staunch resistance.[24]

Several times Webster had the floor to oppose the independent treasury bill, but his thoroughly prepared speech of March 12 attracted the greatest attention.[25] The issues and arguments were familiar, and at the outset he mainly restated views heard before. Again he dwelt upon the duty and power of the government to provide a good currency. Through the years it had performed the function well, usually with the aid of a national bank. Without doubt it had the necessary authority derived from various constitutional provisions, the most decisive being the commerce clause. Presently the administration would abdicate this responsibility by insulating public from private finance. The senator also attacked again the notion of an exclusive metallic currency, advocated by some of his opponents. He predicted a ridiculous situation if they should prevail: the government would lock up bags and chests of gold in vaults; businessmen and farmers would be expected to move and handle unwieldy batches of coins. To avoid that nuisance, at least in private transactions, they would resort to depreciated paper money or use checks on bank deposits, neither of which would concern a heartless government.

Webster underscored in this speech the extent of his worry about the status of currency by saying that, lacking a national bank, he preferred the existing state-bank depository system to an independent treasury. These state banks could supply an adequate volume of money on the basis of the public funds they held. Because of his alarm about the current proposal, he went so far as to deny there had recently been an overexpansion of bank notes, a position strikingly inconsistent with what he had often said before.

Beyond reiteration of his thinking on currency, he expounded his general economic ideas. This part of his speech reflected fresh detail and conceptualization. To be sure, his dominant theme continued to be the economic progress of the nation, homogeneous, socially mobile, and amazingly prosperous. Citing statistics on commerce, industry, and finance, he portrayed the United States as a land of unique opportunity. Here there were no static classes, no permanently rich and poor, no necessary conflict between labor and capital. In Massachusetts, he said, the remarkable development of manufactures, providing large material benefits to the people and stimulating new enterprise, affirmed the fact that there were no aristocrats. Everywhere, in all sections, persons could improve their circumstances in such a fluid society. Progress was possible because of advances in education, science, and technology—but fundamentally it depended upon public policy. The government had a responsibility to assure the availability of capital, of currency and credit, so that the American promise could be fulfilled. As for credit, which he depicted as a crucial dynamic, banks could supply what was required only if Congress exercised its full financial powers. It must quash this wild dream of divorcing government from banking.[26]

A majority of the Senate had made up their minds to adopt the measure. On March 26, without Calhoun's specie amendment, the bill narrowly passed by a vote of 27 to 25. In the House, where the Whigs were stronger, the issue precipitated lengthy debate, often moving toward the subject of slavery. At the end of the session, however, that body rejected the independent treasury, 125 to 111.[27]

Naturally, Webster felt more than a little relief that Van Buren's project had stalled, perhaps would collapse if the next election went right. Reviewing the history of the controversy before a friendly, grateful gathering at Faneuil Hall when he went home, he predicted that the people would choose correctly.[28] Yet there was no dramatic change in party representation in Congress in the fall election, nor any change in the president's confidence of eventual success. The administration did not press hard in the short session the following winter (to March 1839), but it meant to do so at an opportune time.

The time arrived in early 1840. In January Wright reintroduced his proposal for a subtreasury, as it was usually called. Economic conditions had declined, banks had again suspended specie payment, the safety of treasury funds could be invoked. And prominent opponents were absent from the Senate: not only Rives and Tallmadge but also Webster, who had not yet returned to the capital after travel to England. On the twenty-third, four days before Webster's arrival, the bill went through, 24 to 18. As before, the House was more reluctant, not deciding until late June. But at last it did approve, 124 to 107. It was one of the few cheerful moments Van Buren enjoyed that summer—prospects for his reelection were exceedingly poor—when on July 4, 1840, he ceremoniously signed the measure. Benton hailed it as the "distinguishing glory" of this Congress. Others viewed it as America's second Declaration of Independence.[29]

Whether this hard-won victory would have lasting results depended upon party control of the presidency and Congress, to be determined in a few months. The Whigs had been active for quite a while, really beginning with Van Buren's inauguration, to make certain they would have control. And at first, no Whig was more anxious to take the lead than Webster. Immediately after the Red Fox took office in March 1837, the senator went to New York City for a mass meeting at Niblo's Saloon to set out his opinions on major political topics. Then in the summer his western trip appeared to be as much an electioneering expedition as a pleasant holiday. During the legislative session from December to mid-1838, when the Senate faced the thorny issues of slavery and the treasury deposits, Webster had his eye on the political impact of his activities. He mailed an extraordinary number of copies of his speeches for strategic effect.[30]

Though prompt and serious, his bid lacked the active help of a large circle of friends, in contrast to that of the previous election. True, in Massachusetts Caleb Cushing and Robert Winthrop showed an interest in promoting his cause in the press and the legislature, but before long their enthusiasm declined. The Boston *Atlas* dutifully gave over columns to items favorable to Webster, and the *Advertiser* stood by him faithfully. In Washington, the *Intelligencer* thought well of his candidacy, but also of Clay's. In New York, Hiram Ketchum did what he could until he saw that the state would not nominate Webster. But many who had worked for him earlier were quiet or worse. Governor Everett did little; Abbott Lawrence, the wealthy industrialist with growing political influence, left Webster for Clay; and so did Harrison Gray Otis.[31] Webster realized that, instead of trying to gather state after state into the fold with individual nominations, his best hope lay with a national convention, to which no candidate came with overwhelming strength. Appeal for this procedure had a democratic ring because it would go beyond state cau-

cuses and conventions, like those of 1835 when the party held no national meeting for discussion and consensus. Practically, the advantage
for Webster would be that a front-runner might stumble and delegates
turn to him as a man of the whole Union. So he spread the word, advocating a "deliberative" convention.[32]

The front-runner was Clay. Twice previously a candidate, the preeminent spokesman for economic nationalism, an adept parliamentary
manager, and a magnetic person adulated far and wide, Clay felt that
he and his party could not fail in 1840. Hard times, Democratic diver-
sions, and the president's unsolved problems gave the Whigs an enormous advantage. In nearly every state Clay's supporters were busy, so
that in June 1838 reports indicated his probable nomination by a national convention, now called for December 1839 at Harrisburg. Meanwhile in Congress, the Kentuckian had somewhat moderated his
positions to broaden his base—caution on slavery, adherence to the
compromise tariff of 1833, distribution of funds to the states for internal
improvements rather than federal projects, and a new type of national
bank unconnected with Biddle's institution and located in New York. As
usual, in what he offered there was something for every section.[33]

Webster reacted as one would expect of a rival for leadership of party
and nation. In correspondence and conversation he criticized Clay's political conduct in the last few years.[34] Especially objectionable, he
thought, had been desertion of the protective principle in the tariff of
1833, amounting to repudiation of the American System. He supplied
Ketchum with his recollections of the Clay-Calhoun accommodation
during the nullification crisis, material to be used in the press, as
needed.[35] The Massachusetts senator also somewhat distanced himself
from Clay on concessions to the slave states, on new federal internal improvements, and on the character of a national bank. On the last of
these, he pointed out to Biddle the self-serving motive behind the proposal for a national bank in New York City. Though attempting to undermine Clay's standing, he avoided a visible rupture of relations, which
could severely damage the party.[36]

Nothing had much effect. When he assessed his chances in the summer of 1838, he saw little to encourage him. To be sure, Clay also had his
difficulties, particularly in New York, where the Whig chieftain Thurlow Weed argued that the Kentuckian had accumulated too many liabilities. Still, Webster realized that the same objection could apply to
him.[37] Again Harrison, the man demonstrating popular, if vague, appeal, emerged as a strong contender. Better Harrison than Clay, Webster concluded. He therefore calmly accepted, even encouraged,

pro-Harrison sentiment in New England and elsewhere. In September the *Atlas* was praising Harrison; and though these kudos probably appeared on the initiative of the editor, they drew no criticism from Webster, the known sponsor of the paper. In any event, he had lost interest in his own candidacy. Thereafter he remained the passive, formal choice of Massachusetts but only to promote Harrison and stop Clay, who might otherwise gain the state.[38]

Through 1839 he seemed detached from presidential politics, including the Whig national convention in December. Early in the year he accepted reelection to the Senate, despite some recurrent thought of devoting full time to his personal affairs.[39] Soon plans to travel to England diverted his attention. Before leaving in May, he drafted a letter formally withdrawing from the field he had already abandoned in fact. But he did not release the letter until he was in London, on June 12; and it did not appear in the American newspapers until early July. Expressing appreciation for being nominated by a Massachusetts convention, he withdrew as a contribution to party unity, he wrote.[40] Thereafter he made no more public statements.[41] On December 4, while he was still in England, the convention met to select one of three candidates: Clay, holding a narrow lead; Harrison, close behind and gaining; and General Winfield Scott, a late addition with support from Weed and Seward. This three-way competition and a series of convention decisions adverse to Clay ended in the choice of Harrison. So when Webster returned to the country in January 1840, the scene was set for a contest between old Tippecanoe, as the onetime Indian slayer in the Wabash Valley was known, and the besieged Magician in the executive mansion.[42]

"Good intelligence pours in upon us from all quarters. If Genl. Harrison lives, *he will be President,*" Webster predicted. At sixty-seven, Harrison would be the oldest person yet elected to the office, but the senator had no special reason to worry that the candidate's age or health might indeed prove to be important.[43] As he assessed the probable course of the campaign, he felt confident that the Whigs could not fail if they avoided a very bad misstep. "The cry of the nation is for change," he declared, "wafted on all the breezes, borne from every quarter."[44] The people demanded a change of measures, possible only by a change of men.[45] He viewed Harrison as the man of the hour. Honest and amiable, the general could provide necessary leadership without the defects of "obstinacy & ignorant presumption" characteristic of Jackson, and would "bring good men about him" for a successful administration. Webster implied that he would be one of the advisers.[46] In letters and public statements he denied ever having a negative opinion of the Ohioan, even during their competition for the presidency four years before.[47] Admittedly, the problem was to counteract the image of a mere military chieftain, to emphasize positive qualities of patriotism and judgment. Webster felt comfortable about doing so, for he did have a friendly relationship with the candidate. Though not closely associated with each other, the two had had congenial contacts in Washington for many years, Webster had enjoyed a visit in North Bend during his recent western tour, and now their correspondence seemed cordial and relaxed. In fact an intimate letter from Harrison had just arrived, complimenting Webster on his favorable reception in England, profusely thanking Massachusetts for its support of the nomination, and more than incidentally asking help to get a personal loan in Boston.[48]

Webster's optimism soared when he considered the vulnerability of Van Buren, renominated by a rather gloomy, discordant Democratic convention in May 1840. Known for his sure hand in organization and tactics, the president appeared to be a transformed person, defensive, peevish, withdrawn. Instead of energetically mobilizing the party in his customary fashion, he dug in at the White House to ward off the Whig offensive. His principal effort went into composing a long document exhorting his followers to work hard, to be alert to fraudulent voting practices by the opposition. He seemed to harp on the differences between the Democrats' Jeffersonian tradition and the Whigs' Federalist antecedents without attending to the real tasks at hand. A plausible slogan circulated: "Van, Van is a used up man."[49]

Whigs, on the other hand, had learned from past defeats what techniques were effective in the politics of the common man. Their campaign featured the log cabin, allegedly the residence of old Tippecanoe, and hard cider, allegedly his favorite beverage.[50] All very democratic, if stretching the truth about the son of a Virginia aristocrat and the holder of numerous high offices, whose spacious house overlooking the Ohio was hardly a cabin. Webster conceded that the general had put up an addition to his cabin.[51] At any rate, the Massachusetts senator recognized the value of a broad appeal. Mass meetings, stump speeches, parades, songs, catchwords, and down-to-earth language would stir popular interest and deliver a victory. As for his role, he did not hestitate in participating. But skilled orator and dedicated nationalist that he was, he blended his populism with his economic ideology. It was as if he revised his Senate speeches to come across with greater clarity and color. He continued to attack the Democratic record on the same ground— ruinous financial policies had brought the country to its existing sad condition. His theme was not different, but its expression was more in accord with the times.[52]

From May to October he gave priority to electioneering. Invitations to speak came in ever larger numbers from New England, New York, the South, even the West.[53] While Congress was in session he confined his efforts to the vicinity of the capital. On May 4 he went to Baltimore for a Young Whig convention, where a huge gathering of the faithful ratified Harrison's nomination, paraded, sang, cheered, and otherwise displayed their enthusiasm. There were log cabins for authentic effect, and plenty of hard cider.[54] He crossed the Potomac on June 11 to address a Whig festival in Alexandria, which offered an opportunity to call for southern support.[55] Just before Congress adjourned he headed home and was in Barre, Massachusetts, for the Fourth of July. An estimated five thousand people heard him berate Jackson and Van Buren and then say that if the Whigs lost this election, he would retire from public life, fold his arms, and wait for the vessel to go aground.[56] Three days later, on the seventh, at least fifteen thousand gathered at Stratton Mountain, in southern Vermont, for two days of talk. Webster spoke, ate his food on a shingle, and slept before an open fire.[57]

In mid-August, while he was in Saratoga for a case in court, ten thousand listened to him in the open air for three hours. In addition to discussing issues of the election, he strayed from his subject to certify his own humble background: "Gentlemen, it did not happen to me to be born in a log cabin; but my elder brothers and sisters were born in a log cabin, raised amid the snow-drifts of New Hampshire, at a period as early that, when the smoke first arose from its rude chimney, and curled over the frozen hills, there was no similar evidence of a white man's habitation between it and the settlements on the rivers of Canada. Its remains still exist. I make to it an annual visit. I carry my children to it, to teach them the hardship endured by the generations which have gone before them. I love to dwell on the tender recollections, the kindred ties, the early affections, and the touching narratives and incidents, which mingle with all I know of this primitive abode."[58]

The largest rally in which he took part was held in Boston on September 10 and 11. According to a somewhat inflated report, 50,000 people assembled for what was called a general convention of New England Whigs. On the first morning the multitude assembled on the Common to form a procession: 150 truckmen in white frocks; 1,000 mounted men; fifty barouches and carriages, some with veterans of the Revolutionary War; innumerable dignitaries; squads of marchers carrying banners. Column after column, four miles long, moved through the streets, across the Charles, and to Bunker Hill. It took two hours for all of them to pass any one point. There were so many at Bunker Hill that no speaker, not even Webster, could reach everyone; so, as president of the convention, he wrote a declaration of principles, read to separate groups and circulated in print. Later a series of meetings occurred at Faneuil Hall, Webster presiding, and elsewhere.[59]

Ten days afterward, he was on Long Island, at Patchogue. In plain and partisan terms he charged the administration with being much more aristocratic than the Whigs. That generalization applied to himself, notwithstanding slurs to the contrary. "Now, my friends," he declared, "it would be very strange if I, who have grown up among the people, and, as it were, of the people, should at any time of life take a fancy to aristocracy. I have ploughed, and sowed, and reaped the acres that were my father's and that are now mine." He warned his audience that he was being trailed by opponents (chiefly Silas Wright), who would contradict what he told them. Be ready for some falsehoods, he advised. "The man that says I am an aristocrat—is a liar!"[60] In contrasting style, he came in to Wall Street for a sober but hard-hitting address on standard financial topics. It was a merchants' gathering, and there were no allusions to log cabins.[61]

In the final phase he traveled to New Hampshire, especially worrisome because it had been a Democratic stronghold. His native state must not stand out as the solitary dissenter to New England's hearty support of the Whig cause. Stopping at several towns along the Connecticut to deliver his message, he intended to finish at Franklin, near his farm. But on October 22 his physical resources gave out. Exhaustion, a severe cold, loss of voice put him to bed; and he regretfully concluded that further appearances, even at Franklin, were impossible.[62]

A lasting criticism of the "log-cabin campaign" of 1840 has been that it gave full scope to emotional, irrational excesses at the expense of meaningful discussion of substantive issues. The only constructive feature of this colorful, exciting election, as usually portrayed in historical writing, was its strengthening of a valuable two-party system.[63] There is no denying that Webster sought an image different from the familiar one of serious-minded expounder of political principles. With alacrity, he plunged into the work of recruiting votes by resort to homespun phrases and exaggerated statements, by adopting some techniques of an ordinary stump speaker. In doing so, he conformed to the requirements of party strategy. Thus time and again he seemed to have an overwhelming desire to demolish the notion that he was an aristocrat, a friend of the rich, contemptuous of common folk.

A complete reading of Webster's speeches during this campaign, however, shows that he mixed the arts of everyday politics with exposition of his ideas on fundamental problems. Invariably he reviewed recent events and policies involving banking and currency; and he penetrated financial intricacies as deeply as the setting allowed. A topic he developed in detail was the status of American labor in the depressed economy. Democrats, he contended, would accept, yes encourage, deflation of wages if they could impose a hard-money policy. Other subjects also received attention: the current proposal to set up a national program for training state militia (very disturbing, he thought), the condition of state and national debts, and abuses of patronage for partisan purposes (an ever reliable point of attack).

Through early November, returns from the ballot boxes across the land showed, as expected, that the Whigs had won decisively. Harrison carried nineteen states, with 234 electoral votes; Van Buren, seven states, with 60. In Massachusetts the total popular vote was: Harrison, 72,874; Van Buren, 51,944; Birney, of the Liberty party, 1,621.[64] Webster shared the elation expressed in a flow of letters from friends near and distant. He firmly believed the country had experienced a peaceful revolution and thereby passed through a great crisis. Whether such an assessment was valid remained a question to be answered after March 4.[65]

Well before the election, Webster thought he could influence the direction the nation would take afterward. He had in mind some important office, the mission to Britain or probably a place in the cabinet. This early speculation about his own future sprang from absolute confidence in a Whig victory in November 1840. Having decided he would leave the Senate in any case, he felt eager to assume a new role in public affairs.[66]

Harrison never doubted that Webster ought to come into his administration, but he had some difficulty in determining which post the New Englander should occupy. There was the problem of Clay, who also had a very strong claim to an appointment and was visualizing the shape of policies in the months ahead. In November, as soon as the outcome of the contest was certain, the president-elect made a trip to Kentucky as far as Frankfort, undecided whether to risk a visit at Clay's Ashland. The senator had an imperious tendency, which, in the circumstances, might be embarrassing. Clay hurried up to meet Harrison, persuaded him to spend a week in Lexington as his guest, and therefore had a spendid opportunity to offer all the advice which occurred to him. To old Tip's surprise, Clay told him even before being asked that he would not leave the Senate for the cabinet. So Harrison, who had intended to give Clay the State Department, now listened to his host's recommendations about other men, especially Webster. Though Clay freely talked about his disagreements with Webster over the preceding eight years, he supported naming the New Englander to State. That settled one matter, but it was clear that Clay meant to act in the Senate as pilot of the new administration.[67]

On his way home, the general sent Webster the offer of either State or the Treasury Department. "Since I was first a candidate for the Presidency," he wrote, "I had determined, if successful, to solicit your able assistance in conducting the Administration." He did not care which office Webster took, he said, although he broadly hinted the treasury might be better, since it was more difficult to find the right person for it.[68] Webster sidestepped that hint in his response on December 11, accepting the State Department. Much of the activity in the treasury involved dull routine, he believed; and as for the large questions on banking and currency, he told Harrison the whole cabinet ought to discuss and decide them. That would leave Harrison with less to do than even he could accept, inclined though he was toward reduced presidential power.[69]

Harrison arrived in Washington in early February to complete preparations for the transition of power. Shortly, the new cabinet was announced. In addition to Webster, the list included Thomas Ewing in the Treasury, John Bell in the War Department, and John Crittenden as attorney general (all regarded as Clay men), George Badger at Navy (attached to Webster), and Francis Granger as postmaster general. Webster felt satisfied with the whole group—he expected to be a kind of premier among them.[70] On the twenty-second he had resigned from the Senate and was pleased that Rufus Choate, a dependable follower, would succeed him.[71] Meanwhile the general worked on his inaugural address, a rather tortuous exercise, it seemed. Though receiving Webster's advice, especially to stick to broad principles without details on particular measures, he preferred his own turgid prose and countless classical allusions. A later anecdote claims that Webster looked at a draft and killed seventeen Roman proconsuls as dead as smelts. Even so, many other Greek and Roman luminaries remained in the version read at the inaugural ceremony.[72]

Chapter 17

MIDDLE AGE

During the 1830s Webster had reached that point of middle age when his traits were fully developed and fairly stabilized. It was this mature man whose appearance, habits, and mind shaped the reputation of a personality so notable in American history. To an extent, contemporaries and later generations could readily agree in assessing his qualities—unusual intellectual gifts, striking presence, oratorical skill. But as a figure constantly caught up in controversy, he made quite different impressions upon different people. Admirers called him God-like; critics, the opposite. Was his principal achievement a valiant defense of Union and Constitution, or was it mere service to the cause of an elite and the narrow interests of property? In private life he appeared to some a fascinating, truehearted person and to others a disappointingly amoral creature, always yearning for more praise and material satisfaction. Thus an evaluation of his character depends upon how much of each contrasting view one should accept, not whether either is absolutely correct.

Perhaps the most frequently quoted description of Webster came from the pen of Thomas Carlyle: "The tanned complexion; that amorphous craglike face, the dull black eyes under the precipice of brows, like dull anthracite furnaces needing only to be *blown;* the mastiff mouth, accurately closed . . . Webster is not loquacious but he is pertinent, conclusive; a dignified, perfectly-bred man."[1] Another Englishman, writing for a London newspaper at this time, observed, "He is of large and firm stature, and with a head that phrenologists will endorse as the seat of a gigantic intellect. His hair and complexion are dark, and his large deep seated black eyes full of expression. In his impassioned moments he reaches an elevation of eloquence far surpassing anything that I have ever witnessed among his fellow senators and statesmen. His usual manner is calm, collected, and dignified. His voice is clear and sonorous. He uses but little gesture, and that of no remarkable grace. His characteristics are vigor, energy, clearness of arrangement, boldness and directness of logic, with singular simplicity of diction and power of argument."[2] The well-known English traveler Harriet Martineau also saw two images of the same man: "Webster is a lover of ease and pleasure, and has an air of the most unaffected indolence and careless self-sufficiency. It is something to see him moved with anxiety and the toil of intellectual conflict; to see his lips tremble, his nostrils expand, the perspiration start upon his brow; to hear his voice vary with emotion."[3]

It is clear that Webster enjoyed unusually good health throughout a longer than average life span. From his fifties onward, he did suffer from catarrh, a type of hay fever, which laid him low for some days or weeks each fall. Apart from that nuisance and an occasional attack of rheumatism, his health seldom caused him to miss a day of heavy work or active recreation. Martineau's impression of his "indolence" was erroneous; indeed she qualified her comment by speculating that he wished "to conceal the extent of his toils." Webster himself noted his uncommonly sound physical condition on his fifty-seventh birthday, for which, he wrote, "I desire to render the most devout thanks to Almighty God."[4]

He had grown out of his slender physique as a college student to more substantial proportions and showed signs of self-indulgence at the table. Like many other people of the period, he did not worry about the quantity and effects of what he ate and drank. Diets were incredibly heavy— large amounts in numerous courses, a good part being meat and starchy foods. He dined sumptuously at home, more so on social occasions. So he had put on a good deal of weight, concentrated at his midsection and evident also in the fleshiness of his jaws.

As they observed Webster, persons unfriendly to him found proof of dissipation, of intemperate habits. Stories of his showing the effects of alcohol by erratic behavior circulated. Malicious or exaggerated as such tales may have been, they had an element of truth. Even the ever-admiring James Kent remarked in his diary how much Webster had "charmed the party" at a dinner. "He is 57 years old," the chancellor wrote, "and looks worn and furrowed; his belly becomes protuberant, and his eyes deep in his head. I sympathize with his condition. He has been too free a liver. He ate but little, and drank wine freely."[5] Undoubtedly he did like wine, in preference to whiskey or other spirituous liquor. In his house on Summer Street he kept a large supply of many vintages, all listed in a cellar book, which was helpful to reckon the amount of insurance he should carry—he insured his library too.[6]

Nothing in the available evidence proves that Webster was a drunkard or that he allowed drink to interfere seriously with attention to his responsibilities. An early riser, inclined to long hours of demanding work, he must have had a very remarkable ability to hold his liquor if his habits were as profligate as sometimes pictured. At any rate, his drinking had only a long-range effect upon his health and little upon his behavior, public or private.

Though his physical characteristics made an impression upon people, it was chiefly his qualities of mind which determined the image he projected. Undeniably, he was a literate, cultivated person, at ease in the best circles of Boston and elsewhere. An evening in George Ticknor's home provided a setting for good conversation with friends about classical and modern literature or other cultural matters. The scholar-politician Edward Everett, his church's minister John Palfrey, the learned Story, and Josiah Quincy, the president of Harvard, were persons whose company he welcomed.

The fact was that his reading now tended less to belles-lettres than it once had. Public affairs and professional business interfered. And his tastes, so far as time allowed, centered on English authors, some of whom he met while traveling in that country in 1839, rather than on the great American writers of his day. He had nothing to do with Emerson, Thoreau, Hawthorne, or Longfellow and had no regrets about it. In his speeches he made many literary allusions, but largely drew upon a stock amassed much earlier in his life.[7]

As for music and the fine arts, he never paid them much attention. There is no reference in his papers to musical performances, none to the theater or to sculpture. The only artist whose work aroused positive response was Sarah Goodridge, a Boston miniaturist, whom he occasionally visited and even helped with money.[8] On the other hand, he submitted only passively to sittings for a number of portraits by such painters as Gilbert Stuart and Chester Harding.[9] Late in life, he scowled at the daguerreotypist while maintaining the uncomfortably fixed position required by that new medium.

His involvement in the intellectual world ran in a practical direction. A long-standing acquaintance with Noah Webster produced some correspondence, often about the lexicographer's requests for more protection by copyright laws. The senator was well informed on that subject, derived from his legal practice, and he assisted in obtaining stronger legislation. But the two Websters were drawn to each other because of their similar nationalistic political ideas more than because of a mutual interest in the American language.[10] Similarly, Francis Lieber, the rising German-American political scientist formerly of Boston and now a professor of South Carolina College, developed a friendly relationship with him. Lieber, also a committed nationalist, wrote about his scholarly projects, but it is doubtful that the senator ever read much of his writings.[11]

Historical themes and personalities always appealed to him. Pertinent to his concerns in politics and law, central to his patriotism, the history of the United States was both instrumental and inspiring. One topic of which he did not tire was the founding of New England. His bicentennial oration at Plymouth had shown he was well informed about Puritan institutions, and through the years he discussed them in various speeches. In New York City in December 1832 before a gathering of the New England Society, he contrasted the heritage from their forefathers to the doctrines of nullification.[12] He had a still greater interest in the history of the Revolution, earlier demonstrated by the Bunker Hill oration and the eulogy of Adams and Jefferson. In April 1835, at a memorial ceremony on the sixtieth anniversary of the battle of Lexington, he emphasized the advancement of liberty by the patriot militiamen.[13]

In daily life his marriage to Caroline Le Roy now improved his outlook and strengthened his sense of well-being. Fifteen years younger than Webster, the daughter of a prominent New York merchant, his wife added a social dimension to his world. Caroline was more accustomed than Grace had been to mingling with the best society, to numerous calls, visits, and parties. In June 1830, at the close of the congressional session, the Websters arrived in Boston to open their house on Summer Street. The "new mistress" of the household, as her husband called her, had shipped furniture, china, and crystal to dress up the place in anticipation of a good deal of entertainment.[14] Webster's intimate friends welcomed her warmly, though it took her some time to establish all the relationships she wished to have.[15] Generally, he was pleased with his cheerful home life, particularly to have the three children together again under the care of a devoted stepmother.

If adjustments were slow, the reason may have been their long absences from the city. Every year the senator had to spend months in Washington and to travel on professional business elsewhere. When possible, Caroline and the children went along, and their companionship suited him exactly; but too often, he felt, he was alone in a Washington boardinghouse. In these periods he tended to bypass social events for solitary evenings in his room before the fireplace. Extant correspondence with Caroline shows him unhappy with the separations, just as she was. Their letters indicate affection rather than passionate love, with scattered hints of minor problems.[16]

One of his complaints arose from her inclination to visit her family in New York instead of coming to Washington. It was not a matter of any hostility he had toward the Le Roys but simply the depressing loneliness. During the winter of 1840 he repeatedly urged her to join him. When she did not answer, he lost patience: *"Are you coming here, or are you not? My Dear Wife, what possesses you, to act as you do? Why do you not tell me what you mean? I am disappointed—ashamed—mortified— For Heaven's sake, tell me what you mean—I say to every body, that I am looking for you, every day—This must be explained."* The next day his irritation abated, but she stayed in New York that session.[17]

Once in a while, he found her tastes too expensive and chided her about it—an incongruous reaction from one whose own spending habits were unrestrained. Yet she responded to a brisk reminder apologetically, as a dutiful, prudent wife should.[18] In fact she need not have apologized, for her father, Herman Le Roy, had generously provided Webster with a marriage settlement of twenty-five thousand dollars; and he, in turn, had signed an indenture putting the income from the Summer Street property in trust for Caroline's use during her lifetime if she survived him. In 1839, when he sold the house and lots, he substituted the real estate at Franklin (Salisbury) and at Marshfield in a similar trust.[19]

Relations with his father-in-law were very amicable. Old and frail, Le Roy had retired from his mercantile firm but maintained an interest in land speculation and in the enterprises of his sons. Recurrent difficulties, including intricate litigation, led him to consult his son-in-law for advice after giving detailed explanations of his situation. The truth was he greatly admired Webster in addition to embracing him as a valued member of the family. At the Le Roy mansion, 7 Greenwich Street, near Broadway, the Websters were regular visitors, enjoying the company of Caroline's widowed sisters, Catherine Newbold and Cornelia Edgar, and usually one or more of her brothers, Herman, Daniel, and Jacob. Ever concerned about the welfare of his eleven children, the aged merchant was known for his astute handling of money, so that he was no easy mark for anyone, relatives or not, trying to take advantage of him.[20] Webster gained from this association not as much directly in material terms as indirectly in the status it enhanced.

When Webster married Caroline in late 1829, the oldest of his three living children, Daniel Fletcher, was sixteen, nearing the age to enter college. In preparation to do so, Fletcher was tutored by Samuel Walcott, a lawyer of Hopkinton, Massachusetts, and former clerk in Webster's office. Making good progress, he enrolled at Harvard as a sophomore the following August.[21] In his three years there, he revealed what would prove to be lifelong traits. Endowed with average talents, an earnest, compliant son, he constantly sought to fulfill expectations that he do as well as his famous father. He craved approval but realized that he lacked the superior ability many supposed he had. His studies proceeded only passably. "The chief fault is, my dear father," he wrote, "restlessness; I cannot stick to the same thing long, a fault of which I am as well aware, as yourself."[22] In his junior year, the pressure continued to make him uneasy. "I hope that there is more in me than has yet appeared," he said, "for I have done nothing heretofore, and should be very sorry to think that a son of yours was wholly good for nothing; but I fear people think there is more in me than there really is."[23] Though entirely supportive, Webster did indeed expect much of the youngster and was full of counsel on his academic habits, course of reading, and personal conduct. When Fletcher inquired about a good topic for his senior oration, Webster supplied one, the role of labor, and offered hints on how to develop the subject.[24]

After graduation Fletcher moved from one thing to another, seeking the best direction to take. For a while, he read law with Walcott and found the work pleasantly challenging. He reported he had been "tearing the law to pieces" and had "arrived to such a degree of proficiency as to be able to take care of almost any business that presents itself at our office." In addition, he began attending local political meetings and making speeches—a natural area of involvement for one who had grown up in that kind of environment.[25] At this time, the western land fever was spreading and infected some of his friends, and soon his father too. So in 1836 he went out to Michigan and then to Illinois, acted as land agent for Webster, managed a farm for him, and occasionally practiced law. He was now married to Caroline White, daughter of Stephen White and niece of Justice Story. But the depression of the late 1830s and various setbacks caused him to return East after four years, still uncertain about his future.[26]

Webster's daughter Julia was an appealing eleven-year-old schoolgirl when Webster remarried. In her dark hair, large eyes, and facial expressions she resembled her father, who was very fond of her. As she grew older, she kept abreast of Webster's activities and felt boundless pride in the reputation he had achieved. Caroline assumed the responsibilities of a mother quite satisfactorily, mindful of the child's education and social cultivation. In her impressionable teens, Julia became accustomed to the life style of Boston's elite and of New York's leading families during long visits at the Le Roys.[27] In 1839, at twenty-one, she was engaged to marry Samuel Appleton, nephew and partner of Nathan Appleton in the extensive business operations of that prominent merchant-industrialist. Her uncle, William Paige, was also a partner. With meticulous attention to propriety, the suitor had sent Webster a carefully phrased request for his consent to propose to Julia. "I am deeply sensible," he wrote, "how much I ask of you, but I would endeavor by my future conduct never to give you cause to regret having acceded to my wishes." He did not exaggerate when he added, "As to my ability to maintain a wife, I believe I may say with perfect confidence, I am in a situation so to do." The senator approved without hesitation.[28] That September, Julia and Sam were married in London during the Websters' English tour.

Two years younger than Julia, Webster's son Edward had different characteristics. Possibly he was pampered because of his age, but he seemed to be a free spirit in any case. As a boy he had an impetuous, demonstrative streak; and later, in the Latin School, he often tried the master's patience, a tendency reflected in monthly reports with numerous marks for misconduct.[29] At fourteen he went off to Phillips Exeter and after three years to Dartmouth in 1837. He was less than a dedicated student, prone to play rather than to read, a little careless about money. Letters from his father centered on his expenses, personal habits, and minimal commitment.[30] He did not write home often enough; and when he did, Webster found what he read uninformative and sloppily put together. In one instance he issued a sharp reprimand about misspellings, incorrect punctuation, faulty capitalization. "Write me, immediately, a more careful, & a better, letter," Webster demanded.[31] When Edward confessed to having run up a debt in Hanover, Webster was upset, the more so when he felt his son had misrepresented the circumstances. "My first feeling was to withdraw you from College, & to let you take care of yourself hereafter. But your letter shows an apparent spirit of repentance, & if I were sure that I could trust *that*, I might be induced to overlook the enormity of your misconduct." To this lecture Edward replied with a full confession—he had spent the money on candy, cigars, knives, horseback riding, and "some *wine* a very little of which I can say with a clear conscience I drank myself."[32] Pacified by Edward's repentance, Webster sent him the funds. In the summer of 1839 he left Dartmouth to join the family in England, then went to the Continent, where, under Everett's supervision, he was to fill in some gaps left by his college education.[33]

In the early thirties the Websters considered the house on Summer

Street their home, despite periods in Washington and elsewhere. Conveniently located near the center of the city, thus a short walk to the senator's office, the unpretentious brick structure projected dignity. The neighborhood was still being developed; houses were going up on new lots, and streets were being added or changed. Over the years Webster acquired a number of these lots, mainly for speculative profit but also for more breathing space. He kept a parcel of land next to his residence unoccupied for that reason. Next to it were the Paiges, with whom the Websters, young and old, had a happy relationship. Until 1839, when Webster sold this house, he spent a few months here every year.[34]

He never gave up his property in New Hampshire. Indeed he steadily expanded and improved his holdings in Franklin, the new name of the town of Salisbury. After Ezekiel's death he became the sole owner of much of the old Webster farm, the Elms, enlarged in 1831 by a purchase from nephew Charles Haddock. Later, with the aid of his brother-in-law Israel Webster Kelly, he bought more land from neighbors until he owned a sizable estate.[35] He concentrated on producing corn and potatoes but also had a great deal of livestock, mainly cattle and sheep. An absentee proprietor, he needed a manager. For years John Taylor, a rugged Yankee, performed that function and in return received half the income.[36] Webster himself took an active part in deciding even detailed questions through a regular flow of letters back and forth about upgrading soil fertility, planting and marketing crops, and building up larger, better herds of animals.

Taylor's family occupied the main house while reserving a remodeled east wing for the Websters' use whenever they decided to come up for a few days or weeks. There were parlors on the ground floor and two bedrooms on the second, from which the senator could look out upon the beautiful mountains on the horizon, the bottomlands of the Merrimack, and the little cemetery where his parents and other relatives were buried. Returning to this place restored his health and spirits and reminded him of his youth in many ways.[37]

Gradually he had become more and more interested in summer trips to Marshfield, a town south of Boston about ten miles from Plymouth. Beginning in 1824 the Websters had gone there frequently, always staying at the farmhouse of John Thomas.[38] It was an excellent area for hunting, fishing, and boating, for walks in the pine forest or along the splendid Duxbury beach. At the closest point, at the outlet of Green Harbor River, the ocean was only about a mile from the house. The neighborhood had a history dating back to Pilgrim days, to the time when Plymouth's governor, Edward Winslow, was awarded a large tract for settling a new town. In 1699 his grandson had built a handsome residence, still standing a few hundred yards from the Thomas house. Nathaniel Ray Thomas had erected the house just before the Revolution, only to lose it when, as a staunch Tory, he had to flee the country. The emigrant's son, patriot Captain John Thomas, had taken over the property and had held it ever since.[39]

Thomas, now old and pressed for money, was anxious to sell out; and Webster was anxious to buy. Both parties were satisfied: Thomas would receive $3,650 and have the right to live there; his sons, Ray and Henry, would be employed to help run the farm; at a bargain price Webster could have an estate which he had long admired and could enjoy to his heart's content. So in April 1832 the captain signed a conveyance, and the thing was done.[40]

To the original 160 acres, Webster added many more by purchases of bordering land, including the historic Winslow place, and the Soule and Baker farms.[41] Eventually he owned over 1,200 acres (conveyed in twenty-three deeds) and thirty buildings, seven of them houses. He employed twenty-five laborers and at least a half-dozen house servants.[42] Spending a huge sum for improvements, in addition to the amounts laid out for the land itself, he had an investment so large that it was nearly impossible to realize a profit. In fact he never did. If pressed, he could have contended that his profit, though not monetary, was psychological and therefore real enough. Presiding over what might justly be called a spectacle, he derived infinite pleasure from his ideal retreat. He liked the challenge of developing a productive farm out of the sandy soil and spreading salt marshes, his role of country squire, and the manifold outlets for the sportsman he had become.

When he bought it, the Thomas house was a rather ordinary frame building with two full floors and a third with dormers. From time to time, he remodeled and added to it, chiefly a large west wing, whose high-pitched roof displayed strange-looking double dormers projecting at angles. Altogether, there were nine rooms on the first floor alone. One could hardly say it was elegant, but it had a certain imposing and comfortable character. In front was a ringed driveway, to which a long avenue led from the road. And all around, he had profusely landscaped the grounds with trees, shrubs, and flowers.[43] Near the house he had a one-room office for legal and political business.[44]

The overseer at Marshfield, Henry Thomas, kept busy carrying out instructions, laid down in a stream of letters, as well as making decisions himself. At first there was a great flurry of tree planting as the senator shipped in enormous batches of saplings and seeds, many of them from a

Washington nursery. Webster was determined to transform the barren-
ness of the place into a verdant network of groves and fields.[45] Then
Thomas undertook a diverse array of other improvements, barriers
along the beach and dams in the creeks, a causeway across the marshes,
a new barn and other outbuildings. Ceaselessly, Webster sought to make
the stubborn soil more productive. Each time he wrote to Thomas, he
urged an intensified effort by application of various fertilizers: barnyard
manure, kelp, mussel, herring, marl, or any other promising substance of
which he had learned. Crop selection, he knew, was vital. Besides rota-
tion, he insisted upon diversification by limiting acres planted to grain
and putting more into potatoes, beets, and particularly turnips after observing their popularity in England. Like the Elms, Marshfield also had
ever more extensive herds of blooded cattle, swine, and sheep.[46] He fan-
cied himself a scientific farmer and was so bold as to lecture on agricultural topics.[47] What a change there had been from the boy who had had
so little interest in his father's farm in Salisbury! And how strange it
seemed that the great advocate of financial and industrial development
should become absorbed in these agrarian concerns.

Still, Webster loved Marshfield as a haven for rest and recreation even
more than as a progressive farm. The sea and Green Harbor River offered endless opportunities. Within months after taking title to the
place, he directed Thomas to have a boathouse built, sending along his
specifications; thereafter he never lacked a craft when it was needed.
Hunting waterfowl in the marshes remained a favorite pastime, or sailing off the coast in his yacht, *Calypso* (a gift from Stephen White), was
just as pleasurable. "Commodore" Hatch had the responsibility of keeping the boats in repair and ready for launching at short notice. Considered an expert angler, Webster spent long hours fishing, either on the
ponds he had established or at sea.[48] Often he turned from these sports
and merely tramped over the estate, pausing to talk easily with a hand
about some commonplace or current project, exploring remote corners
of his domain while allowing his thoughts to wander as they would. It
was common to see him approach, clothed in linsey-woolsey, high boots,
and broad-brimmed hat. His relations with everyone were amiable and
considerate, though there was a suggestion of the lord of the manor.

The large sums Webster put into his farms at Marshfield and Franklin
would cause him endless trouble, but this was only one aspect of his general financial condition. Although it is impossible to reconstruct his accounts fully, he was obviously running deeply into debt by the
mid-1830s. His income, derived from professional fees of fifteen to
twenty thousand annually and from his farms and investments, came to

an impressive sum. He held stock in a number of corporations, including
the Ellsworth Land and Lumber Company in Maine (he was president
of the board of directors) and the Galveston Bay and Texas Land Company. In both he was an associate of the Democratic spoilsman Samuel
Swartwout.[49] He tended toward ventures involving land or minerals instead of the new manufactures—his small holdings in cotton textiles are
indicative.[50] That he ever gained a great deal from stock dividends is
doubtful. Then there was his compensation as senator, which in those
days was quite modest, normally no more than two thousand a session.[51]
Nevertheless his entire income proved insufficient for his needs, at least
to the extent he generated them.

Notwithstanding the political perils of being charged with improper
connections with the BUS, he relied upon it heavily to mollify his creditors. His relations with the institution transcended routine transactions
at the local branch. An obligation of ten thousand, the advance for services in handling French claims, remained on the bank's books for a long
time.[52] Often he went to the Boston cashier or to the main office to discount notes he negotiated with personal lenders. Of these, many were his
friends. Thomas Perkins, Nathan Hale, Rufus Choate, George Blake,
and Caleb Cushing were only a few of those who helped.[53]

Periodically, money came from funds subscribed by admirers who
wished to keep him on the political scene because they believed he was
making a great financial sacrifice by remaining in public service. In 1834
Everett persuaded Thomas Ward, the Boston agent of the English
banking house of Baring, to solicit a fund of a hundred thousand dollars
for such a purpose.[54] Some years later Ward again took the lead, this
time in enabling Webster to sell his mortgaged Summer Street house
and to travel to England. The fund raisers did not get as much as they
sought, but they apparently provided substantial contributions.[55]

However precarious Webster's financial condition had been through
the years, he entered a period of higher risk in the spring of 1836, when,
like many others, he began investing large sums in western land and
stock. Such activity amounted to nothing less than a boom, highly speculative, irrationally optimistic, increasingly volatile. For about a year
the senator bought heavily in hope of making quick profits to sustain an
affluent life.

A young lawyer in Chicago precipitated the sequence by which Webster moved into the speculator's world. Fisher Harding, his former law
clerk and Fletcher's Harvard classmate, wrote him in March 1836 about
the splendid opportunity to invest in land, especially along the route of
the projected canal connecting Lake Michigan and the Illinois River.

Now an agent for purchasers, Harding offered to put whatever funds Webster could send him into choice tracts which were bound to sell for much more than they cost. The best course, he advised, was to take government land at the minimum price of $1.25 an acre and soon dispose of it as its value climbed. In April Webster told him to go ahead, with permission to spend $2,000 but to be prudent.[56] Meanwhile Fletcher had become intensely interested in what was happening in the West and, with his father's approval, decided to go there at once. His son's involvement influenced Webster to commit himself on a larger scale. He authorized Harding to invest more money and to collaborate with Fletcher, who would shortly arrive in Chicago.[57]

Concurrently he had commissioned another agent in Detroit, Phineas Davis, to purchase land, three-fourths of the five thousand dollars being provided by his wealthy friend Thomas Perkins. A merchant and wide-ranging entrepreneur, Davis was a nephew of Webster's Whig colleague in the Senate, who was also supplying funds. In some ventures Webster and Perkins would be partners; he and John Davis in others.[58]

In a circuit through the West, Fletcher first stopped in Detroit in May. Here he joined Phineas Davis to search out desirable purchases in southern Michigan and to pool their thoughts about various projects. Fletcher was impressed by his fertile-minded associate and liked Detroit very much, in fact concluded he would settle there to practice law and make his fortune. But first he meant to travel farther into this new, exciting country, alive with settlers, builders, promoters, and opportunists of all sorts.

Fletcher's enthusiasm about what he was observing infected Webster. He instructed several agents as well as his son to buy good agricultural land, chiefly from the public domain, well located near a line of communication. If town lots were too expensive, he added, look for areas where towns might develop. "In all your operations," he counseled Fletcher, "you should appear to be acting for yourself; or at least, for yourself & me," and should behave "as if you were already a Western man."[59]

In June, Fletcher rode into Chicago and with his friend Harding traveled through northern Illinois and Wisconsin. The two purchased parcels of farm land, which might also yield minerals, and a few town lots; but they were convinced that they should invest a great deal more as soon as possible. Back in Chicago Fletcher wrote to his father from Harding's office, filled with noisy men talking of land, horses, and canals. The atmosphere was infectious, and innumerable plans raced through his mind. Apart from financial prospects, every day had brought adventure to the youthful New Englander—fording rivers, steering across the prairies by compass, sleeping on cabin floors with his saddle for a pillow. Brown as a nut from the summer's sun and enraptured by this rugged life, he could hardly be happier.[60]

Soon he returned to Detroit for another round of transactions with help from Phineas Davis. Though there were acquisitions at the land office, the chief decision was to subscribe five thousand dollars to the Gibraltar Company, a newly formed venture with Davis as secretary-treasurer. Situated near Detroit at the mouth of the river which connects Lakes Erie and Huron, Gibraltar would become a very prosperous town, Davis predicted, and Webster's stock would produce a profit of 1,000 percent or more. Fletcher was just as confident that his father's shares, one-eighth of the total issued by the company, would be enormously valuable and that he ought not to sell now, despite a demand for them. But Gibraltar, for the time being, was a promotional idea which had not progressed beyond the marketing of stocks.[61]

Fletcher headed East in July to spend some time at home but more at Tonawanda, New York, near Buffalo. The family's friend Stephen White lived here, and Fletcher married White's daughter Caroline. With his bride he returned to Detroit at the end of the year, scratched for fees in a law office, but mainly dreamed of imminent wealth and bought such land as Webster authorized. As for Gibraltar, he was still optimistic, notwithstanding mounting proof that Davis' bookkeeping was careless or worse.[62]

Reconstruction of the story of Webster's land operations is difficult, not only because of gaps in the sources but also because they proceeded simultaneously in several states by arrangement with several agents working independently of each other. Spotty communication with agents and his own irregular attention to details further obscure the record. Nevertheless, a survey of various items for each of the five states involved—Michigan, Indiana, Ohio, Wisconsin, and Illinois—indicates the general character of his foray into speculation.

In Michigan, Phineas Davis bought at least two thousand acres of public land for Webster across the southern part of this new state. Webster also subscribed to stock in companies organized by Davis and associates. Altogether, according to one tabulation, he laid out over twelve thousand dollars to this agent alone.[63] Joseph Williams, a former law student of John Davis, purchased sizable tracts for him in the same region.[64] Fletcher, using capital provided by his father, acquired more, some of it entered in his own name.[65] At first these young men assured him that the property would bring him many times its cost in the near future. But after the Specie Circular of July 1836, demand for cash at land offices slowed business substantially; and their mood sobered. When Fletcher returned to Detroit late in the year, he discovered that all was not well with the Gibraltar Company. An assessment, half the original price of shares, had to be paid to dig a canal and build waterfront facilities. Then the directors found that Davis, the secretary, had mishandled funds, in fact had mortgaged assets for his personal use. Could the enterprise recover from this?[66]

In Ohio, Joseph Williams drew upon Webster both for farm land and for lots in Toledo, a place he said would be a metropolis greater than Detroit or Chicago. He tried unsuccessfully to buy an additional eighty acres in Toledo for subdivision and an estimated profit of 300 percent.[67] Holdings in Ohio were less extensive than in Michigan because the area had been open to sale longer. This was the case in Indiana too, where the senator bought relatively little; he bypassed Williams' ambitious proposal to obtain twenty thousand acres along the northern edge of the state. He briefly had some town lots in Michigan City and some stock in a railroad company there.[68]

Early on, Webster thought that Wisconsin offered an unusual opportunity. Fletcher's reconnaissance of the territory in company with Fisher Harding confirmed an impression that good public land, much of it valuable for minerals and lumber, was plentiful; and so he began buying actively. As elsewhere, Webster shared some commitments with Perkins and John Davis, later with his admiring friend from Newburyport, Caleb Cushing.[69] A knowledgeable agent in Wisconsin was George Jones, native westerner and currently territorial delegate to Congress. James Doty, enterpriser extraordinary and Jones's successor in Congress, also represented him. Jones and Doty bought a huge quantity of land of every type: much of it for agriculture, some for lumber, minerals, and town lots. It included a site at the junction of Iowa, Illinois, and Wisconsin on the Mississippi opposite Dubuque (where Jordan's Ferry was established), desirable plots along the Wisconsin River, parcels in the city of Madison and farther north at Winnebago, even at Superior, in the extreme northwest. Jones estimated the total value to be about eighty thousand, more than the purchase price but reflecting a major investment.[70] In addition, John Haight, a son of the sergeant at arms in the Senate, got him three thousand acres near Rock River. There were acquisitions too for Cushing, whose affairs were becoming entwined with those of Webster.[71]

Northern Illinois proved to be the area to which he gave the most attention. Within a year after beginning purchases there, Webster had acquired large holdings in Rock Island City, up Rock River northeastward, and around Peru, on the Illinois. Several persons, including Jones and Harding, acted for him, but his principal agent was Henry Kinney. About the same age as Fletcher, Kinney had moved west with his family in 1830 and while quite young showed uncommon initiative and self-confidence. In 1834, at age twenty, he helped found the town of Peru, set up a store, and started speculating in land. Afterward he was very interested in construction of the Illinois-Michigan canal—its terminal would be at Peru—and secured contracts from the state to dig sections of the waterway.[72] His relationship with Webster probably arose by way of Harding in Chicago, for when the senator's former law student first suggested buying land, he referred to excellent opportunities along the projected canal and especially at its connection with the Illinois River. In April 1836, about the time that Harding received Webster's authorization to invest, Kinney did too and then asked him to honor a five-thousand-dollar draft to pay for tracts he would take up. Webster agreed, thus commencing a flow of credit amounting to tens of thousands.[73] This response was understandable, for Kinney was an unsurpassed optimist who could also inspire optimism in others. He told Webster about the superlative returns on his own investments, the immense promise of the region, and the large profits, 100 percent a year, to be gained from speculation.[74]

Webster's association with Perkins provided capital for Kinney to purchase hundreds of acres for the two men in mid-1836. By agreement, Webster could draw as much as twenty thousand upon Perkins' company and take one-fourth of the lands while recording three-fourths in Perkins' name. Though the precise character of the arrangement is unclear, it appears that Webster was, in effect, borrowing his quarter part from the merchant, in return for which his agents were acquiring for Perkins property whose value was likely to rise. If this was indeed a loan, it is also unclear when or whether Webster repaid it. At any rate, in this way both of them got land in Michigan, Wisconsin, and Illinois. Webster's draft upon the company for five thousand went to Kinney to buy tracts in and around Peru. For other purchases in Illinois, the senator found different sources.[75]

Though he obtained most of his land for speculative profit, the area a mile or so to the west of Peru had a special character, for he meant to develop a farm here on a grand scale. Beginning with 160 acres, he added neighboring parcels, some coming from Kinney, who had to convey it as his own financial situation worsened.[76] This farm he called Salisbury, in the hope that it would be another Marshfield or Elms where he could carry forward the same kind of improvements he had in the East. He talked of retiring from politics and moving to this new estate as a gentleman farmer. Meanwhile, he depended upon Kinney to look after the place, plant crops, and put up buildings.[77]

Regardless of long-range plans, Webster's thoughts more often centered on short-run profits from speculation. Early in 1837, in the final phase of pursuing that goal, he made his largest investments. In Wisconsin and northern Illinois, George Jones was particularly active in buying for him.[78] But probably Webster's most extensive commitment was to take a great number of town lots in Rock Island from the expansive speculator Levi Turner and others. For these he promised to pay sixty thousand dollars. Kinney may have had a role in arranging this transaction, and one of the persons who helped the senator in the venture was Cushing.[79] At this time, too, Webster heavily subscribed to stock in the Clamorgan Land Association, a risky enterprise though a potential bonanza. The company claimed 458,000 acres in southeastern Missouri and northeastern Arkansas on the basis of an old Spanish grant. To exploit the claim, Webster and his fellow stockholders would have to get legislative and judicial confirmation of the original grant. He felt the chance of success in those efforts was good enough to justify borrowing the capital he provided. Perhaps he could resell the stock for a handsome gain without waiting for the project to mature.[80]

While he was rapidly buying both stock and land, the country's financial situation grew ominous. The Specie Circular of mid-1836, requiring cash for the sale of public land, not only roused him politically but also threatened him personally. His land agents reported how difficult it was to obtain the necessary specie. "Real estate operations are dull in this part of the country," Harding told him in September. "Money is exceedingly scarce."[81] Though quite aware of the problem, Webster still managed to do some business at the government land offices, but now more with individuals and companies, with Turner, Kinney, Jones, and his Clamorgan associates. By the spring of 1837 this option had also dwindled. In April he concluded that "money is too scarce, & the times too *really distressing,* here [Washington], to think of raising any more at present for western operations." Banks and mercantile houses were faltering, he observed, and the outlook was gloomy. Within a few weeks, in May, the panic struck New York, then other places. So he might become a victim of the hard times for which, as a politician, he blamed the administration. His principal hope had to be that he could benefit from his present holdings. "If I am not mistaken," he had written, "my purchases, already made, will afford me the means of spinning out the short remainder of my thread of life."[82]

The status of this property, however, became less and less secure, for it depended upon the complex, shaky arrangements of his western land agents. And one after another they fell into trouble, in each case involving Webster as well.[83] His relationship with Levi Turner turned out to be especially damaging. Among several land deals managed by Turner for the senator, the most important had been acquisition of a large package of lots in Rock Island. He had accepted Turner's drafts; but when they came due, Webster could not pay them. Moreover, Turner had himself taken the land on credit and could not pay the people he owed. Pressed by creditors, both Turner and Webster tried to extricate themselves in a number of ways, so intricate that they defy understanding. What is known is that there was a series of drafts of each man on the other, as well as notes, mortgages, bonds, endorsements, and assignments—all exercises in credit—without reducing their debt.[84] They were sued or threatened with suit for nonpayment of at least thirty thousand dollars, even though lawyers such as Hamilton Fish felt reluctant to pursue a person of Webster's eminence.[85] The most persistent creditor was Ramsay Crooks, president of the American Fur Company and agent of the Chouteau Company of St. Louis, from which Webster had obtained the Clamorgan land. For it, too, he had used drafts, totaling twenty thousand to purchase his stock and more for Turner and Kinney. Relentlessly Crooks squeezed out the first installment of a settlement, but the senator could not meet the next deadline.[86]

He handled, really postponed, problems of this sort with liberal help from the Bank of the United States, currently a state bank of Pennsylvania. However uncomfortable his condition may have been, he still believed his western property was quite valuable. If Biddle could give him credit, things would surely improve in a while. As he explained to the banker, "In the hope of realizing such advances, as would enable me to live without carrying the Green Bag any longer. I put every thing I could rake & scrape, cash & credit, in lands, at Government price, in Illinois & Wisconsin, in 1836. I am quite sure that the investments were well made, & that as soon as times turn, even a little, these lands will sell at from five to ten times their cost. But at present, I can only sell on long credit, & have preferred not to sell at all."[87] Biddle and other BUS officers responded positively. Cashier Joseph Cowperthwaite provided discounts to tide him over on obligations involving Kinney and Turner, including the Clamorgan tangle; and other credit was forthcoming when he was cornered. Indirectly, Biddle assisted by identifying sources of loans outside the bank—prominent persons in Philadelphia and New York. And in one instance, he facilitated matters by requesting the cashier at the former BUS branch in Washington to discount a note. Furthermore, Samuel Jaudon, the bank's representative in London, assumed the task of finding English buyers of stock and land.[88]

He also looked elsewhere for credit. At the Merchants' Bank in Boston, for example, Franklin Haven could be relied upon for loans and discounts and took a flexible view toward overdrafts, due dates, and collateral in his case. Webster's relationship with Haven would be very satisfactory in the years to come, and so one can assume that he was more careful than usual to honor obligations.[89] Apart from banks, there always seemed to be friends willing to come to his rescue—men such as Roswell Colt, the merchant-banker in New York and an associate in the Clamorgan venture.[90]

Within months after the economic downturn had begun, Webster's attention gravitated toward Peru. The principal reason was that Fletcher had decided to move there. His son's brief residence in Detroit had not gone well, perhaps because it was ill timed; his legal practice was not yielding enough, and the cost of living proved to be higher than he could tolerate. In long letters to his father, Fletcher explained his difficulties and proposed a new start at the Salisbury farm and in a law office in Peru.[91] Despite Webster's hesitancy, Fletcher set out for Illinois on November 1, 1837, with Caroline and their infant daughter. Henry Kinney, managing Webster's affairs in the Peru area as well as carrying on his own extensive operations, welcomed them warmly. According to plan, Fletcher assisted Kinney in attempting to get the farm on a paying basis and in shoring up the sagging Webster-Kinney interests. Through the winter he reported quite cheerfully about his situation, but obviously the colonel, as he referred to Kinney, faced almost insuperable problems. Fletcher felt he was a splendid fellow, kind and energetic, but caught in a vise of delinquent debtors and insistent creditors. It was only fair, he cautioned his father, not to blame the colonel for whatever was going wrong.[92] For his part, Kinney assured Webster that he truly had the senator's welfare in mind but that he needed money badly.[93] After months of delay, he decided he must come East to work something out.

When Kinney arrived at the capital in May 1838, he said he needed funds, and Webster replied that he did too. Each had property (then almost impossible to sell) which either could transfer to the other, if the transaction could be discounted as a bank loan. Naturally Webster preferred to be rid of some land if he had a choice. So he asked Biddle to find someone to take a bond on the sale of his land to Kinney.[94] Biddle answered that just now his bank had a "ferocious indisposition to lend," but to come to Philadelphia and he would see what he could do.[95] After a conference the banker decided to discount Kinney's notes to Webster and to credit Webster's account for sixty thousand. No land was mortgaged or sold, and Webster's mere endorsement of the notes provided a large sum, some of which the senator probably made available to Kinney.[96] If so, Webster ended up with an undetermined remainder and more rather than less land, because Kinney was still conveying tracts to him. The Peru farm alone expanded from four hundred to eleven hundred acres.[97]

This arrangement, hazy as it was, would benefit no one, Kinney, Webster, or the bank, if the Peru property continued to be unprofitable. It was therefore imperative to develop the farm as soon as possible. In fact an intensive effort had been under way as early as March 1838, when Webster sent out Ray Thomas of the Marshfield family as manager. His instructions were to equip and stock the place, get more crops in, employ labor.[98] Fletcher would assist him and live in the house on the premises. Kinney gave up his responsibility to oversee the work. Experienced and capable, Thomas would succeed if anyone could. In the spring and summer he bought implements and livestock, put new plots under cultivation, and repaired neglected buildings.[99] Since Thomas had to travel a good deal to carry on business, he often left matters to Fletcher, who soon concluded that despite improvements, the enterprise was impractical because of large expenses and poor economic conditions.[100]

Webster had also asked Thomas to survey the status of all his western holdings and to sell or, if necessary, exchange whatever he could. These included acquisitions in Ohio, Michigan, and Wisconsin, a huge amount, though the exact extent was uncertain. Thomas had to go to Toledo, Detroit, and other towns; to confer with Phineas Davis, Fisher Harding, Benjamin Kercheval (a Detroit businessman who was holding thousands of acres jointly with Webster); and to straighten out numerous titles and contracts. His reports to Webster were discouraging; he found agents and associates in bad shape and no one interested in buying land. One of many disconcerting items was his discovery that a tract at St. Joseph, Michigan, costing two thousand was completely under water. In December 1838 he had amassed the best information he could and then headed East to deliver it to Webster.[101]

As he reviewed his situation, the senator grew ever more anxious to liquidate his western property. Thomas' report dampened hopes, affairs in Peru seemed unpromising, he needed cash for travel to England. Apparently on the advice of his New York circle, he formed a plan to put his lands and stock in trust with the New York Bank of Commerce as security for a loan. Writing to Samuel Ruggles of that institution in March 1839, he said: "I should be glad of $50,000, but could get along with 40,000. I shall have with me satisfactory evidences of value, & clear exhibits of title; & what I have thought of proposing, is, that some few friends should join in a security to your New Bank, & let a conveyance be made of the property, in trust, to be sold in reasonable time."[102] In mid-May 1839 Ruggles had arranged the loan, underwritten by Fitzhenry Homer of Boston and "other persons." The sum was twenty-eight thousand instead of fifty, for a term of two years. He conveyed to the trust about forty-five hundred acres of land as well as corporate stock, to which he would add property when he perfected title to it. Thus the commitment could include nearly all his holdings in the West.[103]

Notwithstanding bleak prospects, Fletcher stayed in Peru for another year and a half, until 1841. Now he was on his own in representing his father, for Thomas did not return and Kinney fled his dreadful circumstances. Priority went to diagnosing the financial situation following the colonel's departure. After looking into Kinney's many investments across the state and in the vicinity, as well as the indebtedness clouding much of it, he knew that recovery depended upon significant changes. Two indispensables were completion of the canal and improvement of economic conditions. Meanwhile he built up the farm and tried to be philosophical. But it became increasingly difficult to feel that way. Only a small fraction of the hundreds of acres was planted; and prices for crops, beef, and pork were outlandishly low. Too often he had to draw bills upon Webster, and too often he had to report setbacks in dolorous terms. As for his law practice, it did not amount to much; indeed, sometimes he was counsel for himself as defendant in actions of debt. His consolation lay in his famiy—there was a second child, named Daniel—and in Illinois politics, with the possibility of election to the legislature or even a federal appointment if the Whigs won in 1840.

Webster and his son were nearly convinced that they should give up on the Illinois farm.[104] One event leading them to this conclusion was the death of Ray Thomas, who might have rescued the undertaking. Thomas had come to Washington in March 1840 to confer with Webster about land titles before going West. But he came down with a recurrence of an illness from the previous year, called bilious fever according to the uncertain medical knowledge of the time. For three weeks Webster and others attended him almost continuously during his decline, ending in death. Deeply affected by the loss of his loyal young friend, the senator may have agreed with Fletcher that the western country was a rather unhealthful place where one was apt to contract such diseases as Thomas had.[105]

Even more decisive was the news that Illinois had discontinued construction of the canal and would probably not soon resume it—a bad blow to the prospects of Peru. Of course, the cancellation of the project was a direct result of the depression, which also seemed to prohibit the Websters holding out any longer. As Fletcher remarked, "I was unfortunate in coming here. I came on an *ebb tide* and things have been going backward ever since."[106] The truth was his father had plunged into the whole business of western land speculation on the ebb tide, and the only question now was how to cut his losses as much as possible. In January 1841, Fletcher, Caroline, and children were back in the East to stay.

During February Webster did close out almost all of his western interests. Again it was the Bank of the United States that answered his plea. Though no longer president, Biddle influenced the corporation's decision to make a settlement; and the details fell to Herman Cope, superintendent of Suspended Debt and Real Estate.[107] Webster felt anxious to conclude the business before the new administration began the next month. He needed money, but he wished to avoid the embarrassment of accepting any favors after he became secretary of state.[108] Wasting no time, Cope got the bank's approval to take almost all the western property as satisfaction of Webster's debts to the institution, amounting to $114,000.[109] Half consisted of the Kinney notes, with the remainder including many overdrafts and various loans. Toward the end of February 1841, the lands had been appraised, though at a much lower figure than real value. Cope and Webster then signed an agreement, concluding a sad chapter in the story of the senator's finances. Still, it did not end his troubles, for he never fully recovered from his setbacks as speculator.[110]

He had resorted to this arrangement with the bank after everything else had failed. Among his attempts to liquidate western investments had been an effort to sell his holdings by traveling to England nearly two years earlier, in May 1839. He had thought that perhaps there, despite hard times and English disenchantment with American debtors, he might market some land and stock. So he had asked Samuel Jaudon, the bank's representative in London, to look into possibilities, which were predictably reported as slight.[111] But together with a remote chance of success, other considerations influenced his decision to go. He had a long-standing interest in visiting England, whose men and institutions he very much admired. Briefly, too, he had the impractical idea that Van Buren would send him on a mission to settle the northeastern boundary dispute. His Democratic adversary soon made it plain that the administration did not need his services.[112] Not getting funds for the trip from this source, he raised money for expenses with help from Boston friends, the loan from Ruggles' bank, and probably a little from his father-in-law and Biddle. With this in hand, he sailed from New York on May 18, 1839.[113]

Webster and his family were in Europe for six months, a period as pleasurable socially as it was disappointing financially. With him were Caroline, Julia, sister-in-law Harriette Paige, later joined by Edward and by Sam Appleton, Julia's fiancé. The party landed at Liverpool but went immediately to London. They spent most of the time here, involved in a whirl of entertainment and sightseeing, broken by a trip through the countryside as far as Scotland and by an interlude on the Continent. When they returned home in December, all of them had many memories of interesting places and people; for Julia and Sam the visit was particularly important, for they were married in London.

The Americans settled in comfortably at Brunswick House, near Oxford and Regent streets, a location convenient for moving about the city each day. Move they did. There were countless calls and invitations from those who knew or wished to know Webster. Persons such as Charles Bagot, Charles Vaughan, and Stratford Canning were well acquainted with the senator from their residence in Washington as diplomats. Minister Andrew Stevenson, Samuel Jaudon, and Joshua Bates, who had been born in Massachusetts but now held a partnership in the Baring firm, saw them frequently, often to make introductions. As the weeks passed, hardly a politician, businessman, or literary figure in London of any prominence missed the opportunity to meet the Defender of the Constitution. Palmerston, Peel, Wellington, Disraeli, Gladstone were only a few of those who befriended him. Carlyle, Wordsworth, Dickins, Moore, Coleridge, and other literati also received him warmly.[114]

Webster's daily routine began with a ride to some point of interest—the carriage and coachman were made available by his friend John Evelyn Denison, Viscount Ossington, then out of town but eager to be of service.[115] He would go to the Tower, Westminster Abbey, the financial district, the courts, or quite regularly the houses of Parliament to follow proceedings. "I have attended the debates a good deal, especially on important occasions," he said. "Some of their ablest men are far from being fluent speakers. In fact, they hold in no high repute the mere faculty of ready speaking, at least not so high as it is held in other places."[116] In the afternoons he would often make calls, and later he and his party would be dinner guests somewhere. Concerts and various social events filled out the evenings.[117] A highlight was being received by the young queen at a ball. For the occasion, he was outfitted in smallclothes, diamond knee and shoe buckles, and a ruffled shirt.[118]

When he traveled outside London, agricultural conditions fascinated him. The squire of Marshfield discovered how far ahead the English were in their progress toward a scientific stage. Their sheep and cattle were better bred, their fields better fertilized and drained, their crops better selected. For future use, he wrote memoranda and drew sketches of what he encountered.[119] "I think I have learned something," he remarked. "The English are better farmers than we are. *Turnips have revolutionized English agriculture.* The sheep are thick as flies, & mutton is dear."[120] It is suggestive of his interest to notice that he paid no attention to English mills or the life of the industrial working class. And though he carefully avoided public speeches, which might have embarrassing repercussions on either side of the Atlantic, he did deliver one formal address. At Oxford on July 17, 1839, he spoke to a large meeting of the Royal Agricultural Society, almost entirely about the great improvements in farming he had observed. Advances in England, he declared, had significant international effects, in light of the financial and commercial leadership exercised by the country. And America, particularly, benefited from the scientific revolution under way by borrowing from British experience.[121]

Though he found his stay in London enjoyable and instructive, he did not forget his main object, the sale of his western property. With the aid of Jaudon and Bates, week after week he sought some way of disposing of it for cash. As expected, he encountered immense obstacles, tightness of British money and credit, lack of interest in further commitments in America, and active hostility toward defaulting debtors, including state governments, in the United States. After a frustrating effort of four months, Webster complained, "Money matters have been in a most horrid State here all summer. Everything American, stocks and land, are perfectly flat. Nothing can possibly be sold. By great exertions, I have done enough to pay expenses, so as to go home no poorer than I came, that is about all."[122] He had even less success in selling his shares in the Clamorgan land company. Relying upon Virgil Maxcy in Brussels and Jaudon in London, he could do nothing with them at the moment. But the contacts he made may have helped him later when he unloaded them in return for bank stock and at last salvaged something.[123]

Webster probably gave as much assistance as he received. In October Jaudon faced a serious problem concerning nonacceptance of BUS paper in Europe. A crisis passed when English bankers, possibly influenced by Webster's pleas, provided support. If that was the case, the senator could feel satisfaction in being able to reciprocate a favor to his steady friend Jaudon.[124] Another good deed involved the worrisome situation of bonds of states, then in bad repute because of their inability to fulfill obligations during the depression. Webster tried to counter the difficulty by writing a legal opinion for the Barings, the states' agent for bond sales in England. Contrary to assertions in some quarters, he argued, the American states could constitutionally contract such debts abroad; furthermore, it was a mistake to assume that these governments would not honor their promises to pay. To do so would bring on unbearable disgrace and public displeasure.[125] Legal theory notwithstanding, Webster had to convince investors that the bonds were desirable investments. With respect to those in which he himself had the greatest interest, the issues of Massachusetts, he did promote a few sales.[126]

These financial matters had delayed Webster's plan to cross to the Continent for a short tour. His family had left for the Low Countries, Germany, Switzerland, and France in September after the wedding of Julia and Sam, but he did not get away until mid-October. So he could not cover the ground they did and had to be satisfied with a brief time in Paris. Here Minister Lewis Cass arranged for a reception by King Louis Philippe, who seemed amicable and talkative.[127]

Back in England in November, he laid plans to sail home, though tempted to stay longer. Undoubtedly a shortage of funds as well as the necessity of attending the Senate, however late, forbade any postponement. As it was, passage was slow and rough, so that he did not land at New York until December 28 nor arrive in Boston until January 2.[128] Before going down to Washington, he could take a few days to get affairs at home in order as well as to think about his interesting, satisfactory visit abroad, the only one he would ever take. He had been welcomed by many English friends and admirers, had been entertained lavishly, had seen places he had long hoped to see. True enough, his financial circumstances had not improved much, but he had established relationships, such as that with Alexander Baring, Lord Ashburton, which would be significant in the future.[129] Just now, of course, he could not know how this would be so.

Chapter 18
VETO

As Harrison's term began, expectations of sudden improvement in the state of the Union had reached a peak. Among many anticipated changes the first step seemed to be wholesale turnover of personnel. However ironic it may have been, the now dominant Whigs, long accustomed to deploring a Jacksonian spoils system, lost no time in replacing incumbents with their own partisans everywhere, from cabinet departments to unimportant offices. Apart from a conviction that thorough reform demanded responsiveness to popular will as recently expressed, the necessity of rewarding log-cabin campaigners and adherents soon overwhelmed the leadership at Washington, Webster included.

So in March 1841 the new secretary of state spent long hours handling patronage, fewer shaping foreign policy.[1] He had already selected his son Fletcher as chief clerk, an important post in the days before assistant secretaries of state. Then with help from Thurlow Weed and William Seward, Webster persuaded the president to stand by a preinaugural commitment to install Edward Curtis as collector of the Port of New York, despite Clay's spirited protest. Currently one of Webster's inner circle, Curtis could control a force of five hundred employees—a choice plum.[2] The secretary gave a great deal of attention to Pennsylvania too. Here Biddle frequently volunteered advice about appointments, much of which Webster passed on to Secretary of the Treasury Thomas Ewing with positive effect.[3] As for the old Antimasonic element, Thad Stevens gave his views at length on taking care of it.[4] And a wealthy friend in Philadelphia, Isaac R. Jackson, solicited a diplomatic assignment while Webster was arranging a loan from him to help buy a house in Washing-

299

ton. Jackson later went to Denmark as chargé d'affaires.[5] Of the many selections made by the administration, Webster had the most to say about consulates abroad and federal judgeships at home.[6]

Reminiscent of Jefferson's hopeless effort to balance partisan appointments with some evenhandedness, the administration issued statements promising more than it could deliver.[7] Webster sent a presidential directive to all departmental secretaries that it was "a great abuse to bring the patronage of the general government into conflict with the freedom of elections; and that this abuse ought to be corrected wherever it may have been permitted to exist, and to be prevented for the future." The circular warned that "partisan interference in popular elections" by public employees "or the payment of any contribution or assessment on salaries or official compensation for party or election purposes, will be regarded by [the president] as cause of removal." It was a high-sounding if ineffective declaration, allowing removals of Democrats and in no way abolishing the spoils system.[8] In any event, three weeks after taking office, Webster showed the strain always besetting dispensers of patronage. "I am almost worn down," he remarked; "never did I fall into such a business, as surrounds us here, while attempting to get under way."[9]

On Capitol Hill, Clay concentrated on more elevated matters of policy. His interpretation of a voters' mandate would require launching an economic program immediately, both to lift the country out of depression and to stimulate its development. Well before the inauguration, he had pushed a reluctant Whig caucus toward the idea of a special session; Webster had been one of those brought into line.[10] Still, after Harrison took over, some resistance to this strategy continued. When the Kentuckian sent a note on the subject to the executive mansion and enclosed a draft proclamation, old Tip briskly replied that he must take advice from others as well. The fact that the exchange was written rather than oral revealed tension as well as hesitancy to follow the party doctrine of executive deference to Congress.[11] Probably the Treasury's shortage of funds caused Harrison to comply; at least Webster said that was the reason.[12] On March 17 the president called a special session to meet at the end of May.[13]

Unfortunately he did not live that long. At the White House during the night of April 3 after an illness of a few days, he died, surrounded by officials and family members. Though sixty-eight and somewhat worn down by his new duties, he had appeared to be in good health until he contracted a fatal case of pneumonia. The shocking event, unprecedented in the first half-century of national history, left leaders of the administration in an uncertain position. Vice-President John Tyler was at home in Williamsburg, Congress was not in session, and so the cabinet—that is, the five out of six who were present—felt they had the responsibility of acting. Throughout the day of the fourth, Webster and his colleagues were busy issuing announcements to the public, dispatching letters to civil servants across the country and in foreign posts, organizing an elaborate funeral and procession to the congressional burying ground on the seventh. Thus ended the shortest term of any American chief executive, precisely one month. If the people grieving at Harrison's death had then known the political consequences, they would have grieved even more.[14]

The cabinet through Webster had also immediately notified the vice-president of the "melancholy tidings," carried to Williamsburg by Fletcher as special messenger.[15] Tyler hurried to the capital, arrived on the sixth, took the oath of office, and met with the cabinet, all of whom consented to his request that they remain in office.[16] Two days after the funeral, in a message to the people on the ninth, he asked for support in these unusual circumstances but showed that he would unhesitatingly assume full presidential status and expressed his opinions on a range of national problems. Besides endorsing Whig policy on removals from office and urging strict economy in governmental operations, he emphasized the serious financial situation, especially an unsatisfactory independent treasury. A better system of performing fiscal functions had to be found, he said, to correct disarrangements of the currency, presumably in the coming special session.[17]

Despite his noncommittal language on what kind of system he preferred, Tyler had a long, well-known record on banking. An aristocratic, states' rights Virginian, he had repeatedly spoken and voted against the Bank of the United States over a twenty-year period in Congress. In 1832 he had supported Jackson's veto of the recharter bill on constitutional grounds. Yet his independent spirit and opposition to strong executive power had led him to disapprove removal of governmental deposits the following year. By this route he had joined the new Whig party, an anti-Jacksonian coalition of a minor segment of southern strict constructionists with nationalists such as Webster and Clay. When the party nominated Harrison in 1840, it added Tyler to balance the ticket, never anticipating that he would become president.

Now Clay, still suffering from injured pride, would have to deal with a chief executive unlikely to share his estimate of the nation's needs. True, he occupied a powerful base in the Senate, for his colleagues acknowledged his leadership, he controlled an active caucus and the selection of committees, and he cited party dogma of strictly limited presidential power. On June 7, a week after the special session began, the Kentuckian laid down an agenda in a series of resolutions favoring a national bank to replace the subtreasury, a higher tariff, distribution of proceeds from land sales to the states, and a bankruptcy law.[18] But would the antique-republican president cooperate?

Whether to charter a bank was the central question. During the recent campaign Tyler had said nothing specific about it, but in private conversation he left the impression that he opposed the revival of a national bank, the very thing Clay wished.[19] In his address to the public on April 9 he had ominously observed that in deciding the issue, he would "resort to the fathers of the great republican school for advice and instruction." His discussion of banking in a message to Congress on May 31 restated what Clay had already been hearing.[20] There must be a new approach rather than a return to the same sort of corporation repudiated by the people in Jackson's time or continuance of an independent treasury so plainly discredited. Though he professed respect for legislative judgment about an alternative, his flourishing of the veto power seemed quite un-Whiggish. He reserved the right to disapprove not only an unconstitutional bill, he said, but also one which would "otherwise jeopardize the prosperity of the country."[21]

Though Clay adhered to his own notions, he had at least to make the cooperative gesture of putting through a resolution requesting Secretary of the Treasury Ewing to present the administration's recommendation. Ewing complied promptly. This plan represented what the secretary thought would satisfy Tyler. Locate the main office of the corporation in the District of Columbia, where Congress had clear constitutional power to legislate, he suggested, and allow branches only in those states consenting to their admission. Referred to a select committee headed by Clay, this proposal at once encountered the senator's hostility. As expected, he reported on it adversely and instead offered his own model, a bank with unrestricted branching privileges.[22] His unyielding, imperious manner revealed something more fundamental than disagreement upon a particular issue. He was fighting a political duel with Tyler over general policymaking, indeed over the next presidential nomination.

Following the controversy closely, Webster sought some compromise to avoid failure of all legislation and disintegration of the party. He had no doubt that Congress had power to create another Bank of the United States with all the features of the earlier one; yet he would take half a loaf rather than none in the existing situation. So he set out to persuade the cabinet, Congress, and the public that this was the only practical option. He kept Ewing in line and even attempted to get his colleague to limit a bank's functions to dealing in interstate and foreign exchange but not local discounts of promissory notes; he sensed that the president was shifting to this narrower view.[23] Meanwhile he exploited his connections with the legislative branch, especially the Massachusetts men Caleb Cushing in the House and Isaac Bates and Rufus Choate in the Senate, who mirrored his thinking during the long summer's debate. Then, to influence public opinion and indirectly the politicians, he recruited the press. The *Intelligencer* was his primary outlet. Through June and July it carried editorials, letters, and clippings urging accommodation of the two sides. As he had often done, he wrote a number of the editorials, which Gales and Seaton printed with few, if any, revisions.[24] In Wall Street his devoted friend Hiram Ketchum carried out his instructions to put the New York papers on the right track with an appeal to the common sense of businessmen. By way of Ketchum he sent draft editorials for the *Commercial Advertiser,* designed to blunt the *American*'s pro-Clay stance, including charges that the cabinet had surrendered to the president.[25]

Webster's theme was pragmatic: the nation's desperate economic condition demanded action. It was folly to insist upon a program which Tyler's constitutional scruples would not permit. Take the Ewing formula now as the best obtainable, for it could be improved if necessary. Otherwise the Whig party would fall victim to internal dissension, the very outcome desired by the Democrats; and the country would be the worse for it. In fact, he contended, locating the bank in Washington and restricting its functions would work out very well. Most states, he predicted, would readily admit branches because of the substantial financial advantages they would bring.

The campaign for compromise was failing. In the Senate early in July, William Rives moved an amendment to Clay's bill that amounted to a substitution of the Ewing plan. In the middle of debate on it, Choate warned that without such a provision, a bill could not become law. He really meant that the president would veto it. Clay angrily demanded that Choate explain how he knew this and implied that the New Englander was speaking for Webster. The usually self-assured orator replied a little lamely but did not confess to having any private information from the cabinet. Nevertheless, Clay prevailed in the vote against the Rives-Ewing option.[26]

Through mid-July Clay then attempted unsuccessfully to gather enough votes to pass his own bill by lecturing the caucus and cajoling or intimidating individual senators. Finally he realized he could not put together a majority. Yet perhaps he might preserve the substance by confecting it with slight concession. It was maverick John Minor Botts, congressman from Virginia, who provided a promising solution to the problem. Formerly a political friend of Tyler but now a Clay man, Botts visited the president to discuss his idea. Permit branching of the bank in any state which did not disapprove in its first legislative session after passage of the national statute, he proposed. Just what Tyler said to that is unclear. Botts told Clay that the chief executive agreed; Tyler later recalled that he did not. At any rate, Botts's report seemed to justify an attempt to pass his amendment, Clay concluded. The senator would not go any further to pacify the president; and if he vetoed, so be it. When the Botts proviso came up, it passed by one vote, with approval of the main measure the next day, July 28, by a margin of only three. The House concurred on August 6.[27]

Tyler held the bill for the maximum ten days, a period of speculation and rumor about what he would do and what the consequences might be. One signal had been Rives's negative vote, since he was consistently the president's legislative advocate and adviser. Still, Webster and the rest of the cabinet had no direct indication of intentions and in fact did not discuss the question with Tyler for several days. Though pessimistic, the secretary of state inclined to think he would sign. His opinion was that he surely ought to do so—if not, "a great commotion will doubtless follow."[28] In the meantime he generated some pressure. The *Intelligencer* and the Boston *Advertiser* urged approval, probably with his prodding; and he brought his friend Richard Blatchford, a New York lawyer representing banking interests, to Washington for useful information from that quarter. But on the eleventh, he knew there was no hope after a five-hour session in which the cabinet found Tyler adamant against their counsel.[29] Thereafter the task must be to contain the damage as much as possible.

In his veto of August 16, the president advanced two objections. First, the Botts amendment obstructed a state's right to decide upon admitting a branch, for interpretation of legislative silence as implied consent would not accurately register that state's considered judgment; nor would the obligation to disapprove in the first session after congressional enactment, because the timing of elections and the complex structure of government would obscure popular will. The reasoning here became finespun. Second, Tyler surprisingly cited a more fundamental defect, the bank's privilege to discount local notes. If this had bothered him when Ewing framed his proposal, Tyler had been unclear about it. During the Senate debate, Webster had suspected that the president opposed local discounts and preferred only business in interstate and foreign exchange. Perhaps it was a new position in reaction to Clay's behavior. In any case, the present message spoke approvingly of exchange operations and just the opposite of discounting. Expressing regret that he must withhold his signature, Tyler inserted a characteristic declaration of duty to follow his conscience at all hazards.[30]

Webster felt deeply disappointed but clung to the possibility of recouping. "On the whole," he remarked, "we have an anxious & unhappy time, & I am sometimes heart sick." While he disagreed with Tyler about the constitutionality and policy of the vetoed measure, he conceded the president's right to define his own obligations. Though the situation had become difficult, Webster saw no reason to resign; and the entire cabinet had so decided. To pick up the pieces, he invited a number of congressional Whigs to his house the day after the veto "to keep them in good temper."[31] Coincidentally an editorial he had drafted appeared in the *Intelligencer,* arguing that Tyler ought to have deferred to Congress but calling for a renewed effort toward agreement either at this session or preferably at the next. Above all, everyone should stay calm and cool.[32]

Clay was definitely not cool. In a scorching speech on August 19 he vented his disgust with executive duplicity, usurpation, and grievous errors. Contrary to the ground upon which the Whigs had been elected, inconsistent with his early public statements in April, incompatible with the terms of the bill as adjusted to suit him in June, Tyler had ignored a popular mandate to restore a national bank. When the president said he would follow the teachings of the republican school, did he not know that one of the fathers of that faith, Madison, had approved a bank in 1816 because of the test of experience? If he was so misguided about an issue upon which there was a constitutional consensus, he should have allowed the bill to pass without signature—or he might resign (doubtless Clay's preference). The Kentuckian went directly to Tyler's motive, which was, he charged, to set up a new party in his own interest for the next election. As proof, he pointed to the small band already maneuvering toward that object. He did not mention names but had in mind Henry Wise, Thomas Gilmer, William Rives, Abel Upshur, Beverly Tucker, and Duff Green, a nefarious "corporal's guard." When Rives responded in detail, Clay depicted him as one of this cabal. At the moment, the violent attack made no difference in a vote which did not come close to overriding the veto.[33]

Clay had delayed delivering this philippic until his Whig colleagues could frame a second bank bill which Tyler might accept. On the very day of the veto, August 16, Alexander Stuart, a Virginia representative, had called upon the president for what appeared to be productive discussion about specific provisions. With a copy of the vetoed bill before them, Tyler pointed to sections requiring revision. They agreed to delete a clause authorizing the bank's local agencies to discount promissory notes so that their main function would be to handle bills of exchange. Then, to meet his objection to the Botts amendment allowing creation of branches or agencies, Tyler penciled in a prohibition against them where forbidden by state law. On that subject the two men left their understanding rather unsettled. Oddly, Tyler did not insist upon the original Ewing requirement of prior state consent to branching. His suggestion, fuzzy and hasty, was to make branching dependent upon whatever state policy might exist at some time or another. Having in mind a recent Supreme Court decision, he would permit the new institution to operate in any state on the common-law principle of comity toward out-of-state corporations if conformable with that state's positive law. This was a dubious extension of the judicial rule on state corporations to a national one. An additional problem was that Stuart objected, saying that it was unnecessary and implying that it was undesirable. Tyler replied he would think about it but suggested that, in the meantime, Stuart see Webster for help in drafting a new bill. If the congressman found a solution, the president declared, "I will esteem you the best friend I have on earth."[34]

Stuart failed to find Webster available and without waiting talked with John Sergeant and John Berrien, chairmen of the appropriate House and Senate committees, as well as with Clay and other Whigs. The next day, the seventeenth, and again the eighteenth, Sergeant and Berrien met with Tyler, who outlined his views but only in general terms. Later in the morning of the eighteenth the president discussed the whole matter with the cabinet.[35] Webster, continuing to play a leading role as pacificator in these tangled events, claimed in his recollections of the occasion that Tyler insisted upon an institution prohibited from discounting notes but permitted to deal in exchange. "And for such a Bank," the secretary wrote, "he did not intimate that he requested the assent of the States."[36]

Now worried about entrapment and conveniently retreating to a stance of noninterference with the legislative branch, Tyler asked Webster and Ewing to see Sergeant and Berrien, to describe the kind of measure they thought he would accept, but not to pledge him to do so. As for himself, he would hold no further conversations with congressmen. Some of the cabinet, probably not including Webster, concurred in this unwise cutoff of direct communications. The likelihood of misinterpretation had increased, for what Tyler had told Stuart he did not tell

306

Webster and Ewing; and what they conjectured Tyler might do could not guarantee how he would respond when a bill reached his desk. But Webster complied with the president's request, rode immediately to the Capitol, and went over the provisions with the lawmakers without absolutely promising that the chief executive would approve them. Within forty-eight hours, on August 20, Sergeant introduced his bill in the House.[37]

When Webster got a copy, as he recalled, he read it to the president, who once more did not demand state assent to a branch or agency dealing merely in exchange. To satisfy Tyler on less important aspects, Webster changed the name of the institution to "Fiscal Corporation" instead of "Bank" and decreased the amount of its capital stock. From his perspective, Congress would have a measure carefully tailored to fit the presidential framework; and he believed it would accomplish everything needed.[38]

Then the arrangement unraveled. The day before Sergeant brought in his bill, Clay had delivered his diatribe against the veto of the earlier plan. The thin-skinned Tyler felt maligned by imputations of dishonorable conduct, of reneging on the first bank proposal, of scheming to wreck the party, of building a new one for his own election in 1844. At the same time, an offensive letter by Botts surfaced. Intending it as a private report of politics in Washington to his fellow club members in a Richmond coffeehouse, this pro-Clay partisan alleged Tyler's aim to be a coalition with the Locofoco Democrats. But the Whigs would "head" that attempt, Botts predicted. The item would have gone unnoticed if one of the president's friends had not copied it and sent it northward. Tyler was incensed and showed it to Webster when he reviewed his complaints in a visit to the latter's office on August 20—and he was even more so when Botts's letter came out the next day in the *Madisonian.* In Webster's opinion, Tyler's irritation was such that from this moment little chance for agreeing upon a bank proposal remained.[39]

Tyler tried to head off action on the bill. Even before the House passed it on August 23 and until Senate approval on September 3, he repeatedly let it be known that he wished postponement of the matter until the next session. Recognizing the certainty of a veto, Webster urged congressional friends such as Bates and Choate to delay. Clay, more interested in bringing down Tyler than in anything else, would not countenance a course he deemed supine. Let the bill go forward, he ordered; and it did. In this fashion the climax of the weird drama arrived.[40]

As adjournment approached, Tyler sent up his veto.[41] The provision on exchange did not suit him, for, like Rives and others, he now saw ways in which bills of exchange could be used in credit transactions much as discounted promissory notes were and would thus bypass his basic objection to loans. He had never discussed that possibility with Stuart, Berrien, Sergeant, Ewing, or Webster. Furthermore, in the absence of a provision on state consent to admit an agency, he feared the fiscal corporation could operate not just in the federal district but throughout the Union.

He had not insisted upon state consent in most of his previous conversations, except with Stuart. Still, the bill he had before him stipulated that agencies could engage in operations "not being contrary to law." And that phrase, despite Tyler's qualms, could comprehend state as well as national law.[42] As before, the president regretted having to follow his conscience rather than give his signature, but he was determined not to let an unconstitutional and also an unwise measure pass. A last-minute attempt to override failed as decidedly as the effort on the first bill had.

That evening, September 9, Secretary of the Navy George Badger invited the cabinet to his house to assess the situation. All except Postmaster General Francis Granger came, and several must have been startled when they found Clay also there. Would he dictate their future course? When the time for serious conversation came, the senator went into another room for a visit with the Badger family, but with every reason to be confident about the outcome of the conference. Webster, also knowing what was going to happen, left for home. His four colleagues then agreed they could no longer remain in office and decided upon the grounds and timing of resignation. They indicated their intention to the president the next day during a cabinet session, and on Saturday, the eleventh, two days before congressional adjournment, their formal letters arrived at the executive mansion. Granger, dissatisfied with the way patronage had been handled but chiefly responding to sentiment of New York politicians, decided also to resign. This left Webster as the only undeclared officer.[43]

Ewing vigorously and explicitly laid out reasons for his decision. Although he had opposed the first veto, he could understand why Tyler disapproved a bill materially amending the original Treasury plan. The second veto was a different matter. It reversed an earlier assurance, Ewing contended, that this kind of measure was satisfactory after he, Webster, Sergeant, and Berrien had written it to meet the president's stipulation on an exchange function without discounting. Ewing was positive that there had been no insistence upon state consent for agencies, particularly when Webster had correctly argued that such a limitation would interfere with countrywide fiscal operations to be performed for the Treasury. But Tyler changed his mind, Ewing charged, at the time Botts's coffeehouse letter appeared and perhaps because of it. Though Ewing had still cooperated by seeking postponement of congressional action, Tyler did not confer with him about a veto; and he first saw the message when it went to Congress. So beyond the substantive issue of a bank, the thing most disturbing to the secretary of the treasury was unjust personal treatment.[44] In a short letter John Crittenden merely alluded to the veto and other, unspecified, events. If he had been less cautious about the political impact, the attorney general could have shown that his conduct and views resembled those of Ewing. Always a compromiser, perhaps he hoped for reconciliation of elements of the party.[45]

A little later, on September 18, Badger published an explanation concurring with Ewing on all points, particularly the president's unfair relations with his associates. John Bell soon released a long account, much the same on the bank question but cryptically mentioning "pre-existing causes" for the rupture. All the cabinet statements demonstrate a consensus that Tyler capriciously rejected his own bill.[46]

Because the resignations did not come in until Saturday, with adjournment scheduled for Monday, the thirteenth, a prediction circulated that time would not permit selection and senatorial approval of replacements, so that the administration might collapse. Tyler himself doubted that an unconfirmed cabinet could serve on an acting basis.[47] Aware of the possibility of resignations for quite a while, however, he had prepared for the event by identifying new secretaries, some of whom he may have already approached. His list included Walter Forward, Treasury; John McLean, War; Abel Upshur, Navy; Charles Wickliffe, postmaster general; Hugh Legaré, attorney general. Encountering no difficulty about last-minute confirmation in the Senate, Tyler soon got acceptances from all except Justice McLean. Despite Webster's plea, the ever-calculating judge declined, giving as his reason the unpromising character of humdrum work in the War Department.[48] Then the president turned to John Spencer of New York, whose appointment carried the advantage of approval by the Weed-Seward forces. He accepted.[49]

Meanwhile congressional Whigs were savagely attacking Tyler not only for his opinions but also for inconsistency and treachery. Simultaneously with the cabinet resignations, a caucus met to assert its intense dissatisfaction, to be expressed publicly through an address drafted by a committee. On September 13, the fifty or so who had not left town approved the document, which was presently distributed far and wide.

Harrison and Tyler had won election, the address declared, because of well-known party commitments on economic policy; and when Harrison died, the vice-president had had an obligation to promote that policy. Instead, he had obstructed it by his bank vetoes, deriving less from constitutional scruples than from personal motives. He had misled and mistreated his own advisers. Consequently, the party could no longer be responsible for Tyler's conduct. This was a way of reading him out of the party, though it was felt he had already detached himself. Concluding on a constructive note, the address referred to significant enactments of the session (preemption and distribution, related to sales of public land; abandonment of the independent treasury; and bankruptcy legislation). What remained for the party was to combat abuses and to establish a badly needed fiscal agent.[50]

During the four-day period from the presidential veto (the ninth) to the day of adjournment and the Whig manifesto (the thirteenth), Webster was deciding whether to resign, then publicizing the reasons for his decision. On the tenth, after the cabinet gathering at Badger's home, he explored opinion in his own state. "Do the Whigs of Mass.," he asked a friend there, "think I ought to quit—or ought to stay?" The answer was what he wanted to hear: stay.[51] He reinforced his inclination to remain by calling a meeting of the state's congressional delegation at his house. He led off with a review of events culminating in the cabinet's determination to resign but his belief that Tyler had been deterred from signing the fiscal-corporation bill mainly by Botts's letter. Oddly enough, Webster had no complaints about his relations with the president and felt that there was still a good chance of later passage. Hearing this, the group acquiesced in his remaining in office.[52] John Quincy Adams went along with this advice but continued to enter sour comments about the secretary in his diary.[53] Both Robert Winthrop and Rufus Choate worried about the political wisdom of Webster's course but did not oppose it outright.[54]

When he called on the president the next morning, a reluctance to follow his cabinet colleagues and Clay must have been obvious. Tyler's manner at first seemed hesitant; in fact there are stories of doubtful merit that he had either planned to dismiss Webster or wished he could.[55] The account of the occasion which is quoted most often—the memoir by Tyler's son—pictures the president as reserved early in the conversation. To the secretary's question what he ought to do, the chief executive replied that Webster himself must decide. After the New Englander said he would stay, Tyler supposedly exclaimed, "Give me your hand on that, and now I will say Henry Clay is a doomed man from this hour." Webster himself left no record of the conversation. Both the context and credible evidence indicate that Tyler never overlooked the essential value of retaining Webster and was pleased by his decision to stay.[56]

On September 14 Webster's letters of explanation for not resigning appeared in the press. Writing to Gales and Seaton of the *Intelligencer,* he declared he saw no justification for dissolving the cabinet. First, the president would cooperate with Congress, he believed, in establishing an institution to aid the government's fiscal operations and to assure the nation of a good system of currency and exchange. It would only be possible, however, if the Whig party remained unified. Second, "If I had seen reasons to resign my office, I should not have done so without giving the President reasonable notice, and affording him time to select the hands to which he should confide the delicate and important affairs now pending in this Department."[57] In New York, Ketchum received a similar letter and had it published in the *American* the same day.[58] It is noteworthy that Webster's first reason related to domestic politics and the second to foreign affairs—probably reflecting his estimate of their relative importance, though he and others would later reverse that order. There were also reasons he did not care to express for present purposes. One was rivalry with Clay. He privately remarked to Ketchum that resignation would appear to be "a combination between a Whig cabinet and a Whig Senate to bother the President."[59] He could have said truthfully that he did not wish to join Clay in such a combination because it would surrender his own claim to party leadership. Another consideration, possibly, was personal: resistance to giving up the honor and perquisites of an office so recently assumed and to uprooting himself from the newly acquired, handsome residence at the capital.[60]

Through the fall he became involved in a controversy about the cabinet and the veto. Writing an aggressive piece for the proadministration *Madisonian* on the cabinet's statements about resigning, he ridiculed them for lack of a common ground. It was an unfair, inaccurate indictment of his ex-colleagues, ending with the assertion that "there was *no* plain, substantial cause, for breaking up the Cabinet, such as the public mind can readily understand & justify."[61] Then, to counter what he charged had been a dishonorable tactic of the cabinet in revealing details about confidential executive meetings on which the president could not comment, he drafted another partisan item for publication.[62] In short, the strange events of the summer of 1841 pushed Webster toward an adversary role in relation to Whig associates.

An analysis of the Tyler-Clay confrontation must naturally emphasize their fundamental disagreement about constitutional principles and economic policy, differences well known before the Virginian moved into the White House. The president devalued a half-century of executive behavior, congressional legislation, and judicial decisions validating the kind of bank he opposed. To be sure, there was also a background of opposition to a national bank; and, as Tyler said, the politics of the 1830s affirmed Jacksonian objections. To this, Clay replied that the economic disaster of recent years and the election of 1840 had at last disposed of such narrow ideas. The answer to the constitutional question was therefore not entirely settled, but it surely inclined toward Clay's views. As for the economic dimension, the fiscal needs of the Treasury and the state of the economy, even in Tyler's opinion, demanded that something be done.

What it should be became very difficult to establish, once the personal element rose to such importance. The president was so ultrasensitive about his own reputation and rights that he became suspicious and negative; the senator had such an expansive estimate of his own power and rectitude that he became arrogant. Both men knew they would have to compromise, regardless of the merits of the issue, to arrive at a solution. Yet neither communicated clearly or adjusted sufficiently to do so. In terms of accepted Whig doctrine, Clay occupied solid ground in calling for executive deference to legislative decisions, for abandonment of sweeping vetoes in the manner of the Jackson administration. Here Tyler got into trouble by ineffective, misleading intervention in legislative formulation of the two bank bills, while insisting upon his ultimate right to veto any bill for reasons of policy as well as constitutionality. If he embraced that formula of veto power, then he had done a poor job of conveying his views to Congress, indeed of exercising presidential leadership.[63]

Webster and the rest of the cabinet were caught in the line of fire between these two combatants. They repeatedly sought a practical outcome instead of an ideological victory. While that painful process was under way they were handicapped by Tyler's vagueness and changeability. That he did shift on the first bill with respect to the discounting function and on the second with respect to exchange operations and state consent to agencies is hardly to be denied. The reason was partly his reaction to the violent attacks of Clay, Botts, and company but also the growing influence of his states' rights advisers such as Rives and Wise.[64] Naturally the cabinet felt circumvented—even mistreated; and it is strange that Webster, the cabinet officer in the center of all this, came out of the episode with no complaint against Tyler's personal conduct, but instead with criticism of his colleagues.[65]

312

VETO

When Congress reconvened in December 1841, hard feeling had not subsided in the slightest degree. Neither congressional Whigs nor the president returned to the capital with any intention of making substantial concessions, beyond superficial gestures, to put through a positive program. Everywhere Tyler's opponents attacked him as an apostate and an obstructionist, whereas he felt persecuted only because he had placed the good of the country above partisanship. In many respects Webster also thought this criticism unfair; at least it threatened to stall any constructive action. In an editorial written for the *Madisonian* he asked that the press print the president's forthcoming annual message in full so that the people could judge its contents for themselves. Conceding that Tyler might be a man without a party, Webster predicted that adoption of his recommendations would be beneficial.[66] When the message came out a few days later, it thoroughly surveyed the state of the Union, especially problems of Anglo-American relations and of public finance.[67] Yet the likelihood of legislative-executive harmony in dealing with the latter was either slim or nonexistent.

The chief executive outlined a plan for a fiscal institution which, as promised, he had developed in the weeks since his veto and which he would submit to Congress upon request.[68] Shortly afterward, a House resolution did call for it, and Tyler went to Webster for help. The secretary drafted both a bill and an explanatory message, incorporating the ideas of the president and revisions by an approving cabinet. They went out over the name of Walter Forward, now in the Treasury, on December 21, 1841.[69]

To be named the exchequer, the projected institution would be a limited governmental body instead of a private corporation such as the old Bank of the United States. Not having a corporate charter or the usual stock subscription, it could be remodeled or discontinued whenever Congress saw fit. A board of three presidential appointees, together with the secretary of the treasury and the treasurer of the United States, would direct the exchequer's operations. Like the independent treasury it would receive and disburse moneys for the government; but it would also perform other functions. On the basis of deposits of specie (up to fifteen millions), it could issue notes to circulate as paper currency, always redeemable in gold or silver. It could also buy and sell interstate exchange at its several agencies, subject to regulations which states might impose. But consistent with Tyler's position of the preceding summer, it could not make loans by discounting or otherwise.

Whether it might fail to attract sufficient deposits as backing for an adequate currency without the ordinary incentives and whether its functions would be impeded by the numerous banks then operating

313

under less restraint were serious questions. Yet Webster's note of trans-
mittal sought to quiet doubts. Admittedly the plan was a modest effort,
he wrote, to find a practical alternative to an old-style bank or an independent treasury, both having been rejected. Give it a trial, he asked, for
the time had come to settle a long controversy, to promote essential
confidence in a financial system. However conciliatory the language
may have been in this document and in Tyler's annual message, the proposal presented no compromise, though the administration was vaguely
telling Congress it would accept reasonable modifications.

In both houses, opponents were unmoved. Committees reported revised bills; however, there was very little debate on the subject and never
a vote during the session. The strategy was to delay on the exchequer
until a decision on the tariff, not coming until the last days. And by that
time tempers had become so hot that nothing could pass. Clay Whigs
insisted upon a traditional bank. Democrats, currently flirting with the
president, balked. They would take nothing but an independent treasury, which many of them joined to a hard-money policy, certainly not
one permitting paper issued by the government. Postponement of the
issue amounted to quiet burial of the Tyler formula.[70]

It was the tariff that brought on another confrontation of president
and Congress. It occurred because circumstances virtually demanded
legislative action on the subject before adjournment. On July 1 the ten-
year period of gradual reduction of rates would end, with all rates over
20 percent to go down to that maximum, as required by the compromise
of 1833 during the nullification crisis. According to the prevailing interpretation of that statute, for collection of any duties after mid-1842 a
new bill was necessary; and low-tariff people also thought the compromise morally obligated Congress not to return to a protective system by
exceeding 20 percent when it did set up a schedule. Another urgent consideration was the worrisome condition of the Treasury, its pressing need
for more revenue, owing to lingering effects of the depression. This situation might push customs over 20 percent, the very thing protectionists
wished and their opponents dreaded. Further complicating the problem,
measures had been hurriedly enacted in the recent special session raising
some rates temporarily and establishing a system of distributing to the
states the proceeds from sales of public land—but only if the tariff
stayed below 20 percent.

As Tyler prepared his annual message in December 1841, he drew
upon Webster's help with the section relating to these problems. Deeply
interested in the direction of tariff policy, the secretary gave a good deal
of attention to his task. He came up with a long paper carefully mixing

the president's well-known opinions with his own firm beliefs in protectionism. Like others, he believed that the terms of the compromise of 1833 now required a new act to permit the government to collect any duties. And to placate Tyler he referred approvingly, more so than he would have preferred, to the desirability of honoring the compromise. Nevertheless, he continued, some rates might have to go above the 20 percent maximum because of the tight fiscal situation. In any event, he contended, within a revenue framework some levies designed specifically for "incidental" protection of American manufactures were highly beneficial to labor and capital. Seizing the opportunity, Webster also argued for specific instead of existing *ad valorem* duties, as he had often done before. He saw even greater reason for them now because the procedure of valuation after 1842 was supposed to depend upon decisions at each port of entry in the country, with the result that some ports would have an unconstitutional advantage.[71]

The president incorporated only a part of Webster's draft in his message and added some of his own ideas. He did endorse the euphemism of "incidental" protection, but he made it clear that he stood by the principle of revenue first. Besides, he was more intent than the secretary on staying within the maximum of 20 percent, set by the compromise of 1833. And though calling for some way of avoiding port-to-port variation of valuation, he did not accept specific instead of *ad valorem* duties. In a move that would soon prove relevant to events, Tyler added a warning that there must be no distribution of land revenues to the states if rates climbed above 20 percent (as provided in the law of 1841).[72]

Clay did not care what the president recommended. Despite his major role in writing the compromise of 1833, he would abandon it for a protective tariff well above the present maximum. Moreover, he insisted on repealing the proviso of 1841, which made distribution contingent on adherence to that maximum. For months Congress did not do anything important, probably to force the administration to approve a distasteful bill near the deadline of July 1. In the meantime Secretary of the Treasury Forward and Tyler himself felt another pressure, the growing need for more revenue. Indeed by March the chief executive told the lawmakers he thought some rates would have to go higher than 20 percent.[73]

The delay stretched into June. Doubtful that a new law could be enacted by July 1, Whigs in the House passed a stopgap bill extending the old rates and postponing for a month the reduction to 20 percent; but in doing this, they included a provision that in effect repealed the limitation on distribution.

This was the point that caused Tyler to set his teeth. Despite a new willingness to accept higher rates and despite his own clear record of supporting distribution, he saw no sense in scrambling for revenue from the tariff while donating funds from land sales to the states. And as for the deadline of July 1, he had obtained an opinion from the attorney general advising him that he need not worry about it; the rate of 20 percent could be collected whether there was new legislation or not.[74] So on June 29 he vetoed the temporary measure. He would not approve unrestricted distribution in order to get more revenue.[75] It was a position taken on ground of policy, not constitutionality.

At last, in early August Congress sent him a bill for a permanent system, quite similar to the one he had just vetoed. In the interim Webster had vainly tried to dissuade legislators from connecting *unlimited* distribution (that is, repeal of the proviso of 1841) to a new tariff. In his judgment, a return to some degree of protection was more desirable than insisting on distribution, even though he had always advocated it too. He knew that Tyler would not accept such a connection.[76] True enough, for the president had made up his mind to stand fast and only as a matter of courtesy asked Webster for his reaction to a draft veto. As he had for some time, the secretary bent as far as he could toward concurring with Tyler and conceded it was undesirable to link changes in distribution and tariff. Nevertheless, he argued for approval. "I would give almost my right hand if you could be persuaded to sign the bill," he lamented.[77] But the president would not bend. His veto again rested almost entirely on an unbudging commitment to conditional distribution.[78]

The outcome was that Congress felt compelled to retreat, to pass a separate, fairly protective tariff without mentioning distribution. This bill the president signed, but the price was a deeper rupture within the party and disappearance of any hope of getting an exchequer or other domestic legislation he wanted.[79] It might have been worse if Clay, who had resigned in March, had still been in the Senate. The Kentuckian did urge his successor John Crittenden and others to insist upon distribution, but they decided they ought not. Even so, the tariff of 1842 passed by only one vote in each house.[80]

This long, futile session marked a turning point for the Whig party. Taking office only a little over a year before, the new administration had been buoyant and determined to reverse Jacksonian policies. After the death of Harrison, the independent but ineffectual action of Tyler guaranteed trouble, the more so when Clay sought ascendancy. As a consequence of interbranch warfare, nothing important, except a somewhat higher tariff, could be accomplished to set the nation on a new course. Clay was now out of the Senate and the leading presidential candidate of the party, but the Whigs would never again have such an opportunity to establish their economic program as they had in 1841.[81]

As for Webster, he had mixed feelings about the future. "I hope for better times," he remarked, "but the present darkness is thick and palpable."[82] Possibly the administration could redeem itself by success in foreign relations. He would know soon, for he was currently completing important negotiations in Washington with a special British minister.

Chapter 19

ANGLO-AMERICAN ISSUES

When Webster became secretary of state on March 4, 1841, he had to familiarize himself with a wide range of administrative business, often more time-consuming than critical diplomatic issues. To his desk in the executive building at Fifteenth and Pennsylvania came a stream of mail from individuals requesting information or assistance—reference to the papers of George Washington as proof of military service for pension claimants, issuance of passports, help in citizens' problems involving foreign governments, distribution of public documents, and many matters which in a later period would be handled by other governmental agencies not then existing. As an instrument of official communications, the department transmitted presidential appointments and instructions, such as those to United States attorneys and marshals, authenticated executive papers, responded to inquiries from congressmen, and in general provided the liaison necessary for day-to-day operations.[1]

To take care of all this, he had what would now be considered a scanty staff of a few clerks, two or three having diplomatic expertise and the rest assigned to routine duties, particularly the endless chore of copying correspondence and records. Throughout his two-year tenure, his son Fletcher had the post of chief clerk and was soon entrusted with some fairly important work, including the role of acting secretary in Webster's absence.[2] But the secretary himself devoted a great deal of time to details having nothing much to do with high-level policy.

The size of the foreign service was growing, though modest by modern standards. In principal European capitals there were American ministers, not yet called ambassadors, with chargés d'affaires sent to other countries on that continent or in Latin America. Then there were many consuls in these areas to look after commercial interests. Despatches, reports, and private, off-the-record letters came in from abroad, while formal instructions and more off-the-record letters went out from Washington.[3]

Through the spring and summer of 1841 the incumbent minister to Britain, Andrew Stevenson, stayed on until a successor could be appointed. A firm Democratic states' righter from Virginia, Stevenson centered his attention on the formidable problem of illegal African slave trade, complicated as it was by questions of maritime rights and slavery itself.[4] The administration encountered delay in arranging the minister's replacement, in part because John Sergeant deliberated for a period before declining a nomination and in part because of the turmoil of the special congressional session.[5] All along, Webster was thinking about some appointment for Edward Everett, who had been thinking about it too. Everett would have been satisfied with any one of several places in southern Europe, but once he learned Webster would not go to London, he preferred that assignment. So Everett, then visiting Italy, was chosen and confirmed before the Senate adjourned in September, though he did not arrive in England until November.[6] Intelligent, cultivated, well liked by the British, he collaborated usefully with his friend at home during the delicate negotiations the following year. It turned out that the main scene was in Washington after Ashburton went over as special envoy, but Everett assured an excellent channel to the Foreign Office.

In another direction, relations with Congress, the secretary could also depend upon support. At first the loyal Caleb Cushing chaired the House Committee on Foreign Relations; however, in December 1841 John Quincy Adams, the most knowledgeable American diplomat then living, took over. Never approving Webster's personal character and less yielding than the secretary on the Maine boundary, the ex-president nonetheless concurred with him on most aspects of Anglo-American relations.[7] And in the Senate, William Rives, former minister to France and an influential adviser of Tyler, headed the committee which would sympathetically receive and report on any treaty the administration might send to the upper chamber.

Webster's own background and views would be major elements in determining the course of international relations. Though he had not previously held a diplomatic position, during his thirty years in politics he had developed ideas on foreign affairs, and his notions were unlikely to change much. As a first principle, he rejected war as an instrument of policy. The spirit of the age, he felt, demanded that civilized nations settle their differences by conciliation, by recognition of the legitimate interests of one another, by reason rather than emotion, by moral precept rather than by narrow advantage. The War of 1812, which he had strenuously opposed, should be the last armed conflict involving this country, just as Europe seemed to have entered an era of lasting peace after the Napoleonic years. Closely related to this belief, his emphasis upon economic growth ruled out damaging dislocations caused by war. His concern for the prosperity of merchant, industrialist, and worker affected every calculation of desirable action. For the United States of the 1840s, the greatest peril to material welfare and cultural improvement was an irrational, self-destructive impulse toward territorial expansion. He would not employ force to extend national boundaries around new regions or even a few square miles. On this subject his outlook on the Maine boundary, Texas, New Mexico, and Oregon resembled that on Louisiana forty years previously.

These generalities affected his approach to Anglo-American relations, the focus of diplomacy in 1841 and 1842. Several vexatious issues had arisen, but fair negotiation could resolve them. Mutual concessions promised more than an inflated sense of national honor, which could lead only to bellicose rigidity. Webster's personal perspective of England undergirded that conviction. Ever since the Jeffersonian era, when Federalists had disapproved embargo and war, he had highly valued the British commercial connection. As a lawyer, he benefited from fees for service to the banking house of Baring and other English clients. In addition, since the 1820s he had enjoyed the friendship of a number of Britons, such as John Evelyn Denison and Edward Stanley. He admired English institutions, the way of life of the English gentry, the classics of English literature. No wonder, then, that his first visit to England in 1839 had been a highlight, a time of observing at first hand and gaining more friendships.[8]

If Webster inclined toward an amicable strategy, so did Britain. True, for a few months, from March to September 1841, Lord Palmerston continued as an unaccommodating foreign secretary. But a new Tory government, led by Sir Robert Peel, came to power at that point, and the more flexible Lord Aberdeen succeeded Palmerston. An experienced diplomatist, anxious to avoid war with the United States, conscious of the financial and commercial costs of a conflict, Aberdeen set in motion a policy of defusion, culminating in a treaty a year later.[9] Before that happened, the two nations had to overcome several dangerous obstacles.

One source of worry was the agitated condition along the Canadian border. Long a source of friction, it worsened with an abortive rebellion in 1837 against the government of Canada. Led by William Lyon Mackenzie, the insurgents sought more home rule within the empire and greater civil liberty. Though soon forced to flee into western New York, Mackenzie made remarkable headway in recruiting American supporters. Thousands joined Hunters' Lodges, called themselves Patriots, gathered large stores of arms, marched around on their side of the Great Lakes, and talked bravely about an invasion of Canada. A force of more than five hundred did occupy a patch of British soil, Navy Island, a mile up from Niagara Falls. Here they set up a provisional government and fired their cannon at Chippewa on the nearby shore. To supply this outpost, they contracted for a small steamboat, the *Caroline*, to bring in food, ordnance, and more troops. After runs to the island on December 29, the *Caroline* came over to Schlosser on the American side to dock for the night. About midnight small boats carrying a British-Canadian party surprised the steamer's crew and took control. During a brief struggle several Americans were wounded; and one, Amos Durfee, was killed. Then the attackers towed the *Caroline* into Niagara River, set it afire, causing it to sink, and returned to Chippewa.[10]

Across the land anger approached the boiling point. Politicians and editors condemned the attack as flagrant aggression, an invasion of American soil without justification. But the Van Buren administration soothed feelings as much as it could by sending General Winfield Scott to the border as a calming influence. Then ensued a long exchange of notes and conversations with the English minister, Henry Fox, in Washington. Britain and the United States disagreed on the right to pursue the *Caroline* into American territory; but throughout the dispute, both proceeded on the assumption that the attack was a public act authorized by the government, not a foray conducted by individuals upon their own responsibility. Despite this implicit understanding, Palmerston did not reply formally to Secretary of State Forsyth's protest of May 1838. The issue remained unresolved as Van Buren's term was coming to a close; and he had no hope of British apology or reparations. To press the matter would risk a war he did not want.[11]

Border unrest continued while the diplomats seemed stymied, with no abatement after Webster came to office in early 1841. He fretted about it all that year and half the next. Often his mail brought alarming reports about the Patriots and Hunters' Lodges stretching from New England as far west as Detroit, of plots, caches of muskets, and some violence.[12] Like Forsyth, he relied upon a show of Scott's uniform (lacking an adequate federal military force), exhortations to United States attorneys and marshals, and whatever help he could get from state governors. He had no more luck with enforcing the national neutrality law than his predecessors had.[13] Meantime the British built up their defenses, including new naval units beyond limits of the Rush-Bagot Agreement of 1817.[14] There were also more boundary crossings, including the case of James Grogan, abducted from Vermont by Canadian raiders in September 1841, though released after a protest.[15]

This volatile situation would probably continue as long as the problem of the *Caroline* remained unsettled. And the outcome of that dispute largely depended upon the fate of a prisoner sitting in the jail at Lockport, New York. The husky, red-bearded man impatiently awaited trial for the murder of Amos Durfee and for arson, both indictments connected to the *Caroline*'s destruction three years earlier. Alexander McLeod, a deputy sheriff of Upper Canada, had been arrested on November 12, 1840, and charged with committing these crimes while participating in the raid at Schlosser. Minister Henry Fox and Secretary John Forsyth had traded protest and rejection of protest, but it appeared that a local jury would deal with McLeod's future first. Fox objected on the ground that an individual could not be punished for obeying orders of his government in such a military operation. Forsyth replied that in this country it was a criminal case falling within state jurisdiction and that he could not interfere. That was a predictable response from the states' rights secretary, who did not intend to challenge New York, particularly during his final weeks in office.[16]

So in March 1841 Forsyth left Webster a hot issue. In looking over the file of despatches from Andrew Stevenson, the new cabinet officer found that the case had deeply stirred English opinion. Stevenson reported that members of Parliament and newspapers urged a policy of demanding McLeod's immediate release and, if refused, of summoning Fox home. Palmerston justified the *Caroline* attack as legitimate retaliation but stopped short of sending a formal note to Washington acknowledging it as a public act. Stevenson wrote that Britain was pushing military preparations, and he advised his government to do the same. Still, the English mood became somewhat calmer once the Harrison administration began, because mutual understanding now seemed possible, especially with Webster in office.[17]

In his first written communication to Webster, on March 12, Fox laid down the British position, in effect reiterating what he had said to Forsyth. The minister remarked that his superiors had instructed him to send this note. McLeod must be set free, he demanded, because the operation against the *Caroline* had a public character, derived from governmental authority and not admitting individual responsibility. It occurred because "a band of British rebels and American pirates," who were permitted to organize on American soil, had invaded Navy Island, Her Majesty's territory. Even if the counterthrust were unwarranted, he contended, the question must be treated by the two nations, certainly not by the courts of New York. To say that the federal government was legally powerless would not do, for Britain could negotiate only with it, never with separate states of the Union. Fox added that in any event he did not concede that McLeod had participated in the raid.[18]

Despite the stern tone of Fox's note, Webster was pleased to receive it. He now had a clear declaration of public responsibility which he could use to persuade New York not to try McLeod. To be sure, Fox had already told Forsyth the same thing; but the former secretary had obscured the point by adhering to the technicality that he had not received a formal note from Palmerston. And the British secretary had intentionally neglected to send one so as to shelve the *Caroline* issue. Indeed he waited until he left office in late August before giving Stevenson the long-delayed statement.[19]

On March 15, immediately after hearing from Fox, Webster, with Harrison's approval, sent Attorney General John Crittenden to Albany to talk with Governor William Seward. He gave Crittenden written instructions, describing the background of the question and enclosing copies of the relevant diplomatic documents to be distributed to Seward and others. As for Fox's note, Webster continued, the president conceded the legal point that McLeod ought not be held individually responsible for the public act of destroying the *Caroline*. Though the administration could not stop the proceedings in the New York courts, the secretary observed, "If this indictment were pending in one of the courts of the United States, I am directed to say that the President, upon the receipt of Mr. Fox's last communication, would have immediately directed a *nolle prosequi* to be entered." He wished Crittenden to find out Seward's views and hoped, of course, that the governor concurred with him. Webster's acceptance of the British argument regarding responsibility for the attack was therefore an important reversal of the Democratic Van Buren–Forsyth stance; he hoped that Seward, a Whig, would see the light.

After Crittenden had talked with Seward, he was to proceed to Lockport and look into the legal defense of McLeod. Though the attorney general himself should not represent the accused, he must see that an "eminent counsel" did and should provide the defendant with copies of diplomatic correspondence as evidence. Finally, he should tell McLeod's attorney that if his client were found guilty, the case ought to be appealed to the Supreme Court.[20]

Webster knew that Crittenden had only a faint chance of persuading

Seward to release McLeod. In his office lay the governor's recent letter to Forsyth, insisting upon a trial and complaining about British refusal to pay reparations for the *Caroline* incident.[21] But the secretary sought somehow to soften this attitude. In addition to sending the attorney general on his mission, he dispatched a letter to Albany on March 17. It was phrased to appeal to Seward's patriotism and vanity. A report had arrived, Webster wrote, that Seward had decided not to prosecute McLeod because Britain had avowed the *Caroline* attack to be a public act. "The President directs me to express his thanks for the promptitude with which you appear disposed to perform an act, which he supposes proper for the occasion, and which is calculated to relieve this Government from embarrassments and the country from some dangers of collision with a foreign power."[22] Promptly Seward replied that the president was entirely misinformed—he had never contemplated stopping prosecution of McLeod, and he had now explained this and all his views to Crittenden. The case posed a judicial question which he must leave to the courts.[23] What the governor did not say was that public opinion in New York would not tolerate the prisoner's exemption from trial. Actually he believed that McLeod would be found innocent; and if not, he inclined toward pardoning the Canadian. He did not tell Webster this but was more candid in conversation with Crittenden. In general, he did not foresee war with Britain unless McLeod was executed.[24]

On the surface, relations between Seward and Webster were polite, with touches of friendliness. Underneath, there was bad feeling. The governor thought the administration should have consulted him before reversing Forsyth's acquiescence in a trial of McLeod, and he may have had valid ground for believing that he had been treated unfairly.[25] For his part, the secretary was more than a little irritated. "He is a contemptible fellow—& this is the end of it," Webster later exclaimed. "We may perhaps yet have a *war*, on account, or by reason of the conduct of this small piece of political character."[26]

While Webster attempted to change Seward's mind on holding a trial, he postponed answering Fox's note of March 12. Then there was further delay because of Harrison's death and Tyler's moving into office. At length, on April 24 he handed the minister his reply, which reflected what he had been unable to do with New York but showed the British that he wished to be reasonable. In fact he enclosed a copy of his instructions to Crittenden, which said that the United States had adopted the principle of no individual responsibility with regard to the *Caroline*. He now repeated that view. What else did the British government expect the administration to do, he asked? It could not comply with a demand for McLeod's release, for he was imprisoned under state judicial process and could be freed only by judicial process. As in England itself, in such a situation only certain options were open. One was to move a *nolle prosequi* (a desire not to prosecute on an indictment), but New York would not do that and the federal government could not. Another was to ask for a writ of habeas corpus, which could result in a judicial ruling against trial. Though he did not elaborate, he knew that the prisoner's counsel would explore this possibility. So he was informing Fox that at this stage McLeod would have to look to the fairness of the state's criminal-justice system, which, he wrote, was above question. On the larger issue of the *Caroline*, he held fast to the American protest against territorial invasion. Rather too confidently, he pronounced that the national government was capable of maintaining order along the frontier without foreign intervention. Here he threw in some animated passages, perhaps to blunt domestic criticism that he had caved in to the British.[27]

Meanwhile McLeod's case proceeded slowly. Originally scheduled for hearing in March, it lay on the docket until May while the court and attorneys threaded their way through technicalities in drawing a jury and gathering evidence.[28] At first the defendant had two lawyers of modest standing, opposed by state prosecutors including the New York attorney general. Then the reputable Joshua Spencer joined defense counsel on a retainer by the British government. Three days later, Spencer received appointment as United States attorney for that district. To this situation Seward reacted strenuously, believing that Spencer's two roles, as federal district attorney and as defender of McLeod, had been intentionally combined by the administration. An exchange of argumentative correspondence between the governor and the president (advised by Webster) followed. Seward protested that Spencer, in the pay of a country perpetrating the *Caroline* outrage and now a federal officer, improperly mixed two adversary relationships. Tyler answered with a mechanical distinction between them. Like others in such an office, he said, the United States attorney could carry on a private practice, and anyway he had been appointed without reference to the McLeod case.[29] Webster's letters to Spencer before and after the appointment, his official instructions combined with personal advice on how to conduct the defense against the state, do not verify Tyler's distinction.

Spencer and his associates, with Webster's collaboration, went to the state supreme court in mid-May for a hearing on habeas corpus, which could stop McLeod's trial. Supplying copies of extensive diplomatic correspondence as evidence, the secretary followed proceedings closely and during a three-day argument was in New York City, where the court sat. Professing noninterference, insisting he was merely making documents available, he took a more active part than he admitted. He was satisfied with Spencer's contentions that this tribunal ought to rule against a trial on the grounds that destruction of the *Caroline* was a public act, that McLeod had merely obeyed orders, and that the question involved international relations wholly within federal jurisdiction.[30] But the court put off its decision until July 12, when Justice Esek Cowen, for a unanimous bench, held against McLeod's motion. He accepted the state's position that the defendant could be tried for violating the law of nations, according to Vattel, Burlamaqui, and English precedents (both parties had cited these authorities to arrive at opposite conclusions). Besides, Cowen concluded, the "unwarranted" *Caroline* attack had been "mixed" warfare, partly public and partly private. New York could prosecute the accused for committing a crime as a private act, but at trial the jury could determine that it was a governmental responsibility.[31]

Webster seemed more upset than British officials. Fox confined his comment to hazy warnings of a crisis, while Palmerston would wait for the trial itself and probably do nothing drastic unless McLeod was executed.[32] But Webster found Cowen's opinion contemptible—"hollow, false, & almost dishonest from beginning to end." He urged Joseph Story to write a critique exposing its errors.[33] Though the justice did not, Daniel Tallmadge, a New York City judge, brought out an adverse review in a pamphlet which was widely circulated and reprinted in the official reports of Cowen's own court. Especially heartening were attached letters of James Kent, Ambrose Spencer, and other distinguished jurists complimenting Tallmadge.[34]

During the three months before the trial opened in October, the defense counsel carefully prepared their case. The first question they faced was whether to appeal Cowen's decision to the state court of errors and to the United States Supreme Court, if necessary. McLeod had had enough of his jail cell and dreaded the delay such a course would involve. He and his lawyers felt that his innocence was unassailable and preferred an immediate trial. Somewhat reluctantly Webster agreed, despite a wish to demolish the doctrine now laid down. For a time Webster maintained the pretense of official noninterference by giving what he described as his "private opinion." Then at presidential direction (on his request), he instructed Spencer to proceed with the trial and to emphasize that the attack had been a public act.[35] As for the evidence, Spencer felt confident it would clear McLeod, for according to depositions from Canada the accused had not been on any of the attacking boats of the boarding party. Other witnesses could confirm his alibi by testifying that he had spent the night of December 29, 1837, in a house near Chippewa.[36] Still, Webster disliked reliance upon an alibi, a strategy which sidestepped the critical legal point.[37]

At last, on October 4, the trial opened. In the absence of Chief Justice Samuel Nelson, who had intended to sit, the circuit judge presided. Though handling the difficult proceedings fairly over the next week, the judge did exclude the plea that the *Caroline* incident was a public act; thus McLeod had to depend upon his alibi. That proved easier than feared, and on October 12 the jury acquitted the defendant after deliberating only twenty minutes.[38]

Although the tension caused by this affair subsided in late 1841, the principles underlying the dispute about the *Caroline* remained. It was not enough, Americans believed, for Britain to declare that destruction of the vessel had been a public act instead of an individual crime or that it had invaded American territory only to defend its own soil. As the president observed in his annual message in December, the British government had never admitted committing a wrong. And that was precisely the point Webster would soon have on the table when negotiations for a general settlement between the two nations began.[39]

Within a month of McLeod's acquittal, in November 1841, a violent incident in another quarter further irritated Anglo-American relations. The brig *Creole*, carrying 135 slaves, was sailing from Virginia to New Orleans when 19 of them seized control and forced the ship into Nassau, in the British Bahamas. They killed one person and wounded several others. The American consul at the port vainly sought help from British colonial officials to extradite the mutineers and to return the brig to the captain with everything else as it was before the uprising. All he achieved was detention of the 19 blacks, with further action delayed until the governor could get instructions from London. The rest of the slaves, encouraged by magistrates and guards, made for shore in Bahamian boats which had menacingly surrounded the *Creole*. As in previous instances of American vessels coming within local jurisdiction after mishaps, the slaves were declared free on authority of the parliamentary emancipation act of 1833.[40]

These events intensified sectional feeling about slavery in the United States. Fearful that recurring insurrections threatened the institution itself, southerners preferred to defend it against such British meddling on grounds of maritime rights and national honor. They could therefore expect more support by the North and deter uncomfortable discussion about slavery. Northern abolitionists, however, did talk about slavery, supplied as they were with a topic attracting national attention. So they disapproved any American move for redress by England and furthermore cheered the freedom gained by *Creole* slaves.[41] Whatever diplomatic position Webster took would have to reckon with these domestic differences.

With this in mind, the secretary proceeded cautiously. Not until January 29, 1842, did he send instructions to Everett. Even then, his protest followed a middle path and seemed tentative. Leaving no doubt that he disapproved official conduct at Nassau, he contended that the ship had involuntarily broken its legitimate voyage between two American ports, whereupon it encountered interference instead of assistance there. While the *Creole* lay in harbor, the captain had violated no British law against slavery, because he and the passengers had not been subject to local jurisdiction. This was the old doctrine that American ships were American soil. As for the mutineers, Webster could not appeal to an existing treaty for extradition but believed the colonial governor should hand over those slaves according to the elusive concept of comity under international law. Because he realized that would probably not happen, he was attempting to establish a basis for indemnification. Similarly, he did not call for the return of the rest of the blacks but argued for compensation because of their irregular emancipation. Overall, he left the matter somewhat open, not absolutely demanding anything.[42] In March he learned that Aberdeen, on advice from crown attorneys, had concluded that all the slaves must go free. He would have to see what could be done with the special British envoy soon to arrive in Washington.

Besides compensation for emancipated blacks and indemnification for damages by mutineers, Webster wanted a new agreement like an expired section of Jay's treaty of 1795 on extradition. Apart from such occasional incidents involving coastal slave ships, the more common problem concerned fugitives across the Canadian border. In the months after he took office, while unrest prevailed along the boundary, he faced a number of cases in which persons had fled from or to Canada to escape criminal charges by one or the other country. In New York Seward, either by direct communication with the governor general or with the help of the State Department, delivered up fugitives to Canada and recovered some who had fled northward. Webster approved both procedures, despite the absence of a treaty and the possibility that the Supreme Court would prohibit state action.[43] Still, a treaty with Britain could clarify the process of federal extradition for most crimes. He had no idea of trying to include runaway slaves, however, because of the furor such a move would cause.

An additional problem, one directly relating to slavery, had plagued British-American diplomacy. How could the two nations stop an active but illicit traffic in slaves from Africa? Since 1808, statutes of the United States had forbidden it, even declared it to be piracy. The Treaty of Ghent obligated the signatories to suppress it, but later efforts to fulfill that pledge had failed, chiefly because joint action might allow the British navy to infringe American rights on the seas, perhaps to impress sailors again. By the 1830s, too, the ever more sensitive slavery interest of the South conjured up other alarming possibilities. At any rate, after adopting the emancipation act of 1833 covering its colonies in the West Indies, England had strengthened its patrols off the African coast and in the Caribbean to search and seize slavers, some of them American. The fact was that operating these carriers of misery became increasingly profitable. A complication derived from the widespread display of the flag of the United States by traders not registered there. As a result, a British naval captain could not be certain when he saw the American colors whether a suspected slave runner was falsifying its identity or not. If not, and if he boarded and searched the vessel but discovered it to be genuinely American, his government soon received a stiff protest from Washington.[44]

Under fire from Minister Andrew Stevenson on this question, Palmerston yielded only a little in their dialogue from the late 1830s through the summer of 1841. Whereas the British secretary had warmly defended the search of suspected ships, including those of Americans, and justified sending them to prize courts, he was retreating to a more moderate position—to "visit" a vessel by boarding it and examining its papers to determine their authenticity was indispensable, he contended, because the mere show of a flag was insufficient proof of identity.[45] The new foreign secretary, Aberdeen, felt obliged to maintain the same ground, though appearing more conciliatory.[46] Stevenson, a proslavery Virginian aroused by the controversy, retorted that the distinction between search and visit was meaningless, for neither was authorized in peacetime under international law and one necessarily led to the other. Nor could England rectify the wrong upon discovering a ship was American by making reparations. Aberdeen was perfectly willing to make reparations because he now claimed no right to visit any vessel with bona fide American papers, even one obviously carrying slaves. Even this concession was unsatisfactory, Stevenson declared, because that very determination depended upon a visit, ordered by a naval officer with discretionary power. Though Stevenson took the initiative in these exchanges without much, if any, instruction from the State Department, Webster was writing the minister that he approved his line of reasoning.[47]

Finding that he and Stevenson, as well as the new minister Edward Everett, were repeatedly going over the same sterile ground, Aberdeen hoped to resolve the issue by drawing the United States into a five-power treaty just then concluded. France, Austria, Prussia, and Russia would join Britain to suppress the slave trade by mutual search, a policy previously adopted through several bilateral agreements. In Paris, American minister Lewis Cass, a leading northern Democrat aspiring to the presidency and solicitous of southern popularity, began a campaign to discourage French ratification of the treaty and to prevent the United States from becoming a signatory. In February 1842 he published a pamphlet toward those ends, and without instructions from Washington he sent Guizot a protest on the subject. He argued that mutual search would surely violate maritime rights and forward the long-standing British effort to rule the waves. As support, he cited Tyler's annual message to Congress, disapproving search as an intolerable practice.[48] Collaborating with Cass was Henry Wheaton, chargé to Prussia then visiting France, a recognized authority on international law, who issued a similar commentary and wrote long letters to Webster urging him to rebuff the British overture.[49] At the same time, Duff Green, the Calhounite former editor of the *Telegraph* and currently a trusted friend of President Tyler, came to Paris, where he published a series of essays not only attacking the five-power treaty but charging that abolitionist-minded Britons desperately sought to undermine the security and material welfare of southern planters because emancipation had been an economic failure in the competing West Indies.[50]

These sallies by Americans in the French capital put Webster on the spot. In his judgment, Cass had proceeded entirely on his own, seemed determined to be hostile toward England, and interfered in a matter for which he had no responsibility. But Tyler thought otherwise, understandably in view of his states' rights, proslavery convictions as well as the diplomat's reliance on the president's own words to Congress. So he directed Webster to send Cass a note approving his conduct—unpleasant medicine for the secretary to swallow. Meanwhile the French chamber refused to ratify the treaty, though probably not because of the minister's propaganda.[51] At this juncture, movement on the slave trade question stalled, so that Webster and the arriving British envoy would have to address it along with other problems.

Of these remaining questions, the most troublesome had been uncertainty about the northeastern boundary. Difficulty began as early as

1783 as a result of an unclear article in the treaty for independence. In it, the negotiators provided for "a line drawn due north from the source of the Saint Croix River to the Highlands; along the said Highlands which divide those rivers that empty themselves into the river St. Lawrence, from those which fall into the Atlantic Ocean, to the northernmost head of the Connecticut River; thence down along the middle of that river, to the forty-fifth degree of north latitude; from there, by a line due west on said latitude, until it strikes the river ... [St. Lawrence]; thence along the middle of said river into Lake Ontario ..."[52] Ill informed about the geography of this remote area, the peace commissioners themselves were unsure where the highlands were or even which of several branches of the rivers were the main ones. Little wonder that it took sixty years for Britain and the United States to agree upon this boundary between the northeastern states (Maine, New Hampshire, Vermont, and New York) and Canada's New Brunswick (formerly part of Nova Scotia) and Quebec.

The two countries disagreed about the entire line and solved only a minor part of the puzzle before Webster's arrival in the State Department.[53] In 1798, through a commission under Jay's treaty, they did fix the source of the St. Croix as the westernmost of several branches. As a result they could now draw the due-north line. But where were the highlands to which it would run? There was no very prominent, continuous ridge extending in a bell shape from northeastern to northwestern Maine, because the watersheds were, in many cases, just slightly elevated swamps. Besides, the most contentious issue turned upon the requirement that the highlands of the treaty must be the starting point for streams flowing into the Atlantic Ocean. Was the Bay of Fundy, into which the important St. John emptied, the ocean? Or was it merely an interior arm of the sea? If the latter, as the British argued, then the highlands and therefore the particular streams coming from them would be farther south than the Americans said. In fact they were more than a hundred miles farther, such as at Mars Hill, forty miles up from the St. Croix (in present-day Maine) instead of somewhere north of the St. John. Lesser questions involved selecting the main branch feeding the upper Connecticut (in northern New Hampshire) and rectifying a surveyor's mistake, detected in the 1820s, in marking the forty-fifth parallel. This error meant that, for the time being, the strategically placed American fort at Rouse's Point, New York, at the head of Lake Champlain sat on Canadian soil, according to a true east-west line.

From Jefferson's presidency to Tyler's, recurrent diplomatic efforts failed. In 1804 a compromise negotiated in London collapsed in Wash-

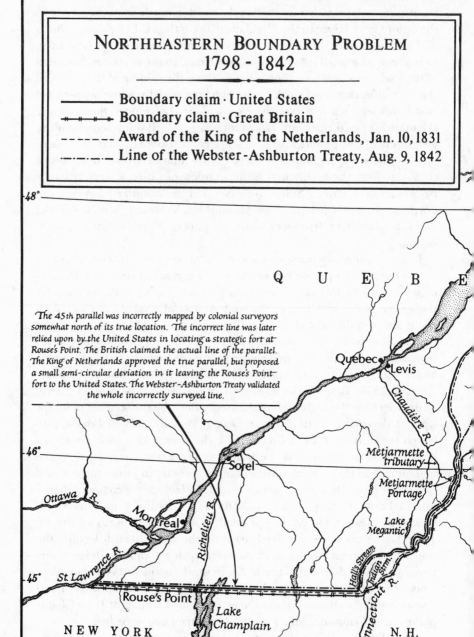

NORTHEASTERN BOUNDARY PROBLEM
1798 - 1842

———— Boundary claim · United States
+—+—+—+ Boundary claim · Great Britain
- - - - - - Award of the King of the Netherlands, Jan. 10, 1831
-·—·—·— Line of the Webster - Ashburton Treaty, Aug. 9, 1842

48°

Q   U   E   B   E

*The 45th parallel was incorrectly mapped by colonial surveyors
somewhat north of its true location. The incorrect line was later
relied upon by the United States in locating a strategic fort at
Rouse's Point. The British claimed the actual line of the parallel.
The King of Netherlands approved the true parallel, but proposed
a small semi-circular deviation in it leaving the Rouse's Point
fort to the United States. The Webster-Ashburton Treaty validated
the whole incorrectly surveyed line.*

Québec
Levis

Chaudière R.

46°

Sorel

Metjarmette
tributary

Metjarmette
Portage

Ottawa R.

Lake
Megantic

Montreal

Richelieu R.

St. Lawrence R.

45°

Hall's Stream

Indian Stm.

Connecticut R.

Rouse's Point

Lake
Champlain

NEW YORK

VERMONT

N. H.

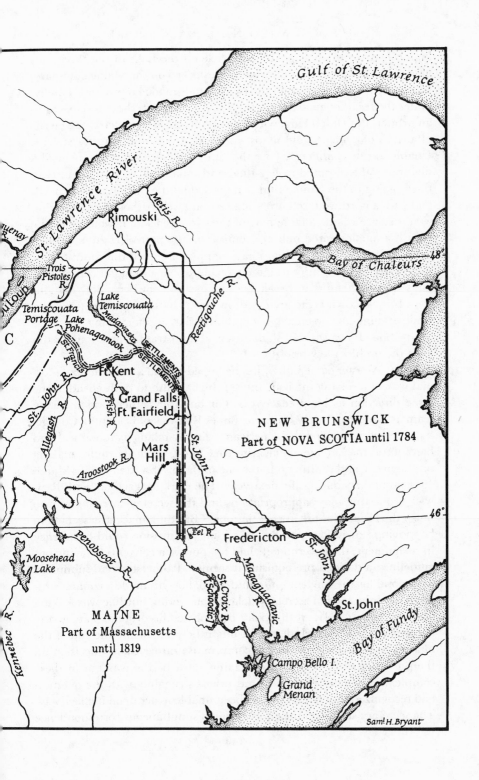

Gulf of St. Lawrence

St. Lawrence River

Rimouski

Metis R.

Bay of Chaleurs

48°

Trois
Pistoles
R.

Restigouche R.

Lake
Temiscouata

Temiscouata
Portage Lake

Madawaska R.

Pohenagamook

C

St. Francis R.

Ft. Kent

SETTLEMENTS

SETTLEMENTS

St. John R.

Allegash R.

Grand Falls

Fish R.

Ft. Fairfield

NEW BRUNSWICK

Part of NOVA SCOTIA until 1784

Mars
Hill

Aroostook R.

St. John R.

46°

Penobscot R.

Eel R.

Fredericton

St. John R.

Moosehead
Lake

Magaguadavic R.

MAINE

Part of Massachusetts
until 1819

St. Croix R.
(Schoodic)

St. John

Bay of Fundy

Kennebec R.

Campo Bello I.

Grand
Menan

Sam! H. Bryant

ington because of an unpalatable article on the Lake of the Woods region.[54] In 1822 a mixed commission deadlocked on the Maine boundary; subsequent approaches from the two capitals made no progress. Finally, under the terms of an article in the Treaty of Ghent, the subject went to an arbiter, the Dutch king, who from 1829 to 1831 pondered the merits of a mass of evidence, old maps, correspondence, and long statements. Unable to rule confidently for either side, the monarch recommended a division of the disputed twelve thousand square miles, with about two-thirds going to the United States, bounded by the St. John in the north and with a northwestern border above that river. Although this solution would assure Maine a large part of the contested soil, it would give the British a much desired military route from the port of Halifax to Quebec.[55] President Jackson would have happily accepted this formula, but the Senate did not ratify it, largely owing to New England complaints. Subsequent attempts to break the impasse got nowhere. Both nations were busy surveying the area and, in effect, hardening their positions, while arguing how to create a new commission and foreseeing still more arbitration. In truth, the Van Buren administration and Palmerston gave the problem low priority.

When Webster came into office, he hoped to find a more direct, informal way of resolving the issue but felt he had also to push ahead in the same direction as his predecessors. For one thing, there was a survey team at work, headed by Professor James Renwick of Columbia College. As expected, it verified the American claim by taking astronomical and barometric measurements, clearing the forest along its route, making profile maps, and drafting reports, one of them submitted in late March 1841 and others during the next year. The work dragged on, with Renwick requesting more appropriations and the secretary pressing him to finish the project for use in negotiations.[56] But diplomacy also seemed to be moving slowly forward. Before a joint commission could commence its assignment, the governments had to approve a convention laying out guidelines, a difficult prerequisite, it seemed. Palmerston had submitted a proposal for the convention in mid-1840, Forsyth made a counter proposal, and the foreign secretary delayed answering until he was leaving office in August 1841. At this point he repeated his original plan, giving Webster reason to conclude that it might be years before the end of the matter. Now it was clear that a compromise rather than a decision on the pure merits of the respective claims must be the way out of these complexities. Since Jefferson's time, others struggling with the question had recognized that truth but had been unable to act upon it effectively. The secretary sustained the effort through simultaneous correspondence and conversations, achieving slow progress toward formation of a new commission.[57]

Meanwhile Webster had begun a campaign to persuade Maine to accept a compromise. The point of departure was a conversation in May 1841 at his house in Washington with a fascinating young man from Portland. Francis O. J. Smith, otherwise known as Fog, was an aggressive politician and entrepreneur with varied experience: banker, speculator, partner with Morse in developing the telegraph, congressman, and, most of all, irrepressible promoter. Smith explained his thinking on the boundary to Webster, who found it corresponded to his own—the desirability of abandoning fruitless surveys, commissions, or arbitrations and finding a give-and-take prescription, necessarily to be supported by Maine in advance. Reviving an abortive proposition he had made to President Van Buren in 1837, Smith warmly recommended it to the new administration. What must be done, he declared, was to influence public opinion in Maine and thereby cause the legislature to approve compromise before action in Washington. Do not start at the wrong end, he warned, and thus present the state with a settlement likely to be rejected out of hand. Specifically, he volunteered as an agent of the State Department, traveling through Maine to talk with people about the general principle and necessary details, getting signatures on petitions to the legislature in support of compromise, and of course lobbying in the state capital as well. The newspapers must be put on the right course, he advised, by strategically placed and widely reprinted editorials; thus he would "adjust the tone and direction of the party presses, and through them, of public sentiment." When he referred to "party," he meant both parties, Democratic and Whig, then in nearly perfect balance in Maine, with the object of removing the boundary question as a partisan issue between them. In the past, neither party had dared risk popular displeasure by straying from rigid insistence upon complete satisfaction of the state's claims. For all this, Smith said he would take an annual compensation of thirty-five hundred dollars plus expenses, as well as a fee for disbursing federal money to Maine and more fees for several assistants.[58]

Webster accepted the plan. Upon request, Smith wrote out what he had said so that the secretary could get Tyler's approval, including authority to draw money from the secret-service fund (a discretionary account the president could use for expenses related to foreign affairs).[59] Webster then reviewed with Smith the terms he should advocate for settling the boundary question, but it was agreed that he should not reveal he was a paid agent of the government. So the undertaking amounted to propagandizing, secretly sponsored by the federal government, in a state

335

of the Union, a technique scarcely compatible with the ways of a democratic society.

Smith set to work at once. Within weeks he visited several counties,
talked with many people, secured long lists of signatures for memorials
to the legislature. As he and Webster had agreed, the package he offered
rested first on an unqualified assertion of Maine's right to all disputed
territory but willingness to make adjustments for the sake of peace if
Britain made equivalent concessions. In return for a good military route
from Halifax to Quebec along the upper St. John, Britain must guarantee free American access to the river, a valuable privilege for lumbermen
and farmers shipping products through New Brunswick. Another equivalent might be cession of a narrow slice of land west of the St. John and
east of the treaty's north-south line down to the Eel River. And quite
important, there must be a sum of money, probably from the United
States government, to compensate Maine for its loss of land. During the
winter, from November 1841 to February 1842, Smith put anonymous
articles in the Portland *Christian Mirror,* a religious and pacifist paper,
urging this policy; and they were soon reprinted throughout the state.[60]
The effect could not have been more heartening. Reflecting a conciliatory public mood, politicians avowed their willingness to try this approach. So reported Peleg Sprague, former senator from Maine and
now a federal judge, who traveled to Augusta with expenses paid out of
the president's contingency fund.[61] After such news, Webster felt optimistic about ending the protracted boundary controversy satisfactorily.

A breakthrough came not so much from these developments as from
some in London. Taking over in the fall of 1841, the new ministry with
Aberdeen in the Foreign Office had no faith in plodding along indefinitely. By Christmas, Aberdeen had arranged a special mission to the
United States, empowered to settle all outstanding questions—Canadian boundary, slave trade, extradition—and perhaps to quiet dissatisfaction over the *Caroline* and *Creole.* Everett learned of this on December
twenty-sixth, and the *Times* announced it on the thirty-first.[62]

Alexander Baring, Lord Ashburton, would be the envoy. In Webster's
opinion, no one could have been better; and Aberdeen knew this when
he made the selection. At sixty-seven, the white-haired aristocrat had
had a lifelong connection with America, highlighted by his marriage to
one of the Pennsylvania Binghams in the 1790s, by extensive land holdings in New England, and by firm financial and personal relationships.
He had succeeded his father as head of the banking house of Baring,
which was heavily involved in transatlantic economic affairs and which
often acted as agent of governments, state and national. Since 1832 he

had been retired from business but had been active in Tory politics. He had always been sympathetic to American interests, as when before the War of 1812 he criticized British maritime policies. Webster shared Ashburton's commitment to Anglo-American commerce. Furthermore, the services he had rendered as legal counsel for the Barings in this country had led to close relations with Thomas Ward, their representative in Boston, and with American-born Joshua Bates, current head of the firm in England.[63]

While the delighted secretary of state awaited Ashburton's arrival, he made such preparations as he could for an enthusiastic reception and for accommodations in the sumptuous style to which the British aristocrat was accustomed.[64] Weeks passed before the envoy's departure while the cabinet at Whitehall considered what his instructions ought to be. Aberdeen's early version told Ashburton to ensure a good military route along the St. John but to go beyond the river to the northwest as far as the Dutch king's award of 1831. Some equivalents could be offered: generosity on the Lake of the Woods area, American retention of Rouse's Point north of the true forty-fifth parallel, and probably free navigation of the St. John. Later, the Duke of Wellington's insistence upon more British space northwest of the St. John for military defense forced the foreign secretary to tighten the instructions accordingly. Still, he and the envoy understood the need for much negotiating flexibility once talks began.[65] A question was whether Webster could also be flexible. In March, Ashburton and a large retinue boarded ship in the hope that he and his American friend could reconcile differences.

Chapter 20
ASHBURTON

Ashburton's arrival in America in the first week of April 1842 was an event exciting interest. On the fourth, HMS *Warspite* came up the Chesapeake to Annapolis, where the special minister and his party disembarked. There were three secretaries, five servants, a carriage and horses, and extensive impedimenta, seeming testimony to the importance of his mission. Soon people at the capital learned that Ashburton and his entourage had taken up residence at Sixteenth and H, close to Webster's house, and that he had presented his credentials to the president. They would often hear of his being host or guest at an elaborate social affair. And they could see the tall, thickset Englishman moving about Washington with an active step and a genial air.[1]

What could be expected from such a full-scale diplomatic effort to solve the large array of problems then disturbing Anglo-American relations? The envoy left no doubt that he would approach them as pragmatically as possible. Acting on the belief that the two countries had too many common interests to allow momentary disagreements to damage those interests, he would concede nonessentials in the cause of conciliation. "For my part," he said, "what seems most important is that there should be a settlement of some sort, and I do not attach all the importance which some do to the precise terms."[2] Perhaps his outlook reflected his lack of diplomatic experience, so that he was unburdened by some of the usual restraints and preconceptions. In any case, he favored informal, relaxed negotiations, just as Webster did. The process may have been disorderly, as one historian has remarked, but it moved along well.[3] For this to happen, the minister required freedom to maneuver,

Alexander Baring, Lord Ashburton, by George P. A. Healy, 1843

provided by a government having confidence in him; and Foreign Secretary Aberdeen gave him large scope because he shared Ashburton's commitment to rapprochement.[4]

On both means and end, the secretary of state agreed. In the modern world, he thought, nations no longer entered treaties merely to make or conclude war but also to secure the just rights of all, consonant with moral and religious principles, not to mention commercial benefits.[5] So he foresaw harmonious collaboration with a like-minded counterpart, "a man of business, & of apparent candor & frankness." Indeed he worried more about obstacles in the United States than about British positions.[6]

For one thing, he felt he must deal with Maine circumspectly, though

Edward Everett, by George P. A. Healy, 1842

attentively. His arrangement with Francis Smith had launched a campaign as early as the summer of 1841 to soften the state's attitude, to put it into a mood for accepting a compromise on the boundary. By the time the secretary learned of Ashburton's mission in January 1842, he knew that Smith had made good progress and was continuing his work with the press and the politicians. Coincidentally he recruited the help of Judge Peleg Sprague, Maine congressman Albert Smith, and a boundary agent of that state, Charles Daveis. All traveled to Augusta to sway opinion.[7] Now that he knew Ashburton would come with authority to settle upon a line, Webster himself began pressing Reuel Williams, Democratic senator from Maine. The state legislature, he recomended, should approve sending commissioners to attend the forthcoming talks with the special minister. Though Williams did confer with Democratic Governor John Fairfield and inclined toward a degree of cooperation, the leadership in Maine refused to act until Ashburton arrived and made the first move.[8] Webster had more success with Governor John Davis of Massachusetts, who in February sent a message to his legislature encouraging it to authorize a commission.[9]

As soon as Ashburton came to Washington, the secretary formally proposed to him that state commissioners participate, an idea which the Englishman did not relish but accepted. Then on April 11, Webster invited Governors Fairfield and Davis to send representatives to the capital for consultation on a boundary compromise. No other procedure, such as the ineffectual attempts of the past, was promising, he contended; moreover, he did not wish to send any treaty to the Senate for ratification without previous assurance that the two states were satisfied.[10] There was no difficulty with Massachusetts; and in Maine, Fairfield showed the effects of months of propaganda by issuing a call for a special session to meet on the question May 18. Pleased with this news, Webster followed through with a plea that Maine confer full power upon its commissioners; they should not be bound by any special terms and their decisions should not be subject to legislative reversal. Meanwhile he maintained his lines of influence upon political opinion in the state.[11]

As the date for the special session of the legislature neared, he decided to play a trump. On May 14 he came to Boston, mainly to confer with Jared Sparks, the Harvard historian, about an additional tactic in his strategy for Maine. He immediately sent his carriage to bring Sparks to Paige's house in Summer Street for a long talk about old maps of the northeastern boundary and their relevance to the pending negotiations.[12]

Throughout the preceding year Webster had been reviewing cartographical evidence contemporaneous to the treaty of independence of 1783.[13] There were many maps from that period, collected by the two governments to support their versions of the boundary as intended by the peace commissioners at the close of the Revolution. The Dutch arbiter had a number of them before him in 1829 but had decided that none unquestionably established the true line. Afterward the search for a definitive map continued and now intensified. So far, however, the connection between a map and the commissioners' understanding of the terms of the treaty could not be convincingly documented.[14]

Sparks had recently discovered information which might do so, but unfortunately it verified the British position. During the previous winter, while carrying on research in the archives in Paris, he had happened upon a letter from Benjamin Franklin, who had been one of the American peace commissioners of 1782–83, to the French foreign minister. "I have marked with a strong red line, according to your desire," Franklin wrote, "the limits of the United States as settled in the preliminaries [for the treaty]." The professor's search in the archives also yielded a map with a red line drawn upon it. "Imagine my surprise," he declared, "on discovering, that this line runs wholly south of the St. John, and between the head waters of that river and those of the Penobscot and Kennebec. In short it is exactly the line now contended for by Great Britain, except that it concedes more than is claimed." Sparks thought circumstances indicated that Franklin had drawn this red line, but he also believed he had seen materials in England supporting the American version of the boundary. After pondering the significance of his findings, he reported them to the secretary of state in February, sending along a copy of the French map.[15]

For three months, until his trip to Boston in May, Webster had not given much thought to the Sparks-Franklin map. One reason was that he already had one showing a similar line. He had bought it in 1838 from an heir of Friedrich von Steuben, the Revolutionary War general, who supposedly had obtained it from John Jay. Like the Sparks-Franklin map, it had a red-line boundary (thought to have been drawn by Jay, another peace commissioner in 1782), and it corresponded with the current British claim.[16] To bring either map to the negotiating table would only help Ashburton. But the secretary had found another use for them. They could be shown to reluctant officials in Maine, who might see that if they did not cooperate in the coming discussions for compromise, Britain might stiffen its stand, once it knew about the Franklin and Steuben maps.

By agreement with Webster in mid-May, Sparks would hurry to Augusta, show Fairfield the maps as well as other materials, and remove any hesitation about sending a commission to Washington. When he set out, he carried a letter from the secretary to the governor, with a warning that the contents must be kept absolutely secret.[17] After talks with Fairfield and with members of the legislature, he wrote Webster that nearly everyone seemed cooperative; he did not say how many people had seen the maps.[18] One may guess that, except to the governor, he spoke only generally about the need to compromise before England strengthened its case with certain new evidence. Whatever Sparks did pleased Webster, who remarked that though the problem of Maine was difficult, "I have attended to that business thoroughly."[19]

Strange to say, he had help from none other than his opposite in the negotiations, Lord Ashburton. While he was waiting impatiently for Maine to make up its mind, the envoy learned from Webster how important it was that the state concur in any settlement. So he provided money to compensate the historian for his mission, an unknown sum in addition to what the State Department paid from the secret-service fund. How much Ashburton himself then discovered about the maps is unclear. Soon afterward he did say that "I have some reason to suspect that Webster has discovered some evidence, known at present to nobody, but favorable to our claim." He hoped to "get at it." Still later, he told Aberdeen that "my informant [perhaps Webster] thinks that without this stimulant [Sparks's effort] Maine would never have yielded." Beyond this expenditure, the minister may have laid out as much as fourteen thousand dollars to smooth the way for a treaty.[20] The probable target was Maine, though the specific transactions cannot now be identified. One modern view is that Webster might have been the intermediary and kept some of the money; yet there is no proof of such misconduct.[21] Outright bribery, if employed, would probably have involved people at the state level, maybe with assistance by Francis Smith's continued intensive lobbying. This, too, however, is an unproven speculation.

When it did address the issue, the legislature seemed well disposed. Governor Fairfield sent a message declaring the justice of Maine's claim to all the disputed area but suggesting the desirability of adjustment if Britain would offer equivalents (free navigation of the St. John had been widely favored).[22] Within a week the lawmakers passed resolutions which authorized appointment of four commissioners to go to Washington, required their unanimous agreement on a treaty, and demanded fair equivalents. The senate approved, 30 to 1; the house, 177 to 11. The appointees to the commission were two Democrats, William Preble and Edward Kavanagh, and two Whigs, former governor Edward Kent and John Otis.[23] In the first week of June they came to Boston, where Webster met with them, and Sparks too, no doubt with maps at hand. Here they encountered the three Massachusetts commissioners, Abbott Lawrence, Charles Allen, and John Mills. They also conferred with the British consul, Thomas Grattan, whose involvement in the diplomacy of the boundary extended back to his presence at the Dutch arbitration of 1829. So well did the Maine representatives think of Grattan's knowledge that they recruited him to accompany them to Washington—an obvious conflict of interest for an adviser in the employ of England.[24] Then the commissioners moved on to New York, where they spent time with Professor Renwick, head of the American survey team and advocate of accommodation.[25] They arrived in Washington by mid-June and found Webster there, at last ready to begin.

During the previous two months, while waiting for the state commissioners to be appointed and to join him, Webster had formulated ideas on a boundary compromise. Anxious for agreement, he would concede a good deal of the American claim to lands north and west of the St. John if he could get reasonable equivalents. He recognized a legitimate British need for space northwest of the river for a military road to Quebec and would put up little resistance to drawing a line near or even along that waterway. Furthermore, he would go below it at the north in the Madawaska area, since there were Canadian residents there. In return, he would ask for free navigation of the entire St. John down to the town of that name on the Bay of Fundy. And he would propose that the United States get new land east of the present due-north boundary and west of the river, extending northward from the Eel to Grand Falls, where the St. John then crossed the due-north line. This was the so-called narrow strip. On April 25 he sketched these propositions in a note to Everett in London, to be handed to Aberdeen.[26] Webster corresponded regularly with Everett, with some effect upon the foreign secretary's instructions to Ashburton, despite the slowness of communication across the ocean. From Everett he learned roughly what room he had for give-and-take.[27]

In this period Ashburton also developed his position. As he familiarized himself with the situation, he found circumstances reinforcing his initial willingness to accommodate. He could see the necessity of getting something done before American political conditions interfered. If possible, he must prevent the conflict between the president and his congressional adversaries from demolishing prospects for a treaty, a hazard which again demonstrated the unstable character of all democratic governments, he thought. Then those state commissioners, worst of all the stubborn Preble of Maine, both bewildered and irritated him. Perhaps it was best not to push them too far. Webster showed little capacity, he feared, to keep them under control, indeed appeared weak and timid on that score. Consequently, the envoy hoped for a relaxation of his instructions on obtaining everything northwest of the St. John, as Wellington had insisted, for that area seemed to him nonessential. More valuable was the Madawaska area south of the St. John, which Webster surprisingly would give up. Why not cede the narrow strip as an equivalent?[28]

Reacting to Ashburton's notes and Everett's conversations through May and June, Aberdeen set new guidelines for negotiations. Never as aggressive as the military on the northwestern sector, he told his minister that after a first attempt for the maximum, following the St. John, he could fall back to the line of the Dutch arbiter (above but closer to the river than the line the Americans claimed). In the north, though not as convinced of the desirability of having all of Madawaska as Ashburton was, he directed him to ask for it but did not say it was indispensable. On one point, the narrow strip, Aberdeen would not budge. His colleagues in the cabinet refused to hand it over to the United States. Still, he concluded, Ashburton must have discretionary power, for time and distance demanded it. Let him do the best he could and be the judge of it.[29]

After preliminary conferences reviewing the long controversy, the British minister presented his proposals on June 21. He asked for everything his instructions had prescribed. Let the boundary run up the St. John from the point where it intersected the due-north line to one of its sources in the northwest. But allow Britain to hold all the Madawaska settlement, south as well as north of the St. John. In return, leave Rouse's Point within the United States by not redrawing the erroneous forty-fifth parallel, and permit American navigation of the St. John. He said nothing about the highlands, upon which he felt the two countries could not agree.[30]

Webster then relayed these proposals to the state commissioners. The men from Maine found them wholly unacceptable and told the secretary so in a note of June 29. It was the possibility of giving up southern Madawaska which most aroused them. If Ashburton insisted upon that condition for a treaty, the negotiations must end, they declared, for they would never consent. In taking their stand, they could not resist throwing in the inflammatory remark that the residents in that area did not especially wish to remain under British rule anyhow and had settled there to escape harsh imperial treatment. As for the rest of the minister's proposed boundary, they also opposed giving up everything above the St. John. Instead they wished to draw a northwesterly line from it near the outlet of the Madawaska River to the highlands and then across to the Connecticut.[31]

Over the next two weeks both sides worried that their differences were so serious the talks would collapse. Ever more clearly Webster realized that success depended on more than two reasonable men sitting down together and disposing of some of these details in friendly fashion. He and Ashburton at an early stage were probably not far apart—on Britain's having southern Madawaska, the United States' getting the narrow strip, and neither caring much about the northwestern sector. But when

Maine would not hear of cession of Madawaska and when Aberdeen vetoed giving up the narrow strip, elements other than an easy understanding between the two diplomats clouded the scene. What he could
not know was the large degree of flexibility Ashburton's superiors had
allowed him.[32] Meanwhile the summer weather in Washington had
reached its notorious worst, with oppressive heat and humidity making
life miserable. This factor in itself depressed the negotiators, Ashburton
most of all. The minister wrote an ill-humored, unfair note to the secretary, one often quoted later. "I contrive to crawl about in this heat by
day & pass my nights in a sleepless fever. In short I shall positively not
outlive this affair if it is to be much prolonged. I had hoped that these
Gentlemen from the North East would be equally averse to roasting.
Could you not press them to come to the point and say whether we can
or can not agree? I do not see why I should be kept waiting while Maine
& Massachusetts settle their accounts with the General Government."[33]

Just now Webster was not ready to push the commissioners openly.
His response of July 8 to the minister corresponded exactly to their position; and to show that it did, he enclosed a copy of their letter to him. In
any event, he had to go through the routine motions of arguing the
American case: refusal to give up southern Madawaska, placement of
the northwestern boundary along the highlands above the St. John, and
the equivalents Ashburton had offered. He did not attempt, however, to
obtain the land due north of the river to the highlands, as claimed, nor
the narrow strip in the east as an equivalent.[34]

As a matter of fact, the English envoy had known the full contents of
the Maine commissioners' paper of June 29 as soon as Webster did, and
that very day had written to Aberdeen about it. Instead of resistance to
the state's demands, he preferred concession, and without delay. He
would have to abandon his effort for Madawaska, he told the foreign
secretary, and probably for the advanced northwestern line as well.[35] So
almost immediately after receiving Webster's note of July 8, he responded with one of his own, suggesting a compromise in which he
might trade off his proposal on Madawaska for a more moderate
American stand in the northwest. Tediously reiterating the merits of
Britain's claims over the years, his tone was more grudging than grace-
ful.[36] Privately, he was even more upset than he revealed in this reply. In
his judgment, Webster could not control the obstreperous representatives of Maine and had shifted ground taken early in the talks. "I have
attached too much importance to his concessions which I thought worth
something but which he is wholly unable to realize," he lamented.[37] To
rescue the mission from unprofitable written exchanges, possibly to re-

duce the states' influence, he recommended that he and Webster resume informal conferences like those soon after his arrival.

That suggestion suited Webster's preference on how to proceed. The two diplomats met frequently and within four days arrived at a mutually acceptable formula. In a note to the Maine commissioners, the secretary outlined its features, marked on an enclosed map, and advised approval because no better, nor perhaps any other opportunity for settlement would arise. The map showed a boundary from the due-north line westward along the St. John past the Madawaska to the St. Francis, then up that river to Lake Pohenagamook. In the northwest, the line would not go as far as the Dutch arbiter's award. Of the 12,000 square miles in dispute, Webster said, 5,000 would be British—893 more than they would have received if the Dutch king's recommendation had been accepted. But besides the previously offered equivalents from Britain, the two states would each receive $125,000 from the federal government.[38]

In addition to sustained off-the-record persuasion, the approval of the Massachusetts commissioners helped convince the Maine delegation that they must acquiesce.[39] On July 22 the latter sent Webster an argumentative paper, restating the justice of their long-held views but closing with an unenthusiastic assent to what had now been arranged. There were other matters to handle, but the secretary knew he would soon have a treaty.[40]

By this time Webster and Ashburton had also disposed of the much easier question of the Canadian boundary through the Great Lakes to the Lake of the Woods. Earlier efforts in 1804 and 1818 had left it unresolved, chiefly because of a dispute about several thousand square miles in northern Minnesota. Without argument, they agreed upon terms in their conferences, and Ashburton then put them into written form. Here Webster fared very well. The minister gave up the sizable, fertile St. George's or Sugar Island at the head of Huron. And most important, he concurred on a boundary from the western shore of Superior by way of Pigeon River, Rainy Lake, and various portages to the Lake of the Woods; from there it dropped down to the forty-ninth parallel running to the Rockies. Here and there the negotiators provided for mutual rights of navigation through narrows and shifting channels connecting the Lakes. The United States got sixty-five hundred square miles of contested land, of which a part, the Vermilion area, would one day yield valuable iron deposits. But Webster had no definite idea of that potential.[41]

With the entire boundary identified, the secretary was able on July 27 to write the precise terms, which Ashburton promptly accepted. After tracing the line, he referred to free American access to the St. John River for transporting timber and agricultural goods without discriminating regulations. He added that a survey commission would make the boundary according to the treaty. He also promised the states federal compensation for land they gave up and further payment to Maine for expenses incurred as a result of recent conflict along the border.[42] The sum provided for the land would amount to about ten cents an acre if Maine had a right to all it claimed, and fifty cents an acre for the forested and swampy tract it could have acquired from the Dutch award. The second figure approximated its current market value.[43]

While attempting to settle the boundary controversy Webster had to handle the other pending issues, one of them the illegal African slave trade. In April 1842, when Ashburton arrived, this problem had reached a diplomatic impasse. In its active effort to stop the traffic, Britain adhered to its perceived right to visit suspected vessels to determine nationality, while the United States contended that visit necessitated search of American ships and violated international law. In London, Everett, like Stevenson before him, continued to protest and argue the matter.[44] In France, Cass was still agitating against the stalled quintuple treaty for mutual search, much to Webster's discomfort.[45] To the American minister's warning that he must not concede rights of visit and search in the treaty with Ashburton, Webster crisply replied he was "not intending to surrender any point of national interest, or national honor" but would assure the United States' fulfillment of its duty to stop the slave trade.[46]

Soon after their talks began in Washington in April, the secretary and the British envoy agreed to deemphasize the question, involving as it did the whole range of maritime rights. They would include nothing about these rights specifically in the treaty but would find a practical alternative for combating the slave trade. This was a system of joint naval patrols off West Africa, an idea advanced as early as the 1820s. Neither country would then lose face by retreating from now hardened positions. So Webster got information and advice from American naval officers with experience on the African station and arrived at an understanding with Ashburton early in their negotiations.[47] Each government would maintain cruisers off the African coast with an armament totaling at least eighty guns; and its commanders could cooperate with those of the other in suppressing the traffic but would visit and search only vessels of its own nationality.[48]

Underlying the slave-trade dispute about the rights of visit and search, the old British practice of impressment inescapably became a topic of discussion, for Americans believed that the drafting of sailors from their merchant ships into the Royal Navy was the inevitable consequence of searching them. Though not used afterward, it had been a sore griev-ance leading to the War of 1812. Cass's view reflected the persistent worry that some day, perhaps after getting approval to visit and search slavers, England would revive impressment. For this reason, he and others hoped that Webster would get a pledge in the treaty not to do so. But Ashburton had no instructions on the subject—British opinion would not allow such an overt concession even though resumption of im-pressment appeared highly unlikely. So he and the secretary wished to play down the question as much as possible. As a result, they resorted to an exchange of notes about it, thereby avoiding the difficulties that would have inevitably arisen during the ratification process if they had included it in the treaty. This device would still give Webster an oppor-tunity to restate long-standing policy for home consumption.[49]

In early August, at the conclusion of negotiations, Webster therefore presented a forceful written argument against impressment, reviewing its history, contending that it violated international law, and declaring that the United States would never submit to it. Especially objection-able, he said, was the doctrine of indefeasible British citizenship, applied to the many immigrants coming to America to improve their lot.[50] True, proof of naturalization would always be difficult; nevertheless, when sailors served on ships of this nation, they must be immune from capri-cious decisions by English naval officers. The sound rule, then, was that the ships were American territory, just as Secretary of State Jefferson had contended years ago. Rephrasing that rule, Webster proclaimed that "in every regularly documented American merchant vessel the crew who navigate it will find their protection in the flag which is over them."[51] Ashburton went as far as he could go. He repeated that he had no authority to treat on this issue; yet, in his opinion, resumption of the practice could not occur "under present circumstances." In a concilia-tory gesture, he promised that his government would give the secretary's paper its most deliberate consideration.[52]

Still more sensitive than the problems of slave trade and impressment, that of the *Creole* worried the diplomats all through the summer's discus-sions. Before Ashburton had left London, Webster sent off his note of late January, protesting emancipation of slaves on the vessel brought into Nassau by mutineers. Yet the British envoy had received no in-structions to cover such questions in the treaty and was told to pacify American excitement as best he could, a charge he knew would be diffi-cult to carry out. The secretary of state also found himself in an uncomfortable position, flanked as he was by British refusal to return the emancipated slaves or to extradite those connected with murder on the one hand and by southern concern about racial uprising on the other hand. There were, moreover, the abolitionists, praising the liberation of blacks on the *Creole*. When he took middle ground by not demanding return of the slaves but by asking for compensation, he did not fully satisfy either side. Antislavery people complained that he thereby countenanced the evil of slavery; the proslavery element sensed an insult to national honor. Aberdeen, apparently surprised that Webster did not take a stauncher stand on returning the slaves, seemed slow to focus on the actual point he was trying to make.[53]

In the final round of talks throughout the first week of August, the negotiators resorted to an exchange of notes on this issue also. Instead of concentrating on the single case of the *Creole,* Webster discussed the general question of British interference with a number of American ships forced into port by weather or violence. In a lawyer's argument, he relied upon the doctrine that these vessels had extraterritorial status and as such were protected from boarding parties which would upset personal relationships of passengers and crew. He conceded the necessity of some municipal regulations for health and safety, but observed that slavery had the sanction of the United States Constitution. Since Ashburton could not enter into a stipulation by treaty, could he, at least, put in writing a statement which would prevent recurrence of these episodes?[54]

The minister complied. In fact he even gave Webster a draft for suggested revisions; and it also went to Tyler, who took special interest in the subject. In final form, the note did somewhat reflect the president's reactions, enough to satisfy him as well as other southerners later.[55] Though saying the matter could be better handled in London, Ashburton pledged a policy of neighborliness and restraint. He promised that colonial governors would be instructed "that there shall be no officious interference with American vessels driven by accident or by violence into these ports."[56] Although that assurance had no basis other than an individual opinion at the moment, afterward the United States had less cause for complaint. As for the *Creole,* a commission would one day award damages for interference.[57]

In part because of British refusal to extradite the nineteen mutineers from Nassau on the ground there was no treaty authorizing it, Webster proposed an article on extradition of fugitive criminals. But he saw a still greater need for a way to handle many instances of flight across the Canadian border in both directions. Some states, especially New York, were encountering difficulties in either recovering or returning such persons.[58] That the forthcoming treaty should provide for extradition Ashburton readily agreed, since it would help Canada as well. His only objection related to slavery, for Britain had no intention of acting as slave catcher or relaxing its West Indies emancipation law.[59] At an early stage, Webster got Story's advice on terms of an article, which the justice modeled after the expired provision in the Jay Treaty. Extraditable crimes would include murder, arson, forgery, and other nonpolitical offenses, with a requirement for judicial hearing before delivering up persons demanded by either country.[60] Though Webster and Tyler wished to add the crime of mutiny (as in the *Creole*), the British envoy refused, despite an initial inclination to do so.[61]

Of the items left for resolution in the final days of negotiation, the *Caroline* affair had been the most bothersome. Now, nearly five years after a Canadian force had destroyed this ship supplying rebels from the American side, the diplomats closed a major dispute. An exchange of notes, representing the outcome of informal talks, again seemed the best procedure. Webster began with a brief statement of his nation's complaint, to which Ashburton responded with a full review of the facts of the raid from Britain's perspective. In a key passage, while rejecting the idea of reparations, the envoy came as close to an apology as he could. It was regrettable, he wrote, that, at the time of the incident, Britain had not offered an explanation and apology. But he and the secretary both emphasized their agreement on the principle of international law governing such cases.[62] In his final comment, Webster expressed that rule as limiting a nation's forcible penetration of another's territory to a situation in which the necessity of self-defense is "instant, overwhelming," with "no choice of means, and no moment of deliberation." He admitted that the two countries disagreed about the application of the principle to the *Caroline;* but to claim American satisfaction, he seized on Ashburton's blurred language expressing regret that an apology had not been made. For present purposes, it was the next best thing to an outright apology.[63]

Webster and Ashburton completed their business on August 8 after the exchange of notes on impressment, the *Creole,* and the *Caroline.* Deciding not to include these subjects in the treaty proper, they then put twelve articles of agreement in final shape and signed the document on the ninth.[64] In them they covered three main topics: the Canadian boundary from Maine to the Lake of the Woods, naval patrols to suppress the slave trade, and extradition of criminals. There were less important features, such as American access to the St. John for transporting lumber and agricultural products, United States compensation to Maine and Massachusetts for claimed territory given up (raised to $150,000 each), and a future survey to mark the boundary.[65] It was an unusual achievement to settle such a variety of long-standing, vexatious problems in one effort. To be sure, there were then and would later be assertions that, because of Anglophilism and personal circumstances, Webster had given up too much. He did concede more on the boundary than strict justice required. Yet on the other side of the Atlantic, criticism of Ashburton was equally severe. Nevertheless, the course of history suggests that the significance of the Webster-Ashburton treaty transcended tracts of land or promises on this or that detail. The major outcome was improved relations between the two countries.[66]

Chapter 21
DIPLOMACY AND POLITICS

Before he sailed for England, Ashburton decided to see some of the country whose character and growth had interested him for so many years. Leaving Washington on August 20, he visited Philadelphia, then traveled north as far as Boston, and ended his circuit at New York. All along the route, people welcomed the minister approvingly. A highlight was his stay in Boston, where he received praise for strengthening the bonds of Anglo-American friendship, to which the Englishman responded with handsome reference to Faneuil Hall as the cradle of liberty. Here and at Harvard, speeches portrayed him as a peacemaker.[1] In New York City the theme also emerged at an affair at the Astor House, featuring a series of toasts, among them one to President Tyler and another to Queen Victoria. Reportedly, silence followed the first, cheers the second.[2] Everywhere Webster's role won recognition too, but he had stayed in Washington to take care of business at the end of the congressional session. In fact the secretary could not see Ashburton off when he boarded the *Warspite* on September 3 but did get a friendly note from the envoy, saying he hoped that Webster would visit him. It must be soon, he added, because "my taper is burning away fast."[3]

After the negotiators had signed the treaty on August 9, the next task was to get ratification by the Senate. Within two days Tyler sent it up to Capitol Hill with a message, at least partly drafted by Webster. The president commented on each important provision, beginning with the boundary settlement, a necessary compromise of the two positions unreconciled for such a long time, he said. Naturally, he emphasized the equivalents gained by this country: access to the St. John, retention of

353

Rouse's Point, and substantial acquisitions in the upper lakes area. He viewed the arrangement to stop the slave trade by joint cruising as a rejection of British visit and search of American ships. And like Webster, he interpreted Ashburton's remarks on the *Caroline* as an apology, thus vindicating national honor.[4]

William Rives, chairman of the Committee on Foreign Relations, guided the treaty through several days of debate. In addition to the public documents, he now had a copy of the Franklin-Sparks red-line map, supplied by Webster. As a clincher to his argument for approval, he warned his colleagues that if they refused to ratify, Britain could use the map to demand more than it would obtain in this treaty. He did not, however, rest his case on the absolute validity of Sparks's findings. Whether senators were swayed by this reasoning is quite doubtful.[5] From a later perspective, it seems clear that the Webster-Rives tactic was not only unnecessary but also of questionable propriety, employed as it was for domestic purposes without any application to the preceding negotiating process. Furthermore, the fact that Webster kept the map under cover until he secretly sent it to Rives for use in his Senate committee bred unnecessary suspicion of sharp dealing. Even if Rives had shown it only to his committee, it was likely the word would have got out, and certainly so when the senator revealed it to the entire Senate. Rives had sufficient grounds for success on the merits of the treaty.[6]

Benton, the leading opponent of approval, did not think so and spoke with his customary fire and verbosity against each article, as well as against display of Sparks's map, a "solemn bamboozlement," he declared. His complaint was that Webster had affronted the Senate by bringing in the map covertly, by trying to bind that body to secrecy while playing upon its worries about an imagined danger of war. In any case, he continued, the map was not much of a discovery, for he himself had found another one, given by Franklin to Jefferson and later deposited in the Library of Congress, which showed a red-line boundary identical to that of the Sparks version. Neither was valid, he argued, for the American claim up to the highlands near the St. Lawrence was entirely sound. So Webster had needlessly and shamefully handed over valuable territory.[7] Equally deplorable was the way he had done it, by resort to private conversations with Ashburton instead of proceedings regularly recorded and susceptible to public scrutiny. The Missourian faulted every provision of the treaty with the same partisan intensity but chiefly depended upon recruiting southern opposition to the slave trade patrols and the *Creole* note.[8] When Calhoun spoke, Benton knew this strategy would fail. While voicing some concern about these points, the South

Carolinian urged ratification as the best path to peace and to improved economic relations; he even had a good word for the secretary's note protesting emancipation of the *Creole* slaves.[9]

Nearly all Whigs and many Democrats accepted the treaty. Among the holdouts were James Buchanan, Levi Woodbury, and, disappointingly, Reuel Williams of Maine. A Democrat, influenced by the background of intensive political conflict in his state as well as by a plain reluctance to give up anything Maine had claimed, Williams had cooperated with Webster in setting up negotiations but now charged that the boundary concessions were unjustified. Still, he did not reflect prevailing sentiment, for the legislature and the press approved the settlement.[10] At nine o'clock on the evening of the twentieth, when the ayes and nays were counted, the secretary of the Senate announced an affirmative vote of thirty-nine to nine.

Webster expected ratification, but not by such a margin. Believing that he had achieved a general settlement not only beneficial to the nation but popular as well, he felt very satisfied and warmly thanked those who had also had a part in the work—Rives in the Senate, Everett in England, and particularly the president.[11] His mood was exuberant as he attended to formalities, Tyler's signature and exchange of ratifications at London. His clerk, William Derrick, sailed to England for that purpose immediately. "He will be back with the Queen's ratifications," he told the chief executive, "by the time I have done making *chowder*—at Marshfield, & we can then have a treaty published & proclaimed."[12] In fact the process did move along nicely; and in two months' time news of British approval arrived.

Some problems, however, persisted. There seemed no way to placate the querulous minister to France, Lewis Cass, whose Anglophobic views on the slave trade become more vocal than ever. Having pressed the French government not to ratify the quintuple treaty and his own government to get British renunciation of visit and search, Cass reacted strongly to the Ashburton treaty as soon as he learned its provisions in mid-September. Indeed he could have known about the joint-patrol article even before Webster officially told him about it, for he had had other sources of information on negotiations.[13] At any rate, he now asked to be relieved of his post and soon expressed his objections in the first of an animated exchange of notes with the secretary. At the threshold of discussions with Ashburton, he contended, Webster ought to have insisted upon a provision forbidding British search, because the cruising agreement implied American consent to the practice. Since he had so consistently stated his stand against it, he said, the treaty amounted to

repudiation of his effort. It had placed him in a false, embarrassing position, so that he could not stay there.[14] To this, Webster responded that a
formal concession by Ashburton had been unnecessary. The United
States had rejected arguments by Palmerston and Aberdeen long before
the treaty and would do so in the future. Now the commitment to station vessels off the African coast handled the problem of the slave trade
in such a way as to avoid further diplomatic debate. Point by point, he
called the minister's remonstrance a "tissue of mistakes." Besides, Webster replied, Cass meddled in a matter that was none of his business. His
responsibility to represent America did not give him freedom to comment from his Paris hotel on negotiations in Washington with another
country.[15] In December, after arriving home, Cass renewed his protest;
and Webster reiterated his disapproval and Tyler's of the diplomat's irregular, mistaken course.[16] The dispute lasted until March, with more
letters from Cass and with Webster's publication of their correspondence. Certain that the Michigan Democrat's motive was to promote
himself for the presidency by playing up to the South, Webster felt more
than a little annoyed.[17]

Meanwhile, controversy about the boundary agreement recurred. In
the Senate, Benton and others attacked the treaty in early 1843 and
could now put their case more effectively because the proceedings of ratification, which had supposedly been secret, were published. In criticizing Webster's compromise, they contended he had improperly used the
Franklin-Sparks map to get the consent of Maine and the Senate to a
bad bargain, since it erroneously upheld the British claim. Concurrently, in England the complaint spread that, to be fair, the secretary of
state ought to have shown the map to Ashburton during negotiations.
Very sensitive to that charge, Webster answered that no diplomat is obligated to reveal evidence helping the other side. And Ashburton, who
had possibly known something about Franklin's letter and red-line map
anyway, agreed there was no such obligation. But Webster's better argument emphasized his reliance directly upon the terms of the treaty of
1783 concerning highlands and rivers, not upon old maps, undepend-
able and contradictory as they were. Best of all was his argument that
the time had come to compromise rather than to haggle about
technicalities any longer. What he said seemed sensible, yet his selective
use of Sparks's findings left an impression of opportunism.[18]

Sparks felt uncomfortable about all this talk questioning his scholarly
probity. In February he began writing an article on the subject for the
North American Review, which might vindicate both Webster and the
Harvard professor himself. "I doubt if anything would have induced me

to furnish the information [about the map]," he lamented, "if I could have foreseen that my name would have been bandied about in the senate in the way it has been."[19] Pleased with the idea of an article, Webster sent Sparks information and advice, including his opinion that Franklin had erroneously interpreted the peace commission's intent when he drew his red line.[20] When the article came out in the April issue of the *Review,* it was a cautious, learned exposition of the map problem and of leading features of the Ashburton treaty. Even today, it serves as a profitable essay in diplomatic history. Its theme, however, was unreserved approval of Webster's peaceful settlement. After surveying most of the maps then known, Sparks concluded that the one he had discovered in the French archives was probably authentic but that the weight of all cartographical evidence inclined toward the later American version. Having said this, he endorsed the current resolution of a debatable issue for the larger good.[21]

Just after Sparks's article appeared, the public learned that still another map had turned up. It was one used by John Jay, a peace commissioner in 1782, and after his death in possession of his sons. Now, in early April 1843, old Albert Gallatin had it; and as president of the New York Historical Society, he was preparing a lecture focusing on this interesting discovery. Former representative at the Dutch arbitration in 1829, Gallatin was well informed and had settled opinions about the historical background of this latest development. Accepting an invitation to attend the society's meeting in New York City on the fifteenth, Webster, too, would have the opportunity to discuss his treaty and the boundary.

A large audience, crowding into the chapel of New York University, strained to hear Gallatin's feeble voice as he delivered a long discourse affirming the American position, founded upon conditions and policies from the 1760s to the present. Jay's map proved what had been claimed, he pointed out, with a red line running up the Madawaska River and thus north of the St. John to the highlands. Along the boundary Jay had written "Mr. Oswald's line," referring to his British counterpart in the negotiations in Paris. Gallatin could not show that the final treaty of 1783 in fact adopted the line proposed by Oswald; but he had no doubt that it did. Certainly, he declared, here was better evidence than the Franklin-Sparks map. Yet like Sparks, after exploring the merits of opposing arguments Gallatin ended by praising the Ashburton treaty on practical grounds, the equivalents given by Britain and the advancement of peace.[22]

Webster listened attentively. The lecture may have dealt with maps more than he would have liked, but he did not mind hearing these words

of approval. So he was in good spirits when he rose to make some remarks, mostly to justify his work of the previous summer but also to stir
the patriotism of his audience. Like Gallatin, he thought the history of
the boundary showed that as early as 1763 England placed it close to the
St. Lawrence. And Jay's map simply added to other strong support of
the American claim, so that, strictly speaking, the United States had the
edge in the protracted controversy. Nevertheless, he preferred to defend
his treaty as an essential concession to Britain for its military road while
obtaining other concessions from that country. Navigational rights on
the St. John and retention of the strategic fort at Rouse's Point were
more valuable than an unpromising tract in the north woods. Above all,
the secretary insisted, the agreement decidedly improved diplomatic
and commercial relations between the two nations.[23]

As in the United States, the treaty became an inexhaustible source for
comment in England. From the time that Webster and Ashburton
signed the document in August 1842 until the following May, the British
press and politicians analyzed its every dimension. Palmerston wrote articles for London newspapers, unsparingly attacking it as outright surrender of national rights by an inexperienced, softheaded negotiator.
But he confronted a prevailing public opinion thankful for the settlement. Peel and Aberdeen had the advantage over those Whigs of the
opposition willing to follow their irascible leader on the issue: Palmerston was complaining about a *fait accompli* after the queen's ratification
on October 13, and all he could do was to capitalize on the treaty's defects for some long-range purpose. Everett's reports to Webster from
London assessed the former foreign secretary's effort as only a minor
nuisance.[24]

Full-scale debate began when Parliament assembled in early 1843.
Palmerston immediately took the offensive by attacking the ineptitude
of Ashburton in agreeing to provisions on the slave trade and the Maine
boundary. With respect to the first, he contended that the British minister had, in effect, abandoned the rights of visit and search as well as endangered current efforts to establish a multinational system to suppress
the trade. Not so, said Peel. Yet in the long run Palmerston's position
was rather close to the truth. As for the boundary article, the former foreign secretary was overpowered by Peel's defense of the treaty. It seemed
strange that Palmerston could complain about a line which gave
England more than the Dutch arbiter would have, in view of the fact
that when in office he would have accepted that decision. Furthermore,
Peel surprised everyone by revealing that he himself had looked over
maps in the archives in Paris, had seen Sparks's discovery there, and

knew it was dated too early to have been the one Franklin had marked. Indeed, the prime minister announced, he had uncovered a map in the Foreign Office itself, marked by the British negotiator Oswald and confirming the American claim. Why had not Palmerston made this known, since he had undoubtedly seen it? Anyway, Peel concluded, no map was decisive, for all of them merely showed what the commissioners of 1782 proposed, not what they had agreed upon.[25]

It goes without saying that these developments gratified Webster immeasurably. Through winter and spring, as they were occurring, he interpreted them, as described in Everett's frequent despatches, to be justification of his diplomacy. Everett, who did not know about the Sparks map until after the negotiations but had long suspected there was a map such as Oswald's, was fascinated by the whole business and theorized about it for a long while.[26] But Webster stuck to his position—similar to that of Peel, Aberdeen, and Ashburton—that the decisive thing had not really been evidence from maps nor even the terms of the treaty of 1783, but the advantages of reciprocal concessions by the United States and Britain.[27]

While Webster gave primary attention to relations with Britain, he faced increasingly important issues concerning the far Southwest. Most of them involved Mexico, its vast but tenuous holdings in New Mexico and California and its now detached state of Texas. Complicated by chronic instability of the Mexican government and by an expansionist surge in the United States, these questions would eventually lead to war. Generally, Webster shared prevailing preconceptions that Mexico had not yet arrived at a stage of enlightened and free republicanism, that its political leadership was weak and unreliable in either domestic or international fields. Still, unlike a growing number of Americans, he did not see these defects as legitimate reasons for expansion at its expense. On the contrary, he believed, territorial acquisition would undermine the nation's institutions.

Mexican-American relations were difficult. There was the problem of Texas, still an independent republic recognized by the United States but claimed by Mexico, perhaps coveted by England. As he had since the revolution of 1835, Webster firmly opposed annexation, while Tyler became increasingly tempted to achieve it, with the effect of widening a gap between the two men. Yet continuance of the existing status of Texas invited trouble along the border, such as illegal commerce southward, and occasional filibusters. In one instance, farther west, in Santa Fe, an American expedition fell captive to the Mexicans; and it took an unusual effort for the secretary to obtain release of some persons who

359

had been marched to Mexico City and imprisoned. Moreover, through-out his time in office, Webster worried about the lack of progress of a claims commission established under a treaty of arbitration but dead-locked on awards. And out in California the Mexican hold on the area was so weak that it seemed only a matter of time before the United States would take it. A naval officer, Thomas A. C. Jones, tried to do just that in 1842 by occupying the fort at Monterey in the belief that war with Mexico had commenced, a move that he had to reverse by evacua-tion the next day when he learned otherwise. But it was the harbor of San Francisco which appeared most attractive to Americans, even to Webster, who sought vainly to negotiate an arrangement to use it. All these concerns remained when he left office and would be on the agenda of his successors.[28]

Through the months after the Ashburton negotiations, from summer 1842 to the following spring, though busy with issues of international relations, Webster played an active role in politics at home. But his po-sition became more and more untenable now that hope for executive-congressional cooperation had vanished. Tyler showed signs of moving over to the Democrats, at least to the states' rights wing; or if he did not end up there, he might head a new party of his own making. In addition to Whig setbacks on tariff and banking as a result of Tyler's categorical stand, the president's yen for Texas and other points west alarmed Webster. Would his own political interest, not to mention conscience, allow him to stay in the cabinet? He inclined to say no. Still, where should he go? To join in the current Whig enthusiasm for Clay as presi-dent seemed not only degrading to his own aspirations but also poor strategy. To leave public life altogether seemed unappealing, an igno-minious retreat from the field where he had gained so much popularity and enjoyed so many perquisites. His indecision dragged on as he searched for some attractive option; and unfortunately his conduct of diplomacy, often mingled with these considerations, took on a self-serv-ing quality.

He did not lack advice. As he neared the time for signing the British treaty, he began getting opinion both ways, to leave the administration immediately in justice to himself or to stay on as its only ornament. One Massachusetts commissioner during the negotiations, Abbott Lawrence, counseled the first; another, John Mills, the second.[29] Among his inti-mate friends, Everett urged him to remain, while Jeremiah Mason ar-gued that his own character did not permit further association with an "almost universally detested" chief executive.[30] The secretary confided to Everett that he felt very unhappy about the presidential vetoes and

360

had told Tyler so. He would probably resign, he said, but had not determined when. Unwilling to be rushed, he would go home to Marshfield at the end of the congressional session and think about it. Perhaps he could go to France as replacement for Cass, who was now resigning, but he did not know the language. Or possibly to England, though he quickly added he hesitated to dislocate his friend. Anyway he could not afford the expenses of a foreign mission.[31]

He felt stronger pressure to say or do something when the Massachusetts Whig convention assembled on September 14, 1842. Besides nominating candidates for state offices, this gathering might declare its support of Clay for president. In Webster's judgment, that course would be foolish, for it would sanction the Kentuckian's behavior in congressional action on banking and tariff. In any case, he declared, *"He has no degree of reasonable prospect of being elected."* Webster doubted that even Clay's own state would vote for him.[32] But the hundreds of delegates arriving in Boston assessed the situation differently. They followed the lead of Abbott Lawrence, the conservative manufacturer-politician who was threatening Webster's hold on the party. A confirmed Clay man, he had been disappointed when Harrison, backed by Webster, obtained the party's nomination in 1840; he had written off Tyler as an apostate early in the conflict at the capital; and he now criticized the secretary of state for clinging to office. In truth, the Webster-Lawrence disagreements had developed into a nasty feud promising to last for some time.

Predictably, the convention did come out for Clay and added John Davis as running mate, on top of his selection as gubernatorial candidate. As for the current administration, a resolution called for a "full and final separation" from the besieged president.[33] It amounted to a demand that if Webster expected to remain a Whig, he must also separate. In light of this display of party discipline, the convention's perfunctory approval of his diplomacy could hardly mollify him.

He would shortly have an opportunity to react publicly to this slap on the wrist. A group of the city's elite had invited him to a meeting on September 30 to honor him for negotiating the Ashburton treaty.[34] Upset as he was after the state convention, he hardly knew what he ought to say on the occasion. His anger rising, he finally decided upon a very powerful counterblow, not only as self-defense but also as chastisement of his critics.[35] In late morning of this autumn day, then, he mounted the platform in Faneuil Hall, projecting poise and power, dressed in customary blue coat with brass buttons, to face the three thousand spectators squeezed into the room.[36] Thanking the mayor for his lengthy, laudatory introduction, speedily disposing of the main topic at hand, the new treaty, he concentrated on the question of resignation from the cabinet. His emphatic tone revealed wounded feelings and inflexible determination. As he had the previous year when the first cabinet had resigned, he still believed he could serve the country by staying on. When he found he could not, he alone would decide what to do. "I am, Gentlemen, a little hard to coax, but as to being driven, that is out of the question." Despite the presumptuous demand of the recent state convention that Whigs should separate from the president, he would not let anyone set up such a test of his relationship to the party. "I am a Whig, I always have been a Whig, and I always will be one; and if there are any who would turn me out of the pale of that communion, let them see who will get out first. I am a Massachusetts Whig, a Faneuil Hall Whig, having breathed this air for five-and-twenty years, and meaning to breathe it, as long as my life is spared."[37]

The speech provided a catharsis for Webster himself but further alienated his critics and discomfited his friends. Lawrence, for example, interpreted it as evidence of stubbornness and of thwarted presidential aspirations. Even those upon whom he could always count for approval, such as Otis, Story, and Hone, regretted his sour mood and apparent endorsement of Tyler's conduct. But after venting his feelings, he had no second thoughts.[38]

On his way to Washington a month later, on November 4, he stopped in New York City for a huge public reception which would allow him to add political comment if he wished. Planned to express gratitude for the Ashburton treaty, the affair attracted thousands to Battery Park, where gun salutes were fired, and to City Hall, where for hours he greeted people individually and then spoke briefly. Deciding that he had no more to say about politics, at least from this visible platform, he talked only about the treaty.[39] Later in the day, however, he was the guest of honor at a private dinner at the Astor House, given by a few of his closest friends, Hiram Ketchum, Moses Grinnell, Richard Blatchford, Philip Hone, and others. Sitting at the table after dinner, he spoke informally about a range of subjects, briefly about his connection with the Whig party. According to Hone, he said, "I was christened at its font, and have continued firm in its faith. I am too old to change my politics or my religion."[40]

In the same month, news of Whig losses was arriving from across the land. Election day varied from state to state; but when Webster was lauded, wined, and dined in New York, he already knew the party would lose more than its share of congressional and state contests.[41] Presently he learned that the Whigs had also lost in Massachusetts. Here Lawrence's candidate for governor, John Davis, lost to the Democratic veteran Marcus Morton—the latter's victory made possible, in part, by a good showing of the new Liberty party. The secretary felt gloomy but not surprised. This downturn, he believed, came because of the unjustified warfare of Whig congressmen against Tyler—and because the party had prematurely and unwisely tied its future to Clay's claim to the presidency.[42] Though in an overstatement he said that the party was "broken up," he took comfort in the possibility that the administration might now attract fragments of both parties.[43]

Through the middle of November he had still not decided whether to resign. One day, he inclined to; the next, he did not. "A few days will decide," he wrote, "whether I shall stay here till spring, or, differing from migratory birds, take an autumnal flight to the north."[44] What, if anything, Tyler said to him about this matter is unknown. Certainly the president made no overt move to push him out, as some people maintained. At last, Webster understood that Tyler wanted him to remain, if for no other reason than that Congress would soon assemble. By the twenty-third it was announced he would continue through the session ending in March. One element in determining what he would do seems to have been Tyler's abandonment of the thought, for the time being, of a general reorganization of the cabinet.[45]

He did not stay in office just to look after miscellaneous items of diplomacy and keep hands off politics at home. As soon as the presidential message went to Congress in early December, he began writing editorials for the administration's organ, the *Madisonian,* to persuade the legislators, the press, and the public that they ought to give Tyler a fair chance. If he was a man without a party, then judge him on his merits, one of Webster's pieces urged. Above all, reexamine the proposal for an exchequer, renewed in the executive message. Dogmatic adherence to an old-fashioned national bank or to a Locofoco independent treasury amounted to folly, in contrast to a realistic acceptance of this modest plan to improve the condition of currency and exchange.[46] Congress did give it a little attention, but with no sign of approval. On this issue especially, Webster placed heavy blame upon Clay, no longer in the Senate but insistent that his party stand fast on a bank. In general, the lame-duck secretary extended himself to speak for the administration. A typical argument ran as follows: while the *Globe* and Benton assail Tyler on one flank, and the *Intelligencer* and Clay's partisans on the other, "the great mass of patriotic citizens, who have no selfish interests in the squabble of parties, will be very likely to think him about right."[47] There may have been a certain logic in such an estimate, yet the subsequent course of politics did not verify it.

The question of Webster's resignation continued to be a popular topic of speculation month after month. Besides its political significance, it affected the way he approached diplomatic problems; indeed it became so mingled with handling of Anglo-American affairs that personal motives and policymaking were almost indistinguishable. To be sure, several matters of interest to the two nations were left unsettled by the Ashburton treaty, yet the possibilities of dealing with them seemed entwined with Webster's indecision about his own future.

The most important pending issue concerned the Oregon boundary. Ashburton's instructions had not permitted him to cede territory farther north than the Columbia, and so the subject was dropped during the negotiations of summer 1842. Webster did not object to the line of the Columbia except for the fact that the United States would then have no adequate harbor on the Pacific coast, because sandbars at the outlet of the river prevented navigation for a large part of the year. Thus he had the idea of connecting an Oregon agreement with access to San Francisco, if Mexico could be persuaded. An antiexpansionist, he did not care about getting a line at the forty-ninth parallel, as others believed desirable, for the whole region was rather "poor country," he thought. But he was also interested in acquiring a port in Puget Sound, with a narrow corridor running along the coast down to the Columbia as connection to United States territory by land.

From an early point, he considered going to England on a special mission to fix the boundary, as well as to treat other questions, such as trade with the West Indies and possibly with Britain itself. Not only could he remove obstacles still hindering complete Anglo-American understanding, but he could also extricate himself from an increasingly uncomfortable situation in Washington.[48] Attractive though this might be, it created an embarrassing problem. What of his friend Everett, now the minister at London? Well liked by officials there for his urbanity, respected for his intellect and information, Everett felt confident he could take care of Oregon without help from a special envoy, even Webster. Through the fall and winter of 1842, he frequently reported to the secretary his conversations with Aberdeen and Ashburton about the far northwestern boundary. Britain was quite anxious to arrive at an agreement as soon as possible, he said; and despite continued mention of the Columbia as the proper line, he believed the forty-ninth parallel was possible. He himself wished to get that much. Typically, Everett would defer to Webster either on a special mission or on being replaced as regular minister; yet in correspondence with others back home, he complained how unfair it was to be pushed aside for personal or political reasons.[49]

Webster was undoubtedly aware of Everett's feelings and also of British reluctance to receive a special mission. Still, in late January 1843 he asked the minister to propose the idea to Aberdeen. As for possible terms of a treaty, he repeated earlier features: the Columbia River, a corridor north to a port at Puget Sound, and a tripartite arrangement with England and Mexico, now ceding all of California, in return for which the United States would assume its citizens' claims and therefore help the Mexican treasury. British claims against that country would also be paid.[50] The foreign secretary replied that he still opposed a special mission because it would be more vulnerable to politicial opposition in America and, if it failed, would leave the Oregon question in worse shape. Better to use regular diplomatic channels, which meant better to negotiate with Everett. And with respect to the tripartite package, Britain would not combine the subjects of Oregon and California in the same treaty but did not object to American acquisition of Mexican territory. Aberdeen did not close the door on a mission, however, and said that if the United States thought one necessary, he would receive it.[51]

Even with such poor prospects, the secretary did not give up. Denying his desire or ability to go over, he added the qualification that he might if a high sense of duty impelled him.[52] By this time the president liked the plan, possibly to provide Webster an exit from the cabinet and to facilitate annexation of Texas somehow. So in late February, near the end of the congressional session, he sent papers on a mission to the House Foreign Affairs Committee, where Adams and Cushing were supportive. Not so the other members; and when the committee disapproved, the administration dropped the idea.[53] Thereafter, the secretary talked of opening negotiations in Washington.[54]

All along, an alternative to a special mission was Webster's replacement of Everett as regular minister. Both men were thinking about this as soon as Ashburton had left Washington; and in their correspondence it is difficult to say which option seemed to prevail at a particular moment. Of course, Everett disliked one as much as the other. Moving Everett out became more practicable, however, in late December 1842, when Tyler sent a message to Congress recommending a mission to China. Britain had recently imposed a treaty on that country opening several ports to commerce; and the United States therefore ought to obtain equal privileges, the chief executive said. The message, written by Webster, expanded upon benefits to be gained from extending American contact with this large, hitherto isolated empire beyond existing access to only one port, Canton.[55] Webster and Tyler concluded that Everett would be an ideal appointee for the mission. Webster claimed that Tyler mentioned the possibility first; but undoubtedly somebody had suggested it to the president.[56] At any rate, after some preliminary signals from Webster, Everett learned in March that Congress had approved the mission on March 3, the last day of the session, and that the Senate, with maximum speed, had confirmed his nomination as commissioner.

When the secretary notified the minister, he strained to assure him there had been no devious purpose in this move. "I wish you, therefore, to feel that, as far as I am concerned," he insisted, "your appointment to China had not its origin in any degree in a desire that your present place should be vacated. If it were vacant now, or should be vacated by you, there is not one chance in a thousand that I shall fill it."[57] But in writing to another person, after professing disinterest he added that he would not go unless he could achieve some substantial good.[58] Anyway, it became an abstract question, for after two exchanges of letters across the Atlantic, Everett told Tyler that his personal affairs prevented him from accepting the assignment.[59]

Webster and the president then decided to appoint Caleb Cushing, one of the proadministration Corporal's Guard in Congress and a recently rejected nominee as secretary of the treasury. Capable and interested in strengthening ties with the Orient, Cushing proved to be an excellent choice. Yes, but Cushing's selection by his debtor, Daniel Webster, was more than a little suspicious, observed a good many cynics on Capitol Hill.[60] At any rate, he soon set off on his long voyage, with instructions and a letter to the emperor, composed by Webster, and with Fletcher Webster as his secretary.[61] Though these events did not take exactly the direction Webster had foreseen, he felt pleased. It was more than a coincidence that his last act as secretary was to sign Cushing's papers.

After a long period of indecision, on May 8, 1843, he sent Tyler his resignation with polite words of a personal sort, to which he received a reply of thanks and praise.[62] That Webster had less than totally positive feelings is clear in an editorial he drafted for the *Intelligencer* a few days later. In it, he accused the chief executive of changing parties and of seeking the Democratic nomination by rewarding greedy office seekers. Though he did not cite Massachusetts, he had that state in mind especially.[63] After this salvo, he left Washington for what would be a fairly lengthy retirement from public office, the first in twenty years.

Chapter 22
WHIG PROBLEMS

After resigning from the cabinet in May 1843, though not holding office for some time, Webster stayed active in politics. Victimized by disarrangement of the party system, he left an administration which was neither Democratic nor Whig. At first he could not repudiate it without repudiating his past relationship to it, but gradually he moved toward reinstatement as a bona fide Whig. In the process, issues and elections occupied a good deal of his attention; and by public speeches, private conversation, and correspondence, he tried to influence the direction of his party on both state and national levels.

He worried almost as much about patronage as about policies. Tyler's appointments were consistently going to Democrats; and to expedite the shift from Whiggery, there were many removals. In August he sent the president a long letter of complaint and advice, emphasizing the hopelessness of getting support from the Van Burenite Locofocos. Adhere to the constituency which gave the Harrison-Tyler ticket a victory in 1840, he counseled, for it was still possible to emerge with a favorable reputation. Webster surely knew how unlikely that was after more than two years of intraparty contention, yet the current course was the worst possible, he believed.[1] In cases directly affecting himself, he felt particularly unhappy. For example, when Fletcher had sailed on the Cushing mission earlier in the summer, Webster learned that the president planned to return his son's predecessor to the post of chief clerk, a person who had criticized administration of the department. After getting a stiff protest from the ex-secretary that this would amount to disapproval of his record, Tyler backed down.[2] Equally disturbing had been the selection of Massachusetts Democrat David Henshaw as acting secretary of the navy. Before the Senate refused to confirm him at the next session, Henshaw had ousted a number of Whigs from office in his state. In an editorial for the *Intelligencer,* Webster expressed disapproval of the trend in patronage quite plainly—he called it "lamentable."[3] Yet personally he remained on friendly terms with Tyler, continuing to correspond with him and to visit at the White House when he came to Washington. Once he unsuccessfully recommended his close friend Hiram Ketchum, the Wall Street lawyer, for a vacancy on the Supreme Court.[4]

During this transitional period he mixed some unfinished diplomatic business with a new foray of the most unpredictable sort. It was to secure agreement with Britain on reciprocal reductions of customs. While in the cabinet he had begun some discussions with the Foreign Office in order to help American merchants and farmers who would profit from better access to the British market. Though nothing had resulted, he continued to think and talk about it through the summer of 1843. Perhaps he could head a mission to London on the subject or, more likely, serve on a commission at Washington. Apart from whatever benefits the country might derive, he must have speculated about some for himself, politically speaking. His following in the South and West might grow, even in the East with the mercantile interest, if he successfully advocated some reasonable, cautious adjustment of the tariff. Yet as months passed, he could see nothing but a dead end. By September in a speech at Rochester he was extolling the advantages of a home market for farmers as any orthodox protectionist would.[5]

Stepping back from reciprocity coincided with greater involvement in party affairs as the state election approached. Hostile as the Lawrence faction was toward him, Webster understandably gave no help to Lawrence's ally, John Davis, for nomination as governor; in fact he may have influenced a move behind the scene which caused Davis to withdraw in favor of George Briggs, Webster's preference. Briggs won in November.[6] Furthermore, just before the election Webster had an opportunity to vindicate his record and reiterate his party regularity. He accepted an invitation by the antislavery merchant Stephen Phillips and the conservative Professor Moses Stuart to address a Whig county convention at Andover on November 9. An open-air gathering of five thousand, stimulated by bands, banners, and military formations, heard him review the standard topics: banking, tariff, and land policy. On each he returned to the reliable argument that protection helped labor as well as capital, without suggesting schemes of reciprocity. As for his relation to the party, he went over recent history, his reasons for not resigning from the cabinet earlier than he did, his doing so as soon as he completed diplomatic business, and his ringing affirmation of Whig loyalty at Faneuil Hall the previous year.[7]

He did not refer to Clay at Andover, but he was edging toward acceptance of the Kentuckian's claim to the presidential nomination. Through the fall and winter of 1843 his correspondence reflected stages of that movement, beginning with cautious probes by friends of the two Whig chieftains. Governor Robert Letcher of Kentucky, no doubt with Clay's knowledge, wrote Webster several times on the importance of closing ranks with the main column of the party. After complaining about past events and perceived injustices, Webster acquiesced, though reluctantly.[8] In New York a Clay lieutenant, Peter Porter, talked with some Webster men, one of them probably Hiram Ketchum, who floated the possibility of Webster's running for vice-president. Porter relayed Clay's refusal to make promises; and in any case, Webster himself had no interest whatever in second place, despite urging by Ketchum and Biddle.[9] As expected, some people hoped to see him as the presidential candidate, including a number of the faithful in New Hampshire, where the idea of presenting his name to the national convention made progress. It was a temptation, but after waiting until January 1844, he replied that "at the present moment, the tendency of opinion among those to be represented in the convention is generally and strongly set in another direction. I think it my duty, therefore, under existing circumstances, to request those who may feel a preference for me not to indulge in that preference."[10] Notwithstanding a deep-seated belief that Clay's prospects of election were slim, in public he now talked as optimistically as any other politician.[11] His reconciliation with Clay got an impetus, too, from an improvement of personal relations when he and the Kentuckian joined other prominent Whigs in February for a dinner in Washington, intended to soothe feelings.[12]

The national convention met in Baltimore on May 1, 1844. Webster had not planned to attend and was in New York on the way home when the delegates assembled. But to demonstrate party unity, the leadership sent him a last-minute call to come down. So he arrived during the night after the convention had unanimously nominated—one should say ratified the nomination of—Clay and had chosen Theodore Frelinghuysen of New Jersey for vice-president.[13] The next day, joining the customary long procession of speakers, he made a few remarks endorsing the nominees with outward enthusiasm. As for Clay, he admitted he had differed with him about particular measures but gave greater weight to their common principles. It must have seemed odd to his listeners that he talked so much about Frelinghuysen, even odder that he elaborated upon the glorious history of Frelinghuysen's state, New Jersey. At any rate, good humor prevailed and increased that evening as a jovial group, including Webster, celebrated at the home of Reverdy Johnson.[14]

Later that month, Democrats came together for what became one of their most tangled conventions. Ex-president Van Buren had been decidedly the foremost contender for nomination among other veterans such as Cass, Buchanan, and Calhoun; but it was his unhappy fate to encounter two formidable barriers, the rule requiring a two-thirds vote for selection and the mounting issue of Texas. The second made the first more serious. Recently Van Buren, like Clay, had announced his opposition to annexing Texas, a statement which alienated expansionists and especially the proslavery wing. Thus he came close to, but did not get, two-thirds of the votes. Maneuvers and arrangements eventually led to nomination of James K. Polk, Jackson's longtime disciple and fellow Tennessean. These circumstances made it still easier for Webster to work for the Whig ticket. For years he had fought this party-line wheelhorse in Congress, whose surprising selection, he observed, marked "a low stage, in the downward progress of things connected with the genl. Govt."[15] For a while Tyler had reconnoitered his chances as an independent but then threw in with the Democrats. An added complication came from the Liberty party, composed of advanced antislavery people, who were not numerous but could make a difference if the two major parties were evenly balanced. It had made a crucial difference in Massachusetts state contests and could now do likewise in New York and other places. Everything indicated that this would be a very close election.[16]

From May to November requests to Webster to speak streamed in from various localities. Though declining many, he consented more often as the campaign intensified—and made a better effort too.[17] At the start, he seemed to go through the old motions without much substance or fire. Then in early September he fought his annual bout with catarrh, a worse case than usual which almost silenced his voice. Near the end, he displayed vigor and eloquence in an exhortation for the cause. He traveled around the Northeast, to New York, New Jersey, Pennsylvania, and towns in New England, chiefly in Massachusetts. In May he had attended state conventions in Boston and Portsmouth ratifying the nomination. Late in August, he spoke to an enormous rally in Albany in the open air—estimates of the size of the crowd ran up to fifty thousand. On October 1 and 3 he appeared at huge gatherings in Philadelphia and Valley Forge. On the eve of the election he concluded his arduous part of the campaign by addressing a mass meeting in Boston.[18]

Generally he gave his audiences what he thought they wanted to hear; a familiar recitation of Whig economic theory, designed to expedite economic development of the nation. The keystone was a protective tariff for fostering growth of industry, not only assisting enterprise but indispensable to a better life for working men and valuable to farmers because of an enlarged home market. Seldom did he allude to reciprocity as encouragement of foreign commerce. On banking, he assumed that restoring an old-style institution, active in local discounts, was now impossible; so he would be satisfied with a limited central bank, dealing with state-chartered ones as necessary to maintain a uniform currency and dependable exchange operations. As for land policy, he would revive the attempt to distribute proceeds to the states, in the hope, he added, of helping them pay their embarrassing existing debts. His speeches closely resembled what Clay would have said if he had been on the same platforms, except perhaps the matter of a limited bank. Yet Webster hardly ever discussed Clay's qualifications, indeed usually did not mention his name.

A far smaller portion of his speeches concerned foreign policy, a surprising circumstance in light of his own recent experience. But as the weeks passed he paid increasing attention to Texas. A vote for Polk was a vote to annex Texas, he warned, with all the inevitable consequences of dividing the sections, exacerbating the slavery question, precipitating war, and ultimately undermining American institutions. Still, he did not reveal the full extent of his worries about annexation in these campaign speeches, probably because Clay himself was presently straddling the question.

Clay lost by the narrowest margin. Two states had been pivotal, and he carried neither. In Pennsylvania, Polk had deftly muted protectionist opposition by hedging on the tariff and had gained also by the fact that his running mate, George Dallas, was from this state. He carried New York by only five thousand votes. James Birney, candidate of the Liberty party, deprived Clay of some antislavery Whig support there, maybe enough to cause his defeat. "Mortified" at the outcome, Webster had his own explanation. In part, he thought, Texas had hurt Clay, because he had waffled on an early declaration against annexation; and that cost him in western New York, an antislavery stronghold. But another problem lay in Clay's personality, his short temper and arrogance, which had also contributed to his failure in earlier elections.[19]

More than a year earlier, discussion of Webster's return to the Senate had begun. A reason besides consideration of his own future was Rufus Choate's well-known lack of interest in holding office any longer. Often in ill health and never caring for either legislative routine or the political

371

turmoil surrounding the position, Choate preferred reading the classics in his study or dazzling a jury with his silver oratory and had been ready at any time to make room for his respected friend. But in early 1844, amid rumors he would do this, he decided to stay on until the end of his term, March 1845. Possibly there were not enough pro-Webster votes in the legislature at the moment. In any case, Webster himself felt disinclined to take over while the Tyler administration, of which he had been a part but which he had now abandoned, was still in power. Besides, his financial condition was even worse than usual, and he needed to give more attention to his legal practice.[20]

As 1844 closed, however, the likelihood of his once again becoming senator increased. He was busily engaged in politics and had convinced himself that he had an obligation to stop the alarming trend of the times, the deplorable Democratic comeback and the expansionist rage sweeping the country. "Nobody," he thought, "has more genius than Choate; but his health is frail, he has no spirit of endurance, & a single effort is apt to lay him up."[21] Webster would supply a firm hand. As for the vexatious financial problem, merchant David Sears and other wealthy admirers in Boston were handling that. A movement to raise a hundred thousand progressed well, and this fund would compensate him for the sacrifices he must make while in public service.[22] Accordingly, in January Choate sent in his resignation; and the legislature acted promptly, with little opposition, to replace him with Webster.[23]

Whatever satisfaction his return to the Senate may have given him soon subsided when he observed the latest turn the issue of Texas had taken. On March 1, 1845, just before the close of Tyler's administration, Congress had passed a joint resolution authorizing steps to bring the Lone Star Republic into the Union as a state. This decision marked the climax of a sequence of events beginning with Texan independence a decade earlier. As senator and as secretary of state, Webster had repeatedly taken a strong antiannexation position. Thus he favored an independent Texas while he dealt with Mexican-American problems, despite Tyler's wish to acquire the area. But his successor in the State Department, Abel Upshur, one of the president's inner circle of proslavery, states' rights Virginians, moved ahead in negotiating for annexation in the latter half of 1843 and until the following February. Almost ready to submit his treaty with Texas to the Senate, Upshur died from an explosion on a naval vessel. Through March, there was delay until the new secretary, Calhoun, could take over and handle the last phase of the process. In the Carolinian's view, one thing to be done was to warn off Britain from interfering with slavery in Texas. No doubt he magnified the possibility, though that country did wish to see an independent Texas without slavery. Calhoun therefore sent the British minister a bristling note extensively defending a vital institution. As a result, when the treaty went to the Senate on April 22, 1844, the connection of Texas with the expansion of slavery had become explicit. That connection had induced Clay and Van Buren, the prospective presidential candidates to come out against the policy on the twenty-seventh. The political impact proved to be important: Van Buren lost the Democratic nomination to Polk; Clay may have lost the November election because of that issue as much as any other. Though the Senate overwhelmingly rejected the Upshur-Calhoun treaty in June, the push for annexation did not abate.[24]

It was in this context that Massachusetts politics often focused on Texas through 1844 and 1845 and materially influenced Webster's own course. A wing of the Whig party developed here around the question, which symbolized the more fundamental problem of slavery itself. Mostly a new generation, these antislavery men would prod, perhaps shove aside, the conservatives to infuse a moral purpose into the organization. Abbott Lawrence and Nathan Appleton expressed the cautious attitude of the dominant industrial interest which the young Whigs challenged. In the latter's view, the established leadership acted as it did because of the economic relationship between cotton planters of the South and textile magnates of New England. Accordingly, the rising element devised the labels Cotton Whigs and Conscience Whigs. One of its leaders was Charles Francis Adams, Webster's former law student and son of the ex-president. Others were Stephen Phillips of Salem; Charles Allen, a judge at Worcester; John Palfrey, Webster's onetime minister in Boston; Henry Wilson, a Natick shoe manufacturer; and the urbane, increasingly zealous Charles Sumner. All of them wished to stay in the party and reform it but had to reckon with the more radical abolitionists, notably William Lloyd Garrison, who would discard any party, if necessary.[25]

What should Webster do? With respect to Texas, he had no trouble identifying with the Conscience Whigs, in light of his consistent record on the subject. Moreover, opposition to annexation pervaded the state. So popular a sentiment could not only provide him with a means of rebuilding his own currently uncertain status but could also be the common ground for a unified party. Almost all Whigs, including the Lawrence-Appleton conservatives, opposed annexation. Yet he sensed difficulties. If the Conscience Whigs, swayed by abolitionists, became too extreme, if they went beyond the specific matter of Texas toward an assault on the South and slavery itself, then a complete rupture with the Cotton Whigs would follow. Webster's whole political life had depended upon collaboration with the entrepreneurial class, and he would not at this late hour change that. Personal relations intensified the cohesive force of these connections. Paige, his brother-in-law, was a partner of Nathan Appleton; and Julia, his daughter, had married another Appleton. So he must follow his own conscience, to be sure, on Texas; but he would not break off from gentlemen of reputable standing and power while doing so. If both factions showed some restraint, perhaps everything would turn out right.

In March 1844, when it was known that the Upshur-Calhoun treaty would soon go to the Senate, the time for action arrived. Webster consented to publication of a letter he had written earlier to citizens of Worcester County, opposing annexation. His main argument was constitutional. Though ordinarily a loose constructionist, he could not justify incorporating foreign territory into the Union, either by the treaty or the war clause. Only the region belonging to the United States at the time the Constitution was adopted was eligible for statehood, he contended. Aside from the inherent weakness of this interpretation, Webster had to account for precedents to the contrary. Both Florida and Louisiana had become territories by treaty after 1783, and states had later been admitted from these regions. To treat these differently from Texas, he reasoned dubiously, was allowable because they had been colonial dependencies of European nations, whereas Texas was an independent nation.[26] One wonders, by the way, if he recalled the judicial opinion in *American Insurance Company* v. *Canter* (1828), in which he had served as counsel and in which Chief Justice Marshall had upheld the full power of acquiring territory by treaty.[27] Proceeding to his other objections, Webster voiced his long-felt concern about expanding the republic to remote areas difficult to assimilate and therefore injurious to American institutions. Furthermore, and here he made a telling point, taking Texas would precipitate war with Mexico, for that country still claimed it. His view seemed more persuasive on practical than on constitutional grounds. Even so, he avoided the practical matter of slavery. Adding a partisan flavor to his letter, he supplied an introduction (not to appear as his own writing): "We believe Mr. Tyler wishes to strike a great blow on the subject, in order to gratify the South, & give him some chance of an election to the Presidency, notwithstanding he seems now to have so little hope. Mr. Calhoun's appointment to the Department of State, is another very fearful omen, in regard to Texas. We hope New England, &

all the North will rise up, like one man, to oppose this abominable project."[28]

During the weeks following publication of his Worcester letter until the Senate rejected the Texas treaty in late April, he initiated or supported a variety of moves to help accomplish that defeat. As usual, he wrote editorials to persuade the public, several appearing in the *Intelligencer* and the New York *American.*[29] He urged Robert Winthrop to introduce resolutions and to speak on the issue in Congress.[30] He advised Massachusetts legislators to adopt a protest. And his conversation and correspondence tended to dwell on the dangers of the current policy of the administration.[31] Upset about the aggressive proslavery statement which the secretary of state sent to Britain, he declared, "Never did I see such reprehensible sentiment, & unsurpassed nonsense, united. I am utterly astonished at Mr. Calhoun. What must he suppose this age will think of him & of us, too, if we adopt his sentiments?"[32]

After defeat of Calhoun's treaty, he felt the peril had not lessened; indeed he intensified his warnings. In his campaign speech in Philadelphia in October 1844, he predicted that annexation would prolong the evil of slavery; and for that reason, he opposed it "without condition and without qualification, at this time and all times, now and for ever."[33] Through the winter he objected to the extension of slavery as much as to the unconstitutionality of acquiring territory.[34]

Polk's election, viewed by expansionists as a popular mandate, generated another attempt at annexation even before the new president took office. In January the lame-duck Congress had before it, instead of a treaty, a joint resolution needing only approval of a majority of the two houses. Immediately Webster and his anti-Texas friends set to work in calling a state convention to meet in Faneuil Hall on the twenty-ninth. The highlight would be approval of a statement to be published in time to influence congressional voting. Charles Allen and Webster collaborated in writing the document—Allen to deal with the extension of slavery and Webster with the constitutional aspects. Though he had to leave for Washington to handle cases before the Supreme Court and could not attend, he felt confident the convention would have positive effect. After sitting through the preliminaries, the six hundred delegates from towns across the state listened to the proposed address.[35] For his part, Webster repeated what he had said about the rejected treaty the previous spring. He contended that the Constitution did not allow annexation of foreign territory and its incorporation into the Union as new states. Again he advanced a narrow, unconvincing view of the questions. Only when he moved to the pending joint resolution did he reach solid ground. Texas was a foreign nation, he said, and could be brought in, if at all, only by treaty. Having said that, he recurred to his argument that annexation was unconstitutional either by treaty or by joint resolution.[36]

After hearing the address, the delegates witnessed a lively struggle among factional leaders concerning strategy. Garrison heatedly criticized the document as far too timid. Wishing to condemn slavery totally and to threaten secession if Texas were annexed, he would force the conservatives beyond their moderate stand. In response, many of the latter walked out of the hall. During a second session the next day, a majority adopted the address over abolitionist protests. Allen, Stephen Phillips, and Charles Francis Adams had achieved an ostensible victory, holding Conscience and Cotton Whigs together; but the episode suggested more trouble ahead.[37]

The joint resolution for annexation passed, but in the senate narrowly (twenty-seven to twenty-five), on March 1, 1845; yet the controversy did not end. A few days later, in executive session of the Senate, Webster vainly voted for a resolution to reverse what had been done. And on through the year until Congress met in December, he clung to the slight possibility that the legislators would then disapprove the proposed Texan constitution and thereby prevent statehood.[38] In Massachusetts, opponents of annexation did not give up. Adams mounted a desperate drive, in the fall headed a group known as the Texas Committee, began editing a newspaper and working strenuously for the cause. He recruited a variety of like-minded persons—Sumner, Wilson, other Conscience Whigs, the clergy, and literary figures. Now he welcomed aid from the Garrisonians, with whom he still disagreed about the breakup of the party, but who could be a good counterweight to the conservatives. The latter, persons such as Lawrence, Appleton, and Winthrop, believed that further agitation would be useless and probably damaging.[39]

The outcome Webster had wanted to avoid threatened to happen, however skillful Adams had been so far in preventing it. Conflict between Cotton and Conscience Whigs could destroy the party, and proliferation of the Texas question could radicalize many moderates. He determined to keep a foot in each camp. To pacify the conservatives, he maintained close communications with Winthrop, now influential in the House. He did not worry about Appleton, for connections with him were firm. And assisted by Appleton's mediation, he exchanged letters of reconciliation with Lawrence, both cryptically saying they would let bygones be bygones.[40] But to assure the Texas Committee that he had not abandoned his position on annexation, he gladly presented batches of petitions to the Senate in December. When the new Texas constitution came before that body, he spoke vigorously against approval, repeating all his arguments though realizing the contest was lost.[41] As he said the next day while presenting still more petitions, they were "a little late for Texas, but they may do for Cuba."[42] If not Cuba, other issues involving expansion of slavery would demand congressional attention during this session.

Chapter 23
EXPANSION

When Webster returned to the Senate in December 1845, he found that nearly everyone was talking about Oregon. Realization of its importance had been growing for more than fifty years, beginning with the first voyages of American ships to the outlet of the Columbia. There followed an expanding maritime commerce, the lucrative fur trade tapping the interior, missions to Indians, and, recently, ever larger numbers of hardy souls going by transcontinental trail to what they believed was an incomparable savanna. Three thousand had arrived in 1844 alone, mostly south of the Columbia, and more than doubled the American population. The far outnumbered Englishmen and Canadians in Oregon lived north of the river, and the once dominant Hudson's Bay Company had now moved its headquarters up to Vancouver Island, above Puget Sound. So the flow of immigration would strengthen American claim to the area at the expense of British rights. Since 1818 the two countries had postponed a decision on sovereignty by agreeing to joint occupation, terminable on one year's notice by either. But the new president, whose platform before election had called for "reoccupation of Oregon," seemed determined to extend the boundary as far north as Alaska, to the 54°40' parallel. At his inauguration in March, Polk asserted a clear title to Oregon, presumably to that advanced line; and in his annual message to this session of Congress, he recommended terminating joint occupation.[1] The question could not be put off any longer. Overheated emotions could lead to war if diplomacy failed.

It was difficult for Webster to understand why the issue of Oregon should have inflated so much. In addition to opposing expansion generally, he had always looked upon this region as unpromising, not worth risks and commitments. In the Ashburton negotiations, after brief discussion, he left the subject unresolved with little regret. The United States should be satisfied with a line along the Columbia, he felt, if it acquired a good Pacific port somewhere, either at Puget Sound or at San Francisco.[2] But while he had been out of office, he worried about the mounting Oregon fever, which could lead to rash action in the name of national honor, to the folly of wrecking relations with Britain. He was particularly concerned about the disastrous impact upon commerce. Almost as bad as war over an insignificant matter, he believed, was speculation that war might come. "It confounds and confuses men in regard to their own business plans. What we want is settled peace, and the conviction that peace will remain until there is some just and sensible cause for war."[3]

A few days after he took his Senate seat, debate on Oregon began with a resolution by Cass that the appropriate committees ought to inquire into military readiness. Quite unnecessary to instruct these committees to do what they would ordinarily, Webster said. The only result would be intensified alarm within the business community, which would unsettle maritime trade. Cass, whose good judgment Webster suspected anyhow, merely worsened the situation by ranting about the probability of war.[4] Still more reprehensible was Polk's zigzagging, first blustering about all of Oregon, then showing willingness to compromise. This president, he privately remarked, had a stubborn, unreasonable streak in his character, for he urged national unity but identified it with uncritical support of his erratic conduct of foreign affairs. "He seems to have expected that he would have been indulged in a *monopoly* of patriotic professions, and self gratification."[5] Polk and his friends talked "loud and large" about war, yet they did not intend or wish war. In the end, Webster predicted, the scare would evaporate.[6]

Through February and March 1846, the Senate grappled with the presidential recommendation to terminate joint occupation. Leading those who favored that policy, William Allen, the bellicose chairman of the Foreign Affairs Committee, encountered resistance not only from Whigs such as Webster but also from a number of Democrats headed by Calhoun. This step could be an impetus to conflict, they believed. If the notice had to be given, it should be delayed until negotiations failed, or at least phrased in conciliatory form, as in John Crittenden's amendment. Webster spoke several times, repeating his opinions of December and calling for compromise. Previous American approaches, as far back as 1826, he said, had offered the forty-ninth parallel, above the Columbia but nowhere close to fifty-four-forty; and England would probably agree to it in existing circumstances. Webster himself was moving northward from the river, which he had thought a fair boundary, to an extension of the present line of forty-nine degrees (between the Lake of the Woods and the Rockies) westward to Puget Sound. It was more than this country ought to have expected, since few Americans lived beyond the Columbia. At length, Allen prevailed on the main question of notice, but Crittenden's moderating amendment passed. So closed a sequence of maneuvers whereby Polk tried to place the responsibility of decision upon Congress, and that body responded by leaving the decision to him.[7]

Though unhappy about the administration's aggressive attitude, Webster could be optimistic about a settlement, since both countries had good reasons to avoid war. In England, as in the United States, commercial relations were a significant influence. American cotton and grain supplied the needs of industrial Britain, a market which benefited farmers, planters, and merchants on this side of the Atlantic. A reflection of that fundamental fact was concurrent reduction of tariffs at this very time. Politically, the Peel ministry preferred a pacific solution of the Oregon question and fortunately got a pledge from the Whigs not to interfere. In America, despite the exhilarating cry of manifest destiny, Polk would face powerful opposition if he pursued an inflexible course and especially if he asked for a declaration of war on this issue. Furthermore, he had enough on his hands in dealing with Mexico, a crisis simultaneously reaching climax. As it turned out, he let Britain know that, under certain conditions, he would take the forty-ninth parallel if offered. The Foreign Office did dispatch the offer, just before it received Polk's formal notice to terminate and before it learned the Mexican War had started. Owing to luck as much as to diplomatic strategy, the president was able in early June to submit a treaty to the Senate for its "previous" advice (an unusual but face-saving procedure). When the Senate approved and Polk then signed the document, the country could feel relieved; but other problems of territorial expansion lay ahead.[8]

For Webster, the Oregon crisis had precipitated a bitter controversy involving his own diplomatic record and personal integrity. In early February 1846, while the House was debating whether to terminate joint occupation, the veteran Democrat Charles Ingersoll of Pennsylvania delivered a long, expansionist speech. What distinguished it from the other oratory was his particularly sharp attack upon Webster. The country had fallen into its existing difficulty about Oregon, he argued, because of enormous concessions to England in the Ashburton treaty; and now critics of the administration's policy would hand over even more to that nation, encouraged to grab territory as it had been in 1842. Contention with Webster had long since become habitual for this pugnacious congressman, extending back to their first days in Washington during the War of 1812 through the Jacksonian years when they had consistently been on opposite sides. During Tyler's administration he had often condemned the secretary of state for mishandling international relations. Now chairman of the House Committee on Foreign Relations, Ingersoll felt he had new evidence of Webster's errors, or worse.[9]

He laid down several counts of his indictment. First, he had learned alarming facts about the McLeod case of 1841. Though he did not say so, his source was William Seward, New York governor when the Canadian had been arrested and tried for participating in the *Caroline* raid. Too anxious to please England, the congressman declared, Webster had demanded that Governor Seward release McLeod immediately, before trial, or else "see the magnificent commercial emporium of New York City laid in ashes" by the British fleet. Seward's refusal, accompanied by an indication that he would pardon McLeod if the latter was convicted, did not stop Webster's efforts. He interfered by arranging for United States Attorney Joshua Spencer to serve as McLeod's counsel and by providing him a fee. Second, the Pennsylvanian restated his complaint that the Ashburton treaty abandoned rightful American claims to land in Maine. And third, Webster would have done the same thing in Oregon, the speaker predicted, if he had been able to go on a special mission to negotiate the question. Fortunately, the House committee on which Ingersoll served had quashed his request to undertake that assignment.[10]

Except for a rejoinder by Winthrop, for a time not much more was said about the charges in the House. Later in February, however, Daniel Dickinson, a New York Democrat, brought up the topic in the Senate during debate on Oregon. As Webster heard him review Ingersoll's allegations, he spiritedly objected that they were totally false.[11] Thus confronting a direct assault upon his reputation, Webster began gathering materials in his defense. He was very angry. To clarify the McLeod matter, he asked Tyler what his recollections were about correspondence with Seward; and the ex-president answered that he, not Webster, had clashed with the governor and on only one point, the role of the district attorney as defense counsel.[12] Then the Massachusetts senator had his New York friend Richard Blatchford write to Seward himself to inquire about the subject. He had readily given Ingersoll information, Seward replied, because it had already been published as a state document and was open to anyone. Still, he had had no idea why the congressman wanted to know about it, he protested. In any case, he summarized twenty-three letters on the McLeod case, now in print, and then explained his position regarding the case, which he characterized as dissatisfaction with the Tyler administration's view of it. In his conversation with Attorney General John Crittenden, Seward recalled, he had insisted upon trial of McLeod, though saying he would pardon the defendant if convicted. In sum, Seward's letter vindicated himself more than it did Webster but did not establish any wrongdoing.[13] Meanwhile the senator searched for further support. From Caleb Cushing he got a little help on the charge that he had asked for a special mission; but he could prove only that he had not formally asked the House committee to authorize it, for he had talked with Adams about the matter.[14] And to document his work on the treaty, he obtained a Senate resolution requesting Polk to provide copies of correspondence with Ashburton.[15]

After collecting all he could and taking several weeks to prepare a rebuttal, Webster delivered a full-scale speech in the Senate on April 6 and 7.[16] In part, it was a capable discussion of all phases of the Ashburton negotiations, a kind of lecture on diplomacy. In part also, it was a hard-hitting, exculpatory statement, laced with partisan passages. As he spoke hour after hour, he paused for colloquies, especially with Dickinson, whose reiteration of Ingersoll's attack in the House provoked his wrath. It was very discourteous of the New Yorker to nourish these falsehoods, amounting to a "foul calumny," he thundered.[17] One by one, he rejected various complaints about interference with the McLeod trial as untrue. His version of communications with Seward and with District Attorney Spencer underplayed his concerted efforts to block McLeod's trial, then to direct strategy of the defense. He could dispose of the assertion that he had provided for Spencer's fee—Seward's correspondence indicated the British government had done that.[18] With respect to the criticism that he had sought a special mission to England for an Oregon treaty, he stood on thin ice, for the truth was he had promoted it orally though not in writing. Beyond these particulars, he was most emphatic in condemning Ingersoll's personal character.[19] "I say the mind of the man seems to be grotesque—bizarre. Why it is rather the caricature of a mind than a mind itself." There is a saying about such people, he exclaimed, that " 'There is a screw loose somewhere.' In this case the screws are loose all over."[20]

Ingersoll reacted immediately. The next day, he went to the State Department to consult whatever records he could find to substantiate his charges. Here the disbursing officer, Edward Stubbs, allowed him to look through the files. He had got some help from Stubbs earlier, but now he was able to see more of Webster's correspondence, and, in his view, very damaging evidence in the accounts of the contingency funds. As he turned the pages, he became convinced that the ex-secretary had been guilty not only of bad judgment but also of illegal use of public funds. So on April 9 he rose in the House, summarized his discoveries, and called upon his colleagues to act against shocking misdeeds.[21]

He reported that he had found conclusive proof that Webster had wrongly interfered with McLeod's trial and sought creation of a special mission on Oregon, which he himself would undertake. Besides filling out information to support these arguments, which he had advanced in February, he could say that Webster had spent money from the secret-service account to corrupt the party press in Maine and otherwise induce that state to give up its just claims. He referred especially to the activities of Francis Smith adjusting the tone of newspapers there, as Smith had put it. Because of this unlawful conduct, Tyler "discharged" his secretary of state, the congressman reasoned. So he presented resolutions for requesting the president to send these records to the House. Whether that body would then decide to impeach Webster "will remain to be considered."

This thrust set off a lively discussion.[22] There were more speeches criticizing Ingersoll than lending him aid. Many representatives suspected that personal vengeance instead of concern for public ethics motivated him. They felt he was casting a dragnet to come up with something somewhere to destroy his adversary's reputation. Several were Democrats who disagreed with Webster politically but detected no misbehavior. Doubting the wisdom or the legality of opening up these confidential papers, especially the secret-service file, quite a number still hesitated to vote against an inquiry and tended toward a more limited one than Ingersoll wished. Though few examined the implications of impeachment, Thomas Bayly of Virginia, the most talkative of these critics, believed it impossible to impeach a person such as Webster. As senator, he was not a civil officer of the United States (as prescribed by the Constitution) but an elected representative of a state and therefore could not be removed from his seat by that process. Accordingly, straight expulsion from the Senate would be the only available procedure. John Quincy Adams disagreed. In his view Webster, as a former cabinet officer, could be impeached for past conduct in that office and, if convicted, could be disqualified from holding another such position. But like most Whigs, Adams did not think Webster ought to be impeached for any offenses alleged by Ingersoll.[23]

After looking through the papers requested by the House and consulting his cabinet, the president decided it was illegal and improper for him to reveal details about the secret account of the contingency fund.[24] So on April 20 he sent up a reply explaining his refusal, though he did discuss the general nature of that fund and did report that $5,460 had been spent from it during Webster's tenure of office. But no law shielded the papers on McLeod, and he did forward them.[25] Ingersoll believed that they verified his charge on that count.[26] Yet he must find a way to get the accounts of the secret fund, which he himself had seen, before Congress formally.

In the House a week later, on April 27, he restated his case, now entirely related to this financial aspect. On the basis of what he had learned, Ingersoll said, Webster was guilty on three grounds. First, as secretary he had made unlawful use of the contingency fund. Instead of following the usual procedure of drawing upon it for specific purposes by a presidential certificate to the departmental disbursing officer, he had drawn a large sum, $17,000, to his own account starting in early 1841. Then he had paid out smaller sums to various persons from time to time, receipted by vague vouchers coming in as late as mid-1842. The president had certified expenditures for secret service of $5,460. As for the larger sum of $17,000, Webster had eventually returned $5,000 and disbursed some for ordinary diplomatic expenses. For quite a period, therefore, he had had a great deal of money at his disposal and could have used it, until final accounting, for his own purposes. Turning to his second point, Ingersoll charged the ex-secretary with corrupting the party press in Maine by way of Francis Smith's propaganda. Compensated with $2,500, Smith had influenced newspapers to favor negotiations with Britain, said Ingersoll, according to Smith's own correspondence. Third, the congressman charged Webster with having left office in May 1843 in default of $2,290—money paid out for which there were no vouchers. Only in the last months of Tyler's administration and only after presidential pressure had he produced some receipts, but even then left at least $1,000 unaccounted for.[27]

At the close of debate, the House voted to create two investigatory committees: one to inquire into the charges against Webster, the other to report how Ingersoll had gathered his facts.[28] On balance, Ingersoll was satisfied, for this action would bring the whole matter into the open and could result in impeachment.

From late April to early May, Webster was absent from Washington on a trip home and stayed longer than he might have otherwise in order to escape this scene of contention. Nevertheless he followed closely what was happening at the capital. Fletcher and Winthrop talked with him in Boston and took some notes he drafted back to Washington to be used as needed during committee hearings.[29] In a four-page memorandum, he countered each of Ingersoll's charges about the secret-service fund. Never had he had a large sum, such as seventeen thousand, at his personal disposal, he said, but spent small amounts periodically for legitimate purposes. Tyler had authorized everything; and since, by law, the fund was completely left to the president's discretion, his approval was the end of the matter. Thus there was no need to go into details. Yet Webster did, to an extent. The notes indicated that some vouchers had come in slowly and that others never did, but the nature of the fund did not require strict auditing, he emphasized. One can believe he did not take money for personal use, even temporarily; but it seems obvious that his procedures were careless—more so than Tyler preferred. Proceeding to other charges, Webster defended use of funds for Smith's work, though he erroneously said it was in Washington rather than Maine. As for the charge of default after leaving office, he answered that the outstanding balance merely reflected oversights in getting vouchers for perfectly proper expenditures.[30]

The five-person committee investigating the charges sat during late May, and nothing could have gone more favorably for the embattled senator. First to testify was Stubbs. He explained the administration of the contingency fund and brought in his records. They coincided with what Ingersoll had reported, but he interpreted them differently. According to Stubbs, there had been delay in receiving vouchers; and more than a year after Webster left office, the president had told him to ask the ex-secretary to settle the account. Able to supply only some missing vouchers, Webster had put up his own money—indeed provided a net amount of a thousand dollars. When Tyler left the White House in 1845, there were no loose ends, he concluded.[31] Next to appear, Francis Smith described his campaign to build support for negotiations with Britain. Denying he had bribed anyone or paid anything to editors in the state, he justified both the project and his compensation out of the secret fund as indispensable.[32] Last, ex-president Tyler came in, principally to assure the committee that he had authorized all expenditures, as law required, and that no wrongdoing had occurred.[33]

Reporting in early June, the committee (four to one) cleared Webster on all charges. Tyler's unusual decision to give him, instead of Stubbs, oversight of the contingency fund fell within statutory authority; and the procedure of certifying secret expenditures was proper. Furthermore, the majority of the committee found that Webster had not defaulted but had merely been late in submitting vouchers. It dismissed the allegation of corrupting the press with a flat statement that such corruption had not occurred. The report was intentionally brief, for the committee thought the details ought to be kept secret, just as Polk had said.[34] Jacob Brinkerhoff, the only dissenter on the committee, thought Ingersoll right about Smith and the Maine press, though the House would have to decide if efforts to influence a state government with federally financed propaganda was an impeachable offense. Likewise, he believed much of what Ingersoll had said on the question of Webster's defaulting.[35] Still, the only thing Brinkerhoff achieved was to force printing of some testimony, though much of it remained sealed against publication.[36]

Both formally and, to a large degree, practically, Webster came out of the distasteful episode with a vindication. Never did Congress or its committee show an inclination to disapprove or reprimand, let alone impeach. Whigs and many Democrats, and apparently the public as well, believed that Ingersoll's attack reflected personal animosity. Technically, the Pennsylvania congressman lacked a strong position in terms of either diplomatic policy (a matter of judgment) or legal grounds. The secret fund did not require the kind of accountability needed for his case. Yet that very flexibility and secrecy did permit Webster to operate even more loosely than usual when money was involved. As in the exploitation of the Sparks map, he did not have to use secret or indirect methods to accomplish public purposes.

While the Ingersoll charges led to a congressional investigation in May and the Oregon question moved toward resolution, Webster paid slight attention to events having more serious consequences than either. They involved a crisis in Mexican-American relations. As he well knew from experience as secretary of state, Mexico had never acknowledged the independence of Texas, indeed had carried on intermittent warfare to regain it. After Polk's election in 1844, expansionists had finally succeeded in annexing Texas, a policy which he had heartily opposed down to the last formal action by Congress at the start of the current session. Polk had made a gesture of pacifying Mexico by a diplomatic mission, which failed; meanwhile he stationed troops near and then within a disputed zone on the Mexican border. Pressures, missteps, and presidential boldness culminated in fighting there in early May 1846. And on the twelfth, Congress responded to Polk's message with a declaration of war.[37] Webster's correspondence and speeches provide no indication that he believed the Mexican problem would lead to war when it did, though he had consistently warned that annexation of Texas could do so sometime.

When Congress voted for war, he was still absent on an extended trip to New England and therefore did not go on record concerning the specific resolution adopted. Though there were many other senators like

Webster who believed the country could and should have avoided the conflict, they discovered it nearly impossible to cast a nay. Attached to the declaration were provisions which said that war already existed by act of Mexico and which appropriated funds for military operations. So the vote in the Senate, forty to two, did not accurately register the sentiment of that body. If war already existed, it might be the result of Polk's incitement, not of Mexican action. Still, if the nation was in peril it was unwise and unpatriotic to deny essential money and arms. How Webster would have voted is an interesting but unanswerable question. He might have felt compelled to support a war already in progress and voted yes, like Winthrop; he might have refused to vote, like Calhoun; or he might have voted no, like the other Massachusetts senator, John Davis. Perhaps the best guess is that he would have abstained.[38]

Though he focused on this war a little late, he soon explained his view of correct policy. Regrettable as the situation was, he would now defend national rights and security, would assist the administration but not if the goals were to promote personal ambitions or to acquire territory. The objectives seemed mixed, however, and so the true course would be difficult.[39] In a way, his problem resembled what he had encountered years before during the War of 1812; now as then, he would oppose more than approve, complain more than praise, yet try to avoid the stigma of disloyalty.

He did not lack ideas about how to prosecute the war. For the first several weeks he thought mainly of diplomatic implications. Believing that the president had badly managed relations with Mexico, he wished to see a new and better effort to negotiate with that hapless country. The United States had an obligation to deal sympathetically with the weak, unstable republic and ought to be able, with patience, to maintain American rights in the process. Why not attempt a new diplomatic mission? Mexico, he concluded, was receptive, for it could not stand a costly war; nor would the United States profit by humiliating it or annexing its territory.[40] Webster alternately predicted that this would be a brief contest or a protracted one, but he hoped that it would end quickly.[41] Then he thought of California, the tenuously held Mexican territory coveted by expansionists. If overland or naval expeditions seized California, as seemed likely, would not Britain strongly react to protect its own interests there? And would not that reaction hinder agreement on Oregon? Soon it became clear that England would not interfere in California and would sign an acceptable treaty on the Pacific Northwest. Webster felt pleased with this improvement in relations with Britain, though he still opposed territorial acquisitions.[42]

Political considerations affected his view of the military phase of the war. A needless conflict such as this should not become a war of conquest. In his judgment, that was unfortunately the tendency, as Congress deliberated about authorizing reinforcements to General Zachary Taylor, perhaps enough to march on to Mexico City. Webster preferred defensive action along the border until saner heads could prevail. There was no need for military conscription or for calling out the state militia for compulsory service to mount an invasion. In fact, that policy would subvert the constitutional purpose of the militia. To the extent that more troops and more commissioned officers were necessary, he wished Congress, not merely the executive, to act—understandably he would not give this president more power and patronage.[43]

Given the limited, short war Webster visualized, the financial commitment should also be minimal. Yet military expenses were already running to half a million each day and would undoubtedly climb. He would not deny support for what must be done, Webster emphasized. But the administration seemed to have a weak grasp of fiscal essentials, largely because it allowed its Democratic preconceptions to determine measures. Thus it would lower the tariff and reduce land prices on the dubious theory that these steps would bring in more money through increased imports and land purchases. He was convinced that such would not be the result. Then, too, it would issue a large volume of treasury notes, amounting to paper money, at the same time that it wanted an independent treasury requiring a hard-money system. Huge expenditures were incompatible with Polk's financial program, the senator reasoned. Inescapably, the public debt would soar, and heavy taxes would have to be levied.[44]

The Senate did not get to the tariff until July. Business on Oregon and the Mexican War had delayed it; and, of course, financial legislation had to originate in the House. There the secretary of the treasury, Robert Walker, submitted a plan for extensive revision, chiefly downward from protection of American products toward a predominantly revenue-producing system. The secretary had been at work gathering economic data in order to determine how to obtain maximum revenue while cutting rates; but the House, as usual, adopted numerous amendments to accommodate various interests having political leverage. When the bill arrived in the Senate, prospects for passage were uncertain, owing to a near balance of party strength. Indeed a count of low- and high-tariff members indicated the possibility of a tie vote, which would compel Vice-President George Dallas of Pennsylvania, a protectionist stronghold, to break it. Democrats hoped, however, that he would defer to the White House and help pass the measure.[45] The fluid situation, involving abandonment of the fairly high schedule in the law of 1842, caused Webster to move energetically on this question, more than on any other during the session.

Debate lasted two weeks in late July, and in view of the long history of argument and legislation on the tariff, few new insights emerged. Democrats adhered to dogma on the exploitative effects of protection, while Whigs resurrected reasoning familiar for decades in behalf of economic development. Whigs attempted time and again to amend and postpone, with Democrats defeating them by thin margins. The struggle demonstrated that party regularity had become firmer on such issues.[46]

Aroused as always when he believed the protective system was endangered, Webster concentrated all his resources on defeating the Democratic bill. He urged businessmen to supply information on manufactures, imports, costs, and prices to be used in debate. And he encouraged a flow of petitions to express opinion, which he then presented to the Senate. So poor was the chance of killing the bill outright that he was willing to compromise by reducing rates 25 percent. But his fellow Whigs were unreceptive. In his two-day speech he objected to many features of the measure: an *ad valorem* schedule susceptible to fraud as well as to the damaging effects upon patterns of commerce, upon the flow of raw materials for manufacturing, and especially upon the welfare of labor. The Senate was about evenly divided, but last-minute pressure by the administration carried the bill through by one vote.[47]

Immediately after adopting a lower tariff, the Senate debated another fundamental of the Jacksonian faith, restoration of an independent treasury. With maximum pressure from Polk, a bill had come over from the House to reestablish a federal depository for public funds instead of selected state banks. Also reflecting past politics, an important feature provided that financial transactions involving the government would require specie payment.[48] The Whigs had less hope of defeating this bill than the one on the tariff. All they could realistically expect was to change its shape somewhat, soften the specie requirement, and perhaps postpone the date when the new system would begin operation.[49]

On August 1, as the Senate was ready to act, Webster made a speech with no effect except to record his dissent. Like the Walker tariff, this measure was ill timed, he argued, for it would interfere with fiscal functions, including the floating of loans for war expenditures. Besides, the existing depository banks were performing quite well. The speech reflected a marked shift in his views since the days of the Jacksonian "pets."[50] But the old objection to separating the government entirely from the nation's banks and currency was still valid, he believed. "I had heard of 'Polk, Dallas, and the tariff of 1842,' but I really never did expect to hear of 'Polk, Dallas, and the old dead sub-treasury.' "[51] Over Whig complaints, the bill passed and revived the institution for a long second life.[52]

On the last day of the session, August 10, an ominous episode occurred. To expedite negotiations with Mexico, the administration had pushed through the House an appropriation of two millions, designated cryptically for extraordinary expenses but meant for territorial acquisition. David Wilmot, a Van Burenite Democrat, representing dissatisfaction of that wing of the party with Polk's willingness to allow extension of slavery, had proposed an amendment, which carried. It would forbid extension of the institution into any Mexican cession. In the Senate, less than an hour was available for discussion of the bill before adjournment; and Webster's colleague, John Davis, an opponent of the war, had the floor. Though promising to stop in time for a vote and conference with the House committee, he was still speaking when word arrived that the House had adjourned, making any action impossible. It was unlikely that the Wilmot amendment would have carried anyhow, yet the flurry underscored an ever deepening division of North and South on the spread of slavery. Webster said nothing at the moment and had no opportunity to vote. He would have supported the nonextension provision; but in his view it would be far better not to acquire any territory and thereby to prevent this dangerous issue from developing further.[53]

It did develop. After a respite from politics through the summer of 1846, Webster confronted the issue at home in September. On the twenty-third, the party held its convention in Faneuil Hall to nominate state candidates, approve a platform, and listen to animated speeches until late in the day. Again the division of Conscience and Cotton Whigs threatened unity. Differences between the two wings on how to oppose slavery became very clear when Charles Sumner and Robert Winthrop clashed. Handsome, eloquent, and aggressive, Sumner stirred his audience with a call to battle against slavery in a moral cause, rooted in the Declaration of Independence and affirmed by national ideals. The party must focus upon this evil, being spread as it was with help not only from current expansionists but also from weak-kneed conservatives. Here he was striking at congressmen such as Winthrop, who professed opposition to the war but voted for appropriations to prosecute it. For some time, Winthrop had been annoyed by Sumner's attitude, changing from friendship to discourtesy to political hostility.[54] But when he spoke, he did not stray from the substance of the discussion into a personal rejoinder and emphasized the necessity for all Whigs to combat the Democratic economic program on tariff and public finance. He insisted that he thoroughly disapproved the war and extension of slavery, yet he would not rashly assail the South and its institution only to destroy the party or endanger the Union. It was a matter of tactics and degree, he thought. Thus these two exemplars of Boston's elite represented the choices thrust upon all who were interested in public affairs.

The Conscience Whigs acquiesced in nominations for governor and lieutenant governor but contested the proposed conservative platform. A mere statement against the war and new slave territory was insufficient, they felt. Instead they favored amendments, presented by Stephen Phillips, urging abolition of slavery in the District of Columbia and prohibition of interstate slave trade—both of which, they believed, lay within jurisdiction of Congress. Furthermore, the party must select only candidates who could accept their platform.

At this juncture excitement built when Webster entered the hall, arm in arm with Abbott Lawrence, his Cotton Whig rival. Obviously they intended the maneuver as a symbol of unity, not just of conservatives but of the whole party. For the moment, Webster merely took a seat on the stage, his visage rather melancholy but helping to cool the heated atmosphere. Late in the afternoon after more rhetoric, Phillips' amendments failed. The total vote was small, for many delegates had left and others abstained; but it was at least a nominal victory for conservatives.[55] Webster attempted to smooth over residual differences with a few general inspirational sentiments. Though it was impossible for Whigs to be unanimous on all questions, he conceded, the party remained the best vehicle for progress. "I see in the dark and troubled night which is now upon us, no star above the horizon, but the intelligent, patriotic, *united* Whig party of the United States."[56]

Webster realized he must go as far as he could to mollify the young Whigs, for reasons of expediency as well as principle. Though avoiding mention of slavery, he broadened his condemnation of the war to the limit when appearing before a preelection rally in early November. "The Mexican War," he asserted, "is universally odious throughout the United States, and we have yet to find any Sempronius [Gracchus] who raises his voice for it."[57] Polk had started it, he continued, by ordering troops into a disputed border area, really Mexican soil. By thus inciting a conflict, the president had presented Congress with the accomplished fact of war, thereby usurping that body's power. It was "a clear violation of his duty; in my judgment it is an impeachable offence." This was not the learned constitutional lawyer speaking but the politician warmed by an election. In closing, however, he hinted broadly that radicals must

consider their course carefully, for, he said, Whigs had no excuse for ig-
noring or rejecting the Constitution. His loose version of impeachment
left the senator himself open to the same advice.[58]

He repeated his theme in a setting more visible nationally, at a public
banquet in Philadelphia on December 2. Here he made an address of
nearly four hours, diligently prepared and widely circulated, at an elaborate affair in his honor.[59] He said he was belatedly fulfilling a promise
to meet with friends in the city; but his speech seemed to be an implicit
announcement of his availability for the presidency. He reiterated his
charge that Polk had usurped congressional power by instigating war,
and now he explicitly connected the conflict with an effort to extend
slavery. Ever since the Texan revolution, he had taken a stand against
that, he recalled. At any rate, the remedy now must be an early peace
without aggrandizement of the national domain. Significantly, he said
nothing about the Wilmot Proviso, introduced in the previous session to
prohibit slavery in any Mexican cession. Nor had he done so in statements earlier that fall. As proof that he had more on his mind than the
war and slavery, he devoted the larger part of this detailed survey of the
political scene to raking the administration's policies on Oregon, the
newly created Independent Treasury, internal improvements, and particularly the tariff, a subject interesting to a Pennsylvania audience. On
each, he summarized his arguments set forth in the Senate, but now
more systematically, so that all could see where he stood on every issue.[60]

During the congressional session beginning in December 1846, he was
remarkably quiet. He did present resolutions against territorial acquisitions and for generous American terms in a treaty.[61] But senators were
busy approaching the problem from a different perspective. They had
before them a measure known as the Three-Million Bill, providing funds
which might be used for obtaining Mexican land or for other purposes—the language was vague. Attached to it, as it came from the
House, was the Wilmot Proviso. As a result, the Senate paid more attention to that proposal than to Webster's resolution on no acquisitions.
The parliamentary situation was such that John Berrien offered a no-
acquisition amendment—the same as Webster's resolution—to the
Three-Million Bill. The climax came on March 1, when talk ran on to
two o'clock in the morning, and voting on key questions occurred. The
Berrien amendment did not carry, and now the only limitation which
might be placed on negotiations for peace appeared to be the proviso.[62]

During this last stage of the debate, Webster got the floor for a general
comment on the situation.[63] After a jab at the president for launching
the war, he read resolutions adopted by the Massachusetts legislature,

declaring that slavery was "an immense moral and political evil, which ought to be abolished as soon as that end can be properly and constitutionally attained; and that its extension should be uniformly and earnestly opposed." The legislature protested "against the acquisition of any additional territory, without an express provision by Congress that there shall be neither slavery nor involuntary servitude in such territory." Despite his endorsement of the resolutions, they did not advance the policy he preferred, for they would accept new territories if accompanied by a Wilmot Proviso, whereas he wanted no acquisitions in order to be certain there would be no problem of slavery in those regions.[64] That this was his preference he demonstrated as he lashed northern Democrats who had supported the war, voted against the Berrien amendment, but voted for the Wilmot Proviso. No such proviso could forestall future trouble, he contended. In some fashion, once there were new territories, controversy about slavery would surround them. Though having indicated less faith in the proviso than the Massachusetts legislature had, he did vote for it that night. But this amendment also failed, followed by passage of the Three-Million Bill. Thus the Senate endorsed expansion without legislative strictures, whether Webster's or Wilmot's.[65]

Chapter 24

SLAVERY IN THE WEST

As early as the spring of 1847, circumstances of the war stimulated serious talk about the next presidential election. Zachary Taylor, popular commander of forces in northern Mexico, advanced to the foreground as an attractive alternative to several well-known aspirants to office. For a while the general appeared to be a likely candidate of either party, for he had no affiliation and was in fact a political innocent. The Whigs claimed him with somewhat more confidence, however, because of his antagonistic relationship to the Democratic president. And they could not forget that the formula of a military hero had been productive, first with Jackson against them, then with Harrison for them. No one could have been more aware of this fact than Webster after the two decades of party warfare. "The probability now is," he remarked, "that General Taylor will come in President with a general rush. He would, certainly, were the election now to come on. It is in the nature of mankind to carry their favor towards military achievement."[1] Though characteristically disturbed by this tendency, he recognized that Taylor had some redeeming traits—"large foresight, & a comprehensive grasp," together with "his sensible manner of writing."[2] Still, for the presidency the senator did not have the slightest doubt that experience and ability in politics were indispensable. And who had them in greater measure than he?

If the movement toward Taylor were to be halted, it had to be done in the South. Old Rough and Ready was especially popular there, partly because the section strongly supported the war, partly because he was a Louisiana slaveholder. So after Congress adjourned, Webster began planning a southern tour as far as Georgia and perhaps over to the lower

Mississippi Valley. Delayed in Washington by legal business, he did not leave until April 28 and could not go as far as he had hoped.[3] He traveled by railroad to Richmond, Raleigh, Charleston, Savannah, and other cities of the Southeast, then on a steamer homeward in early June, a circuit taking him into a part of the country he had never seen and providing a great deal of personal pleasure.[4] It also allowed him to test the political waters of the region. He found that people showered him with attention, whether it was the hospitality of prominent families or the curiosity and admiration of crowds on public occasions. But he also found everywhere that the name most often mentioned for the presidency was that of Zachary Taylor. It may have been for this reason that he cut short his tour, originally intended to include Tennessee and Kentucky, though ostensibly an illness caused him to change his plans. He avoided comment on current issues and seemed more interested in observing the way of life, the rice and cotton fields, the status of transportation than in delivering addresses.[5] In Charleston and Savannah he did speak to large audiences, but on safe topics: the common heritage of the South and New England extending back to the Revolution, the sentiments surrounding the Union, the compromises of the Constitution, the promise of national growth. Nothing about the Mexican War or the extension of slavery.[6] Altogether, he encountered much good will, some adulation, but little encouragement about the next year's election.

In addition to the difficulty of making headway in other sections, Webster encountered a problem even in his own state, where he had to have a loyal following. Factionalism involving Cotton and Conscience Whigs continued to rack the party there. His pursuit of the presidency reached a critical point when the state convention met in Springfield on September 29, 1847. He found the Lawrence conservatives working hard for Taylor and, as before, opposing any stand which would alienate the South. On the other hand, Conscience Whigs—Charles Francis Adams, Charles Sumner, Stephen Phillips, John Palfrey—found the prospect of nominating Taylor, a slaveholder, intolerable and a timid stand on slavery equally so. Between these blocs were a great many Websterites, who took middle ground on extension of slavery, preferring a no-territory policy to the Wilmot Proviso. Above all, they wanted this convention to declare for Webster as president.

At the first stage of proceedings, the Conscience Whigs took the initiative by offering resolutions which could carry only if they played the Lawrence and Webster groups against each other. Phillips moved that there be no declaration on the presidency and came close to winning approval, but failed by a vote of 242 to 232. Though not quite enough, support for Phillips' resolution came from the Taylor men hoping to stop Webster. Then Palfrey moved that the party should support only candidates committed against extension of slavery, but a combination of Lawrence and Webster delegates defeated that resolution as an unwise irritant to southerners.[7]

While the nominating committee met, Webster came to the platform to make a forceful speech, inclining toward the Conscience wing though blending conservative qualifications into his argument. This was his strongest indictment of Polk for inciting an unjustifiable war. The pretended cause of the conflict, he said, was response to an attack shedding American blood on American soil and therefore a defensive action. In truth, the president knew that the border zone into which he had ordered troops had been occupied by the Mexicans and was, at best, disputed soil. The fact that he had allowed the sometime dictator Santa Anna to return to his country from Cuba so that a more amenable Mexican regime would consent to American territorial acquisition was additional proof that Polk had been dishonest about the real object of the war. All the evidence convinced him that the president had violated the Constitution by usurping congressional power to declare war. As for the remedy, he would be severe: ". . . unless the President of the United States shall make out a case which shall show to Congress that the aim and object for which the war is now prosecuted, is no purpose not connected with the safety of the Union, and the just rights of the American people—then Congress ought to pass resolutions against the prosecution of the war, and grant no further supplies."[8]

As advanced as this antiwar dissent was, he seemed defensive when referring to the Wilmot Proviso. Again he favored prevention of territorial acquisitions in the first place instead of hoping to keep them free of slavery later. Nevertheless, he had consistently supported the doctrine of nonextension, he pointed out. "Did I not commit myself in 1838 to the whole doctrine, fully, entirely? And I must be permitted to say I cannot quite consent that more recent discoverers should claim merit, and take out a patent. I deny priority of their invention. Allow me to say, sir, it is not their thunder."[9] After he finished, the last item of business in the convention was the presidential nomination. Apparently Webster had helped his cause among Conscience Whigs, perhaps among some Lawrence conservatives, because he was nominated by acclamation as the choice of Massachusetts for president. On the surface everything had ended as Webster wished, yet he realized his home base was not solid, a condition which seriously undercut his strength elsewhere. Conscience Whigs were a determined element, failing to achieve all their goals at present but intending to influence the future course of politics. And Cotton Whigs had by no means lost their taste for a Taylor ticket.[10]

During the early months of 1848, as the time of the Whig national convention approached, no broad movement for Webster materialized. He could count on votes only from Massachusetts, probably a few more from New England, and none likely beyond that. His friends in New York City made a brave though faltering effort and even considered backing Taylor to counter a trend toward Clay. Disapproving this tactic, Webster depended upon a few loyalists, such as Hiram Ketchum, Moses Grinnell, and Richard Blatchford, to keep his hopes alive. Generally he was inactive, out of the running unless the Taylor craze subsided or some dramatic change occurred.[11]

At the national convention in Philadelphia on June 7 to 9, early balloting centered on Taylor and Clay. The general led but lacked a majority because of several other nominations, including those of another military figure, Winfield Scott, and of Webster. The senator received all the votes of Massachusetts and New Hampshire, all but one of Maine, ᐧ but no others. By the fourth ballot Taylor had more than enough, Clay slipped badly, Webster lost one of the twelve votes from his state and most of those in the other two delegations.[12] He was never close to winning, nor was there any sign the tide might later turn his way. Conservative delegates such as Rufus Choate remained firm for him but afterward were happy to support the nominee.[13] Conscience Whigs Charles Allen and Henry Wilson vowed they would never accept a slaveholding candidate and talked of an independent antislavery ticket. Furthermore, these free-soilers complained that the convention had not adopted a platform, particularly an antiextension statement. Finally, the gathering selected a vice-presidential candidate. Surprisingly, they chose the cautious New York politician Millard Fillmore instead of Abbott Lawrence, recognized as a Taylor man through and through. It was probably because of that link with the general that Lawrence's expected nomination collapsed owing to hard feelings in the Clay camp.[14] The story circulated that Websterites had deprived Lawrence of the honor, but that claim does not seem to be true.[15]

The Democrats had nominated Lewis Cass two weeks earlier. Recently deferential to southern opinion, the Michigan senator could claim a national constituency on the basis of his Jacksonian orthodoxy over a long political career. Yet this selection did not conceal a serious division of the party, in which New York antislavery forces figured large. These so-called Barnburners, chiefly followers of Van Buren, were defeated in their state convention, sent a rival delegation to the national meeting, were dissatisfied with a ruling that they share voting power with the regulars (Hunkers) of the state, and then left the convention in a furious temper after nomination of Cass. Returning home, they met again to present Van Buren as an independent candidate.[16] Already there were reports that a new party of free-soilers would emerge, including Van Burenites and other such Democrats, Conscience Whigs of Massachusetts and elsewhere, and Liberty party men. There was even mention of Webster as a likely head of such a coalition.[17]

These speculations seemed to have substance, for Taylor's nomination had bothered him a good deal. Initially, his reaction was emotional. When a group from a party meeting in Washington on June 12 came to his door that evening and tried to call him out for a few remarks, unlike other Whig leaders who so responded at their own houses, Webster did not appear. The *Intelligencer* explained that he could not "apparel himself for encountering the night air before the crowd departed," an excuse which must not have satisfied his callers.[18] His nonappearance was undoubtedly intentional: he had decided, for the time being, to "stand quite aloof" and let others do the work.[19] As he got reports from the convention he felt mistreated, betrayed by northerners who had not insisted upon a candidate from their section instead of the South and who, still worse, had helped put up one who might not be a true Whig. To document the injustice, he urged Ketchum to write an account of the proceedings, expose the abominable conduct of these northerners, and circulate the piece widely.[20]

Soon he saw how difficult it was to stay aloof while his intimate friends declared for Taylor. George Ashmun, for instance, had extended himself unreservedly for Webster at the convention and had also been irritated by a submissive northern attitude; but he accepted the decision because the nominee was a declared Whig and would defer to Congress on slavery in the territories. Robert Winthrop was reconciled to the choice because of the general's great popularity. Even Everett, often thinking of Webster first and himself second, advised him to suppress his anger at the outcome. Would not Taylor need an able secretary of state just as Harrison had? From Georgia, John Berrien wrote that it would have been far better to have selected Clay or Webster, both proven statesmen, but it was essential to concentrate on winning this election, in which Whig principles were at stake.[21] Pro-Webster newspapers, the *Intelligencer,* the Boston *Atlas,* and others, counseled unity.[22] On June 16, Whigs in Boston held a ratification meeting, sounding the theme of reconciliation and cooperation. Naturally Lawrence and Appleton expressed enthusiasm for the nominee. George Lunt, the only Massachusetts delegate who had changed his vote to Taylor, did too. Even Rufus Choate, notably faithful to Webster, delivered an eloquent plea for party regularity. In short, Whig leaders in the state, except those of the Conscience wing, endorsed the convention's decision.[23]

Although he continued his silence, Webster realized he would presently have to "fall in." Less than a week after the nomination he told Fletcher, "The run is all that way. We can do no good by holding out. We shall only isolate ourselves. Northern opposition is too small & too narrow to rely on. I must say *something, somewhere* soon." At the opportune time, he concluded, he must acquiesce, not praising Taylor's qualifications but advocating the Whig cause and particularly resisting the election of such an impossible person as Cass.[24] Yet the summer passed before he did so, thus leaving some people in doubt and many others critical of his attitude.

An interesting consequence of the senator's delay was the interpretation Conscience Whigs gave to it. Over the past few years they had welcomed his antiexpansionist, antiwar pronouncements regardless of his well-known conservative connections. In a sense, he had been a third force between them and the Cotton Whigs, sometimes an ally as in his opposition to Taylor. Several who had been delegates to the national convention had adhered to him through every ballot. If he acted logically, would he not now join them in their movement for free soil? They held a meeting at Worcester on June 28, 1848, to proclaim their disapproval of the Whig nominee, indeed to plan for a broad national undertaking through a new party. Watching their proceedings with more than a little interest, Fletcher attended as an observer but attracted attention himself. Henry Wilson, Charles Allen, and Rockwood Hoar could be seen talking earnestly with the senator's son, presumably inviting approval of their course. Before adjournment, the meeting adopted a resolution praising Webster for withholding an endorsement of Taylor, implicitly an appeal for his positive aid.[25]

In early August delegates from Massachusetts went to Buffalo for a national convention of the new Free Soil party. The nucleus was the New York Barnburner element attached to Van Buren, to which additions came from states across the North. All agreed to one thing: unrelenting opposition to extension of slavery into any American territory. Some were Democrats, such as Salmon Chase of Ohio and the younger Van Buren, Prince John; others were Whigs, such as the Massachusetts delegation and Joshua Giddings of Ohio's Western Reserve; still others were Liberty party men who had pioneered antislavery politics eight years earlier. Predictably, the Free-Soilers nominated Van Buren for president and then recognized the importance of Conscience Whigs by selecting Charles Francis Adams for vice-president.[26]

Organizers of the new party in the Bay State hoped Webster would give them an endorsement, though they must have understood that the odds against it were large. One of them, young Rockwood Hoar, whose family had been quite friendly with the senator, wrote on August 13, praising him for a speech in Congress the previous day and asking for a statement supporting the movement. "It is utterly impossible for me to support the Buffalo nomination," he answered; "I have no confidence in Mr. Van Buren, not the slightest." He pointed out the Red Fox's earlier accommodations with the slavery interest, only recently reversed for the sake of expediency. At least Taylor was honest and therefore more trustworthy on this very issue. In contrast, Webster emphasized his own consistency, however misunderstood it may have been. "There are those," he complained, "who will not believe that I am an anti slavery man unless I repeat the declaration once a week."[27] To be sure, one obstacle to an endorsement was the antipathy between Van Buren and Webster. Ordinarily, the New Yorker took pride in amiable personal relations with his strongest adversaries, but Webster stood out as an exception. And the latter reciprocated in full measure.[28] Nonetheless, even if there had been no such personal feeling, Webster could not endorse a man who symbolized everything against which he had fought: the Independent Treasury, low tariff, states' rights. Besides, though he remained silent through this period, he had concluded he could not contribute to disruption of the Whig party by backing this unpromising venture.[29]

At last, on September 1, he spoke out. He chose his own neighborhood to do so—his Marshfield property at the old Winslow house. It was not the usual campaign address lavishing praise on a candidate but a plea to vote for Taylor because he was the party's nominee. Because the general lacked experience in public affairs, one must support him because of personal qualities, his honesty, courage, and disciplined mind. Without doubt, declared the senator, he was a Whig, despite widespread suspicion to the contrary; and he could be counted upon to oppose further expansion of territory or extension of slavery. Disposing of Taylor's qualifications hurriedly, Webster emphasized reasons for opposing Cass and Van Buren. The Democratic candidate, with his long history of rash behavior concerning both domestic and foreign policies, was quite dangerous. But it was Van Buren upon whom the speaker dwelt. The Red Fox's belated switch to antislavery made him far less reliable than a true Whig—here Webster cited his own record as evidence. Reviewing the New Yorker's career, he found much to condemn, particularly the position of his northern friends in favor of annexing Texas and Mexican soil.[30] Webster was right about Van Buren's proexpansion friends but did not do justice to the candidate himself in view of his stand on Texas in the election of 1844. Notwithstanding a determination not to speak again during the canvass, he did twice, at the nearby town of Abington in early October and in Faneuil Hall the twenty-fourth. Saying about the same things, he gave more weight to issues than to personalities, more to the tariff and banking than to slavery.[31]

The election went to Taylor, though it was certainly not a landslide. The outcome showed the effects of Van Buren's candidacy, especially in New York, where the electoral vote was precisely the difference between the national totals of Taylor and Cass. There, as anticipated, Van Buren drew heavily from Democratic districts and ran second to Taylor in the field of three. In a number of states the Whig general did not get a popular majority even though he gathered the electoral votes. Webster's reluctant endorsement could hardly have been decisive. In Massachusetts too, Taylor's popular total was less than that of the other two combined; yet a great many of those casting Free Soil ballots were antislavery Whigs who would never have accepted Cass if he had been the only alternative to Taylor.[32] All things considered, Webster felt mildly pleased but not thrilled. The question now was whether Old Rough and Ready would use his common sense and take some good advice.[33]

The possibility that he would be an adviser seemed remote. Apart from any hesitation he might have had about entering the administration, the incoming president was not likely to bring in a person as critical of him as Webster had been. It is difficult to know whether the senator was genuinely reluctant. There was a veiled indication of interest; he watched the formation of the cabinet closely and commented upon the process often. "I am old, and poor, and proud," he wrote. "All these things beckon me to retirement, to take care of myself—and, as I cannot act the first part, to act none. This is exactly my feeling; without being pressed to say what I would or would not do, in case of the arising of an exigency, in which those who have been friendly, and are entitled to best regards from me, might think I could be of essential service." In fact that exigency did arise, for numerous friends wished to see him return to the State Department, and it was the decision on that office which interested him.[34] John Crittenden, Taylor's trusted counselor and strategist during the general's rise to power, could have had it if he wished. Yet he declined any appointment, to forestall the charge of bargaining.[35] When the new president arrived in Washington in late February 1849, it appeared he would select John Clayton for State; but still he delayed acting. On the twenty-fifth, Webster visited Taylor on a pleasant courtesy call and got no hint about any appointment. The old soldier seemed indecisive, he thought. He "means well, but he knows little of public affairs, & less of public men. He feels he must rely on somebody; that he must have counsel, even in the appointment of his counsellors." Finally, Clayton received the nomination. It was clear that if Webster were to have influence, it would have to be from his seat in the Senate.[36]

He showed no disappointment about being an outsider as far as his own future was concerned, but a great deal when his energetic effort to get something for Fletcher fell through. After a so-so law practice, interrupted by service as his father's chief clerk in the State Department and as Caleb Cushing's secretary on the China mission, Fletcher anxiously sought the office of United States attorney in Massachusetts. Webster wrote and spoke to the president, the new cabinet officers, and various friends back home in an attempt to place his son. The matter dragged on for two months after Taylor's inauguration. On his father's advice, Fletcher got members of the bar and leading Whigs in Boston to testify to his qualifications, but the effort was useless. Taylor's answer was that his managers at the Whig convention had promised the position to George Lunt, the only Massachusetts delegate to have dropped Webster for the general on a late ballot. Very upset about this choice, the Websters let everyone know that Lunt was quite unfit to be district attorney.[37] Nothing else came up for Fletcher at the moment, though he later became surveyor of the port of Boston and remained so for a decade. Only scattered appointments went to persons associated with the senator, an outsider still.[38]

While the country was electing a new president in 1848 and then awaiting his inauguration the following March, Webster attended two congressional sessions. Nearly all the important questions before him and his fellow senators concerned the war, its conclusion in early 1848 and its long-range impact upon the far Southwest and slavery. Well before a proposed treaty arrived in Washington in February, the fighting had stopped after a victorious march upon Mexico City by Winfield Scott's army. But time passed while a new Mexican government, able and willing to negotiate a treaty, could be formed. For the United States the responsibility of making the peace rested with Nicholas Trist, chief clerk of the State Department, who had endless trouble, not least of which was his recall by Polk before completing his mission. Nevertheless, he defied that order, achieved terms conformable to his original instructions, and dispatched the document to Washington. In it, the defeated nation agreed to cede California, New Mexico, and the disputed borderland of Texas for fifteen millions. Despite getting as much as he had told

Trist to obtain, Polk was enraged that his envoy had not come home when ordered. But he could hardly afford not to submit the treaty to the Senate; and he did on February 23, 1848. As for the upper house, a number of its members, including Webster, feared that this enormous acquisition of land would be a source of sectional division and the ruin of national institutions.

Debate on the treaty entailed proposal of countless amendments and a long procession of speeches before the Senate gave its advice and consent on March 10, thirty-eight to fourteen. Predictably, Webster voted with the minority. His principal attempt to defeat the treaty consisted of a resolution to send a commission to renegotiate terms with Mexico and thereby stop the projected cession of territory. Polk had been tempted to renegotiate because of Trist's regrettable behavior but would not welcome Webster's prescription for a settlement. In any case, the resolution failed. Some other amendments met the same fate, including one to annex more territory than Trist had gained and another to annex nothing. Webster supported the second. The final vote to ratify would have been closer, even negative, if all those dissatisfied with some provision had opposed the whole treaty; but a consensus to end the war and expand westward prevailed.[39]

After Senate approval, discussion of the purpose and consequences of the war persisted. For one thing, it was not altogether certain that the Mexican government would also ratify, especially in light of certain revisions to the treaty. Just in case it did not, the administration asked for more money and troops to resume military operations. These measures furnished members with an opportunity to repeat publicly what they had said during the secret executive session. Webster had the floor twice for detailed comments largely recapitulating his settled views.[40] Again he traversed the events and conditions leading to war, to a policy unwisely and unconstitutionally adopted by the president. He charged the chief executive with arbitrary actions during the odious conflict, with transforming it into an invasion to grab huge tracts from a prostrate neighbor, with augmenting presidential power alarmingly, and with issuing unjustifiable executive orders on the pretext of military necessity. Now, the senator contended, even after dictating a peace, Polk wanted to spend more and to enlarge an already oversized army. The country had suffered and would even more as it confronted the vexing problem of creating many new states out of this barren, worthless land of the Southwest. Webster knew his complaints would be ineffectual, as they had been before; yet at least he vented deep-seated frustration while exploring his own course in the postwar period.

He had good reason to think about it, because at this very moment

Congress had on its hands the highly explosive question of slavery in the new territories. Through the session of 1848 lasting into August, the entire spectrum of options became clear to all—from one extreme favoring the North to the other favoring the South, across a variety of potential compromises between them. Still very much alive, the Wilmot Proviso would prohibit slavery in the entire Mexican cession of California and New Mexico (including several present-day states west of Texas). The Free Soil coalition of this election year demonstrated growing northern approval of a policy of nonextension. Against it, southern resolve to protect slavery from this lateral attack stiffened; and as a principal contributor to victory in the war, the South felt justified in claiming equal access to the territory acquired. Indeed it was developing a constitutional and moral rationale for protecting slavery in territories as well as in states. Well equipped with arguments, Calhoun headed an active southern rights' movement.

During this session the Senate considered several formulas which might reconcile these extremes. The first was popular sovereignty, the idea that people in the new territories, not Congress, should decide about slavery. Daniel Dickinson, a New York Democrat, introduced a resolution to that effect. Attractive as the pure concept seemed and durable though it would be in the years ahead, it did not appeal to the South in these circumstances, for a decision by first settlers in the far West, unlikely to be slaveholders, would probably take the free-soil direction. Enough senators thought so to table Dickinson's resolution, though Cass adhered to the position during his try for the presidency. Concurrently, Polk and his cabinet sought to quiet mounting disagreement by merely extending the Missouri Compromise line of 36 °30′ latitude to the Pacific, creating two sizable areas for separate northern and southern emigration. With backing from the administration and from southern members, the proposal passed the Senate twice, in June and August, but the majority of the House rejected it. Toward the close of the session, John Clayton, the Delaware Whig who would soon become Taylor's secretary of state, reported for a special committee on the problem. It was a legal, judicial question, he said, and should therefore be determined by the courts. Congress should permit federal judges to entertain such suits as slaves might file concerning their status. That notion, like popular sovereignty, would amount to a decision by Congress not to decide, an appealing alternative to worried politicians. It foreshadowed what the Supreme Court would do in the famous *Dred Scott* case some years later. Eager to find a way out in this session of 1848, the Senate passed a Clayton bill too, with the same negative reaction by the House.[41]

Webster showed no inclination to approve any of these proposed compromises. In fact his thinking had moved toward free soil. He spoke on the question during debate on a bill organizing the Oregon territory. An amendment to that measure by Stephen Douglas would provide that this region be free of slavery because it was north of the 36 °30′ line. Here was an attempt, by indirection, to establish that line in New Mexico. Since no one expected slavery to take hold in Oregon anyway, Webster and others opposed the Douglas amendment because of its implications for the Mexican cession. Referring to slavery, the senator held that it existed only by local legislation. In the existing southern states, it was untouchable; but Congress had full power, he said, to prohibit it in all federal territories. And that is what the legislators ought to do, for slavery there would discourage free settlers from coming in. Employing an argument soon to be familiar, he reasoned that the two labor systems could not thrive side by side, because free men would feel that the peculiar institution degraded the character of work. "I have made up my mind, for one," he concluded, "that under no circumstances will I consent to the further extension of the area of slavery in the United States, or to the further increase of slave representation in the House of Representatives." His determination would be tested later; but now, with adjournment at hand, the Senate gave in to the House and passed the Oregon bill without the thirty-six-thirty amendment.[42]

When Webster returned to Washington in December 1848, he heard more oratory on slavery in the territories, though few people expected legislative action during the interim before Taylor's inauguration in March. The Little Giant, as Douglas of Illinois was called, again played a prominent role, this time in attempting to pass a bill which would create one large state from the entire Mexican cession. Though he deserved credit for a mighty effort, he failed in his impractical project. More to the point was the rather pressing need for some kind of government for the area merely to maintain order until a more comprehensive policy could be adopted. For this purpose Webster proposed an amendment to the annual appropriations bill which would authorize temporary military government and some caretaker functions there. One clause specified that until a regular territorial government was formed, "existing laws" would stay in effect. That expression meant Mexican law, which prohibited slavery, and its effect could be to push future policy toward free soil, especially if the congressional deadlock continued. Posed against Webster's amendment was one by Isaac Walker to extend the Constitution, or as much of it as the president found suitable, to the region and therefore to abrogate existing laws. A protracted colloquy ensued between Webster and Calhoun. The latter contended that the Con-

405

stitution would automatically extend to the territories, regardless of Walker's proposal, and would protect slave property. Not true, replied Webster. Territories were entirely subject to congressional regulation and were covered only by such parts of the Constitution as Congress decided. Thus slavery could go into a place only if Congress allowed, not because of a constitutional imperative. In this exchange the two old adversaries were scouting the central political question of the 1850s.[43]

The Senate did not dispose of the matter until the last minute of the session on March 3, 1849—in fact not until seven in the morning of March 4, some hours after the technical deadline for adjournment. In a parliamentary tangle of protest and exasperation, the exhausted solons discussed various amendments by Webster, Walker, and others, and amendments to amendments. At last they detached the territorial provision from the appropriations bill to allow the federal government to operate next year. And they enacted nothing on the territories.[44] All would wait for the new administration and for an important chapter in the history of Congress.

Chapter 2 5

COMPROMISE

The deadlock on slavery in the western territories seemed all the more immovable when Congress assembled in December 1849 for the first time after Taylor took office. Sectional feeling had risen to a degree not only hindering the process of government but threatening the very existence of the Union. Throughout the North nonextensionist sentiment abounded. Though not electing a president in 1848, the new Free Soil party had made a good showing and won a number of seats in the House. Of greater importance was the determination of most northern Whigs and some Democrats to oppose the spread of slavery into the Mexican cession. In the South an excited mood reflected an equal determination to maintain constitutional rights as people there defined them. Taking the lead, Calhoun had drafted a southern address identifying the danger and recruiting a number of like-minded congressmen to the cause. And just before this session, the movement had begun for a southern convention, which would meet at Nashville in June 1850 to consider strategy, perhaps secession. While Whigs of the region were cautious about following the South Carolina Democrat, the fact was that the pull of sectional interests weakened national party ties. Had the nation reached the point where politics would array North against South, not Whig against Democrat?[1]

The difficulty of selecting a speaker in the House indicated that such a realignment was occurring. For nearly three weeks neither Howell Cobb, Democrat of Georgia, nor Robert Winthrop, Whig of Massachusetts, won a majority. To be sure, the presence of Free-Soilers as a third force contributed to the stalemate, but significantly some representatives

407

voted according to section rather than party. Finally, on the sixty-third ballot, Cobb became Speaker as much because southern Whigs supported him as because the House resorted to election by a plurality. That this could occur demonstrated the predominance of the slavery issue over economic policies, such as tariff and banking, which had long delineated party loyalties. As the vigor of national parties diminished, the peril of sectional conflict grew.[2]

Webster's usual tardiness spared him the trouble of sitting idly in the Senate to wait for the House to organize. Coming into the chamber on December 21, the day before the parliamentary stall had ended, he met veteran colleagues whose actions he could confidently predict, as well as members of a younger generation who would influence the outcome of this crucial session. There were Clay and Calhoun, with whom he was associated in the public mind as a triumvirate of American statesmen. The Kentuckian had returned to the Senate after an absence of seven years and at seventy-two retained his charm, wit, and boldness—Webster would add some less complimentary traits in evaluating his character. As for his constant opponent from Carolina, Calhoun showed the ravages of age and ill health, but remained as resolute and mentally acute as ever. Others on both sides of the aisle reminded him of countless battles of earlier days: Cass, Benton, Bell, Berrien, Mangum. Among younger men rapidly becoming visible were Douglas, the superb tactician heading the key committee on territories; Jefferson Davis, an articulate defender of slavery; and Seward, well-known for his control of the Whig organization in New York and linked with the White House in his views on current issues.

On Christmas Eve, now that Congress was ready for business, the president sent up his annual message. A straightforward unionist document, it sought to divert the lawmakers from exciting topics and to address those which could be handled practically. Avoiding abstract formulas, Taylor recommended doing the task which could not be postponed, the admission of a new state, California. Certainly something was necessary, for the discovery of gold had precipitated a rush of immigrants so that the area required civil government and already had a population justifying admission to the Union. The sooner the better, the chief executive had reasoned, because bypassing the ordinary territorial stage would also bypass a certain controversy about congressional legislation on slavery there. Let Californians proceed to write a state constitution and thus present an accomplished fact to the national legislature. Actually, they had already done so, with the president's strong encouragement by way of representatives he had sent out. Though the document had not yet been received in Washington, it would be a free-state plan. Whigs might think it strange that Taylor had deviated from the party doctrine of deferring to Congress in making policy; and conservatives might worry that his advisers, apparently including Seward, were promoters of a pronorthern, free-soil solution. Referring also to New Mexico, he favored the same swift procedure of admitting it as a state, as his agents were now urging. Obstacles existed there, however; the region was thinly populated, and neighboring Texas menaced New Mexico by claiming a good deal of the borderland, as far as the Rio Grande and the capital of Santa Fe. Yet the president did not elaborate much on either California or New Mexico and promised a special message about them soon. In effect, the administration hoped to quiet sectional argument by a popular decision of westerners themselves and thereby to sidestep several controversial aspects of slavery.[3]

On January 21, 1850, when the more detailed message on California arrived, Clay decided it was time for a surer hand to take hold.[4] That evening the Kentuckian, now somewhat frail, made his way through the wintry weather to Webster's house to discuss his ideas about a general settlement of the questions facing the country. He said he intended to introduce a set of resolutions acceptable to North and South and designed to eliminate once and for all the friction caused by their several complaints. In his judgment, the republic faced such dangerous problems that it might not survive. Would the Massachusetts senator lend his support? With little hesitation, Webster assured Clay he would, at least on the principles involved, and would study the particulars sympathetically.[5] At two other moments of national trial, when Clay, the pacificator, managed the Missouri Compromise of 1820 and the tariff-nullification adjustment of 1833, Webster had opposed concessions to the South; but he felt they were necessary this time.

On January 29 Clay presented his resolutions to the Senate, briefly explaining each and pleading for conciliation to prevent disunion and a bloody civil war. His formula, he emphasized, would protect the interests of both sections, with neither conceding anything vital. California would come in as a free state, in recognition of the recent course of events. New Mexico would be organized as a territory with no mention of slavery by Congress—that is, unaffected by a Wilmot Proviso. The Texan boundary would be adjusted eastward, allowing New Mexico to have much of the disputed zone; and in return Texas would receive federal compensation to help pay its debts. The slave trade in the District of Columbia, obnoxious to northerners, would be prohibited, but Congress would not exercise its power to prohibit slavery itself there. He would also enact a fugitive-slave law stricter than the existing one. And as further assurance to the South, he would declare, in conformity with a Supreme Court decision a few years before, that Congress had no power to legislate on the interstate slave trade.[6]

Interest in this package of proposals, as well as in the Kentuckian's known eloquence and sense of drama, ensured that his speech of February 5 and 6 would be a highlight of the session. Characteristically, he made the most of the opportunity. As so often in the past when he had displayed his unique talents of expression and argumentation, he made a deep impression upon the hundreds squeezing into the Senate chamber and its adjacent corridors. His theme focused on the indispensability of accommodation at this hour of peril. Put aside the violent spirit of party and localism, he advised. Rely upon common sense, reason, and mutual understanding. To do so required reconciling all the competing interests of free and slave states rather than taking piecemeal action, as in the president's project. True, he endorsed the immediate admission of California, but he would handle the New Mexico–Texas situation differently. The first step must be fixing a boundary instead of pushing statehood ahead and depending upon some future judicial decision on the line, or perhaps upon an unfortunate contest of federal and Texan arms. Then the area should be organized as a territory, without congressional stipulation on slavery. Here he gave great weight to existing Mexican law against the institution and even greater weight to climate and geography unfavorable to the system of slave labor. He did not doubt that Congress had the constitutional power to legislate on the matter, but it was entirely unnecessary to use it. To the North he said, "You have nature on your side." Clay's prescription was a type of popular sovereignty, as those of Taylor and Cass were, but he did not adopt the doctrine specifically; indeed, in his opinion the *territorial legislature* (prior to application for statehood) should not deal with slavery at all. Thus he left the point slightly hazy, and it would continue to be a source of confusion. In general, the senator's comprehensive plan had drawn attention away from the president's recommendations and laid out an agenda for protracted debate.[7]

For some time, Webster did not think the situation was serious. Through January and much of February 1850, he believed that angry speeches on both sides of the question had no productive purpose and only diverted Congress from more important business, especially revision of the tariff. "All this agitation, I think, will subside, without serious result, but still it is mischievous, & creates heart burnings," he wrote. "But the Union is not in danger."[8] In his opinion, nothing new had been said, and the debate now merely inflamed emotions without advancing peace and progress. So he did not take much interest nor feel it worthwhile to say anything himself. He spent many of his days in the Supreme Court, where he had a number of cases. In the meantime his mail brought letters pressing him to assume an active role, though they did not agree on what it should be. From New York and Boston, the message from his conservative friends centered on maintaining the Union by essential compromise.[9] In contrast, others who remembered his sustained opposition to extension of slavery hoped he would continue to resist it in the name of human liberty.[10] However much that course appealed to him, an intensified antislavery agitation disturbed him deeply, and nothing more so than the resolutions adopted by the Garrisonian Massachusetts Antislavery Society at a meeting in Faneuil Hall. The members declared themselves "the enemies of the Constitution, Union, and Government of the United States" because these political institutions shielded the evil of slavery.[11] Such a view appeared in an abolitionist petition arriving in the Senate, calling for a dissolution of the Union. Webster joined the argument for nonreception, and it was so voted, fifty-one to three. Since the days when he had firmly upheld the right of memorializing Congress on slavery, his position had changed.[12] As he said in answer to one plea from an antislavery correspondent, "The effect of moral causes, though sure, is slow," so that it was best to rely upon a gradual operation of Christian principles to dissolve the evil.[13]

Repelled though he was by the clamor about him, he thought it would subside as second thoughts and cooler tempers prevailed. Even after Clay's speeches for dealing with all issues, he predicted that Congress would admit California as a state and postpone everything else. As late as mid-February he believed the Union was safe; yet now he thought about taking the floor to promote reason and calm.[14] Within a few days, however, his optimism gave way to alarm. On February 24 he lamented, "I am nearly broken down with labor and anxiety. I know not how to meet the present emergency, or with what weapons to beat down the Northern and Southern follies, now raging in equal extremes."[15] This sense of crisis, though coming late, confirmed his decision to enter the debate and to give "an honest, truth telling speech, a Union speech"—a signal that he would come out for a general compromise.[16]

Before he did, he knew that Calhoun intended to have his say, which would, of course, be a defense of the South and a rejection of Clay's plan as wholly inadequate. Scheduled to speak on March 4, the South Carolinian was so ill that he often had to take to his bed rather than come to the Capitol; and he had arranged for James Mason of Virginia to read

411

his address to the Senate, though he would attend. Webster predicted what his longtime adversary had in mind as a kind of farewell statement of his credo: "It will be in his usual [vein] of dogmatic assertion, & violent denunciations of the North."[17] Nonetheless, as Calhoun's death seemed imminent, Webster felt personal sorrow at the passing of a man whose intellectual qualities and character he admired. On March 2 he made one of several visits to Calhoun's sickroom, where they talked at length both about former days and about what each would say in the Senate. Although the southerner did not agree with Webster, he showed uncommon pleasure in learning the extent to which his opposite would go to preserve the Union through concession.[18] Word got back to Webster that Calhoun exclaimed that if he should live, he might vote for him for president![19]

Calhoun sat impassively, emaciated but very alert, as Mason read his speech on March 4. It was probably his ablest production of a forty-year career, a valiant defense of the South at midcentury. More an overview and philosophical analysis than a comment on specific measures, it set forth a thesis that the Union was unfortunately endangered by the loss of a North-South equilibrium and that this, in turn, had led to injustices to his section. Over the past fifty years, Calhoun said, the North had gained the balance of power in population and geographic area. This ascendancy was now more serious because the numerical equality of free and slave states would disappear if California were admitted with its proposed constitution. Also as a result of northern preponderance, the South had suffered various wrongs. One had been economic exploitation, notably by a protective tariff. Another was the frightening growth of power of the national government at the expense of states to the point that a federal republic had become "a great national consolidated Democracy." And presently a deplorable consequence might be deprivation of southern rights in the territories. Blame must attach to antislavery fanatics, emboldened by a weak southern position. These agitators, not the defenders of the peculiar institution, were the villains. Already the promise of this nation was disintegrating, as one by one the cords binding it together were snapping: the churches into sectional segments, political parties also, and other relationships as well. The remedy, Calhoun asserted, was not to cry, "Union, Union, the glorious Union," nor to invoke the memory of Washington (as Clay had done), but to stop this agitation and do elemental justice to the South. Protect the constitutional right to hold slaves in all territories, reject Wilmot Provisos and popular sovereignty as unconstitutional, and restore the equilibrium beween sections by an amendment to the Constitution. In short, concede what the slave states asked. If the North refused, southerners would protect themselves. Having traveled to this extreme, the senator closed by swearing his unshakable allegiance to the Union, which he hoped would survive and prosper.[20]

Early on the morning of March 7, people began to gather at the Capitol in anticipation of Webster's speech. The gallery of the small Senate chamber could accommodate only a fraction of those anxious to hear. More managed to move into the members' seating area; and, as usual on such occasions, senators gave their places to women in the audience. At noon, the formalities of opening the day's proceedings began. Then Isaac Walker of Wisconsin, who had the floor to finish his remarks of the previous day, immediately announced he was yielding to Webster, "the one man, in my opinion, who can assemble such an audience."[21] With notes and materials at hand, the senator from Massachusetts began in a low key but with a distinct delivery reaching every listener, proceeded methodically through his main points, and near the end of his three-hour oration rose to heights of patriotism and emotion.[22] Throughout, Calhoun sat in his chair, nearly concealed by those at the front of the room, following the course of argument closely, and interjecting comments several times.[23] The New Englander seemed to direct his words toward the Carolinian, as he had so often in legislative debates of days past.

"I wish to speak to-day, not as a Massachusetts man, nor as a Northern man, but as an American, and a member of the Senate of the United States," he announced. Perceiving a national crisis, he declared, "I speak to-day for the preservation of the Union."[24] His exordium introduced the theme to which he would repeatedly recur: sectional controversy had reached a serious stage in which disunion and war were clear, present dangers. Conditions therefore dictated reconsideration of old, divisive ideas in order to achieve the greater good of peace. All else was secondary. If his premise that this kind of crisis existed was valid, then the logic of compromise would appear strong; but assessments of the situation varied significantly. Furthermore, in Congress and across the land a substantial number of Americans questioned the desirability of union at any price.

Webster relied upon history to build his case. Starting with the immediate background, he reviewed the expansionist character of the recent war, resulting in the acquisition of Mexican land in the Southwest. After Congress had failed to provide a government for California and after the gold rush began, the people there had drafted a free-state constitution and sent representatives and senators to Washington. These events, as well as conditions in New Mexico, aroused the South because it seemed unlikely that slavery would enter the region. That southerners felt this way was attributable to changing views on the institution. It had existed since ancient times and had been justified on various bases. Even the Bible was vague about it, leaving it to individual conscience. In America when the Constitution was adopted, both North and South had disapproved slavery, at least in long-range terms. But the southern position had shifted to positive defense for two reasons. During the 1790s the rising production of cotton had magnified its economic importance; later, an aggressive antislavery movement in the North had caused a strong reaction in its support, actually portraying it as a blessing to mankind.

Thus Webster placed much of the blame for the existing confrontation upon dogmatists attacking slavery as immoral and contrary to religious principles. Picking up Calhoun's allusion to the sectional division of the Methodist church, he regretted the lack of understanding and charity responsible for this rupture. Such persons, he said, "are disposed to mount upon some particular duty, as upon a war-horse, and to drive furiously on and upon and over all other duties that may stand in the way ... They deal with morals as with mathematics; and they think what is right may be distinguished from what is wrong with the precision of an algebraic equation."[25] Still more unfortunate, he thought, was the mischievous agitation of abolitionist societies, in whose activity he found nothing helpful. Opinion on both sides had polarized, a fact illustrated in the excesses of the newspaper press. He conceded that the South had legitimate grievances about antislavery hostility, but he pointed out that the government lacked the constitutional power to interfere with free expression.

Though finding fault with northern extremists, he claimed that the South must also bear responsibility for precipitating the crisis. Calhoun had been wrong, he contended, in charging the North with exploiting the South by means of a congressional majority. The fact was, continued the senator, the slave states stood as a bloc and always had northern sympathizers to advance their interests, particularly by a series of territorial acquisitions, Louisiana, Florida, Texas, and recently the Mexican cession. Had not the Carolinian, when he was secretary of state, connected Texan annexation with slavery? And had not Van Burenite Democrats assisted in that enterprise, only later to advocate the Wilmot Proviso? As for himself, Webster painstakingly vindicated his record. He cited and quoted his speeches from the 1830s onward, from his remarks at Niblo's Saloon through his anti-Texas effort and his no-territory stance during the Mexican conflict. He may have pressed the matter of

414

consistency too far, however, for in his Senate speech of August 1848 he had vowed "that under no circumstances will I consent to the further extension of the area of slavery"; and now, about to endorse Clay's compromise, he seemed to be doing so.[26] In any case, his point was that the South had committed numerous offenses, not only insisting upon expansion of slavery but also resorting to fire-eating rhetoric, making insulting comparisons of slavery and factory labor, and imprisoning black sailors coming into port.

Having completed his excursion through this broad terrain, he addressed the issues before the Senate. With respect to California and New Mexico, he asserted, "I hold slavery to be excluded from those territories by a law even superior to that which admits and sanctions it in Texas [where he would leave it untouched]. I mean the law of nature, of physical geography, the law of the formation of the earth. That law settles forever, with a strength beyond all terms of human enactment, that slavery cannot exist . . ." While not doubting for an instant that Congress possessed power to exclude slavery in the Southwest, he concurred with Clay that there was no need to exercise it there. "I would not take pains uselessly to reaffirm an ordinance of nature, nor to reenact the will of God. I would put in no Wilmot Proviso for the mere purpose of a taunt or a reproach."[27]

He would also join Clay in passing a stricter fugitive-slave law, conformable to a northern constitutional duty. If he could have foreseen the costly impact of that measure, he would probably have been more careful and explicit in discussing it. He merely promised to support a bill coming out of committee, "with some amendments to it"—what sort of amendments he did not specify.[28] At the moment, the Senate was not paying much attention to this highly sensitive subject.

Though willing to accommodate the South in every possible way, Webster could not countenance the extravagant pronouncements of proslavery radicals. How unfortunate it was, he said, to hear talk of dissolving the Union. "Secession! Peaceable secession! Sir, your eyes and mine are never destined to see that miracle." A disruption would produce "such a war as I will not describe, *in its twofold character,*" a hint of racial insurrection, which the South most feared. Besides, he saw practical obstacles making secession impossible. Where would the boundary line be? Could the vital artery of the Mississippi be cut? What would become of the army, the navy, the common property of all the states? Yet a southern convention would soon meet in Nashville to consider the awful step of secession. How could a gathering at that place contemplate "the overthrow of the Union over the bones of Andrew Jackson"?[29]

In looking beyond the immediate questions, Webster proposed federally compensated emancipation. He said the money could be raised from land sales in the Old Northwest, as much as two hundred millions; and to quiet southern uneasiness about racial relations, he favored colonizing freedmen elsewhere. Colonization was a plan that had shown little success over the past thirty years. Perhaps he deserved credit, however, for discussing some ways to deal with slavery in the states other than to exchange condemnation and response.

His peroration was a latter-day version of the one in his reply to Hayne twenty years earlier. Rejecting secession and extolling the republic's values, he pleaded for reconciliation, for dedication to the two ideals of liberty and union. This beneficent government, whose jurisdiction ran from ocean to ocean, was the most dependable vehicle to attain those ideals, he concluded. Though not his best flourish, it was good enough to stir his audience deeply. Indeed the speech as a whole did not measure up to many others for which he was known. Not designed to expound great constitutional, economic, or moral principles, it aimed at the goals of building a bridge between angry sections, of forestalling the threat of secession and war, and therefore of deemphasizing those principles.

Webster's own view of the speech was quite positive. To be sure, he attempted to maintain a certain modesty about it and was well aware of the widespread criticism it provoked.[30] Nevertheless, he came to feel it was "probably the most important effort of my life, and as likely as any other to be often referred to."[31] The best indication of his self-estimate appeared soon afterward when he and his friends began distributing copies on a mass scale. With him in Washington, Edward Curtis arranged for printing and sending out pamphlet editions under Webster's frank and raised money to do so. Curtis solicited at least seven hundred dollars from his connections in New York, while Peter Harvey attempted to match the sum in Boston.[32] Webster felt it was especially desirable to blanket Massachusetts, the members of the state legislature and the bar, the clergy, and other influential persons.[33] More than two hundred thousand copies of the speech were printed in Washington alone, about half distributed free and the rest sold at a penny apiece. More editions came out in Boston and elsewhere. Then, of course, there were reports of the text by innumerable newspapers. For weeks, Webster was revising printer's copy and handling a heavy correspondence generated by the speech.[34]

Popular response encouraged him to believe he had taken the correct course. Mail from all parts of the country brought approval of a patriotic attempt to save the Union by compromise; and though he was pleased to be identified as a spokesman of national harmony, he had a special interest in the impact upon his own state. As is always the case where the shaping of opinion is concerned, sentiment in Massachusetts was influenced by leadership (to an extent, by Webster himself). Boston newspapers, particularly the *Advertiser* and the *Courier,* reported his speech and its aftermath at length and favorably.[35] Edward Curtis and Peter Harvey followed through with their extensive distribution of pamphlets. Then there was a public letter, written by George Ticknor Curtis, commending Webster's contributions in the current crisis. Published on March 25, this letter was signed by eight hundred Bostonians, including Thomas Perkins, Rufus Choate, Franklin Haven, Oliver Wendell Holmes, George Ticknor, Josiah Quincy, and Jared Sparks.[36] At Andover Seminary, Professor Moses Stuart produced an antiabolitionist tract defending Webster against his critics.[37] In the state senate, a resolution criticizing him was debated and defeated decisively. From the rest of New England, the Middle Atlantic states, the South, and the West, favorable comment arrived.[38] Old Ike Hill, his inveterate political foe in New Hampshire, sent praise. So did Joel Poinsett and Francis Lieber of South Carolina, ex-president Tyler of Virginia, and others in Tennessee and Alabama.[39] His New York friends of the commercial world gave him a handsome gold watch.[40] And best of all, the Washington banker William Corcoran canceled his notes of indebtedness.[41]

When he answered letters, he underscored the necessity of North-South understanding to carry the nation through troubled times. Whether to admit slavery into New Mexico, he said, was an irrelevant abstraction; abolitionist agitation must stop; the government should attend to pressing business, by which he meant economic legislation associated with orthodox Whiggery. He tended to depict his position as one of independence, even self-sacrifice, in the midst of angry sectionalism and ideological extremism. Despite the predominantly laudatory character of his incoming correspondence, he knew there were many people who thought just the opposite but who did not write to him.

That he would have trouble at home had already become evident. For one thing, the state's delegation in Congress, including John Davis in the Senate, did not support the compromise. The only exception seemed to be George Ashmun. Even the dependable Winthrop preferred Taylor's plan and regretted Webster's stand. Back home, solidly conservative Edward Everett expressed reservations about his speech, though politely complimenting him with generalities. As for specifics, Everett disliked the scope and arbitrary procedures of the fugitive-slave bill; and as if he were a Free-Soiler, he favored a territorial measure prohibiting slavery. While assuring Webster that he would assist in countering harmful agitation, he warned that there was much dissatisfaction in Boston.[42]

Everett reported correctly. The speech had stimulated an active opposition. Free-Soilers such as Charles Francis Adams and Henry Wilson
waited a while before commencing an attack so as not to alienate more
conservative groups; but on March 25 they met in Faneuil Hall to lay
out their protest. In unrestrained language, they condemned the senator's concessions to slaveholders as unworthy of a wise and good statesman. They suspected that he was bowing to southern demands in order
to promote his presidential ambitions and to placate the lords of the
cotton loom.[43] Through the spring, severe criticism came from Horace
Mann, former secretary of the state school board and now a Free-Soil
representative in Congress. Dismayed that Webster had deserted the
nonextensionist cause, Mann called him a "fallen star." Using the columns of the Boston *Atlas,* which had recently become unfriendly to the
senator, Mann wrote articles finding fault with the plan for opening the
territories to slavery and for returning alleged fugitive slaves without
jury trial. In Webster's defense, Professor Stuart wrote his antiabolitionist pamphlet, and George Ticknor published rejoinders to Mann in the
Boston *Courier.* All this upset Webster so much that he searched for a
way to prevent Mann's reelection.[44]

The indictment of Webster charged him with violating moral and religious principles. It was Theodore Parker who most eloquently and relentlessly put the case on that ground from the time of the meeting in
Faneuil Hall until a famous discourse on Webster's character after his
death. The reformist clergyman spoke of the brilliant talents of this
great man, his consistent opposition to the spread of slavery up to 1850,
and the sudden collapse of his resolve because of the presidential lure.
How tragic it was, Parker declared, that despite all his gifts Webster
lacked an essential humanitarianism, a true religious feeling.[45] The senator himself had discussed the relevance of religious principle in his
speech but concluded that the problem of slavery must be left to individual conscience, not settled by national policy.[46] The antislavery answer
was that this stance would not do, for leaders of the nation had a solemn
obligation to root out an enormous evil. To nourish the evil was a grievous sin. As the Quaker abolitionist John Greenleaf Whittier wrote:

> So fallen! so lost! the light withdrawn
>   Which once he wore!
> The glory from his gray hairs gone
>   Forever more!
> . . . . .
>
> All else is gone; from those great eyes
>   The soul has fled:
> When faith is lost, when honor dies,
>   The man is dead![47]

A present-day assessment of the speech on March 7, 1850, must start with the existing situation. At a perilous hour Webster defended continuance of the Union as America's highest priority, though not denying the importance of many other values. If the United States faced only a choice between a compromise such as Clay proposed and civil war, there is much to be said for his reasoning. Although he did not at first diagnose that kind of crisis, he undoubtedly did by late February when he decided to deliver the speech. From his viewpoint, then, it made sense to avoid argument over slavery in New Mexico, where it would not take hold anyway. His perception of conditions in 1850 caused him to abandon in this instance his nonextensionist position of the preceding dozen years. Although there is of course no way of knowing what would have happened if there had been no compromise, no certainty that secession and war would have come anyway, it is fair to say that Webster's motive was constructive. It was to assure the survival of the nation.[48]

Many northerners did not believe the threat of disunion to be great enough to justify such concessions. In the Senate that belief was often and credibly set forth. Moreover, both Webster's adversaries there and his critics in New England thought the senator was not altogether candid in explaining why he took the direction he did. Was he not conciliating the South mainly to attract support for the presidency? Hints that this was a factor appear in the correspondence of some of his friends, but the evidence that his ambition was the main dynamic of his conduct is too thin to be convincing.[49] Another element, however, did influence him. As he had throughout his career, he gave much weight to the economic basis of national unity. Endless argument about slavery in some far-off region interfered with formation of essential policies affecting the economy. As he remarked during the controversy, "All important public measures are worse than stationary. The tariff, for instance, is losing friends, thro the irritation produced by these Slavery Debates."[50] Revealingly, he wrote to the conservative Bostonians who had sent him the public letter of approval in late March that it was indispensable to avoid these distractions so that the government could resume its normal operations. A harmonious Union would give its attention to improvement of its material welfare.[51] In his judgment, the idea of nationalism and the process of economic development were mutually dependent.

Webster's greatest miscalculation was his devaluation of moral principles in politics. Instead of being diversionary, they were and would be a mighty force. Perhaps slavery would not be practical in New Mexico in any event, but the fact was that the question had become the focus for larger, long-range considerations. There was a rising belief that the time had come for the country to assert its faith in freedom and that to fail to do so would be a surrender of its fundamental ideals. Webster might think this to be false symbolism, but he underestimated the vitality of these moral convictions. Theodore Parker had a point, his personal denunciation notwithstanding.[52]

Northern senators opposing the compromise based their argument largely on moral grounds. Four days after Webster's speech, William Seward entered the debate with a long-prepared, much publicized plea for nonextension of slavery. At the other end of the spectrum from Calhoun, he rejected Clay's plan for the territories just as vigorously as the southerner had. Congress had power to legislate against expansion of the institution, he said, and must not hesitate to do so because of bluffs about leaving the Union. But the passage in Seward's remarks which caught attention went beyond practical politics or the usual precincts of constitutional law: "There is a higher law than the Constitution which regulates our authority over the domain and devotes it to the same noble purposes." Instead of relying upon the law of nature (that is, geography) as Clay and Webster would, Seward invoked a universal principle of justice deduced from natural law.[53] No less committed to that doctrine, the Free-Soil leader John Hale of New Hampshire also spoke repeatedly for nonextension. And in the course of his comment, he dwelt upon Webster's abandonment of antislavery, for which he had declared so unequivocally as late as 1848. As any public figure might, Webster warmly denied any inconsistency but seemed unconvincing.[54]

The Senate spent the first two weeks of April arguing about how to proceed on Clay's resolutions. One question was whether to act on statehood for California separately and immediately or to include the provision on it in a comprehensive bill concerning New Mexico and Texas. Clay opposed combining the issues and derisively labeled that kind of measure an omnibus. But Henry Foote, the short, pugnacious senator from Mississippi, demanded an omnibus and received support from southerners who suspected that if California were admitted now, northerners would make no concessions on slavery in the territories later. Benton fought the idea of combining the several items. And Webster agreed with him that separate disposition of California should precede anything else, though he did stay true to his commitment to settle all outstanding issues in this session, one by one. Over the opposition of Clay, Benton, and Webster, those favoring a combined bill succeeded in getting the Kentuckian's resolutions referred to a special committee of thirteen, chaired by Clay and including a reluctant Webster. Days were spent on whether and how to instruct the committee, with Webster becoming more and more restive about lack of progress. Vote on the substantive issues without delay, he exclaimed, so that Congress could move on to other important subjects. But that did not happen.[55] Benton tirelessly attempted to limit the committee's task; Foote continued to insist upon an omnibus. Eventually their feelings reached such a pitch that Benton advanced upon the Mississippian, who, fearing physical attack, pulled out a pistol. "Let the assassin fire!" Old Bullion cried. The incident led to a prolonged investigation by a committee, which finally condemned both hotheads.[56] Meanwhile, in late April and early May, the committee of thirteen did its work.

Believing that referral to this committee would be unproductive, Webster attended only preliminary meetings, and decided to go home while it prepared a report. Late in the afternoon of April 29, he arrived by carriage at the Revere House in Boston's Bowdoin Square, where he was received by an enthusiastic crowd. Standing in his carriage, into which bouquets of flowers had been tossed, occasionally looking up at spectators waving from windows of neighboring buildings, he responded briefly to a welcoming speech by Benjamin Curtis. He affirmed his intention to support compromise, to calm "excited feelings," to enable government to discharge "the proper business of the country." Alluding to the duty of Massachusetts in the crisis, he emphasized the constitutional obligation to return fugitive slaves.[57] Already he was aware how explosive that topic could be. During his stay, he felt he made headway in promoting a conciliatory spirit by conversations with influential people of the city, with editors of newspapers and members of the legislature. Indeed in that body, resolutions criticizing him and instructing him to vote for nonextension failed by a substantial margin.[58] On his way back to Washington he stopped in New York for more meetings to the same end. The trip north had strengthened his optimism about adoption of the compromise.[59]

On May 8, shortly before Webster returned to the Senate, the committee of thirteen presented recommendations exactly corresponding to Clay's original resolutions—little wonder, for, as chairman, he wrote the report mostly on his own. His one concession—and a large one—was to employ the device of omnibus by uniting California statehood with territorial status for New Mexico and Utah and with a contracted Texan boundary, sweetened by federal payment to that state. A fugitive-slave bill and the prohibition of slave trading in the federal district were separate items. Webster had nothing noteworthy to say about the report until early June, when a lively debate and voting on amendments occurred.[60]

The New Mexico–Utah proposal prohibited the territorial legislatures from acting on slavery in any manner, and thus greatly diminished the likelihood that slavery would be recognized by the state constitutions (the latter to be accepted by Congress with whatever policy on slavery the inhabitants approved). Everyone understood that the direction a new state took would depend upon whether slavery had been allowed during the formative, territorial stage. And Clay's plan, with which Webster concurred, would not admit the institution then. So in the proceedings of June, amendments to change this prohibition appeared. One by Salmon Chase, the Ohio Free-Soiler who would be a cabinet member during the Civil War, would prohibit these territorial legislatures from establishing slavery but seemed to allow a free-soil law. Another by Jefferson Davis, now the most energetic proslavery senator, advanced the opposing option, empowering them to protect slave property.[61] Webster spoke in favor of Clay's proposal on this prestatehood stage because, he reasoned, it postponed the time of decision until it would be representative and fair. But he said that he would vote for the Chase amendment since it would make no difference in the outcome. Douglas and Cass disliked all these limitations on territorial legislatures, for they thought it was at this period that their formula of popular sovereignty could work best. A colloquy between Webster and Cass demonstrated the vigor with which northern Democrats would propound their view, in the long run successfully. Yet at the moment, all amendments failed—those of Chase, of Davis, and another attempt with the Wilmot Proviso by Seward.[62]

On other parts of the omnibus, Webster helped fight off amendments too. Against an effort to uphold the advanced Texan claim to a boundary along the full extent of the Rio Grande, he contended that New Mexico must have much of the disputed land if it was to become a viable state. Texas must check its appetite for a vast territory and take federal compensation, he said. Above all, Congress must fix a line so as to avoid future conflict. He could see that this question might be the crucial one in passing the omnibus.[63] As for California, he also went with the majority in beating back a southern attempt to carve out a slave state in the lower half, arguing that the state must be large because it would never be heavily populated.[64]

In general, the debates of June indicated that a compromise resembling Clay's plan would eventually pass the Senate. So Webster thought as he assessed the parliamentary situation during the series of votes in which the procompromise bloc held together well. His main worry was whether a pivotal group of moderate southerners would continue to cooperate; and that might depend upon the effectiveness of the strategy of an omnibus, still in doubt. But unionists had bought time both in Washington and at the Nashville Convention, where postponement on southern action posed a setback for fire-eaters.[65]

Considered from the perspective of later events, the Senate did not pay as much attention to the fugitive-slave issue as one might expect. Early in the session, in January, James Mason of Virginia had introduced a bill providing for federal mechanisms to return runaways, but senators said little about it. To be sure, Clay had included such a concession to the South in his resolutions, and Webster had supported it on March 7. The problem, in the view of compromisers, was that under the existing statute of 1793 recovery of fugitives depended upon state courts and officers, neither able nor inclined to assist. With the rise of antislavery opinion, many states had passed personal-liberty laws forbidding their judges and magistrates from helping.[66] In 1842 the Supreme Court had decided that this was a federal responsibility, that in fact any state legislation might be unconstitutional.[67] In 1850 many southerners felt the need for a new, separate system of national action, while a good many northerners looked upon "slave catching" as abhorrent and, in some cases, a way to kidnap free blacks.

Webster recognized how controversial the subject was but believed Congress should do something about it. Even Everett qualified his praise of the senator's speech of March 7 by warning that the pending bill might be so arbitrary as to excite northern feeling greatly. Other mail brought the same message.[68] And Horace Mann's hostile articles in the Boston *Atlas* mercilessly attacked him for abandoning human rights on this question. He did get support, such as from the future Supreme Court justice Benjamin Curtis in remarks at his reception in Bowdoin Square in late April. George Ticknor Curtis, a brother, also aided him by responses to Mann in the *Advertiser*.[69] Moses Stuart, the admiring professor at Andover, came to his defense as well.[70] Webster himself made a full statement of his position in mid-May when he wrote a public letter to people in Newburyport. Reviewing the historical and legal dimensions, he found that as early as the colonial period there had been provisions for rendition of runaway servants. Then and in 1793, when Congress enacted the current law, northerners had readily affirmed slaveholders' rights. When antislavery agitation began, however, free states had seriously interfered by popular resistance and by crippling legislation. The South, he concluded, therefore had a legitimate complaint that the fugitive-slave clause of the Constitution (Article IV, section 2), one of the original constitutional compromises, had become a nullity. As for the commonly voiced criticism that a federal law must provide for a jury trial (neither the old statute nor the present bill did so), Webster confidently declared that none was necessary, since return of fugitives was neither a criminal nor a common-law action in terms of the Bill of Rights.[71]

However much the senator declared his certainty that summary procedure was perfectly valid, he had already shaped a proposal for jury trial. In February, soon after the Senate bill had been reported, he had drafted an amendment so providing, though he had not mentioned it on March 7 in calling for a new law.[72] Through May, he continued to say that a jury trial was not constitutionally required, though thinking it would be expedient. Meanwhile he consulted Justice John McLean on the details of his amendment and got some suggestions from the Ohioan, who had a good deal of experience with these cases on the circuit. But he waited a while longer before introducing it.[73]

At last, during general debate concerning the compromise on June 3, he introduced his proposal, representing, he revealed, the advice "of a high judicial authority." Unfortunately he simply presented it without explanation or argument; nor did he speak about it later.[74] Perhaps he reasoned that others were also working for a jury clause and could take the lead, while, as a friend of accommodation, he should avoid undue irritation of the South. If so, he underestimated the negative effect of his silence in the North, where his amendment was unnoticed or soon forgotten.[75]

While Congress was immersed in seemingly endless talk about the compromise, an unexpected event changed the situation drastically. The president died. On Independence Day, Taylor had sat in the hot sun during a long ceremony at the Washington Monument and, returning to the White House, had consumed a great deal of food and cold liquids. Whether this sequence had caused his illness the next day or whether he had contracted cholera his physicians were apparently unable to determine. The president died the evening of the ninth.[76] Then ensued congressional resolutions and appointment of committees of arrangements, the swearing in of the vice-president, and the inevitable eulogies. Playing a prominent role in the process, Webster had cause to reflect upon the past and present.[77] Publicly he showed more than perfunctory regret at the death of the chief executive. His remarks in the Senate, laudatory as the occasion demanded, expressed a sincere sentiment, doubtless shared by many Americans, that the old soldier had performed his recent duties with ability and integrity at a time of trial and, though Webster did not say it, more effectively than he had predicted.[78] The senator could never forget the disappointment he had felt when the politically innocent general had won this office; nor had he ever established any useful line of communication with him as president.[79] But appointments to office had been better than he had feared, even though he perceived some as mistakes.[80] More important was Taylor's position on the current slavery controversy. Seeking to avoid sectional antagonism by limiting national action to the minimum, thereby inclining toward the free-soil side, he was known to oppose the comprehensive Clay compromise and would almost certainly have vetoed it. Whatever his personal feelings about the president's death were, Webster knew that the prospect for an overall settlement had definitely brightened.

Millard Fillmore, the new chief executive, posed no problem about compromise. A conservative friendly to Webster and Clay, he could be counted on to use the power of his office to pass the measures. He was an experienced, cautious politician up from the ranks in New York, with several congressional terms behind him. For now, one fundamental fact stood out: he had long been an intraparty adversary of the Seward-Weed wing. For this reason alone, he would have nothing to do with a higher-law doctrine on slavery in the territories and would not irritate or frighten moderates north or south.[81]

As the fate of the compromise shifted from Taylor's hands to Fillmore's, Webster's role in events was also about to change. The very evening Taylor died, Fillmore decided to appoint Webster secretary of state, though nearly two weeks passed before he did so. Anxious to ensure strength to his administration, beginning as it did in worrisome circumstances, he probably selected Webster for his domestic more than for diplomatic contributions.[82] The move also resulted from his conclusion that he must completely reorganize the cabinet, whose usefulness had already been declining. Indeed, Taylor himself had contemplated replacements.[83] In launching this general overhaul, Fillmore had to take some time to choose and recruit persons for the departments. From the start, Webster assisted, advising about some posts and acting as an intermediary. The outcome was formation of a conservative Whig cabinet, including Thomas Corwin in the Treasury and John Crittenden as attorney general, all likely to agree on pending questions.[84]

Webster welcomed a return to the State Department, despite a few protestations. The only difficulty was the additional personal expenses he felt he would incur, expenses he could not afford.[85] Immediately his well-to-do friends in Massachusetts and New York came to the rescue. Franklin Haven, James Mills, the Grinnells and Griswolds, Morris Ketchum, and various other merchants, industrialists, and bankers, forty altogether, each pledged five hundred dollars to a fund for his benefit. By now, subsidization had become a pattern. In view of his great services and his sacrifices to perform them, it was just and desirable to ensure that he not be troubled about mere money.[86] On July 22 he received and accepted his appointment. The transfer satisfied him all the more when he heard that Winthrop would replace him in the Senate and that a true adherent of compromise, Samuel Eliot, would take Winthrop's seat in the House.[87]

Soon after Webster left the Senate to become secretary of state, the omnibus was put to the test and failed. In an intricate sequence of moves, its opponents of various persuasions dismantled it a piece at a time, beginning with its most vulnerable part, the provision of the Texas–New Mexico boundary. An amendment to determine the line by a commission and to permit temporary occupation by Texas, followed by a countermove to secure the rights of New Mexico, led to detachment of the bill's section on that territory. This move permitted blocs dissatisfied with sections on Texas and California to strike them too, so that by July 31 nothing remained in the omnibus but the Utah territorial bill. At this juncture the harassed Clay left for a respite in Newport, where he remained through most of August. During these critical weeks Douglas directed an effort to put through the compromise by dealing with its elements separately; and his parliamentary skill materially contributed to success. When Clay returned, everything except the measure on slave trade in the District had passed the Senate, with the House falling in line by September 17.[88]

Anxiously watching these events, though no longer a major participant, Webster nevertheless exerted some influence upon their course. He helped move along the Texan boundary bill, which was the first part of the compromise to pass the Senate on August 9. The dispute between New Mexico and Texas about their common boundary had worsened to the point that military conflict seemed possible. New Mexico was trying to establish a state government, with the help of the commander of a United States Army unit at Santa Fe, while Texas contemplated sending in troops. In an exchange of letters with Texan Governor Peter Bell, Webster apparently deterred rash action until Congress decided what to do; and in documents he drafted for Fillmore to send up to Capitol Hill he spurred legislative action. Soon both houses had agreed to a boundary bill, giving New Mexico plenty of territory and Texas ten millions to pay its debt. Though there is no evidence that he had them in mind, the holders of Texas bonds, who were lobbying busily, may also have paved the way toward this arrangement.[89]

Little is known about the tactics Webster used to persuade the rank and file of Congress to adopt a compromise, but undoubtedly there were conversations and pressures, including the patronage, as well as the very presence of this prominent advocate of adjustment in the administration.[90] What is clear is that he sought support particularly from the eight Massachusetts representatives, with dismal results. Reconciling himself to solid opposition from the two senators, John Davis and Robert Winthrop, he continued to hope through mid-September that members of the lower house would finally see the light. He found it embarrassing, disheartening, to fight the battle alone. Northern Whigs, infected with free-soilism and abolitionism, were acting as dishonorably, he remarked, as southern disunionists. He knew that Horace Mann would vote against every concession to slaveholders, but he deceived himself in thinking that most of the others from the Bay State would be reasonable.[91] When voting occurred, he found that his estimates had been far too optimistic. Only one of eight voted for the fugitive-slave bill—three abstained. Only two of the delegation were generally for the compromise. One of these was Samuel Eliot, the recently elected member from Boston as Winthrop's replacement. George Ashmun, whom Webster had consistently classified as very reliable, did not cast a vote on any question except the relatively unimportant measure against slave trading in the District.[92] Obviously the secretary's relationship to the Whig party in Massachusetts had entered another troubled period.

On September 20 the president signed the last of the bills into law. Though they had come to him by a somewhat different route than expected, they strongly resembled Clay's resolutions of eight months earlier. California was a free state; New Mexico and Utah were organized territories; the Texan boundary was set; a strict fugitive-slave law was in effect; slave trading in Washington was now illegal. But they represented the work of Douglas and moderate Democrats as well as of Clay and moderate Whigs. Congress had shuffled off the controversial question of slavery in the territories to the people there at the time of admission to statehood, as Clay had recommended; but Douglas had deleted all restrictions on the power of territorial legislatures over slavery, so that at this early stage popular sovereignty could operate. That was the Douglas-Cass formula, a Democratic solution, which would be extended to Kansas four years later. Every measure in the package of compromises had passed separately, with different kinds of majorities for each (just as Webster had predicted they might). Clearly the Compromise of 1850, as a recent historian has said, was not a general, lasting agreement of North and South at all but only a patchwork, at best an armistice, to postpone vexing problems for a little while.[93]

Chapter 26

CHARACTER

When Webster became secretary of state the first time, in 1841, he was approaching his sixtieth birthday; and through the next decade of active involvement in public affairs, his interests, values, and habits largely remained the same as they had been in middle life. He continued to experience the satisfactions of fame and well-being, together with disappointments and misfortunes. Conscious of his status as a popular, powerful figure on the political scene, perhaps unavoidably he acted out his part in the ways expected of him. The natural consequence of attaining a God-like image was to reinforce his self-esteem, with the result that he often appeared too solemn and pompous, too prone to overdramatize. Yet a fuller view of the man revealed warmth in social relations, a willingness to listen to and profit from what others had to say, indeed an acute awareness of his own frailties. His character encompassed contrasting virtues and defects, both derived from standards of behavior established in his earlier years.

Webster's physical features—the thickset body, massive head, cavernous eyes and dark complexion, an overall indication of vigor and will—continued to make an impression upon people. To be sure, overindulgence at the table had further increased his bulk, new lines furrowed his face so that his visage was all the more somber, and his once coal-black hair was graying and thinning.[1] Yet how imposing he was! When he spoke to the Senate, the Supreme Court, or the public at some interesting moment, he wore his usual blue coat with gilt buttons and a buff waistcoat, which had become a kind of trademark.[2] His presence was as striking as ever, his voice strong and sonorous, his manner completely

Caroline Le Roy Webster, by George P. A. Healy, ca. 1845

assured. Observers felt that more often now, when debate dragged on or the setting seemed uninspiring, he lapsed into detachment, but he had done that when he was younger.[3]

That he continued to be so energetic resulted from his uncommonly good health. He escaped serious illness until he was seventy. As he had for a long while, each fall he suffered from catarrh, which brought on inflammation, interminable sneezing, and watering of the eyes—an inconvenience for some weeks, though by no means life-threatening. He allowed it to bother him a good deal, searching unsuccessfully for medicinal remedies and fleeing to the New Hampshire hills for relief. Frequently he resorted to a secretary for writing, even for reading to him.[4] He complained occasionally of rheumatism, too, but it did not interfere with fishing, hunting, and tramping around Marshfield. More ominous

Daniel Webster, daguerreotype by Albert Southworth
and Josiah Hawes, 1850

was the beginning of trouble with diarrhea in 1851, which could signal
difficulty in vital organs.[5]

Though giving major attention to politics and law, he did not altogether neglect the world of the mind. Among his friends were the intel-
lectuals George Ticknor, Edward Everett, and Rufus Choate, with
whom he often enjoyed an evening's conversation about literature, classical or modern. But his chief interest lay in history, which he habitually
used in his legal and political argumentation. He even thought of writing a three-volume history of the United States from the Revolution
through Washington's administration, but never proceeded beyond a
brief outline. His approach to historical writing, however, appears in an
address he delivered to the New York Historical Society in February
1852, when he spoke of the relevance of history to existing social conditions and issues, including the peril to the Union posed by radicals.[6]

Webster's occasional addresses reveal much about his character, for
they provided him a broad scope for expressing his ideas. His most notable speech of this kind during the 1840s commemorated the battle of
Bunker Hill when the monument there was completed. On the anniversary of that battle, June 17, 1843, he returned to the site where in 1825
he had spoken to thousands who had assembled for the laying of the

cornerstone.[7] Again he had an opportunity to review the history of America, its progress and its principles, before an enormous audience and to convey his thoughts on this grand theme also to his fellow citizens across the country, indeed to future generations. Perhaps this did not rank as high as several of his famous speeches, nor quite equal the first one at Bunker Hill; but it closely resembled them in its eloquent statement of nationalism.

Local residents had good reason to celebrate not only the anniversary of the Revolutionary battle but also the completion, after twenty years of planning, fund raising, and agonizingly slow construction, of the stone obelisk rising two hundred feet from the hilltop. Thomas Perkins and a few others who had led the effort could remember the arguments about design, the ingenious methods of quarrying Quincy granite, the pioneering use of a horse railroad to carry the material to boats which would convey it to Charlestown. Now it seemed fitting to recognize that achievement with a ceremony more elaborate than Bostonians had ever witnessed and with another oration by the city's leading statesman. And so they did.[8] The progress of the affair resembled that of previous grand events. In early morning the Common overflowed with people—militia units, musicians, labor and commercial groups, diverse associations and societies, public officials, President Tyler and his cabinet. After a few hours they started moving through the narrow streets, across the Charles, and to the monument. It was midafternoon before Webster began speaking to the vast assembly of about a hundred thousand, perhaps only half of them able to hear even his powerful voice.[9]

He began still more modestly than was his custom by taking a good bit of time to remark upon this wondrous memorial and to recognize those who had contributed to its construction, as well as other prominent guests.[10] He paid a special courtesy to Tyler, who was currently making a circuit of northern states and getting a cool reception from the disenchanted everywhere.[11] Then on to a brief résumé of the British attack against the redoubt on the hill, bravely defended by the patriots of '75. It was here, he said, that the principles of American liberty had been at stake, soon to give life to this nation. With his turning point identified, Webster dropped back to early colonial years and explored the origins of these principles. He was on familiar ground, for he had surveyed it often since his Plymouth oration of 1820 and his first speech here in 1825. In many phases of colonial growth—commercial, religious, intellectual, legal, and political—he found the threads of freedom's fabric. Of all of them, he prized representative government most, as in the Virginia House of Burgesses and the New England general courts. But as a lawyer

431

he also greatly valued the doctrine of equality before the law, the judicial process, and, of course, the protection of property. For these institutions there were English antecedents, he conceded, but America itself advanced them.

Whether the principles would survive depended upon a strong attachment of all sections and interests to the Union. And to maintain that national commitment, the people could find no better inspiration than the character of Washington. This allusion enabled the speaker to move to his ready supply of praise of the first president. He followed the custom of the day in consulting the example of Washington on almost any political question. At the summit of these expressions of nationalistic sentiment, he exclaimed that every young person who saw this monument ought to cry out: "Thank God, I—I also—am an American!"

The Bunker Hill ceremony was a true spectacle, probably more extensive and colorful than any such celebration in the United States until then. Observers felt that they had experienced something unique, yet it was no more than an advanced version of what was happening throughout the young republic. Whether in town halls, courthouse squares, or city parks, Americans gathered to watch and listen, to feel the impact of speeches recalling their past and predicting national growth and prosperity. The scene on many occasions elsewhere must have resembled to some degree the one that William Plumer saw at Bunker Hill: "The great mass of people were on their feet standing still with all eyes intent upon the speaker; and every now and then the whole mass was in action, moving backwards and forwards . . . connected with the orator, and responsive to his action on the minds of his hearers."[12]

Webster's relationship to his family affords another perspective on his character. The 1840s were years of both genuine happiness and deep sorrow for Webster and his wife Caroline. Notwithstanding what seemed to be inescapable debts, they enjoyed material circumstances which were not only very comfortable but, in some ways, luxurious. Imposing homes, excellent food, and a staff of servants contributed to the pleasures of their lives. In Washington and at Marshfield a constant flow of visitors and guests suited them both. Their marriage was sound and generally smooth. Now past forty, tall and slender, Caroline was not judged to be beautiful, but she dressed elegantly and projected a refinement suggestive of her upper-class background.[13] Her father, the prominent New York merchant Herman Le Roy, died at an advanced age in early 1841, the very time of Harrison's fatal illness and Tyler's takeover, so that Webster traveled back and forth between the capital and Manhattan in the following months.[14] As for the estate, he and Caroline ap-

parently did not inherit much. There had been a generous marriage settlement years ago; besides, the Le Roy family was a large one.[15] Busy at
the State Department and trying to outfit a new house in Washington,
the secretary lost patience with her for staying in New York longer than
he wished.[16] But that was nothing new, for she often left him alone while
she went off to that city to visit relatives and friends. In truth, she cared
little about the concerns of politicians and lawyers. Because only a few of
their letters to each other survive, their relationship necessarily remains
obscure. One can infer that it was satisfactory, seldom quarrelsome, but
only moderately affectionate. By the standards of the day, she appeared
to be a good wife, as a companion and manager of a household, as well
as a thoughtful stepmother.

Of Webster's three living children, Fletcher was the closest to him.
After a disastrous effort to make his fortune in western land speculation
and running an Illinois farm, the young man gave up in 1841 and became his father's chief clerk in the State Department, an inconsistent use
of patronage by a Whig who had attacked the Jacksonian spoils system.
When Webster was leaving office in the spring of 1843, he not only set
up the appointment of Caleb Cushing to head the mission to China but
also placed his son as Cushing's secretary. For two years Fletcher was out
of the country but sent frequent letters with interesting details of travel
to East Asia.[17] Upon his return he struggled with a law practice and
hoped something would turn up, with good prospects when the new
Whig administration of Taylor came to power in 1849. Webster tried
hard to obtain the office of district attorney in Massachusetts for him;
though he failed, his influence must have had an effect, for his son later
became surveyor for the port of Boston. So Fletcher had repeatedly relied upon him to get ahead and seemed still under his wing. Though
having only average talent, Fletcher was dependable, indeed a mainstay
for Webster. Father and son, with some similar qualities, had an easy,
positive relationship.

Fletcher had married Caroline White, daughter of the Websters' well-
to-do friend Stephen White and niece of Justice Joseph Story. In the late
1830s and the 1840s, six children were born, one named Daniel and another Caroline after their grandparents.[18] Webster was delighted with
this growing family; and since they lived in Boston and Marshfield, they
became virtually part of his expanded household. More and more, he
counted on Fletcher to carry on his name and reputation.

His daughter Julia, still in her twenties, lived in Boston with her husband, Sam Appleton, nephew of Nathan, the Whig merchant-manufacturer. Their family also grew rapidly, with five children born in seven
years—one named Daniel and another Caroline, matching Fletcher's

tribute to their parents.[19] Webster continued to be proud of Julia, a gifted young woman, intelligent, considerate, and quite religious. In physical features she resembled her father, in personal traits her mother, Grace.

Edward, his other son, had all the advantages a young person could wish.[20] A graduate of Phillips Exeter and Dartmouth, he had gone to England with the family and spent a year and a half on the Continent, mainly in Italy under the tutelage of Edward Everett. After coming home, he studied law in his mildly committed fashion until 1843. As Webster was leaving the cabinet, he arranged something for Edward, just as he had for Fletcher. For nearly three years, his son worked with the Maine boundary commission, to survey the line of the Ashburton treaty and to assist in writing the report.[21] By this time the Mexican War had begun, and he decided to join the Massachusetts Volunteers. Caleb Cushing became the colonel of the outfit, Edward a captain. Owing to antiwar sentiment in the state legislature, Cushing's troops got little support, financial or otherwise. So when the contingent sailed for Texas in early 1847, dissatisfaction prevailed from top to bottom.[22] Through much of that year, these troops had garrison duty along the Texas border, though Edward contracted a fever and came back to Marshfield for a while in the summer. Not long after returning south, he marched with his men from Veracruz to Mexico City and arrived in December after that place had fallen to the Americans. All along, Webster had sought to advance his son's status by using contacts with Cushing, with the secretary of war, and even with General John Wool in northern Mexico. Though Edward did not obtain a better assignment, he was promoted to major and fared well enough for a military neophyte.[23]

It was ironic that he had taken up arms in a war which his father had feared and opposed throughout its progress. Still, Webster did not complain about his joining up; nor did he worry much about his being a casualty in combat. As if he had a premonition, he told Edward that "what I fear most of all, is the *climate*. Pray study to guard agt the effects of climate, in every possible form."[24] When his son came home on sick leave, his concern appeared justified. Later, in February 1848, he received an alarming letter from Edward's servant, Henry Pleasants, from a camp near Mexico City. Pleasants wrote that he had been tending the young officer during a serious illness (later identified as typhoid).[25] Soon a report arrived that Edward had died on January 23. "I hardly know how I shall bear up under this blow," Webster wrote. "I have always regarded it as a great misfortune, to outlive my children ... But the Will of Heaven be done in all things." He may have agreed with Julia's reaction: "He went forth to a wicked & cruel war, & there he has died, like many before him."[26] Through the following weeks, as he waited for the body to arrive home, he was deeply affected. One solace was that George Healy painted a portrait of Edward as he had appeared as a boy. Webster judged it beautiful and vowed to "keep it before my eyes as long as I live."[27]

Soon a second blow fell. Julia, always somewhat frail, had become ill in December not long after giving birth to her fifth child; and her condition, at first thought to be a cold, was worsening. It was severe respiratory trouble, probably tuberculosis, to which the family was vulnerable. Eventually Webster realized that there was little hope of stopping the steady course of the disease; she died on April 28. May 1 was a heart-rending day, for it was the day not only of Julia's funeral but also of the arrival of Edward's body from Mexico. In front of his house at Marshfield Webster planted two weeping elms in memory of his son and daughter.[28]

His farm remained his principal residence, as it had been since the early thirties. Having expanded it to a large estate of hundreds of acres and steadily improved its appearance and productivity, he looked upon Marshfield as an indispensable outlet for personal interests, most of them outdoors. Nearly every day he was there, moving around the property from the pine forest on the west to the splendid white beach along the ocean a mile to the east. The barns and small structures for recreational purposes, a pond with ducks and geese, the salt marshes, the fields of corn, oats, potatoes, and turnips, the cattle, swine, and sheep roaming the broad pastures—all came into view as he walked about. He could see much of the scene from the highest point at Bascom Hill, where he had put up a hundred-foot pole to display the flag on special days.[29] Whenever he could, he and a favorite helper, red-shirted Seth Peterson, sailed offshore to fish for cod and haddock. Rising at four in the morning, spending the day in sport or supervision of farm work, he had dinner in late afternoon with such guests and members of the family as were on hand. Afterward they would sit on the front piazza, cooled by the evening breeze, then go into a parlor or the library, a new addition on the west side of the house.[30]

Not much changed as the years passed, except extension of his acreage northward, continuing enlargement of the old house, and construction of the Old Colony Railroad down from Boston. When the Senate was not in session, when business at the State Department slackened, or when cases in court did not interfere, he spent most of his time at Marshfield. Being there buoyed his spirits and allowed him to relax.

With farm managers, housekeepers, and servants, he was as amiable and communicative as with Philip Hone or Richard Blatchford or some other important visitor.[31] A good conversationalist, he was full of humorous anecdotes and information without being overbearing. Early in the morning, he often broke into song when the freshness and beauty of the new day put him in a good mood.[32]

Equally proud of the Elms, his farm in New Hampshire, he also sank money into improvement and expansion there. Every year he went up for a few days, occasionally for a couple of weeks, to stay at this place near the Merrimack and the surrounding hills. All the memories associated with it made such trips particularly pleasant. In his later years, looking upon the cemetery adjacent to the house or the site along Punch Brook where he was born led him to recall his youth, his parents, and events a half-century ago. Here, too, a good many visitors from a distance and from the neighborhood added interest to his leisure hours.[33] One time, he gave a party for several hundred people at a pond close by. Fishing, lively conversation, and an ample supply of chowder made the affair quite agreeable—no doubt Webster used his special recipe for the occasion.[34] Perhaps the greatest change affecting Franklin resulted from construction of the Northern Railroad. Laid out to connect Boston with other lines in the Connecticut Valley and on as far as Montreal, the road would give a decided impulse to New Hampshire's economy. So Webster thought. It would resemble the Erie Canal, he predicted, in stimulating agriculture and industry, because it facilitated transportation in New England dramatically. For example, he could now ship large quantities of wood to Boston at seven and a half dollars a cord.[35] Even so, the railroad created a personal problem, for it ran just fourteen feet from the corner of his house. Nothing to do but move the structure, he felt; but in a few months he decided to tolerate the noise and smoke, a small price for progress.[36]

Though he sometimes seemed to value his farms mainly for the personal satisfaction they provided, he did not overlook agricultural operations. To his managers, John Taylor at the Elms and Porter Wright and Seth Weston at Marshfield, he sent unending instructions on all matters, however small: what crops to plant in what fields, how to fertilize the soil, which cattle to keep and which to slaughter or market, what part of the land to use for pasture, and so forth.[37] The scale of farming got larger—perhaps more so in livestock than in crops—and so did the capital investment. Toward the end of the depression during the early 1840s, he had to cut back for a while. And again in 1850 he felt uncommonly pressed for money as past miscalculations caught up with him.[38]

With regret, he left his country home each year to spend several months attending the Senate, and longer during his two periods as secretary of state. Until 1841 he had taken rooms at a boardinghouse or hotel at the capital; but when he entered the cabinet, he decided to buy a house. He found one available at Sixteenth and H, facing President's Square (later known as Lafayette Park). It had belonged to the late Walter Swann, one of Webster's fellow lawyers in the Supreme Court, and was large and expensive in terms of property values then. The price was fifteen thousand, which he raised by borrowing. A handsome building, it had an unusually attractive garden and a carriage house. Months passed before all the remodeling and refurnishing Caroline had planned were completed.[39] Having such an establishment, the Websters entertained a good deal, especially during the Ashburton negotiations. Yet it seemed that almost as soon as they were settled, he began thinking of leaving the State Department and did so in spring 1843. This decision compelled them to give up the place. Unable to sell, he finally managed to rent it to Richard Pakenham, the British minister, but wondered when he could get rid of the mortgage.[40]

Upon returning to the Senate in December 1845, he rented a modest two-story house on quiet Louisiana Avenue, just north of the Capitol; and this remained his Washington residence for the next seven years. Though he described it as being the size of "two pigeon-boxes," he felt it was adequate, probably more than that, for he and Caroline often gave sizable dinner parties there. Nonetheless, they never looked upon any living quarters in the District as permanent. Marshfield was their home.[41]

Notwithstanding Webster's essential happiness in his later years, his financial condition never ceased to bother him. As he had since he was a young man, he spent more than he earned, owed more than he could pay, and moved from one problem to another, ever deeper in debt. His high standard of living and unshakable habit of overcommitment constantly left him in difficulty. In addition to expenditures on the huge establishment at Marshfield, on the Elms farm, and on residences in Washington, his disastrous speculative ventures in the thirties put him in a situation from which he could not recover. Handsome professional fees and income from salaries of office could not offset these liabilities. Month after month, his account books showed more borrowing, usually at short term, to satisfy creditors; or it was a matter of renewal of notes, sometimes of waiting until he faced legal action for default.[42] It was depressing. It nagged at him. "A great portion of all the ills which I have felt in my life, except family misfortunes," he lamented, "have arisen from too great a carelessness about saving & investing my hard earnings."[43]

He had hoped that his agreement with the Bank of the United States, just before he entered Harrison's cabinet in March 1841, would allow him to recoup. By taking more than thirteen thousand acres of his western land holdings, the bank erased his debt of $114,000 at its offices.[44] Though he thought this settlement was final, he soon learned otherwise. Instead of being in good order, as Webster had stipulated, many land titles turned out to be defective because of missteps of registry or were not negotiable because of liens or tax delinquency. Periodically he had to ransack his trunk of papers at home to supply corrected lists of the property. When the bank closed its doors the next year, the trustees, who were seeking to liquidate whatever they could, insisted he observe the agreement strictly.[45] And then the always sympathetic Biddle died, further increasing his difficulties. During the mid-1840s Samuel Jaudon, his close friend who had previously been associated with the BUS, stepped in to straighten out the tangle and to raise money from sources in New York. "I am ashamed, & mortified to have given you & other friends so much trouble," Webster wrote. "I begin to feel a sense, if not of humiliation, yet of regret, & awkwardness, at what has occurred."[46] At last, in December 1847, he had done all he could or would do and, probably with justification, felt he had fulfilled his obligations.[47] But he did promise to pay a new debt of $38,000, arising from a foreclosed mortgage.[48]

Trouble about his western lands seemed interminable. Although he had transferred much of them to the BUS, he kept some, including the eleven-hundred-acre farm in Peru, Illinois. After the depression, its value rose; and in 1849, with completion of the Illinois-Michigan Canal and projection of the Illinois Central Railroad, Webster thought he would finally realize something from the property.[49] He could not expect a net profit, however, for he had been compelled, time and again, to take care of debts left by Henry Kinney, his agent in that area in the late thirties and now a promoter in Texas. Through the 1840s his old endorsements of Kinney's notes forced him to pay thousands of dollars, while the irrepressible Kinney wrote him unabashedly for new assistance, such as a federal appointment.[50] He also retained some holdings in Wisconsin, though not nearly enough to make up for all he had invested there. He calculated that purchases by one agent alone, not the most active of several, had resulted in a loss of five or six thousand dollars.[51] Indirectly, by way of that agency, he had a filmy claim to 250,000 acres in Tennessee. Here, too, the outcome was disheartening because of contested and faulty titles.[52]

Of all his joint speculations, those with Caleb Cushing proved the most embarrassing. As a young follower of Webster in the 1830s, Cushing had provided large sums for western acquisitions, one of them a sizable part of the new town of Rock Island, Illinois. Taking advantage of this friendship, Webster postponed the debt for years. Finally Cushing's patience gave way, and he pressed Webster for payment. The latter responded with a waiver of the statute of limitations on the obligation, which in 1848 was reckoned as $4,400 on the Rock Island tract, though the total of all loans was larger.[53] Hearing that the town had begun to grow more rapidly, Webster conveyed his portion to Cushing as payment, only to learn that it had been sold for taxes. If Cushing would go west, however, Webster thought his associate could buy off the tax claim and come out all right. Later he did so but reported that the property was worth much less than believed.[54] Through 1851 and 1852 Cushing's pleas for a settlement of the entire debt brought apologies and delays. Meanwhile Webster sent him a six-month note for $2,500, which he could not pay off when it became due.[55] In September 1852 Cushing showed his complete exasperation by writing, "I have never been able to conceive why for so many years you have refused [to settle] . . . Why, out of the large estate you have, you should be unwilling to do this, I cannot conceive." Whereupon Webster sent him another note for $2,500, with the hope Cushing could turn it "to some account."[56]

Another dream of immense profits which went unfulfilled involved stock in the Clamorgan association, claiming an extensive area in Arkansas and Missouri. After the depression set in, Webster tried through the agency of Virgil Maxcy to market his shares abroad. Maxcy found no foreign buyers but sold a minor part of them to James Murray, a New York merchant. In 1840 Murray paid Webster about twenty thousand, though most of it was in stocks of the moribund national bank and the state of Illinois. This transaction proved to be rather lucky, since the price of the stock plunged soon after he received and unloaded it. Murray complained that he had overpaid Webster as a result of transferring the stock to him in advance of the installment dates.[57] On the other hand, Webster's endorsements of notes by Kinney and Levi Turner for purchase of Clamorgan stock left him with a debt of ten thousand when they defaulted. Attempting to evade the burden, he was sued; and after a vigorous but fruitless defense in the courts, he was ordered to make the notes good.[58] Whenever possible, he disposed of his stock for what little it would bring and suffered a substantial loss.[59]

The full story of Webster's financial trials might fill a volume. If so, a leading aspect would be the repeated and complicated mortaging of his homes. When he took the Swann house near the White House in 1841, he agreed to pay about fifteen thousand for it, almost all by borrowing. His arrangement at first was with the Bank of the Metropolis in Washington, but he then got help from his connections in New York, notably Moses Grinnell and Richard Blatchford, to finance the deal.[60] When he vacated the house in 1843, he could not sell it, struggled with the mortgage, and required several rescues by his friends.[61] Finally, in 1849 the Washington banker William Corcoran, a dependable source of money, bought the house for his own use.[62] As for Marshfield, there may not have been a time when it was unencumbered by a mortgage. He used it often as security for loans at the Boston branch of the BUS, and these debts lasted longer than the bank itself. A problem in mortgaging Marshfield was that the property was already pledged to fulfill the terms of the marriage settlement by Le Roy of twenty-five thousand in return for a life estate for Caroline. A conflict with that obligation could be troublesome.[63] There were mortgages on the Elms farm, too, but he managed to pay them off.[64]

The list of his debts did not stop here. One which particularly worried him was a mortgage of five thousand on a house and lots in Hoboken (acquired in exchange for some western lands).[65] He also had recurrent payments to make in his land operations with David Webster in Maine and New Brunswick.[66] Creditors and alleged creditors were forever demanding satisfaction; some sued when he did not comply.[67] Webster's papers include enough items of this sort to demonstrate a permanent condition of financial disarray.

If his debts were always large, he did not lack means of obtaining funds. In the 1840s his income as a lawyer averaged more than fifteen thousand annually, several times his salary as senator and much more than he received as secretary of state.[68] An important retainer came from Barings of London, formerly headed by Lord Ashburton. Webster helped the Barings by urging the states to pay their debts during the depression; and as secretary of state, he was partial to their bank by having it act as the agent for the United States government in Europe and Latin America. In turn, it helped him financially through its Boston agent, Thomas Wren Ward. In 1845 it collaborated with him when, in behalf of Maryland, he sought to sell the state's bonds to complete the Chesapeake and Ohio Canal.[69] Another way in which he tried to increase his professional income, in 1848 and afterward, was to present claims against Mexico before a commission set up under the treaty of that year. Characteristically, his expectations exceeded the outcome. Land companies whose cases he took gave him their scrip, which was worth far less than face value. Still, he used some of it as collateral in borrowing from banks.[70]

In Boston he usually went to Franklin Haven's Merchants' Bank for credit and seldom failed to get what he needed. His security would sometimes be his note endorsed by a well-to-do person, such as merchant James Mills, who was glad to accommodate him.[71] But there were others, among them Isaac Davis, Rufus Choate, Caleb Cushing, and Peter Harvey. By the late 1840s Harvey had Webster's power of attorney to facilitate raising cash in the city when he was absent.[72] No one was overlooked—he even borrowed from Fletcher.[73] In New York a wide circle of friends was supportive: the Grinnells and Griswolds, Blatchford, Charles Stetson of the Astor House, Samuel Ruggles, Roswell Colt, Samuel Jaudon.[74] In Baltimore, Nathaniel Williams, a wealthy merchant, loaned a great deal over a long period; and Webster used his influence to get him appointed collector of customs there in 1841 and appraiser in 1851.[75] In Washington, William A. Bradley of the Patriotic Bank and Richard Smith of the Bank of the Metropolis were standbys. More and more, however, he conducted his business with the firm of Corcoran and Riggs. It was Corcoran who bought his Washington house in 1849 and canceled his notes in approval of the speech on March 7.[76]

Besides income and loans, he needed still more money; and twice within a few years, in 1846 and 1850, persons in Boston and New York established annuity funds for him, the first for thirty-seven thousand and the second for twenty thousand.[77] On at least one occasion he asked permission to draw his installment early because he was so strapped.[78] Contributions to these funds came readily from those who would not permit his leaving office because of financial difficulties.

Though the fact of his shortcomings in managing his affairs is plain, less clear are its implications in relation to both political behavior and personal ethics. The flow of credit and subsidies he received could have undermined his public integrity for the benefit of those who provided such help. Expediency could have overshadowed principle. Webster's contemporaries and later historians suspected as much.[79] Undeniably, his responsiveness to mercantile and industrial interests was strong from his first years in Washington onward. A protective tariff up to the mid-1820s threatened commercial profits, and he opposed it; afterward it was judged indispensable to the growth of manufactures, and he supported it. So he thought in 1833 when he would not reduce rates to pacify nullifiers, and so he thought in 1850 when he compromised on slavery in the hope it might then be possible to raise the tariff. Yet his ideas on the relationship between government and the economy were so firm that no loan or subsidy was required to sway him. He would have approached broad policies of that kind as he did, in any event. There were always those, knowing his views and ability, anxious to keep him in office. If

441

they influenced him, they did so in a more particular sense. He did not agree to confer a favor upon anyone in exchange for money (that is, for a bribe), but he did remember those friends when appointments were made or when individual interests were at stake. Still, among his numerous financial helpers over many years, comparatively few derived such benefits.

In his personal business he did not behave much differently from many others of that day. People then were free and easy about credit and speculation, permitting their optimism to prevail over a more realistic perception of their situation and reasonable prospects. Nor were they altogether punctual in paying their debts.[80] Nevertheless, after acknowledging the typicality of his conduct and other ameliorating factors, one must say that Webster not only projected the wrong image but did in fact compromise his own character as a result of the way he handled money.

Chapter 27

JUDICIAL
ADJUSTMENTS

Webster's ongoing law practice entered a new phase in the mid-1830s when a significant change occurred on the bench of the Supreme Court. John Marshall and two other former justices were gone, Congress increased the number of judges from seven to nine, and near the close of his presidency Jackson appointed five to fill the vacancies. These, added to the two he had selected earlier, transformed the Court from the conservative, nationalistic body it had been under Marshall to one with a states' rights, Democratic orientation.[1] This composition endured for the remaining fifteen years of Webster's active membership in the bar, and for some time afterward. Roger Taney became chief justice, to Webster's disquiet, and began a long period of service during which his leadership gave a distinctive cast to the high tribunal. All for the worse, thought the Massachusetts senator, who had stood against this Jacksonian stalwart in recent political battles such as the bank controversy. Despite all the efforts of Webster and his Whig colleagues to defeat confirmation, Taney was presiding when the annual term began in early 1837. Though Webster never ceased to believe that the new chief justice was unfit to succeed the great Marshall, many contemporaries as well as later students of constitutional law came to recognize his ability and achievements. There would be a day, as the Civil War approached, when Taney would be roundly denounced for a proslavery decision in the *Dred Scott* case, but generally the course he set for the new Court was constructive and not revolutionary, revisionist and not radical.[2]

Such has been the long-range verdict. Although these Jacksonian jurists certainly did adjust doctrine to conform to their states' rights

443

commitment, they invoked a kind of federalism in which national power remained a vital element in American government. Less inclined than their predecessors to use the largely dormant authority of Congress to strike down state legislation, they favored distribution of powers at the two levels to allow maximum concurrent operation when and if Congress got around to exercising those belonging to it. As for questions involving property rights, they did not turn out to be agrarian extremists as forecast. Though sustaining their opposition to special privileges, particularly monopoly, conferred by government, they reconciled economic growth, corporate development, and even vested rights with their precepts of equal opportunity and public interest.

Webster nevertheless felt that the Taney Court went much too far in its adjustments. His friend Justice Story, now more and more pushed to dissent because of his adherence to old patterns, agreed. "He [Story] thinks the Supreme Court is *gone,*" the lawyer remarked, "& I think so too; and almost everything is gone, or seems to be rapidly going."[3] In his professional work at the capital he was losing more cases and feeling greater dissatisfaction with the new order. Yet he had to admit that on a given issue he might prevail in an argument for nationalism or property rights, because there was in fact a Story wing on the bench and a middle group who could be persuaded.[4] This very mobility of judicial positions seemed to fragment the Court, when viewed in relation to its rather monolithic condition in past years, and to produce, in Webster's judgment, a rash of concurring and dissenting opinions adding up to confusion. Expression of separate lines of reasoning did not disturb Taney, however, who felt, somewhat as Jefferson had, that a republican society required his associates to exercise individual responsibility.

Democrats often complained that the Court had expanded its power too much, at the expense not only of the states but of other branches of the national government as well. To an extent, Taney and his colleagues counteracted what they believed to have been a tendency to do so. In exercising judicial review they inclined to defer to legislators and to give limited scope to their own decisions. Better to do so, the theory ran, than to proclaim absolutes and universals unnecessarily. It was a sort of self-restraint with a pragmatic footing, in contrast to the broader approach taken by Marshall and favored by Webster. Appropriately enough, the new chief justice also found an opportunity to lay down an enduring precedent which reserved an area not susceptible to review by this tribunal at all. In *Luther* v. *Borden* (1849) he set forth a doctrine with antecedents in Marshall's day and known as political questions.[5] Paradoxically, as counsel in that controversy Webster expounded this rule of judicial restraint.

The *Luther* case arose from a protracted struggle in Rhode Island concerning revision of its constitution. Dating back to 1663, the state's fundamental law was the colonial charter, though industrialization and urbanization now made some provisions anachronistic and unfair. Reformers attacked two injustices: (1) overrepresentation of rural towns in the assembly, relative to that of the heavily populated factory towns; and (2) an illiberal suffrage requirement for land holding, which disqualified large numbers of the working class. After repeated failures to get a more democratic constitution by regular procedure and led by an upper-class lawyer, Thomas Dorr, they called a people's convention to write a new document in late 1841, whereupon the established, charter government called one too. Thus Rhode Island had two proposed constitutions, both similarly addressing the old problems. In subsequent referendums the Dorrite version carried and the other narrowly failed. Still acting without approval by the old legislature, the People's party, as it was known, held elections for governor (Dorr won) and for representatives to the new assembly, then vainly sought to take power.[6]

The situation by the spring of 1842, misleadingly labeled the Dorr War, caught national attention, with Whigs tending to disapprove and Democrats to sympathize with the grass-roots movement. Dorr unsuccessfully appealed to Tyler for support but enjoyed moral backing in parts of the Northeast. From the governor of the charter administration came repeated requests for federal intervention against domestic violence; each time, the president refused to send troops until it was absolutely necessary. In his response, however, he recognized the legitimacy of the old government, indicated his willingness to protect it if it was actually in danger, and thereby helped tip the scales in this unusual controversy.[7] Through April and May while this was happening, Webster, though busy with the Ashburton negotiations, kept informed and lent advice to the chief executive. Unhesitatingly he came down on the side of the law-and-order, charter forces. He did urge compromise and concession to end the conflict, however, by way of intermediaries in Rhode Island.[8] Toward the end of the year, excitement had subsided, the Dorrites had scattered, and voters had approved another constitution just as liberal as the People's party had demanded.

Out of this affair came *Luther* v. *Borden.* A Dorrite, Martin Luther, sued Borden and other militiamen for trespass upon his property while acting under martial law imposed by the charter assembly. This move raised the issue of which constitution, the old charter or Dorr's document, was legitimate. In the federal circuit court, Story and fellow judge John Pitman, both clearly hostile to the irregular conduct of the People's party, certified the case to the Supreme Court; and after long delay it was argued there in January 1848. The main question had more to do with ideology than with the substance of constitutional reforms. As it had been since the height of the conflict in 1842, the focus was upon the process by which the people can change their government. Was the cherished doctrine of popular sovereignty sufficient justification for a majority peaceably to set aside one government for another, if the existing one did not approve the procedures for doing so?[9]

A topic of such importance, in addition to the lingering notoriety of the Dorrite movement, drew much attention to the Supreme Court hearing. For Luther, and thus for the People's party, Benjamin Hallett bolstered his argument with a mass of material on the state's population, voting, suffrage requirements, and so forth, all to show that Dorr's constitution justifiably replaced the old charter. The change, he contended, was truly an affirmation of the Declaration of Independence and the political faith upon which the republic was built.[10]

In answer, Webster made an extraordinary effort in behalf of Borden, and thus of the charter government. He did not deny that popular sovereignty was the foundation of the constitutional system. But he reasoned that though the people were the source of all powers, they had delegated authority to their legislative representatives to establish qualifications and procedures for voting not only in elections but also for alteration of the fundamental law. To avert the constant dangers of haste, emotion, and manipulation, the people have chosen to limit themselves, he concluded. As interesting as this discussion of political theory may have been, his other points would have more weight with the Court. Uncharacteristically, he called for judicial restraint in this case. Determination of legitimacy of a state government, he held, was not a justiciable matter. On this matter, the Court must defer to the existing state legislature, as the Rhode Island supreme court had already decided. If the national government had any responsibility to act, as it might under the constitutional clause guaranteeing the states a republican form of government and protecting them from domestic violence, then that responsibility rested with either Congress or the president, not with the Supreme Court. Accordingly, Congress had passed statutes empowering the chief executive to call out the militia to suppress disorder; and Tyler had been ready to do so in this instance, though finding it unnecessary. The proper rule should therefore be that this was a political question outside judicial competence. Adding a practical point, probably persuasive if immeasurable, he called attention to the enormous disarrangement which would follow if the Court threw out all the official acts of the Rhode Island government from 1842 to the present.[11]

Carrying the case over to the 1849 term, the Court then decided unanimously that this was indeed a political question. On this point Taney's opinion followed Webster's brief closely, though the chief justice did not venture into the broad realm of political philosophy as counsel had invited him to do.[12] Although this was not the first instance in which the Court had declared that an issue must be handled by another branch or level of government, the *Luther* decision became a landmark of constitutional law. Drawing the line between justiciable and nonjusticiable zones has always been an elusive exercise, depending as it does upon sensitivity of the subject; yet it involves the same difficult choice of alternatives characterizing the whole judicial process.[13]

In another area of jurisprudence, however, both Webster and Taney contributed to the growth of federal judicial power. This was the specialized but important field of admiralty law. Since the beginning of his practice in federal courts, Webster had handled a substantial number of cases involving maritime questions—prizes, piracy, neutrality violations, concerns of shipping. He felt at home in such litigation, as might be expected of a lawyer situated near active commercial ports; and he favored a broad definition of admiralty jurisdiction, in large part because it fell to federal rather than state courts and seemed more dependable for his clients' interests. By midcentury, bench and bar had developed a system suitable to American circumstances and substantially different from the English one which had long prevailed in this country.[14]

One of Webster's cases influencing this trend was *New Jersey Steam Navigation Company* v. *Merchants' Bank* (1848). Besides having legal significance, it related to a horrifying marine disaster that attracted popular attention. In January 1840 the steamboat *Lexington* was making a regular run across Long Island Sound with passengers and a cargo of baled cotton. Sparks from the smokestack fell on the cotton and set the entire craft aflame. An inexperienced, excited crew lost control and scrambled overboard to escape. Soon the *Lexington* sank; and 138 people, all but three of the crew and passengers, lost their lives in one of the worst of many steamboat disasters of that day. Also lost was a crate of gold and silver coin being transported for the Merchants' Bank of Boston.[15] Webster's young friend Franklin Haven, the president of the bank, retained him to argue the case before the Supreme Court in 1847.[16] There were several questions for the judges to decide (negligence, liability of common carriers, the character of the contract), but the main one was jurisdictional. Had the claim of the bank for damages been brought to the proper court, the United States district judge sitting in admiralty?

In maintaining jurisdiction, Webster urged modification of ancient doctrine so that a contract concerning maritime commerce, such as the bank's arrangement for transporting the specie, could be a subject over which the admiralty court had cognizance. No matter, he contended, that the English rule had been that only contracts *made* as well as performed on the sea fell to that jurisdiction. In this instance the bank's contract had been made on land, he conceded, but it was the character rather than the place of the contract that ought to be decisive. Gaining this point would be a big step toward a quite different setting for future litigants. The lawyer's grounds included the unqualified language of the Constitution on admiralty cases, the difference between the economic and geographical circumstances of nineteenth-century America and early England, and a congressional act of 1845 granting such jurisdiction over shipping on inland lakes and rivers (rather than within the ebb and flow of the tide, as prescribed by precedents).[17] All these arguments might not have been enough to convince five of the nine justices if in another case during that term, *Waring* v. *Clarke,* a rationalization had not been fabricated to extend admiralty well up the Mississippi River. As it was, he had to repeat his argument at the next term before winning his case.[18]

This line of admiralty decisions was only one example of the Court's willingness to extend national judicial power. In other areas too, such as in contract and commerce cases, it assumed a larger role in declaring the general law of the nation. In a system of federalism, some umpire had to draw the line between national and state powers. Though the Jacksonians subscribed to states' rights, judicial definition and protection seemed necessary. So the Court took on more responsibility in deciding what the boundaries were between two levels of authority, as well as between state power and an untouchable private sector.

Conservatives such as Webster, Story, and Kent worried about the security of property as soon as the Taney Court assembled for its first term in 1837. Would the new justices overturn precedents of Marshall's time shielding vested rights from state infringement? Legislative grants, corporate charters, debtor-creditor relations, hitherto protected by the contract clause of the Constitution, might be imperiled. Webster would soon learn whether they were, for a long-pending case raising this very question was due for reargument.

Charles River Bridge v. *Warren Bridge* was not only a highlight of constitutional history but also the culmination of an intense controversy in Massachusetts. In 1785 the legislature had chartered a company to build a bridge across the Charles River from Boston to Charlestown, and for years it had prospered as increasing traffic brought in ever larger toll receipts. Stockholders profited many times their investment in the next forty years, while complaints, especially from people in Charlestown and the countryside, rose to a high level. During the 1820s the matter became a focus of attention in the legislature. Politicians tended to divide for or against the bridge along partisan lines, Federalists for and the growing Jacksonian coalition against. Finally, in 1828 discontent reached the point that a law was enacted to build another structure, the Warren Bridge, to be located closely parallel to the old one, about a city block away at the Charlestown end, and to become toll free in a short time. While it was under construction, the proprietors of Charles River Bridge went to the state supreme court for an injunction against this project certain to ruin their interest. Webster and Lemuel Shaw were their counsel over the next year and a half but failed to get the judicial relief requested. Warren Bridge was opened late in 1828; and with litigation continuing until January 1830, no injunction was issued.[19]

Then Webster carried an appeal to the Supreme Court, where in 1831 he argued the case strenuously but could not persuade the required four of seven justices to hand down a decision.[20] So years passed before the Court disposed of the case. During that interval there were vacancies and absences on the bench owing to illness; and all the while the lawyer waited impatiently and became pessimistic about the outcome. The only hope appeared to be a compromise back home by which owners of the old bridge would obtain state compensation in return for surrendering their charter—a solution they had sought from the first. But the legislators and the corporation could not agree upon terms, much to Webster's disappointment.[21]

When the Court, now headed by Taney, did rehear the case in 1837, the attorney and his associate developed every possible line of argument: (1) Charles River Bridge succeeded to the common-law and statutory rights enjoyed by an old ferry at that place; (2) the state had unconstitutionally exercised its power of eminent domain by taking the company's property without just compensation; and (3) the corporate charter conferred an implied privilege of exclusive service, now revoked. Of these points, the last proved to be pivotal for the decision. Webster contended, as his clients always had, that the construction of a new, free bridge amounted to confiscation of property, the essential right to take tolls. And such a right rested on a contract, the charter, whose obligation the Massachusetts law had impaired, contrary to the contract clause of the Constitution. It was a plea for a loose, generous interpretation of the charter's provisions, for no specific language in it provided for a monopoly. If charters were not so interpreted, Webster warned, investors

449

would not risk capital for economic development of the country. Law must not depend upon vagrant, excitable feelings. The whole affair, he exclaimed, "began with a clamor about monopoly—that all bridges were held by the people—and that what the State wanted it might take. That was bad enough in taverns and bar rooms and garrets in Essex County and was very little better when dressed with more decorum of appearance, and advanced in this Court." He urged that an independent judiciary see that justice was done.[22]

But, as he feared, he lost the case. Speaking for a majority, Taney refused to adopt Webster's rule for interpreting charters. Because the state had not explicitly granted an exclusive right, he held, none could be inferred from the charter. Drawing from English and American precedents, as well as from a strong argument by Harvard professor Simon Greenleaf for Warren Bridge, the chief justice expressed the proper guideline to be "Nothing passes by implication." In a period of rapid development by this nation, he emphasized, new enterprise (such as railroads) must not be hindered by excessive generosity to old interests (such as turnpikes, canals, or bridges).[23] Story objected in a scholarly but animated dissent, predicting frightful consequences if government did not respect vested rights of property. Instead of encouraging economic improvements, he reasoned, the Court would discourage new investment of capital if there was no assurance against capricious shifts of policy. More convincingly than Taney, Story supported his opinion by the common law of England and the United States.[24] Yet the position of Taney did not differ markedly from that of Story and Webster on legal precedent. All would have to agree that statutory language must be read, in some degree, in light of reasonable implications.[25] Where they differed was on the question of which economic policy—strict or flexible interpretation of corporate grants—would be more likely to promote desirable growth. Story and Webster looked to established interests; Taney would not let them obstruct progress. Still, it was noteworthy that he adjusted rather than overturned legal doctrine: he did not overrule but added a proviso to Marshall's *Dartmouth College* precedent that a corporate charter was a contract in the constitutional sense.[26]

That Taney's colleagues did not take his aphorism, "Nothing passes by implication," very seriously was later demonstrated in *Planters' Bank of Mississippi* v. *Sharp* (1848). The state had passed a statute prohibiting banks from transferring promissory notes of their debtors by endorsement. Citing its charter, which authorized discount of notes, a bank claimed that the statute impaired the state's contractual obligation and was therefore unconstitutional. In this instance the corporation had to

450

depend upon a flexible reading of its charter on notes. It so happened that Webster represented the party on the other side of the question and relied upon the statute. So he contended for narrow interpretation of the charter on bank operations, and thus for the law's validity. But the Court struck it down as destructive of an implied bank privilege and therefore violative of the contract clause. Consistent with his former position, the chief justice dissented, holding to strict construction. Not only was the decision a good indication that something does pass by implication, but it was very interesting that nobody, judges or Webster, so much as mentioned *Charles River Bridge*.[27]

There were ways other than strict reading of a corporate grant for states to cope with existing franchises when they wished to promote economic improvements. During the antebellum years they began exercising the power of eminent domain, of revising or revoking a grant if it interfered with progress, as long as just compensation was awarded. Thus taking property by this power could include property in a corporate franchise. But was not such an application contrary to the contract clause of the Constitution? That was the question in *West River Bridge* v. *Dix* (1848). Webster represented a bridge company whose franchise the state of Vermont had set aside to build a new highway. Here was Taney's example of old interests giving way to new in order to encourage progress. The lawyer attacked the idea with as much vigor as he had in *Charles River Bridge*—in which eminent domain had been lengthily discussed during argument. A franchise, being a contract, was immune from subsequent revocation, he insisted. If he prevailed, a corporation which had a charter (constituting a contract with the state) would have more protection than an individual. The more the better, for he visualized all kinds of radicalism seeping into policy if the dangerous power of eminent domain were unchecked. Nevertheless, the Court had no such qualms and upheld the state's action. A franchise, it ruled, was always held subject to this inalienable authority.[28]

The Taney Court was taking middle ground between corporate rights and state power. Recognizing the necessity of a legal climate favorable to enterprise, it evolved a constitutional and common-law basis for business to operate effectively in a modern economy. Yet it also recognized the necessity of adequate public control, largely by the states, of the conduct of business. There is no better example of this judicial balancing than the *Alabama Bank Cases* (1839). The decision dealt with a fundamental issue of law and economics in remarkably pragmatic fashion.

Webster represented the Bank of the United States, now incorporated by Pennsylvania after expiration of its national charter, in an appeal

from the federal circuit court in Alabama. There the decision had gone
against the bank in a case involving a state policy hostile to foreign
(out-of-state) corporations. Reflecting a tendency in the country, Alabama had adopted measures favoring its own banks by excluding any
coming in from other quarters, just as some states had attempted to do
during the time of the national bank. Both financial localism and suspicion of powerful corporations underlay a policy of this kind. A question
in the present cases, of which Webster's was one (*BUS* v. *Primrose*), was
whether Alabama's exclusion of out-of-state banks included a prohibition on their merely dealing in bills of exchange—there was no provision on that specifically. The broader question was whether a state could
constitutionally restrict or prohibit these banks from doing business
within their jurisdictions.

Nicholas Biddle, still head of the BUS, had consulted Webster when
the controversy began and retained him now to combat what he felt to
be a serious threat to the interstate operations of his institution. For his
part, the lawyer believed such obstacles entirely unjustifiable.[29] In his
argument he advanced two principal objections to state action against
foreign corporations, the first on constitutional and the second on common-law grounds. A corporation, he said, was legally a citizen, as the
recent trend of doctrine indicated. He pointed out that a corporation
could sue and be sued in the federal courts on the basis of diversity of
state citizenship under Article III of the Constitution. If it could sue on a
matter involving a state other than the one in which it was chartered,
could it not also do business there? If not, the right to sue was meaningless. Moving from that premise, he turned to Article IV of the Constitution to contend that its assurance of privileges and immunities of citizens
of one state in another comprehended corporate citizens as well.[30] Carried to the extent Webster would have preferred, his version of privileges
and immunities would be an absolute prohibition of any state discrimination against foreign corporations.[31] Besides this line of constitutional
reasoning, Webster also urged application of the principle of comity
under both international and common law. That principle, for which
there was plenty of precedent, would allow persons or companies of one
nation, or in this case one state of the Union, to transact business in another.

The Court handed down a decision favorable to the bank.[32] It did not
go as far as he hoped, for Taney did not accept Webster's full-blown
constitutional argument on privileges and immunities. The chief justice
would not strip a state of all power to legislate on foreign corporations—his Jacksonian ideology would not allow such a sweeping conces-

sion.[33] But he did uphold the principle of comity as advanced by counsel. The well-established usage of one country admitting corporations from another country should apply with even greater force to states of the Union, he ruled. Then to pacify nervous states' righters, he continued by holding that a state could enact some discriminatory restrictions on such business.[34] If it did not adopt a specific statute, however, its silence would be presumed to be consent. No matter that Alabama soon passed a law of the sort (the Court had decided the former measures had not covered bills of exchange); politics, self-interest, or inattention would ordinarily provide much freedom of movement for out-of-state corporations. The decision substantially encouraged business of nationwide scope.[35]

A case equally favorable to interstate enterprise was *Swift* v. *Tyson* (1842), which also involved a question of the legal status of bills of exchange, this time in New York.[36] Precedents on the subject in that state's courts differed from those of other jurisdictions. When a case came to a federal judge, as this one did, must he follow the state rule, or should he not have uniform guidelines? Webster argued for a general commercial law instead of a maze of disparate state systems. To make his point, he had to construe congressional legislation on the federal judiciary supporting his cause. The statute of 1789 had obligated federal judges to follow the "laws" of the states as rules of decision. Unlike many others, Webster took "laws" to embrace only state legislative enactments, not state judicial precedents. That interpretation would often allow national courts to go their own way, a rule which, in Webster's opinion, was indispensable to interstate commerce. Anyway, he added, the commerce clause of the Constitution implied as much. Justice Story eagerly disposed of the case accordingly, and over the next century there was a federal commercial law exclusive of state systems.[37] If Story and Webster had been living in the 1930s, they would have deplored the Court's overturning of *Swift* after a long controversy. All things considered, the Story-Webster position on uniformity was probably the soundest option.[38]

In both *Swift* and the *Alabama Bank Cases,* the Court conceivably could have paid more attention to the constitutional clause on interstate commerce, for they involved economic activities of persons in more than one state. Webster touched upon the possibility in his arguments, and Justice John McKinley in a separate, dissenting opinion in the bank controversy expressed alarm that the majority had really rested its decision on an expanded national commerce power.[39] Yet these were minor aspects of the cases, mainly because few people looked upon transactions in bills of exchange as interstate commerce. Even though the paper certainly served as an *instrument* of commerce, buying and selling it were thought to constitute local business. Perhaps this construction indicates how limited the definition of interstate commerce was then.

Throughout these years the high tribunal continuously confronted commerce questions—and was having a difficult time drawing constitutional boundaries around state and national powers. Taney and his associates inherited the problem from their predecessors. Contrary to the opinion of many experts as well as much of the public, John Marshall had left unanswered the fundamental question: is the power to regulate interstate and foreign commerce exclusively national or concurrently state and national or partly concurrent?[40] All he had decided in *Gibbons* v. *Ogden* (1824) was that the New York statute on the steamboat monopoly conflicted with a federal statute, thus violating the supremacy clause of the Constitution (Article VI). He did not rule on a situation in which no national law clashed with a state law. If he had, he would have defined the commerce clause on congressional power itself (Article I, section 8). Similarly, in *Brown* v. *Maryland* (1827) and *Willson* v. *Blackbird Creek* (1829), the great judge had sidestepped this basic issue by confining his decisions to particular factual circumstances rather than laying down a general formula going to the heart of federalism. So in 1837 the Court had unfinished business on its hands.

During that term it decided *New York* v. *Miln*. The issue was the constitutionality of a state law requiring reports and bonding on arriving alien passengers by masters of vessels. Only three of the seven justices could agree that New York was rightly exercising a concurrent power over foreign commerce. They postponed the central problem by labeling the legislation a proper regulation of police to protect internal health and safety, not a regulation of commerce. This judicial construct, the police power, would often be a way around similar difficulties.[41]

Contemporaries and later scholars believed that the Court's hesitancy to adopt a general formula arose from possible connections of the commerce power and slavery. If this national authority were broad, then what would stop antislavery forces from using it to interfere with the South's peculiar institution? Especially worrisome to southerners was the vulnerability of the interstate slave trade and existing policies restricting black sailors coming into port. These considerations had probably influenced the Marshall Court too in its uncharacteristic caution in earlier decisions. Actually, the slavery interest had little to fear. That this was so became apparent in *Groves* v. *Slaughter* (1841), a revealing if little-known case. Mississippi had a provision in its constitution prohibiting importation of slaves for sale within its boundaries. Was the state invading the sphere of congressional power over interstate commerce? Webster was among the prominent lawyers appearing for argument and represented the party challenging the measure's validity.[42] His ingenuity in reconciling his loose-constructionist view of the commerce clause with a politician's avoidance of trouble about slavery is interesting. Of course, he said, this Court had long since decided that the power was exclusively national. (That claim was untrue, and one wonders how he and other learned participants in these commerce cases could have ever said so.) The sheer power, being exclusive, forbade state action, he asserted. Yet Congress itself could not tamper with the slave trade either, because slaves were a kind of property altogether untouchable by the national government.[43] The silence of federal legislation affirmed the principle of freedom of this type of interstate commerce. What better outcome could the South hope for? Dormant and unusable national power somehow created a highly protected zone. Other counsel discussed this and a variety of other aspects; and so did the justices, who, as often in this period, split off in several directions in their opinions. None of them, however, believed that Congress could interfere with the interstate slave trade by commercial regulation. In addition to this significant revelation of their thinking, the attorneys and judges had a chance to analyze the commerce clause at great length.[44]

Six years later, in the *License Cases* (1847), Webster participated in another exercise in exploration and disputation with inconclusive results. Representing a liquor retailer in Massachusetts, he attacked a state statute prohibiting sale of spirits in small quantities without a license, in effect a temperance policy. As he would at each opportunity, he pressed for adoption of the exclusive-national-power rule, but failed.[45] All the justices sympathized with the state purpose of protecting the health and morals of its citizens. Some would call it an application of concurrent state commerce power, others a police power, in the total of nine opinions on this and related cases from New York and New Hampshire. Two justices favored exclusive national power, two preferred fully concurrent state power, and others in the middle were ready for some kind of compromise.[46]

Webster's last effort in this drawn-out search for common ground came in the *Passenger Cases* (1849). Massachusetts and New York, encouraged by *Miln*, had gone further in addressing what they deemed the danger of diseased and poor immigrants coming into port in larger numbers. As a filter, they levied a head tax, to be paid by shipmasters. This time Webster won his case, five to four, but only after arguing it in four successive terms and only with a proliferated answer from the bench.[47] McKinley, for example, oddly based his opinion on the slave-trade clause of the Constitution (Article I, section 9), which by implication, he said, conferred exclusive power over immigration upon Congress.[48] To other judges of the middle group, the fact that a tax was laid proved that the states were not using their legitimate police power but were unconstitutionally regulating foreign commerce.[49] For Webster, despite the disappointment in not establishing a general formula, the cases did bring in a large fee, plus more from his merchant friends who sued to recover tax payments.[50]

While he was secretary of state and was handling fewer cases, the Court finally arrived at a durable guideline in *Cooley* v. *Wardens* (1852). Justice Benjamin Curtis, whose recent appointment Webster had helped arrange, spoke for a clear majority in holding that a state had partially concurrent power. In this case Pennsylvania had regulated pilotage, an aspect of interstate and foreign commerce not requiring a "uniform rule," he said. Those which did would demand exclusive national regulation. In a given case, the Court would have to consider the nature of the subject being regulated. Though open-ended, the rule must have been quite satisfactory to Webster. From the time of the steamboat case in 1824 onward, he had been willing to settle for exclusive national power in the "higher branches," notwithstanding his sustained advocacy of totally exclusive congressional authority.[51]

During the thirty-eight years of his practice in the Supreme Court, Webster participated in almost all the leading constitutional cases decided there. Altogether, he appeared as counsel in twenty-four whose issues involved an interpretation of the Constitution, though some were actually decided on nonconstitutional grounds; and he won thirteen of the twenty-four. His success was greater in the favorable setting of John Marshall's tribunal than in that of Taney.[52] There were only a few significant cases which he did not argue—*Sturges* v. *Crowninshield* (1819), *Brown* v. *Maryland* (1827), *New York* v. *Miln* (1837), and *Briscoe* v. *Bank of Kentucky* (1837). Thus for the period as a whole, he was in the first rank of those attorneys who shaped constitutional law. The substance of his briefs and the force of his oratory show the strength of his impact in the early years. In contract and commerce cases particularly, the trend of nationalism and vested-rights protection coincided with his arguments time and again. Later, in the Jacksonian era, he encountered judicial resistance to carrying precedents toward a more advanced point; yet for the most part Taney and his associates adjusted rather than rejected earlier Court decisions. Federal power remained substantial, the best example being regulation of commerce. Though Webster's effort for an exclusive congressional power fell short of acceptance, it came close in the ultimate *Cooley* formula of uniform rule. As for the rights of property, there were disappointments over the *Charles River Bridge* rule of strict interpretation of corporate charters and the *West River Bridge* expansion of eminent domain. Still, these were modifications rather than overrulings.

In terms of landmark cases his practice in lower courts may have been less memorable than that in Washington; yet considered as a whole, it reflected a greater investment of time and perhaps an equal contribution to the legal system. Every category of the law was changing as the institutions of society changed. Industrial innovation, the expansion of the market to national dimensions, new ways of handling capital and organizing business demanded a new body of law, different from that of a former agrarian and commercial age. In the courts, attorneys like Webster were fashioning rules adapted from the common law and stimulative to economic growth. The primary characteristic of this developing system was its emphasis upon individual will and responsibility, upon arrangements made at one's risk, instead of upon considerations of order, fairness, and paternalistic oversight by government. This process generated litigation on a wide range of subjects: privileges and liabilities of corporations, employer-labor relations, eminent domain, the modern conception of torts.[53]

An illustration of the kind of problem the courts now faced was the rapid buildup of controversies involving patents. Though he had a pioneering case concerning this topic before the Supreme Court,[54] Webster appeared as counsel in a more important one in the federal circuit court of New Jersey, where he made the last oral argument of his career. It was *Goodyear* v. *Day* (1852). Charles Goodyear had developed a means of vulcanizing India rubber to make products commercially feasible, but he had no end of trouble with competing interlopers. Holding patents from the national office, he became involved in dozens of suits to maintain his right to exploit the invention. This one, heard at Trenton, was so crucial that he retained Webster for the handsome sum of ten thousand plus a five-thousand-dollar contingency fee, with the merchant George Griswold, the lawyer's friend in New York, promising more.[55] The secretary of state could not afford to pass this up and indeed gave his client all the help he needed to win the case. Well prepared for the hearing, Webster not only framed a persuasive brief on the technical points but also convinced the judge to assume the task of ruling on bewildering questions of fact instead of leaving them to a jury. Equity procedure, resorted to as a result, permitted such a judicial role and usually would be safer for a patent holder than trial by a jury, whose members were likely to be fearful of exploitative monopoly.[56] During his time as counsel Webster went to the courthouse each day in a carriage drawn by splendid black horses. In fact he received one as a gift and appropriately named it Trenton.[57]

A number of his cases came up in New York City, and for a while he even kept a small office there to conduct such business. One of these seemed reminiscent of the recent Senate debates on the Compromise, in particular Calhoun's lamentation about sectional division of the nation's churches. In this suit he was counsel for the Methodist Church South, which had filed a bill against the northern branch.[58] Other work related to the vast land holdings of John Jacob Astor and to a charitable bequest for a home for retired sailors.[59]

Naturally, he practiced in the federal and state courts of Massachusetts to a much greater extent. The *Charles River Bridge* case (1831), the most noteworthy one, he had to appeal to Washington, much to his disgust. More often, however, he found the state supreme court of Chief Justices Isaac Parker and Lemuel Shaw, both tried and true conservatives, to be friendly territory. In the 1840s, as questions about franchises and rights of way mushroomed, he had a number of railroad cases there. In *Providence Railroad* v. *Boston* (1844) he represented the city, defending against the company's petition to stop the sale of land on which its depot was located. Despite vigorous argument, he lost his cause on the point that the disputed land had been dedicated to "public use," that is, the railroad's.[60] Other clients were the Boston and Lowell and the Boston and Worcester railroads.[61] They were reminiscent of *Charles River Bridge* because of recurrent questions about original grants and new enterprise. His record in maintaining vested rights was good.

Among the large assortment of his Massachusetts cases, one attracting attention concerned alleged embezzlement by a bank president in Charlestown, William Wyman. Webster and several associates were compensated generously, so much so that the district attorney remarked on it in court. "They want to know what's become of the money," the prosecutor declared. "Five thousand to one counsel, three thousand dollars to another, two thousand dollars to another." That ignited an angry exchange. After three trials Webster's client escaped conviction, even though the legislature had hastily passed a new embezzlement law during proceedings. The court took the finespun position that because the bank had never formally authorized Wyman to take custody of the funds, he could not have mishandled them.[62] Two other much discussed cases involved wills. In *Sanborn* v. *Cooke* (1838) Webster successfully represented a young man claiming a share of the estate of wealthy Nathan Tufts.[63] And in the Oliver Smith case (1847) he proved the authenticity of the will of another well-to-do person, giving a large sum to the town of Northampton.[64] Preparation for such work was necessarily different from that required for appellate cases; it demanded careful strategy, skillful use of evidence, and personal rapport with juries.

In conducting all his professional business he maintained his main office in Boston at Court and Tremont in the center of a thriving financial district. There he was fortunate in having reliable associates, chiefly John Healy for this period. While he was in Washington, his correspondence with the younger man about clients, points of law, and fees was heavy and reflected a productive arrangement.[65] That he thought well of Healy's ability was shown when, as secretary of state in 1850, he arranged his appointment as federal district judge in California.[66] In the late 1840s his son Fletcher took care of some cases too, mostly in Boston.[67] Increasingly, Webster used a one-room building at Marshfield to prepare his briefs for court or legal opinions on questions submitted to him. A respectable library of commentaries and reports served well for these purposes; besides he could combine work with recreation here during times of escape from the political scene. As pleasurable as excursions with rod and gun were, he did not neglect his practice to the extent of impairing his income. Up to the time he entered Fillmore's cabinet he took in an average of seventeen thousand dollars annually.[68] Although he could not handle as many cases afterward, those he did take were lucrative—in the *Goodyear* case he earned over fifteen thousand.

Webster had cause for satisfaction with his practice of law. As a young man he had quickly attained a reputation as one of the leaders of the American bar; and in later life he enjoyed a status which could safely be called preeminent. His professional career, spanning nearly a half-century, involved every branch of the law, though as the country experienced great changes, so did the legal system. From specialization in debt collection and in maritime and land cases, he moved into areas of practice developing from economic growth and diversification. His attendance at each term of the Supreme Court, where his best-known cases came, was compatible with his political activity. But in the lower courts also, both federal and state, he played a part in transforming the law, generally to protect and encourage enterprise.

Then and later, some assessments of his professional record were more critical. His services went to high bidders, moneyed people who could provide good retainers and whose interests the lawyer firmly supported. In a sense, he was Tocqueville's lawyer—a guardian of order, a spokesman of conservatism, an ally of the upper class, as the famous French traveler characterized the American bar at the time.[69] Yet such a perspective understated the thrust for change accomplished by lawyers such as Webster. Like others in the legal profession, he was not attempting merely to hold the line by maintaining the inherited law. Though he highly valued old principles and institutions, he sought substantial adjustments to facilitate progress, as his generation defined it. And, on the whole, he achieved that purpose. If his efforts in party politics had been as successful as they were in his legal career, he could have had few regrets.

Chapter 28

DIPLOMATIC FRUSTRATIONS

When Webster was sworn in as secretary of state on the morning of July 23, 1850, he returned to a familiar and congenial post. "I write this," he remarked in a letter that day, "at my old high table in my little room."[1] Leaving the conflicts of loquacious senators, he was happy to be back in the executive branch. He found business in the department more stimulating and better suited to his intellectual interests, and he enjoyed the prestige of first place in the cabinet. Remembering the satisfaction of completing the Ashburton negotiations in 1842, he hoped that he could contribute to the luster of another administration led by a former vice-president. An indispensable condition was surely an end to the current sectional crisis, for domestic politics very much affected the conduct of foreign relations. The present trend of events promised a lasting settlement of the slavery issue. Then it would be essential to carry out policies at home and abroad affirming national unity and prosperity.

From the start, he was pleased with the way Millard Fillmore handled the presidency. He is "a good-tempered, cautious, intelligent man, with whom it is pleasant to transact business," Webster observed. "He is very diligent, and what he does not know he quickly learns."[2] Possessing these qualities, the chief executive would no doubt take advice from his experienced secretary of state. To be sure, the New Yorker had spent years in state and congressional service, had impeccable credentials as a conservative Whig and political professional, and would usually pursue a course very similar to that of Webster. Allowed a good deal of latitude owing to Fillmore's respect for his capacity, Webster influenced the direction policy would take on important questions. Not passive, the president in-

461

formed himself about issues and options, followed the secretary's work closely, and made the necessary decisions. The two men collaborated well because they communicated with each other effectively and shared the same outlook.[3]

The scale of the department's operations continued to be modest, compared to what it would become. Webster had two competent assistants: William Derrick had been in the office during the Tyler period and now held Fletcher's former post as chief clerk; William Hunter commanded a good fund of knowledge as well as linguistic skills. As for other personnel, there were two intelligent young secretaries, as well as copyists and translators.[4] This small staff could hardly keep up with the growing demands upon them.[5] In foreign countries the United States had a handful of full-fledged ministers—Abbott Lawrence in England and William Rives in France, for example—but a good many chargés d'affaires, consuls, and lesser officers. The number of personnel seemed quite enough when applications for appointment accumulated and had to be sifted.[6] As a rule, Webster spent long hours at his desk each day, usually from early morning to midafternoon, to keep up with the incoming stream of papers.[7] More often now, however, he fled to New England for respite, especially in late summer and fall when hay fever struck. Even then, he took care of essentials by mail or telegrams with assistance from a secretary, to whom he preferred to dictate rather than to write with his own hand.[8]

Directly or indirectly, much of his work involved Britain or France. Through most of this period, the English minister was Sir Henry Bulwer, a middle-aged aristocrat who had come to Washington from an assignment in Madrid and had recently negotiated a treaty with the former secretary, John Clayton, chiefly on possible lines of transportation across Central America. He and Webster would focus on that area in the coming months and, in the process, develop a warm friendship, the kind of personal diplomacy that appealed to the secretary.[9] In London, Minister Abbott Lawrence, onetime Whig rival in Massachusetts, now seemed on good terms with Webster and supplemented negotiations going forward in Washington, particularly those on Latin America. In contrast, the veteran William Rives in Paris could act on his own a good deal, though he could not do much constructive while that unstable republic drifted toward the new empire of Louis Napoleon. Franco-American relations would be less than smooth.[10]

An overview of Webster's diplomacy reveals some guidelines he consistently followed. One was a deep-seated belief that it was not in the national interest to acquire more territory. His forty-year record of opposing such expansion, from the War of 1812 through the Texas episode to the Mexican War, ensured his adherence to that view. Now, in the 1850s, the Young America movement for acquisitions seemed to him even more reprehensible than earlier versions.[11] He would reject any notion of annexation in Latin America or the Pacific. When the Sandwich Islands (Hawaii) became the target of American annexationists, he discouraged that course, though he took the positive step of warning off French penetration. His policy consisted in respecting Hawaiian independence by Britain, France, and the United States, just as he had declared in 1842 during his earlier time in the department.[12] He also opposed American hunger for Mexican, Nicaraguan, and Cuban soil, despite the constant problems all three places posed.

A second guiding principle of foreign relations was to avoid intervention in the internal affairs of other nations, although he gave it greater weight with regard to Europe than elsewhere. Thus the perennial Irish question ought not to induce American intrusion, notwithstanding pressures from Irish Americans.[13] Now and then he did hint of military action in some troubled spots—in Haiti,[14] even in Hawaii if the French menace persisted. Intervention by means other than armed force was another thing; and application of this principle to the Hungarian uprising would be criticized.

Third, he would promote American economic interests abroad, though not in a purely imperialistic sense. This was certainly the case with Hawaii, where a valuable export trade lured capital. He also hoped to secure further advantages in the East, now that China had removed some restrictions in the Cushing treaty (1844).[15] It would be equally desirable to persuade Japan to open its doors to American commerce, and he would take steps toward that objective.[16] In Mexico and Nicaragua, he would support companies developing interoceanic transportation, while in other parts of Latin America he would nourish closer economic connections.[17]

Fourth, his diplomacy had an ideological dimension. Relations with other countries, large and small, provided occasions to explain American institutions, achievements, and ideals. Constitutional government here stood out as an exception in the nineteenth century; monarchies predominated in Europe and a variety of authoritarian regimes existed elsewhere. A democratic republic, created by its people and responsible to them, must therefore provide an example to other nations. As for the domestic effects of foreign policy, Webster believed that the United States in 1850, passing through a sectional crisis as it was, needed some rallying point of Unionism. And what would be better than a bold statement of national unity in the course of communicating with other governments? Perhaps that strategy could calm popular excitement stirred by domestic quarrels.

Webster did not have to wait long to make such a nationalistic statement. In September 1850, just two months after assuming office, he received a brisk protest from the Austrian chargé, J. G. Hülsemann, against American policy sympathizing with the recent Hungarian revolution. Webster's answer laid down the principles of his government which in his view justified that policy. A protracted dispute between the United States and Austria followed, culminating in a visit to this country by the exiled Hungarian leader, Louis Kossuth, whose immense popularity soon dwindled.

This strange episode originated during the Taylor administration with a brave but futile uprising against the old Hapsburg empire, one of a number of European revolutions in 1848. President Taylor sent a special mission to determine if the Hungarians had established de facto independence. Secretary of State John Clayton in June 1849 instructed the agent, Dudley Mann, to recognize them as a new nation if he found they had done so, and to negotiate a commercial treaty as well. Mann reported Kossuth's failure and therefore did nothing further. But Prince Felix von Schwarzenberg, the foreign secretary of Austria, surreptitiously obtained a copy of the instructions to Mann, took umbrage at their unfavorable comparison of Austrian "iron rule" with American republicanism, and generally was upset with what he judged intolerable interference in the empire's internal affairs. He told his chargé, Hülsemann, to complain. Clayton compelled Hülsemann to withdraw a written protest because it would have revealed that Austria had irregularly obtained the copy of Mann's instructions. Still, a lengthy oral exchange between the two ensued. When President Taylor made public various documents, including the instructions, on call from Congress in March 1850, Schwarzenberg and Hülsemann were again aroused; yet the chargé delayed filing a formal protest through the summer, during which time the chief executive died and Webster came into Fillmore's new cabinet.[18]

A familiar personality at the capital, Hülsemann had been with his legation for a dozen years and would be for a dozen more. Despite a good understanding of American politics, he suffered from two handicaps, his own supersensitiveness and his reactionary home government.[19] Even so, he had been reluctant to push the current issue too far and thereby damage relations with the United States permanently. As soon as Webster took over as secretary, he received a conciliatory message

464

from Hülsemann expressing confidence that the two could make a fresh start in removing difficulties. Schwarzenberg, however, insisted that the chargé make a formal protest, which Hülsemann did on September 30.[20] In a written communication, he complained that the Mann mission had violated international law by meddling in Austrian affairs and, moreover, had been inconsistent with the doctrine of nonintervention often pronounced by the United States. Mann's instructions, he declared, insulted his government in several offensive passages, especially in their reference to an "iron rule" in Vienna. Throughout, he intimated serious consequences: treatment of that sort of emissary as a spy and retaliation against American trade.[21]

Though Webster decided at once to answer Hülsemann, it took nearly three months to prepare the document. In the afternoon of October 3, as he was about to leave for New England, he talked with his clerk, William Hunter, about the contents. Going over the main points he had in mind, he told Hunter to make a draft and send it to him, which was done by the fifteenth. This thirty-two-page paper followed the secretary's outline but filled it out with argument and historical detail similar to the final version.[22] When Webster received it during a visit to his New Hampshire farm, he wrote Edward Everett on the twentieth, asking him to make a draft too. Everett had at hand materials Webster had sent him, probably including what Hunter had written. A collation of the two drafts reveals many features in common. After only three days Everett forwarded his production to the secretary, who made literary revisions and inserted several passages, mainly on the contrast between American republicanism and Austrian autocracy. Webster sent the reworked copy to an approving Fillmore but did not then or later mention the collaboration of Hunter or Everett. After his friend's death, Everett caused his own role to be known, indeed had a pamphlet printed with parallel columns of his draft and the final text of the note. Though he had second thoughts and did not distribute the pamphlet generally, in fact much of it was soon known to the public. Everett may indeed have had a valid complaint about not receiving proper credit, but in the pamphlet he did not acknowledge Webster's initial structure, laid out in the conference with Hunter, nor Hunter's draft on the basis of it.[23] Regardless of who contributed what to the document, the reply to Hülsemann represented what the secretary wished to say. Everett characteristically complimented Webster on the "éclat" of the later revisions; but in his private journal he called them "too fierce and bitter."[24]

The note went to Hülsemann on December 21, 1850.[25] It denied the

465

right of Austria to take diplomatic notice of Taylor's message to Congress reporting on the Mann mission, on the ground that it was an internal matter. The United States would not feel entitled to criticize Austrian communications with its provinces, Webster pointed out. In any case, he continued, his predecessor had dispatched Mann to Vienna merely as a fact finder on the Hungarian situation (though actually the instructions revealed a broader purpose if Hungary had achieved de facto independence). As support for the propriety of the mission, the note cited precedents such as the dispatch of agents to former Spanish colonies in Latin America after their revolutions. Thus instead of meddling, reasoned the secretary, his government had carefully observed the law of nations. If Austria had treated Mann as a spy, he asserted, it would have incited immediate hostilities by the United States.

Having covered these and other predictable points, Webster proceeded to the topic he wished to emphasize: the superiority of American republicanism to the European monarchical system. This nation, founded on popular consent and dedicated to civil liberty, offered a model to the oppressed everywhere. It had a rapidly increasing population, a flourishing commerce, sound public credit, and amply protected personal and property rights. "The power of this republic, at the present moment," he proclaimed, "is spread over a region one of the richest and most fertile on the globe, and of an extent in comparison with which the possessions of the House of Hapsburg are but as a patch on the earth's surface."[26] No wonder, then, that America had an interest in movements abroad, such as in Hungary, following its example. It was a matter of legitimate interest and legitimate sympathy, not of abandoning the settled policy of the United States to avoid intervention in the military and political affairs of Europe. Webster did not pause to consider how fine the line between sympathy and intervention might be.

He left no doubt about his motives in expanding into this broad exposition what would normally have been a rather tedious state paper. As he remarked in the note itself, he felt it necessary to answer Hülsemann because "the occasion is not unfavorable for the expression of the general sentiments of the government of the United States."[27] Or, as he later recalled, if the note was "boastful and rough," it was because he wished "to write a paper which should touch the national pride, and make a man feel *sheepish* and look *silly* who should speak of disunion."[28] He exploited the first chance he had after the recent crisis of sectional politics to shore up American nationality. He also believed that the conservative Whigs needed to counter the aggressive Young America movement, centered in the Democratic party.[29]

The Hülsemann note did not have a major impact. Perhaps no diplomatic paper in these circumstances could have accomplished what Webster would have liked. A few letters endorsing his statement came in during the following weeks, the Pennsylvania legislature passed a resolution commending it, and newspapers gave it some space.[30] From Britain, Abbott Lawrence wrote that he had circulated a pamphlet edition among public figures there, apparently at his own expense.[31] But in the Senate, Clay spoke against interference in the domestic affairs of foreign nations and helped defeat a motion to print ten thousand copies of the note.[32] As for Austria, it adhered to its objections against American policy on Hungary; and on March 11, 1851, Hülsemann gave Webster a note saying so.[33] Anxious not to damage Austro-American relations further, Fillmore made sure that Webster's response would be short and pacific.[34] The result was an interlude of quiet until another development revived excitement about the Hungarian cause.[35]

This occurred late in the year, when Kossuth came to the United States. Having been interned in Turkey after suppression of the Hungarian revolution, he arrived in New York aboard an American naval vessel as a result of arrangements Webster had made for an asylum in this country. But not content to spend his days in a quiet haven, he took advantage of an outpouring of popular sympathy to renew his struggle for national independence, much to the dismay of the administration. In December he was in Washington for a meeting with the president, an address to Congress, and an elaborate banquet. On that occasion the secretary tried to pick his way carefully in a speech he made to a large audience, but some of his phrases clearly indicated support for Hungary's national existence. Hülsemann reacted vigorously with a note of protest about Webster's remarks and soon afterward left the country, announcing that he would not return until Fillmore dismissed the secretary of state or until a new administration came in after the next election. For his part, Webster would not retract what he had said and was in no danger of being dismissed. In a little while Kossuth defeated his own cause as he traveled across the land and collected funds benefiting him more than his homeland.[36]

The Kossuth affair attracted much popular attention, but it was in Latin America rather than in Europe that most of Webster's diplomatic problems arose. One of them concerned Cuba. Ruled by Spain for more than three centuries, this island remnant of a once vast empire suffered from nearly intolerable economic and political conditions. Its sugar-staple, slave-labor economy was in deep trouble; its harsh government laid oppressive taxes and ignored civil rights. Many Cuban refugees in the

United States hoped for a revolution in their homeland, a goal shared by a significant number of Americans who contributed money or joined filibustering expeditions to overthrow the Spanish regime. Such was the case in the South, where proslavery leaders tended to look toward places like Cuba as natural, desirable areas for expansion.

The most prominent organizer of an invasion was a Cuban, Narciso Lopez, who led two expeditions. The first ended in his successful retreat by ship to Key West. The second was disastrous. His force of four hundred was captured, many of them executed, and the rest sent to Spain for imprisonment. Webster sought to do what he could to assure humane treatment and even succeeded in getting their release. Generally, however, his effort to enforce the neutrality law against filibusters failed because local sentiment in this country prevailed over available federal measures of control. Cuba would remain a source of trouble for years to come.[37]

Webster's strategy in dealing with Mexican problems seemed to center on use of money, which was extremely scarce in that country. To deal with the persistent unrest along the Texan boundary, which the United States had pledged itself to prevent in the treaty of 1848, he proposed to buy off this obligation, thus forcing Mexico itself to be a more active peacekeeper. But nothing materialized. Then he suggested withholding payment of the installments of the American indemnity of fifteen millions, stipulated in another provision of the treaty, to exert leverage on Mexico. But he had no more success with that idea.[38]

Unrest and payment of the indemnity, however, were secondary to the major question the two nations confronted, construction of an interoceanic railroad across southern Mexico. American interest in some isthmian route, by canal or rail, had grown as a result of the acquisition of California, the subsequent gold rush there, and increased commercial activity in the Pacific. Work proceeded on a railroad across Panama, a project Webster had strongly supported in the Senate. But another route, thought to be practical, would begin at the mouth of the Coatzacoalcos River, ascend to a plateau, then run through deep valleys in the mountains to a harbor at Tehuantepec, on the west coast, altogether a distance of 143 miles. Surveys showed that a railroad could be built here; the main problem was how to win Mexican consent.[39]

A Tehuantepec railroad depended upon two conditions. First, private capital must come in to build and operate it, with assurance that it would be safe under Mexican law. A grant of right of way, augmented by cession of more land and by various legal privileges, must encourage the undertaking in the form of a contract. By 1850 these arrangements seemed in order. Recently the New York company of Peter Hargous believed it had got such a contract, acquired indirectly from an original grant to José de Garay in 1842. It was true that Garay had not completed a transit within the specified time, but Hargous relied upon several extensions of the deadline by the government. He calculated that a wide swath of land, ceded along the route, could be developed to pay for the costs of construction. Second, the project required a treaty between Mexico and the United States to protect the contract. Webster's predecessor, Clayton, and the Mexican foreign secretary had drafted such a treaty, ready for ratification in June 1850. It guaranteed the neutral character of the area, dealt with toll setting, and provided for American intervention if Mexico could not maintain security and requested aid.[40]

When Webster took over in July, he received complaints from Hargous that the draft treaty did not go far enough in protecting workers and settlers, in allowing the company sufficient rights in setting tolls, and especially in authorizing American intervention if Mexico did not invite it. So the secretary instructed his minister in Mexico City, Robert Letcher, to renegotiate these terms.[41] Soon Letcher reported that opinion there was so distrustful of American intentions, perceived to be too much like those during the Texas dispute, that he could not extract further concessions, indeed feared that the national legislature might not ratify any treaty. Later the new president, Mariano Arista, told Webster the same thing, despite friendly professions.[42] Webster concluded that the best solution he could obtain was acceptance of Clayton's treaty, to which Arista agreed on January 25, 1851. As for the necessary ratifications, the Senate quickly assented, but time passed without action by the Mexican congress. Worse yet, that body nullified the Garay-Hargous grant on the grounds that deadlines for the work had passed and that an acting president had exceeded his authority in giving an extension in 1846.[43]

Meanwhile Hargous had combined with a group of investors in New Orleans, headed by Judah Benjamin and operating under the name of the Louisiana Tehuantepec Company. It had sent engineers and laborers to the isthmus to begin construction and was already making land grants to settlers along the right of way. In mid-1851, proceeding on its invalidation of the original contract, Mexico expelled these persons and barred company access to the terminal ports. An able, influential figure, Benjamin exerted all the pressure he could upon the Fillmore administration to rescue the venture. He did get a sympathetic hearing on the wrongs done to the enterprise.[44] At one point the president even considered sending Benjamin to replace Letcher as minister.[45] But both

Fillmore and Webster refrained from extreme steps. The former declared that he was "not willing to see the nation involved in a war with Mexico to gratify the wishes or cupidity of any private company."[46] The latter agreed, refusing to promise Benjamin intervention by force. "If the parties concerned, see fit to prosecute their plans, in defiance of Mexico," he said, "they must be regarded as acting at their own risk." In light of this policy, Benjamin and his associates changed their minds about ordering armed resistance by their own people.[47]

For the time being, the secretary merely protested cancellation of the contract, albeit very vigorously. He still hoped for legislative ratification of the treaty in Mexico by January 1852, within the one-year period allowed. He instructed Letcher to apply all available leverage, including hints of holding up the next indemnity and of paying extra money to buy off the American obligation to monitor the border. A country guilty of such unprincipled conduct, he observed, might respond to dollars if not reason.[48] He did worry that Mexico might now make a new grant to British interests, contrary to an American claim to hemispheric priority (a suggestion of the Monroe Doctrine).[49] Though he generally approved Letcher's efforts and had long been quite friendly with the Kentuckian, Webster was concerned when he left his post at Mexico City for an extended visit home. Maybe it would be well, he thought, to send a special agent to do what the minister could not manage. Yet a last-minute move to do that made no difference.[50]

The deadline for Mexican ratification passed, and so did an extension to April 1852. The possibility of saving the project collapsed, and thereafter relations between the two nations consisted chiefly of justifications and recriminations. A Fillmore-Arista exchange thinly covered some of the hard feeling. And in Congress there was the inevitable committee investigation, but its recommendation to the Senate for some sort of retaliation was tabled.[51] Letcher fumed and scolded in Mexico City, then gave way to a replacement. Fillmore remained determined not to risk war, despite great disappointment at the outcome.[52] Webster believed the true Mexican character had again showed itself. "Nothing can exceed the folly of their conduct," he growled.[53] In an aftermath of the affair, another company secured a grant but laid no track, and another treaty was negotiated but not ratified.[54] The United States would have to use the Panama Railroad, completed in 1855, and try to establish other isthmian connections for its shipping.

An alternative might be a canal across Nicaragua. Concurrently with the Tehuantepec negotiations, Webster pursued that possibility as far as the confused situation in Central America allowed. To succeed, he would have to deal not just with one country but with several, including in this instance a major power, Britain. A positive element was the geography of the area. On the Atlantic coast, the San Juan River provided access to the sizable Lake Nicaragua, and from there it was a short distance to the Pacific. This route lay near or at the southern edge of Nicaragua, which had shown its willingness to have a canal dug and its natural waterways improved. In 1849 the Atlantic and Pacific Ship Canal Company, headed by Cornelius Vanderbilt, had obtained a contract from the government for the project; and the American chargé got a treaty to protect the contract. But Nicaragua could not conclude this arrangement by its own decision. At the eastern terminal, the outlet of the San Juan, Britain controlled Greytown as a protectorate of the Mosquito Indians. These people—an amorphous combination of fugitive black slaves, wandering whites, and native Americans—claimed much of the coastal section but had neither the strength nor unity of a tribe, let alone a nation. So Britain had moved into Greytown two years earlier, evicted a Nicaraguan force, and declared a protectorate for the Mosquitoes. Though also having a commercial interest in the region, Britain insisted it did not intend to hold the place any longer than necessary for some stable native authority to take over. That would probably be Costa Rica, Nicaragua's southern neighbor, which not only claimed the town but also contended that its national boundary followed the river and lake, well to the north of Nicaragua's version.[55]

Britain showed no intention of preventing the construction of a canal. As proof of that attitude, it had signed a treaty with the United States in April 1850 guaranteeing the two countries free access to any line of communication in Central America. The English minister, Henry Bulwer, and Secretary of State Clayton had no difficulty on this point, though they failed to dispose of the larger question of conflicting jurisdictions along the projected isthmian transit. The Clayton-Bulwer treaty, then, left much to be done by the diplomats after Webster became secretary in July.[56]

Despite persistent efforts over the next year and a half, Webster and Bulwer could not solve the boundary problem. At the beginning, Britain offered to withdraw from Greytown in favor of Costa Rica and somehow compensate both Nicaragua and the Mosquitoes. The United States would affirm Nicaraguan sovereignty at the port, make concessions to Costa Rica on the boundary, and leave the Mosquitoes to fend for themselves.[57] The secretary soon developed a very friendly relationship with the British minister, reminiscent of the one with Ashburton. There were hardly any formal notes, but much private talk with maximum flexibility. In June 1851 they conducted business in Capon Springs, Virginia, between fishing forays.[58] Their early approach to the rival Latin American nations was mediation by the two powers, though as the months passed their commitment to their respective clients decreased. They found it unproductive to negotiate with Felipe Molina of Costa Rica and José Marcoleta of Nicaragua—the latter, in fact, lost his accreditation after a change in his home government. So Webster and Bulwer concluded that they must first discover some formula satisfactory to themselves and then see that the two small nations accepted it. In Bulwer's words, it would be necessary to "knock some common sense in them."[59] Yet in December 1851 the prospect of settlement was poor.[60]

During the winter Bulwer had been back in England and finally decided to resign his post, a move which Webster regretted because of their amicable relations. Nevertheless, Bulwer's successor, John Crampton, in cooperation with the secretary, addressed the tangled Central American situation energetically. Countering the unrest of a growing number of arrivals at Greytown, most of them Americans, the new minister and Webster jointly warned the populace that they must obey regulations of the British protectorate, pending an immediate change of government.[61] For the long term, they sought a plan with a greater sense of urgency. On their own, they would decide what ought to be done, for diplomatic contact with the new Nicaraguan government was interrupted, and Costa Rica's attitude seemed more negative than ever before. Webster's patience wore thin. If he could only get a well-protected canal, he declared, he wished to have as little to do with these miserable Central American states as possible.[62]

In late April 1852, Crampton and Webster arrived at a proposed quadruple treaty. Nicaragua would get Greytown, as well as most of the so-called Mosquito kingdom, which would be compensated and given a reservation. The Nicaraguan–Costa Rican boundary would be the San Juan River. The Atlantic and Pacific Canal Company would be assured its rights, as granted in its earlier contract. About as evenhanded as they could be, the proposals offered something to both Central American republics and, Webster believed, promoted the vital interests of all four countries, particularly by advancing construction of a canal.[63] Costa Rica was brought around, but Nicaragua rejected the terms. The new regime there was not disposed to cooperate with either Costa Rica or the canal company, and thus would probably have opposed almost any proposition the diplomats put forward. In time, Nicaragua would have the boundaries Webster and Crampton offered, but never a canal. Acceptance of the treaty and completion of an interoceanic waterway would have brought some political and economic benefits; though, if later experience is a guide, no complete remedies.[64] As for the United States, the failure of these negotiations contributed to a half-century delay in obtaining a water transit to the Pacific.

As isthmian diplomacy was winding down, another Latin American question came to the foreground. It involved a strange substance found on the Lobos Islands, about twenty miles off the Peruvian coast. On these barren rocks seabird droppings, called guano, had collected over many centuries to a depth of thirty feet and had recently been found to be a valuable fertilizer. In the 1840s American farmers were increasingly interested in guano; Webster himself paid a high price for it to improve the fertility of his fields at Marshfield. An international market had developed and was increasing. The Peruvian government, perennially pressed for revenue and hampered by a backward economy, decided to award a monopoly on collection, sale, and shipment to a British firm. Besides shutting out competing shippers, this move raised the price. A New York group sought help from the State Department, asserting that the Lobos, being uninhabited, belonged to no nation and ought therefore to be open to their vessels. Too quickly, the secretary approved and even had a naval vessel dispatched to protect the trade. Now the whole situation exploded. The Peruvian minister in Washington demonstrated clearly that the Lobos were Peruvian soil and that his nation would not tolerate interlopers. Slowly Webster realized his mistake, had to withdraw his commitment to protect a large number of American ships headed for the islands, and confessed to the president that he had been misinformed. It was a discomfiting episode.[65]

While Webster was trying to extricate himself from this tangle he also faced a problem relating to the northeastern fisheries. As a New Englander, he felt keenly the importance of that industry and showed the extent of his concern when Britain threatened it with a new policy in summer 1852. In July word from London arrived that henceforth Britain would more rigorously enforce the rule against fishing within the three-mile limit of the Canadian provinces and that it would close off a large area within the Bay of Fundy and the Gulf of St. Lawrence altogether. This revived the long-standing disagreement about the "liberties" which British-American treaties had granted fishermen of this country. They were actually irrevocable rights, Webster said, and he vowed to protect them "hook and line, and bob and sinker." Nevertheless, through July and August he and Fillmore sought to calm strong reaction in New England while urging England to reconsider. The British were willing to accommodate in return for some tariff concessions. These were difficult for the administration to promise, and a mere truce persisted for the remainder of Webster's tenure as secretary. Two years later, American fishing rights and trade concessions to Canada were secured, satifying both sides.[66]

On the fisheries questions as in all the diplomatic problems arising while he was secretary of state, domestic interests and opinion influenced Webster's conduct of foreign affairs as much as or more than they have influenced others holding that office. The Hülsemann note had little or no effect upon Austria, but its purpose was to arouse a feeling of national pride to counter political sectionalism. Relations with Mexico and Central America pivoted on the establishment of an interoceanic railroad or canal to meet the new needs of an expanding United States. And the abortive venture in guano diplomacy reflected a desire to improve conditions in shipping and agriculture. Although in each instance the outcome was not all he wished, existing circumstances did not permit the kind of success he had enjoyed a decade earlier in framing the Ashburton treaty. Those who came after him would share his realization that one country, however strong, cannot always control what others do.

Chapter 29

COMPROMISE
ON TRIAL

Though Webster's primary duties as secretary of state concerned foreign relations, he remained a major figure on the domestic political scene. Having a relationship of mutual confidence with the president, he could influence policymaking on any issue the administration faced. As pro-Compromise, conservative Whigs, the two men stood together on constitutional and economic grounds, on recent sectional accommodations to preserve the Union, and on the kind of nation they wished the United States to be. Fillmore respected Webster's judgment, took his advice, gave him large scope, but did not automatically defer to him. For his part, the secretary did not overstep his position. Personally and politically, he got on with the chief executive smoothly, even when they moved into an unusual contest for the presidential nomination of 1852.[1]

When he came into the cabinet in the summer of 1850, he hoped that as soon as Congress disposed of slavery questions, it would get busy on what he regarded as the more important task of economic legislation. "There has been such a vast loss of time, that I know not whether any important business can be accomplished at this session," he remarked; yet perhaps the House could take the first step by "some decided expression of opinion" on revision of the tariff. Though he talked with lobbyists and congressmen on the subject before adjournment, he found that little could be done until next year.[2] "If we had three or four of those precious weeks which were spent in making Speeches on the Wilmot Proviso, the revenue of the Country might be settled, I think, on a satisfactory foundation."[3] Actually, he worried more about protecting manufactures than about increasing public revenue. It was a great disappointment that the low tariff of 1846 remained untouched through subsequent sessions. Another measure he supported was a homestead bill, giving 160 acres of public land to a settler who would cultivate it for five years. For some time he had favored such a policy, and currently he joined Andrew Johnson and others who advocated it.[4] On this, too, Congress failed to act. An exception to legislative inaction was the Illinois Central Railroad law of 1850, subsidizing that project with a federal land grant and thereby promoting economic development. Compatible with his firm principles, this stimulus also promised something for his farm at Peru.[5] Otherwise old Whig proposals for national growth stalled, partly because slavery had become the focus of political debate.

In truth, the party system itself seemed to be disintegrating. One reason had been the Whigs' failure to exploit a rare opportunity in the early forties to put through their program. Since the divisive struggle of the Tyler period, their party showed ever less vigor, the election of General Taylor in 1848 notwithstanding. As for the Democrats, who did not wish much federal intervention in the economy and never sponsored a positive alternative to Clay's American System, their rallying cry faded once their target of opposition deteriorated. Then by 1850 the heated debate over slavery further undermined party strength, for sectional alignments, instead of Whig and Democratic loyalty, prevailed. Despite support of a few Whigs from the North such as Webster, voting by that party on the Compromise split into northern and southern segments.[6] Webster feared this damage might be permanent unless Whigs who had opposed the fugitive-slave and territorial bills forgot the past and acquiesced in all adjustments. In his judgment, there was no room in the party for those who stubbornly adhered to free-soilism or agitated the slavery question. Should reconciliation be impossible, he predicted a new party system, composed of pro- and anti-Compromise people, of unionists and antislavery activists on opposing sides.[7] Already he was sending friendly signals to old adversaries, to Cass (Democratic presidential candidate of 1848), even to Daniel Dickinson, the New York senator who had abetted Ingersoll's personal attack upon him a few years ago.[8] If the problem of slavery continued to overshadow tariff, banking, and internal improvements, then political associations must be reshuffled to defend the Union.

In the northeastern states, particularly Massachusetts, such a realignment seemed likely. Here a good many persons would not accept at least one part of the Compromise, the fugitive-slave act. Through the fall and winter of 1850 they showed a strong determination to resist its enforcement under any circumstances. From Boston pulpits, the abolitionist

476

press, meetings in Faneuil Hall and on the Common, the call to battle went out. Charles Francis Adams, Theodore Parker, Wendell Phillips, and Charles Sumner fervently protested slave catching. They contended that the government of a free republic and a society founded on religious principles should have nothing to do with such inhumane behavior. Because slaves were wrongly held in the first place, any runaway reaching free territory deserved protection, not return to the lash.[9] Though the argument was fundamentally moral, though it would not have approved any kind of statute, it denied the constitutionality of this one. The law, it was said, exceeded the limits of federal power, for the Constitution's clause on the subject obligated the states to give over fugitives on the basis of a compact of comity, but did not authorize congressional action. Besides, the commissioners who examined the owners' claims and ordered rendition of slaves performed a judicial function but did not have the constitutional characteristics of federal judges. They lacked tenure of office for life and good behavior and had no fixed compensation. Nor did they observe the rules of due process—rights of defendants to be tried by jury, to present evidence, and to appeal commissioners' orders in higher courts, all guaranteed by the Constitution but bypassed in the statute. Thus the antislavery position advanced some persuasive objections.[10]

In October 1850, shortly after passage of the measure, both verbal and physical resistance emerged in several places. Federal commissioners and judges encountered formidable difficulties requiring support from Washington. Such was the situation in Philadelphia, in the circuit of Supreme Court Justice Robert Grier, who asked Fillmore for troops to put down disorder. Cautious though he usually was, the president wasted no time in acting. He had already resolved doubts about the law's validity after getting the attorney general's favorable opinion, and he was convinced that executing it rigorously was indispensable to upholding the Compromise.[11] Webster thought so too. Because he was in New England, he could not participate in the initial decision. Yet in an exchange of several letters with the chief executive, he fully endorsed a presidential authorization for judges and marshals to invoke military assistance where necessary.[12] "There must be no flinching, nor doubt, nor hesitation," the secretary declared. "The thing should be done as mildly & quietly as possible; but it must be done."[13]

During the following weeks Webster repeatedly affirmed the administration's policy of strict enforcement. In letters addressed to groups or individuals and then published, he took a hard line. The fugitive-slave act, he said, represented majority will and must therefore be obeyed as a

"Christian duty." "No man is at liberty to set up, or affect to set up, his own conscience as above the law, in a matter which respects the rights of others . . ."[14] Deprecating false appeals to a higher law, he warned that they could lead to bloodshed and disruption of basic institutions. Furthermore, he saw no merit in the contention that this statute was unconstitutional. To be sure, he would have preferred the amendment for jury trial he had offered in the Senate, but the fact that it was not adopted did not cause him to doubt the validity of this legislation. Let it be tried, he advised; and if wrongs occurred, Congress could then revise it. He knew that some federal judges, including Supreme Court justices, and some sound lawyers had expressed their opinion that the law was constitutional; but like those on the other side of the question, he gave greater weight to nonlegal factors. At this moment, observance of the Compromise to maintain the Union overrode all else.[15]

He was not dealing with an abstract question, nor one merely affecting people at some distant location, for the center of opposition was Boston. As the administration's policy evolved and as he warmly defended it, controversial cases arose in the Massachusetts capital. The first one involved two fugitives from Georgia, William and Ellen Craft. They had been in the city for some time and had been given haven by antislavery leaders, who now did everything they could to prevent a ruling by the federal commissioner for the slaves' return. Threats of violent resistance, as well as obstructive steps by defense attorneys, represented a strategy agreed upon beforehand. Such tactics promised success in a setting where the United States attorney, George Lunt, felt no interest in executing a law in which he did not believe and where the federal marshal showed little energy or bravery. The case reached a climax in mid-November 1850 when Webster was in town.[16] Meeting with the marshal, he plainly told him to do his duty or announce his reasons for not doing so. At the last minute, when it finally appeared that the Crafts would be handed over to the owner's agent, they were spirited away on a ship bound for England, much to Webster's dismay.[17]

A still bolder defiance of the law occurred the following February. A fugitive from Virginia, Shadrach, was brought before the commissioner, George Curtis, for an immediate hearing on the claimant's affidavit. Several antislavery lawyers, including Richard Henry Dana, volunteered to defend him; accordingly, Curtis ordered a delay in proceedings. But at that juncture a large crowd rushed into the courtroom and rescued the slave, who was soon on his way to freedom in Canada. Leading the intervention were Elizur Wright and other prominent antislavery men, all easily identified.[18] Webster felt there could not have

478

been a more flagrant piece of lawlessness. It was nothing short of treason, he believed.[19] The federal marshal, from whose custody Shadrach escaped, had been out of town during the affair. As in the Craft case, he had not prepared for such trouble. At the secretary's brisk request, he filed a full report on what had happened and on what corrective action would be taken.[20] Fillmore, working closely with Webster, acted on the situation without delay. In a proclamation to all federal officers and citizens in the vicinity of a slave capture, he directed full compliance with the terms of the law.[21] And to the Senate he sent a long message, reviewing the facts and recommending improvements in the system. Both he and the secretary blamed the marshal for negligence.[22] Webster also lectured District Attorney Lunt for being too slow in prosecuting those who had led the rescue—he told him he particularly wished to punish Wright. Having little confidence in Lunt, he tried to add Rufus Choate and other trusted lawyers to counsel for the prosecution; but Choate, who also disliked the district attorney, made an excuse and did not serve.[23] At any rate, there were eight men indicted, three (including Wright) were tried in the United States District Court, but the jury was hung, and all eventually went free. This outcome presaged many others like it throughout the country.

Meanwhile Webster pressed those in authority in Boston to prevent a repetition of such episodes. The mayor and city council seemed ready to do so, but Parker and Phillips continued to call for resistance, even by force. It was unclear which side would prevail.[24]

The test came in early April on a claim for another runaway, Thomas Sims of Georgia. This time Commissioner Curtis adjourned the hearing until the state chief justice, Lemuel Shaw, could rule upon a petition of habeas corpus for Sims's release. Around the courthouse several hundred militiamen, deputy marshals, and city police stood guard; a huge chain encircling the building warned off interlopers from the surrounding crowd. The atmosphere was explosive. But the defenders thwarted plans by Parker and his associates to rescue Sims.[25] And Chief Justice Shaw ruled that he could not intervene in the case because the prisoner had been rightly recovered under the fugitive-slave act. There was a national power, to which states must defer, of giving effect to the clause of the Constitution on this matter, he ruled. Nor could he accept antislavery objections that the commissioners were performing a judicial function without having the characteristics of judges.[26] Webster was in the city to watch these events approvingly, most of all his friend Shaw's decision. The next morning before dawn, April 12, 1851, Sims was hurried aboard a ship for return to Savannah.

Meanwhile, controversy about returning fugitive slaves had become widespread. In Christiana, Pennsylvania, claimant Edward Gorsuch was killed in September 1851 when he sought to recover a slave; and the next month in Syracuse, New York, where an abolitionist convention had gathered, a crowd freed the runaway Jerry McHenry. Webster insisted upon prosecuting a number of people for treason in both incidents, but it was impossible to convict them on that charge.[27] In general, violent resistance or threats of it and ingenious countermovements by defense counsel made punishment of those assisting fugitives virtually impossible. In New England, after the Sims case only one other runaway was returned during the next decade.[28]

In the North as a whole, however, resistance was not significant in terms of numbers. Altogether in the 1850s, the commissioners received 191 claims, of which they upheld 80 percent. But these claims represented perhaps only 2 percent of the number of slaves fleeing northward; and a very small fraction of all slaves in the South did take flight. So in the relatively few instances in which owners did press their claims, most federal and local officials complied with the law. And most northerners were not inclined to resist it, even if they felt it was wrong.[29]

Committed to the Compromise as he was, Webster became ever more convinced that the fugitive-slave law was right. In May 1851, while the Shadrach trials were pending, he denounced the fanatics, as he termed them. They were like the Fifth Monarchy people of Cromwell's day, he declared, talking of a higher law revealed only to them.[30] A year later in a public letter he unreservedly pronounced the law constitutional. He relied upon long-standing acceptance of the earlier statute of 1793, the opinions of various judges and lawyers upon the present legislation, and his own interpretation of the words in the relevant clause of the Constitution. But his argument was more that of the politician than of the careful constitutional lawyer meeting specific objections or developing ideas systematically. He seemed dogmatic and aroused to the danger at hand. This measure, he said, was "entirely constitutional, highly proper, and absolutely essential to the peace of the country. Such a law is demanded by the plain written words of the Constitution, and how any man can wish to abrogate or destroy it, and at the same time say that he is a supporter of the Constitution, and willing to adhere to those provisions in it which are clear and positive injunctions and restraints, passes my power of comprehension." At last, he had come to the point of equating loyalty to the Union with support of the statute.[31]

Throughout his time in the cabinet he emphasized the necessity of preserving the Union, which, he believed, remained endangered on both flanks by northern extremists and southern fire-eaters. He acted as if the nation was still in a crisis, even though the recent Compromise may have somewhat lessened the gravity of the peril. His correspondence and speeches dwelt upon this theme. If the "institutions of our fathers" were maintained, he said, then the future of this dynamic republic would be bright; if not, he saw nothing ahead but retrogression and conflict.[32] Sensitive to condemnation by antislavery critics, he tended to defend his own course while defending the Union. Such a mixture of personal and general interests was, of course, not unique in the world of politicians; but as an aspirant for the presidency, he had special reasons to identify one with the other.

If the United States disintegrated, the cause would be southern secession, followed by civil war; it was that specter which had pushed people like Webster to compromise. So his primary complaint against northern radicals rested on the possibility that they would drive their southern counterparts to that extremity. Presently, this consideration lay behind his staunch position on the fugitive-slave act, for it was the principal concession to the slaveholding states; and they would regard noncompliance with that compromise as good and sufficient grounds for severing ties with the free states, he thought.[33] In speaking to the South, therefore, he promised that section that the executive branch would enforce the law and that people in the North would obey it. Nevertheless, he would place responsibility on southerners, too. Not long after assuming office as secretary of state, he drafted a circular to federal officers about their duty to uphold the Constitution. By their oath of office they must faithfully execute the laws passed in accordance with that document. In the American system of divided state and national power, the laws, treaties, and Constitution of the United States were supreme, state laws to the contrary notwithstanding (Constitution, Article VI). And federal courts could safeguard that supremacy. In this brief exposition of constitutional law, Webster's circular would remind all officers what specific types of judicial help were available in event of state obstruction of national authority. It would further remind them that states were incompetent to dissolve the Union in any regular, peaceful fashion.[34] Reminiscent of what he had often argued in the Senate, the draft seemed a little too nationalistic for at least one member of Fillmore's cabinet, Secretary of the Interior Alexander Stuart. Not wishing to stir up old coals, Fillmore did not approve sending it out.[35]

The president's decision did not discourage Webster from continuing his effort against secessionism by assurances and warnings to the South, assurance that the Compromise was safe and warning that it must not be so foolhardy as to try to break up the perpetual Union.[36] His old friends Joel Poinsett and James Petigru kept him informed about the situation in South Carolina, where the danger of secession had always been especially worrisome.[37] In mid-1851 he appeared at a dinner in Capon Springs, Virginia, in honor of his part in the Compromise. In his address, later published and widely read, he deplored southern restiveness, which, he hoped, would soon "blow over." But if secessionists dared to infringe the Constitution in any way, he vowed that the administration would act vigorously.[38] A few days later, on the Fourth of July, he spoke at a well-reported ceremony for laying the cornerstone of an addition to the Capitol and again rapped the knuckles of southern states' righters. Praising the American system of government and the immense progress the country had made in this century, he declared that extremists would "have their eyeballs seared as they beheld the steady flight of the American eagle, on his burnished wings, for years and years to come."[39]

More often he defended the Compromise against antislavery attack in the North. Whether correctly or not, Webster personally symbolized the policy and therefore was constantly called upon to write or say something for it. A great many invitations to attend Unionist gatherings across the land arrived in the mail; and though it was impossible to accept more than a few, he frequently sent a letter to be read at a meeting and then published. In such statements his plea was to uphold the fugitive-slave law and to reject senseless, categorical free-soilism and inflammatory invocations to conscience or the vagaries of higher law. Stand fast behind the original terms of the Constitution, which are indispensable to the Union, he advised.[40] Now and then he did speak on the subject—at the Pilgrim Festival in New York, at a convention in Annapolis, at a session of the Pennsylvania legislature.[41] Even in his discourse on history to the New York Historical Society, he related his generalizations on the uses of the past to the great question of the moment.[42]

His best opportunity to counter antislavery opinion came in May 1851. The president asked him to join an official party traveling the five-hundred-mile route of the new Erie Railroad in celebration of its opening. For two weeks, beginning on the fourteenth, Webster moved from one town to another, from the Hudson Valley to Lake Erie. When the group reached Dunkirk on the Lake, the westernmost point of the road, he parted company with Fillmore and returned on his own. It was a delicate situation, for both the president and the secretary of state spoke frequently along the way and seemed now to be probable contenders for the Whig nomination next year. Besides, Webster had been reluctant to undergo the physical ordeal of travel and public appearances day after day, morning till night. Still, upstate New York, an anti-slavery stronghold, was the very place to make inroads in behalf of the Compromise. Altogether he made eleven set speeches and many more brief remarks, largely on his return from Buffalo via Rochester, Canandaigua, Auburn, and Syracuse to Albany. Contrary to his fears, he ended the trip in good health and spirits.[43]

He said about the same thing wherever he stopped, and what he had been saying for some time. The burden of his argument was that the nation's troubles resulted from a long series of mistakes concerning slavery in the West. With this review he blended a justification of his own position through the years. Much of the controversy about extension of slavery derived from missteps in acquiring new territory, he said, beginning with Louisiana and Florida and including Texas and the Mexican cession. As he had often said before, he opposed such expansion when it led to adding new states to the Union. Indeed, he still believed that to be unconstitutional. Citing his record on the acquisitions of the thirties and forties, he reasoned that if his view had prevailed, the crisis of 1850 would not have arisen. As it was, there had been expansionists in Congress, some from New York, who had become free-soilers and therefore aggravated the difficulty they helped to create. Fortunate it had been, he said, that the Compromise had provided for sectional accommodation. Much as Lincoln would later express it, Webster observed, "If a house be divided against itself, it will fall and crush everybody in it." As for his own role in averting catastrophe, his account was unblemished by modesty. Recounting his speech of March 7 the previous year, he asserted, "I cared for nothing, I was afraid of nothing, but I meant to do my duty . . . And, Gentlemen, allow me to say here to-day, that if the fate of John Rogers had stared me in the face, if I had seen the stake, if I had heard the faggots crackling, by the blessing of Almighty God I would have gone on and discharged the duty which I thought my country called upon me to perform. I would have become a martyr to save the country."[44] Stirring rhetoric, but not very accurate testimony.

When he talked to a sizable crowd in Syracuse, he spent more time than usual on the fugitive-slave issue. Again, he recalled his jury-trial amendment in the Senate; yet the law was fair and necessary without it, he believed. Knowing he faced an audience composed of many persons discontented with the new procedure for returning runaways, realizing, as he remarked privately, that here was the laboratory of abolitionism, he put his case in the strongest terms. Resistance to this law was treason. A few months later he would test that idea by prosecuting, unsuccessfully, the rescuers of the slave Jerry McHenry.[45]

Old topics also recurred in the addresses, though given less attention than before. In Buffalo he elaborated upon his familiar perception of a burgeoning America, so well illustrated by this new western city, whose commerce and industry had grown spectacularly. He added an interesting element here, approval of the flow of immigrants to the region. In contrast to his previous suspicions of foreign-born Americans, he now showed he would have nothing to do with the rising tide of nativism. But generally he was absorbed in dealing with the multifaceted problem of slavery.[46]

Upon his return to the East, he conferred with his friends about presidential politics and concluded that the western tour had been so satisfactory he ought to circulate his recent speeches widely. Both he and Fillmore had been very much aware of the implications of this tour; and despite traces of concern about appearing to challenge the president for the nomination while remaining in the cabinet, the secretary decided to print thousands of copies of a pamphlet in a "handsome edition."[47] The time had arrived to get the movement underway.

The first step toward candidacy would have to be taken in Massachusetts, which by its endorsement could influence other states to do the same prior to a national convention the following year. Because of the political turmoil there, getting the process in motion would be more difficult than ever before. The truth was that he faced opposition within the party at his home base. It was the old problem of a division between Conscience and Cotton Whigs, for discontent with Webster's role in the Compromise as well as his recent insistence on stiff enforcement of the fugitive-slave act promised trouble. In Boston, the *Atlas* attacked him regularly, though he was pleased with continued assistance from the *Courier* and the *Advertiser*.[48] Horace Mann and many others of the congressional delegation were arrayed against him. Even federal officeholders, especially Collector Philip Greely, were unfriendly.[49] And on the Whig central committee, there were some members dissatisfied with his course.[50] So when the state convention met in October 1850, it was no surprise that a resolution calling for revision of the fugitive-slave law passed, reflecting a general coolness toward the secretary. In the November election, the Whigs suffered a blow when the combined Democratic and Free Soil vote exceeded that of the Whigs. Too many in the party were beguiled by extremist notions, Webster believed.[51]

When the legislature met in early 1851, Democrats and Free-Soilers struck a deal, since together they outnumbered the Whig members. Control of the state administration would go to the Democrats, while the Free-Soilers could have the Senate seat long held by Webster and after him by Robert Winthrop on a temporary basis. Webster and his friends were extremely upset by what they described as an unprincipled coalition of two elements not agreeing on anything except to deprive the leading party of office. Nevertheless, this alliance of convenience had trouble electing a senator. Though the state senate presented no difficulty, Whigs were stronger in the house and had some conservative Democratic help. It was a protracted contest of three months. Whigs voted for Winthrop; the coalition, for Charles Sumner. Webster would have gladly accepted a unionist Democrat but could generate no enthusiasm for that idea. Although Winthrop had not fully supported the Compromise, Whigs felt he was preferable to a Democrat and certainly to a radical such as Sumner. Finally, in April, Sumner won by one vote in the lower chamber. What a disgrace, conservatives complained, to have this unstable doctrinaire, with no experience in public office, supplanting Webster![52]

Another unpleasant event occurred in April. Webster, who was at home through much of the month, received an invitation from his supporters to speak at Faneuil Hall on the seventeenth.[53] In response to the agitation surrounding the Sims case just before this, and in anticipation of the trials of those who had rescued Shadrach, when Parker and his antislavery associates were arousing public opinion by proclaiming resistance, the board of aldermen voted to close Faneuil Hall to speakers who might further excite disorder. To be consistent, the board also refused use of the hall to Webster's group. A furor ensued. The common council unanimously reprimanded the aldermen for this insult to Boston's leading citizen.[54] Webster himself took great offense, despite the council's sympathetic declaration. Even after the aldermen reversed their ruling, he declared in his best style that he would not speak in the hall now, not "till its gates shall be thrown open, wide open, not with impetuous recoil, grating harsh thunder, but with harmonious sound, on golden hinges moving."[55] Instead he addressed a crowd in Bowdoin Square on the twenty-second and looked very much like a martyr to the cause of free speech and the Union.[56] He did not return to Faneuil Hall for a year.[57]

A few weeks after the affair, in early June 1851, an ad hoc group calling itself the Central Committee, including Everett, Choate, George Curtis, Harvey, and Haven, set to work on the presidential nomination. Dissatisfied with the regular party committee because of its free-soil leanings, they decided to bypass the usual procedure and sent out a circular to people in each school district of the state, suggesting that petitions be signed and delegates to a convention be selected. In charge of all

this, Everett reported success in a short while.[58] There was a question
whether to combine the nomination with the annual party convention
in September. Webster and his advisers decided against it, for they still
distrusted the state leadership of the party.[59] On the twenty-fifth of that
month, a special Webster nominating convention assembled in Boston.
The secretary continued to look toward new alignments, a collaboration
of all unionists, Whig and Democratic, and persuaded Everett so to
phrase a nominating address to be approved by the gathering and to go
out to the country. Those who had known Webster over many years
would have been astonished if they had known he made a conciliatory
motion toward the old Jacksonian boss, David Henshaw. Regardless of
these impractical thoughts about strategy, Webster was nominated, as
planned, after a day's proceedings. They were highlighted by Choate's
rhetorical flights, one being a reference to the "golden hinges" of Faneuil
hall swinging open.[60] Taking this independent route toward nomination
was probably unnecessary, though it did avoid an overt confrontation
between Websterites and free-soil people in the state. What mattered
now was the response from other quarters, particularly from the South.

In late 1851, by the time the Webster movement got under way, it was
clear that General Winfield Scott would be a strong contender. Senior
officer in the army, with notable service beginning in the War of 1812
and extending through the war with Mexico, Scott was the sort of candidate whom the Whig party, prone to nominate military heroes for the
presidency, might select. He was no novice in politics, however, for he
had been involved in problems of high policy, such as those along the
Canadian border in the late 1830s and early 1840s. And having spent
years in the War Department, he knew the workings of government and
the ways of politicians at Washington well. His massive physique and
commanding presence were assets attractive to a nation looking for a
popular leader. For his part, Scott had shown a lively interest in the office and had gathered substantial support for attaining it in earlier elections. One source of strength had been the Weed-Seward machine in
New York, which would now be the prime mover in advancing old Fuss
and Feathers toward the White House. Since Seward's wing of Whiggery stood for free soil and other antislavery principles, Scott seemed to
represent that position too, even though he had favored passage of the
Compromise, inconspicuously to be sure.

As a Scott boom developed through 1851, the president watched with
mounting alarm. In light of the continuing conflict with Seward's forces
in the Empire State, Fillmore interpreted what was happening as another assault upon him personally. The election of Scott would have a

deadly effect upon any future he might have as a public figure, he believed. The senator's power at home and at the capital would be overwhelming. Just as unpalatable, if not more so, would be repudiation of the Compromise, which Seward had opposed, and soon a rupture of the Union itself. Someone must stop that from occurring, and the president felt he might be the only person who could do it.

Still, he did not wish to come out openly for another term, even privately. In the year and a half before the party's convention in June 1852, he and Webster did not discuss the subject. The two were amused by gossip that they conferred regularly about their respective candidacies.[61] Publicly, the secretary was particularly anxious not to appear to be politicking in the course of making numerous speeches, for example in the tour of upstate New York along the Erie route. Neither let slip any indication of ambition or rivalry with the other in their harmonious personal relations. Yet beneath the surface both were very aware that they had become opponents. As early as May 1851 Webster wrote, "I have no doubt Mr. Fillmore will try his chances if he shall think he has any."[62] When the convention in Boston nominated him, he regretted that the president did not offer his support or at least say he would not run himself. He hoped for such a statement in the annual message to Congress in December, but there was none. The weeks went by, Fillmore was silent, and silence seemed to be acquiescence in a growing sentiment for his candidacy, particularly in the South. And if Webster did not pick up commitments there, he would not be a national candidate, indeed could not get the party's nomination. Also disturbing was an endorsement of Fillmore by Clay, now nearing death but still an influential Whig voice.[63]

The secretary considered resignation from the cabinet, for it did not seem proper to challenge the leader of an administration of which he was a part. Yet throughout his career he had often talked of resigning office without doing so, and he followed the same course now. His advisers urged him to stay; even Cass, his old Democratic adversary, did so, probably because the Compromise had brought the two men closer together.[64] In any event, there were other things to be attended to. Among them, priority must go to a wide circulation of his speeches. Fortunately, that progressed nicely. A new six-volume edition came off the press and included a very good memoir by Everett. In editing the set, his friend had frequently conferred with him about revisions and deletions of references to persons once arrayed against him but now not to be offended.[65] Besides this promising publication, he was pleased to see a heavy flow of pamphlets reporting his recent speeches, such as the one at the ceremony

487

for the Capitol addition and another in Albany during his New York tour.[66] Like many other politicians, he had confidence in the influence of the printed word upon the public mind. As for getting a nomination, he still wondered if new alignments might replace old party divisions. Could he not appeal to all upholders of the Compromise and the Union, whether Whig or Democratic, and thereby combat secessionism and abolitionism? A passage in Everett's address to the Boston nominating convention in November 1851 had taken that tack. Webster himself remarked, "I take it as certain that there can be no *entire Whig Ticket* nominated for President & Vice President."[67] Despite some weakening, party ties held. By the following March, he realized his only chance lay in selection by the approaching Whig convention.[68] One adjustment he had made was to repudiate nativism, to put aside his earlier complaints about ignorant, corruptible foreign voters. So he showed no interest in a new nativist party, nor in recruiting people of that persuasion into Whig ranks.[69]

Experienced in electioneering as he was, he understood the importance of organization in a campaign. Yet he was never able to establish an effective countrywide network of leaders and workers down to state and local levels. His strength did not extend much beyond the Northeast; and even there, it was scattered and questionable outside Massachusetts. Moreover, recent events there kept him from feeling completely secure about his home state. Around him were a few dedicated men who directed the movement: Hiram Ketchum, Charles March, Edward Curtis, and George Griswold of New York; his son Fletcher, Peter Harvey, Franklin Haven, and George Ashmun of Massachusetts. They came to Washington from time to time to talk over the situation and decide upon action, though they always gave him a far more optimistic impression of prospects than warranted, because they allowed their admiration of the great man to prevail over the facts. Ashmun worked especially hard in seeing that delegates to the national convention from the Bay State were loyal, and he drew upon his congressional experience to move about Washington in search of support by persons from other sections.[70] Haven, a novice in politics but valuable because of his connections as a banker, had recently joined Webster's inner circle. He was useful in propping up the secretary's personal financial condition as well. Ketchum, the Wall Street lawyer, had been a tireless promoter of Webster's presidential ambitions for years. The same was true of the prosperous New York merchant Griswold. Harvey, March, and Curtis were deeply committed to him but hardly up to assembling a national organization. The group, as a whole, listened as much as they advised, set up local meetings, brought out pamphlets reporting speeches, raised a little money, but faced obstacles they did not quite understand.

The main effort unfolded in New York, where the odds against success seemed to be great, owing to Seward's control of the party and his active promotion of Scott's candidacy.[71] An added problem was that the upstate area was an antislavery stronghold. It was that quarter which Webster and Fillmore invaded in their speaking trip along the Erie Railroad. But the chief hope, faint as it may have been, lay in the City, where Webster drew sizable backing from the business community. Here was the field of operations for Ketchum, Edward Curtis, the Griswolds, the Grinnells, and March (who assumed an unofficial role as coordinator). Headquartered at Charles Stetson's Astor House, they called meetings, gathered petitions, collected some funds, and conferred with the secretary whenever he passed through town.[72] The erratic editor Watson Webb added his support and began writing Webster long letters of advice.[73] In February 1852 the secretary came for several speeches—before the Historical Society, at City Hall, and to a gathering in honor of James Fenimore Cooper. On each occasion, he sidestepped specific issues for generalities on the Union and on sectional understanding.[74] On March 5, Websterites held their own nominating convention and sent out a circular, featuring an eloquent address in praise of their experienced, able candidate.[75] But the impact upon New York was discouraging. A legislative caucus declared for Scott, delegates pledged to him were being selected, and it looked as if Seward had maintained his hold on political affairs unimpaired. The best Webster could get was vague promises of second-choice support if the convention did not select Scott.[76]

The situation was the same in other northeastern states. Pennsylvania would have been a valuable prize if the secretary could have somehow overcome Scott's early advantage. He did have a following in Philadelphia, through which he usually traveled to Washington and where his links with businessmen were strong. His address to the legislature in Harrisburg represented an attempt to quiet antislavery feeling, though it seemed unavailing. But by spring 1852, a state convention had gone for Scott and chosen delegates to the national meeting accordingly.[77] In neighboring New Jersey, where he also had some strength, Webster likewise could get only second-choice assurances.[78]

New England was more encouraging. Worries about Massachusetts lessened as the effort to solidify support progressed, and those votes would at least prevent total embarrassment. Rhode Island and Connecticut seemed safe, notwithstanding some dissent and more disorganization.[79] Webster himself had visited and written to groups in New Hampshire and felt optimistic about his native state.[80] From this section, then, he should have a dependable bloc of thirty to forty votes with which to work at the convention.

Elsewhere, prospects were bleak. There seemed no possibility of first-ballot votes from the West. As elsewhere, a few suggestions of interest in these states would not add up to anything unless the Scott cause withered. The spottiness of support here was surprising in light of Webster's positive record on western issues. Perhaps the reason was simple default, a failure to advance his candidacy with any energy.[81]

More and more, the South appeared to be Fillmore territory. In Kentucky persons such as Robert Letcher and Attorney General Crittenden were friendly, but the president was the state's preference, with Webster second.[82] The Southeast and the Gulf states were going for Fillmore as the one safest on slavery and the Compromise, despite all that Webster had been doing to assure them on those grounds.[83] This was the most upsetting development, for he had gone a long way, too long to suit many northerners, to placate the South. Yet his success seemed to hinge upon Fillmore's withdrawing from the contest and asking the South to vote for the secretary. Whether he would do that and whether Webster would actually get the votes were difficult questions.[84]

The two parties held their national conventions in Baltimore in June 1852. Meeting first, the Democrats had little trouble in agreeing on a campaign position. To keep sectional feelings as calm as possible, they would adhere to the Compromise, an understandable course given the fact that they had been primarily responsible for its adoption. At the beginning of balloting for a presidential candidate, there was no consensus on any of several prominent figures—James Buchanan, Lewis Cass, William Marcy, or Stephen Douglas. After protracted voting they turned to Franklin Pierce of New Hampshire, an attractive, second-level politician whose principal asset was the fact he had not built up many enmities and would probably not do so if nominated and elected.[85]

The 294 Whig delegates who assembled in the hall of the Mechanics' Institute on the sixteenth had a similar problem, though a good deal worse. They, too, sought common ground to unify party and nation; and they faced a difficult task in picking one of three candidates, none of whom could count upon a majority at the outset. In addition, however, they had been dangerously weakened by internal conflict over the past few years. In fact it was quite possible that the Whig party was moribund.

Three days passed before the convention began balloting for the nomination. Preliminaries were more time-consuming and perhaps more important than usual: seating delegates, handling other organizational chores, and adopting a platform. In all these, the small band of delegates pledged to Webster fared well, mainly because they might tip the balance toward Fillmore or Scott, each estimated to have about the same number of votes. So the Websterites had an opportunity to get the kind of platform they favored. As chairman of the committee on resolutions, Webster's representative, George Ashmun, reported a platform fully subscribing to the Compromise "as a settlement in principle and substance, of the dangerous and exciting question they embrace." That included the fugitive-slave act, which must be strictly enforced.[86] During debate, Rufus Choate delivered a characteristically ornate and emotional speech, not only urging approval of the report but also implying that Webster was the best person to uphold the Compromise.[87] The Fillmore delegates concurred on the first point, if not the second, so that a majority of the convention would vote that way. Many Scott delegates thought otherwise, but Seward, who headed that contingent, could see that the general's nomination depended upon concession here. His advice to Scott was to forget about such small matters, accept the resolutions, and thereby attract some Webster and Fillmore delegates. This is what happened, and the pro-Compromise platform passed, 227 to 66. Only half the Scott delegates opposed it and were the only ones who did.[88] Upon hearing of this decision, the president felt pleased and seemed to care less whether he got the nomination.[89] Webster was pleased too and continued to hope for some dramatic shift of votes on the nomination.

That evening, the eighteenth, balloting for selection of a candidate began. With 147 required to nominate, the count was Fillmore, 133; Scott, 131; Webster 29. Fillmore received nearly all the southern votes and a scattering elsewhere; Scott, most of the West and many in the East; Webster, much of New England, hardly any from other sections.[90] On through the next day's session, forty-six ballots failed to produce a decisive change—Fillmore and Webster lost a few votes, but Scott did not have enough. It was now Saturday afternoon, and the convention adjourned to try again on Monday. Meanwhile there were talks and maneuvers. A combination of all the Fillmore and Webster votes would be enough to stop Scott; but neither group inclined to help the other. "My friends will stand firm," Webster declared.[91] Then his managers met with the southern Fillmore people and thought they found a way to break the deadlock in their favor. Robert Toombs and Alexander Stephens of Georgia told them that if they could recruit enough northern delegates to give Webster a total of 41, then the southern vote would go for him. Until proceedings resumed on Monday morning, they busily attempted to reach that goal, but with doubtful results.[92] In communication with them by telegraph from Washington, the irritated secretary concluded that it was impossible to pick up the extra northern votes because even old friends, such as members of the New Jersey delegation, stubbornly adhered to Scott.[93] Besides, he must have realized that if he did obtain the stipulated 41, not all the southerners would shift from Fillmore to him but would probably add at least the few votes Scott needed for a majority.

At nine on Monday morning, he sent a telegram to Ashmun in Baltimore, saying that Fletcher and others were leaving at that moment for the convention, presumably with a message.[94] To the president he sent a note stating that Fletcher's instructions were "to have an end put to the pending controversy" and predicting that the chief executive would be chosen by one o'clock.[95] Fillmore immediately replied, "I have intimated to my friends, who left last evening and this morning, a strong desire to have my name withdrawn, which I presume will be done unless the knowledge of your communication shall prevent it. I therefore wish to know whether your friends will make known your communication to mine before the balloting commences this morning? If not I apprehend it may be too late to effect anything."[96]

One can hardly imagine a stranger mix-up. The president and the secretary failed, as they had all along, to discuss the situation in time to form the coalition indispensable to give one of them the nomination. Before the convention met, even after the first few ballots on Friday, they could probably have done so and defeated Scott. The arrangement most likely to have succeeded would have been an early request from Webster to his followers to support Fillmore. As it was, balloting resumed on Monday before all the delegates got the messages. Furthermore, at that stage the Websterites wanted to test their strength, however pessimistic the outlook; and they ignored Webster's instructions anyhow because they would not go on record for anyone else. Likewise, most of the Fillmore people ignored the president's request, for they knew that the probable outcome would now be Scott's nomination. On the fifty-third ballot, the general went over the requisite number, with Fillmore and Webster each having lost just a few—the secretary received twenty-one.

Losing this, doubtless his final, bid for the presidency affected Webster profoundly. Of course, he concealed his feelings as much as he could when he spoke to groups calling upon him at the capital the next day. "The result has caused me no personal feeling whatever, nor any change of conduct or purpose," he assured them. "Circumstances or opponents may triumph over my fortunes, but they will not triumph over my temper, or my self-respect."[97] But to his close friends he seemed utterly despondent at first, then bitter. He felt badly mistreated by the South, for which he had sacrificed so much over the past two years and endured so much as a result of vicious attacks in the North. He believed it to be unmitigated treachery.[98] Consolation from his followers that the consequence was a loss to the country, not to him, that he did not need this office to add to his matchless reputation, was unavailing.[99] Indeed, he had doubts about the fairness, even the constitutionality, of the convention system in the electoral process.[100]

To compensate for the injustice and to demonstrate an undiminished attachment to Webster, the citizenry of Boston honored him with a huge reception when he returned there on July 9. A committee, including George Curtis, Harvey, and Haven, met him at Roxbury and in an elaborate procession escorted him through crowded streets to the Common. How often had he seen such a setting! Throngs of people, cheers, showers of bouquets, a laudatory address, the gift of a cane made from the hull of the USS *Constitution,* all signified enthusiastic approval. Then Webster spoke. His remarks were brief, confined to time-tested allusions to Boston's glorious past, with nothing said about recent political events. However accustomed he was to such occasions, his emotions had never been more deeply stirred.[101]

Staying at Marshfield much of the time in the following weeks, he pondered the future. A possibility, one he had frequently contemplated through the years, was the mission to England. Abbott Lawrence had resigned, dissatisfied with the administration's habit of conducting negotiations with Britain in Washington and of failing to keep him informed. Fillmore told the secretary he could have the post of minister if he wanted it. But by late July, Webster decided he did not. It would be a descent from the status to which he had been accustomed, he said, though the attendant expense and his precarious health may have been his real reasons.[102] The other possibility was to resign. His disgust at the recent decision of the convention and a conviction that the fall election would go to the Democrats led him to consider seriously leaving the cabinet now. So he tendered his resignation but with such provisos as to leave what should be done to Fillmore. The president, remaining as cordial to Webster as ever and valuing their official relationship with no abatement, urged him to stay, even if he might be compelled to be ab-

493

sent from Washington for long periods. In the end, probably because of reluctance to give up the income and prestige of the office, he said he would remain until the close of the term next March.[103]

As the late summer days passed, he was also thinking about events of the past two years. On the whole, he took pride in upholding the Compromise, including the controversial fugitive-slave act, during a grave crisis. It had saved the Union, in his opinion, despite the upheaval through which the nation had gone. How unappreciative his party had been not to acknowledge this service and again to deny him the high honor to which he aspired. The Whig party was disintegrating, he felt, and with it any opportunity he might have to advance the safety and prosperity of the country. Sectional controversy seemed headed for a devastating civil war. His forebodings of trouble grew out of a correct assessment of conditions, and perhaps his self-esteem regarding the part he had played was pardonable. Yet some needless concessions to slaveholders' interests and an underestimate of the moral dimensions of public policy had flawed his own role, whatever his positive contributions had been. Built into the Compromise he had so earnestly upheld were explosive elements likely to precipitate other crises in the years ahead.

If Webster felt that his last opportunity to gain the presidency had slipped away, some irrepressible supporters did not. A pathetic epilogue began in July 1852, when a hardy group met in Boston to propose Webster as an independent candidate. They rejected the idea of another military chieftain heading the Whig ticket and contended that the party had fallen under control of dangerous foes of the Compromise. Safety of the Union required leadership of a better-qualified person, they believed.

The organizers of this dubious, last-minute venture were relatively inexperienced people who had not been active in politics and perhaps had little to risk. Better known than the rest, yet unseasoned too, was the secretary's young friend George Ticknor Curtis; still he had liabilities, notably controversial service as fugitive-slave commissioner. A striking feature of the movement was the refusal of prominent Websterites—Everett, Choate, Ashmun, Harvey, Edward Curtis, Moses Grinnell, and others—to have anything to do with it. These were the persons who had conducted the late campaign from first to last, on through the Baltimore convention. They could see the hopelessness of holding out any longer and the damage an independent candidacy would inflict, not only upon the party but upon the cause for which Webster himself had fought. It would badly tarnish the historical reputation of the great Defender of the Constitution, they warned.[104]

Pressure on Webster to approve this effort increased as appeals arrived in his mail.[105] While he remained at Marshfield, only a few people could reach him directly; and he felt thankful they could not, yearning for escape and quiet as he did. But on August 4, just before he left for Washington, George Curtis came down to talk. After advancing reasons for opposition to the Scott ticket, Curtis got a firsthand reaction. It was negative, though not absolutely prohibitive. Webster agreed that the Whig party stood in mortal danger and that Scott was not a fit candidate, not one whom he could endorse. Nevertheless, he wished his friends would abandon any thought of presenting him on an independent ticket. He hedged a bit, however, when he added that he could not prevent anyone from voting for him, notwithstanding his disapproval of a revolt. His firm intention, he emphasized, was to be silent.[106]

So far the project appeared to be local, confined to Massachusetts and New York.[107] But immediately after Curtis' visit, an interesting letter arrived from Georgia. The writer spoke for two influential Whigs, Alexander Stephens and Robert Toombs, both determined to prevent Scott's election on the ground that he would repudiate the Compromise. No longer able to cooperate as they had with conservative Democrats, Stephens and Toombs had called a convention at Macon for August 18 to nominate an independent unionist. Would Webster consent? Adhering to his position of silence, he did not answer. On the other hand, Stephens' separate approach to George Curtis got an enthusiastic response. Certainly, Curtis replied, Massachusetts welcomed this initiative because it would help make the movement national.[108]

Thus encouraged, a gathering at Boston's Tremont House on August 16 selected a committee, including Curtis, to arrange a nominating convention. Two days later, the Georgia unionists met and declared for Webster as president and for Charles Jenkins, one of their number, as vice-president. Whereas Whig regulars such as Winthrop and Seward had discounted the potential of an independent bid, they now feared that something might come of it, at least a party division allowing Democratic victory.[109] It might accomplish more than that, predicted Fletcher, who reported a heartening momentum to his father. "I am a little provoked," Webster retorted. "I have no advice to give my friends, either to act, or not to act ... Let me at last [be] believed when I say I shall do nothing and say nothing one way or the other."[110]

The Boston *Advertiser* of September 9 announced that those favoring a Webster ticket would assemble in Faneuil Hall the following week. It printed the names of hundreds of persons, very few of them active politicians, joining in the call. On the next page, the masthead showed Winfield Scott to be the paper's choice for president. Despite his unflagging attachment to Webster over the years, editor Nathan Hale agreed with his brother-in-law Edward Everett about the current situation. This irregular sally would not gain many votes for Webster outside the state, perhaps only enough to elect Franklin Pierce.[111] However true that might be, on September 15 the Webster convention conducted its business harmoniously and optimistically. Speeches and resolutions rejected Scott as a mere military figure and asserted Webster's talents to be indispensable to party and nation at this perilous hour. A young lawyer, Archelaus Wilson, delivered the principal address, saying all this and appealing also for a just recognition of Webster's distinguished services. For vice-president, the meeting endorsed Georgia's choice, Charles Jenkins. In these proceedings George Curtis played a leading part, the only intimate friend of the secretary who did.[112]

At this point a question, either previously not considered or judged to be negligible, came to the foreground. It was the status of Webster's health. At seventy, he had continued to be free of serious problems, to be quite active at work and out of doors. Of course, each fall a siege of hay fever came on for a few weeks, and occasionally he had some other minor complaint. Just this spring, he had had an accident on the road down to Plymouth when a wheel of his buggy had broken loose, throwing him to the ground and painfully spraining his wrists. Though he had had to wear a sling for a while and may have made more of it than justified, he seemed back to normal during the summer.[113] After arriving in Washington in August, he remarked that he felt "uncommonly good."[114] But by the time he came home in early September, there was a decided change. Difficulty with diarrhea, previously only an occasional trouble, worsened to the point that his doctor suspected something fundamentally wrong in the abdominal area, in his intestine, stomach, or liver. As the days went by, he had increasing pain, now suffered from constipation, and vomited with traces of blood. On the sixteenth, the day after his nomination by the convention in Boston, he wrote the president about his downward turn: "My diet is milk with half lime-water, water gruel, and sometimes, a little thin soup."[115] Still, he managed to move about Marshfield, handling details on the farm. There was the usual stream of guests, among them Professor Cornelius Felton, Haven, and Ticknor, to whom he gave a host's attention. He spoke of plans to go fishing and to return to the capital. And when he had a chance to purchase a neighboring parcel of land, he did. In short, he acted as if he would soon recover.[116]

The trend was just the opposite. On September 20 he went to Boston to see a doctor, who prescribed stern measures, including complete rest, new medicine, and altered diet. When he called on Ticknor, those present were shocked at his appearance, his ashen complexion, drawn features, and obvious weakness.[117] In early October he was spending most of the time upstairs in his bedroom, the symptoms grew more ominous, his doctors came more frequently and held out less hope.[118] He himself now recognized that he might not survive this illness. One day, he instructed Tom Hatch, his farm helper, to raise a lantern on the mast of his small boat (his "home squadron") on the pond behind the house. He wished to see the boat's flag at night from his window when he could not sleep, he said. "My light shall burn & my flag shall fly as long as my life lasts."[119] Though he was now more detached from the outside world, he did answer the incoming mail by dictating to his secretary, George Abbot. Often he sent notes to Fillmore about his condition and got solicitous replies. But he did not wish the public to know the full extent of the sickness—they should believe he only had another bout of catarrh. Such a piece of news as his serious condition could not be kept secret, however, and many people soon realized this might be the end.[120]

In New York his friends—Grinnell, Evarts, Webb, Stetson, and others—were sorry to hear of his decline. But they were also concerned about the independent movement for him, threatening the regular Whig ticket as it did. Could he not break silence, disclaim such foolishness, and fall in step with the party? On September 24 they wrote a letter pleading with him to do so, but did not send it until October 9, probably because they understood how delicate the subject was. If he allowed the Boston nomination to go forward, the New Yorkers warned, "we can see no prospect of any other issue, than a most false record of the state of feeling in the Country towards you, an issue most unfortunate for the Country, and gratifying only to that faction whom your patriotism and great public services have made your enemies." Just as Webster would have expected from the Scott wing if the convention had selected him, he ought to declare his support of the general's nomination.[121]

His reaction showed how delicate the matter really was. The next day he dictated a bristling answer, refusing to do any such thing as requested. If he complied, it would gratify "that great body of implacable enemies, who have prevented me from being elected President of the United States," he declared. "No earthly consideration could induce me to say anything from which it might be inferred directly or indirectly that I concur in the Baltimore nomination, or that I should give it, in any way the sanction of my approbation. If I were to do such an act, I should feel my cheeks already scorched with shame by the reproaches of

497

posterity." He said what he meant, but for the time being he did not mail the reply.[122]

The truth was that those around his sickbed were debating his options. Edward Curtis arrived from New York to persuade him to accommodate Grinnell's request. He even drafted a response, which would have an effect opposite to that of Webster's statement. Curtis advised him to reply that he had nothing new to say beyond his known views on party allegiance, such as he had expressed in 1842 and 1848. Anyone turning to these references would find Webster's affirmation of Whig loyalty. And that, translated into a position for 1852, would be acquiescence in Scott's candidacy.[123]

Leaning in that direction, Abbot wrote Everett a note suggesting that he, too, draft a statement. As expected, on October 14 Everett supplied one in which Webster would disapprove the independent movement, since it would have no other effect than to deprive the regular Whig nominee of votes. He should bow to the decision of the Baltimore convention, Everett thought. Agreeing with Edward Curtis on what ought to be done, Everett merely phrased his draft in more elegant prose. Yet none of the three drafts, that of Webster, of Edward Curtis, or of Everett, went out.[124]

Growing restless as the election neared, Grinnell and his associates followed up with a second plea. Again Edward Curtis pressed for a reply.[125] George Curtis, William Paige, and Fletcher opposed doing so, owing to Webster's critical condition.[126] Abbot, who had earlier favored a declaration of party loyalty, felt that everyone ought to stop hounding a dying man, who no longer showed any interest in the vagaries of politics. Grinnell's behavior, Abbot remarked, resembled offering twenty pieces of silver, each worth a thousand dollars. There was some truth in this, in light of the vast financial help these wealthy men had provided Webster.[127] But all along, the secretary was convinced that the Whig party was falling to pieces and that it would be pointless, as well as demeaning, to endorse its ticket. Actually he thought highly of the Democratic candidate, Franklin Pierce, and advised his assistant, Charles Lanman, and Harvey to vote for him; but he never went beyond these conversations in embracing the party he had always inalterably opposed. It is doubtful that he ever would have.[128] At any rate, when Grinnell's second letter came, he had stopped worrying about the affairs of politicians. Even George Curtis, the mainspring of the independent movement, could see how useless and unfair it was to bother him further. On October 21 he ordered the Webster Executive Committee in Boston to suspend activities. There would be no other announcement from Marshfield concerning the election.[129]

As his condition deteriorated, Webster resigned himself to the prospect of death. During the week of this minor flurry of presidential politics, his thoughts ran to his personal affairs, his home, family, friends, financial situation, and to his fundamental religious faith.[130] To the end, he found deep satisfaction in his surroundings at Marshfield. Confined to the house, he could look out the windows on these beautiful autumn days toward the marshes and beach, the fields, farm buildings, and livestock. Once, he ordered his prized oxen driven along the front avenue and watched proudly from the parlor.[131] Around him was gathered a contingent of relatives and friends, who listened attentively to what he had to say when his pain abated but sorrowfully shook their heads as the situation looked more hopeless. His servants, the Bakers, William Johnson, Sarah Smith, Monica Carty, and the rest, assisted him constantly and were much affected, for their relations with him had been close. Caroline attended him most of the time, yet seemed overshadowed in the midst of so many others.[132]

One thing requiring attention was a new will. He must provide for his surviving family, in spite of persistent financial difficulty, by making more up-to-date arrangements. On October 18, George Curtis came down to help prepare the document. Webster outlined to Curtis what he wished to say in the will, yet worried about a problem involving the Marshfield estate. Since 1830 he had been obligated by a marriage settlement with the Le Roys. In return for a sum which Caroline's father had conferred upon him, she had a life estate in his property, first in Boston and later at Marshfield. But he wanted to leave it to Fletcher if a fair equivalent could be found to buy out his wife's claim. Could payments from his Boston annuity fund, set up by friends in 1845 to encourage him to return to the Senate, be continued after his death, thereby supporting Caroline? Curtis replied he would go to the city to find out. When he did, John Thayer, the first person he consulted, told him to look no further. Webster's wishes would be carried out. Thayer's generous impulse resembled that of the elder Samuel Appleton, who stuffed a roll of bank notes in Curtis' hands to take care of whatever expenses had arisen. Hurrying back to Marshfield, Curtis drew up the will. It provided that the farm and other property there (and the Elms too) would go to Fletcher if money to pay for Caroline's life interest were raised. There were terms also on other possessions, such as the library and personal papers, going to his son, who was named one of the executors and, as Webster said, would be "the prop of my house." Typically optimistic about how he stood, he remarked to Curtis that he thought there would be enough assets to pay all his debts.[133]

Each day now, Webster seemed on the threshold of death. There were recurrent attacks of nausea and vomiting, alleviated as much as possible with morphine administered by John Jeffries, the doctor who attended him continuously. On the twenty-third, everyone, Webster included, sensed he would probably die within hours. And so the last scene of his life became a dramatic one, a solemn occasion when he uttered a final message to those hovering around his bed. George Curtis sat nearby, listening and taking notes as if reporting a speech at Faneuil Hall or in the Senate. Later he would report in a widely read biography what he had witnessed.

Most of Webster's words concerned his religious faith. Affirming unshakable belief in an omnipotent but merciful God, redemption by Christ, and the doctrine of immortality, he would commit his soul to his maker.[134] He recited the Lord's Prayer, then added, "Peace on earth, and good-will to *men—that* is the happiness, the essence—*good will toward men.*" Aware of the importance of his words to his grieving listeners, he asked, "Have I . . . said anything unworthy of Daniel Webster?" One and all responded, no.

The relationship between consciousness and death obsessed him. What would one experience at the final moment? Would he know that death had occurred? One time, he faded away into unconsciousness, and when he roused, cried out, "I'm dead, I'm dead!" It was a question he repeatedly discussed with his doctor. During the long night of the twenty-third, breaking the silence of the vigil, he exclaimed, "I still live!" No more than a reflection of his confusion about experiencing death, these final words would later take on a much broader meaning to many people. Shortly afterward, a little before three on Sunday morning, October 24, he died.[135]

Through the following week, from Boston across the nation, Webster's passing brought on a massive display of sentiment. Every day the newspapers were full of details about his life and the innumerable events commemorating him. There were eulogies, memorials, and resolutions of all sorts. General gatherings at Faneuil Hall, meetings of Boston merchants and of the bar dominated attention. For the funeral at Marshfield on October 29, ten thousand people crowded around his house and filed in long lines past his coffin set out in front. A religious ceremony inside was followed by a slow procession to Winslow Burying Ground, a short distance away; and there on an elevated site, near the place where a Pilgrim meetinghouse had stood two centuries before, he was buried in a family plot.[136] From this point, one could see his farm, the ocean, and many scenes closely associated with this extraordinary man.

Chapter 30
ADVOCATE
OF NATIONALITY

The story of Webster's life is incomplete until it is set in historical perspective. Unless his undeniable prominence in antebellum America reveals something worth knowing about his times and something relevant to later generations, the record of what he did does not deserve much notice. Such an assessment must take into account the variety of roles he played during fifty years of change in the young republic. Not merely a politician of the first rank, he had a comparable reputation in law, diplomacy, and oratory.

The starting point, however, must be an understanding of his personal character. And a fundamental fact is that he had uncommon natural ability. As even his severest critics conceded, it was his good fortune to have a keen and fertile mind. Laying aside the point impressing nineteenth-century phrenologists, that his brain was larger and weighed more than almost any other on record, one is struck by his mental capacity—his remarkable ability to absorb, analyze, and conceptualize information. Early on, he learned the value of dealing with intricate subjects in a direct and meaningful fashion; and he perfected that technique as few others did. His studies in college and law offices helped him to develop this skill; but mainly it was his continuing experience, his self-education, which did so.

His high-level energy allowed him to work at full speed every day from early morning on, preparing legal cases and speeches or wading through stacks of papers on his desk. Contrary to a widespread impression that he tended to be lethargic and often detached, his habit was to be methodical and industrious. Though he worked hard, he also relished recreational outlets. Nothing pleased him more than a respite outdoors for sailing, fishing, hunting, or tramping around his beloved Marshfield. Close attention to agricultural details there also provided satisfaction.

A driving force was his fondness for things material, for the luxury enjoyed by the wealthy. In contrast to his condition as a youth, his elevated status in later life brought him handsome homes, large tracts of real estate, servants, and fine food and wines. He constantly yearned for the assurance a great fortune could give him; and many of the people he most admired belonged to the upper class. He was continuously on the lookout for some triumph of speculation, a windfall which would eliminate once and for all a nagging worry about money. He was repeatedly disappointed in this hope and never out of trouble, for his extravagance kept him deep in debt. A low point came after the panic of 1837, when his overinvestments in western land purchases overwhelmed him. To be sure, the Bank of the United States and a number of friends came to his aid, but even such help was not enough for him to recoup his losses. He could never close the gap between his uncontrolled expenses and his sizable income. This incapacity was all the more regrettable because it raised a question about his integrity, about his relationship with well-to-do rescuers. The distinction between his personal transactions and public business was a very fine one. Though he did not take bribes nor alter his positions on important political issues because of these relations, he was culpable of serious impropriety.

This dependence upon others went beyond the matter of his financial woes. It also reflected a more attractive characteristic, his sociability. Though he projected an image of brilliance and self-reliance, he needed and fostered close associations. Until Ezekiel's untimely death in the 1820s, his brother was a mainstay. For most of Webster's adult life, Edward Everett remained an intimate; among numerous others were Joseph Story, Jeremiah Mason, George Ticknor, and Peter Harvey. To such friends and to his domestic circle, he was open, lighthearted, and considerate, with none of the aloofness or pomposity frequently attributed to him.

However vulnerable he may have been to charges of unethical, even amoral conduct, he firmly adhered to his own norms of right conduct. The key word for Webster and for a great many contemporaries was respectability. The newspapers and correspondence of his day made heavy use of that term. It connoted personal stability, social conformity, and a certain economic standing. Like other respectable people, Webster observed prevalent rules of behavior, disapproving departures from what was established and embracing values of the great majority. Indispensable was an acceptance of basic religious tenets; for him, this meant the old and safe way of the Congregational faith, more conservative than the Unitarianism of his day. Similarly, most prescriptions for social reform seemed to him misguided and futile, for he held to a doctrine of individual responsibility. Abolitionism, temperance, and other humanitarian movements were more than unpromising—they could undermine order and justice. He probably had too much confidence in the power of individual conscience and self-discipline.

The public estimate of his character was mixed. If exaggerated, stories about his excessive drinking and shortcomings in handling his financial affairs abounded. His closest friends recognized these defects, even at a time when such weaknesses were not unusual. Public awareness of his failings tended to lower confidence in his probity, to create some distrust of his motives. Yet there was the countervailing factor of his popularity, ranging from immense interest to outright adulation. As the years passed, the adjective "God-like" was increasingly joined with his name in the public's perception. In turn, this admiration of his talents significantly affected his personal style.

One of these talents was his superb oratorical skill. Students of rhetoric have ranked him at or near the top among public speakers in the nation's history. Though others, such as Choate, Everett, Clay, Sumner, and Wendell Phillips, were acknowledged masters, none equalled Webster. Avoiding complex or ornate diction, he spoke clearly and logically, here and there with a handsome phrase or magnificent flourish. In every setting—legislative debate, occasional address, expository discussion, courtroom argument, electioneering—he excelled. His eloquence was an invaluable asset. The only drawback may have been that it inflated his self-image and encouraged a tendency to pose. What else could be expected of one who deeply moved the feelings and sustained the attention of fifty thousand at Bunker Hill or Boston Common for two or three hours?

Yet the substance of what he had to say was more important than his power of expression. At a time when economic ideas counted for a great deal, Webster emphasized the theme of progress at every opportunity. In a land of great promise and free institutions, according to a dominant axiom, the United States would surpass the Old World in growth and prosperity. A prime condition for this to occur was protection of property rights. As he contended in his bicentennial oration at Plymouth, the freehold tenure of land equalled the founding of the church and school in promoting welfare and happiness. Drawing from his legal learning, he reiterated the proposition whenever he could: security of property rights encouraged enterprise.

During the first phase of his political life, through the War of 1812

and for a while afterward, he registered the opinion of a largely mercantile section and was partial to commerce. As late as 1824 he opposed
protective tariffs on most goods, except for some help for cotton textiles.
He then shifted from a laissez-faire position to Clay's protectionism because, he explained, New England had adjusted by investing its capital
in manufactures; a new situation required a new response. Thencefor-
ward he remained faithful to the industrial interest, even when Clay arranged an accommodation with antiprotectionists in the nullification
crisis of 1833.

Like other National Republican–Whigs, he reasoned that industrialization benefited all parts of the economy—agriculture with a home
market, commerce with stimulated exports and internal trade, manufacturing with growth and profits, labor with more jobs and higher
wages. He dwelt on the last of these, the advantages to the worker. Protection helped labor by maintaining price levels and thereby prevented
depression of wages to the low level accorded to the "pauper" labor of
Europe. Everything hinged on the principle of harmony of interests:
what aided capitalists also aided their employees. And this economic relationship rested on the continuance of a homogeneous society, indeed
on the political system known as republicanism. Thus it was a logical
step for Webster to underscore the connection between the welfare of
labor and civil liberty. As America developed economically, so would
the rights of all its citizens. He saw no static classes in this free environment. A factory hand or a small farmer could readily attain a greater
stake in society. While speaking in the Senate during the Bank War of
the 1830s, he declared that he knew this to be the case in Massachusetts.
Critics then and later disputed the soundness of such an outlook by
pointing to the quite evident limits to social mobility.

The American System of Clay and Webster comprehended not only a
protective tariff but other measures of economic nationalism as well. Internal improvement of transportation, of waterways, roads, and railroads, depended upon benevolent subsidies by the national government.
As it turned out, such projects suffered setbacks from the 1820s onward,
inflicted by Monroe's and Jackson's vetoes, by Tyler's rejection of provisions for federal distribution of land-sale proceeds, by Polk's adamant
opposition to national involvement. Similarly, their valiant efforts in
behalf of a national bank failed in the face of Jackson's stern action and
of Tyler's blows both to Clay's pure national bank and to Webster's
proposed compromises. Just as disheartening, during Polk's administration the tariff moved to a low, revenue level. The Jacksonians had
thwarted Webster and his friends on each issue. Still, from its revival

during the Civil War to the present day, the rationale of such stimulative policies would be a leading element of conservative thought.

Webster's definition of the Union meshed with his political economy, and here, too, he underwent a transformation. At first, as a young Federalist opposing Jeffersonianism, he defended the rights of a New England minority. He spoke of state interposition against the hated embargo and later war measures, believed them unconstitutional, and, despite disclaimers, approved the proceedings of the controversial Hartford Convention. In the 1820s he became a leading exponent of nationalism. In this federal structure of divided state and central authority, he contended, the sovereign people had delegated powers to two levels of government and maintained a direct relation to both. So the Union was the creation of the whole people, not of the member states. It was, moreover, a perpetual Union, not to be disrupted by any state or group of states claiming the right to rescind an original compact. National authority must be supreme within its sphere, state laws to the contrary notwithstanding. And defining the boundaries of that sphere was the primary responsibility of the Supreme Court in deciding appropriate judicial cases, though Congress and the president had roles too. This Union, Webster exclaimed in his reply to Hayne, promoted popular liberty, did not menace it. "Liberty and Union, now and forever, one and inseparable."

Apart from such partisan applications as he often gave to this definition, it was his greatest contribution to the country. The idea was not novel; its antecedents went back as early as the Constitutional Convention and included a classic statement by the Supreme Court in the national bank case in which Webster participated as counsel. And it took into account years of constitutional development. Nevertheless, the states' rights, compact theory of Calhoun had an equally long history and a substantial following. Lincoln would restate Webster's position, and the Civil War would vindicate it. Afterward it would be a valuable heritage and a fundamental idea of modern America.

Webster's economic and constitutional thought infused his work as a lawyer. In *McCulloch* v. *Maryland* (1819), he and William Pinkney successfully argued for broad national powers by a government of the people and for their benefit, precisely as he would later argue in the Senate. In the steamboat case of *Gibbons* (1824), he contended for broad, flexible congressional power over commerce, with states having some authority but not equal to or fully concurrent with that of the nation. A quarter-century later, he could be satisfied with a general judicial rule laid down along those lines. In several cases involving the contract clause, which prohibits state impairment, he had an opportunity to influence the country's economic direction. The best example is the *Dartmouth College* case on property rights of corporations. Despite losing *Charles River Bridge* in Taney's Court, he could be pleased that by midcentury a body of precedents would amply shield enterprise from excessive state regulation. As a politician, he often drew upon these judicial doctrines to deal with various issues; and well he might, for he had participated in shaping this constitutional law. Furthermore, in his practice before lower courts he helped adapt the old common law to new principles stimulating economic growth. The subjects of banking and marine insurance are examples. Actually, he would have liked the legal system to have gone further toward protecting and encouraging business than some judges believed the public interest would tolerate.

Serving twice as secretary of state, he applied his economic nationalism to foreign affairs. In Latin America particularly, he set policy with this in mind, notably in relation to the railroad project across southern Mexico and to plans for an interoceanic canal in Nicaragua. Pressing these countries to honor contracts with American companies, he believed, conformed to economic needs of the growing United States. He could not, however, mount sufficient pressure to achieve his ends. Although he felt that extolling American nationalism in his letters to Hülsemann had a good effect at home during the sectional crisis of 1850, his assessment proved to be more optimistic than was justified.

There were limits beyond which he believed an aggressive approach should not go. He strongly opposed resort to force as an instrument of policy. In his own conduct of Mexican, Cuban, and Central American affairs, he avoided even a hint of military action, and Fillmore proved to be still more cautious. None of this was surprising strategy for a secretary who had staunchly opposed two American wars. An additional consideration was that war could add more territory to a nation already troubled by the issue of slavery in the Mexican cession. Webster's avoidance of war and territorial acquisitions accorded with Whig, conservative, pro-business doctrine. He usually managed the process of diplomacy efficiently, but it was his fate to encounter several insuperable obstacles.

Without doubt, the most important and most difficult cluster of problems concerned Anglo-American disputes, including those about the Maine boundary, the *Caroline*, the *Creole*, and the slave trade. Again the overriding element in his thinking was his determination to avoid war or other rash remedies. And his lack of interest in more territory, especially what he regarded as worthless swampland in northern Maine, influenced his pacific course. Obviously, too, his long-term friendliness toward Britain and personal connections with its leaders and bankers ensured a conciliatory effort. He negotiated with Ashburton on a relaxed basis, while worrying a great deal more about opinion in his own country and the best way to control it. The treaty did not give the United States as much as it ought to have obtained ideally. Nevertheless, it decidedly promoted rapprochement with Britain; and in the years ahead that would be highly advantageous to both parties.

However salient the diplomatic, legal, and oratorical aspects of his career, Webster remains best known for his involvement in politics over nearly a half century. The main contours are familiar, but a number of interesting questions remain less than fully answered. Among others, they include the following: Was he an effective practical politician, compared to adepts such as Martin Van Buren? Why did he and his party fail to put across the program they advocated? Why did he not win the presidency he pursued for so long? What was his long-range impact upon history?

The point of departure is knowledge about the political parties of the early nineteenth century. During the early phase of Webster's career, from the first decade of the 1800s to the twenties, the so-called first party system prevailed. The Federalists and Republicans, forming in the early 1790s on issues separating Hamilton and Jefferson and their followings, contested elections up to 1820, with Republicans gaining ascendancy when Jefferson came to power and with Federalists steadily losing ground until their last bastion became New England. It is now clear that Webster's party, declining though it was, did not differ as much from the Republicans on strategy and techniques as was once believed. Young Federalists like Webster were not ideologues detached from realistic factors and ways of dealing with them. To be sure, they stood for their own principles, as they demonstrated by their opposition to American policy toward England, to the embargo, and to the war in 1812. Yet they used the newspaper press, mass meetings, caucuses and conventions, stump speaking, local committees, and a network of correspondence much as the Republicans did. National events and opinion, particularly those concerning the war, weakened the party and ultimately brought about its demise. In Massachusetts the Federalists continued to be dominant through the mid-1820s. Afterward much the same leadership and alignments assumed a different name.

The temporary anomaly of a no-party situation was best illustrated in the strange election of 1824, decided in the House for Adams instead of for Jackson and Crawford, all calling themselves Republican but not necessarily taking a common position on issues. Webster had an important role in recruiting enough congressional votes for Adams' narrow, controversial victory. During that period, his view of parties resembled that of many other people; he deplored them for their divisive, factional tendencies and hoped they would not reappear. This view indeed had had strong currency from the moment the first party system arose. Few people felt that parties, unmentioned in the Constitution, were consonant with the nature of the republic.

That persistent idea, however, did not correspond to current developments. When two coalitions, the friends of the Adams administration and the Jacksonians, confronted one another, a second party system developed. In the forefront, Van Buren, always a frank advocate of party organization, assembled the anti-Adams elements, which became the Democratic party. He resorted to proven tactics he had learned in New York and had observed elsewhere, all to persuade and discipline a variety of groups—he referred to planters of the South and plain republicans of the North, but these terms did not describe all of them. Meanwhile he propounded the positive good of parties. The Democratic commitment must be true to the Jeffersonian doctrines of '98 (the Virginia and Kentucky resolutions), he said. While Adams did not stir to establish his own party, Clay and Webster did. And they also used an improved version of familiar techniques for organization and communications. They were just as alive as Van Buren to the indispensability of a partisan press, campaign funds, the patronage, and national party unity. Though they deplored parties publicly, they were the main architects of the National Republican, and then the Whig party. Careful students of the subject now conclude that the nation's political and constitutional conditions demanded parties as an essential for the working of the government. Van Buren and some few others saw this need, whereas persons like Webster talked one way but acted differently.

The second party system, lasting about twenty-five years, was a blend of the new and old. It was new in the sense that the overpowering personality of Jackson had been a catalyst with respect to issues such as the national bank. It was altered by the existence of a broadened electorate and of popularized values; the device of a national convention reflected this popular trend, or was supposed to. But it remained old in a number of ways, including the conservative character of the leaders of the two parties. As before, some issues, such as the tariff or banking, could be fully ventilated, but some must be muted, notably slavery and other fundamental social problems. As for the points of controversy, Webster and most Whigs tried hard to establish a program of economic nationalism, of a harmonious, self-sufficient American System of bank, protective tariff, and federal internal improvements (or its variant, federal distribution to states for the purpose). The weight of Jackson's leadership was the most significant cause of the Whig failure during the 1830s; and after the log-cabin victory of 1840, the adamancy of the antique states' righter Tyler hastened another failure. It proved to be the Whigs' last chance. In addition to the impact of presidential power, there were other reasons for the defeat, certainly the substantial suspicion everywhere of too much national interference with the states, as well as the skillful work of the Democrats in blocking the program.

A more concrete view of the system emerges from a survey of its operation in Massachusetts and of Webster's involvement in politics there. Jeffersonian Republicans such as Levi Lincoln and Henry Dearborn had been influential in that state in the old days; but Federalists had the decided edge. When Webster arrived in 1816 his party had, if anything, gained ground, the late Hartford Convention notwithstanding. Though he was out of Congress from 1817 to 1823, he was a party leader—in the Missouri crisis of 1819–1820 and in the state constitutional convention the next year. He and other Federalists voted for the reelection of the Republican Monroe, wished to collaborate with the administration nationally, but definitely retained party identity at home. To this Federalist dominance, a challenge mounted: the Middling Interest in 1822 and the advocates of a free Charles River bridge afterward. Still, opponents like Marcus Morton and David Henshaw were not much more than a nuisance; Webster and his friends prospered. His own elections to Congress in the years 1822–1826 and to the Senate thereafter indicated the solidity of support for him. Not only by dependence upon his record at Washington or by speeches at Faneuil Hall, but also by attention to details of organization down to the city's wards, to patronage, and to newspaper editorials (many of which he wrote), he stood at the top of the state party for a long while. Only when the Tyler administration precipitated splintering from the ranks and when Webster held on to his cabinet post did internal problems become acute. Soon disagreement between Conscience and Cotton Whigs undermined a unified party, probably to a fatal degree.

For a time after he moved to Boston, the city was fairly homogeneous in character, a fact which helped to keep politics stable and safe. As time passed, the social structure changed visibly, owing to migration from rural areas and particularly to the arrival of Irish immigrants. Like many other Whig politicians, Webster often attributed losses of elections to fraudulent and ignorant foreign voting. He favored some kind of check upon immigrant influence, perhaps through tighter naturalization laws. But in Massachusetts this factor had a minor electoral impact and none upon the senator directly. It did become more significant across the land by midcentury, with ever-larger numbers of foreign arrivals and a nativist reaction. Recent studies of this phenomenon in its political setting show that it rivaled the slavery dispute in importance. By this time, however, Webster himself had rejected any temptation to court the nativists and was speaking of immigration approvingly, as in his speeches during his tour of the Erie route across northern New York in 1851. Ultimately, then, his reaction to the influx of immigrants was the opposite of what one would expect.

The evidence from Massachusetts suggests answers to some of the questions raised above. Webster was a practical politician, for he was usually effective at least in his home state. His main problem until the late 1840s lay in the Whig failure at the national level to implement the program of the American System. Here presidential action and preference for state over national policy undoubtedly outweighed whatever organizational problems the Whigs may have had in causing that failure. In his final years, however, he did have more than he could handle in trying to reconcile free-soilers and conservatives.

To a large extent, a recognition of the declining appeal of his party's principles also suggests an answer to the always interesting query, why did Webster never win the presidency. Except for the aberrations of Harrison's victory during a depression and Taylor's victory as a war hero, the National Republican–Whigs lost to the Democrats every time from 1828 through 1852. Clay came very close in 1844. But whether Webster, if nominated, could have done better than the Kentuckian then or the party candidates at other times is doubtful. The Whigs were competitive but a minority, as a rule. As for the party nomination, which he never got, the immediate consideration must be the party leaders who actually did the nominating. The sources indicate that these people looked upon him as a gifted, imposing man with some personal defects, with too many enemies, and without the essential quality of availability, that is to say drawing power. Try though he did, Webster never recruited a national base in his bid for the office. The public's perception of his character may have been a deterrent, but negativism within the party hierarchy probably counted for more. His supreme disappointment occurred in 1852, when in the party convention he lost the southern vote to Fillmore despite the concessions he had recently made to slavery. That event is difficult to explain. Perhaps southerners remembered too many instances of disagreement with him, or perhaps they wondered what influence the rising antislavery forces in New

England might have on him. Anyway, nomination would surely have been a worthless prize in view of the Democratic strength demonstrated in the election itself.

Webster's dispirited mood in the months before his death was understandable in light of his setbacks. The direction of policy seemed to him altogether wrong, maybe disastrous. The government, in his judgment, had rejected the true course of commitment to economic nationalism. It looked as if an independent treasury and a low tariff would last indefinitely. And now a frightening controversy over slavery not only smothered action on these important matters but portended disruption of the Union and bloody civil war. His own scars, suffered while rigorously enforcing the fugitive-slave law, signified a larger problem.

Nonetheless, if he had been able to see the future, he could have taken heart. The time was not too distant when national banking, high tariffs, and immense federal subsidies to railroads would prevail. Although there would indeed be a terrible civil war, in which his only surviving son would die, his concept of the Union, one and inseparable with liberty, would triumph over the discredited notion of a loose compact of sovereign states. That was a result in which he would have felt great pride.

BIBLIOGRAPHICAL NOTE

The literature on Webster and on the conditions and events of his time is enormous. I have consulted all items that seemed relevant and have cited them fully in the notes. The preface contains a short discussion on the study of Webster's career.

The number and quality of extant manuscripts by or to Webster exceed those of a great many other prominent persons of the early nineteenth century. A few depositories have sizable collections, with the remainder scattered in small holdings in dozens of locations across the nation and in foreign countries. A major portion of these primary sources can be found at the New Hampshire Historical Society, Dartmouth College, and the Library of Congress; there are also significant segments at the Massachusetts Historical Society, Harvard University, Brandeis University, the New York Public Library, and the University of Virginia. During the early stage of research, I used most of those manuscripts. Then in 1971 the Dartmouth College project for the Webster Papers, under the general editorship of Charles Wiltse, brought out a microfilm edition of forty-one reels, a complete reproduction of manuscripts from libraries everywhere. This resource enabled me to use much material that would otherwise have been unavailable and to collate what I had already used. Wiltse's *Guide* (cited in the list of abbreviations) indexes all the papers in the film edition; it also describes the various collections and previous publications of some of them (pp. 9–18). My citations in the notes include both the depositories of the original material and the reel and frame numbers of the film.

Some of the manuscript sources have already been published in book form, and others will soon be available. In 1902 Claude H. Van Tyne edited a volume of *Letters,* chiefly from the collection of the New Hampshire Historical Society. The next year James W. McIntyre's eighteen-volume compilation, *Writings and Speeches,* reprinted earlier publications of the papers and published others for the first time. Currently the Webster project at Dartmouth is nearing completion of a letterpress edition of selected papers, divided into three series. The volumes I used are cited in the list of abbreviations.

I also used film from the National Archives for the General Records of the Department of State. These consist mainly of instructions by Webster as secretary, despatches to him from representatives abroad, and outgoing and incoming correspondence. Specific designations are found in the list of abbreviations.

As for other government documents, I have drawn heavily from the congressional debates (under the various titles *Annals of Congress, Register of Debates,* and *Congressional Globe*) for each session when Webster was in the House or Senate from 1813 to 1850. A thorough reading of these debates reveals the issues, the character of the arguments, and the legislative history of the measures with which he was involved. Printed committee reports in the so-called congressional serial set yield further information. For judicial aspects, the reports of decisions of the Supreme Court and of lower federal and state courts are essential.

Newspapers of the period have also been helpful. Most important are the *National Intelligencer, Globe,* and *United States Telegraph* of Washington; the *Advertiser, Courier,* and *Atlas* of Boston; and the Concord *Patriot* and Portsmouth *Oracle* of New Hampshire.

N O T E S

Abbreviations

DW   Daniel Webster.

F00/00000   Charles M. Wiltse, ed. *Microfilm Edition of the Papers of Daniel Webster*. Ann Arbor: University Microfilms, 1971. Digits preceding the diagonals indicate reel numbers; those following them, the *first frame numbers of items*. *See Wiltse, ed., Guide and Index to the Microfilm* (Ann Arbor: University Microfilms, 1971). All citations also indicate the locations of depositories of the original manuscripts.

SDNA   General Records of the Department of State. RG 59. National Archives, Washington, D.C. Letters received are labeled Miscellaneous; outgoing correspondence, Domestic Letters. Also specified are outgoing Instructions and incoming Despatches from American ministers and chargés d'affaires, classified by country (such as Great Britain). All are available on microfilm.

WP   Charles M. Wiltse et al., eds. *The Papers of Daniel Webster: Correspondence*. 7 vols. Hanover, N.H., 1974–. Vols. I–V, 1974–82.

WPDC   Webster Papers. Dartmouth College, Hanover, N.H.

WP: Diplomatic Kenneth E. Shewmaker et al., eds. *The Papers of Daniel Webster: Diplomatic Papers*. 2 vols. Hanover, N.H., 1983–. Vol. I.

WPLC   Webster Papers. Library of Congress, Washington, D.C.

WP: Legal   Alfred Konefsky and Andrew King, eds. *The Papers of Daniel Webster: Legal Papers*. 2 vols. Hanover, N.H., 1982.

WPNH   Webster Papers. New Hampshire Historical Society, Concord, N.H.

WS   James W. McIntyre, ed. *The Writings and Speeches of Daniel Webster.* 18 vols. Boston, 1903.

1. Preparation

1. Claude M. Fuess, *Daniel Webster,* 2 vols. (Boston, 1930), I, 17–20; Charles Lanman, *The Private Life of Daniel Webster* (New York, 1852), 48–50. Sydney G. Fisher, *The True Daniel Webster* (Philadelphia, 1911), has a photograph of the tavern on p. 28 and a map of the area on p. 42. Webster's own description of the farm is in "Autobiography," *WP,* I, 6, and in his letter to Richard M. Blatchford, May 3, 1846, *WS,* XVIII, 225–29.

2. Fuess, *Webster,* I, 14–16. Lanman, *Webster,* frontispiece, has an authentic engraving of the frame house at Punch Brook and a reliable description on pp. 10–11. Lanman points out that the engraving in the six-volume edition of Webster's works, published in 1851, is inaccurate because of a printer's error. This mistake caused those reconstructing the cabin, which is now standing, to use the wrong model in the early twentieth century. Webster approved the accuracy of Lanman's engraving. DW to Edward Everett, Oct. 18, 1851, Everett Papers, Massachusetts Historical Society, F25/34937.

3. The best source for tracing the lineage of Webster's family is Mable F. Faling, comp., "The Genealogy of the Webster Family to Which Daniel Webster Belonged" (Boston, 1927), manuscript in New England Historic Genealogical Society. See also unsigned memorandum in Caleb Cushing Papers, Library of Congress, box 260; *New England Historical and Genealogical Register,* 7 (Jan. 1853), 101–3, and 9 (April 1855), 159–60; Fuess, *Webster,* I, 6–7; "Autobiography," *WP,* I, 3–4, showing Webster's uncertainty about the English background of his family and their first years in America.

4. Fuess, *Webster,* I, 7, 11–14; "Autobiography," *WP,* I, 4–6, 14–15; conversations of Charles Lanman with DW, *WS,* XIII, 579–80; Thomas H. Pettengill to Edwin D. Sanborn, Jan. 14, 1853, ibid., XVII, 59–60; undated clipping from New York *Observer* in Portsmouth *Journal,* signed "H.W.," WPNH, I, 2–3; other items on Ebenezer Webster in ibid., 4–8.

5. Fuess, *Webster,* I, 10; DW memorandum, clipping from *Old Eliot,* Eliot (Maine) Historical Society, F12/15026; DW to Charles H. Warren, [Sept. 19, 1852], Montague Collection, New York Public Library, F27/37800.

6. See Faling, "Genealogy of Webster Family," 11, 14, for information on Webster's brothers and sisters.

7. For a contemporary description, see Thomas H. Pettengill to Edwin D. Sanborn, Jan. 14, 1853, *WS,* XVII, 61–63.

8. DW to Richard M. Blatchford, Oct. 29, 1850, ibid., XVIII, 398.

9. Fuess, *Webster,* I, 64.

10. A version of the story about the Indian raid many years later is in Moor Russell to DW, Oct. 10, 1849, WPNH, F21/29576.

11. "Autobiography," *WP,* I, 14–15.

12. Ibid., 7–8.

13. Ibid., 8–9; Fuess, *Webster,* I, 33–38; DW speech on fiftieth anniversary of Abbott's service as principal in 1838, *WS,* XIII, 101–3.

14. "Autobiography," *WP,* I, 9–10; Fuess, *Webster,* I, 40.

15. *General Catalogue of Dartmouth College and the Associated Schools, 1769–1911* (Hanover, N.H., 1911), passim. On p. 59 is a drawing by young George Ticknor in 1803 of the green and the college buildings. Daniel probably had a room in Dartmouth Hall his first three years and in the cottage of Mrs. Sylvanus Ripley, daughter of Eleazar Wheelock, his senior year. Leon B. Richardson, *History of Dartmouth College,* 2 vols. (Hanover, N.H., 1932), I, 280.

16. *General Catalogue of Dartmouth,* passim; Richardson, *Dartmouth College,* I, 250–58.

17. George S. Hillard and Anna Ticknor, eds., *Life, Letters, and Journals of George Ticknor,* 2 vols. (Boston, 1876), I, 5–7; Richardson, *Dartmouth College,* I, 258–61.

18. *General Catalogue of Dartmouth,* 206–11, lists names of graduates during Webster's four years at the college.

19. Richardson, *Dartmouth College,* I, 240–47; Fuess, *Webster,* I, 47–49; Richard Lang's "Student Book" for DW debt at his store, WPDC.

20. Richardson, *Dartmouth College,* I, 246–51.

21. Fuess, *Webster,* I, 50–53; Richardson, *Dartmouth College,* I, 281–82.

22. DW to Moses Davis, Aug. 27, 1799, *WP,* I, 26.

23. For a listing of his contributions, see ibid., 383–87. An example of his essays, the one on deception, is in WPDC, F2/40; one of his poems is in ibid., F2/30. On the relationship with Davis, see his letter to DW, [Jan. 5, 1801], WPNH, F2/9.

24. WPDC, F2/17.

25. George T. Curtis, *Life of Daniel Webster,* 2 vols. (New York, 1870), I, 40–42. As a senior, he was president of the Fraternity.

26. WPNH, F2/42.

27. Incomplete draft of speech in ibid., F2/78; printed version in *WS,* XV, 487–93.

28. "Autobiography," *WP,* I, 10–11; sketch of Ezekiel by his son-in-law, Edwin D. Sanborn, *WS,* XVII, 31–42.

29. DW to Ezekiel Webster, Nov. 4, 1802, WPDC, F2/154.

30. Ezekiel Webster to DW, Nov. 6, 1802, *WS,* XVII, 124.

31. Fuess, *Webster,* I, 66–72; DW to Judah Dana, Dec. 26, 1801, WPDC, F2/87; DW to Samuel Bradley, Feb. 20, 1802, ibid., F2/90; DW to James H. Bingham, Feb. 25, 1802, *WP,* I, 36, and May 18, 1802, *WS,* XVII, 108–11.

32. "Autobiography," *WP,* I, 12.

33. Curtis, *Webster,* I, 52–53; DW to Jacob McGaw, Dec. 18, 1802, WPDC F2/161.

34. DW to James H. Bingham, Dec. 8, 1804, *WS,* XVII, 98–99; Ebenezer Webster to DW, Oct. 6, 1804, WPNH, F2/367.

35. Sally Webster to DW, Dec. 21, 1804, WPDC, F2/428.

36. Illustrative letters are DW to John Porter, Dec. 11, 1803, ibid., F2/248; DW to Thomas Merrill, Jan. 4 and July 30, 1803, ibid., F2/200 and 228.

37. DW to Habijah W. Fuller, Dec. 21, 1802, and July 2, 1803, *WS,* XVII, 126, 140–41; DW to Thomas Merrill, Nov. 30, 1804, WPDC, F2/414; Curtis, *Webster,* I, 51–52.

38. Curtis, *Webster,* I, 96–97. The manuscript of the address is in WPLC, F2/776; printed version in *WS,* XV, 575–82.

39. DW to Habijah W. Fuller, May 3, 1802, Fogg Collection, Maine Historical Society, Portland, F2/124.

40. The Fryeburg pieces are in WPNH, F2/98.
41. Manuscripts of these writings are in WPDC, F2/176.
42. One review discussed Christopher Caustic, "First Canto of Terrible Tractoration," *Monthly Anthology*, 2 (April 1805), 167–70. See *WS*, XV, 533–35; Claude H. Van Tyne, ed., *The Letters of Daniel Webster* (New York, 1902), 19–21 and 21 n. 1, listing other contributions to the magazine.
43. "Autobiography," *WP*, I, 13–14.
44. DW to Habijah W. Fuller, Feb. 20, 1802, Fogg Collection, F2/94; C. D. to DW, Feb. 25, 1802, WPNH, F2/113.
45. DW to Thomas Merrill, Dec. 1803, WPDC, F2/252.
46. DW to Habijah W. Fuller, Oct. 17, 1804, *WS*, XVII, 191, written from Boston, where he met the young woman.
47. DW to James H. Bingham, Sept. 28, 1803, WPNH, F2/240.
48. DW to Thomas Merrill, Dec. 1803, WPDC, F2/252; Samuel Osgood to DW, Jan. 26, 1805, ibid., F2/434.
49. DW to James H. Bingham, May 5, 1802, Van Tyne, *Letters*, 7.
50. DW to Habijah W. Fuller, [1802], Fogg Collection, F2/165.
51. DW to Thomas Merrill, May 28, 1804, WPDC, F2/288.
52. DW to James H. Bingham, Jan. 19, 1806, *WS*, XVII, 221.
53. DW to James H. Bingham, Sept. 3, 1803, ibid., 143; DW to Samuel Bradley, Sept. 24, 1803, WPDC, F2/236; DW to Thomas Merrill, March 16, 1804, ibid., F2/268; DW to James H. Bingham, March 16 and April 3, 1804, *WP*, I, 49–51.
54. DW to James H. Bingham, Oct. 6, 1803, *WP*, I, 47–48.
55. "Autobiography," ibid., 13; Daniel Abbott to Edwin D. Sanborn, Feb. 5, 1853, *WS*, XVII, 64; DW to James H. Bingham, Dec. 21, 1802, ibid., 127. See discussion of legal study in *WP: Legal*, I, 6–7.
56. DW to [?] Cook, Jan. 14, 1803, *WS*, XVII, 131.
57. DW to James H. Bingham, Oct. 26, 1801, ibid., 98.
58. DW to James H. Bingham, Oct. 6, 1803, ibid., 145; Curtis, *Webster*, I, 61–63.
59. Ezekiel Webster to DW, March 10, 1804, WPLC, F2/264.
60. Ezekiel Webster to DW, April 4, 1804, WPDC, F2/272.
61. "Autobiography," *WP*, I, 15–16; DW to James H. Bingham, Aug. 4, 1804, *WS*, XVII, 185.
62. Thomas W. Thompson to DW, Oct. 17, 1804, WPDC, F2/375.
63. Ms. diary, July 17, 1804–March 1805, ibid., F2/315; "Autobiography," *WP*, I, 17–19.
64. DW to Thomas Merrill, Nov. 30, 1804, WPDC, F2/414.
65. Ms. diary, ibid., F2/315.
66. DW to Thomas Merrill, Nov. 30, 1804, ibid., F2/414.
67. Curtis, *Webster*, I, 67–68.
68. DW to Ezekiel Webster, Nov. 5, 1804, WPDC, F2/400; Nov. 9, 1804, ibid., F2/402; Nov. 12, 1804, WPLC, F2/410.
69. DW to Ezekiel Webster, June 10, 1804, *WP*, I, 55; DW to Timothy Farrar, July 12, 1804, WPNH, F2/304.
70. "Autobiography," *WP*, I, 19–21.
71. DW to Thomas W. Thompson, Nov. 30, 1804, Webster Papers, Harvard University, F2/418.

72. DW to Judah Dana, Dec. 29, 1804, *WS,* XVI, 670.

73. Thompson to DW, Dec. 10, 1804, WPDC, F2/423; Dana to DW, Jan. 18, 1805, ibid., F2/433.

74. "Autobiography," *WP,* I, 19; DW to Thomas Merrill, March 10, 1805, WPDC, F2/441.

75. DW to James H. Bingham, May 4, 1805, *WS,* XVII, 206; Fuess, *Webster,* I, 84–85; DW to Ezekiel Webster, May 25, 1805, WPNH, F2/520.

76. DW to Ezekiel Webster, April 25 and April 30, 1805, WPDC, F2/469 and 482; DW to Ezekiel Webster, May 12, 1805, WPLC, F2/493; Ezekiel Webster to DW, May 19, 1805, WPDC, F2/513; DW to Ezekiel Webster, July 28, 1805, ibid., F2/566.

77. Sewall, Salisbury & Co. to DW, Sept. 12, 1805, WPDC, F2/592; Gore, Miller, & Parker to DW, April 1, 1806, ibid., F2/718; Book and Pratt to DW, May 24, 1806, ibid., F2/748; William H. Wilkins to DW, Aug. 6, 1806, ibid., F2/767. For an excellent discussion of his Boscawen practice, see *WP: Legal,* I, especially 63, 72–75, 82–93, 138–39, 157–59.

78. Fuess, *Webster,* I, 89. A recollection of the favorable impression he made in another case is in a newspaper clipping, WPNH, F21/28275.

79. DW to James H. Bingham, May 4, 1805, *WS,* XVII, 206; Jan. 19, 1806, ibid., 220–22.

80. Constitution of the Federal Club, [July 1799], *WP,* I, 25–26.

81. Boston *Columbian Centinel,* Sept. 29, 1804; Boston *Repertory,* Oct. 2, 1804.

82. Review of Tunis Wortman, *A Treatise Concerning Political Inquiry, and the Liberty of the Press* (New York, 1800), reprinted from *Monthly Anthology* in *WS,* XV, 548–51.

83. DW to George Herbert, Jan. 7, 1801, *WP,* I, 30–32.

84. DW to James H. Bingham, May 18, 1802, ibid., 41–42.

85. DW to James H. Bingham, Feb. 5, 1800, ibid., 27–29.

86. His oration at Fryeburg in 1802 illustrates many basic elements of his thinking; WPNH, F2/136.

87. Oration of 1800 at Hanover, *WS,* XV, 475–84; oration of 1806 at Concord, ibid., 537–47.

88. DW to James H. Bingham, May 18, 1802, *WP,* I, 41–42.

89. WPDC, F2/176.

90. WPNH, F2/136.

91. *WS,* XV, 547.

92. DW to John Porter, June [6], 1802, WPDC, F2/128.

93. DW to Ezekiel Webster, June 10, 1804, ibid., F2/292; DW to Moses Davis, Oct. 20, 1804, WPNH, F2/383; Fuess, *Webster,* I, 124–25.

94. DW to Thompson, March 15, 1806, Miscellaneous Bound MSS, Massachusetts Historical Society, F2/707; Thompson to DW, March 10, 1806, *WP,* I, 81–82.

95. Pamphlet reprinted in *WS,* XV, 522–31.

2. Portsmouth

1. DW to James H. Bingham, Feb. 27, 1808, Western Reserve Historical Society, Cleveland, F2/972; DW to Jacob McGaw, Jan. 12, 1807, *WS,* XVII, 224; DW to Ezekiel Webster, Nov. 5, 1807, WPDC, F2/934.

2. Nathaniel Adams to DW, June 9, 1807, WPDC, F2/878.

3. Claude M. Fuess, *Daniel Webster*, 2 vols. (Boston, 1930), I, 94–98; Thomas Bailey Aldrich, *An Old Town by the Sea* (Boston, 1917); Portsmouth *Oracle*, passim.

4. George S. Hillard, *Memoir and Correspondence of Jeremiah Mason* (Cambridge, Mass., 1873); George T. Curtis, *Life of Daniel Webster*, 2 vols. (New York, 1870), I, 86–90; DW eulogy of Mason, Nov. 14, 1848, *WS*, IV, 177–91.

5. Curtis, *Webster*, I, 82–83.

6. Ezekiel Webster to DW, [Dec. 15, 1809], WPDC, F2/1106; DW to Ezekiel Webster, [Feb. 1811], ibid., F2/1226.

7. DW to Habijah W. Fuller, Dec. 2, 1807, *WS*, XVII, 227.

8. Eliza Buckminster Lee, "Sketch of Mrs. G. F. Webster," ibid., 438–44; *New England Historical and Genealogical Register*, 7 (Jan. 1853), 102.

9. DW to Grace Fletcher, Sept. 4, 1807, WPDC, F2/921; William G. Hunt to DW, May 1, 1828, WPNH, F6/7302; *WP*, I, 97n.; Fuess, *Webster*, I, 100.

10. Fuess, *Webster*, I, 100–101; autobiographical note, [1828], WPNH, F6/7355; *WP*, I, 21.

11. Fuess, *Webster*, I, 101–3.

12. Recollections of Webster by Eliza Buckminster Lee, *WS*, XVII, 443; reminiscences of George Ticknor in Curtis, *Webster*, I, 85.

13. Recollections of Lee, *WS*, XVII, 438.

14. Curtis, *Webster*, I, 85; Munroe and Francis to DW, Jan 14, 1810, WPLC, F2/1115.

15. Fuess, *Webster*, I, 117; Noah Webster to DW, Nov. 4, 1809, WPLC, F2/1100.

16. Peter O. Thacher to DW, April 24, 1807, WPNH, F2/863. See, for example, the essay on French language in the *Monthly Anthology* of December 1807, in *WS*, XV, 557–58.

17. DW to Charles B. Haddock, Feb. 7, 1814, *WS*, XVII, 241–42; Portsmouth *Oracle*, March 30, 1811.

18. Enclosure in DW to Thomas Worcester, Aug. 8, 1807, WPDC, F2/800. See also DW to Kingston Goddard, [ca. 1807], Claude H. Van Tyne, ed., *The Letters of Daniel Webster* (New York, 1902), 740–41.

19. *WP: Legal*, I, 185–88, 194–97, 296–300. He served on a committee to revise the state criminal code, but it was not adopted; Samuel Sparhawk to DW, June 26, 1811, WPNH, F2/1253; Peter O. Thacher to DW, July 6, 1811, ibid., F2/1258.

20. Autobiography, Webster Papers, Massachusetts Historical Society, F7/8205.

21. DW to Ezekiel Webster, March 3, 1808, WPDC, F2/979.

22. DW to Nathaniel Gilman, May 16, 1811, *WP*, I, 123–24 and n.

23. DW to Ezekiel Webster, March 27, 1811, WPDC, F2/1236; Ezekiel Webster to DW, April 4, 1811, ibid., F2/1244; and DW to Ezekiel Webster, April 8, 1811, ibid., F2/1247.

24. Thacher to DW, April 24, 1807, WPNH, F2/863; Perkins to DW, Feb. 3, 1807, WPDC, F2/825; Perkins to DW, Feb. 27, 1807, ibid., F2/835; DW to Thomas W. Thompson, Jan. 9, 1808, *WP*, I, 98–99.

25. DW to Ezekiel Webster, Nov. 27, 1810, WPDC, F2/1206.

26. James M. Banner, Jr., *To the Hartford Convention: The Federalists and the Origins of Party Politics in Massachusetts, 1789–1815* (New York, 1970), 3–33,

36-60, 84-121, explains the ideas and grievances of Federalists in Massachusetts. For New Hampshire politics see Lynn W. Turner, *The Ninth State: New Hampshire's Formative Years* (Chapel Hill, 1983), 236-49.

27. Donald B. Cole, *Jacksonian Democracy in New Hampshire, 1800-1851* (Cambridge, Mass., 1970), 17-31.

28. DW to Samuel A. Bradley, June 28, 1808, WPDC, F2/999, and Oct. 20, 1808, ibid., F2/1014; DW to Thomas W. Thompson, July 25, 1808, WPNH, F2/1008.

29. For these years when the party was compelled to adopt more effective political techniques while holding to the old ideology, David H. Fischer classifies Webster as a young Federalist; *The Revolution of American Conservatism: The Federalist Party in the Era of Jeffersonian Democracy* (New York, 1965), 238; for general discussion, see 29-181.

30. "Considerations on the Embargo Laws," reprinted in *WS*, XV, 564-74.

31. Portsmouth *Oracle*, March 9, 1809, March 10, 1810, March 9, 1811, March 7, 1812, and passim.

32. Ibid., March 17, 1810, March 16 and 23, 1811; Benjamin J. Gilbert to DW, April 2, 1810, WPNH, F2/1143.

33. DW et al. circular letter to Federalists, Aug. 1, 1810, WPNH, F2/1186.

34. Portsmouth *Oracle*, July 6 and 13, 1811.

35. Ibid., March 14, 1812.

36. Lynn W. Turner, *William Plumer of New Hampshire, 1759-1850* (Chapel Hill, 1962), 204-15.

37. DW to Timothy Farrar, Jr., July 28, 1812, WPNH, F2/1338.

38. Fischer, *Revolution of Conservatism*, 114-28.

39. Pamphlet report reprinted in *WS*, XV, 583-98; Portsmouth *Oracle*, June 27, July 4 and 12, 1812.

40. Portsmouth *Oracle*, Aug. 1 and 8, Sept. 26, 1812.

41. An early draft, written before the declaration of war, is in WPNH, F2/1344.

42. Final version, reprinted in *WS*, XV, 599-610. A slightly different draft in Webster's hand is in WPDC, F2/1355. He also spoke at the meeting.

43. Autobiography, Webster Papers (Mass. Hist. Soc.), F7/8025.

44. Plumer to John Quincy Adams, Aug. 19, 1812, and Plumer to John Adams, Jan. 2, 1813, Plumer Papers, Library of Congress, Letters, 1791-1817.

45. Concord *New-Hampshire Patriot*, Aug. 25 and Oct. 29, 1812.

46. Portsmouth *Oracle*, Oct. 17, 1812. The meeting's address to the president is in ibid., Oct. 24, 1812.

47. Horace Binney et al. printed circular, Sept. 26, 1812, WPNH, F2/1388; DW to John Pickering, Oct. 15, 1812, Pickering Papers, Massachusetts Historical Society, F2/1403; Timothy Pickering to DW, Oct. 29, 1812, ibid., F2/1405; *WP: Legal*, I, 530-42; Portsmouth *Oracle*, Oct. 31, Nov. 7, Dec. 5, 1812.

48. Turner, *Ninth State*, 279-83.

3. Antiwar Congressman

1. Constance McL. Green, *Washington: Village and Capital, 1800-1878* (Princeton, 1962), passim.

2. Robert Ernst, *Rufus King, American Federalist* (Chapel Hill, 1968), 322–23.

3. James S. Young, *The Washington Community, 1800–1828* (New York, 1966), 88–92, 98–102, 107–9, 250–54.

4. Washington *National Intelligencer,* Jan. 2 and May 25, 1813; Irving Brant, *James Madison,* 6 vols. (Indianapolis, 1948–61), VI, 179; Henry Adams, *History of the United States of America during the Administrations of Jefferson and Madison,* 9 vols. (New York, 1921), VII, 50–51.

5. Donald R. Hickey, "The Federalists and the War of 1812" (Ph.D. dissertation, University of Illinois, 1972), 341–43 and passim; *Annals of Congress,* 13th Cong., 1st sess., 110.

6. Washington *National Intelligencer,* May 26, 1813; Adams, *History,* VII, 53.

7. DW to Ezekiel Webster, May 26, 1813, WPDC, F2/1460.

8. DW to Edward Cutts, Jr., May 26, 1813, WPNH, F2/1457.

9. DW to James H. Bingham, June 4, 1813, *WS,* XVII, 234.

10. DW to Ezekiel Webster, May 29, 1813, WPDC, F2/1476.

11. DW to Charles March, May 31, 1813, WPNH, F2/1478; DW to Timothy Farrar, Jr., June 1, 1813, ibid., F2/1488; DW to Jedidiah Morse, June 28, 1813, Gratz Collection, Pennsylvania Historical Society, Philadelphia, F2/1578.

12. DW to Charles March, June 19, 1813, WPNH, F2/1551.

13. DW to March, June 14, 1813, ibid., F2/1537. See letters of May 31, 1813, ibid., F2/1478; June 19, 1813, ibid., F2/1551; June 24, 1813, ibid., F2/1566; July 6, 1813, ibid., F2/1592; July 10, 1813, ibid., F2/1599; Nov. 20, 1813, ibid., F2/1613.

14. Charles March to DW, May 31, 1813, WPLC, F2/1484, and June 18, 1813, WPNH, F2/1548.

15. Washington *National Intelligencer,* Aug. 5, 1813; Brant, *Madison,* VI, 182.

16. Ernst, *King,* 324; Harry Ammon, *James Monroe: The Quest for National Identity* (New York, 1971), 321.

17. DW to Charles March, June 8, 1813, WPNH, F2/1515.

18. *Annals of Congress,* 13th Cong., 1st sess., 151–52; *WS,* XIV, 3–7; Washington *National Intelligencer,* June 11, 1813.

19. *Annals of Congress,* 13th Cong., 1st sess., 168–82, 185–301.

20. Ibid., 186–200, for Oakley's speech.

21. Ibid., 251–65, for Hanson's speech.

22. Ibid., 169, 171.

23. Ibid., 219–29, for Grundy's speech.

24. Ibid., 303–11

25. DW to Charles March, June 21, 1813, WPNH, F2/1554.

26. DW to Ezekiel Webster, June 28, 1813, WPDC, F2/1582.

27. Washington *National Intelligencer,* July 13 and 14, 1813.

28. *Annals of Congress,* 13th Cong., 1st sess., 435–36, 439, 442, 470–71.

29. Timothy Pickering to Josiah Quincy, June 7, 1813, quoted in Edmund Quincy, *Life of Josiah Quincy of Massachusetts* (Boston, 1867), 322; Jedidiah Morse to DW, July 9, 1813, WPLC, F2/1595; Richard Stockton to DW, July 23, 1813, WPDC, F2/1601; Portsmouth *Oracle,* July 24, 1813; Concord *New-Hampshire Patriot,* July 27, 1813.

30. Bradford Perkins, *Prologue to War: England and the United States, 1805–1812* (Berkeley, 1961), 335–37; Brant, *Madison,* VI, 57, 184–85, 195–96;

Ammon, *Monroe*, 293, 311, 322; William R. Barlow, "Congress during the War of 1812" (Ph.D. dissertation, Ohio State University, 1961), 253-61.

31. Adams, *History*, VII, 55, 67; Barlow, "Congress during War," 154-57.

32. *Annals of Congress*, 13th Cong., 1st sess., 319-28, 330-31, 351-83, 387-98, 405-22, 431-32, 469.

33. DW to Charles March, June 6, 1813, WPNH, F2/1508; DW to Moody Kent, June 12, 1813, WPLC, F2/1531; Hickey, "Federalists and War," 171-72; Washington *National Intelligencer*, July 2, 1813.

34. DW to Charles March, July 6, 1813, WPNH, F2/1592.

35. DW to Ezekiel Webster, July 4, 1813, WPDC, F2/1588; Washington *National Intelligencer*, July 10, 1813.

36. Claude M. Fuess, *Daniel Webster*, 2 vols. (Boston, 1930), I, 160 n. 2.

37. Portsmouth *Oracle*, Dec. 25, 1813, Jan. 1, 1814; Daniel Waldron to DW, Dec. 26, 1813, WPNH, F2/1619; Fuess, *Webster*, I, 119-21.

38. DW to Ezekiel Webster, Dec. 29, 1813, WPDC, F2/1621; DW to Timothy Farrar, Jr., Dec. 30, 1813, WPNH, F2/1623.

39. George S. Hillard, *Memoir and Correspondence of Jeremiah Mason* (Cambridge, Mass., 1873), 73; DW to Isaac P. Davis, Jan. 6, 1814, WPNH, F2/1631.

40. DW to Edward Cutts, Jan. 27, 1814, Boston Public Library, F2/1632a; Autobiography, Webster Papers, Massachusetts Historical Society, F7/8025.

41. Records of House of Representatives, RG 233, National Archives, Washington, D.C., F30/40765 and F30/40770; *Annals of Congress*, 13th Cong., 2d sess., 1150, 1922, 1926, 2009.

42. DW to Edward Cutts, Jan. 27, 1814, Boston Public Library, F2/1632a.

43. Adams, *History*, VII, 396.

44. Washington *National Intelligencer*, Dec. 21, 1813; *Annals of Congress*, 13th Cong., 2d sess., 2031-32, 2034-46, 2048-53, 2055-59.

45. See Webster's speech of January 14, 1814, *Annals of Congress*, 13th Cong., 2d sess., 940-51.

46. Ibid., 1115-16, 1122.

47. Ibid., 824-28, 1941.

48. Ammon, *Monroe*, 324.

49. DW to Isaac P. Davis, Jan. 6, 1814. The item appeared in the Boston *Columbian Centinel*, Jan. 15, 1814, *WP*, I, 160 n.

50. *Annals of Congress*, 13th Cong., 2d sess., 928-79, 1093-94.

51. Ibid., 939.

52. Webster's speech is in ibid., 940-51.

53. Ibid., 934. These are Webster's remarks just before the vote on Sheffey's amendment.

54. DW to Ezekiel Webster, Jan. 30, 1814, WPDC, F2/1633; Portsmouth *Oracle*, Feb. 5, 12, and 19, 1814.

55. Diary of William Plumer, Sr., Plumer Papers, Library of Congress, II (1807-36), 121.

56. Adams, *History*, VII, 384.

57. *Annals of Congress*, 13th Cong., 2d sess., 981-1009, 1018-46, 1060-92, 1093-1113.

58. Ibid., 990-1002.

59. Brant, *Madison*, VI, 248-49; Donald R. Hickey, "American Trade Re-

strictions during the War of 1812," *Journal of American History,* 68 (Dec. 1981), 517–38.

60. *Annals of Congress,* 13th Cong., 2d sess., 1866–68.

61. Washington *National Intelligencer,* April 1, 1814; Adams, *History,* VII, 373–74.

62. *Annals of Congress,* 13th Cong., 2d sess., 1946–47, 1962–65; Charles M. Wiltse, *John C. Calhoun: Nationalist* (Indianapolis, 1944), 80–92.

63. *Annals of Congress,* 13th Cong., 2d sess., 1966–70.

64. Ibid., 1976–78.

65. Ibid., 1979–82, 1985–2000, 2002, 2014. Webster did not vote on repeal.

66. Adams, *History,* VII, 377.

4. Peace

1. Portsmouth *Oracle,* July 28, 1814.

2. Essays by "A Farmer," July 25 and Aug. 1, 1814, Plumer Papers, Library of Congress; Concord *New-Hampshire Patriot,* Aug. 2 and 9, 1814.

3. Concord *New-Hampshire Patriot,* July 19, Aug. 2, and 27, 1814.

4. The *Patriot,* June 7, 1814, reported that Webster "has commenced scribbling in the Portsmouth *Oracle."* He also published "a paragraph" in the Concord *Gazette,* Aug. 16, 1814, on Jefferson's mistakes in diplomacy; *WP,* I, 169, n. 1.

5. Portsmouth *Oracle,* Aug. 13, 1814. See also ibid., Aug. 6, 1814.

6. Ibid., Oct. 1, 1814; William R. Barlow, "Congress during the War of 1812" (Ph.D. dissertation, Ohio State University, 1961), 44–45; Washington *National Intelligencer,* Oct. 20, 1814. Portsmouth voted against Webster, 528 to 348.

7. Claude M. Fuess, *The Life of Caleb Cushing,* 2 vols. (New York, 1923), I, 172–73.

8. Samuel Sheafe to George Ticknor, Nov. 12, 1852, WPNH; printed bill, headed "Attention," ibid., F2/1669.

9. Constance McL. Green, *Washington: Village and Capital, 1800–1878* (Princeton, 1962), 62, 67; Glenn Tucker, *Poltroons and Patriots: A Popular Account of the War of 1812,* 2 vols. (Indianapolis, 1954), II, 552–60, 563–67, 575–79, 582–83; Washington *National Intelligencer,* Aug. 30, 1814.

10. Marshall Smelser, *The Democratic Republic, 1801–1815* (New York, 1968), 261–64; Washington *National Intelligencer,* Sept. 21, 1814.

11. Harry Ammon, *James Monroe: The Quest for National Identity* (New York, 1971), 339–40; Henry Adams, *History of the United States of America during the Administrations of Jefferson and Madison,* 9 vols. (New York, 1921), VIII, 264–66.

12. *Annals of Congress,* 13th Cong., 3d sess., 715, 720–42, 749–50, 753–56, 1838; Donald R. Hickey, "The Federalists and the War of 1812" (Ph.D. dissertation, University of Illinois, 1972), 140–41.

13. Adams, *History,* VIII, 266–74.

14. For Calhoun's position, see *Annals of Congress,* 13th Cong., 3d sess., 712.

15. Washington *National Intelligencer,* Dec. 14, 1814.

16. His speech was not reported in the *Annals of Congress,* but it is in *WS,* XIV, 55–69; and a manuscript copy is in WPNH, F2/1747.

17. *WS,* XIV, 65–67.

18. Ibid., 68.

19. Ibid., 69.

20. *Annals of Congress,* 13th Cong., 3d sess., 800–70, 876–99, 901–29.

21. Ibid., 972–76, 993–94.

22. Washington *National Intelligencer,* Dec. 15, 1814.

23. *Annals of Congress,* 13th Cong., 3d sess., 378–81, 404, 420, 430–52, 458–62, 465–80, 491–94, 697–700, 931–51, 957–72.

24. Hickey, "Federalists and War," 136–38, 182–85; Barlow, "Congress during War," 169–71.

25. DW to [Timothy Farrar, Jr.?], Oct. 30, 1814, WPDC, F2/1727.

26. *Annals of Congress,* 13th Cong., 3d sess., 460–62.

27. Ibid., 465–69.

28. Washington *National Intelligencer,* Oct. 25, 1814.

29. Barlow, "Congress during War," 165–68, 172–76; Hickey, "Federalists and War," 188–91; Adams, *History,* VIII, 252–54, 258–60; Charles M. Wiltse, *John C. Calhoun: Nationalist* (Indianapolis, 1944), 94–96.

30. *WS,* V, 35–47; manuscript copy in WPNH, F3/1787.

31. *WS,* V, 38.

32. Wiltse, *Calhoun: Nationalist,* 98–100; DW to Nathaniel A. Haven, Jan. 21, [1815], WPLC, F3/1841.

33. Washington *National Intelligencer,* Jan. 31, 1815.

34. Adams, *History,* IX, 82.

35. On the background of the convention, see James M. Banner, Jr., *To the Hartford Convention: The Federalists and the Origins of Party Politics in Massachusetts, 1789–1815* (New York, 1970), 294–333; Adams, *History,* VIII, 3–12, 224–29, 287–90.

36. Adams, *History,* VIII, 291–95; Banner, *Hartford Convention,* 334–46. Washington *National Intelligencer,* Jan. 11, 1815.

37. Adams, *History,* VIII, 296.

38. DW to [Lawrence?], [Dec. 1835?], WPNH, F10/12820. Some of the repeated disclamers are DW to Jeremiah Mason, March 2, 1830, *WS,* XVI, 193; Richard Stockton to the editor, Washington *National Intelligencer,* Feb. 7, 1832; DW to James H. Bingham, Aug. 24, 1835, *WS,* XVIII, 11.

39. Webster later recalled that he so advised Gilman because it "would not be wise"—a vague explanation; DW to James H. Bingham, Aug. 24, 1835, *WS,* XVIII, 11. Lynn W. Turner, *The Ninth State: New Hampshire's Formative Years* (Chapel Hill, 1983), 292–93, says Gilman was reluctant anyhow.

40. DW to William Sullivan, Benjamin D. Curtiss Collection, Watertown (Conn.) Library, F2/1704. The second letter is in Norcross Papers, Massachusetts Historical Society, F2/1707. See also DW to [Timothy Farrar, Jr.?], Oct. 30, 1814, WPDC, F2/1727.

41. DW to [William F. Rowland?], Jan. 11, 1815, Webster Papers, Harvard University, F3/1824.

42. Adams, *History,* VIII, 255, 261, 283.

43. DW to Ezekiel Webster, Nov. 29, 1814, WPDC, F2/1744; DW to Moody Kent, Dec. 22, 1814, WPNH, F2/1770.

44. DW to Jacob McGaw, Dec. 31, 1814; original in possession of Lester W. Parker, Brimfield, Mass., F2/1781.

45. DW to [William F. Rowland?], Jan. 11, 1815, Webster Papers, Harvard University, F3/1824; *Annals of Congress,* 13th Cong., 3d sess., 463–64.

46. Washington *National Intelligencer,* Feb. 6, 1815; Adams, *History,* IX, 57–61.

47. Washington *National Intelligencer,* Feb. 16, 1815.

48. Portsmouth *Oracle,* Feb. 18, 1815.

49. George S. Hillard, *Memoir and Correspondence of Jeremiah Mason* (Cambridge, Mass., 1873), 118.

50. Shaw Livermore, Jr., *The Twilight of Federalism: The Disintegration of the Federalist Party, 1815–1830* (Princeton, 1962), 3–26.

51. For a sympathetic assessment, see Hickey, "Federalists and War," 332–40.

52. DW to Moody Kent, Dec. 22, 1814, WPNH, F2/1770; Claude M. Fuess, *Daniel Webster,* 2 vols. (Boston, 1930), I, 116.

53. This was an unsubstantiated suspicion expressed in the Concord *New-Hampshire Patriot,* Jan. 9, 1816.

54. Francis N. Stites, *Private Interest and Public Gain: The Dartmouth College Case, 1819* (Amhurst, 1972), 1–26; Maurice G. Baxter, *Daniel Webster and the Supreme Court* (Amherst, 1966), 65–69.

55. Turner, *Plumer,* 233–39; Concord *New-Hampshire Patriot,* Jan. 2, 9, and 23, Feb. 13, 1815.

56. *Annals of Congress,* 14th Cong., 1st sess., 494–514; Wiltse, *Calhoun: Nationalist,* 108–11.

57. *Annals of Congress,* 14th Cong., 1st sess., 1214–19; Bray Hammond, *Banks and Politics in America: From the Revolution to the Civil War* (Princeton, 1957), 232–43.

58. Glyndon G. Van Deusen, *The Life of Henry Clay* (Boston, 1937), 112; DW to Ezekiel Webster, March 7, 1816, WPDC, F3/1919.

59. *Annals of Congress,* 14th Cong., 1st sess., 1091–94, 1212–13, 1339–43.

60. Ibid., 1219, 1314, 1344.

61. Ibid., 1437, 1440–52.

62. Autobiography, Webster Papers, Massachusetts Historical Society, F7/8025; Webster's memorandum, 1831, *WS,* XV, 100–103; Hammond, *Banks and Politics,* 246–50.

63. George Dangerfield, *The Awakening of American Nationalism, 1815–1828* (New York, 1965), 13–16.

64. Wiltse, *Calhoun: Nationalist,* 115–24; Dangerfield, *Awakening Nationalism,* 15–16; *Annals of Congress,* 14th Cong., 1st sess., 1329–37.

65. DW to James W. Paige, April 1816, Paige Papers, Massachusetts Historical Society, F3/1926; Autobiography, Webster Papers (Mass. Hist. Soc.), F7/8025; *Annals of Congress,* 14th Cong., 1st sess., 1257–63, 1271–73, 1312–13, 1325.

66. *Annals of Congress,* 14th Cong., 1st sess., 1272, 1329.

67. Ibid., 1285, 1312, 1326.

68. Ibid., 1271–72, 1352.

69. DW to John Randolph, [April 1816], WPNH, F3/1939; DW to Randolph, [April 30, 1816], University of Virginia, F3/1838; Randolph to DW, April 30, 1816, WPNH, F3/1939.

70. On the tariff bill there were sixty-three Republicans for and thirty-one

against, twenty-five Federalists for and twenty-three against; Dangerfield, *Awakening Nationalism*, 14.

71. DW to Samuel A. Bradley, April 21, [1816], WPDC, F3/1934.

72. Review of the English *Red Book* for the *North American Review* of December 1816, *WS*, XV, 8.

73. DW to Joseph Story, Dec. 9, 1816, Story Papers, Massachusetts Historical Society, F3/2007.

5. Boston

1. DW to Ezekiel Webster, March 26, 1816, *WP*, I, 196. For his interest in Albany, see Moss Kent to James Kent, March 27, 1816, James Kent Papers, Library of Congress.

2. Autobiography, *WP*, I, 24; DW to Alexander Bliss, June 27 and July 29, 1816, Bancroft-Bliss Papers, Library of Congress, F3/1943 and 1952; Irving H. Bartlett, *Daniel Webster* (New York, 1978), 71–74.

3. For information on Boston in this period, see Walter M. Whitehill, *Boston: A Topographical History* (Cambridge, Mass., 1968); Harold Kirker and James Kirker, *Bulfinch's Boston, 1787–1817* (New York, 1964); Justin Winsor, ed., *The Memorial History of Boston, Including Suffolk County, Massachusetts, 1630–1880*, 4 vols. (Boston, 1882), III and IV; Claude M. Fuess, *Daniel Webster*, 2 vols. (Boston, 1930), I, 197–204; and files of the Boston *Columbian Centinel* and Boston *Advertiser*.

4. Autobiographical Notes, *WS*, XIII, 549–51; Fuess, *Webster*, I, 205–6.

5. John D. Forbes, *Israel Thorndike, Federalist Financier* (New York, 1953), 144–45; Mark A. D. Howe, *Boston, the Place and the People* (New York, 1907), 305; Fuess, *Webster*, I, 206; deeds of conveyance, April 6, 1825, and Sept. 27, 1828, Sang Collection, Brandeis University, F29/39618; another deed, [April 18, 1825], *WP*, II, 40–41; Lewis Tappan to DW, Feb. 14, 1826, ibid., 85–86; George F. Weston, Jr., *Boston Ways: High, By, and Folk* (Boston, 1967), 131; Kirker and Kirker, *Bulfinch's Boston*, 188–89.

6. Edward Pessen, *Riches, Class, and Power before the Civil War* (Lexington, Mass., 1973), 39–40, 48, 66–67, 139, 189–201, and passim; David B. Tyack, *George Ticknor and the Boston Brahmins* (Cambridge, Mass., 1967), 157–59; Paul Goodman, "Ethics and Enterprise: The Values of a Boston Elite, 1800–1860," *American Quarterly*, 18 (Fall 1966), 437–51; Robert Rich, " 'A Wilderness of Whigs': The Wealthy Men of Boston," *Journal of Social History*, 4 (Spring 1971), 263–76.

7. Peter R. Knights, *The Plain People of Boston, 1830–1860: A Study in City Growth* (New York, 1971); Roland N. Stromberg, "Boston in the 1820's and 1830's," *History Today*, 11 (1961), 591–98.

8. DW record of birth dates of children, [ca. Jan. 1, 1825], *WP*, II, 4.

9. DW to Jeremiah Mason, Oct. 29, 1816, WPNH, F3/1995; Grace Webster to James W. Paige, Dec. 1 and 14, 1816, ibid., William Sullivan to DW, Jan. 9 and 11, 1817, ibid., F3/2034 and 2041; DW to Ezekiel Webster, Jan. 19 and 26, 1817, WPDC, F3/2047 and 2054.

10. Eliza Buckminster Lee, "Sketch of Mrs. G. F. Webster," *WS*, XVII, 441–42.

11. Grace Webster to DW, Dec. 4, 6, and 13, 1824, WPNH, F4/4447, 4451, 4485, and other letters in ibid. at the time.

12. John C. Warren to DW, Dec. 13, 1824, Warren Papers, Massachusetts Historical Society, F4/4483; Warren to DW, Dec. 19, 1824, WPNH, F4/4536.

13. James W. Paige to DW, Dec. 19, 1824, WPNH, F4/4533.

14. The poem is published in *WP*, II, 3-4.

15. Among the numerous letters reflecting her grief are the following from Grace to DW: Dec. 29, 1824, WPNH, F4/4555; Dec. 31, 1824, ibid., F4/4581; Jan. 15, [1825], ibid., F5/4686.

16. Grace Webster to DW, Feb. 21, 1825, ibid., F5/4858.

17. Grace Webster to DW, Jan. 26, 1825, ibid., F5/4736; DW to Ezekiel Webster, Feb. 27, 1825, ibid., F5/4886.

18. An illustrative letter is DW to Blake, June 16, 1824, WPLC, F4/4298.

19. DW to Alexander Bliss, [Aug. 29, 1820], Bancroft-Bliss Papers, F3/2909; DW to Henry Cabot, June 4, 1825, Lodge Papers, Massachusetts Historical Society, F5/5001.

20. DW to Fletcher Webster, June 12, 1847, *WS*, XVIII, 257-58.

21. Maurice G. Baxter, *Daniel Webster and the Supreme Court* (Amherst, 1966), 14-15; DW to Nathaniel A. Haven, Nov. 9, 1816, WPDC, F3/1999.

22. DW to Ezekiel Webster, [May 25, 1817], WPDC, F3/2068; John C. Chamberlain to DW, Jan. 12, 1818, ibid., F3/2147; DW to Ezekiel Webster, July 8, 1818, ibid., F3/2488; DW to Ezekiel Webster, Aug. 27, 1818, *WP*, I, 227; DW to Nathaniel A. Haven, Sept. 21, 1818, ibid., 231; George Farrar to DW, Aug. 10, 1818, ibid., 232; Haven to DW, May 4, 1821, ibid., 284; DW to Ezekiel Webster, Nov. 13, 1826; WPDC, F5/5707.

23. DW memorandum, 1828-33, Sang Collection, F29/39819; deeds of conveyance, Oct. 13, 1826, ibid., F29/39640 and 39642.

24. Fuess, *Webster*, I, 341, citing Nathan Appleton, *Introduction of the Power Loom*, 22.

25. DW to Augustus Peabody, June 24, 1823, *WP*, I, 330.

26. DW to James Lloyd, Dec. 20, 1819, Webster Papers, Harvard University, F3/2793.

27. DW to Nicholas Biddle, Jan. 6, 1825, Biddle Papers, Library of Congress, F5/4616; DW to Biddle, Jan. 26, 1827, ibid., F5/5851; DW to Biddle, Nov. 1, 1828, ibid., F6/7291; Washington *National Intelligencer*, Jan. 5, 1829; Boston *Columbian Centinel*, Jan. 19, 1820.

28. DW to Biddle, Oct. 30, 1828, Biddle Papers, F6/7291; Gardiner Greene to DW, Oct. 31, 1828, ibid.; DW to Biddle, Nov. 1, 1828, ibid., F6/7296; Biddle to DW, Nov. 4, 1828, WPLC, F6/7304; DW to Biddle, Nov. 7, 1828, Biddle Papers, F6/7315.

29. Webster's checks, notes, and drafts at the national bank for 1826 to 1834 are in U.S. Fianance Papers, Library of Congress, box 4, accession 6046A.

30. Illustrative letters are DW to Bliss, March 27, 1824, Bancroft-Bliss Papers, F4/4069; DW to Bliss, March 3, 1826, *WP*, II, 94; DW to Kinsman, April 22, 1828, WPNH, F6/7010.

31. George T. Curtis, *Life of Daniel Webster*, 2 vols. (New York, 1870), I, 288. As senator, he was paid $1,720 in 1827, $920 in 1829, $1,624 in 1831. U.S. Congress Papers, Library of Congress, F29/39650.

32. One of his contributions to the *North American Review*, reviewing an

English publication on the civil list, appeared in December 1816; another, on English attitudes toward America, in July 1820; *WS*, XV, 3-7, 76-77.

33. Curtis, *Webster*, I, 334.

34. *WS*, II, 27-40.

35. Printed notice, signed by Josiah Quincy, WPLC, F3/2885.

36. DW to Nathaniel Macarty, Aug. 23, 1820, American Antiquarian Society Archives, Worcester, Mass., F3/2907.

37. Two meetings of historical societies which he and other leading men of the state attended at this time were those of the East India Society and of the Essex Historical Society, both in Salem; Boston *Advertiser*, Oct. 14, 1825 and Sept. 22, 1828.

38. See his Plymouth oration, discussed later in this chapter.

39. DW to Samuel Boyd, Jan. 3, 1822, WPNH, F4/3128; DW to Ezekiel Webster, Jan. 13, 1822, WPDC, F4/3157.

40. DW to John Pierce, May 16, 1822, Corporation Papers, Harvard University Archives, F4/3303.

41. Boston *Advertiser*, Aug. 25, 1824.

42. Tyack, *Ticknor*, 85-126; George S. Hillard and Anna Ticknor, eds., *Life, Letters, and Journals of George Ticknor*, 2 vols. (Boston, 1876), I, 361.

43. DW to Story, April 13, 1828, Story Papers, Library of Congress, F6/6964; Gerald T. Dunne, *Justice Joseph Story and the Rise of the Supreme Court* (New York, 1970), 274-75.

44. DW to Story, [Sept. 5, 1829], Story Papers, Masschusetts Historical Society, F7/8066.

45. In its chronicle of Boston churches, Winsor, *History of Boston*, includes valuable lists of trinitarian and unitarian congregations in the city, III, 415-20, 480-82.

46. See Isaac Parker, DW, et al. to Channing, May [?], 1826, Channing Autographs, Rhode Island Historical Society, Providence, F5/5481, urging Channing to publish his sermons for the benefit of present and future generations.

47. Grace Webster to DW, Jan. 21, 1827, WPNH, F5/5836.

48. Receipt to DW for purchase of pew in Brattle Square Church, signed by Alden Bradford et al., Oct. 18, 1824, Sang Collection, F29/39613; conveyances of pews in St. Paul's, Nov. 28, 1820, ibid., F3/2925 and 2929.

49. Winsor, *History of Boston*, III, 455.

50. Wesley F. Craven, *The Legend of the Founding Fathers* (New York, 1956), 30-32, 82-84, 152.

51. Curtis, *Webster*, I, 192-93, quoting Ticknor's account.

52. Journal of Lewis Tappan, Dec. 26, 1820, Tappan Papers, Library of Congress; Fuess, *Webster*, I, 286.

53. Text of speech in *WS*, I, 181-230.

54. Several years later, Webster privately criticized the intolerance of Puritans in New England (not especially the Plymouth Pilgrims) toward dissidents there; DW to Charles B. Haddock, Oct. 14, 1826, *WS*, XVII, 412.

55. Boston *Columbian Centinel*, Dec. 27, 1820. The rock had been split in two in 1774 in an effort to move it to the town square. Only half remained at its original site in 1820. Later the parts would be rejoined, and the whole moved to another point on the shore. Craven, *Founding Fathers*, 32.

56. Editor's note, *WS*, I, 233-34; printed announcement by Bunker Hill

Monument Association, [1824?], WPNH, F4/3816; Boston *Advertiser,* Jan. 15, Sept. 20, and Oct. 5, 1824.

57. Boston *Advertiser,* Aug. 24, 1824; Hillard and Ticknor, *Life of Ticknor,* I, 345.

58. DW to George W. Warren, March 6, 1825, *WS,* XVI, 107–8; Boston *Advertiser,* June 30, 1825.

59. DW to Ticknor [June 1825], WPDC, F5/5027.

60. DW to Fletcher Webster, June 12, 1847, *WS,* XVIII, 257–58.

61. Review of Henry Dearborn's *Account of the Battle of Bunker Hill* in the *North American Review,* July 1818, *WS,* XV,14–44.

62. Boston *Advertiser,* June 20 and 23, 1825; Curtis, *Webster,* I, 248–50, quoting Ticknor's description of the occasion. The text of his speech is in *WS,* I, 235–54.

63. *WS,* I, 240–42.

64. Ibid., 245–46.

65. Ibid., 254.

66. Webster received some help from Timothy Pickering and borrowed some of Adams' letters from him; Pickering to DW, July 19 and 22, 1826, WPNH, F5/5515 and 5519; DW to Pickering, Aug. 7, 1826, Pickering Papers, Massachusetts Historical Society, F5/5607.

67. Boston *Advertiser,* Aug. 4, 1826; Curtis, *Webster,* I, 274–76, quoting Ticknor's description. Text of speech is in *WS,* I, 289–324.

68. *WS,* I, 309–12.

69. Ibid., 324.

70. One can find evaluations of Webster's oratory, in the context of his times, in the following: Wilbur S. Howell and Hoyt H. Hudson, "Daniel Webster," in William N. Brigance, ed., *A History and Criticism of American Public Address,* 3 vols. (New York, 1960), II, 665–733; Russel B. Nye, *Society and Culture in America, 1830–1860* (New York, 1974), 36–46. For his own thoughts on oratory, see DW to Anna Ticknor, Jan. 17, 1825, *WP,* II, 12–13.

6. Massachusetts Politician

1. James M. Banner, Jr., *To the Hartford Convention: The Federalists and the Origins of Party Politics in Massachusetts, 1789–1815* (New York, 1970), 221–25, 227–30, 235–36, 238–48, 263–65; Shaw Livermore, Jr., *The Twilight of Federalism: The Disintegration of the Federalist Party, 1815–1830* (Princeton, 1962), 81–82.

2. George T. Curtis, *Life of Daniel Webster,* 2 vols. (New York, 1870), I, 161.

3. Harry Ammon, *James Monroe: The Quest for National Identity* (New York, 1971), 374–77.

4. Ibid., 357, 377; Livermore, *Twilight of Federalism,* 51–52.

5. DW to Jeremiah Mason, Feb. 22, 1818, WPNH, F3/2182.

6. Boston *Columbian Centinel,* Nov. 8, 1820; Claude M. Fuess, *Daniel Webster,* 2 vols. (Boston, 1930), I, 307–8.

7. Charles M. Wiltse, *John C. Calhoun: Nationalist* (Indianapolis, 1944), 216–18; Curtis, *Webster,* I, 176–77.

8. Fuess, *Webster,* I, 270–71. The text of the memorial is in *WS,* XV, 55–72.

9. Glover Moore, *The Missouri Controversy* (Lexington, Ky., 1953), 119–24. A

majority of southern congressmen had also bypassed the point during the debates.

10. Robert Ernst, *Rufus King, American Federalist* (Chapel Hill, 1968), 372–73. On December 27, 1819, Webster wrote King that "we have added little or nothing in this memorial, to the view taken by you"; King Papers, New York Historical Society, F3/2798.

11. *WS*, XV, 56–69.

12. Ibid., 70–71.

13. DW to Henry Baldwin, Feb. 15, 1820, WPNH, F3/2827.

14. *WS*, XV, 71–72.

15. *Journal of Debates and Proceedings in the Convention of Delegates, Chosen to Revise the Constitution of Massachusetts* (Boston, 1853), 3–4 [hereafter cited as *Conv. Mass.*]; Merrill D. Peterson, ed., *Democracy, Liberty, and Property: The State Constitutional Conventions of the 1820s* (Indianapolis, 1966), 3–4; Boston *Columbian Centinel*, June 17, Aug. 2, 16, 19, 23, and 26, Sept. 13 and 23, 1820.

16. Boston *Columbian Centinel*, Oct. 11, 18 and 21, 1820.

17. *Conv. Mass.*, 9–48; Boston *Columbian Centinel*, Nov. 18, 1820.

18. DW to Story, [Nov. 20, 1820], Story Papers, Massachusetts Historical Society, F3/2921; DW to Mason, Nov. 12, 1820, WPNH, F3/2920. Peterson, *Democracy*, 6, says the reformers probably had a majority in the convention—an estimate apparently taken from Story—but that is doubtful.

19. *Conv. Mass.*, 410, 664; Peterson, *Democracy*, 11, 59–67. The taxpaying requirement was not abandoned until 1891.

20. *Conv. Mass.*, 249–59, 265–66, 295–97, 299–302; Peterson, *Democracy*, 11–12, 68.

21. *Conv. Mass.*, 258–59, 261–64, 268–71, 273–76, 278–95, 297–99.

22. Text of Speech in *Conv. Mass.*, 305–21, and in *WS*, V, 8–25.

23. *WS*, V, 14.

24. Ibid., 15.

25. *Conv. Mass.*, 512–13, 615–16.

26. Ibid., 616–17; Peterson, *Democracy*, 12–14, 120–21.

27. *Conv. Mass.*, 669–70.

28. Webster's speech in ibid., 160–63. For the general debate, see ibid., 124–25, 163–67, 169–87, 205–7, 665.

29. Committee report, ibid., 136–38; Webster's speeches, ibid., 481–86, 489.

30. *Conv. Mass.*, passim.

31. Boston *Columbian Centinel*, Jan. 10, 1821.

32. DW to Jeremiah Mason, Jan. 12, 1821, WPNH, F3/2947.

33. Story to unnamed person, Jan. 21, 1821, in William W. Story, ed., *Life and Letters of Joseph Story*, 2 vols. (Boston, 1851), I, 395–96.

34. *Conv. Mass.*, 622–32; Boston *Columbian Centinel*, Jan. 17, 1821; Boston *Advertiser*, April 4, 5, and 9, 1821.

35. *Conv. Mass.*, 633.

36. This is the view of Peterson, *Democracy*, 16.

37. Robert A. McCaughey, *Josiah Quincy, 1772–1864: The Last Federalist* (Cambridge, Mass., 1974), 100–106; Ronald P. Formisano, *The Transformation of Political Culture: Massachusetts Parties, 1790s–1840s* (New York, 1983), 181–87.

38. Boston *Advertiser*, May 7 through 18, 1822.

39. Ibid., June 10 through 17, 1822.

40. Ibid., May 31 and June 6, 1822; Rufus King to Christopher Gore, June 2, 1822, in Charles R. King, ed., *The Life and Correspondence of Rufus King,* 6 vols. (New York, 1894–1900), VI, 473.

41. Thomas H. Perkins et al. to DW, Oct. 18, 1822, WPNH, F4/3360; Curtis, *Webster,* I, 197–98; Boston *Advertiser,* Oct. 18, 19, and 22, 1822.

42. Boston *Advertiser,* Oct. 23 through Nov. 4, 1822.

43. Ibid., Nov. 5, 1822.

44. DW to Joseph Hopkinson, Nov. 13, 1822, Hopkinson Papers, Pennsylvania Historical Society, F4/3362.

7. Sectionalism

1. Claude M. Fuess, *Daniel Webster,* 2 vols. (Boston, 1930), I, 311–12; Grace Webster to James W. Paige, March 13, 1824, Paige Papers, Massachusetts Historical Society, F4/4040.

2. *Annals of Congress,* 18th Cong., 1st sess., 22. Historians have had to rely upon Adams' own account of his influence in causing Monroe's retreat. See Charles F. Adams, ed., *Memoirs of John Quincy Adams, Comprising Portions of His Diary from 1795 to 1848,* 12 vols. (Philadelphia, 1874–77), VI, 204–5.

3. Paul R. Frothingham, *Edward Everett: Orator and Statesman* (Boston, 1925), 76–81.

4. "The Ethics of Aristotle . . . ," *North American Review,* n.s., 8 (Oct. 1823), 389–424.

5. DW to Everett, Nov. [?], 1823, Everett Papers, Massachusetts Historical Society, F4/3675; Nov. 16, 1823, ibid., F4/3633; Nov. 28, 1823, ibid., F4/3666.

6. DW to Everett, Dec. 5, 1823, ibid., F4/3700. The article soon to appear in print was "Life of Ali Pacha," *North American Review,* n.s., 9 (Jan. 1824), 106–40. The narrative was probably an "Address of the Committee appointed at a Public Meeting held in Boston, Dec. 19, 1823, for the Relief of the Greeks, to Their Fellow Citizens," published in the Boston *Advertiser,* Jan. 10, 1824.

7. DW to Everett, Dec. 6, 1823, Everett Papers, F4/3704.

8. *Annals of Congress,* 18th Cong., 1st sess., 805–6; DW to Everett, Dec. 9, 1823, Everett Papers, F4/3712.

9. *Annals of Congress,* 18th Cong., 1st sess., 843, 914. The documents are in ibid., appendix, and in the Washington *National Intelligencer,* Jan. 3, 1824.

10. *Annals of Congress,* 18th Cong., 1st sess., 849, 870–74, 917. The report was received by the House on January 16; ibid., 1063–64.

11. Carl Seaburg and Stanley Paterson, *Merchant Prince of Boston: Colonel T. H. Perkins, 1764–1854* (Cambridge, Mass., 1971), 313–14; DW to Everett, Dec. 21, 1823, Everett Papers, F4/3752.

12. Adams, *Memoirs,* VI, 227.

13. Notes in WPNH, F4/3871.

14. *Annals of Congress,* 18th Cong., 1st sess., 1084–99.

15. Adams, *Memoirs,* VI, 227, 230, 233; Poinsett to DW, [Dec. 1823], WPLC, F4/3800.

16. *Annals of Congress,* 18th Cong., 1st sess., 1104–11.

17. Ibid., 1115–16, 1127–39, 1150–55, 1165–70, 1204–13.

18. Ibid., 1111–13, 1181–90.

19. Ibid., 1114–15, 1170–77. Other speeches supporting Webster in ibid., 1116–26, 1139–50.

20. Ibid., 1171.

21. DW to Ezekiel Webster, Jan. 27, 1824, *WP,* I, 350–51; Adams, *Memoirs,* VI, 240–41. Bartlett's speech in *Annals of Congress,* 18th Cong., 1st sess., 1150–55.

22. *Annals of Congress,* 18th Cong., 1st sess., 1190–97; *WS,* XIV, 84.

23. *Annals of Congress,* 18th Cong., 1st sess., 1214.

24. DW to Mason, Feb. 15, 1824, WPNH, F4/3982.

25. In 1827 Russia, Britain, and France signed a treaty affirming Greek independence, and an allied naval force annihilated the Turkish fleet in the Bay of Navarino. In 1829 Turkey recognized Greek independence.

26. Shaw Livermore, Jr., *The Twilight of Federalism: The Disintegration of the Federalist Party, 1815–1830* (Princeton, 1962), 98–100.

27. George T. Curtis, *Life of Daniel Webster,* 2 vols. (New York, 1870), I, 205–6, quotes Webster as explaining his motive in this way when he looked back on his speech in 1831.

28. General descriptions in Frederick J. Turner, *Rise of the New West, 1819–1829* (New York, 1962), 169–73; George Dangerfield, *The Awakening of American Nationalism, 1815–1828* (New York, 1965), 202–8.

29. William Plumer, Jr., "Reminiscences of Daniel Webster," *WS,* XVII, 550; DW to Nathan Appleton, Jan. 12, 1824, WPDC, F4/3862; DW to [Enoch Silsby], ibid., F4/3863.

30. Boston *Advertiser,* Jan. 23, 29, 30, and Feb. 3, 14, 1824.

31. Mason to DW, Feb. 1, 1824, WPLC, F4/3954.

32. George R. Taylor, *The Transportation Revolution: 1815–1860* (New York, 1951), 363. Appleton came to Washington during the tariff debates and consulted with Webster; DW to Appleton [March 29, 1824], Appleton Papers, Massachusetts Historical Society, F4/4077.

33. Perkins to DW, Jan. 26, 1824, WPLC, F4/3936, and May 12, 1824, ibid., F4/4184.

34. Boston *Advertiser,* Jan. 28, 1824.

35. The petition of February 9, 1824, is in Records of House of Representatives, RG 233, National Archives, F30/41226. The enclosed document, the Boston committee report of 1820, is in ibid., F30/41234. Perkins was chairman, and Webster a member, of this committee.

36. Turner, *Rise of New West,* 112–13.

37. A report of the speech by the *Advertiser,* Oct. 11, 1820, is reprinted in *WS,* XIII, 5–21.

38. Ibid., 9.

39. Ibid., 5–6.

40. *Annals of Congress,* 18th Cong., 1st sess., 1679–96, 1859–67, 1880–93. Webster's speeches, ibid., 1695, 1699–1701, 1867, 1869, 1888, 1904.

41. Ibid., 1962–2001.

42. DW to Jeremiah Mason, April 19, 1824, WPNH, F4/4114. Webster's speech in *Annals of Congress,* 18th Cong., 1st sess., 2026–68.

43. *Annals of Congress,* 18th Cong., 1st sess., 2427–30, 2673–75. After losing his motion for indefinite postponement of the conference bill (reconciling House and Senate versions), Webster then did vote for passage—no doubt

because this version, amended by the Senate, was preferable to earlier forms of the measure.

44. DW to Isaac P. Davis, April 11, 1824, WPNH, F4/4091.

45. Chase C. Mooney, *William H. Crawford, 1772–1834* (Lexington, Ky., 1974), 242–44, 248; *Annals of Congress,* 18th Cong., 1st sess., 2431–55, 2713–56, 2770–916; Adams, *Memoirs,* VI, passim; Randolph to DW, [Feb. 19, 1825], copy in Levi Woodbury Papers, Library of Congress, F5/4844; and DW to Randolph, Feb. 25, [1825], ibid.

46. Mooney, *Crawford,* passim.

47. Ezekiel Webster to DW, Jan. 28, 1822, WPDC, F4/3184.

48. DW to Jeremiah Mason, [May 1823?], WPNH, F4/3815.

49. Calhoun to Micah Sterling, March 27, 1823, in Robert L. Meriwether and W. E. Hemphill, eds., *The Papers of John C. Calhoun,* 8 vols. (Columbia, S.C., 1959–), VII, 547.

50. Calhoun to Virgil Maxcy, Aug. 27, 1823, ibid., VIII, 248; Maxcy to Lemuel Williams, Sept. 10, 1823, ibid., 263–67; Calhoun to Henry Wheaton, Sept. 26, ibid., 287; DW to Maxcy, Sept. 22, 1823, Galloway-Maxcy-Markoe Papers, Library of Congress, F4/3593a.

51. DW to Ezekiel Webster, March 1824, in Curtis, *Webster,* I, 218–19.

52. DW to Jeremiah Mason, Nov. 30, 1823, in George S. Hillard, *Memoir and Correspondence of Jeremiah Mason* (Cambridge, Mass., 1873), 276.

53. DW to Ezekiel Webster, Dec. 4, 1823, WPDC, F4/3697.

54. DW to Ezekiel Webster, Feb. 15, 1824, ibid., F4/3986; DW to Jeremiah Mason, Feb. 15, 1824; WPNH, F4/3982.

55. DW to Ezekiel Webster, Feb. 22, 1824, WPDC, F4/4004.

56. DW to Jeremiah Mason, Nov. 30, 1823, *WP,* I, 336.

57. DW to Jeremiah Mason, Nov. 20, 1823, WPDC, F4/3637.

58. Arthur B. Darling, *Political Changes in Massachusetts, 1824–1848: A Study of Liberal Movements in Politics* (New Haven, 1925), 40–46.

59. Livermore, *Twilight of Federalism,* 160–68.

60. Adams, *Memoirs,* VI, 312–13, 316, 332.

61. DW to Ezekiel Webster, April 18, 1824, WPDC, F4/4111.

62. DW to William Gaston, Sept. 8, 1824, WPNH, F4/4411.

63. Boston *Advertiser,* Sept. 30 and Oct. 1, 9, 12, 13, 15, 18, 22, 23, 1824.

64. Ibid., Oct. 14, 1824. At a "republican" meeting in Boston on October 11, Webster was nominated for Congress; of course all those preferring the Federalist label supported him.

65. Arthur M. Schlesinger, Jr., and Fred L. Israel, eds., *History of American Presidential Elections, 1789–1968,* 4 vols. (New York, 1971), I, 409.

66. Boston *Advertiser,* Nov. 2 and 15, 1824.

67. Robert V. Remini, *Martin Van Buren and the Making of the Democratic Party* (New York, 1959), 73–80, 82; Mooney, *Crawford,* 294.

68. He strongly supported an internal-improvements bill, which passed; *Register of Debates,* 18th Cong., 2d sess., 249–52, 254–55. And as chairman of the Judiciary Committee, he drafted a federal criminal code with Story's help; Records of House of Representatives, RG 233, National Archives, F30/40808; *WS,* XIV, 101–2; *U.S. Statutes at Large,* IV, 115–23.

69. Plumer, "Reminiscences of Webster," *WS,* XVII, 553, 556.

70. DW to Jeremiah Mason, Dec. 29, 1824, WPNH, F4/4558.

71. Adams, *Memoirs*, VI, 472.

72. Ibid., 474.

73. DW to George Ticknor, Jan. 20, 1825, *WP*, II, 14-15.

74. In a letter to Joseph Hopkinson, Jan. 29, 1825, Webster accurately listed the states that would vote for Adams; Hopkinson Papers, Pennsylvania Historical Society, F5/4743.

75. Adams, *Memoirs*, VI, 483; essay on the election by James F. Hopkins in Schlesinger and Israel, *Presidential Elections*, I, 376-81.

76. Warfield to DW, Feb. 3, 1825, WPNH, F5/4776; DW to Warfield, Feb. 5, 1825, ibid., F5/4792.

77. Adams, *Memoirs*, VI, 492-93.

78. Ibid., 500.

79. Ibid., 493.

80. Livermore, *Twilight of Federalism*, 177-79.

81. Florence Weston, *The Presidential Election of 1828* (Washington, D.C., 1938), 12-13; Washington *National Intelligencer*, Jan. 31 and Feb. 4 and 5, 1825; James F. Hopkins and Mary W. M. Hargreaves, eds., *The Papers of Henry Clay*, 7 vols. (Lexington, Ky., 1959-73), IV, 165-66.

82. DW to Joseph Hopkinson, May 2, 1825, *WP*, II, 45-46.

83. Washington *National Intelligencer*, Feb. 10, 1825; *Register of Debates*, 18th Cong., 2d sess., 525-27.

84. Livermore, *Twilight of Federalism*, 180-82.

85. John C. Fitzpatrick, ed., *The Autobiography of Martin Van Buren* (Washington, D.C., 1920), 152; Remini, *Van Buren and Democratic Party*, 89-90; John Niven, *Martin Van Buren: The Romantic Age of American Politics* (New York, 1983), 56-62.

86. Adams, *Memoirs*, VI, 502, 505.

87. Washington *National Intelligencer*, Feb. 11 and 16, 1825.

88. Boston *Columbian Centinel*, Feb. 16, 1825; Isaac Parker to DW, Feb. 21, 1825, WPLC, F5/4852.

89. DW to Mason, Feb. 14, 1825, WPDC, F5/4818.

90. Mason to DW, Feb. 20, 1825, ibid., F5/4848.

91. DW to Adams, Feb. 26, 1825, Adams Papers, Massachusetts Historical Society, F5/4878.

8. Friend of the Administration

1. DW to Samuel Jaudon, July 4, 1824, *WP*, I, 362.

2. Charles F. Adams, ed., *Memoirs of John Quincy Adams, Comprising Portions of His Diary from 1795 to 1848*, 12 vols. (Philadelphia, 1874-77), VI, 442, 469; William Plumer, Jr., "Reminiscences of Daniel Webster," *WS*, XVII, 553, 557.

3. Adams, *Memoirs*, VI, 511.

4. DW to Henry Clay, April 7, 1825, Clay Papers, Library of Congress, F5/4952; DW to J. Evelyn Denison, May 2, 1825, WPLC, F5/4965; Jeremiah Mason to DW, May 7, 1826, Mason Papers, New Hampshire Historical Society, Concord, F5/5442; Shaw Livermore, Jr., *The Twilight of Federalism: The Disintegration of the Federalist Party, 1815-1830* (Princeton, 1962), 202.

5. Adams, *Memoirs*, VI, 511.

6. Ibid., VII, 68–70; DW to Jeremiah Mason, Dec. 11, 1825, Mason Papers, F5/5161; Samuel F. Bemis, *John Quincy Adams and the Union* (New York, 1956), 72–73.

7. Adams, *Memoirs,* VII, 84.

8. Parker to DW, Feb. 12, 1826, WPLC, F5/5301.

9. Robert V. Remini, *The Election of Andrew Jackson* (Philadelphia, 1963), 39–40; Florence Weston, *The Presidential Election of 1828* (Washington, D.C., 1938), 85–86.

10. Clay to DW, [ca. Jan. 31, 1826], WPLC, F5/5281.

11. Adams, *Memoirs,* VII, 107, 111.

12. *Register of Debates,* 19th Cong., 1st sess., 1208–19, 1226–1302.

13. Remini, *Election of Jackson,* 40–43.

14. *Register of Debates,* 19th Cong., 1st sess., 2011–22, 2029–49, 2055–59, 2066–87, 2168–82, 2277–2337, 2349–76, 2391–2408, 2415–19, 2423–27, 2433–56, 2511–14.

15. Ibid., 2254–77. For other speeches supporting the administration, see ibid., 2021–29, 2052–55, 2060–65, 2087–98, 2182–2254, 2408–10, 2440–42, 2427–33, 2440–42, 2458–72.

16. Speech of Samuel D. Ingham, ibid., 2366–68. See also the remarks of John Forsyth, ibid., 2303–37.

17. Ibid., 2453.

18. Ibid., 2457–90.

19. Ibid., 2514.

20. George Dangerfield, *The Awakening of American Nationalism, 1815–1828* (New York, 1965), 249–55.

21. Maurice G. Baxter, *Daniel Webster and the Supreme Court* (Amherst, 1966), 228–32; *WS,* V, 150–63, 165–77; *Register of Debates,* 19th Cong., 1st sess., 1148–49.

22. *Register of Debates,* 19th Cong., 2d sess., 732–33, 744–46, 957–86, 1014–29, 1086–87, 1099.

23. For Webster's extensive explanation of his changing position on the tariff, see DW to [William Coleman], Feb. 23, 1827, *WP,* II, 159–63.

24. Robert V. Remini, *Martin Van Buren and the Making of the Democratic Party* (New York, 1959), 135–36.

25. Dangerfield, *Awakening Nationalism,* 276. Among other issues in this session, Webster supported the president's stern position against British policy on the West Indies trade, opposed southern states' rights arguments on the removal of the Creek Indians, and voted at every opportunity for federal internal improvements; *Register of Debates,* 19th Cong., 2d sess., passim.

26. Remini, *Van Buren and Democratic Party,* 148–49.

27. DW to Ezekiel Webster, July 12, 1827, WPDC, F6/6297.

28. John S. Bassett, *The Life of Andrew Jackson,* 2 vols. (New York, 1911), II, 375–81; Robert V. Remini, *Andrew Jackson and the Course of American Freedom* (New York, 1981), 74–115, believes the "bargain" reflected the pervasive corruption of the era. He refers to various corrupt aspects of Webster's career, 397 n. 14.

29. Bassett, *Jackson,* II, 386–91.

30. DW to Clay, April 7, 1825, Clay Papers, F5/4951.

31. DW to Clay, Sept. 28, 1825, ibid., F5/5110.

32. An example is DW to Clay, Oct. 13, 1826, ibid., F5/5674a.

33. DW to Clay, July 24 and Aug. 22, 1827, ibid., F6/6310 and 6343. For context, see Washington *National Intelligencer,* July 12 and 17, 1827; Remini, *Election of Jackson,* 65–67.

34. Remini, *Election of Jackson,* 56; Niven, *Van Buren,* 174–84.

35. Remini, *Van Buren and Democratic Party,* 130–33.

36. Remini, *Election of Jackson,* 49.

37. Remini, *Van Buren and Democratic Party,* 138–44.

38. Ibid., 1–11, 167–68, 186–95.

39. For contemporary views of parties, see Richard Hofstadter, *The Idea of a Party System: The Rise of Legitimate Opposition in the United States, 1780–1840* (Berkeley, 1969), 212–71.

40. David H. Fischer, *The Revolution of American Conservatism: The Federalist Party in the Era of Jeffersonian Democracy* (New York, 1965).

41. DW to Jeremiah Mason, March 25, 1823, WPDC, F4/3465.

42. *Annals of Congress,* 18th Cong., 1st sess., 1171.

43. DW to John Agg, April 2, 1827, WPDC, F5/6062.

44. Livermore, *Twilight of Federalism,* 223 and passim.

45. DW to Jonathan Goodhue, May 7 and July 30, 1825, *WP,* II, 48, 65; Robert Walsh, Jr., to DW, Aug. 22, 1825, ibid., 70–71.

46. DW to Ezekiel Webster, Jan. 29, 1826, WPDC, F5/5274.

47. DW to Jeremiah Mason, March 27, 1826, Oliver Papers, Massachusetts Historical Society, F5/5387.

48. DW to Jeremiah Mason, April 10, 1827, *WP,* II, 184–85.

49. DW to Clay, April 14, 1827, Clay Papers, F5/6098; Clay to DW, April 14, 1827, WPLC, F5/6102; Clay to DW, April 20, 1827, ibid., F5/6109; Clay to DW, May 14, 1827, ibid., F5/6134; Clay to DW, Oct. 17, 1827, ibid., F6/6399; DW to Clay, Nov. 5, [1827], Clay Papers, F6/6424; Clay to DW, Nov. 8, 1827, ibid., F6/6434.

50. DW to Joseph Story, May 12, 1823, *WP,* I, 328; Livermore, *Twilight of Federalism,* 117–19.

51. Boston *Advertiser,* April 4, 1825.

52. Text of speech in ibid., April 6, 1825.

53. Arthur B. Darling, *Political Changes in Massachusetts, 1824–1848* (New Haven, 1925), 46–47.

54. Boston *Advertiser,* March 24–April 7, 1827; DW to Faneuil Hall meeting, March 31, 1827, *Niles' Register,* 32 (April 7, 1827), 103. On the bridge controversy, see Stanley I. Kutler, *Privilege and Creative Destruction: The Charles River Bridge Case* (Philadelphia, 1971).

55. Boston *Advertiser,* April 10, 20, 21, 23, May 8, 10, 1827.

56. Text of Webster's speech of April 20 in ibid., April 23, 1827.

57. Ibid., May 12, 18, 1827.

58. Donald B. Cole, *Jacksonian Democracy in New Hampshire, 1800–1851* (Cambridge, Mass., 1970), 54–56, 63–65; Ezekiel Webster to DW, June 17, 1827, WPDC, F5/6228; DW to Adams, June 30, 1827, Adams Papers, Massachusetts Historical Society, F5/6266; DW to Ezekiel Webster, June 22, 1827, WPDC, F5/6253; Livermore, *Twilight of Federalism,* 227.

59. Caleb Cushing to DW, Aug. 17, 1825, Cushing Papers, Library of Con-

gress, F5/5073a; DW to Edward Everett, Aug. 28, 1825, Everett Papers, Massachusetts Historical Society, F5/5082.

60. Boston *Massachusetts Journal*, Jan. 3, 1826. This was the first number in the first volume, but the newspaper did not come out regularly until September, with issue no. 4 on Sept. 2, 1826.

61. DW to John C. Wright, April 30, 1827, *WP*, II, 197.

62. DW to Philip Carrigain, Oct. 3, 1827, ibid., 243; DW to Timothy Upham, Oct. 3, 1827, ibid., 243 n. 1; David L. Child to DW, Jan. 3, 1829, WPDC, F6/7627.

63. Clay to DW, Aug. 19, 1827, WPLC, F6/6333; DW to Clay, Sept. 28, 1827, Clay Papers, F6/6366; Clay to DW, Oct. 17, 1827, WPLC, F6/6399. He did not buy the type but apparently sent money later.

64. DW to Clay, Oct. 29, 1827, *WP*, II, 248; DW to Clay, Nov. 5, 1827, Clay Papers, F6/6424; Clay to DW, Nov. 8, 1827, *WP*, II, 252-53.

65. Edward Everett to DW, Nov. 18, 1827, Everett Papers, F6/6447. Help went to a Pittsburgh paper (DW to John C. Wright, April 30, 1827, *WP*, II, 195), and to the Baltimore *Patriot;* DW to J. Q. Adams, March 23, 1827, ibid., 172; DW to Nathaniel F. Williams, March 24, 1827, ibid., 174-75; DW to Williams, April 7, 1827, ibid., 183.

66. DW to Henry Clay, March 25, 1827, ibid., 175-77; DW to Adams, March 26 and 27, 1827, Adams Papers, F5/6042 and 6045.

67. Adams, *Memoirs*, VII, 251; Hopkinson to DW, April 13, 1827, WPNH, F5/6092.

68. The first number of the *Telegraph* appeared in February 1826, and Green assumed the editorship some months later. On the political role of this paper and others at the capital, see Erik M. Eriksson, "Official Newspaper Organs and the Campaign of 1828," *Tennessee Historical Magazine*, 8 (Jan. 1925), 231-47.

69. An example of the *Telegraph*'s criticism of Webster is an item in the issue of Feb. 27, 1828, emphasizing his conservatism, egotism, and political immorality. Jarvis and the president's son John fell into a quarrel, highlighted by Jarvis' pulling young Adams' nose at the Capitol; Bemis, *Adams and Union*, 99; *U.S. Telegraph,* May 8, 1828.

70. Bemis, *Adams and Union*, 141-42; *U.S. Telegraph,* May 11, 1826; DW to Agg, April 2, 1827, WPDC, F5/6062, and Oct. 25, 1827, ibid., F6/6406; Agg to DW, Oct. 30, 1827, Russell Jarvis Papers, Library of Congress, F6/6418; DW to Joseph Story, [Jan. 14, 1828], Story Papers, Library of Congress, F6/6615; Anne R. Wharton, *Social Life in the Early Republic* (Philadelphia, 1902), 213, 230.

71. An example of the partisan position of the paper is the issue of May 27, 1828, reviewing events of the preceding congressional session and predicting Adams' reelection.

72. Eber Malcolm Carroll, *Origins of the Whig Party* (Durham, N.C., 1925), 15-23; Adams, *Memoirs*, VII, passim; William Plumer, Jr., to William C. Bradley, Feb. 13, 1826, Plumer Papers, New Hampshire State Library, Concord.

73. DW to Henry Clay, March 25, 1827, Clay Papers, F5/6034.

74. His correspondence on patronage was fairly heavy throughout this term, most of it incoming items asking for help; WPLC, passim. Examples are:

Isaac Parker to DW, Jan. 21, 1826, F5/5232, and Henry Wheaton to DW, April 12, 1826, F5/5406.

75. Livermore, *Twilight of Federalism*, 211-13.

76. In the lame-duck session after the election of 1828, Adams nominated John J. Crittenden for the Supreme Court; and over Webster's objections, the Senate refused to act on the nomination. Speech in Senate, February 1829, *WS*, XIV, 581-83; *Register of Debates*, 20th Cong., 1st sess., 80-81.

77. DW to Henry Clay, June 8, 1826, Clay Papers, F5/5483; Boston *Advertiser*, June 10, 1826.

78. Boston *Advertiser*, Nov. 4 and 8, 1826; Boston *Massachusetts Journal*, Nov. 9, 1826; DW to Henry Clay, Nov. 6, [1826], James F. Hopkins and Mary W. M. Hargreaves, eds., *The Papers of Henry Clay*, 7 vols. (Lexington, Ky., 1959-73), V, 872; Clay to DW, Nov. 10, 1826, WPLC, F5/5702.

79. Washington *National Intelligencer*, Jan. 20, 29, 30, Feb. 5, 13, 20, 1827; George T. Curtis, *Life of Daniel Webster*, 2 vols. (New York, 1870), I, 202-3. Webster received no votes.

80. John T. Winthrop to DW, Jan. 4, [1827], WPLC, F5/5214; DW to Joseph E. Sprague, Jan. 10, 1827, *WS*, XVII, 414; DW to Jeremiah Mason, April 10, 1827, ibid., 418; DW to John Barney, April 13, 1827, WPDC, F5/6088; DW to John C. Wright, April 30, 1827, ibid., F5/6116; Wright to DW, May 24, 1827, ibid., F5/6168.

81. DW to Clay, May 7, 1827, Clay Papers, F5/6125. See also his letter to Clay of May 18, ibid., F5/6146.

82. Clay to DW, May 14, 1827, WPLC, F5/6134; Clay to DW, May 28 and June 7, WPDC, F5/6172 and 6199.

83. A signal was the comment by the Boston *Advertiser*, May 21, 1827, that E. H. Mills and Lincoln were probably unavailable and that support for Webster was solid.

84. DW to Lincoln, Lincoln Papers, Massachusetts Historical Society, F5/6152.

85. Lincoln to DW, May 24, 1827, WPLC, F5/6164.

86. The connection of Lincoln's remaining governor and protecting old-bridge interests is suggested in Nathaniel Silsbee to Clay, May 23, 1827, WPLC, and in Darling, *Political Changes in Massachusetts*, 50-54.

87. DW to Lincoln, Lincoln Papers, F5/6177; DW to Appleton, Appleton Papers, Massachusetts Historical Society, F5/6174; DW to Sprague, WPNH, F5/6180. See also DW to Clay, June 2, 1827, Clay Papers, F5/6181.

88. Boston *Advertiser*, June 8 and 9, 1827.

89. Joseph Story to DW, June 10, 1827, Story Papers, Massachusetts Historical Society, F5/6206; Charles Miner to DW, June 13, 1827, WPLC, F5/6217.

9. Senator

1. DW to Nathaniel Silsbee, Dec. 1, 1827, *WP*, II, 255-56; DW to Sarah P. Hale, Dec. 13, 1827, Hale Papers, Smith College Library, F6/6489; DW to Nathaniel Silsbee, Jan. 4, [1828], WPNH, F6/6553; Washington *National Intelligencer*, Feb. 20, 1828. Grace Webster's illness and death are described more fully later in the chapter.

2. DW to Elijah H. Mills, Dec. 19, 1827, Lodge Papers, Massachusetts Historical Society, F6/6502; Claude M. Fuess, *Daniel Webster,* 2 vols. (Boston, 1930), I, 350–52.

3. Robert V. Remini, *Martin Van Buren and the Making of the Democratic Party* (New York, 1959), 170–85.

4. Israel Thorndike to DW, April 28, 1828, WPNH, F6/7022; William E. Tileston and James M. Robbins to DW, Feb. 18, 1828, ibid., F6/6768; Levi Lincoln to DW, April 19, 1828, ibid., F6/6981; Patrick T. Jackson to DW, Feb. 11, 1828, *WP,* II, 293–94.

5. Lawrence to DW, May 7, 1828, WPNH, F6/7051.

6. Buckingham to DW, May 7, [1828], WPLC, F6/7047.

7. Thomas H. Perkins to DW, March 1, 1828, WPDC, F6/6805; Samuel H. Babcock to DW, May 7, 1828, WPLC, F6/7045.

8. *Register of Debates,* 20th Cong., 1st sess., 750–62.

9. He should have recalled that he had favored increased rates on cotton textiles in 1816 and on woolens in 1824, notwithstanding his opposition to most other provisions of those laws.

10. The perennial problem with *ad valorem* duties was that in terms of their market value, goods were undervalued at customs.

11. *Register of Debates,* 20th Cong., 1st sess., 786. Two days later the House accepted all the Senate amendments and passed it too; ibid., 2714.

12. DW to Joseph E. Sprague, April 13, 1828, WPNH, F6/6963. On May 7, two days before Webster's speech, Adams wrote in his diary that the senator "expressed some doubt how he should vote"; Charles F. Adams, ed., *Memoirs of John Quincy Adams,* 12 vols. (Philadelphia, 1874–77), VII, 534.

13. *Register of Debates,* 20th Cong., 1st sess., 665–68, 674–75, 678.

14. Senate speech of May 2, 1828, on appropriations for federal surveys; *WS,* XIV, 129–32.

15. Ibid., II, 13–24; Clay to DW, June 13, 1828, in George T. Curtis, *Life of Daniel Webster,* 2 vols. (New York, 1870), I, 329.

16. DW to George Ticknor, Feb. 22, 1828, *WP,* II, 301; DW to Eliza B. Lee, May 18, 1828, Curtis, *Webster,* I, 325.

17. For example, Robert J. Walsh to DW, Feb. 25, 1828, WPNH, F6/6787.

18. Adams, *Memoirs,* VII, 468, 474.

19. Ibid., 483, 485, 493, 519, 525–27, 538–39, 544–47.

20. Joseph Story to Jeremiah Mason, Feb. 27, 1828, in George S. Hillard, *Memoir and Correspondence of Jeremiah Mason* (Cambridge, Mass., 1873), 316; DW to Mason, March 20, 1828, WPDC, F6/6888; Mason to DW, March 27, 1828, *WP,* II, 322–23.

21. Extant sources suggest that Webster was more hesitant than Adams and Clay thought he was. Reminiscences of George Ticknor in Curtis, *Webster,* I, 323; DW to James W. Paige, March 13, [1828], Paige Papers, Massachusetts Historical Society, F6/6855; DW to Joseph Sprague, March 22, 1828, *WP,* II, 320.

22. *U.S. Telegraph,* Jan. 19, 1827.

23. Clippings from *Palladium* and *Post* in Boston *Advertiser,* Oct. 13, 1827. They later appeared in *Niles' Register,* 30 (Oct. 20, 1827); and Bailey's denial was also carried here. The *Post* conceded that it might have been wrong about Bailey's role. See also Boston *Advertiser,* Oct. 19, 1827.

24. Clay to DW, Nov. 8, 1827, WPLC, F6/6434.

25. *U.S. Telegraph,* March 20, 1828; Joseph Hopkinson to DW, April 19, 1828, WPNH, F6/6977; *WP,* II, 334 n.; Samuel F. Bemis, *John Quincy Adams and the Union* (New York, 1956), 138-39.

26. DW to Hopkinson, April 21, 1828, Hopkinson Papers, Pennsylvania Historical Society, F6/7002; *WP,* II, 336 n. 1; *U.S. Telegraph,* April 29, 1828.

27. *U.S. Telegraph,* May 5, 1828, clipping item from Philadelphia *National Gazette* and criticizing it.

28. Stockton to DW, May 14, 1828, WPLC, F6/7076.

29. *U.S. Telegraph,* May 28, 1828.

30. DW to Adams, Sept. 13, 1828, Adams Papers, Massachusetts Historical Society, F6/7189. Henry Warfield wrote Webster on March 22, 1830, that he thought the correspondence ought at last to be published; but it was not; WPLC, F7/8582.

31. Shaw Livermore, *The Twilight of Federalism: The Disintegration of the Federalist Party, 1815-1830* (Princeton, 1962), 227-28; Henry A. S. Dearborn to DW, March 7, 1828, *WP,* II, 308-09.

32. DW to Joseph E. Sprague, July 20, 1828, *WP,* II, 355-56 and n. 3; DW to Sprague, [Sept. 24? 1828], ibid., 364. The address was published in the Boston *Columbian Centinel,* Oct. 11, 1828.

33. Livermore, *Twilight of Federalism,* 228-30; DW to Anna Ticknor, March 23, 1828, Curtis, *Webster,* I, 322; William Sullivan to DW, May 12, 1828, WPLC, F6/7068.

34. Ezekiel Webster to DW, March 17, 1828, *WP,* II, 314-15; Washington *National Intelligencer,* March 18, 1828.

35. DW to Ezekiel Webster, March 23, 1828, WPDC, F6/6900.

36. Ezekiel Webster to DW, [March 17, 1828], ibid., F6/6872; DW to Ezekiel Webster, March 23 and April 4, 1828, ibid., F6/6900 and F6/6938. He did run for Congress in March 1829 and was defeated; Ezekiel Webster to DW, Jan. 9, 1829, ibid., F6/7636; *WP,* II, 315-16 n.

37. DW to Samuel Bell, July 29, 1828, *WP,* II, 356.

38. DW to Jeremiah Mason, Aug. 1, 1828, WPNH, F6/7159; DW to Mason, Aug. 4, 1828, Oliver Papers, Massachusetts Historical Society, F6/7163; DW to Nicholas Biddle, Aug. 9, 1828, Morristown (New Jersey) National Historical Park, F6/7167; Biddle to DW, Aug. 14, 1828, Mason Papers, New Hampshire Historical Society, F6/7170; *WP,* II, 357-58 n. Webster was a director of the national bank. Mason's handling of the branch's presidency later led to controversy.

39. Adams, *Memoirs,* VII, 455.

40. Weed to DW, March 7, 1828, WPLC, F6/6835; DW to Ezekiel Webster, March 18, 1828, WPDC, F6/6878.

41. Clinton himself had supported Jackson.

42. DW to Van Buren, Sept. 27, 1828, Van Buren Papers, Massachusetts Historical Society, F6/7219.

43. DW to Jeremiah Mason, March 20, 1828, WPDC, F6/6888.

44. Adams, *Memoirs,* VII, 469-70.

45. Florence Weston, *The Presidential Election of 1828* (Washington, D.C., 1938), 112; DW, Benjamin Gorham, and Edward Everett to Nathaniel Silsbee, Sept. 22, 1828, Webster Papers, Harvard University, F6/7203.

46. Clay to DW, Oct. 24, 1828, WPLC, F6/7281.

47. DW to Nathaniel F. Williams, Sept. 25, 1828, WPDC, F6/7207; DW to Ezekiel Webster, [Sept. 28, 1828], *WP*, II, 367.

48. DW to Clay, Oct. 1 and 23, 1828, Clay Papers, Library of Congress, F6/7235 and F6/7274.

49. Clay to DW, Oct. 24, 1828, WPLC, F6/7281.

50. Robert V. Remini, *The Election of Andrew Jackson* (Philadelphia, 1963), 151-56.

51. Ibid., 102-3, 117-18.

52. Boston *Advertiser,* Oct. 27, 1828, clipping Jefferson's letter and Adams' statement and commenting on the matter; Samuel F. Bemis, *John Quincy Adams and the Foundations of American Foreign Policy* (New York, 1949), 575.

53. *U.S. Telegraph,* Oct. 28, 1828.

54. Boston *Advertiser,* Nov. 3, 1828, including clipping from the *Massachusetts Journal.*

55. Arthur M. Schlesinger, Jr., and Fred L. Israel, eds., *History of American Presidential Elections, 1789-1968,* 4 vols. (New York, 1971), I, 492.

56. Clay to DW, Nov. 30, 1828, WPLC, F6/7331.

57. Ezekiel Webster to DW, Feb. 15, 1829, WPDC, F7/7757.

58. See Webster's manuscript of a newspaper editorial, probably written in August 1829, praising Clay's many qualifications for the presidency. WPDC, F7/8041.

59. DW to Nathaniel Silsbee, Dec. 1, 1827, *WP,* II, 255-56; DW to James W. Paige, Dec. 5, 1827, WPNH, F6/6465; DW to John C. Warren, Dec. 7, 8, and 9, 1827, Warren Papers, Massachusetts Historical Society, F6/6471, 6479, and 6485.

60. DW to Ezekiel Webster, Jan. 8, 1828, WPDC, F6/6585.

61. DW to Jeremiah Mason, Dec. 26, 1827, *WP,* II, 255 and n.; DW to Joseph Story, Jan. 19, 1828, Story Papers, Library of Congress, F6/6629; DW to Ezekiel Webster, Jan. 21, 1828, WPDC, F6/6662; DW to Eliza B. Lee, Jan. 21, 1828, *WS,* XVII, 436; DW to John G. Palfrey, Jan. 21, 1828, Webster Papers, Harvard University, F6/6649; George Ticknor to Story, Jan. 25, 1828, Story Papers.

62. DW to Nathan Hale, [Jan. 23, 1828], Hale Papers, F6/6676.

63. Curtis, *Webster,* I, 314, quoting Ticknor's reminiscences.

64. DW to Cyrus Perkins, Jan. 28, 1828, *WP,* II, 288-89; DW to Jeremiah Mason, Jan. 29, 1828, ibid., 290-91; DW to Joseph Story, Feb. 5, 1828, Story Papers, F6/6708.

65. DW to Anna and George Ticknor, Feb. 22, 1828, *WP,* II, 301.

66. Story to Jeremiah Mason, Feb. 27, 1828, in Hillard, *Jeremiah Mason,* 315.

67. One of his letters that is particularly revealing was written to Fletcher, May 11, 1828, *WP,* II, 344. There are many letters from each of the three children in WPNH.

68. DW to John Agg, June 12, 1828, WPDC, F6/7110; DW to Joseph E. Sprague, July 20, 1828, *WP,* II, 355; DW to Ezekiel Webster, [Sept. 28, 1828], WPDC, F6/7223; DW to Mrs. John Agg, Dec. 4, 1828, ibid., F6/7342; DW to Achsah Webster, March 4, 1829, ibid., F7/7863.

69. Curtis, *Webster,* I, 342-43.

70. DW to Cyrus Perkins, April 17, 1829, *WP*, II, 409.

71. DW to Achsah Webster, May 16, 1829, WPDC, F7/7966; DW to John Agg, Aug. 10, 1829, *ibid.*, F7/8022; DW to Nathan Hale, [Aug. 10? 1829], Webster Papers, Maryland Historical Society, Baltimore, F7/8060; DW to Jacob McGaw, Nov. 18, 1829, WPDC, F7/8137.

72. DW to Stephen Van Rénssalaer, May 15, 1829, WPDC, F7/7962.

73. DW to John Agg, Aug. 10, 1829, ibid., F7/8022.

74. One rumor concerned Maria Parker of Boston. *WP*, II, 428 n. 7.

75. DW to Jacob McGaw, Nov. 18, 1829, WPDC, F7/8137.

76. Curtis, *Webster*, I, 345; Fuess, *Webster*, I, 359-60.

77. DW to Fletcher Webster, Dec. 14, 1829, WPDC, F7/8156; Fletcher Webster to DW, Dec. 20, 1829, WPNH, F7/8174.

10. Lawyer

1. For Webster's relationship with his associates, see the numerous items in the George Bancroft–Alexander Bliss Papers, Library of Congress; copies of Webster–Henry W. Kinsman Correspondence, Library of Congress, originals in possession of Gurdon S. H. Pulford, Los Altos, Calif.; and Letterbook and Register of Kinsman, 1829–1841, WPDC, F6/7365–7626.

2. Samuel F. Bemis, *John Quincy Adams and the Union* (New York, 1956), 95; statement by DW, Sept. 10, 1831, WPDC, F8/9567; DW to Edward Everett, [Nov. 2, 1835], Everett Papers, Massachusetts Historical Society, F10/12654.

3. Record of legal earnings, *WS*, XVII, 291–98; manuscript records by DW for August 1816–August 1818 in Webster Papers, Massachusetts Historical Society, F3/1961, and for September 1833 to April 1837 in Sang Collection, Brandeis University, F9/11142.

4. DW to Henry Kinsman, Jan. 29, 1831, Webster-Kinsman Correspondence, F8/9161.

5. *Laurason* v. *Nickerson* (Mass. Sup. Jud. Ct. 1819), description and documents in *WP: Legal*, II, 344–56; *Ward* v. *Peirce* (Mass. Sup. Jud. Ct. 1822), ibid., 356–78; Thorndike's case, ibid., 378–415.

6. *King* v. *Dedham*, 15 Mass. 447 (1819); *Salem Bank* v. *Gloucester Bank*, 17 Tyng (Mass.) 3 (1820); *State Bank* v. *Welles*, 3 Pickering (Mass.) 394 (1826). All discussed in *WP: Legal*, II, 527–39.

7. William E. Nelson, *The Americanization of American Law: The Impact of Legal Change on Massachusetts Society, 1760–1830* (Cambridge, Mass., 1975); Morton J. Horwitz, *The Transformation of American Law, 1780–1860* (Cambridge, Mass., 1977).

8. For his thoughts as a young man, see his review essay in *Monthly Anthology*, April 1807, reprinted in *WS*, XVII, 552–55.

9. See his role in *C.&O.* v. *B.&O.*, 4 Gill and Johnson (Md.) 1 (1832), with description in Washington *National Intelligencer*, Jan. 13, 1832, and in Carl B. Swisher, *Roger B. Taney* (New York, 1935), 115–17.

10. George T. Curtis, *Life of Daniel Webster*, 2 vols. (New York, 1870), I, 171–75; Webster's summation to the jury, *WS*, X, 177–93.

11. Clipping of Salem *Register*, April 8, 1830, in Boston *Courier*, April 10, 1830.

12. Howard A. Bradley and James A. Winans, *Daniel Webster and the Salem Murder* (Columbia, Mo., 1956), 18–23.

13. Ibid., 24–30; Curtis, *Webster,* I, 378–80.

14. Bradley and Winans, *Webster and Salem Murder,* 96–97, 143–217, for texts and sources; *WS,* XI, 51–105 for version prepared by Webster for his collected works.

15. The fullest report of the case is John D. Lawson, ed., *American State Trials,* 17 vols. (St. Louis, 1917), VII, 395–593. See also 26 Mass. 495–518 (1830), the official report of the state supreme court's hearing and rulings. Also valuable is the full coverage in the Boston *Advertiser,* Aug. 16, 17, 20, 21, and Oct. 1, 1830.

16. Bradley and Winans, *Webster and Salem Murder,* 96–97.

17. Ibid., 221–24; Lawson, *State Trials,* VII, 594–639.

18. Bradley and Winans, *Webster and Salem Murder,* 221–22; DW to Joseph Story, Aug. 11 [?], 1830, *WS,* XVII, 506. The letter to Story was probably written in November instead of August, since the trial of Joseph occurred in November, and the issue of the fees arose in court then. The receipt in Webster's hand for $1,000, dated August 14 and given to Stephen White, is in Webster Papers (Mass. Hist. Soc.), F29/39752. It was for services in the case of "Jno. F. Knapp," thus John Francis [Frank] Knapp.

19. The view that "moral justice" was served can be found in Curtis, *Webster,* I, 378–85, and in Claude M. Fuess, *Daniel Webster,* 2 vols. (Boston, 1930), II, 292–98. Walker Lewis, "The Murder of Captain Joseph White, Salem, Massachusetts, 1830," *American Bar Association Journal,* 54 (1968), 460–66, is helpful on numerous legal points but does not discuss important questions concerning the law of confessions and says merely that "justice was done." Such defects of judicial procedures in criminal cases as appear in the Knapp trials were common in this period; Lawrence M. Friedman, *History of American Law* (New York, 1973), 134.

20. Commentary and documents, *WP: Legal,* II, 415–519. The case on jurisdiction is *Peele* v. *Merchant's Insurance Co.* (1822), discussed in ibid., 474–82.

21. Summary of arguments by Webster and George Blake in *WS,* XV, 279–81.

22. 20 *Federal Cases* 840–51 (1822).

23. *The Antelope,* 10 Wheaton 66 (1825).

24. DW to no addressee, Feb. 24, 1819, WPDC, F3/2654.

25. DW to Joseph Hopkinson, March 11, 1819, *WP,* I, 250.

26. Dudley Pickman and Stephen White to DW, Sept. 10, 1821, WPNH, F3/3049; Nathaniel Gilman to DW, Sept. 3, 1821, ibid., F3/3042; DW to Jeremiah Mason, Jan. 13, 1822, Bancroft-Bliss Papers, F4/3150.

27. Agreement signed by Peter C. Brooks et al., July 27, 1821, WPNH, F3/3028; DW to Jeremiah Mason, Sept. 12, 1821, *WP,* I, 291. The agreement with the Boston claimants provided that Webster's fees not exceed a total of twenty thousand dollars, but this limit was later deleted; Waiver signed by Joseph Wood et al., April 24, 1823, WPNH, F4/3522; Peter C. Brooks to DW, Oct. 10, 1823, ibid., F4/3609.

28. Hopkinson to DW, Oct. 14, 1821, Webster-Healy Papers, Massachusetts Historical Society, F3/3081; agreement signed by DW, John Inskeep, and Jacob Waler, Jan. 3, 1822, WPNH, F4/3131.

29. There are many items in Webster's correspondence describing his commitment to the business. Illustrative letters are: DW to Alexander Bliss, Sept. 7, 1821, Bancroft-Bliss Papers, F3/3046; DW to Edward Cutts, Oct. 8, 1821, Montague Collection, New York Public Library, F3/3077; DW to Willard Peale, Jan. 17, 1822, WPNH, F4/3163; DW to Samuel Jaudon, April 19, 1822, Miscellaneous MSS, New York Historical Society, New York, F4/3269; DW to Bliss, Feb. 23, 1823, Bancroft-Bliss Papers, F4/3428, and May 10, 1824, ibid., F4/4170. A valuable source is *WP: Legal,* II, 175–275, commentary and documents.

30. DW to Jeremiah Mason, May 9, 1824, *WS,* XVI, 85–86; John C. Fitzpatrick, ed., *The Autobiography of Martin Van Buren* (Washington, D.C., 1920), 662–63; *Annals of Congress,* 18th Cong., 1st sess., 2559–75; *U.S. Statutes at Large,* IV, 33–34.

31. The complete list of awards by the commission is in Washington *National Intelligencer,* July 3, 1824; Webster's record of his cases, awards, and fees is in Sang Collection, F4/4245-71.

In the 1830s Webster presented a good many cases to other commissions concerning claims against France, Denmark, and Naples. DW to Henry Kinsman, Jan. 25, 1833, WPNH, F9/10502, and Jan. 31, 1833, ibid., F9/10535; *WP: Legal,* II, 325–27.

32. For a fuller treatment of his practice before the high court see Maurice G. Baxter, *Daniel Webster and the Supreme Court* (Amherst, 1966). A splendid short biography of Marshall is Francis N. Stites, *John Marshall: Defender of the Constitution* (Boston, 1981).

33. 4 Wheaton 52–65 (1819).

34. 7 Wheaton 282–355 (1822).

35. *U.S.* v. *The Pirates,* 5 Wheaton 184–206 (1820). Though Webster's argument is unreported here, it was similar to one he advanced in *U.S.* v. *Smith,* ibid., 156–57.

36. Leon B. Richardson, *History of Dartmouth College,* 2 vols. (Hanover, N.H., 1932), I, 13–63, 112–18, 303–9; John K. Lord, *A History of Dartmouth College: 1815–1909* (Concord, N.H., 1913), 1–61, 69–71; Francis N. Stites, *Private Interest and Public Gain: The Dartmouth College Case, 1819* (Amherst, 1972), 1–22. Stites's monograph is the most valuable study of the case as a whole.

37. Concord *New-Hampshire Patriot,* May 23, Sept. 5 and 12, Oct. 10, 1815, and numerous issues throughout the controversy. The Portsmouth *Oracle* predictably came to the trustees' defense. See, for example, issues of July 29, Sept. 2, Oct. 14, 21, and 28, 1815.

38. Lynn W. Turner, *William Plumer of New Hampshire, 1759–1850* (Chapel Hill, 1962), 233–39, 245–46, 303–4; *Laws of New Hampshire,* VIII, 505–8, 555–56, 584.

39. Richardson, *Dartmouth College,* I, 323–27; Stites, *Private Interest,* 34–38; Concord *New-Hampshire Patriot,* Sept. 3, 1816.

40. John M. Shirley, *The Dartmouth College Causes and the Supreme Court of the United States* (St. Louis, 1879), 2, 116–18, 149–51; 4 Wheaton 518–51 (1819); 65 New Hampshire Reports (Parsons, 1888–89) 473–502, 524–63 (1817).

41. There is no extant report of Webster's brief in the state court; but after listening to the arugment, on October 2, 1817, the defendant Woodward remarked to Governor Plumer about the emotion-laden peroration, probably

similar to Webster's concluding flourish in the Supreme Court the following year; Plumer Papers, Library of Congress.

42. 65 New Hampshire Reports 624-43.

43. DW to Francis Brown, Nov. 15, 1817, WPDC, F3/2093.

44. Compare the manuscript of Webster's argument, ibid., F3/2383-2414, with that of Mason, "Briefs in the Dartmouth College Case," Dartmouth College Archives.

45. Salma Hale to William Plumer, Feb. 7, 1818, Plumer Papers.

46. In addition to Webster's manuscript notes and briefs for the case in the Dartmouth College Library, there is the printed version in *WS*, X, 195-233.

47. Webster relied upon William Blackstone's *Commentaries on the Laws of England*, I, 467-85, and the English precedent, *Phillips* v. *Bury*, 1 Lord Raymond 5 (91 English Reports 900) concerning a college in Oxford.

48. See Thomas M. Cooley, *A Treatise on Constitutional Limitations* (Boston, 1874), 353-54.

49. *Fletcher* v. *Peck*, 6 Cranch 87 (1810); *New Jersey* v. *Wilson*, 7 Cranch 164 (1812). The case decided on general principles was *Terrett* v. *Taylor*, 9 Cranch 43 (1815).

50. Baxter, *Webster and Supreme Court*, 83-84.

51. *WS*, XV, 11-13.

52. Story's description of Webster's argument is in WPLC, XII, 1809-15.

53. Baxter, *Webster and Supreme Court*, 91-93.

54. William Allen to William Pinkney, Sept. 10, 1818, copy in Dartmouth College Archives; Allen to Salma Hale, Oct. 15, 1818, ibid.; Hale to Allen, Dec. 4, 1818, ibid.

55. Baxter, *Webster and Supreme Court*, 94-98.

56. DW to Jeremiah Mason, Feb. 4, 1819, WPDC, F3/2631.

57. DW to Jeremiah Mason, May 27, 1819, WPNH, F3/2737; Shirley, *Dartmouth College Causes*, 204-5.

58. The two justices thought to be hesitant were Brockholst Livingston and William Johnson. Possibly Kent exerted some influence upon Livingston. Johnson, however, would probably have been willing to strike down the New Hampshire legislation on general principles of natural justice, instead of the contract clause, if necessary. See his opinion in *Fletcher* v. *Peck*, 6 Cranch 143-48 (1810).

59. 4 Wheaton 624-54 (1819).

60. Years later, at the entrance of a new building, Webster Hall, the college placed a bronze tablet with the inscription, "Founded by Eleazar Wheelock. Refounded by Daniel Webster." Joseph Hopkinson, his associate in the case, had suggested this be done at the time of the decision in a letter to President Francis Brown, Feb. 2, 1819, *WS*, XVII, 301. See also the items frequently appearing in the *Dartmouth Alumni Magazine* in recent years.

61. Limitations upon state power were not complete, for there were still ways for the states to act—by using the police power, by inserting reservations in corporate charters, and by convincing courts that the language of such charters be narrowly interpreted.

62. Benjamin F. Wright, Jr., *The Contract Clause of the Constitution* (Cambridge, Mass., 1938).

63. 12 Wheaton 213 (1827).

64. *Sturges* v. *Crowninshield,* 4 Wheaton 122 (1819).

65. *WS,* XI, 25-40.

66. 12 Wheaton 254-357 (1827), for opinions of Washington, Johnson, Thompson, and Trimble of the majority and for that of Marshall in dissent.

67. Peter J. Coleman, *Debtors and Creditors: Insolvency, Imprisonment for Debt, and Bankruptcy, 1607-1900* (Madison, Wis., 1974), 286-93 and passim; Charles Warren, *Bankruptcy in United States History* (Cambridge, Mass., 1935), 27-51; *Register of Debates,* 19th Cong., 2d sess., 76-210, 276-88.

There was a second decision in *Ogden,* invalidating an application of the state bankruptcy law. It could not affect contracts between citizens of different states. Now considering a point which had been reserved in the first decision, Justice Johnson joined the three dissenters to make a new majority against the extraterritorial applicability of such state legislation. This was a very significant ruling, usually receiving insufficient attention but not lost upon an elated Webster, because of the increasing proportion of creditor-debtor relations crossing state lines; DW to Alexander Bliss, March 14, 1827, Bancroft-Bliss Papers, F5/5989; 12 Wheaton 358-69 (1827).

68. 12 Wheaton 370-83 (1827).

69. 2 Peters 647 (1829).

70. 8 Peters 591.

71. Elizabeth F. Baker, *Henry Wheaton, 1785-1848* (Philadelphia, 1937), 123-27.

72. 8 Peters 591-95 (1834). For the legal history of the subject, see Lyman R. Patterson, *Copyright in Historical Perspective* (Nashville, 1968); Benjamin Kaplan, *An Unhurried View of Copyright* (New York, 1967).

73. 8 Peters 651-54 (1834).

74. Ibid., 654-58. McLean also found no protection for Wheaton in the common law of Pennsylvania, and it was for this that Webster had been primarily contending.

75. *Swift* v. *Tyson,* 16 Peters 1 (1842), discussed in chapter 27.

76. Ralph C. H. Catterall, *The Second Bank of the United States* (Chicago, 1903), 60-65; Bray Hammond, *Banks and Politics in America: From the Revolution to the Civil War* (Princeton, 1957), 263-64.

77. *WS,* XV, 262-64.

78. Ibid., 265

79. Opinion in 4 Wheaton 400-37 (1819). Compare Pinkney's argument, ibid., 377-400.

80. Ibid., 404-5.

81. Ibid., 431.

82. A far-reaching rule of intergovernmental tax immunity did develop and significantly limited both state and national powers; Thomas R. Powell, "Intergovernmental Tax Immunities," *Harvard Law Review,* 57 (May-July 1945), 633-74, 757-805.

83. 9 Wheaton 739-44 (1824); R. Carlyle Buley, *The Old Northwest: Pioneer Period, 1815-1840,* 2 vols. (Bloomington, Ind., 1951), I, 588-94.

84. Arguments of Webster and his associates are in 9 Wheaton 805-11; Marshall's opinion, ibid., 816-71.

85. Examples are *Finley* v. *BUS,* 11 Wheaton 304 (1826); *McGill* v. *BUS,* 12

Wheaton 511 (1827); *Winship* v. *BUS*, 5 Peters 529 (1831); *BUS* v. *Hatch*, 6 Peters 250 (1832).

86. Maurice G. Baxter, *The Steamboat Monopoly: Gibbons v. Ogden, 1824* (New York, 1972), 3–21; and passim for a treatment of the *Gibbons* case as a whole.

87. *Livingston and Fulton* v. *Van Ingen*, 9 Johnson (N.Y.) 307 (1812).

88. *Livingston* v. *Ogden and Gibbons*, 4 Johnson Ch. (N.Y.) 48 (1819); *Ogden* v. *Gibbons*, ibid., 150; *Gibbons* v. *Ogden*, 17 Johnson (N.Y.) 488 (1820).

89. Gibbons to DW, April 2, 1821, and Feb. 21, 1822, WPDC, F3/2969 and F4/3221.

90. *WS*, XI, 4–23.

91. Ibid., 8.

92. Ibid., 11.

93. Ibid., 4–6, 9–11.

94. Ibid., 12–13. One must bear in mind that his argument concerned interstate commerce, for he conceded that states did have full power over commerce within their own boundaries, the aspect to be known as intrastate commerce. And as for regulation of interstate commerce, Webster would allow state legislation if justifiable under the *police* power, which he discussed specifically, where not permissible under the *commerce* power; ibid., 14.

95. Ibid., 20.

96. The text of the coasting act is in *U.S. Statutes at Large*, I, 305–18. See Kent's construction of the act in *Ogden* v. *Gibbons*, 4 Johnson Ch. (N.Y.) 150–65 (1819).

97. 9 Wheaton 187–221 (1824).

98. Even Thomas Oakley and Thomas Emmet, the losing counsel, thought so. See their arguments in *North River Steamboat Co.* v. *Livingston*, 1 Hopkins Ch. (N.Y.) 149 (1824). And the judges of the New York Court of Errors thought so too; *North River Steamboat Co.* v. *Livingston*, 3 Cowen (N.Y.) 713 (1825).

99. Frederick D. G. Ribble, *State and National Power over Commerce* (New York, 1937), 8–51. There are strong indications that Marshall avoided a ruling of exclusive national power because this would alarm southern states, which feared congressional action on slavery under the commerce clause. See Baxter, *Webster and Supreme Court*, 206–7.

11. Liberty and Union

1. DW to Achsah Pollard Webster, March 4, 1829, WPDC, F7/7863.

2. DW to Ezekiel Webster, March 15, 1829, ibid., F7/7878.

3. DW to H. and J. White, Dec. 24, 1829, John Campbell White Papers, Maryland Historical Society, F7/8189; Irving H. Bartlett, *Daniel Webster* (New York, 1978), 125.

4. *Register of Debates*, 21st Cong., 1st sess., 3–5.

5. Ibid., 22–27. Benton's account of the debates is in his *Thirty Years' View*, 2 vols. (New York, 1856), I, 130–43.

6. *Register of Debates*, 21st Cong., 1st sess., 31–35.

7. Hayne's speech of the twenty-fifth is in ibid., 43–58, and of the twenty-seventh, 82–92.

8. The *Massachusetts Weekly Journal*, Dec. 5, 1829, complained that Web-

ster's foes in New England had collected his speeches and writings, "garbled" them, and sent copies to Washington to be used against him. William B. Lewis recalled that Senator Levi Woodbury of New Hampshire sat beside Hayne while the South Carolinian was speaking and passed him extracts from New England newspapers hostile to Webster; Lewis to DW, March 18, 1852, WPDC, F26/36268.

9. Jackson and his fellow Democrats emphasized the Jeffersonian connection.

10. DW to Jeremiah Mason, Feb. 27, 1830, *WP*, III, 18-19.

11. Washington *National Intelligencer*, Jan. 27, 1830.

12. Margaret Bayard Smith, *The First Forty Years of Washington Society*, ed. Gaillard Hunt (New York, 1906), 309-10.

13. *Register of Debates*, 21st Cong., 1st sess., 35-41.

14. Entire speech in ibid., 58-82.

15. They traced the policy regarding the Northwest to Jefferson's plan of 1784 in the Confederation Congress and therefore credited the South rather than New England.

16. The last sentence paraphrased the opinion of Chief Justice Marshall in *Cohens* v. *Virginia*, 6 Wheaton 264 (1821). For *McCulloch*, see 4 Wheaton 316 (1819).

17. Webster saw other stones in the arch, such as provision for frequent elections, the representative system, and the distribution of powers among three branches of government.

18. *Register of Debates*, 21st Cong., 1st sess., 196-210.

19. Ibid., 129-45.

20. Ibid., 210-20.

21. Ibid., 119-28, 160-68.

22. Ibid., 224-44.

23. Speeches of James Noble, ibid., 168-72; Josiah Johnston, ibid., 277-302; Asher Robbins, ibid., 435-38.

24. Ibid., 247-72. Later, as Jackson's secretary of state during the nullification crisis of 1832-33, Livingston would have a major role in countering South Carolina's position.

25. Benton did not endorse interposition, indeed did not mention it; ibid., 95-119. Woodbury, a future Supreme Court justice, deplored the growth of judicial power but reasoned that a state could only remonstrate against a national measure, not nullify it; ibid., 179-96.

26. The shorthand notes, the transcription, Webster's revised version, and a pamphlet edition of the speeches were placed in the Boston Public Library years later. See Claude M. Fuess, *Daniel Webster*, 2 vols. (Boston, 1930), I, 383 and nn. 1 and 2. Webster's memorandum about preparation for publication is in WPLC, F7/9108, printed in *WS*, VI, 296. His notes, used for delivering his speeches, are in WPNH, F7/8350, and WPLC, F7/8372, printed in *WS*, VI, 81-88, and XV, 98-99. His description of the background and setting of the Senate debates are in WPLC, F7/9104, printed in *WS*, VI, 287-96.

27. Washington *National Intelligencer*, Feb. 23, 25, 27, 1830; Boston *Advertiser*, Feb. 27 and March 8, 1830.

28. Illustrative issues of the *Telegraph* are those of Jan. 26 and 29 and March 16, 1830.

29. Ibid., Jan. 28 and 29, Feb. 1 and 4, 1830. As presiding officer, Calhoun ruled Webster's motion out of order; ibid., Feb. 2, 1830.

30. See issues of late December 1831.

31. Boston *Advertiser,* Feb. 4, 1830, and passim.

32. Various clippings in ibid.

33. Dearborn to DW, Feb. 5, 1830, WPNH, F7/8393; Walsh to DW, March 8, 1830, ibid., F7/8505; Warfield to DW, March 1, 1830, WPLC, F7/8468; Plumer to DW, May 5, 1830, Plumer Papers, Library of Congress, F7/8784; Lincoln to DW, March 17, 1830, *WP,* III, 35; Dutton to DW, March 4, 1830, George J. Abbot Papers, Yale University Library, F7/8482; Davis to DW, June 3, 1830, WPLC, F7/8861.

34. Sullivan to DW, March 23, 1830, WPNH, F7/8588.

35. Mason to DW, March 8, 1830, ibid., F7/8501.

36. Hay to DW, March 10, 1830, *WP,* III, 28–29; DW to Hay, March 12, 1830, Henry Ford Museum, Dearborn, Mich., F7/8522; Hay to DW, March 24, 1830, *WP,* III, 40–42.

37. Lawrence to DW, March 3, 1830, WPNH, F7/8474; DW to [Lawrence], May 22, 1830, George F. Hoar Papers, Massachusetts Historical Society, F7/8829; Lawrence to DW, Oct. 23, 1830, WPNH, F7/8971; Washington *National Intelligencer,* March 3, 1830; Boston *Advertiser,* April 7, 1830.

38. Dane to DW, March 26, 1830, *WP,* III, 43–48.

39. Lieber to DW, [Nov. 20, 1831], WPNH, F8/9672.

40. Story to DW, April 17, 1830, ibid., F7/8670.

41. Charles F. Adams, ed., *Memoirs of John Quincy Adams, Comprising Portions of His Diary from 1795 to 1848,* 12 vols. (Philadelphia, 1874–77), VIII, 193; Samuel F. Bemis, *John Quincy Adams and the Union* (New York, 1956), 233–36.

42. Kent et al. to DW, Feb. 23, 1831, George F. Hoar Papers, F8/9215; text of speech in *WS,* II, 45–65; Webster's notes for speech, WPDC, F8/9398.

43. Irving Brant, *James Madison,* 6 vols. (Indianapolis, 1948–61), VI, 468–500; Madison to Everett, April 2, 1830, Madison Papers, Library of Congress, LXXXIII, 35, and Madison to Hayne, April 3, 1830, ibid., 36–87; DW to Madison, May 24, 1830, WPDC, F7/8842; Madison to DW, May 27, 1830, Madison Papers, F7/8847.

44. [Edward Everett], "Speeches Made . . . on . . . the Resolution Offered by Mr. Foot . . . ," *North American Review,* 31 (Oct. 1830), 462–546. Madison's letter, 537–46.

45. As laudatory to his subject as Claude Fuess is in his biography of Webster, he concludes that the Massachusetts senator was wrong about the formation of the Union, if closer to the truth in his view of later history; *Webster,* I, 380–81. Charles Wiltse, *John C. Calhoun: Nullifier* (Indianapolis, 1949), 62–66, says that Webster's oratory was a masterpiece but that his argument on the nature of the Union was weak. A recent biographer, Bartlett, *Webster,* 165–73, also believes that he may have been wrong about the establishment of the Union. Although this important question will be handled more fully in a subsequent chapter; for the present it ought to be said that Webster's constitutional history was better than that of many of his critics.

46. Wiltse, *Calhoun: Nullifier,* 113–16.

47. John S. Bassett, *The Life of Andrew Jackson,* 2 vols. (New York, 1911), II, 412–18, 458–530; Wiltse, *Calhoun: Nullifier,* 19–23, 67–71. Robert V. Remini,

Andrew Jackson and the Course of American Freedom (New York, 1981), 305–9, says Jackson probably intended to precipitate a break with Calhoun at this stage after a series of disputes with him.

48. DW to Jeremiah Mason, Feb. 27, 1830, *WP*, III, 19; DW to Henry Clay, April 18, 1830, Clay Papers, Library of Congress, F7/8674; DW to John Woods, April 24, 1830, WPNH, F7/8709.

49. James S. Chase, *Emergence of the Presidential Nominating Convention, 1789–1832* (Urbana, Ill., 1973), 146–47, 167, 177–78; Samuel R. Gammon, Jr., *The Presidential Campaign of 1832* (Baltimore, 1922), 38–52. Early indications of some Antimason interest in Webster as a candidate are William W. Irwin to DW, Aug. 25, 1830, WPLC, F7/8936, and Sept. 17, 1830, WPDC, F7/8954, as well as Charles Miner to DW, Dec. 31, 1830, WPLC, F7/9092.

50. DW to Nathaniel F. Williams, Oct. 1, 1831, WPDC, F8/9596; Ambrose Spencer to DW, Oct. 24, 1831, WPNH, F8/9629; DW to Spencer, Nov. 16, 1831, ibid., F8/9659.

51. DW to Charles Miner, Oct. 28, 1831, Miner Collection, Wyoming Historical and Geological Society, Wilkes-Barre, Pa., F8/9553. On Clay's weakness in the West, see DW to Levi Lincoln, Dec. 25, 1830, Miscellaneous MSS, American Antiquarian Society, F7/9075; DW to Nathaniel Williams, Dec. 28, 1830, Montague Collection, New York Public Library, F7/9088.

52. DW to Charles Haddock, March 4, 1830, WPDC, F7/8479. The volume was published: *Speeches and Forensic Arguments* (Boston, 1830).

53. DW to Henry Kinsman, Feb. 25, 1831, Special Collections, Columbia University Library, F8/9219; DW to Clay, March 4, 1831, Clay Papers, F8/9231; DW to Elisha Whittlesey, May 10, 1831, Whittlesey Papers, Western Reserve Historical Society, F8/9452. That Webster had his own presidential prospects in mind is clear from his correspondence of these months. But he detected little support and declared he would "do nothing to brg myself forward"; DW to Charles Miner, Oct. 28, 1831, Miner Collection, F8/9553.

54. DW to Clay, Oct. 5, 1831, Clay Papers, F8/9604.

55. Chase, *Presidential Nominating Convention,* 190–91, 198–205; Gammon, *Campaign of 1832,* 63–71; Washington *National Intelligencer,* Dec. 13–17, 21, 1831; George T. Curtis, *Life of Daniel Webster,* 2 vols. (New York, 1870), I, 404, drawing upon a statement by a delegate, Hiram Ketchum.

12. Killing the Monster

1. Fritz Redlich, *The Molding of American Banking: Men and Ideas* (New York, 1968), pt. 1, 96–145; Peter Temin, *The Jacksonian Economy* (New York, 1969), 25–58; George R. Taylor, *The Transportation Revolution: 1815–1860* (New York, 1951), 310–11. Temin and Taylor say that in some respects this institution was not a central bank, at least by modern standards.

2. Thomas P. Govan, *Nicholas Biddle: Nationalist and Public Banker, 1786–1844* (Chicago, 1959); Walter B. Smith, *Economic Aspects of the Second Bank of the United States* (Cambridge, Mass., 1953), 11–17, 39–40.

3. John S. Bassett, *The Life of Andrew Jackson,* 2 vols. (New York, 1911), II, 584–608; Robert V. Remini, *Andrew Jackson and the Bank War: A Study in the Growth of Presidential Power* (New York, 1967), 41–48, 176–78; James C. Curtis, *Andrew Jackson and the Search for Vindication* (Boston, 1976), 111–14.

4. *Register of Debates,* 21st Cong., 1st sess., app., 98-132.

5. John A. Munroe, *Louis McLane: Federalist and Jacksonian* (New Brunswick, N.J., 1973), 304-16; Carl B. Swisher, *Roger B. Taney* (New York, 1935), 160-71. Livingston thought he had arranged an agreement of Jackson and Biddle on terms for a new charter in February 1832, but failed to do so; William B. Hatcher, *Edward Livingston: Jeffersonian Republican and Jacksonian Democrat* (Baton Rouge, 1940), 373-76.

6. Washington *National Intelligencer,* Dec. 21, 1831.

7. Glyndon G. Van Deusen, *The Life of Henry Clay* (Boston, 1937), 256-57.

8. DW to Biddle, Dec. 18, 1831, and Jan. 8, 1832, Biddle Papers, Library of Congress, F8/9700 and F8/9778.

9. Remini, *Jackson and Bank War,* 75-76; Jean A. Wilburn, *Biddle's Bank: The Crucial Years* (New York, 1967), 20-135.

10. William N. Chambers, *Old Bullion Benton: Senator from the New West* (Boston, 1956), 171-74; Thomas H. Benton, *Thirty Years' View,* 2 vols. (New York, 1856), I, 187-205; DW to Biddle, Feb. 4, 1831, Biddle Papers, F8/9170.

11. *Register of Debates,* 22nd Cong., 1st sess., 114-54.

12. Draft by Webster and smooth copy by Biddle, [February 1832], Biddle Papers, F8/9966.

13. DW to Biddle, [ca. March 1832], Biddle Papers; *Senate Document 98,* 22d Cong., 1st sess.

14. Benton, *Thirty Years' View,* I, 235-41. The reports of the House committee are in *Register of Debates,* 22d Cong., 1st sess., 33-78.

15. Several items in the Biddle Papers show that the BUS president was in Washington most of the time during the congressional debates and supplied information and advice to Webster and others.

16. *WS,* VI, 124-40. Smith, *Second Bank,* 234-63, finds similar positive elements in the bank's operations.

17. *Register of Debates,* 22d Cong., 1st sess., 965, 977-80, 1005-8, 1033-43.

18. Ibid., 980-81, 989, 1008-10.

19. *WS,* VI, 141-48.

20. *Register of Debates,* 22d Cong., 1st sess., 1005.

21. Ibid., 1008-32, 1043-68, 1071.

22. Ibid., 1073-74.

23. Swisher, *Taney,* 190-97; Remini, *Jackson and Bank War,* 81. Robert V. Remini, *Andrew Jackson and the Course of American Freedom* (New York, 1981), 371-73, sees Jackson reshaping the role of the presidency in American government by this veto.

24. *Register of Debates,* 22d Cong., 1st sess., app., 73-77.

25. *WS,* VI, 149-80.

26. *Register of Debates,* 22d Cong., 1st sess., 1240-65.

27. Ibid., 1265-74, 1293-96; Benton, *Thirty Years' View,* I, 254-65. Benton dubbed Webster and Clay the "duplicate senators."

28. Benton, *Thirty Years' View,* I, 262.

29. DW to Biddle, May 14, 1832, Biddle Papers, F8/10049.

30. DW to Biddle, Dec. 21, 1833, ibid., F9/11256. Biddle answered on December 25 that he would delay taking it to the board; *WP,* III, 292.

31. DW to Biddle, [July 4], 1832, Biddle Papers, F8/10171.

32. There was great difficulty about the Connell notes; DW to Samuel

Jaudon, July 25, 1834, Miscellaneous MSS, New York Historical Society, F10/11821; and later letters, Aug. 2, 1834, ibid., F10/11838, and Aug. 6, 1834, ibid., F10/11841.

33. DW to Everett, April 26, 1834, Everett Papers, Massachusetts Historical Society, F9/11636. Everett was a member of the committee.

34. His notes, amounting to fifteen pages, are in WPNH, F8/10197.

35. DW to Story, July 21, 1832, Story Papers, Massachusetts Historical Society, F8/10215.

36. DW to Biddle, Aug. 20, 1832, Biddle Papers, F8/10243; DW to Biddle, Aug. 25, 1832, ibid., F8/10254; DW to Biddle, Sept. 24, 1832, ibid., F8/10272; Gales and Seaton to Biddle, Sept. 27, 1832, ibid.; DW to Biddle, Oct. 1, 1832, ibid., F8/10297; Biddle to John Tilford, Sept. 26, 1832, in Reginald C. McGrane, ed., *The Correspondence of Nicholas Biddle, Dealing with National Affairs, 1807-1844* (Boston, 1919), 197-98; Biddle to DW, Sept. 27, 1832, *WP*, III, 191; and Biddle to DW, Oct. 1, 1832, ibid., 192.

37. John D. Macoll, "Representative John Quincy Adams's Compromise Tariff of 1832," *Capitol Studies*, 1 (1972), 41-58; Samuel F. Bemis, *John Quincy Adams and the Union* (New York, 1956), 241-47.

38. Munroe, *McLane*, 339-50.

39. John D. Macoll, "Congressman John Quincy Adams, 1831-1833" (Ph.D. dissertation, Indiana University, 1973), 65 and passim.

40. Van Deusen, *Clay*, 249-54.

41. Otis to DW, April 11, 1832, *WP*, III, 164-67, and June 12, 1832, ibid., 175-77; Mason to DW, May 27, 1832, ibid., 172-74; William W. Stone to DW, May 25, 1832, WPNH, F8/10065. During the Senate debate Hayne deplored the presence of "lobby members"; Webster retorted that their presence was useful. One of the most knowledgeable and interested textile manufacturers, Nathan Appleton, was a member of the House—he voted for the Adams bill. For Webster's desire for stability, see his speech at Faneuil Hall, Oct. 30, 1830, WPDC, F7/8975.

42. DW to Stepen White, June 28, 1832, WPNH, F8/10151; *Register of Debates*, 22d Cong., 1st sess., 1197-98, 1220-21, 1275-79, 1281, 1286-90, 1293; Macoll, "Congressman Adams," 104-6.

43. Webster's speeches in Senate, *WS*, VI, 89-101; Jackson to John Coffee, Feb. 19, 1832, in John S. Bassett, ed., *The Correspondence of Andrew Jackson*, 7 vols. (Washington, D.C., 1926-35), IV, 406-7, and July 17, 1832, ibid., 462.

44. Van Deusen, *Clay*, 247; Clay to DW, Aug. 27, 1832, WPLC, F8/10256.

45. Samuel R. Gammon, Jr., *The Presidential Campaign of 1832* (Baltimore, 1922), 143-45.

46. *WS*, II, 87-128.

47. Robert V. Remini, "Election of 1832," in Arthur M. Schlesinger, Jr., and Fred L. Israel, eds., *History of American Presidential Elections, 1789-1968*, 4 vols. (New York, 1971), I, 515-16; Gammon, *Campaign of 1832*, 153-54, 170. Remini, *Jackson and Freedom*, 374, says this election was "the one and only time in American history that a major issue was submitted to the electorate for disposition." It was one in which Jackson made an appeal to the moral sense of the people, he continues. Despite this advanced interpretation of good versus evil, Remini does conclude that, in the end, the fundamental issue was Jackson himself (391-92).

13. Nullification

1. Quoted in William W. Freehling, *Prelude to Civil War: The Nullification Controversy in South Carolina, 1816-1836* (New York, 1965), 260-64.

2. Ibid., 266-67.

3. James D. Richardson, ed., *A Compilation of the Messages and Papers of the Presidents, 1789-1897,* 10 vols. (Washington, D.C., 1896-99), II, 640-56.

4. DW to James Kent, Oct. 29, 1832, Kent Papers, Library of Congress, F8/10313; Kent to DW, Oct. 31, 1832, ibid., F8/10323.

5. DW to Levi Lincoln, Dec. 10, 1832, Lincoln Papers, Massachusetts Historical Society, F8/10365.

6. Boston *Advertiser,* Dec. 18, 1832; Washington *National Intelligencer,* Dec. 22 and 25, 1832.

7. DW to Hiram Ketchum, Jan. 20, 1838, Huntingon Library, San Marino, Calif., F12/14579; DW to Ketchum, Feb. 12, 1838, WPDC, F12/14636; George T. Curtis, *Life of Daniel Webster,* 2 vols. (New York 1870), I, 454-55; Glyndon G. Van Deusen, *The Life of Henry Clay* (Boston, 1937), 264-66. Recollections of Clay and Webster in 1839 of the Philadelphia meeting are in *Congressional Globe,* 25th Cong., 3d sess., 182-83.

8. John D. Macoll, "Congressman John Quincy Adams, 1831-1833" (Ph.D. dissertation, Indiana University, 1973), 159-63; DW to Henry Kinsman, Jan. 1, 1833, WPDC, F9/10417; DW to William Sullivan, Jan. 3, 1833, George F. Hoar Papers, Massachusetts Historical Society, F9/10438; DW to Warren Dutton, Jan. 4, 1833, WPDC, F9/10446; Charles F. Adams, ed., *Memoirs of John Quincy Adams, Comprising Portions of His Diary from 1795 to 1848,* 12 vols. (Philadelphia, 1874-77), VIII, 517; DW to Arthur Livermore, Jan. 5, 1833, *WS,* XVI, 225; DW to Warren Dutton, Jan. 15, 1833, ibid., XVII, 530-31; DW to Joseph Hopkinson, Jan. 31, 1833, Hopkinson Papers, Pennsylvania Historical Society, F9/10533.

9. *Register of Debates,* 22d Cong., 2d sess., app., 145-54.

10. Ibid., 244-63, 378-403, 414-30.

11. Ibid., 460-62, 483, 592-95. Forsyth worried about further judicial intervention in the Georgia-Cherokee controversy.

12. Ibid., 311-33, 348-58, 661-87.

13. Ibid., 333-47, 489-92. George Bibb of Kentucky did approve the theory of nullification but thought South Carolina had acted rashly; ibid., 301-12. Stephen Miller, Calhoun's colleague from that state, justified the nullification ordinance in detail; ibid., 433-60.

14. Ibid., 360-77.

15. Ibid., 492-517.

16. Ibid., 602-61.

17. Ibid., 519-53.

18. DW to James Kent, Jan. 28, 1833, Special Collections, Columbia University, F9/10518; DW to Joseph Hopkinson, [Feb. 15, 1833], Hopkinson Papers, F9/10595; *Register of Debates,* 22d Cong., 2d sess., 409-14. Eighty-eight pages of notes on his speech are in WPNH, F9/10598.

19. The text and explanation of Calhoun's resolutions, introduced on January 22, are in *Register of Debates,* 22d Cong., 2d sess., 187-92.

20. *WS,* VI, 182-96.

21. Ibid., 198.

22. Ibid., 205, paraphrasing Chief Justice Marshall's opinion in *Cohens* v. *Virginia*, 6 Wheaton 264 (1821).

23. *WS*, VI, 205–10.

24. Ibid., 211–23.

25. Ibid., 224–27.

26. Ibid., 228–36.

27. Ibid., 237–38.

28. Kenneth M. Stampp, "The Concept of a Perpetual Union," *Journal of American History*, 65 (June 1978), 5–33, reviews perspectives of the Union from 1787 to the 1830s and finds the nationalist idea less developed than that of state sovereignty. He may not give sufficient weight to historical experience, constitutional law laid down by the Supreme Court, or Webster's arguments in 1830 and 1833, though he does say that by that time the idea of a perpetual Union was, at last, developed. Authors who believe that the nationalist position rested chiefly upon sentiment in the early years of the republic are Paul C. Nagel, *One Nation Indivisible: The Union in American Thought, 1776–1861* (New York, 1964); and Major L. Wilson, " 'Liberty and Union': An Analysis of Three Concepts Involved in the Nullification Controversy," *Journal of Southern History*, 33 (Aug. 1967), 331–55. Freehling, *Prelude to Civil War,* 286, in a brief reference to the debate of 1833, says Calhoun "outargued" Webster, who relied upon "lush rhetoric" and a weak historical argument. Sydney Nathans, *Daniel Webster and Jacksonian Democracy* (Baltimore, 1973), 58, believes that Calhoun had the better argument on the Constituton as a compact of sovereign states. Charles M. Wiltse, *John C. Calhoun: Nullifier* (Indianapolis, 1949), approves Calhoun's contribution to the doctrine of minority rights. Though David Herbert Donald, *Liberty and Union* (Lexington, Mass., 1978), ix, 31–33, sees Webster's position on the Union superior, he believes it to have been founded mainly on sentiment, not logic. All these authors underestimate the strength of Webster's constitutional law, logic, and history.

29. Gordon S. Wood, *The Creation of the American Republic: 1776–1787* (New York, 1969), 524–36, is the most thorough and convincing discussion of the close relationship of popular sovereignty and the Constitution. In several constitutional studies published in the first third of the twentieth century, Andrew McLaughlin sets forth impressive evidence much like that of Webster supporting the nationalist view. He emphasizes historical continuity from colonial days and the Revolutionary era onward, showing the importance of popular sovereignty and of federalism. Governmental powers, accordingly, were drived from popular consent and were distributed on two levels. See McLaughlin's *The Foundations of American Constitutionalism* (1932; reprint, New York, 1961), 82–83, 129–54.

30. Madison to DW, March 15, 1833, Madison Papers, Library of Congress, F9/10752. He also praised the speech of his fellow Virginian, Rives.

31. *Register of Debates,* 22d Cong., 2d sess., 600–601, 687–89.

32. Ibid., 750–78, 785.

33. Ibid., 462–73, 481–82. See Merrill D. Peterson, *Olive Branch and Sword: The Compromise of 1833* (Baton Rouge, 1982), on revision of the tariff.

34. *Register of Debates,* 22d Cong., 2d sess., 484–86, 722, 749–50, 785–86.

35. Ibid., 483–84.

36. Ibid., 478-79, 727-29, 801-2.

37. Ibid., 723-24, 727-29.

38. Ibid., 692-703, 703-16, 729-49, 787-808.

39. Ibid., 808-9.

40. DW memorandum, [1838], Huntington Library, F12/15294.

41. Tyler to John Floyd, Jan. 22, 1833, in "Original Letters," *William and Mary Quarterly,* 21 (1912), 11. Nothing survives in the papers of Webster or Jackson to indicate any important direct communication. In a letter, probably on February 21, to Joseph Hopkinson, the senator wrote, "I have only seen him [Jackson] when I went, in turn, to dine at the White House, & then said not a word except about the weather &c, but I hear of his conversation with others"; *WP,* III, 219.

42. Edward Everett's memoir of Webster, published twenty years later, is the source of this story. See Curtis, *Webster,* I, 464 n. 1.

43. Jackson to Joel Poinsett, Feb. 17, 1833, in John S. Bassett, ed., *The Correspondence of Andrew Jackson,* 7 vols. (Washington, D.C., 1926-35), IV, 18.

44. [Seba Smith], *My Thirty Years out of the Senate, by Major Jack Downing* (New York, 1860), 236-41.

45. Washington *U.S. Telegraph,* Dec. 24 and 27, 1832; Feb. 1, 16, and 19, 1833.

46. *Thirty Years' View,* 2 vols. (New York, 1856), II, 122-23. His version of the compromise is in ibid., I, 334-47. For his position on the tariff, see Elbert Smith, *Magnificent Missourian: The Life of Thomas H. Benton* (Philadelphia, 1958), 142-45.

47. John C. Fitzpatrick, ed., *The Autobiography of Martin Van Buren* (Washington, D.C., 1920), 549-65.

48. For its criticism of Webster's Faneuil Hall speech, see issue of Dec. 27, 1832.

49. Hill to Benton, quoted in Claude M. Fuess, *Daniel Webster,* 2 vols. (Boston, 1930), II, 4.

50. Clay to Francis Brooke, March 11, 1833, in Calvin Colton, ed., *The Private Correspondence of Henry Clay* (New York, 1856), 352.

51. Clay to Biddle, April 10, 1833, in Reginald C. McGrane, ed., *The Correspondence of Nicholas Biddle, Dealing with National Affairs, 1807-1844* (Boston, 1919), 202-04.

52. Illustrative letters are Levi Lincoln to DW, Feb. 20, 1833, WPLC, F9/10697; and Ambrose Spencer to DW, Feb. 21, 1833, ibid., F9/10709.

53. Peleg Sprague to Clay, March 19, 1833, in Colton, *Private Correspondence of Clay,* 355; and Harrison G. Otis to DW, Feb. 18, 1833, WPNH, F9/10693. Otis himself was not one of those satisfied with the compromise tariff, but he reported that many others in New England were.

54. Mathew Carey to DW, April 9, 1833, WPNH, F9/10838; DW to Carey, May 14, 1833, ibid., F9/10912; Carey to DW, [May 1833], WPLC, F9/10947.

55. Benjamin F. Perry to DW, April 1, 1833, WPNH, F9/10823; DW to Perry, [April 27, 1833], ibid., F9/10849.

56. Poinsett to DW, March 25, 1833, George F. Hoar Papers, F9/10782; DW to Poinsett, May 7, 1833, Autographs, Miscellaneous American, Pierpont Morgan Library, New York, F9/10898; Poinsett to DW, May 24, 1833, WPLC, F9/10937; John Bolton to DW, May 16, 1833, *WP,* III, 251-52; DW to Bolton, May 17, 1833, ibid., 252-53.

14. Bank War

1. Lewis Cass to DW, April 17, 1833, WPNH, F9/10869; DW to Cass, April 21, 1833, ibid., F9/10878; Boston *Advertiser,* June 21–28, 1833.

2. DW to Joseph Hopkinson, May 8, 1833, Hopkinson Papers, Pennsylvania Historical Society, F9/10902.

3. George T. Curtis, *Life of Daniel Webster,* 2 vols. (New York, 1870), I, 461–64; DW to Samuel Frothingham, [May 1833], Roberts Autograph Collection, Haverford College Library, F9/10982; speech at Buffalo, [June 1, 1833], *WS,* II, 131–33; DW to John G. Camp, June 1, 1833, Webster Folder, Buffalo and Erie County Historical Society, F9/10951; William Armstrong et al. to DW, June 6, 1833, WPLC, F9/10955.

4. DW to Fletcher Webster, July 1, 1833, *WS,* XVII, 538; DW to Clay, June 10, 1833, Clay Papers, Library of Congress, F9/10963; Clay to DW, June 17, 1833, WPLC, F9/10966; DW to Clay, June 22, 1833, *WP,* III, 258–59.

5. *WS,* II, 137–47.

6. Authors who suggest an interest, at least on Webster's part if not on Jackson's, in a coalition are: Eber M. Carroll, *Origins of the Whig Party* (Durham, N.C., 1925), 82–83, 85–117; Norman D. Brown, *Daniel Webster and the Politics of Availability* (Athens, Ga., 1969), 15–52; Sydney Nathans, *Daniel Webster and Jacksonian Democracy* (Baltimore, 1973), 61–66; Irving H. Bartlett, *Daniel Webster* (New York, 1978), 137–38, 140, 144–45. Those who believe that, at most, Webster hoped for some Jacksonian concession on the banking question are: Ralph C. H. Catterall, *The Second Bank of the United States* (Chicago, 1903), 290; Arthur B. Darling, *Political Changes in Massachusetts, 1824–1848* (New Haven, 1925), 148 n. 39; Charles M. Wiltse's editorial note in *WP,* III, 224–25.

7. DW memorandum, [1838], HM 779, Huntington Library, San Marino, Calif., F12/15294. Notice that this is a recollection five years later.

8. DW to [Livingston], [March 21, 1833], WPNH, F9/10766.

9. See note 7 above.

10. Carl B. Swisher, *Roger B. Taney* (New York, 1935), 210–49; Robert V. Remini, *Andrew Jackson and the Bank War: A Study in the Growth of Presidential Power* (New York, 1967), 112–25; John A. Munroe, *Louis McLane: Federalist and Jacksonian* (New Brunswick, N.J., 1973), 375–80, 385–88, 393–404; Thomas H. Benton, *Thirty Years' View,* 2 vols. (New York, 1856), I, 373–79, 381–85.

11. Editorial note in *WP,* III, 283–84; Washington *National Intelligencer,* Dec. 19, 1833; John C. Fitzpatrick, ed., *The Autobiography of Martin Van Buren* (Washington, D.C., 1920), 671–708. John Niven, *Martin Van Buren: The Romantic Age of American Politics* (New York, 1983), 356–58, accepts the vice-president's version of Webster's conduct, but the evidence is thin.

12. DW to Edward Everett, [Dec. 13, 1833], Everett Papers, Massachusetts Historical Society, F9/11216.

13. DW to [Stephen White], Dec. 21, [1833], WPDC, F9/11252. Sometime before the beginning of the session, Webster had drawn up a memorandum on his views on the Union, the tariff, and the currency; WPNH, F9/10977.

14. On July 4, 1833, the Washington *Examiner* began publication and promoted the idea of a unionist party with Webster as its presidential candidate.

15. Biddle to DW, Dec. 15, 1833, *WP,* III, 285; Philadelphia *National Gazette and Literary Register,* Dec. 19, 1833. Webster was wary of an alliance either with Calhoun, because of the nullification issue, or with the administration, be-

cause he feared this would advance Van Buren to the presidency as well as sanction removal of the deposits. For these implications, see Stephen White to DW, Jan. 9, 1834, WPNH, F9/11341; DW to White, Jan. 10, 1834, *WP*, III, 306; and DW to White, Jan. 14, 1834, WPDC, F9/11379.

16. DW to Biddle, Dec. 19, 1833, Biddle Papers, Library of Congress, F9/11242; Biddle to DW, Dec. 20, 1833, *WP*, III, 287–88; Benton, *Thirty Years' View*, I, 387–92.

17. *Congressional Globe*, 23d Cong., 1st sess., 20–21; *National Intelligencer*, Dec. 12, 1833; Benton, *Thirty Years' View*, I, 399–400.

18. *WS*, VI, 250–67.

19. Ibid., 268.

20. Biddle to DW, Jan. 8, 1834, *WP*, III, 301–02.

21. Story to DW, Dec. 25, 1833, in William W. Story, ed., *Life and Letters of Joseph Story*, 2 vols. (Boston, 1851), II, 156; Joseph Hopkinson to DW, Dec. 27, 1833, WPLC, F9/11292; Charles F. Adams, ed., *Memoirs of John Quincy Adams, Comprising Portions of His Diary from 1795 to 1848,* 12 vols. (Philadelphia, 1874–77), IX, 72.

22. *Congressional Globe*, 23d Cong., 1st sess., 83, 152, 156.

23. *WS*, VII, 50–81; Philadelphia *National Gazette*, Feb. 11, 1834.

24. Washington *National Intelligencer*, March 13 and 17, 1834; *WS*, VII, 8–14.

25. *WS*, VII, 15–21; Washington *Globe*, April 11 and 12, 1834. The Jacksonian view of these memorials is advanced by Benton, *Thirty Years' View*, I, 421–22.

26. *Congressional Globe*, 23d Cong., 1st sess., 170; *WS*, XIV, 184–99.

27. Horace Binney to Biddle, Feb. 4, 1834, in Reginald C. McGrane, ed., *The Correspondence of Nicholas Biddle* (Boston, 1919), 220–21; James G. King to DW, March 8, 1834, WPDC, F9/11536.

28. Biddle to DW, Feb. 10, 1834, WPLC, F9/11471.

29. Walter B. Smith, *Economic Aspects of the Second Bank of the United States* (Cambridge, Mass., 1953), 160–67.

30. *WS*, VI, 240–49; Washington *National Intelligencer,* Jan. 20, 1834; White to DW, Jan. 21, 1834, WPNH, F9/11407. The prominent banker Nathaniel Prime wrote Webster on January 26 to recommend a scheme similar to that proposed by White; WPLC, F9/11422.

31. *WS*, VI, 269.

32. DW to Nathan Appleton, Feb. 2, 1834, *WP*, III, 315; editorial in Washington *National Intelligencer*, Feb. 3, 1834, nearly identical to Webster's draft (WPDC, F9/11449); *Congressional Globe*, 23d Cong., 1st sess., 225; *WS*, XIV, 203–12.

33. For the text of his bill, see *Congressional Globe*, 23d Cong., 1st sess., 248–49; for his speech, *WS*, VII, 82–102.

34. Somewhat more than he had previously, he relied upon the commerce clause of the Constitution; *WS*, VII, 97–98.

35. *Congressional Globe*, 23d Cong., 1st sess., 253, 261, 264–65; Washington *National Intelligencer*, March 21 and 22, 1834; DW to Charles G. Loring, March 21, 1834, WPLC, F9/11603; DW to Jeremiah Mason, March 21, 1834, WPNH, F9/11605.

36. Webster wrote to Biddle, probably on February 17, that "if Mr. C. and

Mr. C. would go along with us, we could carry the compromise Bill thro. the Senate by a strong *2 thirds* majority. Can you write to any body to talk with Mr. Calhoun?" Biddle Papers, F9/11616.

37. Calhoun had opposed recharter, but his opposition to everything Jacksonian had pushed him toward the pro-BUS camp.

38. Charles M. Wiltse, *John C. Calhoun: Nullifier* (Indianapolis, 1949), 226-29; Benton, *Thirty Years' View*, I, 434-35; Washington *National Intelligencer*, March 26 and 28, 1834.

39. Thomas P. Govan, *Nicholas Biddle: Nationalist and Public Banker, 1786-1844* (Chicago, 1959), 261.

40. Biddle to DW, Feb. 13, 1834, *WP*, III, 321, and March 15, 1834, WPLC, F9/11581; Govan, *Biddle*, 261-66.

41. *Congressional Globe*, 23d Cong., 1st sess., 264-65.

42. Benton, *Thirty Years' View*, I, 402-14.

43. Washington *National Intelligencer*, March 31, 1834; DW to William King, April 11, 1834, William King Papers, Maine Historical Society, Portland, F9/11617.

44. Washington *National Intelligencer*, April 22, 1834; Boston *Advertiser*, April 26, 1834.

45. Benton, *Thirty Years' View*, I, 425-32.

46. *WS*, XIV, 222-26; ibid., VII, 103-47.

47. Benton, *Thirty Years' View*, I, 428-33.

48. Ibid., 436-58, 470.

49. See Webster's recent speech in Senate, Feb. 22, 1834, *WS*, VI, 271-78.

50. DW to Campbell P. White, March 22, 1834, Miscellaneous MSS, New York Historical Society, F9/11606; *Congressional Globe*, 23d Cong., 1st sess., 401; Benton, *Thirty Years' View*, I, 469.

51. Remini, *Jackson and Bank War*, 170-71; Washington *Globe*, June 12, 1834.

52. *Niles' Register*, 47 (Oct. 18, 1834), 106-8; Swisher, *Taney*, 287-89, 300-301.

53. Swisher, *Taney*, 309-10; Benton, *Thirty Years' View*, I, 470-71.

54. In *WP*, III, 353-57: DW to Biddle, July [7], 1834; "Heads of Inquiry," [July 7, 1834]; DW to Biddle, [July 8, 1834]; Biddle to DW, [July 8, 1834], drafted by DW; Biddle to DW, July 8, 1834.

55. Willie P. Mangum to DW, Sept. 24, 1834, WPNH, F10/11905; DW to Samuel L. Southard, Oct. 12, 1834, Southard Papers, Princeton University, F10/11917; DW to Mangum, Nov. 4, 1834, Mangum Papers, Library of Congress, F10/11953; DW to Biddle, Dec. 10, 1834, Biddle Papers, F10/11999; Biddle to DW, Dec. 10, 1834, ibid., F10/12005.

56. The report was published as *Senate Document 17*, 23d Cong., 2d sess.

15. Jackson's Vindication

1. Samuel F. Bemis, *John Quincy Adams and the Union* (New York, 1956), 306-9.

2. Washington *National Intelligencer*, Jan. 15, 1835; DW to William Sullivan, George F. Hoar Papers, Massachusetts Historical Society, F10/12344.

3. Bemis, *Adams and Union*, 316–18; *WS*, VII, 206–19; George T. Curtis, *Life of Daniel Webster*, 2 vols. (New York, 1870), I, 517. The conference committee bill would still have given the president some discretion on how to spend the money but not on whether to spend it. Jackson left the Capitol late that night, furious that his nomination of Taney as associate justice of the Supreme Court had been rejected; Carl B. Swisher, *Roger B. Taney* (New York, 1935), 311–14.

4. Bemis, *Adams and Union*, 321–22.

5. *WS*, VII, 205–29.

6. Bemis, *Adams and Union*, 322–24. Webster wrote a speech to reply to Adams but never delivered it. See Curtis, *Webster*, I, 532–34, for text. See also the discussion later in this chapter of the impact upon Massachusetts politics.

7. Thomas H. Benton, *Thirty Years' View*, 2 vols. (New York, 1856), I, 528–51.

8. *WS*, XIV, 234–35.

9. Ibid., VII, 200–204, 235–37.

10. Washington *National Intelligencer*, Feb. 3, 8, 18, 1836.

11. Charles M. Wiltse, *John C. Calhoun: Nullifier* (Indianapolis, 1949), 263–64.

12. *WS*, VII, 252–64.

13. Washington *National Intelligencer*, June 2, 1836.

14. *U.S. Statutes at Large*, V, 52–56. Unlike Webster's proposal, the law authorized the secretary of the treasury instead of Congress to demand payment by the states. The Boston *Atlas*, June 30, 1836, somewhat inaccurately said that the law had been Webster's bill.

15. *WS*, VII, 238–46; *Congressional Globe*, 24th Cong., 1st sess., 326–27; Benton, *Thirty Years' View*, II, 14.

16. Records of Senate, RG 46, National Archives, F32/43768 and F32 passim. The petition of the New England Antislavery Society is in ibid., F32/43772.

17. *Congressional Globe*, 24th Cong., 1st sess., 229, 236; ibid., 2d sess., 160. See ibid., 26th Cong., 2d sess., 199 and appendix, for Cuthbert's later attack on February 22, 1841.

18. Glyndon G. Van Deusen, *The Life of Henry Clay* (Boston, 1937), 276–77; Eber Malcolm Carroll, *Origins of the Whig Party* (Durham, N.C., 1925), 123–24, 183–87.

19. Wiltse, *Calhoun: Nullifier*, 230, says Calhoun never thought of himself as a regular member of the Whig party.

20. William P. Vaughn, *The Antimasonic Party in the United States, 1826–1842* (Lexington, Ky., 1983), 184–91; Ronald P. Formisano, *The Transformation of Political Culture: Massachusetts Parties, 1790s–1840s* (New York, 1983), 209–17.

21. Arthur B. Darling, *Political Changes in Massachusetts, 1824–1848* (New Haven, 1925), 105–11; Bemis, *Adams and Union*, 298–300; DW to John Davis, Sept. 30, 1833, Davis Papers, American Antiquarian Society, F9/11138.

22. Darling, *Political Changes*, 181–86; DW editorial in behalf of Davis, WPDC, F10/12276, appearing in Washington *National Intelligencer*, Feb. 2, 1835.

23. Darling, *Political Changes*, 121, 193–94; Charles F. Adams, ed., *Memoirs of John Quincy Adams, Comprising Portions of His Diary from 1795 to 1848*, 12 vols. (Philadelphia, 1874–77), IX, 71–72; DW to Levi Lincoln, Jan. 8, [1834], Lin-

coln Papers, Massachusetts Historical Society, F9/10467; Lincoln to DW, Jan. 11, 1834, *WP*, III, 307–9; DW to John Davis, Aug. 14, 1834, Davis Papers, F10/11858. Vaughn, *Antimasonic Party*, 115–32.

24. Van Deusen, *Clay*, 298.

25. DW to Joseph Hopkinson, [Jan. 27, 1833], Hopkinson Papers, Pennsylvania Historical Society, F9/10513.

26. Charles G. Sellers, *James K. Polk, Jacksonian, 1795–1843* (New York, 1957), 258, 264–65; DW to Samuel L. Southard, April 28, 1835, *WP*, IV, 43–44 and n. 1.

27. Eli S. Davis to DW, March 27, 1833, *WP*, III, 233.

28. DW to Ezekiel F. Chambers, Aug. 6, 1833, Balfe Collection, Washington's Headquarters Museum, Newburgh, N.Y., F9/11017; DW to Caleb Cushing, Feb. 17, 1834, Montague Collection, New York Public Library, F9/11486; William Plumer, Jr., "Reminiscences of Daniel Webster," *WS*, XVII, 558.

29. Sydney Nathans, *Daniel Webster and Jacksonian Democracy* (Baltimore, 1973), 78–83. For subsequent attention to New York, see DW to George W. Lay, Sept. 22, 1834, Lay Papers, Library of Congress, F10/11901; Boston *Courier*, Nov. 7, 1834; William Taggard to DW, Dec. 17, 1834, WPLC, F10/12033.

30. Text of speech in *WS*, XIII, 44–56; Plumer, "Reminiscences," *WS*, XVII, 558–59.

31. [Joseph Story], "Statesmen—Their Rareness and Importance. Daniel Webster," *New England Magazine*, 7 (Aug. 1834), 89–104.

32. DW to Jeremiah Mason, Jan. 1, 1835, *WP*, IV, 4–5.

33. Abbott Lawrence to DW, Jan. 5, 1835, ibid., 10–11; DW to Edward Everett, [Jan. 7, 1835], ibid., 12; Jeremiah Mason to DW, Jan. 8, 1835, ibid., 13; Caleb Cushing to DW, Jan. 9, 1835, ibid., 13–14; DW to Everett, Jan. 10, 1835, WPLC, F10/12206; Cushing to DW, Jan. 16, 1835, *WP*, IV, 14–15; Henry W. Kinsman to DW, Jan. 18, 1835, ibid., 15–17; DW to Mason, Jan. 22, 1835, ibid., 17.

34. Washington *National Intelligencer*, Jan. 26, 1835; Nathans, *Webster and Jacksonian Democracy*, 91–93; Charles P. Curtis to DW, [Jan. 26, 1835], WPLC, F10/12262; DW to Jeremiah Mason, Feb. 1, 1835, *WP*, IV, 24–26.

35. Darling, *Political Changes*, 181–86, 191; Caleb Cushing to DW, Feb. 9, 1835, *WP*, IV, 27–28; Stephen White to DW, Feb. 28, 1835, ibid., 34.

36. Cushing to DW, Jan. 16, 1835, *WP*, IV, 14–15. Cushing published an unsigned essay, "Mr. Webster," *New England Magazine*, 8 (March 1835), 220–28; and he wrote a supportive piece for the *National Intelligencer*, Dec. 2, 1835.

37. Choate to DW, Aug. 12, 1833, WPLC, F9/11066. Winthrop had been the person coordinating the move for the nomination by the legislature.

38. See, for example, the issues of Sept. 14 and 19, Oct. 10, 1834.

39. Webster's opinion on the paper, expressed somewhat later but doubtless unchanged, is in DW to Theophilus Parsons, Jan. 2, [1841], *WS*, XVI, 315–16.

40. DW to Everett, Aug. 1, 1834, Everett Papers, Massachusetts Historical Society, F10/11834; Cushing to DW, Aug. 9 and 10, 1834, *WP*, IV, 361–62; DW to Cushing, Aug. 13, 1834, ibid., 362; John O. Sargent to DW, Dec. 17, 1834, Sargent Papers, Massachusetts Historical Society, F10/12030.

41. DW editorial for *Atlas,* Dec. 17, 1834, in *WP,* III, 380–81; and others in Sargent Papers, F10/12835 and 12840.

42. Webb to DW, [Jan. 3, 1834], WPLC, F9/11330; Webb to DW, Jan. 20, 1835, ibid., F10/12235; DW to Webb, Jan. 22, 1835, WPDC, F10/12241; Webb to DW, Jan. 25, 1835, WPLC, F10/12251; Webb to DW, April 9, 1835, ibid., F10/12447; James L. Crouthamel, *James Watson Webb: A Biography* (Middletown, Conn., 1969), 60.

43. William E. Ames, *A History of the National Intelligencer* (Chapel Hill, 1972), 235–36. See Norman D. Brown, *Daniel Webster and the Politics of Availability* (Athens, Ga., 1969), 102–3 and passim, for an excellent treatment of Webster's effort for the presidency. If the election had gone to the House because no one candidate received a majority of electoral votes, Van Buren could have expected to win because of the Democratic majority there.

44. DW to Charles H. Thomas, March 19, 1835, *WP,* IV, 37–38; see also ibid., ed. note, 35–36.

45. DW to Biddle, May 9, 1835, Biddle Papers, Library of Congress, F10/12517.

46. Washington *National Intelligencer,* Dec. 2, 1835.

47. Brown, *Webster and Politics of Availability,* 113–16, 119–21, 126–28.

48. Henry D. Sellers et al. to DW, November 10, 1835, WPLC, F10/12670; Brown, *Webster and Politics of Availability,* 128, 140–41.

49. DW to Everett, [July 2, 1835], Everett Papers, F10/12555; Nov. 2, 1835, ibid., F10/12657; and Nov. 22, [1835], ibid., F10/12715.

50. Harmar Denny to DW, Nov. 5, 1835, WPDC, F10/12661; Harmar Denny to DW, Nov. 11, 1835, WPLC, F10/12673 and 12676; Joseph Wallace et al. to DW, Nov. 16, WPNH, F10/12688; Everett's draft, revised by DW, to Denny, Nov. 20, 1835, ibid., F10/12694. Related drafts and correspondence are in Everett Papers, F10/12701; WPLC, F10/12702; Buchanan Papers, Pennsylvania Historical Society, F10/12706; and WPDC, F10/12709. On Webster's views, expressed after the request for revision, see William W. Irwin to DW, Nov. 27, 1835, WPLC, F10/12720; DW to Irwin, Nov. 30, 1835, ibid., F10/12732.

51. Brown, *Webster and Politics of Availability,* 128–31, 138–39. Harrison had said he did not believe the national government had the power to act against Masonry. For the political context, see Vaughn, *Antimasonic Party,* 99–114.

52. Washington *National Intelligencer,* Dec. 19 and 22, 1835; Charles Miner to DW, Dec. 17, 1835, WPLC, F10/12781; Brown, *Webster and Politics of Availability,* 141–42. The state Whig convention, meeting at the same time, concurred with the Antimason convention.

53. Webster's views were probably reflected accurately in the Boston *Atlas,* Dec. 18, 24, 25, and 31, 1835. See also Washington *National Intelligencer,* Dec. 28, 1835, and Jan. 18, 1836.

54. Washington *National Intelligencer,* Dec. 8, 1835; DW to Edward Everett, Dec. 7, 1835, Everett Papers, F10/12762.

55. DW to Edward Everett, Nov. 11, [1835], Everett Papers, F10/12659; Luke Tiernan et al. to DW, Dec. 9, 1835, WPLC, F10/12769; Washington *National Intelligencer,* Dec. 23, 1835; Boston *Atlas,* Dec. 29, 1835.

56. Washington *National Intelligencer,* Dec. 28, 1835, Jan. 8, March 1, 7, 8, 1836; Joseph W. Scott to DW, June 6, 1836, WPLC, F11/13325. White received nominations in Tennessee, Georgia, and North Carolina.

57. DW to Everett, Jan. 27, 1836, Everett Papers, F10/12896.

58. DW to Kinsman, Feb. 27, 1836, *WP*, IV; and Feb. 29, 1836, Winthrop Papers, Massachusetts Historical Society, F10/13017.

59. Kinsman to DW, March 9, 1836, WPNH, F10/13044; Washington *National Intelligencer*, March 19, 1836.

60. *WS*, XVI, 272 n.; *WP*, IV, 89 n. 1.

61. Levi Lincoln to DW, Feb. 19, 1836, Lincoln Papers, F10/12988; DW to Everett, Aug. 6, 1836, *WP*, IV, 154 and n. 2.

62. Joel L. Silbey, "Election of 1836," in Arthur M. Schlesinger Jr., and Fred L. Israel, eds., *History of American Presidential Elections, 1789–1968*, 4 vols. (New York, 1971), I, 595–96; Brown, *Webster and Politics of Availability*, 159–60.

63. DW to Nathaniel Silsbee et al., Nov. 15, 1836, in Curtis, *Webster*, I, 538; Silsbee to DW, Dec. 27, 1836, ibid., 539.

64. *Congressional Globe*, 24th Cong., 2d sess., 9, 51, 94, 96; Benton, *Thirty Years' View*, I, 717–27.

65. *Congressional Globe*, 24th Cong., 2d sess., 97–98.

66. *WS*, VIII, 30–35.

67. DW to David Sears, Feb. 5, 1844, *WS*, XVIII, 183; DW to Jeremiah Mason, Feb. 6, 1835, WPLC, F10/12291.

68. Winthrop to DW, Jan. 21, [1837], *WP*, IV, 175–77; DW to Winthrop, Jan. 27, 1837, Winthrop Papers, F11/13988; DW to Everett, Jan. 31, 1837, Everett Papers, F11/14004; DW to James W. Paige, Feb. 3, 1837, WPNH, F11/14017; DW to Henry Kinsman, Feb. 1, 1837, George F. Hoar Papers, F11/14012; DW to Winthrop, Feb. 15, 1837, Winthrop Papers, F11/14062; DW to Winthrop et al., Feb. 23, 1837, ibid., F11/14098.

69. DW to Ketchum, Jan. 28, 1837, WPDC, F11/13996; DW to Ketchum, Feb. 11, 1837, *WP*, IV, 188–89.

70. David B. Ogden to DW, March 2, 1837, *WP*, IV, 201; DW to Ogden, March 4, 1837, WPNH, F11/14139. On Feb. 24, 1837, Webster read and revised the resolutions which would later be adopted at the meeting he would address; DW to Ketchum, WPLC, F11/14100. Text of resolutions in Washington *National Intelligencer*, March 18, 1837.

71. Washington *National Intelligencer*, March 18 and 20, 1837; Benton, *Thirty Years' View*, II, 12; *WS*, II, 189–92.

72. *WS*, II, 192–212.

73. Ibid., 214–29.

74. Benton, *Thirty Years' View*, II, 16–23. Benton believed Webster's speech did provoke the crisis.

16. Depression

1. Reginald C. McGrane, *The Panic of 1837: Some Financial Problems of the Jacksonian Era* (Chicago, 1924), 7–144; Samuel Rezneck, "The Social History of an American Depression, 1837–1843," *American Historical Review*, 40 (Oct. 1936), 662–87.

2. Peter Temin, *The Jacksonian Economy* (New York, 1969), 22–177, argues that Jacksonian policy was a less important factor than the large inflow of capital from England followed by the sharp decline of the cotton market there in 1837.

3. *WS*, II, 233–43. New York banks had suspended specie payment a week earlier, May 10.

4. Claude M. Fuess, *Daniel Webster*, 2 vols. (Boston, 1930), II, 62–65; George T. Curtis, *Life of Daniel Webster*, 2 vols. (New York, 1870), I, 562–64; *WP*, IV, ed. note, 223–24. See the next chapter on the Peru farm.

5. DW to Fletcher Webster, Feb. 12, 1837, *WP*, IV, 189–91; DW to William P. Fessenden, April 8, 1837, Fessenden Family Papers, Bowdoin College Library, F11/14197.

6. D. K. Este et al. to DW, [Feb.?] 1837, Kenyon College Library, F11/14123; DW to John C. Wright, May 27, 1837, University of Virginia Library, F11/14276; Henry Clay to DW, March 28, 1837, WPLC, F11/14179; and F11 passim.

7. Washington *National Intelligencer*, Sept. 20, 1837; Curtis, *Webster*, I, 564; Fuess, *Webster*, II, 63.

8. DW to George W. Jones, June 24, 1837, Jones Papers, Iowa State Department of History and Archives, Des Moines, F11/14314.

9. Speech at Madison, Indiana, *WS*, II, 251–59; at St. Louis, ibid., XIII, 79–87.

10. Ibid., XIII, 98–99.

11. Ibid., 97.

12. *Congressional Globe*, 25th Cong., 1st sess., 4–8.

13. Ibid., 9.

14. James C. Curtis, *The Fox at Bay: Martin Van Buren and the Presidency, 1837–1841* (Lexington, Ky., 1970), 64–94; McGrane, *Panic of 1837*, 145–76.

15. *Congressional Globe*, 25th Cong., 1st sess., 17, 29–30, 32; Thomas H. Benton, *Thirty Years' View*, 2 vols. (New York, 1856), II, 36–39; *WS*, VIII, 55. The law now provided that Congress, not the secretary of the treasury, could recall previous installments.

16. *WS*, VIII, 56–57; Benton, *Thirty Year's View*, II, 33–36; Washington *National Intelligencer*, Sept. 18 and 21, Oct. 11, 1837. Webster favored a minimum of a hundred dollars for a treasury note.

17. *Congressional Globe*, 25th Cong., 1st sess., 147–48; Benton, *Thirty Years' View*, II, 42–56. Webster urged comprehensive legislation on both of these subjects.

18. Webster's principal speech on the independent treasury came on September 28; *WS*, VIII, 62–108; *Congressional Globe*, 25th Cong., 1st sess., app., 167–74.

19. *WS*, VIII, 88–89. On September 26 Wright's resolution that, in the Senate's opinion, a majority of the American people opposed a national bank, passed, twenty-nine to fifteen.

20. *Congressional Globe*, 25th Cong., 1st sess., 96–97, 147–48.

21. Ibid., 2d sess., 55, 74; *WS*, VIII, 109–14.

22. Washington *National Intelligencer*, May 31, 1838; DW speech, May 29, 1838, *WS*, XIV, 256–70.

23. DW speech in Senate, March 30, 1840, *WS*, VIII, 278–96; DW editorial for Boston *Atlas*, [Nov. 1840], Jabez L. M. Curry Collection, Library of Congress, F13/17085; DW speech in Senate, Dec. 16 and 17, 1840, *WS*, IX, 50–54.

24. Curtis, *Fox at Bay*, 111–17.

25. *WS*, VIII, 162–237.

26. Ibid., 165–79. Edward Pessen, *Riches, Class, and Power before the Civil War* (Lexington, Mass., 1973), a study of social structure and mobility in Boston and other cities, finds far less mobility than Webster saw.

27. Curtis, *Fox at Bay,* 126–28, 132.

28. *WS,* II, 267–83.

29. Benton, *Thirty Years' View,* II, 164–67.

30. In WPDC, F10/12109, there is a book of 173 pages, apparently compiled by Webster in 1838 and entitled "Names of persons to send Documents to."

31. Robert F. Dalzell, Jr., *Daniel Webster and the Trial of American Nationalism, 1843–1852* (Boston, 1973), 61–69; Sydney Nathans, *Daniel Webster and Jacksonian Democracy* (Baltimore, 1973), 122–23.

32. DW to Richard Haughton, Feb. 23, 1838, WPDC, F12/14672; DW to Robert C. Winthrop, Feb. 24, 1838, Winthrop Papers, Massachusetts Historical Society, F12/14680; DW to William P. Fessenden, April 21, 1838, WPDC, F12/14865.

33. Glyndon G. Van Deusen, *The Life of Henry Clay* (Boston, 1937), 320–23.

34. DW to [Robert C. Winthrop], Feb. 7, 1838, *WP,* IV, 268; DW to Hiram Ketchum, Feb. 10, 1838, ibid., 268–69; DW to Winthrop, May 10, 1838, ibid., 295.

35. DW to Ketchum, Jan. 20, 1838, ibid., 263–64; and Feb. 12, 1838, WPDC, F12/14636.

36. DW to Biddle, May 24, [1838], Biddle Papers, Library of Congress, F12/14944.

37. Robert G. Gunderson, *The Log-Cabin Campaign* (Lexington, Ky., 1957), 41–53; Van Deusen, *Clay,* 323–31.

38. Nathans, *Webster and Jacksonian Democracy,* 123–24; Boston *Atlas,* Sept. 14, 1838.

39. DW to Samuel Jaudon, Jan. 13, 1839, Miscellaneous MSS, New York Historical Society, F12/15234; Fuess, *Webster,* II, 73 n. 2; Washington *National Intelligencer,* Jan. 21, 1839.

40. Copy of DW draft letter in letterbook of Edward Everett, May 13, 1839, Everett Papers, Massachusetts Historical Society, F12/15495; DW to John P. Healy, June 12, 1839, enclosing DW letter of withdrawal, George F. Hoar Papers, Massachusetts Historical Society, F12/15593; DW to Everett, June 12, 1839, Everett Papers, F12/15589; Everett to DW, July 3, 1839, ibid., 15854.

41. On September 20 he wrote Everett, "I write nothing to America concerning American politics"; *WP,* IV, 394–95.

42. Gunderson, *Log-Cabin Campaign,* 57–66. Harrison had commanded the force clashing with Tecumseh's Indians in 1811 at the juncture of Tippecanoe Creek and the Wabash in Indiana.

43. DW to John P. Healy, Jan. 31, 1840, Webster-Healy Papers, Massachusetts Historical Society, F13/16286.

44. DW speech at convention of Young Whigs at Baltimore, May 4, 1840, quoted in Washington *National Intelligencer,* June 2, 1840.

45. DW to Everett, Feb. 16, 1840, Everett Papers, F13/16352; DW to Stephen White, Feb. 20, 1840, WPLC, F13/16374.

46. DW to Joshua Bates, March 26, 1840, Baring Papers, Public Archives of Canada, Ottawa, F13/16571.

47. DW to editor of Harrisburg *Telegraph and Intelligencer,* March 28, 1840, clipping in Washington *National Intelligencer,* April 6, 1840; DW to Edward Curtis, Feb. 17, 1840, WPDC, F13/16356; DW to Gentlemen of Indiana, April 17, 1840, Webster-Healy Papers, F13/16635.

48. Harrison to DW, Jan. 25, 1840, Morristown National Historical Park, F13/16261.

49. Curtis, *Fox at Bay,* 189-206.

50. The story of the origin of the log-cabin idea is well-known. A Democratic reporter had contemptuously said that the old soldier would be satisfied to live out his days in a log cabin with a barrel of hard cider at his side; Gunderson, *Log-Cabin Campaign,* 74-75.

51. DW speech at Patchogue, N.Y., Sept. 22, 1840, *WS,* XIII, 141.

52. Authors emphasizing his popularized style are Gunderson, *Log-Cabin Campaign,* 173-81; and Nathans, *Webster and Jacksonian Democracy,* 134-42.

53. DW to Charles H. Warren, Aug. 15, 1840, WPNH, F13/16907; George Badger to DW, Sept. 5, 1840, Morristown National Historical Park, F13/16916; DW to John P. Healy, Sept. 25, 1840, Webster-Healy Papers, F13/16938; and F13 passim.

54. Summary of speech, *WS,* XIII, 108-9; Washington *National Intelligencer,* May 6 and 7, 1840; Gunderson, *Log-Cabin Campaign,* 1-7.

55. DW speech, *WS,* XIII, 110-13; Washington *National Intelligencer,* June 13, 1840.

56. DW description of meeting and summary of his speech, July 4, 1840, Webster-Healy Papers, F13/16800; Washington *National Intelligencer,* July 7, 1840.

57. Rebecca M. Samson, "When Webster Spoke on the Mountain," *Outlook,* 129 (Nov. 30, 1921), 521-23.

58. *WS,* III, 30; entire speech, ibid., 4-36.

59. Ibid., 39-52; Boston *Atlas,* Sept. 14 and 18, 1840; Arthur B. Darling, *Political Changes in Massachusetts, 1824-1848* (New Haven, 1925), 262-63. Webster had advised against such a large, unwieldy gathering; DW to Robert C. Winthrop, Aug. 10, 1840, *WP,* V, 52-53. Allan Nevins, ed., *The Diary of Philip Hone, 1828-1851,* 2 vols. (New York, 1927), I, 494-98, is an interesting description of these gatherings.

60. Boston *Atlas,* Sept. 25, 1840; *WS,* XIII, 114-42.

61. *WS,* III, 55-79.

62. DW to Caroline Webster, [late Oct. 1840], WPNH, F13/16965; DW to John P. Healy, Oct. 26, 1840, Webster-Healy Papers, F13/16971; DW to Caroline Webster, Oct. 26, 1840, WPNH, F13/16978.

63. To an extent, an exception is William N. Chambers, "The Election of 1840," in Arthur M. Schlesinger, Jr., and Fred L. Israel, eds., *History of American Presidential Elections, 1789-1968,* 4 vols. (New York, 1971), I, 684, concluding that rational economic issues were important in the campaign. A very informative study of the development of the two-party system at this juncture is Ronald P. Formisano, *The Transformation of Political Culture: Massachusetts Parties, 1790s-1840s* (New York, 1983), 264-67 and passim.

64. Gunderson, *Log-Cabin Campaign,* 252-55.

65. John J. Crittenden to DW, Oct. 27, 1840, WPLC, F13/16985; George Poindexter to DW, Nov. 11, 1840, WPNH, F13/17027; and F13 passim.

66. Edward Everett to DW, May 9, 1840, Everett Papers, F13/16665; DW to Samuel Jaudon, June 23, 1840, Miscellaneous MSS, New York Historical Society, F13/16757.

67. Van Deusen, *Clay, 338; Clay to Francis Brooke*, Dec. 8, 1840, in Calvin Colton, ed., *The Private Correspondence of Henry Clay* (Cincinnati, 1856), 447. George R. Poage, *Henry Clay and the Whig Party* (Chapel Hill, 1936), 15–21.

68. Harrison to DW, Dec. 1, 1840, WPNH, F13/17095; DW recollection in a speech at Boston, Sept. 30, 1842, *WS*, III, 118–19.

69. DW to Harrison, Dec. 11, 1840, WPNH, F13/17116.

70. Washington *National Intelligencer*, Feb. 9 and 13, 1841; Harrison to DW, Dec. 27, 1840, WPNH, F13/17171; George E. Badger to DW, Dec. 17, 1841, Harrison Papers, Library of Congress, F14/17554.

71. Records of Senate, RG 46, National Archives, F35/48182; Washington *National Intelligencer*, Feb. 22, 1841.

72. Text of inaugural in Washington *National Intelligencer*, March 5, 1841; DW to Biddle, Feb. 4, 1841, Biddle Papers, F14/17434; Gunderson, *Log-Cabin Campaign*, 267–68. The story of Webster's revision is told in Peter Harvey, *Reminiscences and Anecdotes of Daniel Webster* (Boston, 1878). William E. Ames, *A History of the National Intelligencer* (Chapel Hill, 1972), 250, says that both Harrison and Webster stayed at the home of William Seaton, an editor of the *Intelligencer*, at this time.

17. Middle Age

1. Quoted in George T. Curtis, *Life of Daniel Webster*, 2 vols. (New York, 1870), II, 21.

2. Boston *Atlas*, July 8, 1839, clipping of letter from London *Herald*, June 4, 1839.

3. Harriet Martineau, *Retrospect of Western Travel*, 2 vols. (New York, 1838), I, 166.

4. Fragments of a diary, published by Eliot (Maine) Historical Society as *Old Eliot;* also in F12/15026.

5. Quoted in Claude H. Van Tyne, ed., *The Letters of Daniel Webster* (New York, 1902), 745.

6. DW cellar book, Nov. 25, 1830–Dec. 27, 1838, Sang Collection, Brandeis University, F7/9016; policy for fire insurance, Nov. 11, 1839, Webster-Healy Papers, Massachusetts Historical Society, F29/39835.

7. A letter indicating his literary tastes is DW to George Ticknor, April 8, 1830, *WS*, XVII, 533–34.

8. DW to Sarah Goodridge, Jan. 4, 1832, WPDC, F8/9742; Dec. 2, 1835, Webster Papers, Massachusetts Historical Society, F10/12745; Jan. 5, 1836, ibid., F10/12849; Aug. 7, 1838, ibid., F12/15149.

9. DW to Isaac P. Davis, March 29, 1830, *WP*, III, 48–49.

10. Noah Webster to DW, May 13, 1831, WPLC, F8/9458; DW to Noah Webster, May 16, 1831, Noah Webster Papers, New York Public Library, F8/9460; Noah Webster to DW, Sept. 29, 1835, WPLC, F10/12631, and March 30, 1837, ibid., F11/14183.

11. Lieber to DW, April 7, 1836, WPDC, F10/18115; *Congressional Globe,* 24th Cong., 1st sess., 312; Lieber to DW, Feb. 15, 1837, George F. Hoar Papers, Massachusetts Historical Society, F11/14065.

12. Washington *National Intelligencer,* Jan. 2, 1833.

13. *WS,* XIII, 57–58.

14. DW to Mrs. John Agg, June 12, 1830, WPDC, F7/8874; Caroline Webster to DW, May 14, 1830, WPNH, F7/8821.

15. DW to Caroline Webster, Jan. 10, 1836, WPNH, F10/12856.

16. Illustrative letters are DW to Caroline Webster, Jan. 24, 1836, WPNH, F10/12886; Caroline Webster to DW, May 4, 1830, ibid., F7/8773.

17. DW to Caroline Webster, March 7, 1840, ibid., F13/16432; but calmer letter of March 8, 1840, ibid., F13/16441.

18. Caroline Webster to DW, May 1, 1830, WPNH, F7/8751; DW to Caroline Webster, Dec. 7, 1835, ibid., F10/12764.

19. Change in terms of settlement, May 18, 1839, with annexation A, Dec. 10, 1830, to original terms, Webster-Healy Papers, F29/39835; DW receipt of payment by Le Roy, July 21, 1830, Bayard-Pearsall-Campbell Collection, Le Roy Family Papers, New York Public Library, F29/39726.

20. Herman Le Roy to DW, Feb. 13, 1830, WPNH, F7/8429; May 2, 1830, ibid., F7/8767; Jan. 20, 1831, ibid., F8/9144; June 29, 1831, ibid., F8/9498; Herman Le Roy to Caroline Le Roy, Feb. 6, 1837, ibid., VII, 8.

21. Fletcher Webster to DW, April 6, 1830, ibid., F7/8645; Samuel B. Walcott to DW, Aug. 28, 1830, ibid., F7/8944.

22. Fletcher Webster to DW, Jan. 3, 1831, ibid., F8/9123. See Josiah Quincy's report to DW, Dec. 27, 1830, WPLC, F7/9085.

23. Fletcher Webster to DW, Feb. 25, 1832, WPNH, F8/9878.

24. DW to Fletcher Webster, July 5, 1833, *WP,* III, 259.

25. Fletcher Webster to DW, Feb. 28, 1835, WPNH, F10/12366.

26. Caroline White was the sister of Harriette, wife of William Paige.

27. Julia Webster to DW, Dec. 25, 1831, WPNH, F8/9713; March 3, 1833, ibid., F9/10741.

28. Samuel Appleton to DW, Feb. 5, 1839, ibid., F12/15360. See also letter of Feb. 17, 1839, ibid., F12/15375.

29. Caroline Webster to DW, Dec. 31, 1832, ibid., F8/10395; Edward Webster to DW, Jan. 1, 1832, ibid., F8/9736.

30. DW to Fletcher Webster, June 5, 1834, ibid., F9/11723; DW to Edward Webster, April 22, 1837, ibid., F11/14226.

31. DW to Edward Webster, Sept. 16, 1837, ibid., F11/14407.

32. DW to Edward Webster, Sept. 8, 1838, WPDC, F12/15190. Related letters are Edward Webster to DW, [Sept. 2], 1838, ibid., F12/15172, and Sept. 13, 1838, ibid., F12/15200; also DW to Edward Webster, Sept. 21, 1838, WPNH, F12/15209.

33. DW to Everett, May 24, 1840, Curtis, *Webster,* II, 45; Everett to DW, Aug. 1, 1840, Everett Papers, Massachusetts Historical Society, F13/16854.

34. DW to Thomas Wigglesworth, Sept. 22, [1831], *WP,* III, 125–26; map of the neighborhood, ibid., 127; conveyance by Samuel Hawes et al., Nov. 10, 1831, Sang Collection, F29/39757; DW mortgage to Wigglesworth, Nov. 17, 1831, WPDC, F29/39762; DW to Henry Kinsman, Jan. 16, 1832, Special Collections, Columbia University Library, F8/9794.

35. DW to Charles B. Haddock, Feb. 6, 1831, WPDC, F8/9180; DW memorandum of real estate 1825–1833, relating also to other New Hampshire property, *WP*, III, 280–81; DW to Israel W. Kelly, Jan. 1, 1835, ibid., IV, 3; Jan. 11, 1835, WPNH, F10/12210; Jan. 29, 1835, ibid., F10/12266.

36. Agreement of DW and John Taylor, Sept. 14, 1835, *WP*, IV, 51–52.

37. Claude M. Fuess, *Daniel Webster*, 2 vols. (Boston, 1930), II, 337–41.

38. Curtis, *Webster*, I, 220–21.

39. Restored in 1920, the Winslow house in Marshfield is now open to the public. Information on the early history of the area, prepared by Cynthia Hagar Krusell, is available there.

40. Conveyance by John Thomas to DW, April 23, 1832, WPDC, F29/39770.

41. DW to Charles Henry Thomas, March 18, 1833, Webster Papers (Mass. Hist. Soc.), F9/10750; Feb. 4, 1836, ibid., F10/12947.

42. Fuess, *Webster*, II, 324–26.

43. Photograph of house is in ibid., 326.

44. The law office was moved to the grounds of the Winslow house in 1966 and, with many of Webster's personal items, is also open to the public. Webster's house was destroyed by fire in the late nineteenth century.

45. DW to Charles Henry Thomas, March 23, 1832, Webster Papers (Mass. Hist. Soc), F8/9948; Joshua Peirce to DW, March 22, 1833, WPNH, F9/10773; DW to Charles Henry Thomas, March 14, [1834], *WP*, III, 330–32.

46. DW to Charles Henry Thomas, Dec. 12, 1833, Webster Papers (Mass. Hist. Soc.), F9/11227; March 25, 1834, *WP*, III, 338–39; Feb. 16, [1835], ibid., IV, 29–30; March 5, 1840, Webster Papers (Mass. Hist. Soc.), F13/16415; Fuess, *Webster*, II, 326–29. Webster's correspondence is filled with many other items on agriculture.

47. An example is a lecture before the Massachusetts legislature in January 1840 on his observations of English agriculture; *WS*, II, 293–307. He was a trustee of the Massachusetts Society for Promoting Agriculture. DW to Benjamin Guild, April 17, 1833, Papers of the Society, Wenham (Mass.) Historical Association and Museum, F9/10868.

48. DW to Thomas, Jan. 4, 1833, Webster Papers, F9/10454, and later letters that month; DW to Thomas, Dec. 11, 1837, *WP*, IV, 253–54; DW to John Davis, Oct. 2, 1838, ibid., 331; Fuess, *Webster*, II, 16.

49. Seth Geer to DW, Jan. 23, 1837, WPLC, F11/13977–79; certificates of sale of stock, March 18, 1837, WPDC, F29/39835–134; DW to Edward Curtis, Jan. 30, 1836, *WP*, IV, 80–81 and n. 2.

50. Conveyance of two shares of stock in Hamilton Manufacturing Company by William Appleton to DW, July 22, 1830, Sang Collection, F29/39728.

51. Records of Secretary of Senate, Pay Receipts, 1814–1836, U.S. Congress Papers, Library of Congress, passim.

52. DW to Samuel Frothingham, Jan. 28, 1836, A. W. Anthony Collection, New York Public Library, F10/12900; DW to John Connell, Nov. 20, 1840, Society Collection, Pennsylvania Historical Society, F13/17048.

53. DW to John P. Healy, June 8, 1840, Webster Papers (Mass. Hist. Soc.), F13/16728; U.S. Finance Papers, Library of Congress, 39730; Herman Le Roy, Jr., to DW, Jan. 25, 1840, WPNH, F13/16265; DW to Nathaniel Wil-

liams, Nov. 1, 1840, WPDC, F13/16997. Throughout Webster's correspondence with Biddle, one finds repeated proof of his dependence upon the BUS.

54. Everett to Thomas W. Ward, Feb. 18, 1834, cited in *WP*, IV, 11–12 n. 1; Arthur B. Darling, *Political Changes in Massachusetts, 1824–1848* (New Haven, 1925), 131–32.

55. Lists of names and amounts, May 1, 1839, *WP*, IV, 359–61. At this time, anonymous friends in Boston advanced a loan by way of Samuel Ruggles' bank in New York on security of Webster's western lands to enable him to travel to England. There may have been a connection between Ward's subscription fund and this loan. The Boston *Advertiser*, Sept. 22, 1840, said that the fund was actually a loan. For the circumstances of the Ruggles loan, see the discussion later in this chapter.

56. Harding to DW, March 16, 1836, University of Virginia, F10/13072; DW memorandum, April 14, 1836, ibid., F10/13136.

57. Harding to DW, May 4, 1836, ibid., F10/13175; DW to Harding, May 16, 1836, Special Collections, Columbia University Library, F10/13225; Harding to DW, June 2, 1836, University of Virginia, F11/13297; July 5, 1836, ibid., F11/13429; abstract of Harding's letters to DW, May–Sept. 1836, ibid., F10/13178; Harding to DW, Dec. 29, 1836, ibid., F11/13699.

58. John Davis to DW, April 10, 1836, WPLC, F10/13122.

59. DW to Fletcher Webster, June 12, 1836, WPNH, F11/13347; DW to Phineas Davis, May 16, 1836, Sang Collection, F10/13214.

60. Fletcher Webster to DW, July 1, 1836, University of Virginia, F11/13417; July 6, 1836, ibid., F11/13438.

61. Fletcher Webster to DW, July 13, 1836, ibid., F11/13458; Phineas Davis to DW, July 18, 1836, ibid., F11/13463; July 26, 1836, ibid., F11/13485; Fletcher Webster to DW, Aug. 1, 1836, ibid., F11/13495; Phineas Davis to DW, July 30, 1836, ibid., F11/13493.

62. Fletcher Webster to DW, Dec. 14, 1836, WPNH, F11/13670; Jan. 23, 1837, ibid., F11/13981; Feb. 16, 1837, ibid., F11/14071.

63. Account sheets of Davis-Webster transactions, 1836, WPDC, F29/39835-95. See several letters from Phineas Davis to DW in May and June 1836 giving specific information on purchases, University of Virginia and F11.

64. Joseph Williams to DW, May 4, 1836, University of Virginia, F10/13182; May 24, ibid., F10/13257; June 6, ibid., F11/13329; June 14, 1836, ibid., F11/13361.

65. Fisher Harding to DW, June 14, 1836, ibid., F11/13358.

66. Fletcher Webster to DW, Jan. 4, 1837, Sang Collection, F11/13727; March 2, 1837, *WP*, IV, 202–3.

67. Williams to DW, July 9, 1836, University of Virginia, F11/13446; Oct. 3, 1836, ibid., F11/13558; Sept. 29, 1836, *WP*, IV, 159.

68. Fisher Harding to DW, May 17, 1836, Alderman Library, University of Virginia, F10/13233; May 21, 1836, ibid., F10/13242; Joseph Williams to DW, [ca. Sept. 28, 1836], ibid., F11/13552.

69. DW to Fisher Harding, June 18, 1836, Special Collections, Columbia University Library, F11/13373; Harding to DW, July 18, 1836, ibid., F11/13468; Aug. 16, 1836, WPDC, F11/13568; Phineas Davis to DW, June 16, 1836, University of Virginia, F11/13367.

70. List of purchases by George Jones, James Doty, and Benjamin Kercheval, 1836, Sang Collection, F29/39835-98; agreement of DW and Jones, March 1, 1837, Jones Collection, Iowa State Dept. of History and Archives, F29/39835-125; Jones to DW, April 22, 1837, University of Virginia, F11/14230; April 16, 1837, ibid., F11/14222; DW to Fletcher Webster, March 24, 1837, WP, IV, 212.

71. John Haight to DW, Aug. 4, 1849, Caleb Cushing Papers, Library of Congress, F21/29483 [later statement by Haight]; Haight draft on DW to pay James Sanderson three thousand dollars, March 4, 1837, ibid., F29/39835-128A; Haight to DW, March 14, 1837, ibid., F11/14156; March 31, 1837, ibid., F11/14187; DW to Cushing April 27, 1837, WP, IV, 213-14; Cushing to DW, July 28, 1837, ibid., 228; DW to Cushing, July 29, 1837, ibid., 228-29.

72. Coleman McCampbell, "H. L. Kinney and Daniel Webster in Illinois in the 1830's," Journal of the Illinois State Historical Society, 47 (Spring 1954), 35-44.

73. Kinney to DW, [April 13, 1836], with DW endorsement of agreement, University of Virginia, F10/13132.

74. Kinney to DW, May 24, 1836, ibid., F10/13253.

75. DW to Perkins and Co., May 16, 1836, Samuel Cabot Papers, Massachusetts Historical Society, F10/13228; June 20, 1836, ibid., F11/13379; June 27, 1836, ibid., F11/13409; Aug. 22, 1836, ibid., F11/13535; summary of purchases in Kinney to DW, Jan. 12, 1837, University of Virginia, F11/13738. In May 1836 Perkins traveled to the West, probably to look for opportunities to speculate in land; DW to B. Bakewell, May 16, 1836, Historical Society of Western Pennsylvania, Pittsburgh, F10/13210.

76. Kinney to DW, June 20, 1836, University of Virginia, F11/13385; July 18, 1836, ibid., F11/13470; July 28, 1836, ibid., F11/13488; Aug. 8, 1836, ibid., F11/13522. Altogether, according to a later investigation of the records, he held over three thousand acres in the area. Louis Worcester to Caleb Cushing Dec. 2, 1851, Cushing Papers, F25/35335.

77. Curtis, Webster, I, 571-72; II, 27; Kinney to DW, Aug. 24, 1837, University of Virginia, F11/14371. Kinney enclosed a sketch of the area, reproduced in WP, IV, 231.

78. Jones to DW, April 1, 1837, University of Virginia, F11/14190; April 14, 1837, ibid., F11/14215.

79. WP, IV, 213 n. 2 and 458 (calendar of correspondence, Feb. 13, 1837, referring to deed no. 321 in book A, Office of Register of Deeds, Rock Island County, Illinois; copy in Library of Congress; also in F29/40348).

80. Editorial note, WP, IV, 220-22. Webster also invested in the Maryland Mining Company, holding coal lands near Cumberland, Maryland. He and some of his associates in that company acquired an interest in the Clamorgan venture.

81. Fisher Harding to DW, Sept. 12, 1836, University of Virginia, F11/13546.

82. DW to Fletcher Webster, April 9, 1837, Special Collections, Columbia University Library, F11/14204.

83. George W. Jones to DW, July 7, 1837, University of Virginia, F11/14326; Fisher Harding to DW, Sept. 12, 1837, ibid., F11/14396.

84. DW to Franklin Haven, Oct. 2, 1837, Webster Papers, Harvard University, F11/14434; Oct. 25, 1837, ibid., F11/14449; DW to Joseph Cowperthwaite, Oct. 31, 1837, Dreer Collection, Pennsylvania Historical Society, F11/14459; DW bond to pay Turner fifty thousand dollars plus interest in ten years, Oct. 30, 1837, Sang Collection, F29/39835–160; DW draft on Turner, Oct. 31, 1837, WPDC, F29/39835–162; WP, IV, 246, editorial note describing transactions; Turner to DW, March 13, 1840, WPLC, F13/16493.

85. Fish to DW, Jan. 19, 1838, Hamilton Fish Papers, Library of Congress, F12/14578.

86. Crooks to DW, Sept. 23, 1837, American Fur Company Papers, New York Historical Society, F11/14424; Oct. 2, 1837, WP, IV, 243; Dec. 20, 1837, ibid., 256–57; DW to Crooks, Jan. 2, 1838, American Fur Company Papers, F12/14556; Feb. 26, 1838, ibid., F12/14693; May 12, [1838], ibid., F12/14927; Crooks to DW, June 19, 1838, WP, IV, 309–10.

87. DW to Biddle, May 24, 1838, Biddle Papers, Library of Congress, F12/14939.

88. Biddle to DW, May 22, 1838, WP, IV, 299; DW to Biddle, [June 16], 1838, Biddle Papers, F12/14951; DW to Joseph Cowperthwaite, July 23, 1838, Gratz Collection, Pennsylvania Historical Society, F12/15065.

89. DW to Haven, Feb. 27, 1837, Webster Papers, Harvard University, F11/14110; March 20, 1837, ibid., F11/14165; [Aug. 1837], WP, IV, 235–36; Feb. 25, [1841], Webster Papers, Harvard University, F14/17675.

90. DW to Colt, Oct. 8, 1838, Colt Papers, Pennsylvania Historical Society, F12/15237; notes of DW to Caleb Cushing, May 8, 1839 and June 29, 1841, Cushing papers, box 56. Webster's correspondence shows extensive business with William A. Bradley, president of the Patriotic Bank in Washington during this period.

91. Fletcher Webster to DW, Aug. 28, 1837, University of Virginia, F11/14380; Oct. 30, 1837, WPNH, F11/14452.

92. Fletcher Webster to DW, Dec. 5, 1837, WPNH, F11/14503; Jan. 8, 1838, ibid., F12/14566; March 3, 1838, ibid., F12/14699.

93. Kinney to DW, Feb. 14, 1838, ibid., F12/14652.

94. DW to Biddle, [June 9, 1838], Biddle Papers, F12/14978.

95. Biddle to DW, June 12, 1838, ibid., F12/14981.

96. Notes of Kinney, endorsed by DW to BUS, Sang Collection, F29/39835–181; DW to John Andrews, Sept. 22, 1838, WP, IV, 328.

97. DW to Nathaniel Ray Thomas, May 11, 1838, WPNH, F12/14920.

98. DW to Thomas, March 5, 1838, ibid., F12/14706.

99. Thomas to DW, April 20, 1838, ibid., F12/14862.

100. Fletcher Webster to DW, July 16, 1838, ibid., F12/15051; Sept. 26, 1838, ibid., F12/15214; April 26, 1839, ibid., F12/15469.

101. DW power of attorney to Thomas, March 5, 1838, Illinois State Historical Library, Springfield, F29/39835–170; DW to Thomas, March 5, 1838, WPNH, F12/14706; Thomas to DW, July 27, 1838, ibid., F12/15115; July 30, 1838, ibid., F12/15119; Dec. 19, 1838, ibid., F12/15271.

102. DW to Ruggles, March 2, 1839, George F. Hoar Papers, F12/15384. The idea probably originated with Richard M. Blatchford, a New York lawyer associated with the BUS, to whom, with Ruggles, Webster did convey his property. Others who may have advised the senator were Philip Hone and Edward Curtis.

NOTES TO PAGES 294–96

103. Agreement of DW with Richard M. Blatchford and Samuel B. Ruggles, May 16, 1839, WPNH, F29/39835–301. In ibid., F29/39835–264, are conveyances of individual parcels of property to Blatchford and Ruggles. Though none of the Boston underwriters is named except Homer, they may have been people who subscribed to the fund currently being raised for Webster by Thomas W. Ward. But the Blatchford-Ruggles agreement was a loan.

104. Fletcher Webster to DW, June 22, 1839, ibid., F12/15704; Dec. 5, 1839, ibid., F13/16198; Dec. 22, 1839, ibid., F13/16202; Feb. 13, 1840, ibid., F13/16344; March 5, 1840, ibid., F13/16423; March 30, 1840, ibid., F13/16590.

105. N. Ray Thomas to DW, Jan. 20, 1840, ibid., F13/16245; DW to Charles Henry Thomas, March 6, 1840, ibid., F13/16428; DW to Caroline Webster, March 9, 1840, ibid., F13/16444; March 13, 1840, ibid., F13/16464; March 19, ibid., F13/16532; DW to Charles Henry Thomas, March 24, 1840, WS, XVI, 324–25.

106. Fletcher Webster to DW, April 16, 1840, WPNH, F13/16614.

107. Biddle to DW, Feb. 7, 1841, Biddle Papers, F14/17459; Feb. 10, 1841, ibid., F14/17477.

108. DW to Biddle, [Feb. 1841], ibid., F14/17735.

109. Cope to DW, Feb. 10, 1841, Sang Collection, F14/17479.

110. Copy of agreement of DW and BUS, Feb. 12, 1841, ibid., F29/39835–295; BUS accounting sheet for DW, Feb. 15, 1841, WPNH, F29/39835–166; DW memorandum, [Feb. 1841], Sang Collection, F14/17740. The final step of approving the agreement came on Feb. 27, 1841; Cope to DW, ibid., F14/17713. Thomas P. Govan, *Nicholas Biddle: Nationalist and Public Banker, 1786–1844* (Chicago, 1959), 389, says, "The Bank lost nothing by this arrangement." Though it covered Webster's debts to the corporation he had other debts, of course, not covered.

111. DW to Samuel Jaudon, Jan. 12, 1839, Miscellaneous MSS, New York Historical Society, F12/15308; March 29, 1839, ibid., F12/15421; April 22, 1839, ibid., F12/15461.

112. DW to Samuel B. Ruggles, March 23, 1839, George F. Hoar Papers, F12/15414; DW to Samuel Jaudon, March 29, 1839, Miscellaneous MSS, New York Historical Society, F12/15421; April 15, 1839, ibid., F12/15454.

113. DW to Samuel Jaudon, Jan. 12, 1839, Miscellaneous MSS, New York Historical Society, F12/15421, saying Le Roy would probably supply a few thousand dollars so that Mrs. Webster and Julia could go along. In a letter of May 5, 1839, Biddle told Webster that he would "try to put something in your way that will help to pay your expences"; Biddle Papers, F12/15493.

114. DW to Edward Curtis, June 12, 1839, WS, XVIII, 49; DW to Edward Everett, June 12, 1839, ibid., 50; DW to Isaac P. Davis, June 24, 1839, ibid., 50–52.

115. John Evelyn Denison to DW, June 5, 1839, Webster Papers, Harvard University, F12/15511.

116. DW to John J. Crittenden, July 31, 1839, WP, IV, 384–85.

117. Charles M. Wiltse, "Daniel Webster and the British Experience," *Proceedings of the Massachusetts Historical Society*, 85 (1973), 67–72. In Webster's correspondence there are a great many social invitations.

118. Palmerston to Andrew Stevenson, June 14, 1839, Stevenson Papers, Library of Congress, XV; DW to Stevenson, June 17, [1839], ibid., F12/15662;

573

June 22, 1839, ibid., F12/15695; June 25, 1839, ibid., F' /15733; Fuess, *Webster,* II, 75.

119. Memorandum by DW, Nov. 8, 1839, WPNH, F13/16156.

120. DW to Charles Henry Thomas, Oct. 14, 1839, ibid., F13/16117.

121. Speech in *WS,* II, 285-89.

122. DW to Charles Henry Thomas, Oct. 14, 1839, WPNH, F13/16117. Though Webster did raise enough money to pay his expenses, he continued to borrow some sizable sums; DW to Samuel Jaudon, Sept. 14, 1839, Miscellaneous MSS, New York Historical Society, F13/16028; DW note to Joseph Travers for five hundred pounds, Nov. 19, 1839, WPDC, F29/39835.

123. DW to Virgil Maxcy, July 1, Aug. 1, and Sept. 25, 1839, *WS,* XVI, 311-12; Maxcy to DW, Aug. 5, 1839, George F. Hoar Papers, F13/15987; statement by James B. Murray at London on purchase of DW Clamorgan stock, [ca. Oct. 1840], WPLC, for $34,800 in three installments over the years 1840-1842, payable in BUS stock. Maxcy, Jaudon, and probably Roswell Colt negotiated the sale. See also Murray to DW, June 29, 1840, and DW to Jaudon, July 30, 1840, *WP,* V, 46, 49.

124. DW to Jaudon, Oct. 1, 1839, Queen's University Library, Belfast, Northern Ireland, F13/16088; DW to Samuel Frothingham, Oct. 14, 1839, Huntington-Wolcott Papers, Massachusetts Historical Society, F13/16114; DW to Edward Everett, Oct. 16, 1839, *WS,* XVIII, 71.

125. DW legal opinion, Oct. 16, 1839, *WP,* IV, 401-2. See Wiltse, "Webster and British Experience," for the context. Webster was attacked for being the instrument of the Barings and the English government and particularly for encouraging the idea of federal assumption of these state debts. Thus charged Calvin Colton, a friend of Clay, in an anonymous pamphlet. It has been erroneously thought that this attack came from Charles J. Ingersoll. In any event, Webster then and later did not favor federal assumption of the debts.

126. Edward Kenyon told Webster in July that he intended to buy Massachusetts bonds amounting to thirty thousand pounds or more; *WP,* IV, 386.

127. Fuess, *Webster,* II, 78-79, drawing from accounts by Caroline and Julia Webster and Harriette Paige of the travel to England and the Continent.

128. DW to John P. Healy, Dec. 29, 1839, Webster-Healy Papers, F13/16212; DW to Caroline Webster, Jan. 3, 1840, WPNH, F13/16225.

129. Alexander Baring, Lord Ashburton to DW, June 12, [1839], Houghton Library, Harvard University, F12/15599; Sept. 22, [1839], ibid., F13/16043.

18. Veto

1. Box 1841-1842, WPNH, passim, is a full file of applications and appointments. See also F15 passim.

2. Probably the main reason for Clay's disapproval was Curtis' opposition to his nomination in the recent election. Peter B. Porter to Clay, Jan. 29, 1841, in Calvin Colton, ed., *The Private Correspondence of Henry Clay* (Cincinnati, 1856), 448-50; Clay to Francis Brooke, Feb. 5, 1841, ibid., 451; Clay to Harrison, March 15, 1841, ibid., 453; DW to Curtis, June 10, 1841, Montague Collection, New York Public Library, F15/19350; Irving H. Bartlett, *Daniel Webster* (New York, 1978), 175.

3. Nicholas Biddle Papers, Library of Congress, numerous letters in 1841;

DW to Ewing, [March 1841], Ewing Papers, Library of Congress, F14/18637.

4. Stevens to DW, March 27, 1841, WPLC, F14/18588.

5. DW to Jackson, Feb. 12, 1841, F14/17499; Jackson to DW, Feb. 15 and March 17, 1841, F14/17523 and 18345; DW to Jackson, March 19, 1841, F14/18380; Jackson to DW, March 20, 1841, F14/18420; DW to Jackson, March 30, 1841, F14/18620; Jackson to DW, April 8, May 10, June 12, 1841, F15/18746, 19052, and 19380; all in James Bayard Papers, Maryland Historical Society. See Kenneth Stevens, "Editing the Papers of Daniel Webster," *Dartmouth College Bulletin,* 21 (Nov. 1980), 20.

6. See Kermit L. Hall, *The Politics of Justice: Federal Judicial Selection and the Second Party System* (Lincoln, Neb., 1979), passim, on appointment of judges of the lower federal courts.

7. See Noble E. Cunningham, Jr., *The Jeffersonian Republicans in Power: Party Operations, 1801-1809* (Chapel Hill, 1963).

8. DW circular to cabinet, March 20, 1841, John J. Crittenden Papers, Duke University Library, F14/18411; see an inquiry about the practice in DW to M. St. Clair Clarke et al., March 27, 1841, *WS,* XII, 216-17.

9. DW to John P. Healy, March 25, 1841, Webster-Healy Papers, Massachusetts Historical Society, F14/18534.

10. Clement Eaton, *Henry Clay and the Art of American Politics* (Boston, 1957), 93-94.

11. George R. Poage, *Henry Clay and the Whig Party* (Chapel Hill, 1936), 26-32. Clay interpreted Harrison's answer as indicating a preference for communication in written form in the future, but that was not the president's intention.

12. DW draft editorial, March 25, 1841, WPDC, F14/18536; see also Washington *National Intelligencer,* March 20, 1841.

13. Text in Washington *National Intelligencer,* March 18, 1841.

14. Ibid., April 5 and 9, 1841; DW circular letter, April 4, 1841, George F. Hoar Papers, Massachusetts Historical Society, F15/18712; DW public announcements, April 4, 1841, Domestic Letters, SDNA. The time of death was 12:30 A.M., April 4.

15. DW et al. to Tyler, April 4, 1841, Domestic Letters, SDNA.

16. Washington *National Intelligencer,* April 7, 1841.

17. Ibid., April 10, 1841; Lyon G. Tyler, *Letters and Times of the Tylers,* 2 vols. (Richmond, 1884-85), II, 18. From the beginning Tyler rejected the status of "acting president."

18. William R. Brock, *Parties and Political Conscience: American Dilemmas, 1840-1850* (Millwood, N.Y., 1979), 72-81; Glyndon G. Van Deusen, *The Life of Henry Clay* (Boston, 1937), 344-45.

19. Tyler, *Tylers,* II, 16-17. Webster believed Tyler would defer to Congress on a bank if it were located in the District of Columbia or if some other way were found to escape the old constitutional question; DW to John Davis, April 16, 1841, Davis Papers, American Antiquarian Society, F15/18825.

20. Tyler wrote Clay on April 30 setting forth his objections to an old-style national bank. See Oliver P. Chitwood, *John Tyler: Champion of the Old South* (New York, 1939), 213.

21. James D. Richardson, ed., *A Compilation of the Messages and Papers of the Presidents, 1789-1897,* 10 vols. (Washington, D.C., 1896-99), IV, 40-51.

22. Texts of Ewing's recommendations and of Clay's committee report in

Washington *National Intelligencer,* June 22, 1841. For Webster's suggestions to Ewing, see his undated memorandum in Ewing Papers, VI.

23. DW to Ewing, July 15, 1841, Ewing Papers, F15/19648.

24. DW draft editorials, June 14, 16, and 17, 1841, Webster Folder, Personal (Miscellaneous) Papers, New York Public Library, F15/19396, 19426, and 19438. They appeared in the Washington *Intelligencer,* June 15, 16, and 17.

25. Covering letter of DW to Ketchum, [July 1841], WPDC, F15/19480; draft editorials in DW to Ketchum, July 16 and 17, 1841, *WS,* XVI, 344–48 and 348–51. The *Intelligencer* clipped items from the *Commerical Advertiser* and the *American.* For Webster's dissatisfaction with the *American,* see DW to Ketchum, July 12, 1841, WPDC, F15/19620. For context, see also *WP,* V, editorial notes on 134, 137, 138.

26. Jean V. Matthews, *Rufus Choate: The Law and Civic Virtue* (Philadelphia, 1980), 59–61; Poage, *Clay and Whig Party,* 50–58.

27. Poage, *Clay and Whig Party,* 59–66; Tyler, *Tylers,* II, 54–64.

28. DW to Caroline Webster, Aug. 8, 1841, *WS,* XVIII, 107–8; Poage, *Clay and Whig Party,* 68–69.

29. Fletcher Webster to Hiram Ketchum, July 28, 1841, WPDC, F15/19797; DW to Thomas Ewing [Aug. 8, 1841], Ewing Papers, F15/19899; Washington *National Intelligencer,* Aug. 7, 1841; Sydney Nathans, *Daniel Webster and Jacksonian Democracy* (Baltimore, 1973), 172–73.

30. Richardson, *Papers of the Presidents,* IV, 63–68.

31. DW to Caroline Webster, Aug. 16 and 19, 1841, WPNH, F15/19933 and 19961.

32. DW draft editorial, Aug. 16, 1841, Webster Folder, Personal (Miscellaneous) Papers, New York Public Library, F15/19937; the editorial is in *Intelligencer,* Aug. 17, 1841.

33. Poage, *Clay and Whig Party,* 74–78; Thomas H. Benton, *Thirty Years' View,* 2 vols. (New York, 1856), II, 317–28. The vote to override was twenty-four to twenty-four.

34. Tyler, *Tylers,* II, 74–79. Chitwood, *Tyler,* 469–70, has the texts of the vetoed bill and the revisions made by Stuart and Tyler. The judicial rule to which Tyler referred had been laid down in the *Alabama Bank Cases,* 15 Peters 519 (1839), in which Webster had participated as counsel.

35. Tyler, *Tylers,* II, 81–82; Poage, *Clay and Whig Party,* 82–83.

36. DW undated manuscript memorandum, [1841], narrating conversations and movements involving the second bank bill, WPLC, F16/21025. This version contrasts with that of the president in Tyler, *Tylers,* II.

37. DW memorandum [1841], WPLC, F16/21025. See also "The Diary of Thomas Ewing, August and September, 1841," *American Historical Review,* 18 (Oct. 1912), 97–112, on this and other aspects of the bill's history. It coincides with Webster's recollection.

38. Tyler later wrote that he had not had a proper opportunity to examine and suggest changes in the bill—a contradiction of Webster's account; Tyler, *Tylers,* II, 86.

39. Chitwood, *Tyler,* 239–40, 266 n. 30; Tyler, *Tylers,* II, 112; DW memorandum, [1841], WPLC, F16/21025. Webster told his wife on August 21 that Tyler was "much agitated"; WPNH, F15/19979.

40. Tyler, *Tylers,* II, 86–88; DW to Bates and Choate, August 25, WPLC, F15/20030. A detailed account of the bill's passage is in Poage, *Clay and Whig Party,* 85–91. Rives was the only Whig to vote against it.

41. Richardson, *Papers of the Presidents,* IV, 68–72.

42. Tyler, *Tylers,* II, 98–102, especially 100 n. 1. The phrase in the bill seems to have incorporated Tyler's proviso that states must be able to regulate out-of-state corporations according to the rule of the *Alabama Bank Cases.*

43. Poage, *Clay and Whig Party,* 100–101; Chitwood, *Tyler,* 272–73. On Clay's presence at Badger's house, see Washington *National Intelligencer,* Sept. 27, 1841.

44. Washington *National Intelligencer,* Sept. 13, 1841. Ewing was also upset by items in the New York *Herald* criticizing the cabinet for having remained in office allegedly contrary to Tyler's wishes. Benton, *Thirty Years' View,* II, 353, emphasizes this point.

45. Crittenden, like Ewing and Webster, had sought to reconcile the opposing positions during the controversy and to persuade Tyler to sign both bills; Albert D. Kirwan, *John J. Crittenden: The Struggle for the Union* (Lexington, Ky., 1962), 149–55. His letter of resignation is in the *Intelligencer,* Sept. 13, 1841.

46. *Niles' Register,* 61 (Sept. 25, 1841).

47. Tyler, *Tylers,* II, 94. There are unverifiable statements that Tyler had planned to dismiss the cabinet, in any event, at the end of the session.

48. DW to McLean, Sept. 11, 1841, McLean Papers, Library of Congress, F16/20202; McLean to DW, Sept. 18, 1841, ibid., F16/20308. Undoubtedly McLean considered this offer of appointment in its relation to his presidential aspirations, as he often did.

49. Glyndon G. Van Deusen, *Thurlow Weed: Wizard of the Lobby* (Boston, 1947), 124. Tyler wrote Webster on October 11: "Each man [of the new cabinet] will go steadily to work for the country—and *its interests* will alone be looked to. I congratulate you in an especial manner upon having such co-workers. I would have each member to look upon every other, in the light of a friend and brother"; WPNH, F16/20535. There was an implied contrast with the old cabinet.

50. Washington *National Intelligencer,* Sept. 15, 1841.

51. DW to [Isaac P. Davis], Sept. 10, 1841, WPNH, F16/20194. For recipient of letter, see *WP,* V, 149 n. See Davis' response, ibid., 152.

52. Charles F. Adams, ed., *Memoirs of John Quincy Adams, Comprising Portions of His Diary from 1795 to 1848,* 12 vols. (Philadelphia, 1874–77), XI, 13–14, 16.

53. It was now that Adams wrote his much quoted characterization of Webster: "Such is human nature, in the gigantic intellect, the envious temper, the ravenous ambition, and the rotten heart of Daniel Webster"; ibid., 20.

54. Winthrop to DW, Sept. 13, 1841, Winthrop Papers, Massachusetts Historical Society, F16/20222; Choate to Theophilus Parsons, Sept. 13, 1841, Chamberlain Collection, Boston Public Library, cited in Kinley J. Brauer, *Cotton versus Conscience: Massachusetts Whig Politics and Southwestern Expansion, 1843–1848* (Lexington, Ky., 1967), 51 n. 3.

55. See Glyndon G. Van Deusen, *The Jacksonian Era, 1828–1848* (New York, 1959), 159, for what little evidence there is of a possible dismissal. The citations are to a letter by William Rives to his wife, August 27, and to Tyler,

Tylers, II, 122 and n. Rives said Tyler offered the office to Louis McLane, who declined; it is very unlikely that he did so at that date or earlier, while Webster was still acting as Tyler's trusted intermediary on the bank question. An appointment of McLane or someone else might have been thought of in case Webster resigned along with the rest of the cabinet. The evidence in Tyler, *Tylers,* rests on a later assertion, probably to bolster the president's reputation.

56. Tyler, *Tylers,* II, 118-23. The narrative quotes a letter by John Tyler, Jr., to Lyon Gardiner Tyler long afterward, January 29, 1883; ibid., 121-23, n. 1.

57. Washington *National Intelligencer,* Sept. 14, 1841.

58. DW to Ketchum, Sept. 11, 1841, WPDC, F16/20198; and New York *American,* Sept. 14, 1841.

59. DW to Ketchum, Sept. 10, 1841, *WS,* XVIII, 110.

60. Persuasive conjectures in Bartlett, *Webster,* 177.

61. DW draft, Sept. 24, 1841, WPNH, F16/20364. See earlier in this chapter for the discussion of these resignations, all grounded on the same objections to the bank vetoes and Tyler's conduct.

62. Claude H. Van Tyne, ed., *The Letters of Daniel Webster* (New York, 1901), 237-38.

63. Chitwood, *Tyler,* 267-68, despite an extensive defense of the president, concedes that Tyler did not "exhibit in his management of the bank question the boldness, wisdom, and firmness that should characterize the policy of a Chief Magistrate." Though disapproving Clay's actions, the author concludes that Tyler "had not fought a good fight." Though dealing with Tyler's presidency favorably, Robert J. Morgan, *A Whig Embattled: The Presidency under John Tyler* (Lincoln, Neb., 1954), 27-45, 57-76, 181-83, criticizes the president's inconsistencies and mistakes in congressional relations and in his use of the veto.

64. Chitwood, *Tyler,* 264, agrees that Tyler may have changed his mind and was affected by Clay's speech and Botts's letter. Even Tyler's confidant, Henry Wise, said that Tyler lost his willingness to accept any compromise after discussions with his closest advisers (apparently including Wise himself); see his *Seven Decades of the Union* (Philadelphia, 1881), 188-90.

65. One must keep in mind that Webster never abandoned his own unqualified preference for a national bank in the fullest sense, though deploring Clay's hard-line strategy.

66. DW draft editorial, [Dec. 4, 1841], WPNH, F16/20785. Also on December 4, Webster asked Edward Curtis to recruit help from the New York press; Montague Collection, F16/20782. Thurlow Weed wrote Webster that he held out hope for reconciliation, Dec. 18, 1841, WPLC, F16/20910.

67. Richardson, *Papers of the Presidents,* IV, 74-89.

68. Ibid., 83-87.

69. Tyler, *Tylers,* II, 131-34. DW draft of message, to be signed by Walter Forward [Dec. 1841], WPNH, F16/20898; DW draft of bill, [Dec. 1841], ibid., F16/20869. Compare these with the published texts in Washington *National Intelligencer,* Dec. 22, 1841.

70. Washington *National Intelligencer,* Dec. 30, 1841, Feb. 17, 22, 24, 25, and 26, 1842; Benton, *Thirty Years' View,* II, 373-94.

71. DW draft, [Nov.-Dec. 1841], WPNH, F16/20758. The Constitution, Art. I, sec. 9, states: "No preference shall be given by any regulation of commerce or Revenue to the Ports of one State over those of another."

72. Richardson, *Papers of the Presidents*, IV, 81–82.

73. Tyler, *Tylers*, II, 164.

74. Ibid., 165–69.

75. Richardson, *Papers of the Presidents*, IV, 180–83.

76. DW to Isaac Bates, July 16, 1842, Kenyon College Library, F17/22896; Bates replied on July 19, 1842, that he felt obligated to vote for unlimited distribution because of Massachusetts' need for revenue and because of instructions by the state legislature; WPDC, F17/22946.

77. Tyler to DW, Aug. 8, 1842, WPNH, F17/23127; DW to Tyler, Aug. 8, 1842, ibid., F17/23123.

78. Richardson, *Papers of the Presidents*, IV, 183–89.

79. Tyler, *Tylers*, II, 181.

80. Kirwan, *Crittenden*, 165–66; Charles M. Wiltse, *John C. Calhoun: Sectionalist* (Indianapolis, 1951), 86.

81. Poage, *Clay and Whig Party*, 114–15; Brock, *Parties and Political Conscience*, 106–13.

82. DW to Everett, May 31, 1842, Webster-Healy Papers, F17/22576.

19. Anglo-American Issues

1. SDNA records for 1841–1843.

2. Another instance of nepotism was the appointment of Webster's brother-in-law, Daniel Le Roy, as despatch agent in New York City; Fletcher Webster to Le Roy, Oct. 4, 1841, Domestic Letters, XXXII, 64–67, SDNA.

3. List of ministers and consuls, May 5, 1843, with printed date of Sept. 10, 1842, WPLC.

4. Stevenson to DW, May 18, 1841, WPLC, F15/19108.

5. DW draft, July 15, 1841, Webster Folder, Personal (Miscellaneous) Papers, New York Public Library, F15/19654; published in Washington *National Intelligencer* of that date.

6. Everett to DW, Jan. 1, 1841, Everett Papers, Massachusetts Historical Society, F14/17232, and April 16, 1841, ibid., F15/18832; DW to Peter C. Brooks, July 8, 1841, ibid., F15/19598; Brooks to DW, July 13, 1841, ibid., F15/19631; DW to Everett, July 24, 1841, ibid., F15/19752; Paul R. Frothingham, *Edward Everett: Orator and Statesman* (Boston, 1925), 185–87; DW to Everett, Nov. 20, 1841, *WS*, XIV, 369–70.

7. Charles F. Adams, ed., *Memoirs of John Quincy Adams, Comprising Portions of His Diary from 1795 to 1848*, 12 vols. (Philadelphia, 1874–77), XI, 36–38, 41–42, 46–47.

8. Charles M. Wiltse, "Daniel Webster and the British Experience," *Proceedings of the Massachusetts Historical Society*, 85 (1973), 58–77.

9. Wilbur D. Jones, *The American Problem in British Diplomacy, 1841–1861* (London, 1974), 1–16.

10. Howard Jones, *To the Webster-Ashburton Treaty: A Study in Anglo-American Relations, 1783–1843* (Chapel Hill, 1977), 20–26; Albert B. Corey, *The Crisis of 1830–1842 in Canadian-American Relations* (New Haven, 1941), 34–38. A thorough study of the *Caroline* affair, from background to impact, is Kenneth R. Stevens, "The *Caroline* Affair: Anglo-American Relations and Domestic Politics, 1837–1842" (Ph.D. dissertation, Indiana University, 1982), upon which the discussion here draws liberally.

11. James C. Curtis, *The Fox at Bay: Martin Van Buren and the Presidency, 1837–1841* (Lexington, Ky., 1970), 170–82; Howard Jones, *Webster-Ashburton Treaty*, 27–32; Alastair Watt, "The Case of Alexander McLeod," *Canadian Historical Review*, 12 (June 1931), 147–52.

12. See Miscellaneous Letters, SDNA, 1841–1842 passim, for numerous letters carrying such information.

13. DW to John Tyler, [July 1841], WPNH, F15/19844; DW to Demas Adams, Sept. 25, 1841, Domestic Letters, XXXII, 55, SDNA; DW to Joshua Spencer, Sept. 9, 1841, ibid., 33; Tyler to DW, July 9, 1841, WPLC, F15/19608.

14. William Seward to DW, Sept. 17, 1841, Seward Papers, University of Rochester, F16/20281; DW to Seward, Sept. 23, 1841, Domestic Letters, XXXII, 52, SDNA; DW to Fox, Sept. 25 and Nov. 29, 1841, in William R. Manning, ed., *Diplomatic Correspondence of the United States: Canadian Relations, 1784–1860*, 4 vols. (Washington, D.C., 1943), III, 151–54, 157–58.

15. Fletcher Webster to William Barrow, Sept. 28, 1841, Domestic Letters, XXXII, 60, SDNA; Henry Fox to Fletcher Webster, Oct. 21, 1841, in Manning, *Diplomatic Correspondence: Canadian*, III, 683. Claiming he had been mistreated, Grogan allegedly had burned property and assaulted persons in Canada in retaliation. Then a Canadian party had come into Vermont to take him away.

16. Howard Jones, *Webster-Ashburton Treaty*, 49–51; Corey, *Crisis of 1830–1842*, 130–32. In his note to Forsyth December 13, 1840, Fox called the raid a *public* act but had no specific instructions from Palmerston to do so.

17. Stevenson to John Forsyth, Feb. 9 and March 3, 1841, Despatches, Great Britain, SDNA; Stevenson to DW, March 9 and 18, April 7, 1841, ibid.

18. Fox to DW, March 12, 1841, *WS*, XI, 247–50.

19. In Despatches, Great Britain, SDNA, are items of Palmerston-Stevenson correspondence: Palmerston to Stevenson, Aug. 27, 1841; Stevenson to Palmerston, Aug. 31, 1841; Palmerston to Stevenson, Sept. 2, 1841; Stevenson to Palmerston, same day.

20. DW to John J. Crittenden, March 15, 1841, Crittenden Papers, Duke University Library, F14/18257.

21. Seward to Forsyth, Feb. 27, 1841, in George E. Baker, ed., *The Works of William H. Seward*, 5 vols. (Boston, 1884), II, 547–54.

22. DW to Seward, March 17, 1841, WPNH, F14/18335. After talking with a young New Yorker, Webster may have been led to believe that Seward would stop prosecution of McLeod. See Stevens, "*Caroline* Affair," 148–51.

23. Seward to DW, March 22, 1841, WPNH, F14/18458.

24. Seward to Eliphalet Nott, Sept. 17, 1841, in Baker, *Works of Seward*, III, 453; Glyndon G. Van Deusen, *William Henry Seward* (New York, 1967), 76–78; Albert D. Kirwan, *John J. Crittenden: The Struggle for the Union* (Lexington, Ky., 1962), 145–46.

25. Seward to Lovell G. Mickells, Aug. 23, 1841, in Baker, *Works of Seward*, III, 451–52.

26. DW to Hiram Ketchum, [July 1841], WPDC, F15/19837.

27. DW to Fox, April 24, 1841, *WS*, XI, 250–62. He defined the rigorous standards justifying an invasion of territory, as he also did in his note at the end of the Ashburton negotiations.

28. Seward to Samuel Nelson, March 18, 1841, Miscellaneous Letters, SDNA; Willis Hall to Seward, April 1, 1841, ibid.

29. DW to Joshua Spencer, April 16, 1841, Gratz Collection, Pennsylvania Historical Society, F15/18831; and April 19, 1841, Domestic letters, XXXI, 395, 400-401, SDNA; Seward to Tyler, May 4, 1841, Misc. Letters, SDNA; Tyler to Seward, May 7, 1841, Domestic Letters, XXXI, unnumbered page in back of volume, SDNA; Seward to Tyler, May 10, 1841, Misc. Letters, SDNA; DW to Fletcher Webster, May 10, 1841, Webster-Healy Papers, Massachusetts Historical Society, F15/19042; Tyler to DW, May 15, 1841, WPLC, F15/19087; Seward to Tyler, May 20, 1841, Misc. Letters, SDNA; Tyler to Seward, May 25, 1841, ibid.; Seward to Tyler, June 1, 1841, ibid.; Fox to DW, April 12, 1841, F0/97/16, Public Record Office, London, F15/18787. The last item refers to the relationship of the British government to McLeod's defense. After the trial the government paid Spencer five thousand dollars; Stevens, "*Caroline* Affair," 239.

30. DW to Gardner and Bradley, April 14, 1841, Domestic Letters, XXXI, 387, SDNA; DW to Fletcher Webster, May 16, 1841, *WS*, XVIII, 104-5; Ogden Hoffman to DW, May 18, 1841, WPDC, F15/19101; Joshua Spencer to DW, July 6, 1841, WPNH, F15/19592. Report of proceedings of court in Washington *National Intelligencer,* May 19 and 21, 1841.

31. Case reported in 25 Wendell (N.Y. Sup. Ct.) 483-603 (1841), with Cowen's opinion on pp. 567-603.

32. Fox to DW, Sept. 5, 1841, F0/97/16, Public Record Office, F16/20139; Stevenson to DW, Aug. 18, 1841, Despatches, Great Britain, SDNA.

33. DW to Story, July 16, [1841, erroneously printed as 1842], *WS*, XVI, 379-80.

34. Pamphlet, "Review of the Opinion of Judge Cowen ..." (New York, 1841), reprinted in 26 Wendell (N.Y. Sup. Ct.) 663-69 (1842) with complimentary letters on pp. 699-705. For Webster's praise of Tallmadge's review, see DW to Edward Everett, Feb. 7, 1842, Everett Papers, F16/21507, and his draft editorial for Washington *National Intelligencer* of Feb. 12, 1842, in WPDC, F16/21531.

35. Spencer to DW, July 12, 1841, WPNH, F15/19628; also July 14, 1841, ibid., F15/19644; DW to Spencer, July 15, 1841, ibid., F15/19652; also Aug. 6, 1841, Domestic Letters, XXXI, unnumbered pages, SDNA, and Sept. 21, 1841, Joseph Hopkinson Papers, Pennsylvania Historical Society, F16/20327.

36. Spencer to DW, Sept. 18, 1841, WPNH. Other letters are Sept. 24, ibid., F16/20389; Sept. 27, ibid., F16/20421; Sept. 29, ibid., F16/20442; Oct. 1, ibid., F16/20478.

37. DW to Tyler, [July 1841], *WS*, XVI, 344.

38. Daily reports of the trial are in Washington *National Intelligencer,* Oct. 9-16, 1841. See also *Niles' Register,* vol. 61, especially Oct. 16, 1841, for counsel's addresses to jury. The most comprehensive report is Marcus T. C. Gould, *Gould's Stenographic Reporter,* 2 vols. (Washington, D.C., 1841), II. The best study of the trial is Stevens, "*Caroline* Affair," 221-40.

39. James D. Richardson, ed., *A Compilation of the Messages and Papers of the Presidents,* 10 vols. (Washington, D.C., 1897), IV, 75-77.

40. Howard Jones, "The Peculiar Institution and National Honor: The Case of the *Creole* Slave Revolt," *Civil War History,* 21 (March 1975), 29-33, 36;

Senate Document 51, 27th Cong., 2d sess., II, 1–46. Compensation for emancipating slaves on ships coming into Nassau prior to passage of the British law had been allowed.

41. Jones, "Peculiar Institution," 34–38; Thomas H. Benton, *Thirty Years' View,* 2 vols. (New York, 1856), II, 411–13; Charles M. Wiltse, *John C. Calhoun: Sectionalist* (Indianapolis, 1951), 62–64, 69–70.

42. DW to Edward Everett, Jan. 29, 1842, *WS,* XIV, 373–81. A copy of Everett's note to Aberdeen setting forth Webster's view is enclosed in his letter to Webster of March 1, 1842, Despatches, Great Britain, SDNA. Webster subsequently asked Story for his opinion on extradition under the law of nations and found that it corresponded to his position in the note of January 29; DW to Story, March 17, 1842, Story Papers, Massachusetts Historical Society, F17/21889; Story to DW, March 26, 1842, WPNH, F17/21984; DW to Story, April 9, 1842, Story Papers, F17/22101.

43. Fletcher Webster to Seward, May 10, 1841, Domestic Letters, XXXI, 422–23, SDNA; Seward to Fletcher Webster, May 13, 1841, Misc. Letters, SDNA; Seward to John Tyler, May 18, 1841, ibid.; DW to Seward, Sept. 16, 1841, Domestic Letters, XXXII, 41, SDNA. In *Holmes* v. *Jennison,* 14 Peters 540 (1840), Chief Justice Taney had written an opinion saying that a state could not extradite fugitives to Canada because this was an exclusive national power; but the justices were evenly divided, and thus the case was not a binding precedent, though suggestive of what the Court might do in the future. See Charles G. Haines and Foster H. Sherwood, *The Role of the Supreme Court in American Government and Politics, 1835–1864* (Berkeley, 1957), 206–17.

44. Hugh G. Soulsby, *The Right of Search and the Slave Trade in Anglo-American Relations, 1814–1862* (Baltimore, 1933), 7–58; Howard Jones, *Webster-Ashburton Treaty,* 71–72. Palmerston could correctly point to weak American enforcement against American violators.

45. Stevenson to DW, May 18, 1841, Despatches, Great Britain, SDNA; Palmerston to Stevenson, Aug. 27, 1841, enclosure in Stevenson to DW, Sept. 18, 1841, ibid.

46. Aberdeen to Stevenson, Oct. 13, 1841, enclosure in Stevenson to DW, Oct. 22, 1841, ibid. See also Aberdeen to Everett, Dec. 20, 1841, printed in Washington *National Intelligencer,* April 22, 1842.

47. Copy of Stevenson to Palmerston, April 16, 1841, Despatches, Great Britain, SDNA; Stevenson to DW, Aug. 18, 1841, ibid.; copy of Stevenson to Aberdeen, Sept. 10, 1841, ibid.; DW to Stevenson, April 12, 1841, Instructions, Great Britain, SDNA, XV, 25; DW to Stevenson, June 8, 1841, ibid., 28. Although the slave trade had been declared piracy by the municipal law of some countries, including the United States, such laws could be enforced by those countries only against their own ships. The slave trade was not piracy under international law; so the American argument was that the only way for Britain to act against foreign ships was to rely upon a treaty. And the United States and Britain had not entered such a treaty.

48. Cass to DW, Feb. 13, 1842, Cass Papers, Clements Library, University of Michigan, F16/21552; copy of Cass to DW, March 12, 1842, Aberdeen Papers, British Library, London, F17/21829; Howard Jones, *Webster-Ashburton Treaty,* 75–77; Tyler's message is in Richardson, *Papers of the Presidents,* IV, 77–78. Interestingly, unlike Stevenson, Cass conceded a British right of visit

(with reparations if the ship was discovered to be American) and concentrated his argument against the right of search.

49. Wheaton to DW, Jan. 26, 1842, WPNH, F16/21405; Feb. 15, 1842, ibid., F16/21590; March 12, 1842, ibid., F17/21849; Washington *National Intelligencer,* March 19, 1842.

50. St. George L. Sioussant, "Duff Green's 'England and the United States,'" *American Antiquarian Society, Proceedings,* n.s., 40 (Oct. 1930), 175–276, has an introduction and the text of Green's essay.

51. Tyler to DW [March 1842], WPLC, F16/21734; DW to Cass, April 5, 1842, *WS,* XII, 17–20. Howard Jones, *Webster-Ashburton Treaty,* 77, says that France had decided not to ratify the treaty before the appearance of Cass's pamphlet.

52. Hunter Miller, ed., *Treaties and Other International Acts of the United States of America,* 8 vols. (Washington, D.C., 1931–48), II, 152.

53. The following summary of the boundary issue through the 1830s is based upon Howard Jones, *Webster-Ashburton Treaty,* 6–18; Frederick Merk and Lois Merk, *Fruits of Propaganda in the Tyler Administration* (Cambridge, Mass., 1971), 40–54; Samuel F. Bemis, *John Quincy Adams and the Foundations of American Foreign Policy* (New York, 1956), 469–78.

54. It was feared that this compromise might reduce rightful American claims to more of the area on the basis of the Louisiana Purchase of 1803.

55. The British wanted the land route because the St. Lawrence froze over and therefore could not be used during the winter.

56. Renwick to DW, March 15, 1841, Misc. Letters, SDNA; March 27, 1841, ibid.; report of the surveyors, March 28, 1841, in Richardson, *Papers of the Presidents,* IV, 113–50; additional reports, Jan. 4 and 25, 1842, ibid., 92–99; memorandum of Renwick, June 4, 1841, Misc. Letters, SDNA; DW to Renwick, March 7, 1842, Domestic Letters, XXXII, 227–28, SDNA.

57. DW to Francis C. Gray, May 11, 1841, WPNH, F15/19053; DW to Andrew Stevenson, July 28, 1841, Instructions, Great Britain, XV, 29, SDNA; Palmerston to Henry Fox, Aug. 24, 1841, in Manning, *Diplomatic Correspondence: Canadian,* III, 678–80; DW to Edward Kent, Dec. 21, 1841, WPNH, F16/20914; DW to Edward Everett, Dec. 28, 1841, Everett Papers, F16/20945.

58. Merk and Merk, *Fruits of Propaganda,* 59–64; text of Smith's earlier proposal to Van Buren, Dec. 7, 1837, in ibid., 131–36.

59. Smith to DW, June 7, 1841, WPNH, F15/19318.

60. Smith to DW, July 2, 1841, ibid., F15/19559, with enclosed copy of petition; Merk and Merk, *Fruits of Propaganda,* 158–72, for texts of three items in Portland paper, Nov. 18 and Dec. 2, 1841, Feb. 3, 1842.

61. Sprague to DW, Feb. 17, 1842, WPNH, F16/21606, and March 26, 1842, ibid., F17/21980.

62. Howard Jones, *Webster-Ashburton Treaty,* 95; Everett to DW, Dec. 31, 1841, Despatches, Great Britain, SDNA.

63. Howard Jones, *Webster-Ashburton Treaty,* 96–100.

64. DW to Everett, Jan. 29, 1842, Everett Papers, F16/21434; DW draft editorial, [Feb. 28, 1842], *WS,* XV, 154–55, for *National Intelligencer,* March 1, 1842; DW to Walter Forward, March 14, 1842, Domestic Letters, XXXII, 236–37, SDNA.

65. Wilbur D. Jones, "Lord Ashburton and the Maine Boundary Negotiations," *Mississippi Valley Historical Review,* 40 (Dec. 1953), 479–83; Howard Jones, *Webster-Ashburton Treaty,* 101.

20. Ashburton

1. Howard Jones, *To the Webster-Ashburton Treaty: A Study in Anglo-American Relations, 1783–1843* (Chapel Hill, 1977), 113–14. Although citations in this chapter are to manuscript and archival materials, most of these sources are now available, along with editorial comment in *WP: Diplomatic,* I, 483–704.
2. Ashburton to Charles Bagot, July 26, 1842, quoted in Albert B. Corey, *The Crisis of 1830–1842 in Canadian-American Relations* (New Haven, 1941), 166.
3. Wilbur D. Jones, *The American Problem in British Diplomacy, 1841–1861* (London, 1974), 17–28.
4. A pioneering and still useful study, based upon archival research, is Ephraim D. Adams, "Lord Ashburton and the Treaty of Washington," *American Historical Review,* 17 (July 1912), 764–82.
5. A typical expression of this view was his speech before the New York Chamber of Commerce, Nov. 4, 1842, *WS,* XIII, 143–49.
6. DW to John E. Denison, April 26, 1842, University of Virginia Library, F17/22264. See also DW to Edward Everett, May 16, 1842, Everett Papers, Massachusetts Historical Society, F17/22460.
7. Frederick Merk and Lois B. Merk, *Fruits of Propaganda in the Tyler Administration* (Cambridge, Mass., 1971), 66–67, 174–76. All were compensated from the secret-service fund, also drawn upon earlier to pay Francis Smith.
8. DW to Williams, Feb. 2, 1842, WPNH, F16/21475; Williams to DW, Feb. 9 and 12, 1842, ibid., F16/21521 and 21548; DW to Williams, Feb. 18, 1842, ibid., F16/21615; Williams to Fairfield, Feb. 28 and April 8, 1842, Fairfield Papers, Library of Congress, box 1828–1844; Francis O. J. Smith to DW, April 13, 1842, WPNH, F17/22153.
9. DW to John Davis, [Feb. 15, 1842], in Claude H. Van Tyne, ed., *The Letters of Daniel Webster* (New York, 1902), 270–71; Washington *National Intelligencer,* March 3, 1842, for Davis' message of Feb. 23.
10. DW to John Fairfield, April 11, 1842, Domestic Letters, XXXII, 288–91, SDNA; DW to John Davis, ibid., 293; DW to Davis, April 16, 1842, WPNH, F17/22169.
11. Fairfield to DW, April 30, 1842, Miscellaneous Letters, SDNA, enclosing copy of proclamation; DW to Reuel Williams, May 7, 1842, Fairfield Papers, box 1828–1844; Francis Smith to DW, April 16, 1842, WPNH, F17/22185; DW to Edward Kavanagh, May 17, 1842, Kavanagh Collection, Roman Catholic Diocese of Portland, Me., F17/22474; Peleg Sprague to DW, May 18, 1842, WPNH, F17/22484.
12. DW to Sparks, May 14, 1842, Harvard University, F17/22450.
13. Thomas Fisher to Fletcher Webster, May 23, 1841, Misc. Letters, SDNA; Jared Sparks to DW, June 7, 1841, Harvard University, F15/19322; DW to George R. Babcock, Dec. 14, 1841, Domestic Letters, XXXII, SDNA, 115; DW to Austin, Lowell, and Adams, Dec. 13, 1841, ibid., 126.
14. There is a comprehensive description of maps of the northeastern

NOTES TO PAGES 342-43

boundary at the time of the Ashburton negotiations in Hunter Miller, ed., *Treaties and Other International Acts of the United States of America,* 8 vols. (Washington, D.C., 1931–48), IV, 403–13.

15. Sparks to DW, Feb. 15, 1842, Harvard University, F16/21582. Franklin had written his letter to Count de Vergennes, who was chiefly interested in the new boundary in the West and South. The map that Sparks copied was published by d'Anville in 1746, and later research has indicated that it is not the one marked by Franklin. It showed a line well down from Canada, probably as claimed by the French against the British before they lost their colonies in that area in 1763; Miller, *Treaties,* IV, 406. The peace commissioners in 1782 used a Mitchell map, 1775 edition.

16. DW to Sparks, March 4, 1842, Harvard University, F17/21777. In Miller, *Treaties,* III, there is a copy of the Steuben map in a pocket at the back cover and a discussion of the map on pp. 338–40, 350–51. General von Steuben had bequeathed the map to his secretary, John W. Mulligan, and died in 1794. In 1838 Mulligan sold it to Webster, who gave it to Charles Daveis, a Maine boundary agent, and then bought it back in 1841 with State Department funds. There was no documentation to prove that it was used at the peace table in 1782.

17. Sparks to DW, May 16, 1842, Harvard University, F17/22471; DW to Sparks, May 16, 1842, ibid., F17/22464.

18. Sparks to DW, May 19, 1842, ibid., F17/22498.

19. DW to Fletcher Webster, May 21, 1842, WPNH, F17/22513.

20. Text of Ashburton-Aberdeen correspondence from Aberdeen Papers, British Library Add. MSS. 42123, in Samuel F. Bemis, *John Quincy Adams and the Foundations of American Foreign Policy* (New York, 1956), 585–88.

21. Bemis, *Adams and Foreign Policy,* 588, concludes that "we may guess that Ashburton had handed the money over to Webster with only a general assurance that it would help out." After reviewing the evidence, Howard Jones, *Webster-Ashburton Treaty,* 128–32, finds no proof that Webster sold the Sparks information to Ashburton or that he handled any of the fourteen thousand dollars. Possibly Thomas Grattan, a British consul with a close connection to the Maine commissioners, may have been involved. But in his *Civilized America,* 2 vols. (London, 1859), I, 384–401, he rather convincingly denies knowing about the Sparks map while negotiations were in progress; if this is true, whatever he may have done with any of Ashburton's money did not relate to that map. Ashburton less convincingly said that he did not see the Sparks map until he had signed the treaty in August; Ashburton to Aberdeen, Aug. 9, 1842, cited in Wilbur Jones, *American Problem,* 488–89. Merk and Merk, *Fruits of Propaganda,* 70–72, is a reliable reference on this entire question. Their conclusion is that the fourteen thousand was somehow used to influence Maine but that it is impossible to tell to whom Ashburton gave it. In any event, they believe both Webster and Ashburton were "undoubtedly guilty of improper use of secret funds in this case."

22. Text of message of May 18 in Washington *National Intelligencer,* May 25, 1842.

23. Ibid., May 30, 1842. Copy of legislative resolutions, May 26, 1842, Misc. Letters, SDNA.

24. Grattan, *Civilized America,* I, 365–66.

25. Ibid., 366-68.

26. Everett Papers, F17/22246. See also notes of April 26 and 28, ibid., F17/22269 and 22292.

27. DW to Everett, June 14, 1842, ibid., F17/22684. In this letter Webster responded to Everett's repeated reference to probable evidence in the form of maps in London favorable to the American claim. He asked Everett to *"forbear to press the search after Maps in England or elsewhere. Our strength is on the letter of the treaty."* This request shows that his own use of maps was intended for persuasion of Americans in Maine or Washington, not for negotiating with Ashburton. See the following letters from Everett to DW, reporting conversations with Aberdeen: May 17, F17/22479; May 19, F17/22491; June 16, F17/22700; June 30, F17/22782; all in Everett Papers.

28. Howard Jones, *Webster-Ashburton Treaty*, 118, 120-21; Ashburton to Aberdeen, April 25, 1842, in William R. Manning, ed., *Diplomatic Correspondence of the United States: Canadian Relations, 1784-1860*, 4 vols. (Washington, D.C., 1943), III, 704-9.

29. Aberdeen to Ashburton, May 26, 1842, in Manning, *Diplomatic Correspondence: Canadian*, III, 711-13; also July 2, cited in Wilbur Jones, "Lord Ashburton and the Maine Boundary Negotiations," *Mississippi Valley Historical Review*, 40 (Dec. 1953), 485.

30. Ashburton to DW, June 17, 1842 [presented June 21], in Manning, *Diplomatic Correspondence: Canadian*, III, 727-33. See also earlier statement of June 13, 1842, ibid., 722-26.

31. William Preble et al. to DW, June 29, 1842, ibid., 734-43; Edward Kent to DW, July 4, 1842, WPLC, F17/22819.

32. For Webster's pessimism and belief that instructions hampered Ashburton, see DW to Edward Everett, June 28, 1842, Everett Papers, F17/22771; DW to Fletcher Webster, July 3, 1842, WPNH, F17/22815; DW to Benjamin W. Leigh, July 7, 1842, University of Virginia Library, F17/22823.

33. Ashburton to DW, July 1, 1842, WPLC, F17/22802.

34. DW to Ashburton, July 8, 1842, *WS*, XIV, 392-402.

35. Ashburton to Aberdeen, June 29, 1842, in Manning, *Diplomatic Correspondence: Canadian*, III, 744-45.

36. Ashburton to DW, July 11, 1842, ibid., 746-52. The minister sent Webster the letter, dated the eleventh, on the tenth and asked him to return it if he found anything objectionable; WPLC, F17/22856.

37. Ashburton to Aberdeen, July 13, 1842, quoted in Wilbur Jones, "Ashburton and Maine," 487.

38. DW to Maine commissioners, July 15, 1842, *WS*, XI, 276-79. He now also asked the congressmen from New Hampshire to approve the proposed boundary affecting their state; Domestic Letters, XXXII, 372, SDNA.

39. Massachusetts commissioners to DW, July 20, 1842, in Manning, *Diplomatic Correspondence: Canadian*, III, 756-58.

40. Maine commissioners to DW, July 22, 1842, ibid., 759-65. News of agreement now reached the public; Washington *National Intelligencer*, July 25, 1842.

41. Ashburton to DW, July 16, 1842, in Manning, *Diplomatic Correspondence: Canadian*, III, 735-55; DW to Ashburton, July 25, 1842, WPNH, F17/22981;

Thomas Le Duc, "The Webster-Ashburton Treaty and the Minnesota Iron Ranges," *Journal of American History,* 51 (Dec. 1964), 476–81. Drafted by Webster, Tyler's message to Congress transmitting the treaty hinted at the possibility of iron deposits. The area, he said, was "considered valuable as a mineral region"; *WS,* XII, 25.

42. DW to Ashburton, July 27, 1842, *WS,* XI, 282–88; Ashburton to DW, July 29, 1842, ibid., 288–89.

43. The calculation is based upon the sum of $150,000 given to Maine and Massachusetts each (raised from the earlier figure of $125,000). The loss of land to Maine, on the basis of the Dutch award, was one-half of 893 square miles, or about 285,000 acres. In a letter of June 11, 1842, the survey commissioner, Professor James Renwick of Columbia, told Webster this land was then being sold for fifty cents an acre; WPNH, F17/22672. Despite Ashburton's objection, Webster included an article in the treaty on federal compensation to the states, though agreeing in a note that the British government had no responsibility on the matter; *WS,* XI, 289–90.

44. Despatches, Great Britain, passim, SDNA.

45. DW to Everett, April 26, 1842, Everett Papers, F17/22270.

46. DW to Lewis Cass, April 25, 1842, Cass Papers, Clements Library, University of Michigan, F17/22243.

47. DW to Charles H. Bell and John Paine, April 30, 1842, Domestic Letters, XXXII, 306–7, SDNA; Bell and Paine to DW, May 10, 1842, Misc. Letters, SDNA.

48. Through the next two decades, the United States did not maintain a force as large as promised, partially because the presidential administrations were not interested. In 1862 it agreed with Britain upon mutual search of suspected slavers; Hugh G. Soulsby, *The Right of Search and the Slave Trade in Anglo-American Relations, 1814–1862* (Baltimore, 1933), 118–76.

49. Howard Jones, *Webster-Ashburton Treaty,* 139–42.

50. Here Tyler made some suggestions, which Webster incorporated in his note; Tyler to DW, Aug. 1, 1842, WPNH, F17/23089; three-page Tyler draft, undated, WPLC, F17/23070.

51. DW to Ashburton, Aug. 8, 1842, *WS,* XI, 318–25.

52. Ashburton to DW, ibid., 326–28.

53. Though not demanding outright the slaves' return, Webster did contend that according to the rule of comity of nations Britain ought to have followed this course; Everett and Aberdeen were exchanging views on the *Creole* for months and found little common ground. See, for example, Aberdeen to Everett, April 18, 1842, enclosed in Everett to DW, May 2, 1842, Despatches, Great Britain, SDNA; Everett to DW, July 18, 1842, Everett Papers, F17/22916.

54. DW to Ashburton, Aug. 1, 1842, *WS,* XI, 303–12.

55. Ashburton to DW, July 31, 1842, WPNH, F17/23061; Tyler to DW, Aug. 7, 1842, WPLC, F17/23112. Attorney General Hugh Legaré told Webster on July 29, 1842, that Tyler was worried that the *Creole* issue was not being handled satisfactorily; Webster-Healy Papers, Massachusetts Historical Society, F17/23027.

56. Ashburton to DW, Aug. 6, 1842, *WS,* XI, 313–17; DW to Ashburton, Aug. 8, 1842, ibid., 317–18.

57. In 1853 the commission, with Joshua Bates of the House of Baring as arbiter, awarded the owners of the *Creole* $110,000 because Britain had not fulfilled its obligation to afford shelter to a ship in distress; Howard Jones, *Webster-Ashburton Treaty,* 150.

58. See the preceding chapter for a discussion of the political and legal problems. Governor Seward of New York wrote Tyler on June 4, 1842, that he hoped there would be an agreement on extradition; Misc. Letters, SDNA.

59. Ashburton to Aberdeen, April 25, 1842, in Manning, *Diplomatic Correspondence: Canadian,* III, 703–4; and April 28, 1842, ibid., 710; Everett to DW, April 15, 1842, Despatches, Great Britain, SDNA.

60. DW to Joseph Story, April 9, 1842, Story Papers, Massachusetts Historical Society, F17/22101; Story to DW, April 19, 1842, WPNH, F17/22221.

61. Of course, the mutineers of the *Creole* were also accused of murder, an extraditable crime under the new treaty.

62. DW to Ashburton, July 27, 1842, *WS,* XI, 292–94; Ashburton to DW, July 28, 1842, ibid., 294–301. Tyler had read a draft of Ashburton's note and unsuccessfully recommended payment of reparations; Tyler to DW, July 26, [1842], WPLC, F17/23009, and Aug. 3, 1842, ibid., F17/23100.

63. DW to Ashburton, Aug. 6, 1842, *WS,* XI, 301–3.

64. At the last minute, in a letter to Webster on August 8, Tyler suggested that there be a separate treaty on each subject, lest opposition to the extradition article kill the whole effort; WPNH, F17/23130.

65. The text of the treaty is in Miller, *Treaties,* IV, 363–70.

66. This treaty may have helped bring about a compromise on Oregon a few years later. Webster and Ashburton gave that issue only casual attention at the moment. For a favorable assessment of the negotiation of the treaty, see the editorial discussion in *WP: Diplomatic,* I, 483–86.

21. Diplomacy and Politics

1. Washington *National Intelligencer,* Aug. 20 and 26, Sept. 2, 1842.

2. Ibid., Sept. 6 and 22, 1842; Allan Nevins, ed., *The Diary of Philip Hone, 1828–1851,* 2 vols. (New York, 1927), II, 143.

3. Ashburton to DW, Sept. 3, 1842, WPNH, F18/23337.

4. James D. Richardson, ed., *A Compilation of the Messages and Papers of the Presidents, 1789–1897,* 10 vols. (Washington, D.C., 1897), IV, 162–69; DW to Edward Everett, Oct. 30, 1851, *WS,* XVIII, 482–83, for his recollection that he wrote the message.

5. Text of Rives's speech in *Congressional Globe,* 27th Cong., 3d sess., app. 59–67. This appendix reports the debate on ratification, made public at the next session of Congress. On ratification, see also George T. Curtis, *Life of Daniel Webster,* 2 vols. (New York, 1870), II, 133–37; and Howard Jones, *To the Webster-Ashburton Treaty: A Study in Anglo-American Relations, 1783–1843* (Chapel Hill, 1977), 161–66.

6. In the early years of the republic, executive sessions of the Senate often remained secret. Even so, reports of many were leaked or later published by order of the Senate; in this instance, both happened.

7. Benton's speech is in *Congressional Globe,* 27th Cong., 3d sess., 1–27. See

p. 16 for his discussion of the Franklin-Sparks and the Franklin-Jefferson maps. On the latter, he pointed out that there was, besides a red line corresponding to the Sparks, a dotted line farther north and doubtless the true line. Rives and Calhoun scoffed at this notion in a substantial rebuttal on the map question; ibid., 50–51, 61.

8. See Thomas H. Benton, *Thirty Years' View*, 2 vols. (New York, 1856), II, 420–56, for his own account and critique of the treaty from beginning to end.

9. *Congressional Globe*, 27th Cong., 3d sess., 49–53.

10. Reuel Williams to John Fairfield, Aug. 21, 1842, Fairfield Papers, Library of Congress, box 1828–1844; Edward Kent to DW, Jan. 4, [1843], WPLC, F16/21230; Washington *National Intelligencer*, Aug. 2, 1842, and March 29, 1843. Governor John Fairfield later complained about the treaty in Senate debates of 1846; *Congressional Globe*, 29th Cong., 1st sess., 644–47.

11. DW to Jeremiah Mason, Aug. 21, 1842, WS, XVIII, 146; DW to William Rives, [Aug. 21, 1842], Rives Papers, Library of Congress, F17/23236; DW to Edward Everett, Aug. 22, 1842, WS, XIV, 405.

12. DW to Tyler, [Aug. 21, 1842], WPNH, F17/23238.

13. DW to Cass, Aug. 29, 1842, WS, XII, 41–42.

14. Copy of Cass to DW, Oct. 3, 1842, Rives Papers, F18/23509.

15. DW to Cass, Nov. 14, 1842, WS, XII, 43–52.

16. DW to Cass, Dec. 20, 1842, ibid., 56–64. For the president's views, see Tyler to DW, [Dec. 1842], WPLC, F18/24013.

17. The Webster-Cass correspondence appears in the Washington *National Intelligencer*, March 18, 21, 23, and 28, 1842, and more fully in *WP: Diplomatic*, I, 710–75.

18. DW draft editorial, Webster Folder, Personal (Miscellaneous) Papers, New York Public Library, F18/24421, appearing in Washington *National Intelligencer*, Feb. 27, 1843; DW to Jared Sparks, March 18, 1843, Harvard University, F18/24309. Many of the sources, as well as editorial comment, on the so-called battle of the maps in the aftermath of the Ashburton negotiations are available in *WP: Diplomatic*, I, 775–95.

19. Sparks to DW, Feb. 8, 1843, WPDC, F18/24309.

20. DW to Sparks, Feb. 15, 1843, Webster Papers, Harvard University, F18/24365; Sparks to DW, Feb. 21, 1843, George J. Abbot Papers, Yale University Library, F18/24388; and Feb. 22, 1843, WPLC, F18/24392; DW to Sparks, March 11, 1843, Webster Papers, Harvard University, F18/24619; Sparks to DW, March 30, 1843, WPLC, F18/24782; Francis Bowen to DW, March 27, 1843, WPDC, F18/24746; and DW to Bowen, April 2, 1843, Webster Papers, Harvard University, F18/24822.

21. Jared Sparks, "The Treaty of Washington," *North American Review*, 56 (April 1843), 452–96. At the time, Sparks and Webster did not know about the Oswald map just then revealed to Parliament. Engish maps, published in 1783 when the treaty of independence was approved, upheld the later American view; and it was only after 1783 that maps pubished in Britain showed a version such as that country would advance. Sparks said nothing about the impact of the Franklin map upon Maine as a result of his own journey there before negotiations. And all that he said about its effect upon the Maine commissioners in Washington was that they were "influenced to a considerable extent."

22. Washington *National Intelligencer,* April 19, 1843, carried a full account of the meeting. Gallatin's speech in "A Memoir of the North-Eastern Boundary in Connexion with Mr. Jay's Map," *Proceedings of the New York Historical Society, 1843* (New York, 1844), 5–53. There is a facsimile of Jay's map here.

23. DW's speech in Gallatin, "North-Eastern Boundary," 54–68, and in *WS,* III, 143–53.

24. Washington *National Intelligencer,* Jan. 26 and Feb. 9, 1843, reprinted some of Palmerston's articles published in the London *Chronicle* in September 1842. Webster wrote an editorial, appearing in the Washington *Madisonian,* criticizing Palmerston's arguments; Curtis, *Webster,* II, 147–49. Everett's glowing reports of English opinion favoring the treaty are in the following letters to Webster: Sept. 1, 1842, Everett Papers, Massachusetts Historical Society, F18/23355; Sept. 19 and Oct. 17, 1842, Despatches, Great Britain, SDNA.

25. *Hansard's Parliamentary Debates* 3d ser. (London, 1843), LXVII, 247–48, 1162–1252, 1290–99. The map that Sparks erroneously thought Franklin had marked was a D'Anville publication of 1746, but the negotiators of 1782 used a Mitchell of 1775. In the 1930s, Lawrence Martin and Samuel F. Bemis found a convincing map in the archives in Madrid, with a boundary marked by the Spanish minister to France in 1782 as he had learned of it and as later claimed by the Americans; Hunter Miller, ed., *Treaties and Other International Acts of the United States of America,* 8 vols. (Washington, D.C., 1931–48), IV, 412–13.

26. DW to Everett, Dec. 29, 1842, Everett Papers, F18/23968; Everett to DW, Jan. 31, 1843, ibid., F18/24209; Feb. 10, 1843, ibid., F18/24332; March 28, 1843, ibid., F18/24750; March 31, 1843, ibid., F18/24805.

27. DW to Everett, April 25, 1843, WPLC, F18/24936.

28. Tyler to DW, Oct. 11, 1841, Lyon G. Tyler, *Letters and Times of the Tylers,* 2 vols. (Richmond, 1884–85), II, 254–55; DW to Waddy Thompson, April 5, 1842, *WS,* XII, 101–14, and June 27, 1842, WPNH, F17/22754; George L. Rives, *The United States and Mexico, 1821–1848,* 2 vols. (New York, 1913), I, 508–11, 516–24.

29. Lawrence to DW, July 30, 1842, printed in Curtis, *Webster,* II, 131; Mills to DW, July 28, 1842, WPNH, F17/23021.

30. Everett to DW, Sept. 1, 1842, Everett Papers, F18/23349; Mason to DW, Aug. 28, 1842, WPNH, F17/23317.

31. DW to Everett, Aug. 25, 1842, Everett Papers, F17/23293.

32. DW to John P. Healy, Aug. 26, 1842, Webster-Healy Papers, Massachusetts Historical Society, F17/23306. A previous letter to Healy, Aug. 24, 1842, avoided personal aspersions and was published in the press after the fall elections; ibid., F17/23278; Washington *National Intelligencer,* Dec. 3, 1842.

33. Report of proceedings in Boston *Advertiser,* Sept. 15, 1842; Kinley J. Brauer, "The Webster-Lawrence Feud: A Study in Politics and Ambitions," *Historian,* 29 (Nov. 1966), 34–59. Lawrence would have liked to succeed Davis as governor if the latter were subsequently elected vice-president.

34. Printed invitation to DW by Harrison G. Otis et al., Sept. 8, 1842, Gideon Welles Papers, Library of Congress, F18/23395-a.

35. DW to Charles P. Curtis, Sept. 15, 1842, *WS,* XVI, 383, and Sept. 17, 1842, WPLC, F18/23444; DW to Fletcher Webster, Sept. 23, 1842, WPNH, F18/23451.

36. Curtis, *Webster,* II, 143-46, is an interesting account because the author was present. The Boston *Advertiser,* Oct. 1, 1842, is a full report. Webster's notes of two pages with headings and key ideas are in his papers at Harvard University, F18/23482.

37. *WS,* III, 124-29.

38. DW to Fletcher Webster, Oct. 2, 1842, WPNH, F18/23501.

39. Washington *National Intelligencer,* Nov. 2 and 7, 1842.

40. Nevins, *Hone,* II, 627-30. Hone reputedly gave the name Whig to the political party in the early 1830s.

41. DW to Fletcher Webster, Oct. 19, 1842, WPNH, F18/23590.

42. Brauer, "Webster-Lawrence Feud," 44-45; Arthur B. Darling, *Political Changes in Massachusetts, 1824-1848* (New Haven, 1925), 302-11.

43. DW to Edward Everett, Nov. 28, 1842, Everett Papers, F18/23779.

44. DW to Harriette Paige, Nov. 18, 1842, *WS,* XVIII, 152.

45. Washington *National Intelligencer,* Nov. 23, 1842, referring also to item in Washington *Globe.*

46. DW draft editorials, *WS,* XV, 159-61, 162-65, appearing in the *Madisonian,* Dec. 3 and 6, 1842.

47. DW draft editorial, [Jan. 1843?], *WS,* XV, 185-88. Though there is no indication on the manuscript in what newspaper this appeared, it probably was the *Madisonian.*

48. DW to Everett, Aug. 25, 1842, Everett Papers, F17/23293; Nov. 28, 1842, ibid., F18/23779.

49. Everett to DW, Sept. 16, 1842, ibid., F18/23423; Sept. 16, 1842, ibid., F18/23437; Oct. 1, 1842, ibid., F18/23488; Oct. 17, 1842, ibid., F18/23568. For Everett's complaints to his friends back home about Webster's idea of taking over the Oregon negotiatons, see Claude M. Fuess, *Daniel Webster,* 2 vols. (Boston, 1930), II, 126; also Everett to Peter Brooks in Paul R. Frothingham, *Edward Everett: Orator and Statesman* (Boston, 1925), 229; to Robert Winthrop, May and June 1842, ibid., 233.

50. DW to Everett, Jan. 29, 1843, Everett Papers, F18/24179.

51. Everett to DW, Feb. 27, 1843, ibid., F18/24430.

52. DW to Robert Letcher, Feb. 21, 1843, John J. Crittenden Papers, Duke University Library, F18/24382.

53. DW to Caleb Cushing, Feb. 24, 1843, Caleb Cushing Papers, Library of Congress, F18/24396; Tyler to DW, Feb. 26, 1843, WPLC, F18/24417; Samuel F. Bemis, *John Quincy Adams and the Union* (New York, 1956), 483-85.

54. DW to Everett, March 20, 1843, Everett Papers, F18/24708; March 29, 1843, Peel Papers, British Library, F18/24772.

55. Richardson, *Papers of the Presidents,* IV, 213-14.

56. In an undated note to Webster, Tyler asked if Everett would like to go to China; WPLC, mounting no. 18109. Webster first mentioned the idea to Everett on January 29, 1843, Everett Papers, F18/24179.

57. DW to Everett, March 10, 1843, Everett Papers, F18/24597.

58. DW to Thomas B. Curtis, March 12, 1843, Cushing Papers, F18/24626.

59. Everett to DW, April 3 and 18, 1843, Everett Papers, F18/24629 and 24889.

60. DW to Cushing, March 27, 1843, Montague Collection, New York Public Library, F18/24742. A detailed description of the background of the mission and of the preceding correspondence between Everett and Cushing

are in Claude M. Fuess, *The Life of Caleb Cushing,* 2 vols. (New York, 1923), I, 399–411. Fuess also gives an account of the mission itself, culminating in a treaty of 1844.

61. Fuess, *Cushing,* I, 421; copy of instructions, Cushing Papers, F19/25045.

62. DW to Tyler, May 8, 1843, WPLC, F19/25057; Tyler to DW, same date, ibid., F19/25063.

63. DW draft editorial, F19/25082, published in revised form in Washington *National Intelligencer,* May 13, 1843. In Massachusetts, the administration was favoring Calhounite Democrats David Henshaw and Robert Rantoul instead of the former Whig power brokers.

22. Whig Problems

1. DW To Tyler, Aug. 29, 1843, Webster-Healy Papers, Massachusetts Historical Society, F19/25330.

2. Tyler to DW, July 18, 1843, Morristown (N.J.) National Historical Park, F19/25299, in response to Webster's letter of July 3, in George T. Curtis, *Life of Daniel Webster,* 2 vols. (New York, 1870), II, 212.

3. DW draft editorial, Webster Folder, Personal (Miscellaneous) Papers, New York Public Library, F19/25586, for Washington *National Intelligencer,* Jan. 18, 1844.

4. Ketchum to DW, Feb. 29, [1844], WPDC, F19/25716. As late as February 9, 1845, Tyler invited Webster and his family to dinner; WPNH, F19/26137.

5. William R. Brock, *Parties and Political Conscience: American Dilemmas, 1840–1850* (Millwood, N.Y., 1979), 116–18; *WS,* XIII, 150–71, 183–92.

6. Robert F. Dalzell, Jr., *Daniel Webster and the Trial of American Nationalism, 1843–1852* (Boston, 1973), 77–78.

7. Text of speech, *WS,* III, 159–85; text of speech and description of setting in Boston *Advertiser* and Boston *Courier,* Nov. 10, 1843. DW revisions of text for pamphlet edition, written on clippings of *Courier,* Miscellaneous MSS, American Antiquarian Society, F19/25423.

8. Letcher to DW, Oct. 2, 1843, WPLC, F19/25367; DW to Letcher, Oct. 23, 1843, John J. Crittenden Papers, Duke University Library, F19/25395; Letcher to DW, Nov. 17, 1843, WPDC, F19/25415.

9. Porter to Clay, Oct. 11 and 13, 1843, in Calvin Colton, ed., *The Private Correspondence of Henry Clay* (Cincinnati, 1856), 478–79; DW to Hiram Ketchum, Dec. 2, 1843, WPDC, F19/25490; Nicholas Biddle to DW, Oct. 9, 1843, and Jan. 9, 1844, Biddle Papers, Library of Congress, F19/25380 and 25577.

10. DW to John Haven, Jan. 3, 1844, *WS,* XII, 217–20, replying to Simeon Veazey to DW, Sept. 30, 1843, WPNH, F19/25349.

11. DW to Hiram Ketchum, Nov. 28 [1843], WPDC, F19/25475; DW to Thomas B. Curtis, Jan. 17, 1844, Webster Papers, Massachusetts Historical Society, F19/25583; DW to Severn Wallis et al., April 29, 1844, WPDC, F19/25804.

12. George R. Poage, *Henry Clay and the Whig Party* (Chapel Hill, 1936), 111.

13. DW to Franklin Haven, April 30, 1844, Webster Papers, Harvard Uni-

versity, F19/25815; Allan Nevins, ed., *The Diary of Philip Hone, 1828-1851*, 2 vols. (New York, 1927), II, 695-99.

14. Text of speech, *WS*, XIII, 196-202; Hone, *Diary*, II, 699.

15. DW to Robert P. Letcher, July 5, 1844, Crittenden Papers, F19/25877.

16. An excellent, compact history of the election is Charles G. Sellers, in Arthur M. Schlesinger, Jr., and Fred L. Israel, eds., *History of American Presidential Elections, 1789-1968*, 4 vols. (New York, 1971), I, 747-98, from which some of the description here is drawn.

17. Caroline Webster to Mrs. Jeremiah Mason, Sept. [5, 1844], Mason Papers, New Hampshire Historical Society, F19/25946. The correspondence on invitations to speak is in F19 passim.

18. The reports of speeches, upon which the following discussion is based, are: Boston, May 9, *WS*, XIII, 203-11; Portsmouth, May 17, ibid., 212-15; Trenton, late May, ibid., 216-38; Boston, July 4, ibid., 238-39; Springfield, Mass., Aug. 9, ibid., 242-51; Albany, Aug. 27, ibid., III, 219-48; Taunton, Mass., Sept. 10, ibid., XIII, 252-53; Boston, Sept. 19, ibid., 254-69; Philadelphia, Oct. 1, ibid., III, 253-73; Valley Forge, Oct. 3, ibid., 277-93; New York, Oct. 9, ibid., XIII, 270-75; Pepperell, Mass., Nov. 5, ibid., 276-300; Boston, Nov. 8, ibid., 301-5.

19. DW to Edward Everett, Dec. 15, 1844, Everett Papers, Massachusetts Historical Society, F19/26022; DW to Chandler Robbins, Nov. 20, 1844, George B. McClellan Papers, Library of Congress, F19/25994; DW to Edward Curtis, Sept. 1 [1844], WPDC, F19/25935. Clay had softened his earlier declaration on Texas by writing the so-called Alabama letters.

20. DW to John P. Healy, Feb. 1, 1844, Webster-Healy Papers, F19/25643; DW to Jeremiah Mason, Feb. 6, 1844, *WS*, XVI, 424-25; Kinley J. Brauer, "The Webster-Lawrence Feud: A Study in Politics and Ambitions," *Historian*, 29 (Nov. 1966), 46-48.

21. DW to Richard M. Blatchford, Dec. 23, 1844, WPDC, F19/26031.

22. He would draw an annuity from the fund.

23. Boston *Advertiser*, Jan. 15-17, 1845. The house vote was 186 for Webster and 64 for Marcus Morton; the senate voted for Webster unanimously; Claude M. Fuess, *Daniel Webster*, 2 vols. (Boston, 1930), II, 149 n. 1.

24. Glyndon G. Van Deusen, *The Jacksonian Era, 1828-1848* (New York, 1959), 177-80, 183, 186.

25. Kinley J. Brauer, *Cotton versus Conscience: Massachusetts Whig Politics and Southwestern Expansion, 1843-1848* (Lexington, Ky., 1967), 84-85, 88-89; Thomas H. O'Connor, *The Lords of the Loom: The Cotton Whigs and the Coming of the Civil War* (New York, 1968), 65.

26. Webster wrote the letter to Bigelow et al. on January 23; DW draft, WPNH, F19/25597. Then on March 13, he told Charles Allen to publish it; George F. Hoar Papers, Massachusetts Historical Society, F19/25745. It was published in the Boston *Advertiser*, March 19, 1844, and in other newspapers. Text also in *WS*, XVI, 418-23.

27. Marshall did what Webster argued could not be done. He inferred the power from the treaty and war clauses of the Constitution, and he used principles of international law to do so; 1 Peters 511 (1828).

28. DW to Charles Allen, March 13, 1844, George F. Hoar Papers, F19/25499.

29. Washington *National Intelligencer,* March 16, 1844; Brauer, *Cotton versus Conscience,* 65–66.

30. DW to Winthrop, March 20, 1844, *WS,* XVI, 426.

31. See reminiscence of George Ticknor in Curtis, *Webster,* II, 230–35.

32. DW to Robert Winthrop, April 28, 1844, Winthrop Papers, Massachusetts Historical Society, F19/25797.

33. *WS,* III, 270.

34. DW to Robert Winthrop, Dec. 13, 1844, and Jan. 11, 1845, Winthrop Papers, F19/26018 and 26069.

35. DW to Robert Winthrop, Jan. 10, 1845, ibid., F19/26066; DW to Charles Allen, Jan. 20, 1845, George F. Hoar Papers, F19/26077; Brauer, *Cotton versus Conscience,* 115–19.

36. *WS,* XV, 192–203; Allen's part of address on pp. 203–12.

37. Brauer, *Cotton versus Conscience,* 120–25; Boston *Advertiser,* Jan. 30, 31, and Feb. 3, 1845. Lawrence and Appleton did not attend the convention, but other conservatives did.

38. DW to Samuel H. Walley, March 8, 1845, Miscellaneous MSS, New York Historical Society, F19/26199; and other correspondence through the year, F19 passim.

39. Brauer, *Cotton versus Conscience,* 135–58.

40. DW to Nathan Appleton, Aug. 8, 1845, *WS,* XVI, 436–37; Appleton to DW, Sept. 11, 1845, Appleton Papers, Massachusetts Historical Society, F19/26439; DW to Appleton, Sept. 11, 1845, WPNH, F19/26443.

41. *WS,* IX, 55–59.

42. *Congressional Globe,* 29th Cong., 1st sess., 93.

23. Expansion

1. David M. Pletcher, *The Diplomacy of Annexation; Texas, Oregon, and the Mexican War* (Columbia, Mo., 1973), 237–41. Polk did not say *all* of Oregon, but that is the way it was interpreted. In his message to Congress in December, he referred to the Monroe Doctrine in resisting British expansion; ibid., 306–8.

2. DW to Edward Everett, Jan. 29, 1844, Everett Papers, Massachusetts Historical Society, F19/25620; DW to Franklin Haven, Feb. 2, [1845], Harvard University, F19/26118.

3. Speech in Faneuil Hall, Nov. 7, 1845, *WS,* XIII, 318.

4. *Congressional Globe,* 29th Cong., 1st sess., 54–57; Pletcher, *Diplomacy of Annexation,* 320. The Cass resolutions passed unanimously.

5. DW to Nathan Appleton, Jan. 20, 1846, Appleton Papers, Massachusetts Historical Society, F20/26633. Polk had offered a compromise at forty-nine degrees in July 1845, but the British minister had rejected it, whereupon the president reverted to a broader claim. See Pletcher, *Diplomacy of Annexation,* 247–49.

6. DW to David Sears, Jan. 17, 1846, *WS,* XVIII, 215. Webster was probably right that Polk did not think much about the long-range possibility of war in his diplomacy of bluff, which shifted to meet the situation immediately at hand.

7. *Congressional Globe,* 29th Cong., 1st sess., 430–32, 567–69; Albert D. Kir-

wan, *John J. Crittenden: The Struggle for the Union* (Lexington, Ky., 1962), 188–92. The fact that the debate on termination stretched out so long, instead of being brief, as Polk expected, weakened his hand; Pletcher, *Diplomacy of Annexation*, 318–51.

8. Pletcher, *Diplomacy of Annexation*, 402–17. Though England sent the offer before receiving formal notice, it knew that notice was coming—or the British ministry could have changed its mind later.

9. William M. Meigs, *The Life of Charles Jared Ingersoll* (Philadelphia, 1897), 247–90 and passim, is slightly useful for understanding Ingersoll's role.

10. *Congressional Globe,* 29th Cong., 1st sess., 343–45.

11. Ibid., 419.

12. DW to Tyler, March 5, 1846, WPNH, F20/26763; Tyler to DW, March 12, 1846, ibid., F20/26772. Before Tyler became president, Webster wrote Seward on March 17, 1841, subtly trying to persuade Seward to release McLeod; ibid., F14/18335. And there were other letters between Webster and Seward on the general problem of McLeod, not recalled by Tyler.

13. Seward to Blatchford, March 23, 1846, ibid., F20/26798.

14. DW to Cushing, March 28, 1846, Cushing Papers, Library of Congress, F20/26811; Cushing to DW, April 4, 1846, ibid., F20/26830; Samuel F. Bemis, *John Quincy Adams and the Union* (New York, 1956), 483–85. Tyler did recommend a special mission, but Adams' committee did not approve.

15. *Congressional Globe,* 29th Cong., 1st sess., 599.

16. The most accurate report of the speech is in *WS,* IX, 78–150; but see also *Congressional Globe,* 29th Cong., 1st sess., 609–11, 616–22, for exchanges with other senators and for Webster's personal allusions to Ingersoll.

17. *Congressional Globe,* 29th Cong., 1st sess., 620.

18. William Seward to Richard Blatchford, March 23, 1846, WPNH, F20/26798.

19. *Congressional Globe,* 29th Cong., 1st sess., 619.

20. Everett told Webster he may have overreacted; April 20, 1846, Everett Papers, F20/26852. George T. Curtis, *Daniel Webster,* 2 vols. (New York, 1870), II, 263, says that the angry passages of the speech were intentionally omitted from the early edition of his collected works. They are published, however, in *WS,* XIV, 294.

21. *Congressional Globe,* 29th Cong., 1st sess., 636, for Ingersoll's speech. The fact that Ingersoll was chairman of the Foreign Affairs Committee facilitated his access to the records.

22. Ibid., 637–43, 648–53, reports the debate.

23. The Constitution, Art. II, sec. 4, provides that civil officers of the United States can be impeached; and Art. I, sec. 4, provides as the penalty for conviction removal from office and disqualification from holding office. In the case of William Blount (1797–1799), the Senate decided it could not try one of its members on impeachment, but it did expel him; John C. Miller, *The Federalist Era: 1789–1801* (New York, 1960), 190–91. In the case of W. W. Belknap of 1876, the Senate decided that it could try the impeached secretary of war, who had resigned; William A. Dunning, *Reconstruction: Political and Economic, 1865–1877* (New York, 1907), 287–88. All things considered, one must agree with Adams that Webster could have been impeached for conduct during past service in the cabinet. But constitutional history shows that impeachable offenses have been redefinable by Congress, often influenced by politics. See

also Howard Jones, "The Attempt to Impeach Daniel Webster," *Capitol Studies*, 3 (Fall 1975), 31–44.

24. Milo M. Quaife, ed., *The Diary of James K. Polk, during His Presidency*, 4 vols. (Chicago, 1910), I, 328, 332–34.

25. Polk's message in *Congressional Globe*, 29th Cong., 1st sess., 698.

26. Speeches by Ingersoll and others, ibid., 699–701.

27. Ibid., 729–30.

28. Ibid., 733–35, 737.

29. DW to Edward Curtis, May 1, [1846], Montague Collection, New York Public Library, F20/26883; DW to Robert Winthrop, May 2, 1846, Winthrop Papers, Massachusetts Historical Society, F20/26885; DW to Fletcher Webster, May 5, [1846], Sang Collection, Brandeis University, F20/26901.

30. DW draft, "Mr. Ingersolls 3 charges," WPNH, F20/26869. Inefficiency and mistakes could have been the fault of clerks working under Webster, but there might have been fewer mistakes if the usual procedure had been followed of entrusting oversight to the disbursing agent rather than to the secretary of state himself. As for the expenditures from the secret fund, though there was no legal requirement that anything but presidential certificates (issued at his discretion) were needed, Tyler required more careful internal accounting by way of vouchers. It was this aspect that caused Webster his difficulty.

31. Testimony of Edward Stubbs, with documents, Records of House of Representatives, RG 233, National Archives, F40/55311–96, with statement by Stubbs, dated April 13, 1846. Much of this material was not printed. Webster had put up over two thousand dollars of his own money but later produced some vouchers, leaving his net out-of-pocket amount at a thousand.

32. *House Report 684*, 29th Cong., 1st sess., 11–35, for Smith's testimony and documents.

33. Extracts of Tyler's testimony, ibid., 8–11. Some testimony of the expresident was not printed and can be found in Records of the House, RG 233, F40/55303 ff.

34. *House Report 684*, 29th Cong., 1st sess., 1–5.

35. Ibid., 5–8, followed by testimony of Smith and some of Tyler, cited above. See also Frederick Merk and Lois B. Merk, *Fruits of Propaganda in the Tyler Administration* (Cambridge, Mass., 1971), 177–214, reproducing documents and discussing the committee's work.

36. *Congressional Globe*, 29th Cong., 1st sess., 946–48, 952, 988, 999–1000, for debate and voting on how much of the committee papers should be published. The other committee, investigating how Ingersoll got his information, reported testimony it had gathered but made no recommendation. The House tabled the report. The answer to the question had already been given by Ingersoll, who, with Stubbs's help, got access to State Department records; ibid., 966–67.

37. Pletcher, *Diplomacy of Annexation*, 352–92; Charles G. Sellers, *James K. Polk: Continentalist, 1843–1846* (New York, 1966), passim.

38. William R. Brock, *Parties and Political Conscience: American Dilemmas, 1840–1850* (Millwood, N.Y., 1979), 169–70; Irving H. Bartlett, *Daniel Webster* (New York, 1978), 228–29.

39. DW to Fletcher Webster, May 20, 1846, WPNH, F20/26969.

40. Speech in Senate, June 24, 1846, *WS*, IX, 156–60.

41. DW to Franklin Haven, May 28, 1846, Webster Papers, Harvard University, F20/26998; DW to Fletcher Webster, June 1 and 13, 1846, WPNH, F20/27023 and 27070.

42. DW to Peter Harvey, May 18, 1846, Sang Collection, F20/26960; DW to Franklin Haven, May 28, 1846, Harvard University, F20/26998.

43. Speeches in Senate, May 26, 1846, *WS*, XIV, 301–3, and June 5, 1846, *Congressional Globe,* 29th Cong., 1st sess., 927–31; DW to Sherrod Williams, [Jan. 1847], WPNH, F20/27575. The Constitution, Art. I, sec. 8, provides that the state militia can be called out to suppress insurrections and repel invasions; and the states have power of appointing officers of the militia.

44. Speech in Senate, June 24, 1846, *WS*, IX, 152–56.

45. Compact discussions of the Walker tariff in Charles M. Wiltse, *John C. Calhoun: Sectionalist* (Indianapolis, 1951), 266–72, and Sellers, *Polk: Continentalist,* 465–67.

46. Report of debates from July 13 to 28, 1846, in *Congressional Globe,* 29th Cong., 1st sess., 1081–84, 1089–90, 1095–96, 1102–3, 1112–13, 1139, 1141, 1144, 1153–58. For Whig cohesion and Webster's orthodoxy, see Joel H. Silbey, *The Shrine of Party: Voting Behavior, 1841–1852* (Pittsburgh, 1967), 73, 176, and passim.

47. DW to Nathan Appleton, July 8, 1846, Appleton Papers, F20/27150; *WS*, IX, 161–243, and XIV, 307–11, 313; Washington *National Intelligencer,* July 29, 1846, and March 13, 1847.

48. But treasury notes and drafts were used in large quantity and were not fully redeemable in specie.

49. DW to Franklin Haven, March 26, 1846, Webster Papers, Harvard University, F20/26838.

50. One of the depositories was the Merchants' Bank in Boston, whose president was Webster's intimate friend, Franklin Haven.

51. Speech in Senate, August 1, 1846, *WS*, IX, 245–51.

52. *Congressional Globe,* 29th Cong., 1st sess., 1176. The Independent Treasury lasted until the creation of the Federal Reserve in 1913.

53. David M. Potter, *The Impending Crisis, 1848–1861* (New York, 1976), 18–22; Chaplain W. Morrison, *Democratic Politics and Sectionalism: The Wilmot Proviso Controversy* (Chapel Hill, 1967), 3–20; *Congressonal Globe,* 29th Cong., 1st sess., 1217–18, 1220–21.

54. David Donald, *Charles Sumner and the Coming of the Civil War* (New York, 1960), 144–45, 148.

55. The account here is drawn primarily from Kinley J. Brauer, *Cotton versus Conscience: Massachusetts Whig Politics and Southwestern Expansion, 1843–1848* (Lexington, Ky., 1967), 190–94; and Martin Duberman, *Charles Francis Adams, 1807–1886* (Boston, 1960), 113–18.

56. *WS*, XIII, 328–29.

57. The Gracchi were popular reformers of ancient Rome.

58. *WS*, XIII, 330–41. The Constituton, Art. II, sec. 4, provides that civil officers can be removed for treason, bribery, and other high crimes and misdemeanors. Webster's prescription would rest on a broad interpretation, sometimes taken in history. In the state election, the Whig candidate, George Briggs, was elected governor.

59. Webster told his son Fletcher that the speech was being circulated as a

pamphlet; Dec. 10, 1846, WPNH, F20/27488. See *WS*, IV, 3-6, editorial note, drawing from an account of the dinner in this pamphlet. Also described in Allan Nevins, ed., *The Diary of Philip Hone, 1828-1851*, 2 vols. (New York, 1927), II, 780-81.

60. *WS*, IV, 7-56.

61. Text of resolutions, presented on February 15, 1847, in *Congressional Globe*, 29th Cong., 2d sess., 422. Winthrop presented a similar measure in the House, but it was rejected; Washington *National Intelligencer*, Feb. 23, 1847.

62. *Congressional Globe*, 29th Cong., 2d sess., 310, 545, and passim for recurring debate during February 1847; Robert F. Dalzell, Jr., *Daniel Webster and the Trial of American Nationalism, 1843-1852* (Boston, 1973), 128-31.

63. Text of speech, March 1, 1847, *WS*, IX, 253-61.

64. Text of Massachusetts resolution, ibid., 255.

65. *Congressional Globe*, 29th Cong., 2d sess., 556. Webster voted against the Three-Million Bill after the proviso failed. Apart from whatever validity Webster's argument for a no-acquisition policy had, it seemed the best way, in his opinion, to reconcile northern opposition to extending slavery with southern sensitivity about the proviso. If he were to get southern support for the presidency, he had to think of that. This factor would become ever clearer in the future.

24. Slavery in the West

1. DW to Fletcher Webster, April 25, 1847, WPNH, F20/27862.

2. DW to Caleb Cushing, June 18, 1847, Montague Collection, New York Public Library, F20/28034.

3. DW to William Paige, Feb. 26, 1847, Sang Collection, Brandeis University, F20/27677; DW to [Edward Curtis], April 24, 1847, Montague Collection, F20/27853.

4. *WS*, IV, 70, editorial note on trip; Claude M. Fuess, *Daniel Webster*, 2 vols. (Boston, 1930), II, 174-78.

5. There are a number of his letters in F20 passim describing his visits along the route—and many invitations to visit other places.

6. Speeches at Charleston, *WS*, IV, 73-92; speech at Savannah, ibid., 99-103.

7. Kinley J. Brauer, *Cotton versus Conscience: Massachusetts Whig Politics and Southwestern Expansion, 1843-1848* (Lexington, Ky., 1967), 218-19; Martin Duberman, *Charles Francis Adams, 1807-1886* (Boston, 1960), 126-27; David Donald, *Charles Sumner and the Coming of the Civil War* (New York, 1960), 157-59.

8. *WS*, XIII, 348-58, 363-64. He did say that opposition to war must be wise and constitutional, recognizing the principle of majority rule; ibid., 346-47. For his full view of the limits of dissent, see his letter to Fletcher Webster, April 24, 1847, Everett Papers, Massachusetts Historical Society, F20/27858.

9. *WS*, XIII, 359.

10. Duberman, *C. F. Adams*, 126-27.

11. Washington *National Intelligencer*, Jan. 31 and Feb. 7, 1848; DW to Richard M. Blatchford, Jan. 30, 1848, *WS*, XVI, 491-92; George T. Curtis, *Life of*

Daniel Webster, 2 vols. (New York, 1870), II, 335–36; DW to Fletcher Webster, May 25, 1848, WPNH, F21/28631. A state convention on April 5, 1848, declared for Clay but would accept the national convention's choice. Webster opened a friendly correspondence with Millard Fillmore, soon to be nominated for vice-president, on April 24, 1848; Fillmore Papers, State University of New York at Oswego, F21/28576.

12. The proceedings were reported in the Washington *National Intelligencer,* June 8–10 and 12, 1848. The votes on the first ballot were: Taylor, 111; Clay, 97; Scott, 43; Webster, 22; others, 6. Fourth ballot: Taylor, 171; Clay, 32; Scott, 63; Webster, 13 (including 11 of 12 Massachusetts votes). See also Curtis, *Webster,* II, 337–39.

13. Jean V. Matthews, *Rufus Choate: The Law and Civic Virtue* (Philadelphia, 1980), 170–72.

14. Washington *National Intelligencer,* June 12, 1848.

15. Writing to Richard Blatchford, June 10, 1848, Webster denied rumors he had interfered with Lawrence's nomination; Appleton Papers, Massachusetts Historical Society, F21/28685. Brauer, *Cotton versus Conscience,* 234–36, suggests that even if Webster did not try to interfere, the mere knowledge that Webster-Lawrence relations were strained may have caused delegates to fear that if Lawrence were nominated, Webster might not support the ticket. They might have thought so, but the main reason for Fillmore's selection was probably his greater acceptability to antislavery Whigs. That perception of his position on slavery was faulty; Robert J. Rayback, *Millard Fillmore: A Biography of a President* (Buffalo, 1959), 184–86.

16. Chaplain W. Morrison, *Democratic Politics and Sectionalism: The Wilmot Proviso Controversy* (Chapel Hill, 1967), 75–173; William R. Brock, *Parties and Conscience: American Dilemmas, 1840–1850* (Millwood, N.Y., 1979), 211–13.

17. Henry Wilson to DW, May 31, 1848, WPDC, F21/28652; Donald, *Sumner,* 169–70.

18. Washington *National Intelligencer,* June 16, 1848.

19. DW to Fletcher Webster, June 10, 1848, WPNH, F21/28690.

20. DW to Hiram Ketchum, June 11, 1848, WPDC, F21/28692.

21. Ashmun's letter to his constituents, Washington *National Intelligencer,* June 14, 1848; Robert C. Winthrop, Jr., *A Memoir of Robert C. Winthrop* (Boston, 1897), 82–83; Everett to DW, June 26, 1848, Everett Papers, F21/28735; Berrien to DW, June 16, 1848, WPLC, F21/28714.

22. Various items in Washington *National Intelligencer* in June 1848, including a clipping of Boston *Atlas,* June 13.

23. Report of meeting in Washington *National Intelligencer,* June 20 and 21, 1848.

24. DW to Fletcher Webster, [June 15, 1848], WPNH, F21/28703. See also letter of June 19, 1848, ibid., F21/28727.

25. Duberman, *C. F. Adams,* 141–42; Henry Wilson, *History of the Rise and Fall of the Slave Power in America,* 3 vols. (Boston, 1884), II, 147–49.

26. Brock, *Parties and Conscience,* 218–27.

27. DW to E. Rockwood Hoar, Aug, 23, 1848, George F. Hoar Papers, Massachusetts Historical Society, F21/28788, replying to DW, Aug. 13, 1848, WPDC, F21/28779; George F. Hoar, *Autobiography of Seventy Years,* 2 vols. (New York, 1903), I, 145–57.

28. John C. Fitzpatrick, ed., *The Autobiography of Martin Van Buren* (Washington, D.C., 1920), 536-39.

29. Unsigned article in New York *Commerical Advertiser*, clipped in Washington *National Intelligencer*, Aug. 4, 1848, probably written by Hiram Ketchum and no doubt reflecting Webster's views. It said the senator had decided to come out for Taylor. The article appeared during the sitting of the Free Soil party convention. See Edward Everett to DW, Aug. 4, 1848, Everett Papers, F21/28760.

30. *WS*, IV, 121-44. DW notes, Miscellaneous Bound MSS, Massachusetts Historical Society, F21/28814.

31. Speech at Abington, Mass., Oct. 9, 1848, *WS*, XIII, 366-80; speech in Faneuil Hall, Oct. 24, 1848, ibid., IV, 147-74.

32. Holman Hamilton, "Election of 1848," in Arthur M. Schlesinger, Jr., and Fred L. Israel, eds., *History of American Presidential Elections, 1789-1968*, 4 vols. (New York, 1971), II, 865-96. On Massachusetts, see p. 918.

33. DW to Richard Blatchford, Nov. 13, 1848, Montague Collection, F21/28887.

34. DW to Richard Blatchford, Dec. 5, 1848, *WS*, XVI, 502. Numerous letters from DW to Hiram Ketchum, Richard Blatchford, and Franklin Haven, from December 1848 through February 1849, F21 passim, show his close interest in what Taylor was going to do. The three were among those hoping he would go into the State Department.

35. Albert D. Kirwan, *John J. Crittenden: The Struggle for the Union* (Lexington, Ky., 1962), 200-23.

36. DW to Richard Blatchford, Feb. 25, 1849, WPLC, F21/29101.

37. DW to Fletcher Webster, March 26, 1849, WPNH, F21/29191; March 27, ibid., F21/29195; March 29, *WS*, XVI, 517-18; April 12, WPNH, F21/29303; and other letters of the time. See also DW to Thomas Ewing, May 1, 1849, with enclosed memorandum setting forth facts and arguments, ibid., F21/29392.

38. DW to Franklin Haven, June 15, 1849, Webster Papers, Harvard University, F21/29433, refers to Haven's appointment as assistant treasurer. On patronage generally, see DW to no addressee, June 24, 1849, WPDC, F21/29450.

39. *Senate Journal*, VII, 303-40. The Senate removed the secrecy of proceedings, though full speeches of senators were not reported. A report of proceedings and votes also appeared in the Washington *National Intelligencer*, June 10, 1848.

40. Speech on Ten Regiment Bill for reinforcing the army, March 17, 1848, *WS*, IX, 262-70; speech on loan bill, March 23, 1848, ibid., X, 3-33.

41. David M. Potter, *The Impending Crisis, 1848-1861* (New York, 1976), 69-76; Brock, *Parties and Conscience*, 210-11; Charles M. Wiltse, *John C. Calhoun: Sectionalist* (Indianapolis, 1951), 325-29, 348-53.

42. *WS*, X, 34-44; *Congressional Globe*, 30th Cong., 1st sess., 1060-61, 1077-80.

43. Potter, *Impending Crisis*, 82-83; *Congressional Globe*, 30th Cong., 2d sess., 259-60, 272-74; *WS*, XIV, 317-24. Webster relied upon the Constitution, Art. IV, sec. 3, para. 2, empowering Congress to regulate the territories. His argument resembled John Marshall's opinion in *American Insurance Co.* v. *Canter*, 1

Peters 511 (1828), in which he had been counsel. Calhoun referred to the Bill of Rights generally, but could have had in mind the Fifth Amendment, prohibiting Congress from depriving persons of property [in slaves] without due process of law. That was the ground of Taney's opinion in *Dred Scott* v. *Sandford,* 19 Howard 393 (1857).

44. *Congressional Globe,* 30th Cong., 2d sess., 392, 682-92.

25. Compromise

1. David M. Potter, *The Impending Crisis, 1848-1861* (New York, 1976), 83-89.

2. Ibid., 90; *Congressional Globe,* 31st Cong., 1st sess., 1-66. See Michael F. Holt, *The Political Crisis of the 1850s* (New York, 1978), for a study of parties.

3. James D. Richardson, ed., *A Compilation of the Messages and Papers of the Presidents, 1789-1897,* 10 vols. (Washington, D.C., 1897), V, 9-24; Holman Hamilton, *Prologue to Conflict: The Crisis and Compromise of 1850* (Lexington, Ky., 1963), 13-18.

4. Richardson, *Papers of the Presidents,* V, 27-30.

5. George T. Curtis, *Life of Daniel Webster,* 2 vols. (New York, 1870), II, 397-98.

6. *Congressional Globe,* 31st Cong., 1st sess., 244-47.

7. Ibid., app., 115-27.

8. DW to Franklin Haven, Jan. 13, 1850, Webster Papers, Harvard University, F22/29740.

9. Charles March to DW, Jan. 9, 1850, WPNH, F22/29728; Edward Everett to DW, Feb. 18, 1850, Everett Papers, Massachusetts Historical Society, F22/29829; and other correspondence of January and February in F22 passim.

10. Illustrative letter from Benjamin D. Silliman, March 5, 1850, WPNH, F22/29872; William Plumer, Jr., "Reminiscences of Daniel Webster," *WS,* XVII, 563.

11. See Curtis, *Webster,* II, 399-400 n. 1, for text of resolutions.

12. *Congressional Globe,* 31st Cong., 1st sess., 328-33.

13. W. H. Furness to DW, Jan. 9, 1850, WPNH, F22/29725; DW to Furness, Feb. 15, 1850, ibid., F22/29810.

14. DW to Peter Harvey, Feb. 13 and 14, 1850, Sang Collection, Brandeis University, F22/29804-5; DW to Edward Everett, Feb. 16, 1850, Everett Papers, F22/29818; *Congressional Globe,* 31st Cong., 1st sess., 375.

15. DW to Fletcher Webster, Feb. 24, 1850, Everett Papers, F22/29848.

16. DW to Charles H. Warren, March 1, 1850, Montague Collection, New York Public Library, F22/29858.

17. Ibid.

18. Charles M. Wiltse, *John C. Calhoun: Sectionalist* (Indianapolis, 1951), 459-60.

19. Waddy Thompson to DW, March 2, 1850, WPLC, F22/29864.

20. *Congressional Globe,* 31st Cong., 1st sess., 451-55.

21. Ibid., 476.

22. An observer, Samuel P. Lyman, published an account in *The Public and*

Private Life of Daniel Webster (Philadelphia, 1890), 154–60. Lyman said Webster had only brief notes in front of him; if so, he probably had drafted and studied the full notes, cited above, beforehand.

23. Wiltse, *Calhoun: Sectionalist,* 469–70.

24. The text of the speech used here is in *WS,* X, 57–99.

25. Ibid., 63.

26. His earlier statement had been made during the debate on the Oregon bill; *Congressional Globe,* 30th Cong., 1st sess., 1077–80. Webster now contended that he was opposing the extension of slavery because the law of nature forbade its establishment in these territories.

27. *WS,* X, 83–84.

28. Ibid., 86. On this point, see the discussion later in the chapter.

29. *WS,* X, 93.

30. DW to George Ticknor, March 17, 1850, ibid., XVIII, 359.

31. DW to Edward Everett, Sept. 27, 1851, ibid., 473.

32. Edward Curtis to Peter Harvey, March 15, 1850, in Claude H. Van Tyne, ed., *The Letters of Daniel Webster* (New York, 1902), 404; March 28, 1850, WPNH, F22/30128; April 12, 1850, Van Tyne, *Letters,* 408; July 3 and 7, Aug. 2, 1850, WPNH. These letters of July and August are not in the film edition of the Webster Papers.

33. DW to Peter Harvey, March 22, 1850, WPNH, F22/30057.

34. DW to Redding and Co., March 15, 1850, WPDC, F22/29998; several proof sheets in ibid., F22/29938; DW to Fletcher Webster, March 21, 1850, WPNH, F22/30049; DW to Peter Harvey, May 11, 1850, ibid., F22/30403; DW manuscript memorandum, ibid., F23/31973.

35. From the time the *Advertiser* published the text of the speech on March 11 onward, it was highly favorable. On the *Courier,* see DW to Peter Harvey, April 15, 1850, WPNH, F22/30257. Webster's friends supplied items which were published in these papers; David B. Tyack, *George Ticknor and the Boston Brahmins* (Cambridge, Mass., 1967), 227, says Ticknor wrote a number of them.

36. Thomas H. Perkins et al. to DW, March 25, 1850, WPNH, F22/30083; among other places, the letter was published in the Boston *Advertiser,* April 3, 1850. Webster's reply of April 9 is in the Sang Collection, F22/30212, and was published in the *Advertiser* of April 13.

37. Stuart to DW, May 30, 1850, WPNH, F22/30491.

38. Much of the correspondence, not cited specifically here, is in F22 passim.

39. Isaac Hill to DW, April 17,1850, Webster Papers, Maryland Historical Society, F22/30270; DW to Hill, April 20, 1850, WPNH, F22/30292; Joel Poinsett to DW, April 10, 1850, ibid., F22/30236; Francis Lieber to DW, May 4, ibid., F22/30379, and June 6, 1850, WPLC, F22/30535; John Tyler to DW, April 17, 1850, transcript in Tyler Papers, Library of Congress, F22/30276.

40. Charles L. Vose et al. to DW, March 28, 1850, WPNH, F22/30142; DW to Vose et al., April 15, 1850, ibid., F22/30259; letter of several hundred New York citizens to DW, printed in Boston *Advertiser,* April 10, 1850; DW letter of thanks, June 19, 1850, *WS,* XVI, 550.

41. Claude M. Fuess, *Daniel Webster,* 2 vols. (Boston, 1930), II, 226–27; DW to William Corcoran, Corcoran Papers, Library of Congress, F22/29878.

42. Everett to DW, March 12 and 22, 1850, Everett Papers, F22/29963 and 30060.

43. Martin Duberman, *Charles Francis Adams, 1807-1886* (Boston, 1960), 167; Henry Wilson, *History of the Rise and Fall of the Slave Power in America,* 3 vols. (Boston, 1884), II, 241-46; Boston *Advertiser,* March 26, 1850.

44. Jonathan Messerli, *Horace Mann: A Biography* (New York, 1972), 512-21; DW to Ticknor, June 1, 1850, *WS,* XVI, 542-44; June 3, 1850, Sang Collection, F22/30521; June 13, 1850, *WS,* XVI, 545-46; June 14, WPLC, F22/30573.

45. Theodore Parker, "Daniel Webster," in *The Works of Theodore Parker,* 15 vols. (Boston, 1908), VII, 317-48.

46. See also the following exchange of correspondence on this subject: Calvin Hitchcock to DW, March 13, 1850, WPNH, F22/29989; DW to Hitchcock, March 17, 1850, ibid., F22/30022; Hitchcock to DW, March 25, 1850, ibid., F22/30079.

47. John G. Whittier, *The Poetical Works of Whittier* (Boston, 1975), 186-87. Though his critical view of Webster, quoted here from "Ichabod," is well known, those familiar with Whittier's work as a whole will recall that in a later poem, "The Lost Occasion," he saw the Civil War as a vindication of Webster's concept of liberty and union; ibid., 187.

48. Webster's friend George Ticknor Curtis vigorously set forth the view that his dominant motive was to save the Union, contrary to charges of Parker and other critics; *The Last Years of Daniel Webster: A Monograph* (New York, 1878). After extensive research in the sources, Herbert D. Foster came to the same conclusion; "Webster's Seventh of March Speech and the Secession Movement, 1850," *American Historical Review,* 27 (Jan. 1922), 245-70. A recent interesting study of the intellectual dimensions of Webster's unionism, with some reference to the crisis of 1850, is Major L. Wilson, *Space, Time, and Freedom: The Quest for Nationality and the Irrepressible Conflict, 1815-61* (Westport, Conn., 1974), 159-77.

49. Although he emphasizes Webster's presidential ambition in his career generally, Robert F. Dalzell, Jr., finds other factors prevailing in this instance; *Daniel Webster and the Trial of American Nationalism, 1843-1852* (Boston, 1973), 188-95.

50. DW to Franklin Haven, May 18, 1850, Webster Papers, Harvard University, F22/30435.

51. DW to Thomas H. Perkins et al., April 9, 1850, Sang Collection, F22/30212. See also DW to Peter Harvey, May 29, 1850, WPNH, F22/30482. Webster referred to the economic implications time and again in correspondence and speeches. Their importance to Webster is recognized in Hamilton, *Prologue to Conflict,* 124-32; David Van Tassel, "Gentlemen of Property and Standing: Compromise Sentiment in Boston in 1850," *New England Quarterly,* 23 (Sept. 1950), 307-19; Eric Foner, *Free Soil, Free Labor, Free Men* (New York, 1970), 187-93; and Dalzell, *Webster and Trial of American Natonalism,* 188-95.

52. William R. Brock, *Parties and Conscience: American Dilemmas, 1840-1850* (Millwood, N.Y., 1979), 296-300, concludes that Webster's insensitivity to the moral question in 1850 helped weaken the Union in the long run. In Webster's behalf it must be said that moral factors, as he defined them, did influence him. And he attributed a damaging moral absolutism to antislavery.

53. *Congressional Globe,* 31st Cong., 1st sess., app., 260–69; Glyndon G. Van Deusen, *William Henry Seward* (New York, 1967), 123–27; Brock, *Parties and Conscience,* 301–6.

54. *Congressional Globe,* 31st Cong., 1st sess., app., 1054–65. Webster's denial of inconsistency is in ibid., 591–92.

55. Ibid., 517, 640–43, 708, 710–14, 721–22, 757, 759, 780–81; Hamilton, *Prologue to Conflict,* 92–94; DW to Willie Mangum [April 12, 1850?], Mangum Papers, Library of Congress, F22/30288.

56. *Congressional Globe.,* 31st Cong., 1st sess., 762–64, 769, 1153–54, 1480–81. The committee did not report until July 30; and Webster, a member, was no longer a member of the Senate then.

57. *WS,* XIII, 386–89; Boston *Advertiser,* April 30, 1850.

58. Myron Lawrence to DW, April 30, 1850, WPLC, F22/30354; DW to Willie Mangum, May 1, 1850, Myers Collecton, New York Public Library, F22/30370; Fuess, *Webster,* II, 225.

59. DW to Peter Harvey, May 11, 1850, WPNH, F22/30403; "A New Yorker" to DW, May 14, 1850, ibid., F22/30417.

60. Hamilton, *Prologue to Conflict,* 95–96; Curtis, *Webster,* II, 440–41.

61. *Congressional Globe,* 31st Cong., 1st sess., 1113–17.

62. Ibid., 1118–22, 1134, 1145–46, 1238–39.

63. Ibid., 1164–65; *WS,* X, 107–12.

64. *Congressional Globe,* 31st Cong., 1st sess., 1279, 1314; *WS,* X, 118–37.

65. DW to Franklin Haven, June 19 and July 4, 1850, Webster Papers, Harvard University, F22/30591 and 30637. For southern opinion, see Thelma Jennings, *The Nashville Convention: Southern Movement for Unity, 1848–1851* (Memphis, 1980).

66. Stanley W. Campbell, *The Slave Catchers: Enforcement of the Fugitive Slave Law, 1850–1860* (Chapel Hill, 1970), 15–17.

67. *Prigg* v. *Pennsylvania,* 16 Peters 539 (1842); Charles G. Haines and Foster H. Sherwood, *The Role of the Supreme Court in American Government and Politics, 1835–1864* (Berkeley, 1957), 121–28. Justice Story's opinion in the case not only invalidated a state personal liberty law but declared an exclusive national power over fugitive slaves, leaving none to the states. But he spoke only for himself and two other justices on the latter point. Since only three of the nine-person Court took such a position on exclusive power, that part of his opinion did not provide precedent for future cases.

68. Everett to DW, April 3, 1850, Everett Papers, F22/30162; H. W. Warren to DW, June 5, 1850, WPLC, F22/30529.

69. Boston *Advertiser,* June 13, 1850.

70. Moses Stuart to DW, May 2, 1850, WPNH, F22/30373.

71. *WS,* XII, 225–37; Boston *Advertiser,* May 31, 1850. Webster referred to the Sixth and Seventh Amendments on jury trial. One might reasonably argue, however, that Congress could make a fugitive-slave question a criminal case by legislation, either as inference from the fugitive-slave clause of the Constitution (Art. IV, sec. 2), or as a regulation of interstate movement of persons under the commerce clause.

72. DW to Peter Harvey, June 4, 1850, WPNH, F22/30522A. In his speech of March 7, he had said he would support the bill coming from the committee, "with some amendments."

73. John McLean to DW, April 6, 1850, WPDC, F22/30187.

74. *Congressional Globe*, 31st Cong., 1st sess., 1111, which includes the text of his amendment. See also Records of the Senate, RG 46, National Archives, F37/51163.

75. The legislative history of the fugitive-slave law, passed in September, is given in Campbell, *Slave Catchers*, 19–25. Of several similar amendments for jury trial submitted, the one of William L. Dayton most closely resembled Webster's; but none passed. So even if Webster had made a great effort to get his amendment through, he would not have succeeded.

76. Hamilton, *Prologue to Conflict*, 106–7.

77. *Congressonal Globe*, 31st Cong., 1st sess., 1362–63, 1365. Webster was appointed to the committee for funeral arrangements.

78. Ibid., 1364–65.

79. DW to J. Prescott Hall, May 18, 1850, WPLC, F22/30431.

80. *Congressional Globe*, 31st Cong., 1st sess., 1125–26; DW to Franklin Haven, Jan. 24, 1850, Webster Papers, Harvard University, F22/29767.

81. Glyndon G. Van Deusen, *Thurlow Weed: Wizard of the Lobby* (Boston, 1947), 180.

82. Robert J. Rayback, *Millard Fillmore: A Biography of a President* (Buffalo, 1959), 242–43.

83. In a scandal related to the so-called Galphin claims, some cabinet members were suspected of improper intervention in behalf of creditors of Georgia; Dalzell, *Webster and Trial of American Nationalism*, 203–5.

84. DW to Fillmore, [July 11, 1850], Fillmore Papers, Buffalo and Erie County Historical Society, F22/30655, containing a list of possible cabinet appointees, partly different from list of actual appointees. See also two letters to Fillmore, both July 19, 1850, ibid., F22/30701 and 30705.

85. DW to Franklin Haven, July 12, 1850, Webster Papers, Harvard University, F22/30664.

86. James K. Mills to DW, July 17, 1850, WPLC, F22/30690; DW to Franklin Haven, July 26, 1850, Webster Papers, Harvard University, F22/30742. For an explanation of the fund and a list of the subscribers, see George Griswold to DW, Jan. 17, 1851, Sang Collection, F23/32199. The list of names is dated August 1, 1850.

87. DW to Peter Harvey, July 21, 1850, WPNH, F22/30690; *Congressional Globe*, 31st Cong., 1st sess., 1432. A few days earlier, on the seventeenth, he gave a kind of farewell speech, outlining the advantages of compromise for each section; *WS*, X, 144–70.

88. Hamilton, *Prologue to Conflict*, 108–14, 135–65; Rayback, *Fillmore*, 250–53.

89. DW to Peter H. Bell, Aug. 5, 1850, *WS*, XII, 153–61; Richardson, *Papers of the Presidents*, IV, 67–73, for message of early August; DW to Franklin Haven, Aug. 10, 1850, Webster Papers, Harvard University, F22/30848; Hamilton, *Prologue to Conflict*, 124–32.

90. He wrote at least one newspaper editorial, arguing for House approval. It appeared in the *Intelligencer*. His draft is in Personal (Miscellaneous) Papers, New York Public Library, F22/30964.

91. DW to George Ticknor, July 28, 1850, *WS*, XVI, 554; DW to Peter Harvey, Aug. 7, 1850, Sang Collection, F22/30807; DW to Franklin Haven, [Sept. 5, 1850], Webster Papers, Harvard University, F22/31034.

92. See Hamilton, *Prologue to Conflict*, appendices, 191, 193, 195–99, for vot-

ing by Massachusetts congressmen, in the tabulation of all congressional voting on key issues of the compromise.

93. Potter, *Impending Crisis,* 114–20. See also David Herbert Donald, *Liberty and Union* (Lexington, Mass., 1978), 35–51; and Hamilton, *Prologue to Conflict,* 168–90.

26. Character

1. Paintings and photographic portraits of Webster can be found in a number of repositories, including the National Portrait Gallery in Washington, which presented an exhibit of portraits during the bicentennial of Webster's birth in 1982. For an early, informative description and reproductions of many portraits, see Charles H. Hart, "Life Portraits of Daniel Webster," *McClure's Magazine,* 9 (May 1897), 619–30. The daguerreotypes dating from the late 1840s up to 1852 show features mentioned in the text here.

2. Webster's friend Philip Hone remarked upon his dress on occasions other then during great speeches, when he seemed fond of a variety of bold colors. "I was much amused a day or two since by meeting him in Wall Street, at high noon, in a bright blue satin vest, sprigged with gold flowers, a costume as incongruous for Daniel Webster as ostrich feathers for a sister of charity"; Allan Nevins, ed., *The Diary of Philip Hone, 1828–1851,* 2 vols. (New York, 1927), II, 728–29.

3. George T. Curtis, *Life of Daniel Webster,* 2 vols. (New York, 1870), I, 182, refers to periods of "solemn repose, amounting to an apparent lethargy, from which in his later years he seemed capable of being aroused only by a strong external pressure."

4. DW to Franklin Haven, Sept. 12, 1850, Webster Papers Harvard University, F22/21073; DW to no addressee, Sept. 15, 1850, WPNH, F22/31118; DW to Millard Fillmore, July 20, 1851, *WS,* XVIII, 449–51; DW to Caleb Cushing, Sept. 1, 1849, Cushing Papers, Library of Congress, F21/29521. Webster wrote Louisa Cheney, September 29, 1845, that "a fellow sufferer, from the same affliction . . . was asked the other day, what in the world he took for it; his reply was that he 'took eight handkerchiefs a day' "; WPDC, F19/26468.

5. DW to Millard Fillmore, Sept. 28, 1851, in Curtis, *Webster,* II, 528–29; Claude M. Fuess, *Daniel Webster,* 2 vols. (Boston, 1930), II, 279; DW to Henry D. Moore, Aug. 28, 1850, Roberts Autograph Collection, Haverford College, F22/30977.

6. DW to Edward Everett, Nov. 28, 1848, Everett Papers, Massachusetts Historical Society, F21/28941; DW draft outline of history, [April 1852], with letter of George J. Abbott to Everett, April 12, 1854, WPNH, F26/36693; text of address, Feb. 23, 1852, *WS,* XIII, 463–97.

7. See the description of the first speech at Bunker Hill in chapter 5.

8. Carl Seaburg and Stanley Paterson, *Merchant Prince of Boston: Colonel T. H. Perkins, 1764–1854* (Cambridge, Mass., 1971), 318–26, 329–30, 333, 336–40.

9. *WS,* I, 257–58; Robert F. Dalzell, Jr., *Daniel Webster and the Trial of American Nationalism, 1843–1852* (Boston, 1973), 1–3.

10. Text of speech in *WS*, I, 259–83. DW draft in Webster Papers, Massachusetts Historical Society, F19/25200.

11. Oliver P. Chitwood, *John Tyler: Champion of the Old South* (New York, 1939), 319–23.

12. William Plumer, Jr., "Reminiscences of Daniel Webster," *WS*, XVII, 560–61. Dalzell, *Webster and Trial of American Nationalism*, 4–19, offers a valuable analysis of the speech, which he thinks well illustrates the chief elements of Webster's political thought.

13. An unfriendly description of Caroline Webster by Justice Daniel is quoted in John P. Frank, *Justice Daniel Dissenting: A Biography of Peter V. Daniel, 1784–1860* (Cambridge, Mass., 1964), 176.

14. Washington *National Intelligencer,* March 29, April 6 and 30, 1841.

15. For Webster's dissatisfaction with the will, see DW to Hiram Ketchum, May 22, 1841, George F. Hoar Papers, Massachusetts Historical Society, F15/19176; heirs to executors of Le Roy estate, [ca. 1841], Bayard-Pearsall-Campbell Collection, Le Roy Family Papers, New York Public Library, F29/39880.

16. DW to Caroline Webster, Aug. 22, 1841, WPNH, F15/20005.

17. Fletcher Webster to DW, Jan. 7 and Feb. 6, 1844, ibid., F19/25568 and 25663. Webster unsuccessfully sought to get a congressional appropriation to make up arrears in Fletcher's compensation; DW to Fletcher Webster, March 3 and 5, 1845, *WS*, XVI, 432–34.

18. Fuess, *Webster,* II, 360–61. An interesting letter of advice from Webster to his grandson, Daniel Fletcher Webster, Jr., on March 6, 1848, is in WPNH, F21/28473.

19. DW to Julia Appleton, Feb. 14, 1848, James W. Paige Papers, Massachusetts Historical Society, F21/28406; Julia Appleton to Caroline Webster, Dec. 22, 1847, enclosed in Caroline Webster to DW, WPNH, F21/28259.

20. Sketch of Edward by Fletcher, quoted in Curtis, *Webster,* II, 318–20.

21. DW to Edward Webster, March 21, 1843, WPNH, F18/24723.

22. DW to Fletcher Webster, Jan. 25, 1847, ibid., F20/27571.

23. DW to Caleb Cushing, April 15, 1847, Montague Collection, New York Public Library, F20/27822; DW to Fletcher Webster, April 27, 1847, WPNH, F20/27867; DW to John E. Wool, April 7, 1847, WPDC, F20/27806. When Cushing was promoted to brigadier general, in command of several regiments, Edward succeeded him as commander of the Massachusetts troops.

24. DW to Edward Webster, Feb. 5, 1847, WPNH, F20/27610.

25. Henry Pleasants to DW, Jan. 12, 1848, Sang Collection, Brandeis University, F21/28309; George Ticknor's reminiscence of conversation with Webster on April 29, 1848, in Curtis, *Webster,* II, 329–30.

26. DW to Fletcher Webster, Feb. 23, 1848, *WS*, XVIII, 271; Julia Appleton to DW, [Feb. 23, 1848], WPNH, F21/28426.

27. DW to Fletcher Webster, March 12, 1848, *WS*, XVIII, 273. This portrait showed Edward as he would have looked in 1830, at the time of the Webster-Hayne debate. Healy probably intended to use it in his famous painting of that debate, which shows the scene in the Senate with a composite of many individuals, some of whom were not in fact present then. The complete painting appeared in 1851.

28. DW memorandum, May 11, 1848, ibid., 558–59; series of letters of DW in early 1848 on Julia's illness, WPNH, F21 passim; Curtis, *Webster,* II, 327.

29. Among various descriptions of Marshfield, see DW to Mrs. Edward Curtis, May 26, 1842, *WS*, XVIII, 129-31; DW to Millard Fillmore, July 23, 1851, Fillmore Papers, Buffalo and Erie County Historical Society, F24/34484; letters by Samuel Lyman, describing his visits there from 1842 to 1848, in his *Public and Private Life of Daniel Webster* (Philadelphia, 1890), 53-148.

30. One visitor describing his time at Marshfield was Philip Hone; Nevins, *Hone*, II, 736-40, 771. For the library addition, see Julia Appleton to DW, July 11, 1842, WPNH, F17/22865; and her own plans for that addition, reproduced in *WP*, V, 224-25. A new kitchen was also added in 1844.

31. For a description of the employees, including house servants, see Curtis, *Webster*, II, 662-65. Some servants had been slaves, and Webster had purchased their freedom—for example, William Johnson, as evidenced in bill of sale, Dec. 16, 1850, Personal (Miscellaneous) Papers, New York Public Library, F29/40452, and DW to David A. Hall, [Jan.] 1851, ibid., F23/32372.

32. Webster's life at Marshfield is also described rather fully in Fuess, *Webster*, II, 333-36; and Curtis, *Webster*, II, 216-22.

33. Lyman, *Webster*, II, 148-59, includes the author's letters describing his visit to the Elms in 1849. Charles Archer also wrote about the Elms and Webster's early life there; these writings were published in the New York *Courier and Enquirer*, then in Lyman's book. Ninety-eight pages of his manuscript are in WPLC, IX, 17152-250. Webster's papers for the years after 1840 include many items on this farm, not cited here.

34. Boston *Atlas*, Aug. 9, 1843.

35. DW speech at Grafton, N.H., Aug. 28, 1847, at celebration of railroad reaching that place, *WS*, IV, 107-11; DW speech in Lebanon, N.H., on a similar occasion, Nov. 17, 1847, ibid., 112-17.

36. DW to Edward Curtis, Oct. 18, 1845, Montague Collection, F19/26490; DW to Seth Weston, Feb. 18, 1846, *WS*, XVIII, 217-19; DW to Caroline Webster, May 3, 1846, Sang Collection, F20/26897.

37. A typical letter among a great many is DW to Seth Weston, Dec. 8, 1842, WPNH, F18/23863.

38. DW to Charles Henry Thomas, April 11, 1841, Webster Papers (Mass. Hist. Soc.), F15/18781; DW to Porter Wright, March 16, 1850, *WS*, XVIII, 357.

39. DW to Caroline Webster, Aug. 16, 1841, WPNH, F15/19933; Richard Smith to DW, March 9, 1844, ibid., F19/25731; Benjamin Perley Poore, *Reminiscences of Sixty Years*, 2 vols. (Philadelphia, 1886), I, 297-98.

40. On the financial aspects of the house until its sale in 1849, see discussion later in this chapter.

41. DW to George Ticknor, Jan. 24, 1846, in Curtis, *Webster*, II, 296; Poore, *Reminiscences*, I, 383-84; Nevins, *Hone*, II, 766-77.

42. Account book, 1844-1847, Webster-Healy Papers, Massachusetts Historical Society, F29/39923; account book, 1847-1851, Sang Collection, F29/40178; box, 1842-1853, and box, Miscellaneous, WPNH. Though the records are extensive, there is no systematic recapitulation by year. Reconstruction of the financial life of Webster on that basis would reveal a great deal but is probably impossible.

43. DW to Franklin Haven, Dec. 23, 1851, Webster Papers, Harvard University, F25/35557.

44. [James D. Doty] to Nicholas Biddle, March 25, 1841, Biddle Papers, Library of Congress, F14/18549; Herman Cope to DW, April 6, 1841, Sang Collection, F15/18728; Richard A. Smith to DW, March 29, 1841, ibid., F14/18606; list of western lands, ibid., F29/39847.

45. Herman Cope to DW, Oct. 5, 1841, Sang Collection, F16/20506; and Sept. 3, 1844, WPNH, F19/25942.

46. DW to Samuel Jaudon, Oct. 12, 1845, Miscellaneous MSS, New York Historical Society, F19/26476; DW to Fletcher Webster, Jan. 30, 1846, WPNH, F20/26672.

47. Samuel Jaudon to DW, Dec. 23, 1847, WPLC, F21/28231; DW to Jaudon, Dec. 26, 1847, ibid., F21/28244.

48. Herman Cope to DW, Sept. 3, 1844, WPNH, F19/25942; itemized account of DW with BUS trustees, Jan. 25, 1846, ibid., F29/39835-193.

49. DW to Fletcher Webster, Feb. 24, 1845, ibid., F19/26162; George Jones to DW, Jan. 21, 1850, ibid., F22/29763; Fletcher Webster to DW, [May 1851?], ibid., F24/33698.

50. DW to Henry Hubbard, Dec. 8, 1842, Hungtington Library, San Marino, Calif., F18/23860; Henry L. Kinney to DW, July 25, 1842, WPNH, F17/22991; Caleb Cushing to Kinney, March 9, 1849, Cushing Papers, F21/29143; Kinney to DW, March 3, 1850, WPNH, F22/29869.

51. John T. Haight to DW, July 11, 1849, Cushing Papers, F21/29463; DW to Haight, Jan. 5, 1850, State Historical Society of Wisconsin, Madison, F22/29707.

52. DW to Virgil Maxcy, May 31, 1842, Galloway-Maxcy-Markoe Papers, Library of Congress, F17/22587; Levi C. Turner to DW, Feb. 16, 1851, WPNH, F23/32555. Webster said he had acquired some of the Tennessee lands from Stephen Haight (father of Webster's land agent), with whom he had been associated in the Wisconsin purchases; see *WP*, IV, 124 n. 3.

53. Agreement of DW and Cushing, Oct. 5, 1848, Cushing Papers, F29/40246.

54. Copy of deed of conveyance and enclosures by DW to Cushing, Nov. 27, 1849, WPLC, F29/40340; DW to Cushing, April 11, 1850, Cushing Papers, F22/30238; Cushing to DW, Sept. 14, 1850, ibid., F22/31113.

55. DW to Cushing, April 8, 1852, Cushing Papers, F26/36463.

56. Cushing to DW, Sept. 11, 1852, ibid., F27/37744; DW to Cushing, Sept. 30, 1852, ibid., F27/37903.

57. DW to James Murray, with enclosure of Virgil Maxcy to DW, June 8, 1842, WPDC, F17/22644; Murray to DW, June 9, 1842, WPLC, F17/22657; DW to Maxcy, June 18, 1842, ibid., F17/22725; Murray to DW, Dec. 22, 1842, ibid., F18/23941.

58. DW to John Healy, Dec. 28, 1841, *WP*, V, 176-77 and editorial note; Healy to DW, Feb. 7, 1843, ibid., 267-68; G. C. Grammer to DW, Feb. 13, 1844, WPDC, F19/25675; document conveying land to Clemens Cox as security for court judgment against DW, March 5, 1844, WPNH, F29/39953; statement by Cox of settlement with DW, April 2, 1846, ibid., F29/40069. The decision of the Massachusetts supreme court is in 6 Metcalf 1 (1843).

59. Agreement by DW to convey land to Francis Price, Dec. 27, 1848, WPDC, F29/40286; DW to Price, Sept. 18, 1849, Loyola University, F21/29547.

60. DW statement, with endorsements by Moses Grinnell, Richard M.

Blatchford, and J. Prescott Hall, June 4, 1842, University of Virginia, F17/22640.

61. DW to Edward Curtis, Feb. 1, [1844], Cromaine Library, Hartland, Mich., F19/25636; DW to Franklin Haven, May 17, 1845, Webster Papers, Harvard University, F19/26365; DW to Richard Smith, July 21, 1845, Jacobs Library, Dayton, Ohio, F19/26421; DW to Haven, April 2, 1846, Webster Papers, Harvard University, F20/26819.

62. William W. Corcoran to DW, April 20, 1849, Corcoran Papers, Library of Congress, F21/29346.

63. Fuess, *Webster*, II, 387, drawing from WPNH, says that in December 1844 his account with the Boston branch showed loans of $17,000 and repayments of $16,186. For later obligation on a mortgage, see DW to Fletcher Webster, June 16, 1848, WPNH, F21/28712. Webster used some Marshfield property as security to purchase a share in a cotton mill nearby; documents of April 12 and Oct. 17, 1851, WPDC, F29/40504, and George J. Abbot Papers, Yale University Library, F29/40567.

64. DW to Mary Ann Sanborn, May 3, 1843, WPDC, F19/25036.

65. DW to Thomas B. Curtis, Jan. 30, 1844, Webster Papers (Mass. Hist. Soc.), F19/25628; DW to [David A.?] Russell, Dec. 18, 1846, WPDC, F20/27503; DW to Edward Curtis, Jan. 16, 1847, Montague Collection, F20/27560.

66. Israel Washburn to DW, March 31, 1846, WPDC, F20/26817; DW to Washburn, April 8, 1846, Washburn Papers, Library of Congress, F20/26832; May 20, 1846, ibid., F20/26968.

67. He did not even fully pay for three volumes of Audubon's *Birds of America*, for which he had subscribed. When John James Audubon, in very respectful terms, said he needed the money, Webster paid some more but not the whole bill; Audubon to DW, Feb. 3, 1843, *WP*, V, 268-69 and n. 1.

68. DW record book of legal fees, May 8, 1843 to March 1847, Webster-Healy Papers, F19/25167.

69. Joshua Bates to DW, May 30, 1843, WPDC, F19/25148; DW to Bates, July 30, 1845, Baring Papers, Public Archives of Canada, F19/26425; DW to Thomas Wren Ward, July 31, 1845, Webster-Healy Papers, F19/26435; DW to Baring Brothers, Oct. 14, 1845, Baring Papers, F19/26477; Dalzell, *Webster and Trial of American Nationalism*, 90.

70. DW to Franklin Haven, March 12, 1850, *WS*, XVI, 536; March 23, 1850, Webster Papers, Harvard University, F22/30071; Dec. 7, 1850, ibid., F23/31764; DW to Thomas Corwin, with Corwin's reply subscribed, Dec. 7, 1850, ibid., F22/31780; W. A. Bradley and Gilbert L. Thompson notes of May 17, 1851, with DW endorsement of July 11, 1851, Personal (Miscellaneous) Papers, New York Public Library, F29/40514; Levi C. Turner to DW, Feb. 16, 1851, WPNH, F23/32555.

71. One of numerous loans by Mills was the note of June 9, 1849, Webster-Healy Papers, F29/40318. See also DW to Franklin Haven, March 9, 1850, Webster Papers, Harvard University, F22/29931.

72. On Harvey's role, see, for example, DW to Franklin Haven, June 13, 1846, Webster Papers, Harvard University, F20/27063. On Choate's easygoing response to Webster's requests, see Jean V. Matthews, *Rufus Choate: The Law and Civic Virtue* (Philadelphia, 1980), 148-49.

73. DW to Fletcher Webster, March 29 [ca. 1850], WPNH, XV, 130.

74. Moses Grinnell gave Webster a great deal of help, such as on the problems of his western lands and of his house in Washington. It was charged that Webster reciprocated by putting through the appointment of Washington Irving, Grinnell's brother-in-law, as minister to Spain. See Grinnell to DW, [Feb. 10, 1842], George F. Hoar Papers, F16/21525, and *WP*, V, editorial note on 189.

75. A typical letter concerning credit is DW to Williams, March 3, 1842, WPDC, F16/21500. Williams was dismissed by the Tyler administration in 1844. On Dec. 7, 1844, Webster told him he had certainly not deserved such treatment; ibid., F19/26014. On April 10, 1845, he wrote: "I feel greatly obliged to you, My Dear Sir, for your kindness in times past; & if at any time, or in any way, I can be useful to you, hereafter, I assure you I should most readily & eagerly be of service to you"; ibid., F19/26296.

76. On Sept. 12, 1845, Webster wrote Corcoran and Riggs about discounting his note and referred to their "well known disposition to oblige me ... At all events do not let a check of mine come back"; WPDC, F19/26452.

77. David Sears to DW, March 21, 1846, *WS*, XVI, 445-46; George Griswold to DW, Jan. 17, 1851, Sang Collection, F23/32199.

78. DW to Peter Harvey, Nov. 23, 1847, WPNH, F21/28198.

79. Sympathetically though Claude Fuess portrays Webster, he concludes that his financial laxity was a blemish on his character; *Webster*, II, 384-94. George Ticknor Curtis, who was not only Webster's biographer but also a close friend, is also critical. *Webster*, II, 214-16. A recent biographer, Irving H. Bartlett, *Daniel Webster* (New York, 1978), 202-9, theorizes that his compulsive spending and poor judgment arose from an effort to gain the wealth and standing his father failed to achieve: he "had never really given up depending on his father, the most powerful influence on his own life." It is difficult to find evidence to support this interpretation. Among the numerous contemporaries criticizing Webster's financial behavior, none was more decided than John Quincy Adams, who wrote that "money, public and private, is the insuperable obstacle to his successful progress"; Charles F. Adams, ed., *Memoirs of John Quincy Adams, Comprising Portions of His Diary from 1795 to 1848*, 12 vols. (Philadelphia, 1874-77), XI, 47-48. Webster himself freely admitted his failings, but only as to private money.

80. The example of Henry Clay might be mentioned. Late in life, he was deep in debt and received contributions from friends and admirers; Calvin Colton, ed., *The Life, Correspondence, and Speeches of Henry Clay*, 6 vols. (New York, 1857), I, 43-44 and III, 40-41.

27. Judicial Adjustments

1. The appointees were James Wayne, Philip Barbour, Roger Taney, John Catron, and John McKinley, confirmed in the years 1835-1837.

2. Illustrative of this view are Carl B. Swisher, *History of the Supreme Court of the United States*, vol. 5, *The Taney Period* (New York, 1974); Bernard Schwartz, *From Confederation to Nation: The American Constitution, 1835-1877* (Baltimore, 1973); and Harold M. Hyman and William M. Wiecek, *Equal Justice under*

Law: Constitutional Development, 1835–1875 (New York, 1982). Not only did the *Dred Scott* decision (1857) damage his reputation, but so did his opposition to many of Lincoln's policies during the Civil War.

3. DW to Caroline Webster, Jan. 10, 1836, *WS*, XVI, 264.

4. Story died in 1845; but from the 1830s through the 1850s John McLean and James Wayne reflected his brand of judicial nationalism, even though they had been Jacksonian appointees.

5. Antecedents indicating judicial self-restraint were *U.S.* v. *Palmer*, 3 Wheaton 610 (1818); *Foster and Elam* v. *Neilson*, 2 Peters 253 (1829); *Cherokee Nation* v. *Georgia*, 5 Peters 1 (1831).

6. Peter J. Coleman, *The Transformation of Rhode Island, 1790–1860* (Providence, 1963), 254–94 and passim, for background; Marvin E. Gettleman, *The Dorr Rebellion: A Study in American Radicalism, 1833–1849* (New York, 1973); William M. Wiecek, *The Guarantee Clause of the U.S. Constitution* (Ithaca, 1972), 87–109; George M. Dennison, *The Dorr War: Republicanism on Trial, 1831–1861* (Lexington, Ky., 1976).

7. Lyon G. Tyler, *Letters and Times of the Tylers*, 2 vols. (Richmond, 1884–85), II, 193–99; Robert J. Morgan, *A Whig Embattled: The Presidency under John Tyler* (Lincoln, Neb., 1954), 97–105. The massive report by a congressional committee, including a variety of relevant materials on the whole affair, is *House Report 546*, 28th Cong., 1st sess., "Interference of the Executive in Affairs of Rhode Island."

8. Joseph Story to DW, April 26, 1842, *WP*, V, 202–3; DW to John Whipple, May 9, 1842, ibid., 207–8; William C. Gibbs to DW, May 12, 1842, WPNH, F17/22440; Tyler to DW, May 28, 1842, Webster-Healy Papers, Massachusetts Historical Society, F17/22547; Dennison, *Dorr War*, 90–99.

9. The Dorrite claim was not based on a natural right of necessarily violent revolution.

10. 7 Howard 3–19 (1849).

11. DW argument, as recorded by a reporter for the New York *Courier and Enquirer*, is in *WS*, XI, 217–42. DW ms. brief, [Jan. 27, 1848], Henry J. Raymond Papers, New York Public Library, F21/28331; printed in Samuel P. Lyman, *The Public and Private Life of Daniel Webster*, 2 vols. (Philadelphia, 1890), I, 289–300. The provision in the Constitution guaranteeing a republican form of government is Art. IV, sec. 4. A full study of its relevance to this case is in Wiecek, *Guarantee Clause*.

12. 7 Howard 34–48 (1849).

13. In *Baker* v. *Carr*, 369 U.S. 186 (1962), the leading modern case on legislative reapportionment, the Court lengthily considered the *Luther* precedent but bypassed it by turning to the equal-protection clause of the Fourteenth Amendment rather than to the guarantee clause of the Constitution to uphold justiciability.

14. The Constitution, Art. III, sec. 2, awards judicial power to federal courts in all cases of admiralty and maritime jurisdiction. One reason that resort to admirality may have seemed preferable was that in such cases there was usually no jury. And in this period, admiralty jurisdiction probably expanded in part because of a constitutonal relationship to interstate and foreign commerce; Milton Conover, "The Abandonment of the 'Tidewater' Concept of Admiralty Jurisdiction in the United States," *Oregon Law Review*,

38 (1958), 34-53; "From Judicial Grant to Legislative Power: the Admiralty Clause in the Nineteenth Century," note in *Harvard Law Review*, 67 (1954), 1214-37. The last two items provide a context for understanding the *Lexington* case, discussed later in this chapter.

15. 6 Howard 345-54 (1848); Traveller, *A Letter . . . on the Causes of the Destruction of the Steamer Lexington* (Boston, 1840); Robert G. Albion, *The Rise of New York Port* (New York, 1939), 160-63.

16. The case came up from the federal district court by way of Story's circuit court and had been decided for the bank. For the Supreme Court hearings in 1847 and 1848 Story was no longer on the bench, a circumstance which Webster regretted. See DW to Franklin Haven, Jan. 10, 1845, and Jan. 29 [1847], Webster Papers, Harvard University, F20/26602 and 27573.

17. DW argument reported in Washington *National Era*, Feb. 4 and 11, 1847, and in 6 Howard 377-78 (1848).

18. 5 Howard 459 (1847), for *Waring* case. Majority opinion in *Lexington*, 6 Howard 378-92. But to make up the minimal five for a decision, two justices concurring on separate grounds had to be counted. They concluded that a tort rather than a breach of contract had been committed; ibid., 394-95, 418-37. In *Genessee Chief* v. *Fitzhugh*, 12 Howard 443 (1852), Taney for the Court held that Congress could extend admiralty jurisdiction almost as much as it saw fit.

19. Stanley I. Kutler, *Privilege and Creative Destruction: The Charles River Bridge Case* (Philadelphia, 1971), 6-50; Maurice G. Baxter, *Daniel Webster and the Supreme Court* (Amherst, 1966), 120-23; 7 Pickering (Mass.), 347-71, 391-402, 427-533 (1828-30). The four judges divided evenly so as to refuse the petition for an injunction.

20. DW ms. brief and notes on arguments of other counsel during the 1831 term of the Supreme Court, totaling 151 pages, Webster Papers, Massachusetts Historical Society, F8/9241.

21. Peter C. Brooks to DW, Jan. 6, 1833, in possession of H. Bartholomew Cox, Oxon Hill, Md., F9/10461; DW to Warren Dutton, Jan. 26 and Dec. 24, 1835, WPDC, F10/12295 and 12791.

22. Simon Greenleaf ms. notes on arguments, Harvard University Law Library; DW ms. brief and notes on arguments of other counsel in 1837, totaling 218 pages, Webster Papers (Mass. Hist. Soc.), F11/13752; DW argument printed in *WS*, XV, 322-47; arguments of other counsel in 11 Peters 428-541.

23. 11 Peters 536-53 (1837).

24. Ibid., 583-650.

25. As Story pointed out, in the very recent English case upon which Taney relied so much, *Stourbridge* v. *Wheely*, 109 English Reports 796, the court had ruled that grantees could claim rights "clearly given by inference."

26. Kutler, *Privilege and Creative Destruction*, 85-95, 155-71; Morton J. Horwitz, *The Transformation of American Law*, 1780-1860 (Cambridge, Mass., 1977), 109-39; William E. Nelson, *The Americanization of American Law: The Impact of Legal Change on Massachusetts Society, 1760-1830* (Cambridge, Mass., 1975), 161-63. The legislature eventually awarded the old bridge company twenty-five thousand dollars as compensation; but for a while, tolls were collected on both bridges. Kutler, *Privilege and Creative Destruction*, 103-14, has a useful section on local events.

27. 6 Howard 301–36 (1848).

28. Ibid., 507–47. On the development of eminent domain, see Horwitz, *Transformation of Law*, 63–108.

29. Biddle to DW, Aug. 13, 1836, *WP*, IV, 154–55; DW to Biddle, Aug. 23, 1836, ibid., 157, and Feb. 7, [1839], Biddle Papers, Library of Congress, F12/15359.

30. *WS*, XI, 111–31; 13 Peters 523–67 (1839). An early case on the right of corporations to sue in federal courts was *BUS* v. *Devaux*, 5 Cranch 61 (1809), and the end case developing the rule was *Louisville, Cincinnati, and Charleston Railroad* v. *Letson*, 2 Howard 497 (1844).

31. On circuit, Justice Bushrod Washington had handed down an opinion with such sweeping implications; *Corfield* v. *Coryell*, 6 *Federal Cases* 3230 (1823).

32. DW to Biddle, Feb. 15, 1839, *WP*, IV, 344.

33. 13 Peters 584–97 (1839). Webster believed that the decision implied that there were even broader corporate rights, such as he had advanced; but his inference was speculative; DW draft editorial, [March 9, 1839], WPDC, F12/15389.

34. President Tyler cited the *Alabama Bank* precedent in 1841 to insist upon state control of branches of a proposed national bank (blocked by his veto).

35. Baxter, *Webster and Supreme Court*, 192–93.

36. Webster argued the case in 1840; and he and an associate submitted a written brief in 1842 when it was decided; File of case in Records of Supreme Court, RG 267, National Archives.

37. 16 Peters 1–22.

38. Swift was overruled in *Erie Railroad* v. *Tompkins*, 304 U.S. 64 (1938). The best study of the *Swift* case and its impact is Tony Freyer, *Harmony and Dissonance: The Swift & Erie Cases in American Federalism* (New York, 1981), taking a favorable view of the ruling. See also William W. Crosskey, *Politics and the Constitution in the History of the United States,* 2 vols. (Chicago, 1953), II, 856–60, also favorable. More critical are Swisher, *Taney Period*, 327–31, and Horwitz, *Transformation of Law*, 245–52.

39. 13 Peters 531–32, 556, 572–73, 600 (1839).

40. Story, McLean, and other nationalists said the Court had decided for exclusive national power; Taney and other states' rights justices contended with equal confidence that the precedents were for full concurrent state power unless there was a clear incompatibility between two statutes. Judges and lawyers participating in the *Gibbons* case repeatedly attributed a broader scope to the decision than was justified. The New York courts, previously upholding the steamboat monopoly, later applied *Gibbons* even to intrastate commerce. Today scholars as well as college students often make similar mistakes; Baxter, *Webster and Supreme Court*, 202–3.

41. 11 Peters 102 (1837).

42. Webster's argument is in 15 Peters 494–96. One of his associates was Henry Clay. An opponent, the rising Mississippi Democrat Robert J. Walker, spoke for four days.

43. Clay and Justice Baldwin interpreted the due-process clause of the Fifth Amendment as a check on congressional action, an early appearance of the doctrine of substantive due process.

44. Justice Thompson delivered what was called the opinion of the Court, holding narrowly that the Mississippi constitution was not self-executing

without a statute. Unlike Webster's argument, his did not rely upon the commerce clause; 15 Peters 496–503; other opinions, ibid., 503–15. Six of the seven justices would allow state regulation of importation of slaves, which Webster opposed.

45. 5 Howard 505–14, 538–39; New York *Tribune*, Feb. 3, 1845; DW ms. notes, [Jan. 1847], WPDC, F20/27588.

46. Opinions in 5 Howard 573–631. Webster contended that the liquor had been imported in foreign commerce and that, since it was still in the "original package," a state could not tax it, according to *Brown* v. *Maryland* (1827). Taney followed the precedent but said that the package had been broken by the retailer and that the liquor was no longer in the flow of foreign commerce. The chief justice and Daniel favored fully concurrent state power, while McLean and Wayne favored exclusively national power.

47. Webster's arguments: Washington *National Era*, March 4, 1847; *WS*, XV, 403–4; and 7 Howard 288–89.

48. 7 Howard 452–55.

49. Several opinions in ibid., 437–572. Webster was interested in national action to regulate immigration; his resolution to have the opinions of the judges in the *Passenger Cases* printed by the Senate to inform his colleagues about the problem failed; *Congressional Globe*, 30th Cong., 2d sess., 482, 550.

50. Webster had arrangements with merchants in New York and Boston for a contingency fee for winning the cases and for 25 percent of the sums paid in head taxes and recovered; DW to unnamed correspondent, Jan. 3, 1849, Montague Collection, New York Public Library, F21/29003; document signed by Harnden et al., Jan. 8, 1849, Webster-Healy Papers, F21/29011; DW to John Healy, Jan. 24, 1849, ibid., F21/29026, and Feb. 21, 1849, Miscellaneous Bound Mss, Massachusetts Historical Society, F21/29089.

51. 12 Howard 299. Webster had used the distinction of "higher branches" in his argument of the steamboat case in 1824. He would not classify pilotage as a higher branch, indeed had looked upon it as subject to the police rather than commerce power.

52. Baxter, *Webster and Supreme Court*, viii and appendix. Of the cases in which the decisions rested on constitutional grounds, he won six of nine in the Marshall period, only two of six in the Taney period. In the years 1814–1852 he argued 168 cases before the Supreme Court.

53. Hyman and Wiecek, *Equal Justice under Law*, 20–54; *WP: Legal*, II, 564–81.

54. *Pennock* v. *Dialogue*, 2 Peters 1 (1829).

55. George Griswold to DW, March 18, 1852, *WS*, XVI, 665 n. 2.

56. 10 *Federal Cases* 678–84; DW brief, March [25], 1852, WPLC, F26/36330. Legal context in Swisher, *Taney Period*, 484–511.

57. Peter Harvey, *Reminiscences and Anecdotes of Daniel Webster* (Boston, 1878), 102–5.

58. DW to Millard Fillmore, April 15, 1851, Fillmore Papers, Buffalo and Erie County Historical Society, F24/33249; DW to Edward Curtis, March 8, 1844, Montague Collection, F19/25729.

59. Both cases were appealed to the Supreme Court; *Carver* v. *Jackson*, 4 Peters 1 (1830); *Inglis* v. *Sailors' Snug Harbor*, 3 Peters 99 (1830). On Webster's handling of *Carver* in the circuit court, see *WP: Legal*, II, 95–115.

60. *WS*, XI, 185–216.

61. Ibid., XV, 373–404; DW brief, [Jan. 20, 1845], WPNH, F19/26080, for Boston and Lowell; DW brief, May 10, 1844, Webster-Healy Papers, F19/25829, for Boston and Worcester.

62. *WP: Legal*, II, 549–64; Claude M. Fuess, *Daniel Webster*, 2 vols. (Boston, 1930), II, 312–14; George F. Hoar, *Autobiography of Seventy Years*, 2 vols. (New York, 1903), I, 136–41; Boston *Atlas*, Aug. 8, 9, 16, and 19, 1843. The crime for which Wyman was charged allegedly involved embezzlement by loose discounting of notes.

63. Fuess, *Webster*, II, 316–17; Harvey, *Reminiscences*, 85–97. Sanborn had supposedly forged a note by Tufts, but Webster and Choate repelled that charge.

64. *WP: Legal*, II, 83–95; Fuess, *Webster*, II, 315–16; Fuess, *Rufus Choate: The Wizard of the Law* (New York, 1928), 149–51; Harvey, *Reminiscences*, 105–10.

65. Webster-Healy Papers, passim.

66. Edward Curtis to [Peter Harvey], Sept. 28, 1850, WPNH.

67. DW to Fletcher Webster, Dec. 10, 1846, in Calude H. Van Tyne, ed., *The Letters of Daniel Webster* (New York, 1902), 344.

68. DW account book for May 1843 to March 1847, Webster-Healy Papers, F19/25167. He often said, however, that he found public affairs more interesting and indicated as much by never withdrawing from politics.

69. Alexis de Tocqueville, *Democracy in America* (New York, Doubleday Anchor ed., 1969), 263–70; R. Kent Newmyer, "Daniel Webster as Tocqueville's Lawyer: The *Dartmouth College Case* Again," *American Journal of Legal History*, 11 (April 1967), 127–47.

28. Diplomatic Frustrations

1. DW to Fletcher Webster, July 23, 1850, WPNH, F22/30732.

2. DW to George Ticknor, Aug. 15, 1850, *WS*, XVI, 562.

3. Webster wrote Moses Stuart that he was also pleased with the composition of the cabinet: "They are all sound men, of fair and upright character, sober minds, and national views"; ibid., XVIII, 383.

4. For much of the time, his secretaries were George J. Abbot and Charles Lanman, both gifted and well educated.

5. For the need of additional personnel and improved procedures, see DW report to Senate, June 30, 1852, *WS*, XIV, 552–54.

6. Illustrative applications for appointments are: H. A. S. Dearborn to DW, Nov. 18, 1850, WPNH, F23/31696; Stephen A. Hurlbut to DW, March 17, 1851, WPLC, F24/32999.

7. Edward Curtis to Peter Harvey, Aug. 2, 1850, WPNH.

8. William Plumer, Jr., "Reminiscences of Daniel Webster," *WS*, XVII, 565.

9. At a dinner party Webster gave Bulwer seating preference, much to the dissatisfaction of the more senior Brazilian minister; George T. Curtis, *Life of Daniel Webster*, 2 vols. (New York, 1870), II, 562–65; DW to Chevalier S. de Macedo, Jan. 27, 1851, WPLC, F23/32302.

10. DW to William Rives, Jan. 12, 1852, *WS*, XIV, 451–52; March 8, 1852, Rives Papers, Library of Congress, F26/36171; Rives to DW, March 31, 1852, ibid., F26/36385.

11. DW to Millard Fillmore, July 13, 1852, *WS*, XVIII, 536.

12. Ralph S. Kuykendall, *The Hawaiian Kingdom,* 3 vols. (Honolulu, 1938), I, 405–10; DW to Luther Severance, July 14, 1851, in Claude H. Van Tyne, ed., *The Letters of Daniel Webster* (New York, 1902), 484–86.

13. Abbott Lawrence to DW, April 23, 1852, WPLC, F26/36597.

14. DW to Robert M. Walsh, Jan. 18, 1851, *WS*, XIV, 411–15; DW to Henry Bulwer, July 5, 1851, Public Record Office, F0/115/117, F24/34295.

15. DW to Millard Fillmore, July 10, 1851, Fillmore Papers, Buffalo and Erie County Historical Society, F24/34362. (All subsequent citations of the Fillmore Papers in this chapter are to this depository.)

16. DW to William A. Graham, May 9, 1851, Domestic Letters, XXXIX, 40–41, SDNA; DW to John H. Aulick, June 10, 1851, Aulick Expedition Papers, Maryland Historical Society, F24/33820.

17. For example, he sought a commercial treaty with Argentina; DW to Robert C. Schenck, April 28, 1852, draft in George F. Hoar Papers, Massachusetts Historical Society, F26/36646.

18. The documents which Taylor submitted in March 1850 included the diplomatic correspondence from 1848 up to that date and are in *Senate Executive Document 43,* 31st Cong., 1st sess. A valuable reference on the whole subject is Merle Curti, *Austria and the United States, 1848–1852* (Northampton, Mass., 1926). For developments up to the spring of 1850, see pp. 150–61. See also Schwarzenberg to Hülsemann, Nov. 5, 1849, Van Tyne, *Letters,* 455–56; John Clayton to DW, Jan. 12, 1851, WPNH, F23/32121.

19. Curti, *Austria and United States,* 144–50.

20. Hülsemann to DW, July 27, 1850, WPNH, F22/30744; Curti, *Austria and United States,* 161.

21. Hülsemann to DW, Sept. 30, 1850, *WS*, XII, 162–64.

22. Hunter to DW, Oct. 15, 1850, with enclosed draft of note, WPNH, F23/31359.

23. WPNH, XX, contains documents and correspondence on drafting the Hülsemann note sent by Webster, including Everett's draft, Webster's revisions, and Everett's pamphlet, *The Original Draft of the Hülsemann Letter* (Boston, 1853). Everett told Fletcher Webster, May 8, 1854, that one copy of the pamphlet had accidentally circulated beyond his control; Van Tyne, *Letters,* 451. See also Paul R. Frothingham, *Edward Everett: Orator and Statesman* (Boston, 1925), 321–24, 359–61. Curtis, *Webster,* II, 535 n. 1, believes Everett used Hunter's draft extensively.

24. Everett to DW, Oct. 31, 1851, Everett Papers, Massachusetts Historical Society, F25/35026; Everett's journal quoted in Frothingham, *Everett,* 324.

25. Text of note in *WS*, XII, 166–78.

26. Ibid., 170. Webster told Hülsemann he was mistaken about the phrase "iron rule" appearing in Clayton's instructions to Mann: "that phrase is not found in the paper." But he told Fillmore the words were actually in the original version of the instructions and were deleted when a copy was forwarded by Taylor to Congress afterward. This proved, Webster said, that Austria had surreptitiously obtained a copy of the original but had never admitted it; DW to Fillmore, Jan. 16, 1851, Fillmore Papers, F23/32179.

27. *WS*, XII, 166.

28. DW to George Ticknor, Jan. 16, 1851, ibid., XVI, 586.

29. Donald S. Spencer, *Louis Kossuth and Young America: A Study of Sectionalism and Foreign Policy, 1848–1852* (Columbia, Mo., 1977), 37–42, discusses this factor but does not make clear that Webster strongly opposed the Young America movement.

30. Henry D. Gilpin to DW, Jan. 22, 1851, WPNH, F23/32230; Francis Lieber to DW, Feb. 13, 1851, WPLC, F23/32527; copy of Pennsylvania resolutions, March 11, 1851, ibid., F24/32909.

31. Lawrence to DW, Jan. 27 and 29, 1851, WPLC, F23/32308 and 32326.

32. Glyndon G. Van Deusen, *The Life of Henry Clay* (Boston, 1937), 415–16.

33. *WS*, XII, 179.

34. Fillmore's revision of DW draft, March 13, 1851, WPLC, F24/32938; final version of DW to Hülsemann, March 15, 1851, *WS*, XII, 180.

35. Webster wrote Richard Blatchford, May 4, 1851: "There never was a time, I think, in which our foreign relations were more quiet . . . I think Mr. Hülsemann is the most satisfied and happy of them all"; *WS*, XVIII, 441.

36. Spencer, *Kossuth and Young America,* passim; DW speech in Boston *Atlas,* Jan. 10, 1852; Hülsemann to Fillmore, Van Tyne, *Letters,* 496–97; DW to Charles McCurdy, June 8, 1852, *WS*, XIV, 503–4.

37. Robert G. Caldwell, *The Lopez Expeditions to Cuba, 1848–1851* (Princeton, 1915); DW to A. Calderon de la Barca, Sept. 3 and Oct. 3, 1850, *WS*, XIV, 419–20; DW to J. Prescott Hall, Sept. 7, 1850, Domestic Letters, XXXVIII, 486, SDNA; and many other letters in ibid., passim, in 1850 and 1851.

38. J. Fred Rippy, *The United States and Mexico* (New York, 1931), 68–84; DW to Luis de la Rosa, Nov. 4, 1851, *WS*, XIV, 447–48; DW to Fillmore, Oct. 10, 1851, Fillmore Papers, F25/34573.

39. *American Railroad Journal,* 25 (April 10, 1852), 236–37.

40. Rippy, *United States and Mexico,* 47–53.

41. Ibid., 53–54; DW to Peter Hargous, Aug. 13, 1850, Domestic Letters, XXXVIII, 384–85, SDNA; DW to Robert Letcher, Aug. 17 and 24, 1850, Instructions, Mexico, XVI, 206–16, SDNA.

42. DW to Peter Hargous, Nov. 25, 1850, Domestic Letters, XXXVIII, 247, SDNA; Mariano Arista to DW, Jan. 25, 1851, WPNH, F23/32277.

43. DW to Letcher, Dec. 4, 1850, Instructions, Mexico, XVI, 231–33, SDNA; DW draft to Mariano Arista, May 1, 1851, Fillmore Papers, F24/33469; DW to Luis de la Rosa, April 30, and Aug. 25, 1851, *WS*, XIV, 520–35.

44. *American Railroad Journal,* 23 (Nov. 2, 1850), 689–90; DW to Thomas Corwin, May 7, 1851, Domestic Letters, XXXIX, 67, SDNA; DW to Robert Letcher, Aug. 16, 1851, *WS*, XIV, 535–36.

45. DW to Fillmore, Aug. 1, 1851, Fillmore Papers, F25/34532.

46. Fillmore to DW, July 19, 1851, WPLC, F24/34437.

47. DW to Fillmore, July 21, 1851, Fillmore Papers, F24/34448.

48. DW to Letcher, Aug. 16, 1851, Instructions, Mexico, XVI, 272–73, SDNA; Dec. 22, 1851, ibid., 298–303.

49. DW to Letcher, Feb. 10, 1852, ibid., 308–9.

50. DW to Fillmore, Feb. 27, 1852, Fillmore Papers, F26/36088; DW to William M. Burwell, March 22, 1852, Instructions, Mexico, XVI, 318–23, SDNA.

51. Rippy, *United States and Mexico*, 61–64. The long committee report, with copies of much of the diplomatic correspondence on the whole affair, is in *Senate Executive Document 97*, 32d Cong., 1st sess.

52. Fillmore to DW, May 20, 1852, WPNH, F26/36870. As on other diplomatic issues, Fillmore was more cautious than his secretary of state. In the president's judgment, the administration had done all it could in behalf of a private company, which could now submit its claim for losses.

53. DW to Fillmore, May 24, 1852, Fillmore Papers, F26/36890.

54. Rippy, *United States and Mexico*, 65–67.

55. Mary W. Williams, *Anglo-American Isthmian Diplomacy, 1815–1915* (Washington, D.C., 1916), 26–66; Wilbur D. Jones, *The American Problem in British Diplomacy, 1841–1861* (London, 1974), 66–79.

56. Jones, *American Problem*, 77–88. Britain got a vague American statement acknowledging British rights in Belize but failed to obtain a trade agreement for Canada. For a renewal of that effort, see the discussion of the fisheries controversy later in this chapter.

57. Henry Bulwer to DW, Aug. 16, 1850, in William R. Manning, ed., *Diplomatic Correspondence of the United States: Inter-American Affairs*, 12 vols. (Washington, D.C., 1932–39), VII, 402–3; Sept. 27, 1850, ibid., 416.

58. Bulwer to DW, June 25, 1851, WPLC, F24/33975.

59. Bulwer to DW, June 27, 1851, ibid., F24/33998.

60. Williams, *Isthmian Diplomacy*, 110–19.

61. DW to Foxhall A. Parker, March 12, 1852, Public Record Office, F0/115/117, F26/36211; DW to William A. Graham, March 17 and 18, 1852, Domestic Letters, XL, 24–27, SDNA.

62. DW to Abbott Lawrence, Jan. 18, 1852, Webster Papers, Harvard University, F25/35803.

63. "Basis of a Convention for the settlement of the difference between Nicaragua and Costa Rica proposed by the United States and Great Britain," *WS*, XIV, 482–87; DW to Abbott Lawrence, May 14, 1852, Instructions, Great Britain, XVI, 131–33, SDNA.

64. For an overview, see Williams, *Isthmian Diplomacy*, 321–30.

65. George I. Oeste, *John Randolph Clay: America's First Career Diplomat* (Philadelphia, 1966), 289–90, 353–403; Juan Y. de Osma to DW, June 22, 1852, *Senate Executive Document 109*, 32d Cong., 1st sess., pt. 1, 1–3; July 3, 1852, ibid., 4; Aug. 9, 1852, ibid., 5–7; DW to Fillmore, Sept. 15, 1852, Fillmore Papers, F27/37764.

66. Boston *Courier*, July 19, 1852; Jones, *American Problem*, 109–11, 113–14; DW to Fillmore, July 17, 1852, Fillmore Papers, F27/37276, and July 30, 1852, ibid., F27/37383.

29. Compromise on Trial

1. Webster remarked to Franklin Haven, Dec. 5, 1850, "The President is a first rate business man"; Webster Papers, Harvard University, F23/31764. The Fillmore Papers, Buffalo and Erie County Historical Society, include many items of correspondence between Webster and Fillmore for this period, none showing anything but an easy, friendly relationship. (All subsequent citations of the Fillmore Papers are to this depository.) Antislavery critics of

Webster erroneously believed that he dominated the president and his cabinet; Henry Wilson, *History of the Rise and Fall of the Slave Power in America*, 3 vols. (Boston, 1884), II, 275–76.

2. DW to Franklin Haven, Aug. 9, 1850, Webster Papers, Harvard University, F22/30832; DW to Peter Harvey, Sept. 13, 1850, typewritten copy in Middlesex County Historical Society, Middletown, Conn., F22/31090.

3. DW to Franklin Haven, Sept. 27, 1850, Webster Papers, Harvard University, F22/31231.

4. DW speech at Buffalo, May 21, 1851, *WS*, IV, 240; Andrew Johnson and Timothy R. Young to DW, Jan. 27, 1851, WPDC, F23/32312.

5. DW to David A. Neal, March 12, 1852, *WS*, XVI, 647–48.

6. William R. Brock, *Parties and Political Conscience: American Dilemmas, 1840–1850* (Millwood, N.Y., 1979), 106–13, 317–40. Michael F. Holt, *The Political Crisis of the 1850s* (New York, 1978), argues persuasively that the vigor of the two-party system depended upon the existence of conflict on a number of issues, though he would place the decline of healthy conflict on economic issues somewhat later than Brock. In any event, the Democratic party seemed in better shape than that of the Whigs.

7. DW to Peter Harvey, Oct. 2, 1850, *WS*, XVI, 568–69; Robert F. Dalzell, Jr., *Daniel Webster and the Trial of American Nationalism, 1843–1852* (Boston, 1973), 214.

8. DW to Dickinson, Sept. 27, 1850, and Dickinson to DW, Oct. 5, 1850, *WS*, XVIII, 392–93. In contrast to his earlier behavior, Cass's reactions to Webster's diplomacy were now supportive. In preparing his works for publication, Webster sought to revise passages which could have emphasized former controversies with Cass.

9. Stanley W. Campbell, *The Slave Catchers: Enforcement of the Fugitive Slave Law, 1850–1860* (Chapel Hill, 1970), 51–52; George T. Curtis, *Life of Daniel Webster*, 2 vols. (New York, 1870), II, 489.

10. Campbell, *Slave Catchers*, 26–48.

11. Carl B. Swisher, *History of the Supreme Court of the United States*, vol. 5, *The Taney Period* (New York, 1974), 573–75; Campbell, *Slave Catchers*, 96–102.

12. Fillmore to DW, Oct. 17, 1850, A. G. Mitten Collection, Indiana Historical Society, Indianapolis, F23/31399; Oct. 28, 1850, WPNH, F23/31558; DW to Fillmore, Oct. 19, 1850, Fillmore Papers, F23/31417.

13. DW to Fillmore, Oct. 29, 1850, Fillmore Papers, F23/31562.

14. DW to F. S. Lathrop et al., Oct. 28, 1850, *WS*, XII, 251–53.

15. DW to Colby, Nov. 11, 1850, ibid., XVIII, 402; DW to B. F. Ayer, Nov. 16, 1850, ibid., XVI, 577–78; DW to Ichabod S. Spencer, Dec. 7, 1850, ibid., 580–81. Justices Robert Grier and Levi Woodbury of the Supreme Court had already made their views known; from earlier correspondence, Webster knew that John McLean approved a federal law of this type; soon Samuel Nelson would so indicate; and it was certain that several justices who were southerners would also. He had good reason to believe that in Massachusetts, federal district judge Peleg Sprague and state supreme court chief justice Lemuel Shaw would uphold the statute. Lawyers Benjamin and George Curtis, followers of the secretary, and other leading lawyers in Massachusetts had declared themselves on the issue.

16. Harold Schwartz, "Fugitive Slave Days in Boston," *New England Quar-*

terly, 27 (1954), 193–94; Jane H. Pease and William H. Pease, *The Fugitive Slave Law and Anthony Burns: A Problem in Law Enforcement* (Philadephia, 1975), 15–16. In these cases defense counsel would often file for a writ of habeas corpus from state courts or bring actions against agents of slaveholders.

17. DW to Fillmore, Nov. 15, 1850, Fillmore Papers, F23/31671.

18. Descriptions of the case are in: Campbell, *Slave Catchers*, 148–51; Schwartz, "Fugitive Slave Days," 194–97; Pease and Pease, *Fugitive Slave Law*, 16–17.

19. DW to Moses Taylor et al., Feb. 20, 1851, WPNH, F23/32591.

20. Curtis, *Webster*, II, 490.

21. James D. Richardson, ed., *A Compilation of the Messages and Papers of the Presidents, 1789–1897*, 10 vols. (Washington, D.C., 1897), IV, 101–6.

22. Ibid., 93–98.

23. DW to Lunt, March 1, 1851, Domestic Letters, XXXVIII, 491, SDNA; March 28, 1851, ibid., 548; Choate to Lunt, March 29, 1851, enclosed in Lunt to DW, April 4, 1851, Fillmore Papers, F24/33175; Lunt to DW, March 21, 1851, enclosed in DW to Fillmore, April 4, 1851, ibid., F24/33164.

24. DW to Mayor John P. Bigelow, March 10, 1851, *WS*, XIV, 623–25.

25. Description of case in Campbell, *Slave Catchers*, 117–21; Schwartz, "Fugitive Slave Days," 197–200; Pease and Pease, *Fugitive Slave Law*, 18–19.

26. Leonard W. Levy, *The Law of the Commonwealth and Chief Justice Shaw* (Cambridge, Mass., 1957), 91–105; Levy, "Sims' Case: The Fugitive Slave Law in Boston in 1851," *Journal of Negro History*, 35 (Jan. 1950), 39–74; report of Shaw's decision, 7 Cushing (Mass.) 285 (1851). On the question of congressional power to legislate, Shaw relied upon the Supreme Court decision upholding the earlier federal law of 1793, *Prigg* v. *Pennsylvania*, 10 Peters 539 (1842). On the question of the judicial character of the commissioners, he held that they were not performing such a function but merely identifying the fugitive, who must then resort to a court in the state of flight for judicial remedy. The fact was that a person wrongly transported there as a fugitive would have trouble in that jurisdiction.

27. Pease and Pease, *Fugitive Slave Law*, 19–21. Gerrit Smith and other prominent abolitionists were involved in the Jerry case. In it, the grand jury refused to indict on a charge of treason and returned a bill only on obstruction of justice under the fugitive-slave law. One person was convicted on that charge.

28. The only one was the case of Anthony Burns in 1854, in which the fugitive was returned with a great show of force against much resistance in Boston; Campbell, *Slave Catchers*, 214–32, 169–70.

29. Ibid., 53–79, 107–9, 199–207; David M. Potter, *The Impending Crisis, 1848–1861* (New York, 1976), 134–40.

30. Speech at Albany, May 28, 1851, *WS*, IV, 270–80.

31. DW to G. A. Tavenner, April 9, 1852, WPNH, F26/36495. The Supreme Court upheld the law in *Ableman* v. *Booth*, 21 Howard 506 (1859), in a controversy that continued for several years before and during the Civil War and involved a confrontation between judges of Wisconsin and of the United States.

32. DW to William Prescott, Nov. 7, 1850, WPNH, F23/31621.

33. DW to Richard Blatchford, Dec. 10, 1850, WPLC, F23/31815.

34. DW draft of "Cabinet Circular," [Oct. 1850], WPDC, F23/31580.

35. Alexander H. H. Stuart to Millard Fillmore, Nov. 11, 1850, WPNH.

36. DW to William Kinney et al., Nov. 23, 1850, WS, XII, 254–55.

37. Joel Poinsett to J. J. Abert, Dec. 12, 1850, Poinsett Papers, Library of Congress, asking Abert to pass information on to Webster; James L. Petigru to DW, Oct. 10, 1851, WPLC, F25/34971.

38. Text of speech, WS, XIII, 429–41.

39. Text in ibid., IV, 293–318; DW draft, George J. Abbot Papers, Yale University Library, F24/34258. For a recollection of an eyewitness, see "Reminiscences of Stockton Axson," Woodrow Wilson Papers, Princeton University Library.

40. DW to Josiah Randall et al., Nov. 14, 1850, WPNH, F23/31666; to James A. Hamilton et al., Jan. 27, 1851, WS, XII, 256–60; to William M. Richards et al., March 21, 1851, WPNH, F24/33044.

41. Speech at Pilgrim Festival, Dec. 22, 1850, WS, IV, 217–26; at Annapolis, March 25, 1851, ibid., XIII, 392–400; at Harrisburg to state house of representatives, April 1, 1851, ibid., 401–4.

42. For this speech, delivered in February 1852, see the discussion earlier in the chapter.

43. Claude M. Fuess, Daniel Webster, 2 vols. (Boston, 1930), II, 275–77; DW to Richard M. Blatchford, May 7 and 11, 1851, in Curtis, Webster, II, 502–3; DW to Franklin Haven, June 4, 1851, Webster Papers, Harvard University, F24/33735.

44. Speech at Buffalo, May 22, 1851, WS, IV, 242–62.

45. Text of speech, WS, XIII, 408–21.

46. Text of speech, May 21, the first of two given in that city, ibid., IV, 231–41.

47. DW to Franklin Haven, June 15, 1851, Webster Papers, Harvard University, F24/33880; to Fletcher Webster, June 16, 1851, WPNH, F24/33904.

48. Webster wrote Secretary of the Treasury Thomas Corwin, Nov. 13, 1850, recommending withdrawal of that department's patronage from the Atlas; Corwin Papers, Library of Congress, F23/31649.

49. DW to Millard Fillmore, Sept. 11, 1850, Fillmore Papers, F22/31068.

50. DW to Edward Everett, Sept. 26, 1850, Everett Papers, Massachusetts Historical Society, F22/31222; Everett to DW, Oct. 5, 1850, ibid., F23/31317; DW to Everett, Oct. 8, 1850, ibid., F23/31330.

51. Dalzell, Webster and Trial of American Nationalism, 219–22; DW to Millard Fillmore, Nov. 13, 1850, Fillmore Papers, F23/31654.

52. Quoted in David Donald, Charles Sumner and the Coming of the Civil War (New York, 1960), 189–203. Webster wrote Thomas B. Curtis, Jan. 24, 1851, suggesting a conservative Democrat; Webster Papers, Massachusetts Historical Society, F23/32245.

53. Caleb Eddy et al. to DW, April 11, 1851, Sang Collection, Brandeis University, F24/33234; DW to George G. Smith et al., April 15, 1851, WPNH, F24/33255.

54. Francis Brinley to DW, April 17, 1851, WPNH, F24/33279.

55. DW to Henry B. Rogers et al., April 23, 1851, WPNH, F24/33337; DW to Francis Brinley, April 19, 1851, WS, XVI, 609–10.

56. Text of speech, April 22, 1851, WS, XIII, 405–7.

57. Speech in Faneuil Hall, May 22, 1852, ibid., 510–24.

58. One of several letters in Webster's correspondence criticizing the regular party committee is DW to Peter Harvey, May 4, 1851, ibid., XVI, 610–11. On the circular, see George Ashmun to DW, [June 1851], WPLC, F24/34039; Everett to DW, June 26, 1851, Everett Papers, F24/33978. There is a good discussion of the movement for a nomination in Dalzell, *Webster and Trail of American Nationalism*, 232–34.

59. Everett to DW, Sept. 2, 1851, Everett Papers, F25/34643; DW to Everett, Sept. 3, 1851, ibid., F25/34658. The regular convention nominated Winthrop for governor, but he later lost the election.

60. Description of the convention and quotation of part of Everett's address in Curtis, *Webster*, II, 579–81. For the mellowed relations with Henshaw, see Webster's letter to him of June 11, 1851, WPNH, F24/33841.

61. DW to Fillmore, [Jan. 1851], Fillmore Papers, F23/32369.

62. DW to Edward Curtis, [May 1851?], Montague Collection, New York Public Library, F24/33691.

63. Robert J. Rayback, *Millard Fillmore: A Biography of a President* (Buffalo, 1959), 333–53; Dalzell, *Webster and Trial of American Nationalism*, 242–46.

64. DW to Franklin Haven, June 11, 1851, Webster Papers, Harvard University, F24/33836; Dec. 13, 1851, ibid., F25/35430.

65. Among many letters on publishing the works are DW to Everett, Sept. 22 and Oct. 4, 1851, Everett Papers, F25/34744 and 34844.

66. Fletcher Webster to DW, Oct. 31, 1851, WPNH, F25/35028.

67. DW to Franklin Haven, Nov. 30, 1851, Webster Papers, Harvard University, F25/35306.

68. Edward Everett to DW, March 8, 1852, Everett Papers, F26/36172; DW to Everett, March 13, 1852, ibid., F26/36215.

69. Remarks welcoming immigration in speech at Albany, May 28, 1851, *WS*, IV, 288–89. Some of Webster's friends would move into the American party in the late 1850s.

70. DW to Franklin Haven, Dec. 14, 1851, Webster Papers, Harvard University, F25/35464.

71. Weed spent much of this period in travel to Europe.

72. Ketchum to DW, May 5, 1851, George F. Hoar Papers, F24/33513; Edward Curtis to DW, May 7, 1851, WPLC, F24/33543; Ketchum to Peter Harvey, Nov. 18, 1851, WPNH; Charles W. March to DW, Dec. 2, 1851, ibid., F25/35327.

73. James L. Crouthamel, *James Watson Webb: A Biography* (Middletown, Conn., 1969), 117; Webb to DW, Feb. 8, 1852, Miscellaneous MSS, New York Historical Society, F26/35931; DW to Webb, Feb. 11, 1852, WPLC, F26/35960.

74. Text of speech at City Hall, Feb. 24, 1852, *WS*, XIII, 498–500. The other speeches are described earlier in this chapter.

75. Printed notice of meeting, Feb. 27, 1852, WPNH; quotation of part of address adopted at meeting of March 5, 1852, in Curtis, *Webster*, II, 582–83. The address was written by William M. Evarts, who adeptly reviewed Webster's accomplishments and capacity for the presidency. Ms. copy of the circular, signed by A. C. Kingsland et al., calling upon leading persons throughout the country to work for Webster's nomination, is in the William

H. Taft Papers, Library of Congress, series 1, box 7, folder, March 1852. This copy went to Alphonso Taft in Ohio; Ketchum to Taft, March 31, 1852, ibid. It was a promising approach but had little effect.

76. Charles W. March to DW, April 8 and 12, 1852, WPNH, F26/36477 and 36517. These letters are informative about the general character of the campaign.

77. Charles W. March to DW, June 21, 1851, ibid., F24/33954; anonymous letter to DW, Oct. 28, 1851, ibid., F25/34999; "A Compromise Whig" to DW, March 3, 1852, ibid., F26/36130.

78. In the spring of 1852 Webster was in Trenton, arguing the Goodyear rubber patent case before the federal circuit court. He spoke to the state legislature on March 26, 1852; text in *WS*, XIII, 509–10.

79. On Connecticut, see Charles J. Lanman to DW, March 4, 1852, WPDC, F26/36135. There were troubles here which would deprive Webster of votes in the national convention. On Rhode Island: DW to Franklin Haven, Feb. 6, 1852, Webster Papers, Harvard University, F26/35917.

80. DW to Millard Fillmore, Oct. 11, 1851, Fillmore Papers, F25/34881.

81. A negative report on Indiana and Ohio is Fletcher Webster to DW, Nov. 29, 1851, WPNH, F25/35298.

82. Charles S. Moorehead to DW, June 11, 1852, University of Kentucky Library, F26/37028; DW to Humphrey Marshall, June 15, 1852, George J. Abbot Papers, F26/37039.

83. Webster had support from some individual politicians of the South, such as John Bell of Tennessee, possibly John Berrien of Georgia and Henry Hilliard of Alabama, but it did not deliver votes; George Abbot to DW, May 15, [1852], original in possession of John R. Morison, Peterborough, N.H., F26/36825; and May 16, 1852, ibid., F26/36845.

84. Webster was receiving optimistic predictions on the eve of the convention; Fletcher Webster, June 4, 1852, WPNH, F26/36957; Edward Everett to DW, June 11, 1852, Everett Papers, F26/37020. But he himself was less optimistic. Writing to Fletcher sometime in May, he complained of talk without action. "Really," he exclaimed, "I am tired of hearing any thing upon this subject, unless it is a proposition *to do something*"; WPNH, F26/36921.

85. The party's two-thirds rule for nomination had effect here.

86. The following account of the convention draws upon Roy Nichols and Jeanette Nichols, "Election of 1852," in Arthur M. Schlesinger, Jr., and Fred L. Israel, eds., *History of American Presidential Elections, 1789–1968,* 4 vols. (New York, 1971), II, 921–57. The platform is printed on pp. 956–57.

87. Claude M. Fuess, *Rufus Choate: Wizard of the Law* (New York, 1928), 200–3.

88. Dalzell, *Webster and Trial of American Nationalism,* 260–66, thinks that though there was probably no specific deal between Scott and Fillmore forces on the platform, the concession by the general helped his eventual nomination.

89. Rayback, *Fillmore,* 357, says that Fillmore was in fact so pleased with the platform that he was ready to withdraw.

90. Webster got eleven of Massachusetts' thirteen votes; most of those of New Hampshire, Rhode Island, and Vermont, but none from Connecticut or Maine; three from Wisconsin; one from California; and two from New York; table of ballots in Curtis, *Webster,* II, 621.

91. DW to Daniel Jenifer, [June 19, 1852], original in possession of John R. Morison, Peterborough, N.H., F26/37083.

92. Fuess, *Webster*, II, 288, says it was Toombs and Stephens who pledged the southern vote if Webster collected the total of forty-one. Dalzell, *Webster and Trial of American Nationalism*, 269-71, uses the Fillmore Papers for his account and shows that not all southerners would have voted for Webster in any case.

93. DW to no addressee, [June 20, 1852], WPDC, F26/37084.

94. DW to George Ashmun and Edward Curtis, June 21, 1852, James Watson Webb Papers, Yale University Library, F26/37087.

95. DW to Fillmore, June 21, 1852, Fillmore Papers, F26/37090. At the top of this note someone wrote that Fillmore received and answered it at 9:30, a half hour later.

96. Fillmore to DW, June 21, 1852, ibid., F26/37095. An endorsement at the top of this item, "not sent but seen," suggests that the two men met and that Fillmore showed Webster the note. The language of Fillmore's note indicates that he still hoped for the nomination with the addition of Webster's votes, if the secretary's instructions arrived at the convention in time.

97. Text of remarks to Whig delegates, June 21, 1852, WS, XIII, 526.

98. DW to Richard M. Blatchford, June 22, 1852, Everett Papers, F26/37099; DW to John E. Wool, June 22, 1852, George J. Abbot Papers, F26/37101.

99. Edward Everett to DW, June 22, 1852, Everett Papers, F26/37104.

100. Curtis, *Webster*, II, 672.

101. Franklin Haven to DW, June 29, 1852, WPNH, F26/37138; DW to Haven, July 7, 1852, *WS*, XVIII, 535; description of event in ibid., XVI, editorial note, 530-32; text of DW remarks, ibid., 532-38; John Stimpson to Edward Everett et al., Nov. 13, 1852, WPNH, F27/37239, on gift of cane. On July 25 a large gathering also honored him at Marshfield, where he spoke about his friendship with neighbors and about the pending fisheries question; Curtis, *Webster*, II, 647; *WS*, XIII, 539-42.

102. DW to Fletcher Webster, July 4, 1852, WPNH, F27/37183; DW to Fillmore, July 25, 1852, Fillmore Papers, F27/37352; DW to Everett, Aug. 14, 1852, Everett Papers, F27/37570. On Lawrence's dissatisfaction, see his letter to Webster, Sept. 30, 1852, J. C. Bancroft Davis Papers, Library of Congress, F27/37910.

103. DW to Fillmore, July 26, 1852, Fillmore Papers, F27/37362; Aug. 3, 1852, ibid., F27/37489. Webster had lingering thoughts about resigning after telling the president he would stay; Curtis, *Webster*, II, 660.

104. Dalzell, *Webster and Trial of American Nationalism*, 285-86.

105. Anonymous letters, signed *, to DW, July 14, 1852, WPNH, F27/37252; C. Fletcher to DW, Aug. 17, 1852, WPLC, F27/37607; Richard J. Mapes to DW, Oct. 10, 1852, WPNH, F27/37993.

106. Curtis, *Webster*, II, 650-51.

107. One of the few prominent Websterites in New York favoring an independent nomination was Hiram Ketchum.

108. John L. Stephens to DW, Aug. 3, 1852, WPLC, F27/37491; Dalzell, *Webster and Trial of American Nationalism*, 287-88.

109. Dalzell, *Webster and Trial of American Nationalism*, 289-92.

110. DW to Fletcher Webster, Aug. 26, 1852, Webster Papers, Harvard

University, F27/37702; replying to Fletcher Webster to DW, Aug. 25, 1852, WPNH, F27/37687.

111. Boston *Advertiser,* Sept. 9, 1852.

112. Ibid., Sept. 16, 1852.

113. DW to Millard Fillmore, May 9 and 12, 1852, Fillmore Papers, F26/36770 and 36794; DW to Franklin Haven, Webster Papers, July 31, 1852, Harvard University, F27/37400. It was suspected, but not established, that internal injuries from the accident contributed to Webster's later decline. Certainly it was not the principal factor.

114. DW to Fletcher Webster, Aug. 10, 11, and 22, 1852, *WS,* XVI, 662–63.

115. DW to Fillmore, Sept. 16 and 28, 1852, Fillmore Papers, F27/37778 and 37895.

116. DW to Richard Blatchford, Sept. 29, 1852, *WS,* XVIII, 555; Curtis, *Webster,* II, 667–80; DW to Franklin Haven, Sept. 29, 1852, *WS,* XVI, 665. He probably bought the land from Edward P. Little.

117. Curtis, *Webster,* II, 670–71; DW to Fillmore, Sept. 22, 1852, Fillmore Papers, F27/37855.

118. Curtis, *Webster,* II, 681–83; George J. Abbot to Peter Harvey, Oct. 11, 1852, in Claude H. Van Tyne, ed., *The Letters of Daniel Webster* (New York, 1902), 540–41.

119. DW to Hatch, Oct. 1, 1852, *WS,* XVI, 668 and n. 2.

120. DW to Fillmore, Sept. 28, Oct. 4, 8, and 15, Fillmore Papers, F27/37895, 37947, 37962, and 38040. Beginning about October 15, Webster's incoming mail indicated many people realized his illness was quite serious. See F27 for this period.

121. Moses H. Grinnell to DW, Oct. 9, 1852, Van Tyne, *Letters,* 541, enclosing Grinnell et al. to DW, Sept. 24, 1852, WPNH, F27/37975.

122. DW draft to [Grinnell et al.], Oct. 12, 1852, WPNH, F27/38000.

123. Curtis draft of DW to Grinnell et al., Oct. 13, ibid., F27/38023.

124. Everett draft of DW to Grinnell et al., [Oct. 1852], George J. Abbot Papers, F27/38095. Everett's draft arrived at Marshfield the fourteenth; Dalzell, *Webster and Trial of American Nationalism,* 299–300.

125. Dalzell, *Webster and Trial of American Nationalism,* 302.

126. Curtis, *Webster,* II, 688–89. George Curtis had opposed a reply anyway because he had feared it would undermine an independent nomination.

127. Dalzell, *Webster and Trial of American Nationalism,* 301, using Abbot Papers; Curtis, *Webster,* II, 686. Abbot probably used the phrase "twenty pieces of silver" in a figurative sense, for there is no indication that Grinnell was offering Webster twenty thousand dollars at the moment. See also Abbot to "a friend," ibid.

128. Lanman to Pierce, Oct. 19, 1852, and Pierce to Lanman, Oct. 21, 1852, copies in WPNH; Peter Harvey, *Reminiscences and Anecdotes of Daniel Webster* (Boston, 1878), 203, makes the suspicious statement that Webster also told him that if he himself were casting a vote, it would be for Pierce.

129. Dalzell, *Webster and Trial of American Nationalism,* 303.

130. Communications with Washington now wholly concerned his declining physical condition; DW to Fillmore, Oct. 18, 1852, Fillmore Papers, F27/38066; Abbot to Fillmore, Oct. 21, 23, and 25, 1852, *WS,* XVIII, 560–62.

131. Curtis, *Webster,* II, 685.

132. Ibid., 688-701.

133. Ibid., 689-97; copy of will, *WS*, XIII, 586-87; DW memorandum as supplement, [Oct. 21, 1852], WPNH, F27/38083. The story of the administration of Webster's estate is a protracted, complex one not discussed here. In general, his supposition that his assets would take care of his liabilities was erroneous. One of his debtors posing particular difficulties was Caleb Cushing. The materials relating to problems after his death are in MS Estate Book, WPDC; Registry of Deeds, Plymouth County, Mass., F27/38149; schedule of property at Elms farm, WPNH, F27/38110; Caleb Cushing Papers, Library of Congress, boxes 56, 62, 72, 75, 76, 79. See Claude M. Fuess, *The Life of Caleb Cushing*, 2 vols. (New York, 1923), II, 84-94.

Caroline Le Roy Webster soon moved to New York City, where she lived quietly for the next thirty years. Fletcher did get Marshfield and lived there until he was killed during the Civil War. His wife, Caroline White Webster, occupied the property until the early 1880s, in fact built a new house after the original one burned down. On this and on Webster's descendents, see an extensive discussion in Fuess, *Webster*, II, 359-63.

134. On October 15, 1852, Webster wrote a brief statement of his religious faith, to be inscribed on his tombstone; text in *WS*, XIII, 592; memorandum by Edward Curtis about a conversation with DW on this topic in Montague Collection, New York Public Library, F27/38043.

135. George Ticknor Curtis, who was present through this period, provides a detailed narrative of the death; *Webster*, II, 689-701. On the twenty-fifth, the day after his death, physicians conducted an autopsy, showing cirrhosis of the liver, likely to have been the alcoholic type, and ascribing death to hemorrhage in the abdominal area; details in Fuess, *Webster*, II, 357-58. A report of the illness and the autopsy was published by his doctor, John Jeffries, "An Account of the Last Illness . . . of Daniel Webster . . . ," *American Journal of the Medical Sciences*, n.s., 25 (Jan. 1853), 110-20.

136. Curtis, *Webster*, II, 703-4; Paul R. Frothingham, *Edward Everett: Orator and Statesman* (Boston, 1925), 326-27; George S. Hillard and Anna Ticknor, eds., *Life, Letters, and Journals of George Ticknor*, 2 vols. (Boston, 1876), II, 284. See also Boston *Advertiser* for late October 1852.

INDEX

Criminal cases, *see* Law cases
Crittenden, John J., 274, 309, 316, 323, 324, 379, 380, 382, 401, 425, 490
Crooks, Ramsay, 291
Crowninshield, Dick and George, 158–61
Cuba: and slavery issue, 122, 377; invasion of, 467–68, 506
Currency reform, 64–65, 234, 237, 243; and depression of 1830s, 262, 264, 266
Curtis, Benjamin R., 421, 423, 456
Curtis, George Ticknor, 417, 423, 478, 479, 485, 493–500 passim
Cushing, Caleb, 249, 250, 267, 285, 288, 290, 303, 319, 365, 382, 434, 439, 441; minister to China, 365, 366, 367, 402, 433, 463
Cuthbert, Alfred, 245

Dallas, Alexander, 57, 58, 61, 64
Dallas, George M., 197, 212, 371, 388
Dana, Judah, 16
Dane, Nathan, 184, 185, 190
Dartmouth College: DW attends, 5–8, 17, 20; Ezekiel at, 8–10; speeches at, 17–18, 19, 26; trustee-president conflict, 63, 77, 166–71
Dartmouth College v. *Woodward*, 66, 77, 166–71, 450, 506
Dartmouth Gazette, 7, 11, 18
Davis, Jefferson, 408, 422
Davis, John, 189, 246, 247, 249, 286, 287, 288, 341, 361, 362, 368, 387, 390, 417, 427
Davis, Moses, 7, 11, 18
Davis, Phineas, 286, 287, 288, 293
Dearborn, Henry A. S., 92, 189, 509
Death(s), DW and: of Grace (daughter), 71; of Charles, 71–72, 113; of Grace (wife), 140, 143, 151, 152; of Ezekiel, 152, 153, 179, 282, 502; of Edward, 434–35; of Julia, 435; contemplations of his own, 499–500; of Fletcher, 511
Death penalty, DW on, 17
Debt-collection cases, 16–17, 459
Declaration of Independence, 18, 83, 84, 85, 218, 446
Dedham Bank case, 157
Democracy, DW on, 19
Democratic party, 444, 445, 508, 509, 510; DW on, 31; and election of 1824, 111, 129, 508; and election of 1832, 194; and BUS, 202, 258, 259; and nullification crisis, 224; and antislavery movement, 240; and election

of 1836, 247; and economy, 261–67, 303, 307, 314, 389; and election of 1840, 268, 270, 272, 273; and election of 1844, 370, 372; and election of 1848, 394, 397–402; and Compromise of 1850, 407; Young America movement, 466; and election of 1852, 484–86, 488, 490, 493, 495, 498
Denny, Harmar, 251, 252
Derrick, William, 355, 462
Dickinson, Daniel, 382, 404, 476
Divina Pastora case, 165
Dix, Timothy, 16, 17, 27
Dorchester, 69, 70
Dorr War, 445–46
Doty, James, 288
Douglas, Stephen, 405, 408, 426, 427, 490
Draft, *see* Conscription
Dred Scott case, 404, 443

Eastman, Gerusha (grandmother), 3
Eastman, Roger (grandfather), 3
Eaton, John, 126, 191–92
Economy, U.S.: bank war and, 235, 254, 258–59; depression, 240, 257, 258–74, 290, 301–17; easy credit, 259, 260, 261, 266; independent treasury debate, 261–67; and foreign policy, 463. *See also* Bank of the United States (BUS)
Education of DW: preparatory, 4–5, 15, 23, 76; at Dartmouth, 5–8, 9, 11, 17, 20; study of law, 9, 10, 13–16, 20; DW's views on, 77–78, 80
Edwards, Ninian, 107–8
Election campaigns, presidential: of 1804, 20; of 1808, 30, 31; of 1812, 32; of 1820, 88, 89, 509; of 1824, 108–17, 127, 131, 133, 507; of 1828, 120, 125–28, 130–37, 141, 146–50; of 1832, 141, 192–93, 194, 203, 207–8, 246, 247; of 1836, 245, 246, 247–53; of 1840, 240, 267–73, 361, 509; of 1844, 305, 307, 317, 356, 369–71, 373, 401, 510; of 1848, 392, 394–402, 407, 476; of 1852, 475, 476, 481, 482, 484–98, 510. *See also* Presidency, DW's quest for
Elections, Massachusetts, 96, 146, 246–47, 248–49, 368, 390; DW for Representative, 97, 112, 131, 133–35, 138, 147, 509; DW for Senator, 138–39, 269, 372. *See also* Election campaigns, presidential; Massachusetts politics